# APPLYING EDUCATIONAL RESEARCH

# APPLYING EDUCATIONAL RESEARCH

## A Practical Guide

### Third Edition

**WALTER R. BORG**
*Late of Utah State University*

**JOYCE P. GALL**
*University of Oregon*

**MEREDITH D. GALL**
*University of Oregon*

**Longman**
New York & London

**Applying Educational Research: A Practical Guide, Third Edition**

Longman, 10 Bank Street, White Plains, N.Y. 10606

Associated companies:
Longman Group Ltd., London
Longman Cheshire Pty., Melbourne
Longman Paul Pty., Auckland
Copp Clark Pitman, Toronto

Acquisitions editor: Kenneth J. Clinton
Sponsoring editor: Naomi Silverman
Development editor: Virginia L. Blanford
Production editor: Ann P. Kearns
Cover design: Michelle Szabo
Text art: Burmar
Production supervisor: Richard C. Bretan

**Library of Congress Cataloging-in-Publication Data**

Borg, Walter R.
    Applying educational research : a practical guide /
  Walter R. Borg, Joyce P. Gall, Meredith D. Gall.—3rd ed.
        p.      cm.
    Includes bibliographical references and index.
    ISBN 0-8013-0486-5
    1. Education—Research—Handbooks, manuals, etc.   I. Gall, Joyce
P.  II. Gall, Meredith D., Date.   III. Title.
LB1028.B59   1992
370'.78—dc20                                            92-20899
                                                          CIP

2 3 4 5 6 7 8 9 10-MA-959493

Dedicated to the memory of
our friend and colleague

Walter R. Borg

# CONTENTS

# REPRINTED STUDIES, BY CHAPTER

# PREFACE

We were saddened by the sudden death of our long-time mentor and friend Walter Borg in 1990. At the time of his death, he was well along in revising the second edition of his book *Applying Educational Research*. We took comfort in the opportunity to carry on Walter's tradition of scholarship by completing the revision.

Walter and Meredith ("Mark") Gall were co-authors of the second through fifth editions of *Educational Research: An Introduction*, a comprehensive text on the design and conduct of research studies. This long-time collaboration led to the decision for Mark to complete the revision of *Applying Educational Research: A Practical Guide*, which concerns the use of published research knowledge to improve educational practice. Mark was joined in this endeavor by his colleague and spouse, Joyce P. Gall.

The third edition continues the tradition of the first two editions of making educational research as accessible as possible to educational practitioners, especially those who will study this subject in a graduate degree program. We have done so by including many examples of research studies that have implications for the improvement of education. Recognizing that educators work in diverse settings, we included research on elementary and secondary education, higher education, and education in the private sector. Throughout the text, we explain ways in which educators can use the findings of educational research to inform the decisions that they make.

This edition maintains the readability and study aids of the book's two previous editions. Most notably, every major type of educational research is illustrated by including the complete text of an actual published research report. There are eleven of these reports, easily identified by their shaded background, each accompanied by comments written by the actual researchers and also a critical review of the study written by us. A feature new to this edition is the inclusion of editors' notes in the reports. Each note provides a nontechnical definition of research concepts and procedures mentioned in the report. Thus, readers are spared the task of searching the textbook to find definitions of terms they have not studied or may have forgotten. Comprehensive forms for evaluating quantitative and qualitative research reports are another new feature.

This edition has expanded coverage of the methods used in educational research. A chapter on research synthesis has been added to help educators find published reports that bring together the findings of many studies on a particular topic or problem. A new chapter on qualitative research introduces educators to the exciting developments that have occurred recently in this approach to educational inquiry. The new chapter on evaluation research describes methods used by professional evaluators and how their findings can improve educational policy-making. Finally, the chapter on action research has been expanded to include more examples in addition to detailed procedures for helping educators carry out their own action research projects.

The book has four parts, each preceded by a brief introduction to orient the reader to its topics. All the chapters include a list of objectives and a set of application problems to facilitate mastery of their content.

Part I consists of a chapter that explains the role of research in improving educational practice and previews the remainder of the book.

Part II concerns sources of educational information. Chapter 2 discusses the steps involved in reviewing educational literature and how to conduct a manual literature search. Chapter 3 describes procedures for carrying out a computer search of various indexes to the educational research literature. Chapter 4 describes procedures for reviewing primary sources (i.e., reports of research written by the actual investigators) and for writing a report of what one has found as a result of the review.

Part III describes methods for evaluating and synthesizing research evidence. Chapter 5 provides guidelines for evaluating each part of a research study. Chapters 6 and 7 discuss more deeply two important aspects of research methodology—measurement and statistics. Chapter 8 discusses the value of using published syntheses of research findings as a guide in making educational decisions. In this and all subsequent chapters, one or more research articles is reprinted in full. As we stated above, each article is accompanied by comments by the original researchers, footnotes explaining technical concepts and procedures, and our critical review.

Part IV includes seven chapters, each describing a different type of educational research. We begin with a discussion of qualitative research in Chapter 9 and explain three common types of this research paradigm: case studies, historical research, and ethnographies. Chapters 10 through 13 describe the four main types of quantitative research: descriptive research (Chapter 10); causal-comparative research (Chapter 11); correlational research (Chapter 12); and experimental research, including true experiments, quasi-experiments, and single-subject research (Chapter 13). Chapter 14 covers the expanding field of evaluation research. Chapter 15 describes action research and shows educators how they can do their own action research to generate findings that apply to their unique situations.

An *Instructor's Manual* is available.

# Acknowledgments

The authors wish to express their appreciation to the following reviewers, whose helpful suggestions and insight contributed greatly to the development of this book:

Doran Christensen, Tennessee Technological University
James Divine, University of Southern Indiana
Stephen Jenkins, Georgia Southern College
William Steve Lang, Georgia Southern College

William Mehrens, Michigan State University
Rita O'Sullivan, University of North Carolina/Greensboro
Susan Rodman, University of West Virginia
William Stallings, Georgia State University
John Tenny, Willamette University

JOYCE P. GALL
MEREDITH D. GALL

# PART I

# THE CONTRIBUTIONS OF EDUCATIONAL RESEARCH

## The Goal of This Book

This book is written primarily for the master's degree student in education who will need to demonstrate the ability to write a research paper, synthesizing and interpreting findings from the educational research literature. It is also intended for educators who at certain points in their work need to investigate the research that has been done on an educational issue or problem and share what they learn with others.

Our aim is not to train you to be an educational researcher. Rather, our goal is to help you learn how to evaluate and interpret educational research and apply its findings to educational practice. This is an important goal because a vast body of information and ideas is contained in the educational research literature. Although educational research rarely results in pat answers, it provides knowledge and insights that are relevant to virtually any practical problem or question in education. If you can locate and interpret research information that relates to the problems that arise in your work, you will be in a position to make sounder decisions than someone who relies only on personal experience or others' opinions.

## The Authors' Assumptions

In this book we have tried to provide the *minimum* skills you will need to locate and evaluate educational research reports on a given problem or to conduct action research. We have made certain assumptions in writing the book. Among them are the following:

1. Most readers are or will become teachers, school administrators, or other types of educators. They are not interested in becoming educational researchers at the time they study this book.

2. Most readers have had little or no previous instruction in research methods, educational measurement, and statistics.
3. The minimum skills needed to use educational research literature and action research as aids to decision making can be learned without extensive training in research methodology, measurement, and statistics.

To achieve our goal, we have cut away all but the bare essentials of research methods, statistics, and measurement. Thus there is virtually nothing in this book that is not important to achieving the goal of becoming an intelligent consumer of the educational research literature. As a result, thorough and careful study of this book is necessary in order to achieve its specified goals and objectives.

# A Study Strategy

Many students find the following strategy effective for studying books like this one:

*1. Read the overview and objectives.* Each chapter begins with a brief overview and a list of objectives. Both are intended to give you an idea of the scope of the chapter and to help you focus on the main concepts that you should learn.

The objectives are stated in roughly the same order in which they are covered in the chapter. Some are concerned with understanding important concepts. These objectives usually require you to state the concept and describe or explain it. Other objectives call for applying what you have learned. They usually state the conditions under which you should be able to apply the principle or skill. Both types of objectives are important.

When you begin each chapter, we recommend that you read the objectives slowly and think about each one after you read it. If you pause and think about each objective for 20 to 30 seconds, you will remember them much longer than if you merely read them and go on. Some students find it helpful to read the objectives two or three times, so that they have them firmly in mind before they start reading the body of the chapter.

*2. Read the body of the chapter.* As you read the chapter, try to locate the main ideas related to each objective. We recommend that you underline or highlight main concepts. Avoid underlining too much. Most of the content explains the main ideas or gives examples that are designed to help you place these ideas into a meaningful context. You will be able to grasp the most important ideas by underlining 10 to 20 percent of the text. After you have read about an important concept, test your understanding by stating it to yourself in a context with which you are familiar. Reflect on and reread the sections about any concepts that are new to you or that you find difficult to grasp.

In reading the text, you probably will come upon research-related terms with which you may not be familiar. If you find a word you do not understand, we suggest that you check it in the Index. The page where you can find a definition of the term is shown in boldface in the Index. In addition, each of the research articles reproduced in this book contains footnotes explaining statistics and research procedures that we feel you might need help in understanding. We also suggest that you ask your instructor or your classmates about terms and concepts that you wish to understand more thoroughly.

*3. Check your mastery.* After you finish reading an entire chapter, go back to the objectives and see if you can state the concepts or carry out the activities as described in each objective. If you find any objectives that you have not mastered, reread the sections related to the objective that you have underlined and then check yourself again. Use class time and whatever free time you have to review the text and discuss it with colleagues, classmates, and your instructor. If you wish to expand your understanding of particular aspects of educational research, read some of the references given at the end of the chapter.

*4. Complete the application problems.* Most of the chapters have application objectives as well as concept mastery objectives. A good way to increase your skill and check your achievement of the application objectives is to complete the Application Problems at the end of most chapters. After you complete these problems, check your answers against the model answers given in the back of the book.

*5. Review previous chapters.* As you progress through the book, review the objectives and the material you have underlined in previous chapters before starting to read a new chapter. You will find that each chapter builds on what you have learned in the previous chapters. If you are to become skillful in locating and interpreting educational research, you cannot afford to skip chapters or to let the main concepts in the early chapters become hazy while studying the later chapters.

*6. Prepare for tests.* If you follow the strategy described above, you will find it easy to prepare for tests. Reread the objectives and underlined material once or twice, and you should be ready. However, you can prepare even better if you work with a classmate as a last step in your study sequence. Go through your underlined material for the first chapter to be covered on the test, and ask your classmate questions. Check her answers and add any ideas that she omitted. For the next chapter, reverse roles and have her ask questions on the concepts she has underlined. This is also a good strategy for getting to know your classmates.

# CHAPTER 1

# USING RESEARCH TO IMPROVE EDUCATIONAL PRACTICE

## Overview

The main goal of this book is to help you become an intelligent consumer of educational research. To achieve this goal, you must develop skills in (1) defining your problem clearly and specifically, (2) locating research literature that is relevant to the problem, (3) evaluating research reports, and (4) interpreting research findings. In this chapter we present an overview of the book and the chapters in which these skills are described. We then compare the use of the educational research literature, and when appropriate your own action research, with personal experience and expert advice to make educational decisions. Also, we summarize the key characteristics of educational research, and describe commonly held views of educational practitioners concerning the benefits and limitations of educational research. Finally, we preview the contents of each chapter and make suggestions to help you get the most value from this book.

## Objectives

1. Describe the skills that must be mastered in order to use the research literature to improve educational practice.
2. Explain the characteristics of educational research.
3. Describe the main benefits and concerns of practitioners in using educational research findings to improve practice.
4. Explain the pros and cons of personal experience, expert advice, review of educational research literature, and conduct of action research as aids in making educational decisions.
5. Understand how each chapter in this book will contribute to your skills as a consumer of educational research.

## Characteristics of Educational Research

Every human being has learned certain skills and information. Also, most of us have received formal education and have contributed to the funding of education through taxes or in other ways. As a result, we have knowledge and opinions about such matters as what students should learn in order to function effectively in society, the characteristics of schools and students, and what teaching strategies are appropriate to achieve a particular objective. Besides this general knowledge, educators receive specialized training in curriculum and instructional methods and in the particular subjects they teach. How does educational research add to or differ from what you already know about education?

Educational research involves the systematic collection of information (sometimes called *data*) to describe, predict, control, or explain the phenomena involved in learning and teaching. These different functions of research can be understood by considering a specific example from research on study skills. Educators, and the public at large, already "know" that students who study effectively are more likely to do well in school than those who have poor study skills. However, knowledge of pertinent research findings allows us to go beyond general hunches or statements about the value of a particular educational practice.

With respect to *description,* researchers investigating the value of study skills might start out by identifying a group of students who get good grades. They might then observe the students in class or during free study periods outside of class, when they are presumed to be reading their textbooks, and record the behaviors in which the students engage. The researchers might find that these high-achieving students take a lot of notes on their reading and that their notes have certain characteristics, for example, definitions of key terms. This is an example of the use of research to *describe* behavior.

Now suppose that the researchers form two hypotheses (that is, educated guesses): first, that students who take a lot of notes on their reading will receive higher grades than students who take few or no notes on their reading, and second, that students whose notes have more of certain characteristics will receive higher grades than students whose notes have fewer of the characteristics. Using trained observers, the researchers record the amount of time each student spends taking notes during a fixed amount of study time. They also analyze the content of the notes and record the prevalence of the characteristics being studied. Then the researchers look at the grades of those students whose note-taking time was above average and compare them to the grades of those students whose note-taking time was below average. A similar analysis is made of the characteristics of the students' notes. If the students who take more notes and more notes of a certain type turn out to have higher grades, the researchers have demonstrated that one can *predict* school achievement by knowing how much time students spend taking notes on their reading.

Suppose the researchers decide next to train students to take notes on their reading, using what they have learned from the descriptive and prediction research to design the training program. They give one group of students extensive training in note taking, and another group of students does not receive training. They compare the two groups following the training period, to see whether the trained students took more notes overall, and more notes having the targeted characteristics, than the nontrained students. At the end of the term they also find out the grades of each group. If trained students took more and better notes and also got better grades, the researchers have demonstrated that one can *control* student achievement by training students in note taking.

Finally, suppose that the researchers seek to theorize why students' note-taking behavior affects their school grades. Based on the researchers' knowledge of learning theory, they reason that the students who took more notes overall and more notes of a certain kind were cognitively processing the information from their textbooks to move it from short-term memory into long-term memory. They thus have used learning theory to *explain* the relationship between note taking and school achievement. This theoretical explanation may stimulate further research to produce more refined descriptions of students' note-taking behavior, better predictions of school grades, and better training in note-taking skills.

Notice that our hypothetical researchers used organized, systematic procedures to define a problem for investigation, to collect information that bears on the problem, and to draw inferences and conclusions based on the information that was collected. For educators to be familiar with and make use of this research, the researchers would also need to publish their findings in scholarly books or journals.

The work of the hypothetical researchers we have described exemplifies three important criteria that educational researchers seek to achieve in conducting research: objectivity, generalizability, and replicability. We will briefly explain what we mean by each criterion.

## OBJECTIVITY

All researchers have certain biases and assumptions, based not only on their personality and demographic characteristics (age, race, socioeconomic status, etc.) but also on their particular experience. However, educational researchers design their research to overcome these biases as much as possible. To be objective, they seek to define clearly the phenomena being studied and to use procedures to study or measure those phenomena that others will agree are reasonable and accurate. The researchers' objectivity can be checked by determining whether other researchers can use the same measures to record similar events and obtain the same results. If other researchers obtain different results with the same measures, we can conclude that there is bias somewhere in the research procedures.

## GENERALIZABILITY

Most of us have limited experience from which to generalize to other settings. We may know what works for us as educators, but we do not know whether it will work for other educators. Researchers overcome this problem by selecting subjects (students, teachers, or some other group) who are representative of the population to which they wish to generalize.

By selecting representative samples, researchers can be more certain that their results will apply to other individuals who are similar to the sample. In medicine, for example, patients can receive medical advice and physicians can be given guidelines for practice based on researchers' generalizations about the risks and benefits of drugs or other treatments found from research studies conducted with a small percentage of cases. Researchers are careful about selecting their samples because they want to learn what is *generally* true rather than what is true of only a few individuals or an individual case.

**REPLICABILITY**

A goal of those who conduct and use educational research is to accumulate evidence over time that can be used to validate, or to disprove, commonly held notions about learning and learners. Researchers thus attempt to design their studies and describe their procedures in such a way that other researchers can replicate their research findings. If other researchers duplicate the procedures used in previous research and obtain similar results, we can have greater confidence in the findings. Conversely, if other researchers obtain different results, we will have less confidence in the original findings.

When conflicting results occur, we need to examine the various research studies to determine whether the original study or replications based on it showed evidence of systematic bias or some unusual conditions. Another possibility is that each study obtained valid but different results because of differences in research procedures or in the characteristics of the sample.

# Benefits and Drawbacks of Educational Research

Unfortunately, much of the useful information that has emerged from educational research is difficult to locate and even more difficult to interpret and relate to the practical problems that teachers and school administrators must address. Although we have little objective information about the degree to which teachers use research in decision making, the evidence that does exist suggests that use is minimal. For example, 88 percent of the in-service teachers surveyed by Reys and Yeager (1974) reported that they seldom or never read research articles. A more recent survey (Owen, Malcolm, & Hall, 1982) supports these findings.

James Shaver points out that many people ignore research results in areas such as the link of smoking to lung cancer and of the nonuse of seat belts to injury in auto accidents (Shaver, 1982). He asks why teachers should be different in their inattention to research. One answer is that, because teachers belong to a profession, they should seek any relevant information that will help them advance in their profession and do their jobs better. In general, physicians do not ignore medical research, and mechanical engineers do not ignore the results of research on the properties of metals and other materials they use to design and build new machines.

In a recent educational research course taught by one of our colleagues at the University of Oregon, students were asked to brainstorm their concerns about educational research and their perceptions of its potential benefits. Most of the students were experienced public school teachers or administrators enrolled in a master's degree program. They identified three major concerns about educational research. First, they felt that educational research was intimidating, either because the terminology and statistics were difficult to understand or because they were not sure how to interpret or apply the results. Second, they felt that the research they had been exposed to had actually *increased* their distrust of educational research. Their reasons included a sense that some researchers were biased and that research findings were removed from practical classroom reality and offered glib answers to difficult problems. Third, they felt educational research actually could decrease their effectiveness as practitioners. Their reasons included fear that they could try something based on positive research outcomes and find that it did not work, that they might be pressured to behave differently as educators because of the political use of research results, and that the findings of research might cause them to distrust their own experience and intuition.

We recommend that you reflect on the extent to which you have these concerns, and others as well. Share your concerns with colleagues who, like you, are examining the possible relevance of educational research to their own work in education. If you have some negative feelings about research, know that you are not alone. We suggest that you keep your concerns in mind when you read research but also that you keep an *open* mind to its potential value.

The students in the course also saw some major possible benefits of educational research. First, they felt that familiarity with research methodology and findings would empower them as educators. Their reasons included a belief that they could use research findings to help them grow professionally. For example, they felt that the study of research could encourage self-analysis, provide alternatives to their standard operating procedures, and help them communicate more effectively with their students as well as with administrators, parents, and school board members. Second, they felt that familiarity with research findings would reduce their isolation as teachers by providing an "outside" perspective on their problems and by serving as a basis for peer collaboration. Third, they believed that educational research would increase their effectiveness as instructors by offering them new ideas and by keeping their teaching dynamic. For example, they thought that the research literature could save them time by pointing out useful procedures and materials they could use instead of reinventing the wheel.

# Methods of Making Educational Decisions

Many educators have succeeded in their jobs for years without ever reading educational research literature or conducting an action research project. They generally have relied on personal experience or expert advice to make decisions and solve problems. Why, then, are we recommending the use of research literature reviews and action research to supplement these methods? To answer this question, we need to consider the pros and cons of each of these four decision-making approaches.

## PERSONAL EXPERIENCE

Most people find personal experience to be an attractive basis for making decisions. We generally are more comfortable with approaches we have tried ourselves, as opposed to those that have been successful for others. Also, personal experience has the advantages of being quick and easy. Thus, when a decision must be made immediately, personal experience may be the only approach available. Or the decision may be too minor to justify a review of the research literature or an action research project, both of which are rigorous and time-consuming.

You should keep in mind, though, that personal experience has serious limitations when important decisions must be made. First, we accumulate personal experience in a very haphazard fashion. In educational situations, there is no reason to assume that the students we teach or the situations in which we teach them are representative. Thus, personal experience with unique groups of students may suggest solutions that will be totally ineffective with other groups of students. For example, in the late 1950s after the Soviet Union had launched *Sputnik,* there was a great clamor to improve the American high school science curriculum. University professors in fields such as chemistry and physics developed new curricula based on their university experience. In most high schools these curricula failed because they were too difficult for all but the brightest students. Personal experience in university teaching did not prove to be a good basis for deciding what to include in high school science courses.

Another shortcoming of personal experience is that our memory of past experience is often faulty. If we are committed to a particular method or program, we are more likely to remember incidents when it was successful than when it failed. Also, making decisions on the basis of personal experience ignores the knowledge and experience accumulated by others. A basic rule in decision making is that the more relevant information decision makers have, the more likely they are to make sound decisions.

## EXPERT ADVICE

Relying on the advice of an expert is usually a better basis for decision making than relying solely on one's own experience. However, this approach has limitations too. Experts usually base their opinions on their personal experience, their knowledge of the experience of others, and, to some extent, the research of others. However, experts' interpretation of the work of others tends to be influenced by their own personal biases.

In effect, experts function as brokers between their client and the researchers and scholars who have contributed relevant knowledge and ideas. This brokering function can be very helpful because the expert is usually better able than the practitioner to weigh and interpret the research evidence. However, if experts are committed to a particular solution or if their experience has been gained in settings that are substantially different from the local situation, their advice may not lead to a sound decision.

Despite the limitations of expert advice, we recommend that you identify and contact experts for information related to the educational problems that concern you. Talking to an expert can save you time and can give you a personal sense of how research is generated, retrieved, and applied. We suggest, however, that you use experts primarily to locate relevant research literature rather than relying entirely on the conclusions that they have reached on the basis of this literature.

## SEARCHES OF THE RESEARCH LITERATURE

When you conduct your own search and evaluation of the research literature, you can be more confident that all relevant findings and theories have been reviewed. If you conduct your search with an open mind, the danger of omitting or distorting a particular point of view is much less than if you rely on personal experience or expert advice alone. In most cases, a literature search for information related to a well-defined local problem will produce information that is recent and relevant. Also, by searching the literature yourself, you will achieve a depth of understanding of the problem that can rarely be gained in any other way.

Careful search of the literature involves considerable effort. However, if it produces a better solution to an important problem in your classroom, school, or other setting, you probably will consider it worth the effort.

## CONDUCT OF ACTION RESEARCH

If a literature search does not produce a satisfactory solution to your problem, you should consider carrying out an action research project. Assuming you are concerned with a specific solution to a local problem, your research sample need only be representative of the local population of students to whom the results will be applied. Also, you need use only the simplest statistical procedures. In fact, many action research projects need no statistical analysis at all to serve their purpose as an aid to decision making.

Action research is a far better basis for decision making than personal experience. Most of the discoveries and progress made by Western civilization during the past two hundred years have been achieved by using the scientific method to attack problems and questions. Action research employs the scientific method to solve the problems of the educational practitioner. Chapter 15 will give you the necessary guidelines for reviewing or conducting an action research study.

# Preview of Chapters 2–15

If you want to benefit from the findings of educational research, you must develop several skills. One of the most essential of these skills is locating documents that report, interpret, evaluate, or synthesize research studies. In recent years the computer has been harnessed to the task of locating documents (books, journal articles, technical reports, speeches, etc.) that relate to a given educational problem. A computer search of the educational literature has eliminated most of the drudgery involved in manual procedures that were necessary in the past. However, the computer is no more efficient than the search plan that is entered into the computer. Therefore, whether you choose to do a computer search or a manual search, you must learn how to define your problem and to develop a search plan for investigating it.

Chapter 2 describes how to define a problem for investigation and discusses useful preliminary sources for identifying relevant research documents. Chapter 3 discusses the advantages of conducting a computer search for research documents and procedures for doing so. Chapter 4 describes how to locate and record information from primary source documents located in your search.

Once you have located documents that relate to your problem or question, you have a difficult task. You must read them, determine how much confidence you can place in the findings, and decide how to apply the findings to your own problem or question. In the past, few educational practitioners knew enough about the research process to interpret the typical research report. Educational researchers reported their findings mainly for the benefit of other researchers and often gave little attention to the application of their findings to practical educational problems. The result has been a serious lack of communication between the researcher and the practitioner. Researchers and practitioners have begun working together to solve this communication problem. For example, Alan Bell (1983) describes how research on understanding mathematics can be applied to mathematics teaching. This type of report can be very useful because it makes explicit the connection between research and practice. Reports like this can save you much time in applying the findings of research to the real-life problems that concern you.

Another solution to the communication problem between researchers and practitioners is to develop the latter's knowledge and skill for reading and applying research. The goal of this book is to help you to do so. For example, suppose that a researcher investigated a sample of students entirely from schools serving middle-class children. If you wish to apply the research findings, you must be aware that the sample is biased in favor of middle-class students, and you must have the skill to interpret the results in terms of their applicability to your own students, who may come predominantly from a different social class.

Obtaining a thorough knowledge of the research process requires much more time for study than most educators have available. In this book you will not learn enough to make sophisticated interpretations of research. However, you will gain the *minimum essentials* that you need to use research to make better educational decisions. Chapters 5, 6, 7, and 8 are aimed at giving you these essentials.

In Chapter 5, you will be introduced to the task of evaluating a research report. You will learn what to look for to identify possible bias and to evaluate the soundness of the study's objectives, hypotheses, research design, and data analysis.

All research involves measurement, and the validity of research results is determined to a great degree by the accuracy of the measures that the researcher employs. Therefore, to interpret educational research and apply the findings to practical school problems, you must have a basic understanding of educational measurement. Chapter 6 describes the use of paper-and-pencil tests, questionnaires, interviews, and direct observations as measures in educational research. If you have taken a course in educational measurement, much of this chapter will be a review for you. If not, Chapter 6 will give you the minimum foundation you need to understand the role of educational measures in research.

Chapter 7 provides an overview of the statistical tools that you need to interpret research findings. Researchers use statistics to measure relationships or differences between the groups they are studying and to draw inferences about the populations from which the researcher's sample was drawn. Most educational researchers have had considerable training in statistics, and most of the quantitative research reports that you will read use statistical procedures to test the researcher's hypotheses. Our goal in writing Chapter 7 was to give you a simple introduction to some of the concepts underlying statistical theory and then to describe in brief, nontechnical language the most widely used statistical procedures. This information will give you some insights into why researchers selected particular statistical tools, how they analyzed their results, and what the results mean. If you find that you want more detailed information, we urge you to read an introductory text in educational statistics. It will better prepare you to interpret the statistical analyses presented in research reports.

A difficulty in applying research findings when making educational decisions is the problem of combining findings from different research studies that represent diverse perspectives and obtain different results. Chapter 8 describes several strategies that you can use to synthesize research findings. In that chapter and in all subsequent chapters in the book, you will find examples of actual research articles that illustrate the type of research covered there. Reading these articles will give you necessary practice in analyzing and interpreting different types of research. The article in Chapter 8 describes a particular statistical approach to combining research findings on a given problem: *meta-analysis*.

Once you have gained a basic understanding of the educational research process, the next step is to learn about the many different types of educational research. Chapters 9 through 15 introduce you to the major research methods represented in the current educational literature. In each of these chapters you will learn about the unique strengths and characteristics of each type of research method and the reasoning processes needed to interpret the findings that it yields.

Chapter 9 introduces you to a type of educational research that is based on a very different paradigm than that described in the remaining chapters, namely, qualitative research. Qualitative researchers are not interested in analyzing or measuring discrete aspects of an educational problem. Rather, their goal is to gain an overall grasp of an educational phenomenon in all its complexity. Observation and interview are the primary research procedures, and statistical analysis is not used at all because only a few examples of the phenomenon are studied. Qualitative research is easier for the educational practitioner to understand because it is based on techniques similar to those that practitioners use in their everyday personal experience. We hope to demonstrate, however, that qualitative research, like the other research methods discussed in this book, is based on a disciplined inquiry that goes well beyond personal experience in investigating an educational phenomenon.

Chapter 10 introduces you to the simplest type of quantitative research, namely, descriptive research. One of the first steps in any scientific discipline is to describe objectively the phenomena of interest. This step is necessary to identify the factors that may be involved in cause-and-effect relationships, which are usually of most interest to researchers.

Education is no exception in the need for descriptive research. Therefore, you will find that much educational research is aimed at describing the characteristics of the students, the teachers, and the educational environment. In discussing descriptive research, we will emphasize the use of questionnaires, interviews, and direct observations—all well-established ways of collecting descriptive data.

Chapter 11 provides an introduction to causal-comparative research. This method involves comparing two groups of individuals who differ in some important characteristic in order to identify possible causes for the difference. Causal-comparative research is useful in studying factors that cannot be manipulated in an experiment, such as the causes of juvenile delinquency, the effects of brain damage on human performance, or the effects of broken homes on the social adjustment of children. Because causal-comparative research is conducted after the fact, that is, *after* subjects have become delinquent or suffered brain damage, it can only be used to explore *possible* causes and effects rather than to demonstrate true causal relationships.

Chapter 12 provides an introduction to correlational research, which is similar to causal-comparative research except for the statistical analysis procedures it employs. For example, researchers using the causal-comparative method to study why some students are at risk of leaving school before completion might form two groups of students: those classified as at risk and those classified as not at risk. They then would investigate whether the two groups differ on certain factors. If differences are found, these factors may be interpreted as potential causes of the at-risk syndrome.

By contrast, researchers using the correlational method would conceptualize and measure the at-risk syndrome as a continuum. In other words, they would assume that the at-risk syndrome is present in most students to varying degrees. In their statistical analysis, therefore, they would relate students' scores on one or more measures of being at risk to their scores on measures of factors hypothesized to be potential causes of the at-risk syndrome. Relationships between sets of scores are determined by computing correlation coefficients. These coefficients are a statistical expression of the magnitude of the relationship between the scores of a group of subjects on one measure and their scores on another measure.

The statistical precision possible in the correlational method makes it more suited for prediction studies than the causal-comparative method. For example, correlation coefficients can be computed to express the magnitude of relationship between the grade point average of college seniors and scores they obtained on the Scholastic Aptitude Test (SAT), taken before starting college. Educators can use these coefficients to predict the grade point averages that future students are likely to earn, based on their SAT scores. The predictions can be used to select and counsel prospective college students.

When educators hear the term *research,* they tend to think of experiments. They may have this association from reading about classic experiments in the physical sciences, and perhaps they have repeated such experiments in laboratory classes. Although education and the other behavioral sciences are far less advanced than the physical sciences, experiments carried out in education have contributed significantly to advances in our knowledge about human learning, motivation, and effective teaching. Chapter 13 introduces you to the experimental research method.

In the simplest form of experiment we hypothesize that a particular teaching method, curriculum, or other intervention (called the *experimental treatment*) will bring about changes in the behavior of the individuals who are exposed to that treatment. Other individuals serve as a *control group,* meaning that they are not given the experimental treatment but their performance is measured in the same way as that of the experimental treatment group. Comparing the performance of the two groups on the measure then permits us to estimate the effect of the experimental treatment. The essential requirement for a "true" experiment is that subjects are *randomly* assigned to the experimental and control groups, meaning that each subject has an equal chance of being in either group.

*Quasi-experimental* research is similar to experimental research, except that subjects are not randomly assigned to the experimental and control groups. Quasi-experiments are common in education because school authorities often do not permit researchers to assign students randomly to the experimental and control groups. Thus, students must be assigned to these groups on a nonrandom basis. For example, Mr. Smith's second-period class is designated the experimental group, and Ms. Johnson's third-period class is designated the control group.

Another variation of the experimental method is *single-subject research,* which involves investigating the effects of an experimental treatment on one individual. This method is especially appropriate for studying individualized teaching methods and curriculum programs. Also, it is used when only a few individuals are available for study, as is the case in special education research with students who have rare handicapping conditions.

The last two chapters in the book describe research methods that have a direct link to the improvement of educational practice. Chapter 14 describes how evaluation research is used to determine the effectiveness of educational methods and materials that are under development or in final form. Chapter 15 is designed to give you not only the knowledge of action research as a type of research reported in the literature but also the essential skills needed to conduct your own action research when appropriate. Whereas most educational research seeks to discover knowledge that can be applied to a broad range of educational situations, action research aims at gathering evidence that relates to a specific local problem. In other words, it gives you a way to apply the scientific method to the solution of local educational problems.

Chapters 9 through 15 include research articles exemplifying each type of educational research. You will have an opportunity to apply what you have learned about educational research by evaluating and interpreting these articles. We selected only articles that are good examples of educational research. Moreover, they deal with topics that are of interest to most educators and that report findings with clear applications to educational practice.

# Chapter References

BELL, A. W. (1983). The design of teaching using research on understanding. *International Reviews on Mathematical Education, 15*(2), 83–89.

OWEN, J. M., MALCOLM, C. K., & HALL, K. C. (1982, April). *Alternative forms of communicated knowledge and their effects on Australian teachers.* (ED 217 535).[1] Melbourne, Australia: Melbourne State College, Tertiary Education Research Unit.

REYS, R. E., & YEAGER. T. (1974). Elementary teachers and research in mathematics education. *School Science and Mathematics, 74*(5), 431–436.

SHAVER, J. (1982, November). *Making research useful to teachers*. Presented at the annual meeting of the National Council for the Social Studies, Boston.

# Recommended Reading

EAKER, R. E., & HUFFMAN, J. O. (1981). *Teacher perceptions of dissemination of research on teaching findings*. (ED 205 501). East Lansing: Michigan State University, Institute for Research and Teaching.

This questionnaire survey examines the perceptions of 105 teachers concerning the use of educational research findings as a resource for instructional improvement. The results generally indicate that teachers believe that research findings have practical classroom applications. A review of the responses given to 40 questionnaire items provides some useful insights into teachers' perceptions and attitudes about educational research.

GAGE, N. L. (1985). *Hard gains in the soft sciences: The case of pedagogy*. Bloomington, IN: Phi Delta Kappa.

Using a clear and interesting style, the author discusses some of the gains made in research on teaching. Nine experimental studies designed to improve teaching through in-service teacher training are reviewed. Of these, eight brought about significant improvement in teaching performance as well as in student achievement, attitudes, or behavior. This finding demonstrates that despite the inertia that can keep teachers doing the same thing decade after decade, real improvement in teaching can be achieved. Finally, a number of models for the study of teaching are described. Students will gain some valuable insights into teaching and its scientific study.

NATIONAL DISSEMINATION STUDY GROUP. (1988). *Education programs that work: A collection of proven exemplary educational programs and practices. Edition 14*. Longmont, CO: Sopris West.

This publication presents an overview of all educational programs approved for national dissemination by the U.S. Department of Education. The programs are divided into the following sections: (1) adult education, (2) administration/organizational arrangements, (3) alternative schools/programs/bilingual/migrant programs, (4) basic skills—language arts/writing, (5) basic skills—mathematics, (6) basic skills—multidisciplinary, (7) basic skills—reading, (8) career/vocational education, (9) early childhood/parent involvement, (10) gifted and talented/technology/special interests, (11) health/physical education, and (12) education/learning disabilities. It can be found on microfiche in most university libraries. Ask the librarian for the *Resources in Education* (ERIC) microfiche ED 296 984. See Chapter 2 for more information about the Educational Resources Information Center (ERIC) system.

ROSNOW, R. L., & ROSENTHAL, R. (1984). *Understanding behavioral science: Research methods for research consumers*. New York: McGraw-Hill.

This small book is an excellent supplement to your text. The sections on the nature of behavioral research and the limits of behavioral research are especially recommended for teachers who want to gain more depth of understanding of the research process in the behavioral sciences.

TRAVERS, R. M. W. (1983). *How research has changed American schools*. Kalamazoo, MI: Mythas Press.

This book will be useful to the student who wants to gain a long-range perspective on the impact of research on American education. It is organized by major research areas, such as the psychology of school subjects, and by the work of important early researchers like Judd and Thorndike. In general, Travers's treatment of early research in education is the best part of the book.

**ARTICLES ON RESEARCH UTILIZATION**

The following articles are examples of the kind of information you can find in the educational literature to help you utilize research results in your teaching.

BROPHY, J. (1988). Research on teacher effects: Uses and abuses. *Elementary School Journal, 89*(1), 3–21.

CARRAHER, T. N., & SCHLIEMANN, A. D. (1988). Research into practice: Using money to teach about the decimal system. *Arithmetic Teacher, 36*(4), 42–43.

EWART, A. (1987). Research in experiential education: An overview. *Journal of Experiential Education, 19*(2), 4–7.

GRIFFIN, G. A., & BARNES, S. (1986). Using research findings to change school and classroom practices: Results of an experimental study. *American Educational Research Journal, 23*(4), 572–586.

ROSS, D. D., & KYLE, D. W. (1987). Helping preservice teachers learn to use teacher effectiveness research. *Journal of Teacher Education, 38*(2), 40–44.

# Chapter Note

1. This number indicates that the reference is available in *Resources in Education (RIE)*. Most college libraries have microfiche copies of all *RIE* documents.

# PART II

# SOURCES OF EDUCATIONAL INFORMATION

To use the findings of educational research in making decisions, you must first find the information you need. The difficulty you face is not a lack of information but rather the great amount of information that is available, and thus how to access it efficiently. You first need to know, therefore, how to find information to help you define your problem and to give you an overview of the relevant research.

The knowledge base in educational research continues to expand at an accelerating rate. Similarly, the computer technology that stores and accesses that knowledge base is changing rapidly. Thus you also need to know how to determine the current availability and content of relevant data bases and how to carry out efficient searches of the research literature. The chapters in Part II are designed to help you locate and use the varied sources of information about educational research that are now available.

In Chapter 2 we discuss the differences between preliminary, primary, and secondary information sources and the value of each. The chapter describes a strategy for finding educational literature that bears on a problem or question that concerns you. It provides suggestions for contacting experts and for reviewing secondary sources to help you define your problem. It discusses procedures for conducting a manual search of the research literature and describes various preliminary sources that you can search. You also will learn a format for preparing bibliographic records to keep track of your information sources.

Chapter 3 describes how to conduct a computer search of preliminary sources to find research literature bearing on your problem. It explains the great advantages of this procedure over the manual search of printed index volumes. Several data bases relevant to education are described. The chapter also discusses how to define your search terms or descriptors to design your computer search. By carefully combining appropriate search terms, you will be able to identify a manageable number of references that relate closely to (1) the topics with which you are concerned, (2) the pertinent characteristics of your target audience or work site, and (3) the period of time in which you are most interested. The chapter also describes how to print your references and options concerning the level of detail that the printed output will include.

Chapter 4 describes the types of publications in which most primary sources appear and discusses how to use your local university library, and other libraries if necessary, to obtain relevant primary sources. The chapter suggests steps for classifying and taking notes on primary sources to help you keep track of information relevant to your problem. It concludes with a suggested procedure for writing a report of your findings. This report can be designed to meet requirements for a course or degree program in which you are enrolled or simply to share with colleagues.

CHAPTER **2**

# LOCATING EDUCATIONAL INFORMATION

## Overview

This chapter discusses the steps you should follow in reviewing the educational literature for research on your problem or question: (1) defining your problem, (2) contacting appropriate experts, (3) reviewing secondary sources, (4) selecting the most appropriate preliminary sources, (5) translating your problem statement into key words, and (6) searching preliminary sources for relevant references.

We also explain three sources of information: primary (original research reports), secondary (reviews of research), and preliminary (indexes of the research literature). We describe the most important preliminary sources to use in identifying primary and secondary sources in education, and we explain how to use them in conducting a literature review. We emphasize the need to use a systematic procedure to record bibliographic data for references you identify.

## Objectives

1. Define a preliminary, primary, and secondary source; give an example of each; and describe how each is used in a review of educational research literature.
2. Describe the appropriate use of secondary sources and of contact with experts as part of your literature search.
3. Given a general problem statement, write a specific problem statement and make up a list of key words or terms.
4. Describe four preliminary sources that are useful for locating publications related to educational problems.
5. Describe how to translate key words into the appropriate ERIC descriptors and *Psychological Index* terms.
6. Describe the steps to take in conducting a manual search of *Current Index to Journals in Education, Education Index, Psychological Abstracts,* and *Resources in Education.*
7. Describe a systematic procedure for writing bibliographic citations and converting them to a single format.

In education, as in the social sciences, research rarely provides final answers for the questions that concern practitioners and researchers. However, research has generated much useful information that can help educators decide on a course of action for nearly any educational problem.

The research literature helps you determine what is known about a question or problem. Then this knowledge can be weighed and interpreted in terms of your local educational situation. Two keys are needed to open the door to this literature. The first key is the ability to locate published research findings that are relevant to your problem. This chapter and the two following chapters will help you develop this skill. The second key is the ability to evaluate the evidence you find and relate it to the question you seek to answer. Chapters 5, 6, 7, and 8 will provide you with the basic tools needed to evaluate and synthesize research evidence. Subsequent chapters will give you experience in evaluating actual research studies.

# Preliminary, Primary, and Secondary Sources

To locate and use educational research, you must be familiar with three major sources of information. Preliminary sources are used to locate books, articles, and other educational documents that relate to your problem. Most preliminary sources are either indexes, such as *Education Index,* which identify the author, title, and publisher of educational documents, or they are abstracts, such as *Psychological Abstracts,* which give the same information as an index plus a brief summary of the document's contents. The documents are usually journal articles, papers presented at professional conferences, technical reports, or book chapters.

Primary sources are documents in which the persons who actually carried out a research study report their findings. In other words, primary source information is communicated directly from the researcher to the reader. Most primary sources in education are found in journals, such as the *Journal of Experimental Education.* Each article in these journals typically reports on a different research project. However, some books contain reports of original research, in which case they are considered primary sources.

Secondary sources are publications in which the author is reporting on research that someone else carried out. The most common secondary sources in education are scholarly books and textbooks. For example, a text in educational psychology will usually discuss the findings of the classical and recent research in areas such as human development, motivation, learning, instructional methods, and assessment. Or a chapter reviewing research on cooperative learning will summarize the findings of many researchers who have investigated this method.

The advantage of secondary sources is that they give you a quick and readable overview of research and opinion related to an educational topic. A potential disadvantage is that the authors may not accurately report and interpret the primary source findings. Since their coverage must be brief, they will surely omit much of the information in the primary sources, and they may select information or interpret the research findings to support their own point of view.

When seeking information about an educational problem, we advise you first to contact appropriate experts and also to read a few secondary sources to get a quick overview of the relevant research. Then use preliminary sources to locate relevant primary sources, and read them to get detailed, current information about your problem. This procedure is described in detail in the following section.

# Steps in Reviewing Educational Research Literature

We will first define each step and then discuss it in greater depth.

*1. Define the problem.* Your problem is the question for which you are seeking an answer. The problem description should be short, specific, and clearly written. (Chapter 2)

*2. Contact appropriate experts for information.* Identifying experts in the topic, both local and located elsewhere, can give you a speedy and personal introduction to research bearing on your problem. (Chapter 2)

*3. Review secondary sources.* Reading a brief discussion of your problem area in one or two secondary sources gives you an introduction to your problem and helps you define it in more precise terms. (Chapter 2)

*4. Select the most appropriate preliminary source(s).* For most educational problems, you can identify one or two preliminary sources that will lead you to information relevant to your problem. (Chapter 2)

*5. Translate the problem statement into key words.* To look up relevant studies in the subject index of the preliminary source you select, you must make a list of key words or descriptors that fit the main concepts related to your problem. (Chapter 2)

*6. Search the preliminary source(s).* You first should decide whether to conduct a manual or computer search. Then, follow a systematic search procedure and make bibliographic citations on primary source references that appear relevant to your problem. (Chapters 2 and 3)

*7. Prepare bibliographic records.* Read the primary sources related to your problem, and make bibliographic records that outline the relevant information in each of these sources. (Chapters 4 and 5)

*8. Write notes on pertinent primary sources,* and organize the notes. The findings from the studies you have reviewed should be interpreted and organized to give you the best available answer to your problem. (Chapters 4 and 5)

*9. Write a report.* Emphasize the studies that contribute most to solving your problem. Interpret each study in terms of its relevance to your local situation. (Chapters 4 and 5)

## STEP 1: DEFINE THE PROBLEM

The first step in locating relevant research is to define your problem as clearly and specifically as you can. It usually is easiest to frame your problem in the form of the question you want to answer.

A broad, fuzzy question such as "What does research say about the effectiveness of teaching methods?" is not very helpful when you start looking into the preliminary sources because more than 40,000 documents published in the past 15 years have something to do with teaching methods. More specific questions related to teaching methods might be these: "Does whole-class instruction or individual instruction result in greater pupil achievement in primary grade classrooms?" "How effective is the skill-centered method of teaching first-grade reading?" "What teaching methods are used by peer tutors in the elementary school?" Narrow your problem's scope until it covers only the specific question you seek to answer.

## STEP 2: CONTACT APPROPRIATE EXPERTS FOR INFORMATION

Many problems that concern you as an educator have been thought about by others. To save yourself time and to make your search for information more personal and rewarding, we recommend that you identify experts who can help you find the information you need. Talk to people in your own institution and ask for referrals to others. If you live near an institution of higher education, examine the catalog for departments and individuals dealing with your topic. At the library, talk to the reference librarian and ask to see directories of organizations that deal with educational issues.

For example, here in Eugene, Oregon, a teacher concerned with teaching students relevant, current information about career choices has a ready resource at hand: the Oregon Career Information System (OCIS), a computerized information system located at the University of Oregon and staffed by many education professionals. By contacting some of these experts, you could obtain a good deal of information about not only this system and the research on which it is based but also other aspects of career education.

Once you have identified appropriate experts, you will need to call, write, or visit them. If you ask appropriate questions, a few contacts may result in a wealth of information related to your problem.

## STEP 3: REVIEW SECONDARY SOURCES

Once you have stated your problem or question in specific terms, it is a good idea to check one or two secondary sources in order to form a general picture of research that has been done on your topic. This step usually requires no more than a half day's reading, and the overview you get provides a framework that can fit your later reading of primary sources into a meaningful context.

To identify relevant secondary sources, you may need first to consult preliminary sources. *Books in Print,* the card catalog at your local library, *Education Index,* and *Psychological Abstracts* are secondary sources that are particularly useful for this purpose. We will describe them before proceeding to a description of some of the best secondary sources to examine for coverage of current educational problems.

***Books in Print.***    Many significant educational questions have not been dealt with recently by any of the major secondary sources described below. If this is true of your problem, your best chance of finding a discussion of recent research may lie in checking recent scholarly books, monographs, and textbooks.

The best source for locating these publications is the most recent edition of the Subject Guide to *Books in Print,* which is available in most libraries and bookstores. Start by looking up specific key terms related to your topic. For example, suppose you are interested in the academic achievement of minority children. In the 1988–

1989 edition, 2 recent books that appear to deal with this topic are listed under the heading Academic Achievement. Under Prediction of Scholastic Success, another relevant book is listed, and under Minorities Education 8 additional titles are listed. Thus, by using this source you would promptly identify 11 potentially useful books, all published since 1986. A quick scanning of the tables of contents of these books would probably locate the kind of overview of your problem that you usually seek in secondary sources.

If you find no scholarly books that relate specifically to your topic, you may find reports of research in a recent textbook on educational administration, child development, educational psychology, or another field of education. For example, a check of three randomly selected textbooks in educational psychology revealed that all of them contained brief discussions of such topics as motivation, reinforcement, sex roles, and reading instruction. Because most textbooks cover a broad subject, discussion of specific questions is usually brief, often less than a page. However, scholarly books cited in *Books in Print* usually deal with a more limited topic, covering it in much greater depth.

**Library Card Catalog.**   The subject card catalog in a university library is another good place to look for secondary sources. Keep in mind, however, that although most libraries purchase as many scholarly books as their budgets allow, their collection usually is not complete.

***Education Index* and *Psychological Abstracts.***   The main use of these preliminary sources is to locate primary source documents. However, they also can be used to locate new professional books in education and psychology.

Many secondary sources contain reviews of research on significant topics in education and related fields. Several examples are listed below in alphabetical order. To identify others, check with the reference librarian at your university library or check the documents listed in the Recommended Reading for this chapter.

***Encyclopedia of Educational Research.***   The third edition of this monumental work, published in 1982, includes the work of over 300 contributors in more than 2,000 pages. The contents are organized in alphabetical order by topic. However, if your topic is not found in the alphabetical listing, it is advisable to check the 12,000 entries in the index. This is an excellent source for getting a brief review of topics related to your area of interest.

**ERIC Clearinghouses.**   The Educational Resources Information Center (ERIC), which publishes two of the main preliminary sources in education described later in this chapter *(Resources in Education* and *Current Index to Journals in Education),* operates 16 clearinghouses and 4 adjunct clearinghouses. The names and addresses of each clearinghouse are presented in Figure 2.1 (p. 27). Each clearinghouse is responsible for cataloging, abstracting, and indexing relevant documents in its subject area. The clearinghouses also publish newsletters, bulletins, annotated bibliographies, and interpretive summaries dealing with high-interest topics. Copies of these publications may be obtained by contacting the appropriate clearinghouse.

***Handbook of Research on Teaching.***    This is an excellent source for students who are interested in research on various aspects of teaching. The third edition, published in 1986, contains 35 articles organized into five main areas: (1) theory and methods of research on teaching, (2) the social and institutional context of teaching, (3) research on teaching and teachers, (4) adapting teaching to differences among learners, and (5) research on the teaching of subjects and grade levels. Extensive bibliographies are provided. A subject index can be used to locate research on specific topics.

***International Encyclopedia of Education.***    Published in 1985, this 10-volume encyclopedia is the first major attempt to present an up-to-date overview of scholarship on educational problems, practices, and institutions all over the world. Where appropriate, research studies form the information base that authors used in describing the state of the art in their area of expertise. The encyclopedia entries are grouped into six major clusters, such as human development, the conduct of education, and evaluation and assessment.

**NSSE Yearbooks.**    Each year the National Society for the Study of Education (NSSE) publishes two yearbooks. Each yearbook covers recent research related to a major educational topic and contains 10 to 12 chapters that deal with different aspects of that topic. The chapters are written by experts in their field. Recent yearbooks of the NSSE are

| | | |
|---|---|---|
| 1989 | Part 1 | From Socrates to Software: The Teacher as Text and the Text as Teacher |
| | Part 2 | Schooling and Disability |
| 1988 | Part 1 | Critical Issues in Curriculum |
| | Part 2 | Cultural Literacy and the Idea of General Education |
| 1987 | Part 1 | The Ecology of School Renewal |
| | Part 2 | Society as Educator in an Age of Transition |
| 1986 | Part 1 | Microcomputers and Education |
| | Part 2 | The Teaching of Writing |
| 1985 | Part 1 | Education in School and Nonschool Settings |
| | Part 2 | The Humanities in Precollegiate Education |

The society also publishes a series of volumes on contemporary education issues. Recent titles in this series include *Contributing to Educational Change: Moral Development and Character Education* (1989), *Perspectives on Research and Practice* (1988), *Adapting Instruction to Student Differences* (1985), and *Colleges of Education: Perspectives on Their Future* (1985). A complete list of volumes in this series may be found at the back of the most recent NSSE yearbook.

**Research Annuals.**    A series of research annuals published by JAI Press covers several topics of interest to teachers, including early education, educational productiv-

CE  ADULT, CAREER AND VOCATIONAL EDUCATION
Ohio State University
1900 Kenny Road
Columbus, OH 43210-1090
(614) 292-4353; (800) 848-4815

CG  COUNSELING AND PERSONNEL SERVICES
University of Michigan
School of Education, Room 2108
610 East University Street
Ann Arbor, MI 48109-1259
(313) 764-9492

CS  READING AND COMMUNICATION SKILLS
Indiana University, Smith Research Center
2805 East 10th Street, Suite 150
Bloomington, IN 47408-2698
(812) 855-5847

EA  EDUCATIONAL MANAGEMENT
University of Oregon
1787 Agate Street
Eugene, OR 97403-5207
(503) 346-5043

EC  HANDICAPPED AND GIFTED CHILDREN
Council for Exceptional Children
1920 Association Drive
Reston, VA 22091-1589
(703) 620-3660

FL  LANGUAGES AND LINGUISTICS
Center for Applied Linguistics
1118 22nd Street, NW
Washington, DC 20037-0037
(202) 429-9551

HE  HIGHER EDUCATION
The George Washington University
One Dupont Circle, NW, Suite 630
Washington, DC 20036-1183
(202) 296-2597

IR  INFORMATION RESOURCES
Syracuse University
School of Education
Huntington Hall, Room 030
Syracuse, NY 13244-2340
(315) 443-3640

JC  JUNIOR COLLEGES
University of California at Los Angeles
Math-Sciences Building, Room 8118
405 Hillgard Avenue
Los Angeles, CA 90024-1564
(213) 825-3931

PS  ELEMENTARY AND EARLY CHILDHOOD
EDUCATION
University of Illinois
College of Education
805 West Pennsylvania Avenue
Urbana, IL 61801-4897
(217) 333-1386

RC  RURAL EDUCATION AND SMALL SCHOOLS
Appalachia Educational Laboratory
1031 Quarrier Street, PO Box 1348
Charleston, WV 25325-1348
(800) 624-9120; (304) 347-0400

SE  SCIENCE, MATHEMATICS, AND ENVIRONMENTAL
EDUCATION
Ohio State University
1200 Chambers Road, Room 310
Columbus, OH 43212-1792
(614) 292-6717

SO  SOCIAL STUDIES/SOCIAL SCIENCE EDUCATION
Indiana University
Social Studies Development Center
2805 East 10th Street, Suite 120
Bloomington, IN 47408-2698
(812) 855-3838

SP  TEACHER EDUCATION
American Association of Colleges for
Teacher Education
One Dupont Circle, NW, Suite 610
Washington, DC 20036-2412
(202) 293-2450

TM  TESTS, MEASUREMENT, AND EVALUATION
American Institutes for Research (AIR)
3333 K Street, NW
Washington, DC 20007-3893
(202) 342-5060

UD  URBAN EDUCATION
Teachers College, Columbia University
Main Hall, Room 300, Box 40
525 West 120th Street
New York, NY 10027-9998
(212) 678-3433

AR  ADJUNCT ERIC CLEARINGHOUSE FOR ART EDUCATION
Indiana University
Social Studies Development Center
2805 East 10th Street, Suite 120
Bloomington, IN 47408-2373

JS  ADJUNCT ERIC CLEARINGHOUSE FOR UNITED STATES-
JAPAN STUDIES
Indiana University
Social Studies Development Center
2805 East 10th Street, Suite 120
Bloomington, IN 47408-2373

LE  ADJUNCT ERIC CLEARINGHOUSE ON LITERACY
EDUCATION FOR LIMITED-ENGLISH-PROFICIENT ADULTS
Center for Applied Linguistics (CAL)
1118 22nd Street, NW
Washington, DC 20037

TA  ADJUNCT ERIC CLEARINGHOUSE ON CHAPTER 1
Chapter 1 Technical Assistance Center
Advanced Technology, Inc.
2601 Fortune Circle East, Suite 300-A
Indianapolis, IN 46241

Figure 2.1  Educational Resources Information Center (ERIC) Clearinghouses (Source: Reprinted from *Current Index to Journals in Education* [CIJE], vol. 23, number 10 and vol. 21, number 9. Copyright 1989 and 1991 by The Oryx Press, 4041 N. Central at Indian School Rd., Phoenix, AZ 85012. Used by permission of The Oryx Press.)

ity, learning and behavioral disabilities, motivation and achievement, reading and language research, and teaching. Each volume typically contains a dozen or more articles by eminent researchers in the field.

**Review of Educational Research.**    The *Review of Educational Research* consists entirely of reviews of research literature on educational topics. It is published quarterly, and each issue typically contains four to seven reviews. Each review includes an extensive bibliography, which may list primary source articles relevant to your problem. For example, the Spring 1989 issue includes a review of research by Steven Stahl and Patricia Miller on the effects of the whole-language and language-experience methods of teaching reading on beginning reading achievement. The text of this article covers 28 pages and cites more than 100 references.

**Review of Research in Education.**    The *Review of Research in Education* is an annual series that was started in 1973. Each volume contains chapters written by leading educational researchers that provide critical surveys of research in important problem areas. For example, Volume 16, published in 1990, includes chapters on student learning in mathematics and science, supply and demand for science and mathematics teachers, and parental choice of schools.

**Specialized Secondary Sources.**    An increasing number of specialized secondary sources on educational topics are available. The *Handbook of Research on Educational Administration* and the *Handbook of Research on Teacher Education* are examples of two recent sources. Check the listings in your university library to determine whether specific sources are available in the topic area or areas into which your problem falls.

## STEP 4: SELECT THE MOST APPROPRIATE PRELIMINARY SOURCE(S)

After you have read one or two secondary sources, you should be able to define your problem in more specific terms. Think about what you have read and how it fits into your initial problem statement. Rewrite your problem statement so that it indicates in clear and specific terms what you hope to find by searching the research literature.

You are now ready to enter your problem statement on a copy of the Manual Search Record Form, in Appendix 1. We recommend that you make several photocopies of this form. Use it to record your research problem, so that you have a clear statement of your problem to guide your search. As you conduct your search, you can use the form to record the sources you have examined and the years or volumes you have checked. You can also use the form to keep track of the key words, index terms, or descriptors that you used to search for sources. The Manual Search Record Form will help you determine the best search terms to use and will enable you to remember which preliminary sources you have checked for what time periods. Having this information will save you a great deal of time if later you need to expand your search.

Figure 2.2 (p. 30) shows a Manual Search Record Form with information filled in for a specific search of a preliminary source on the subject of basal reading programs. Note that the purpose of the search is "To select a new basal reading program for my district." The preliminary problem definition is specified as a question: "Which basal reading program results in the highest level of reading achievement when used with elementary students similar to those in our district?"

You are now ready to select the preliminary source or sources that will be most helpful in locating primary and secondary sources related to your problem. Several preliminary sources are useful to educators. We will describe in alphabetical order four of the most important: *Current Index to Journals in Education, Education Index, Psychological Abstracts,* and *Resources in Education.*

***Current Index to Journals in Education.***     *Current Index to Journals in Education (CIJE)* is published monthly by ERIC. As described earlier, the ERIC clearinghouses provide a comprehensive service that includes cataloging, abstracting, and indexing relevant documents related to education. The primary coverage of *CIJE* is educational periodicals, so it is an excellent source for identifying published educational research. *CIJE*'s coverage is very thorough, providing abstracts of articles from approximately 750 publications, including many foreign periodicals. Most of the sources covered are educational periodicals, but when articles relevant to education are published in other periodicals such as *Time, Nursing Outlook,* or *Personnel Journal,* these are also abstracted in *CIJE*. Many journals peripheral to education, such as the *Journal of Geography* and the *Journal of Family Issues,* are regularly reviewed for relevant articles.

***Education Index.***     Published monthly except July and August by the H. W. Wilson Company, *Education Index* primarily covers educational periodicals, yearbooks, and monographs printed in the English language. Articles from over 400 periodicals related to education are indexed. Coverage in *Education Index* includes only bibliographical data. Therefore, *CIJE* is the preferred preliminary source for searches of educational periodical literature because it also includes an abstract of each document. If you wish to do an exhaustive literature search (one that attempts to cover everything published about an educational problem), we recommend that you use *CIJE* for the period 1969 to date and *Education Index* for the period 1929 to 1968. For most education problems, however, a search that covers the most recent 10 years is sufficient. In this case, *CIJE* is recommended.

***Psychological Abstracts.***     *Psychological Abstracts,* the monthly publication of the American Psychological Association, regularly covers over 950 journals, technical reports, monographs, and other scientific documents—in fact, most of the world's literature in psychology and related disciplines. Books, secondary sources, and articles peripheral to psychology make up about 30 percent of the sources listed. Although there is considerable overlap between *CIJE* and *Psychological Abstracts,* the latter will usually provide more thorough coverage and more detailed abstracts. Therefore, we recommend *Psychological Abstracts* for any educational problem that is related to an area of psychology, such as child development, learning, counseling, or student attitudes.

# MANUAL SEARCH RECORD FORM

| *Mary Alpha* | *Supt. Omega* | *Oct 15 '89* | *Nov 15 '89* |
|---|---|---|---|
| **Your Name** | **Person Requesting Search** | **Starting Date** | **Due Date** |

**Purpose of Search:** *To select a new basal reading program for our district.*

**Preliminary Problem Definition:**

*Which basal reading program results in the highest level of reading achievement when used*

*with elementary students similar to those in our district?*

**Secondary Sources Reviewed:** *Arnell, D. & Browns, F. A guide to the selection and use*

*of reading instructional materials, 1981, Alexander Graham. Hoffman, J.V. (ed)*

*Effective teaching of reading; Research and practice, 1986 International Reading.*

**Preliminary Source Selected:**

*Education Index*

**Instructions: Start with current year and work back. Enter a check mark after you have checked a key word and made up necessary bibliography cards. Enter an "N" If you find no relevant references for a given key word.**

| Key Words, Index Terms of Descriptors (in alphabetical order) | Dates or Volume | | | | |
|---|---|---|---|---|---|
| | *Sept,* 19 *89* | 19 *88-9* | 19 *87-8* | 19 *86-7* | 19 *85-6* |
| *Reading Readiness* ~~Beginning Reading~~ | ✓ | ✓ | ✓ | N | ✓ |
| *Reading achievement,* *Student* | N | ✓ | ✓ | ✓ | ✓ |
| *Comprehension in Reading* ~~Reading Comprehension~~ | ✓ | ✓ | ✓ | ✓ | ✓ |
| *Reading Improvement* | N | N | *drop this term* | ✓ | |
| *Reading Curriculum Evaluation* ~~Reading Programs~~ | ✓ | N | ✓ | ✓ | ✓ |
| *Reading Research* | N | N | N | N | ✓ |
| *Reading Bibliography* | N | ✓ | N | N | N |
| *Reading teaching evaluation* | N | N | ✓ | ✓ | N |
| *Readers evaluation* | N | ✓ | ✓ | ✓ | ✓ |
| *Reading textbooks* | N | ✓ | ✓ | ✓ | ✓ |

Figure 2.2 Manual Search Record Form Filled Out for a Literature Search on Basal Reading Programs for Elementary School Students

***Resources in Education.***   *Resources in Education (RIE)* has been published monthly by ERIC since 1966. *RIE* reviews "report literature," which consists of virtually all educational documents other than journals, including speeches given at professional meetings, final reports of federally funded research, state education department documents, school district reports, and other published and unpublished reports. Early volumes covered only research reports sponsored by the U.S. Office of Education. Other preliminary sources in education generally do not provide abstracts of report literature, so *RIE* is often the only means of locating them.

A typical issue of *RIE* contains bibliographic data and abstracts for approximately 1,000 documents. Each abstract is about 200 words in length and provides enough information for you to judge whether the reference is relevant to your problem. Some reports abstracted in *RIE,* such as final reports of federally funded research projects, are subsequently published in journals. However, the journal version of the report will usually give much less detail, and there is often a two- to three-year lag between completion of a report and publication of the results in a journal. Therefore, *RIE* is the one preliminary source that should be searched regardless of your problem or area of interest in education.

**Other Useful Preliminary Sources.**   The four preliminary sources described above have very broad coverage, and so they are useful for identifying information about most educational problems. However, specialized preliminary sources also may prove useful. For a thorough review, one of these sources should be searched if your problem relates to its field of specialization. Several sources that are commonly used by educators are described below.

Child Development Abstracts and Bibliography.   Articles covered in *Child Development Abstracts and Bibliography* are drawn from about 200 periodicals in medicine, psychology, biology, sociology, and education. Books related to child development also are reviewed. The three issues published each year include abstracts under six major subject headings as well as an author index and subject index. The issues are combined into annual volumes.

Exceptional Child Education Resources.   The Council for Exceptional Children has published *Exceptional Child Education Resources (ECER)* on a quarterly basis since 1969. More than 200 journals are regularly searched for articles concerning exceptional children. The format is similar to that used in *CIJE.* However, many journals searched for *ECER* are not covered by *CIJE.* Each issue contains abstracts of relevant books, journal articles, and dissertations as well as subject, author, and title indexes. The final issue each year contains indexes for the entire volume.

*Foreign Preliminary Sources.*   Both *CIJE* and *Psychological Abstracts* provide extensive coverage of journals published in countries other than the United States. However, for cross-cultural studies or studies in areas where foreign researchers have taken the lead, a check of foreign preliminary sources, such as *British Education Index* and *British Education Theses Index,* may be worthwhile.

*Social Science Citation Index and* Science Citation Index.    Suppose that your literature review identifies some key education references that were published several years ago. You can use the *Social Science Citation Index (SSCI),* which began in 1973, to trace the effects of these earlier studies on subsequent research. *SSCI* covers the literature of education and of the social and behavioral sciences. A companion index, the *Science Citation Index (SCI),* dating back to 1969, covers the literature of science, medicine, agriculture, technology, and the behavioral sciences. Articles in psychology are cited in both *SCI* and *SCCI,* but work in education is most likely to be cited in *SSCI.* By looking up the author of a given reference, you can find where that reference has been cited by later writers. Start your search of *SSCI* with the year that your key reference was published, and check all volumes up to the current one. Under the name of the author of the key reference, you will find bibliographical data for all sources that have cited the key reference. For example, Arthur Jensen's famous article in the 1969 *Harvard Educational Review* entitled "How Much Can We Boost I.Q. and Scholastic Achievement?" was cited in 20 articles in the 1986 edition of the *SSCI.* A review of these articles would give you a clear picture about current thinking in 1986 regarding this controversial topic.

Sociological Abstracts.    *Sociological Abstracts* is published five times each year. Each issue contains subject, author, and source indexes in addition to abstracts that are similar in format and length to *Psychological Abstracts.* The subject index is also similar to *Psychological Abstracts,* typically listing from 3 to 10 phrases that describe the content of the article. The *Thesaurus of Sociological Indexing Terms* is useful in selecting key words for your search. For example, under the broad subject heading Attitudes in the December 1989 issue [*37*(5), 1985] here is a typical entry: "attitudes toward homosexuals, heterosexual university students, US; gender; questionnaire/scale data; 89U9366." Note that this example contains information on the population and methodology employed. This kind of information is often given in the subject index of *Sociological Abstracts.*

As a rule, articles appear more promptly in *Psychological Abstracts* than in *Sociological Abstracts.* Thus, when you are searching areas covered by both sources, such as topics in social psychology, *Psychological Abstracts* is likely to cover a higher percentage of recent articles. However, if you are studying a research topic that cuts across both psychology and sociology, it is useful to look over the tables of contents of an issue of both abstracts and compare the coverage on your topic.

## STEP 5: TRANSLATE THE PROBLEM STATEMENT INTO KEY WORDS

All preliminary sources in education include subject indexes. Thus, an important step in your literature review is to translate the statement of your problem or question as written on your Manual Search Record Form into a set of key words or terms that you can look up in the subject index of the preliminary source you have selected. The method of selecting key words or index terms differs slightly for the different preliminary sources. Let's see what steps we should take for each of the principal preliminary sources.

*1.* For all preliminary sources, start by underlining the most important words and terms in your problem statement. If your problem statement does not express your problem in clear, specific terms, you should think through your problem, read some additional secondary sources, and rewrite your problem statement before proceeding.

*2.* The second step for all preliminary sources is to list the underlined words in pencil in the Key Words section of your Manual Search Record Form. In Figure 2.2 the specific problem has been stated in the form of a question: "Which *basal reading program* results in the highest level of *reading achievement* when used with *elementary students* similar to those in our district?"

*3.* Next, list synonyms and closely related words for each important word or term you underlined in step 1. These three steps are enough to get you started on a search of the subject index section of *Education Index.* The initial selection of key words for the literature search on basal reading programs for elementary school students includes "Beginning reading," "Reading achievement," "Reading comprehension," "Reading improvement," "Reading programs," and "Reading research."

*4.* For *RIE* and *CIJE,* which are the two ERIC sources, an additional step is required. You should consult the *Thesaurus of ERIC Descriptors,* which ERIC publishes, to assist you in identifying key words or terms. This volume, which should be in the reference section of your library, lists all terms used to classify ERIC documents by subject. For a given subject area, it will provide synonyms, narrower terms, broader terms, and related terms. For example, the general search term "dropouts" is further analyzed into "high school dropouts," "potential dropouts," "dropout identification," and "dropout teaching."

You usually will find that some of the key words you have written on your Manual Search Record Form appear in the *Thesaurus* in slightly different form. For example, if you had listed "Racial relations" as a key term, you would find in the *Thesaurus* that the term "Race relations" is listed instead. In such cases, erase the word or term you have listed and enter the *Thesaurus* term.

For many terms listed in the *Thesaurus,* related terms (RT) are given. If any of these related terms seem relevant to your problem, add them to the list on your Manual Search Record Form. If any of the terms you listed are not included in the *Thesaurus,* delete them from your list. Finally, you should look in the most recent monthly issue of *RIE,* where you will find a list of all ERIC descriptors that have been added since the *Thesaurus* was published. Check this list and add to your record form any of the descriptors that relate to your problem. The final result of checking your original terms in the *Thesaurus* will be a list of ERIC descriptor terms that you can use to search the subject indexes of *RIE* and *CIJE.*

*5.* If you have selected *Psychological Abstracts* as a preliminary source, use the *Thesaurus of Psychological Index Terms* to translate your original key words into terms that are used in the subject index of *Psychological Abstracts*. Although this thesaurus was not developed until 1973, the terms you select should be satisfactory for searching earlier volumes because it includes most of the 800 index terms used before 1973. Note that the index term "Bibliography" should always be checked in *Psychological Abstracts*. Under this heading you will find a list of bibliographies on a wide variety of subjects. If you can locate a recent bibliography in your area of interest, it will make your review of the literature much easier.

Because the index terms listed in the *Thesaurus of ERIC Descriptors* are not identical to those listed in the *Thesaurus of Psychological Index Terms,* you will have to use different key word lists if you decide to search both these sources.

## STEP 6: SEARCH THE PRELIMINARY SOURCE

Now that you have a set of appropriate key terms listed on your record form, you can start your search of the preliminary source itself. Here we will discuss how to proceed in a manual search of each preliminary source. If you decide to conduct a computer search, the procedures are given in Chapter 3.

**Searching *Education Index*.** *Education Index* is a combined author-subject index, and it lists only the bibliographical data concerning each item. The year for this index runs from September to the following June. For the current quarter, each of the monthly issues must be searched, but these monthly issues are combined into a quarterly index, and the quarterly issues in turn are combined into a yearly volume for the immediate past year.

In searching all preliminary sources, you should start with the most recent issue and work back. The Manual Search Record Form shown in Figure 2.2 demonstrates a systematic procedure you can follow. Check each of your key words in a volume of *Education Index,* look up the word, and read the titles of articles listed under it. If you find a title that seems relevant to your topic, record the bibliographical data (author, title, and source of publication) on an index card or sheet of paper. An example of bibliographic data is shown in Figure 2.3. A separate bibliographic index card or sheet of paper should be used for each reference. It is often difficult to judge the contents of an article from the title, and therefore many articles for which you prepare bibliographic records will later be found to contain nothing pertinent to your topic. In deciding whether to prepare a bibliographic record and check a particular article, you should generally follow the rule that it is better to check an article that proves to be of no use than to overlook one that may be important. Also, many articles that are peripheral to your topic include background information that will give you a better understanding of the context into which your topic fits. Thus, whenever in doubt, prepare a bibliographic record and check the article in question.

After you read the titles given under your first key word, place a check on the record form, indicating that this word has been checked. Then look up the next key word in the subject index, and continue until you have checked all the terms you listed. Then go through the same process with the next most recent volume of *Education Index*.

*Breznitz, Zvia, and Teltsch, Tamar*
  *The effect of school entrance age on academic achievement and*
    *social-emotional adjustment of children: follow-up study of fourth*
    *graders. bibl Psychol Sch 26:62-8 Ja '89*

Figure 2.3 Sample Bibliographic Record in *Education Index* Format

If you do not find any titles under a descriptor term for the volume you are checking, write "N" (for "no titles") or another symbol in the appropriate box of the Manual Search Record Form. If you have recorded several consecutive "N's" for a descriptor term, this key word can be dropped and not checked in the remaining volumes you search.

To illustrate the process, let us now demonstrate the use of the record form in Figure 2.2 to search five years of *Education Index*. Recall that the specific problem has been stated in the form of a question: "Which basal reading program results in the highest level of reading achievement when used with elementary students similar to those in our district?"

Our initial selection of key words included "Beginning reading," "Reading achievement," "Reading comprehension," "Reading improvement," "Reading programs," and "Reading research." It would be ideal if we could search for studies that include all three of the most important concepts in our problem statement, that is, *reading programs, reading achievement,* and *elementary*. We will see in the next chapter that such searches are possible with a computer, but for manual searches we can look up only one key term at a time. Thus, what we must do in our search of *Education Index* is to look up each term and then judge from the title whether the article is related to our problem. It will be easiest to look up our key terms in alphabetical order. In searching the September 1989 issue of *Education Index,* we find nothing under "Beginning reading" except a notation, "See Reading readiness." Thus we change our first key term to "Reading readiness" and check the articles entered under that term. One pertinent article is listed, so we make up a bibliographic record and then enter a check mark in the first column for "Reading readiness," indicating that we have checked this term and found one or more relevant references. Next we check "Reading achievement" but find nothing, so we enter "N" in the first column. Instead of "Reading comprehension," the term "Comprehension in reading" is used in *Education Index,* so we make this change in our key-word list. Then we check "Reading improvement," but this term is not included in this issue. After checking the headings under "Reading" in *Education Index,* we also change "Reading programs" to "Reading-curriculum-evaluation" and add "Reading-teaching-evaluation," "Readers-evaluation," and "Reading-textbooks."

You will recall that when you fail to find a given term in your preliminary source or if the term fails to produce any relevant references for two or three years, you can drop it, as we have done with "Reading improvement." Notice that we have also added "Reading-Bibliography." It is usually a good idea to include a bibliography heading if one is found in the *Education Index,* because if you are fortunate enough to find a bibliography on your topic you will locate many relevant references with little effort.

Note that even though we found only one relevant bibliography in our search, we retained the term.

To demonstrate the kinds of articles you are likely to find on this problem, five of the references found in this brief search are listed below in the format used in *Education Index:*

> Effectiveness of the DISTAR reading I program in developing first graders' language skills. C.W. Sexton. bibl *J Educ Res* 82:289–93 My/Je'89
>
> How the basals stack up [results of a teacher poll]. R.R. Turner. il *Learn 88* 17[16]:62–4 Ap'88
>
> The evaluation and selection of basal readers. R. Farr and others. bibl *Elem Sch J* 87:267–81 Ja'87
>
> Choosing basal reading texts: guidelines in progress. J. Osborn. por *Curric Rev* 27:9–11 S/O'87
>
> Selecting basal reading series: the need for a validated process. L.M. Clary and S.J. Smith. bibl *Read Teach* 39:390–4 Ja'86

The procedure we have described would provide a fairly complete search of *Education Index* if extended over a 10-year period. However, let us suppose that the purpose of our search was to locate very quickly a few references on the relative effectiveness of different reading programs that we could discuss in a teachers' workshop. In this case we may decide to select only the two or three key terms that seem most likely to produce relevant articles and search only those terms. For example, we may decide to search only "Reading achievement," "Reading-curriculum-evaluation," and "Readers-evaluation."

In other words, the depth of a literature search is determined to a large degree by your purpose. For many of the day-to-day problems that arise in education, sufficient information can be obtained from a brief search that covers only one preliminary source for a period of two or three years. However, if the evidence you find is to be the basis for answering a major question such as "Should the school district adopt an ability grouping program?" a thorough search involving at least two preliminary sources and extending over a 5- to 10-year period is desirable.

**Searching *Psychological Abstracts*.**    Every issue of *Psychological Abstracts* has 16 sections, each covering a different area of psychology. The sections most pertinent to educators are developmental psychology, which includes such topics as cognitive and perceptual development and psychosocial and personality development; and educational psychology, which includes such topics as curriculum and programs, teaching methods, academic learning and achievement, and special and remedial education. The coverage of the 16 areas of psychology is very thorough. For example, many journals such as *Elementary School Journal, Harvard Educational Review,* and *Journal of Reading Behavior,* which are predominantly educational journals, are covered in *Psychological Abstracts*. Many foreign psychological journals are also covered.

Currently, one volume of *Psychological Abstracts* is published each year. Each monthly issue has a brief subject index and an author index. At the end of each volume, there is a cumulated subject and author index for that year. In using *Psychological Abstracts,* you turn first to the index volume to check your key words. The index volume of *Psychological Abstracts* does not contain complete bibliographical data, like those in *Education Index,* but lists only the subject of the article in the briefest possible terms, usually about 10 to 15 words. You will find a number after each of these brief descriptions that refers to the number of the abstract. Write down the numbers of articles that appear relevant to your topic and then look for them in the volume of abstracts.

Suppose that you are an elementary school principal and your school has recently started a mainstreaming program. You want to conduct a very brief search of the literature to learn how teachers can be trained to function effectively in mainstreamed classrooms. This information can help you in teacher placement decisions and also in conducting an in-service program to prepare your teachers for their new role. You should look up "Mainstreaming (Educational)" in the index volumes of *Psychological Abstracts* since this seems to be the most important key term for your problem. In Volume 76 (July–December Index for 1989) you find the following entry:

> mainstreaming teaching program, attitudes towards mainstreaming & classroom management style & student behaviors, elementary teachers with mainstreamed students, 20443

This reference seems very pertinent to your problem, so you look up 20443 in the Abstracts part of Volume 76, where you find

> 20443 *Leyser, Yona.* (Northern Illinois U, De Kalb) **The impact of training in mainstreaming on teacher attitudes, management techniques, and the behaviour of disabled students.** *Exceptional Child,* 1988(Jul), Vol 35(2), 85–96. —30 female prospective elementary education teachers, including 15 teachers trained in special education and 15 untrained controls, were observed while interacting with mainstreamed and matched comparison pupils from a group of 30 1st–6th graders. Findings reveal that training was effective in modifying attitudes toward mainstreaming by experimental teachers. Mainstreamed pupils in control teacher classrooms displayed significantly fewer appropriate classroom behaviors than did their comparison peers. Experimental and control teachers did not differ significantly in the management techniques they employed. Both groups, however, reacted differently toward mainstreamed pupils than toward their matched classmates, showing more approval of on-task behavior and more criticism of inappropriate behavior in mainstreamed pupils.*

Note that in addition to the bibliographical data needed to locate the original article, a brief but informative abstract is provided. These abstracts are very useful because they help you decide whether an article actually pertains to your problem. This

* Reprinted with permission of the American Psychological Association, publisher of *Psychological Abstracts* and the PsycInfo Database (© 1967–1992).

decision is much easier to make on the basis of an abstract than solely on the basis of the bibliographical data found in *Education Index.*

After reading the abstract, you must decide whether the article is pertinent. This abstract indicates that the article is closely related to your problem, so you would list the bibliographical data on an index card or sheet of paper (see Figure 2.2) and continue your search for additional references.

When the research topic is exclusively educational, such as school lunch programs, little is gained by checking *Psychological Abstracts.* However, in areas relating to educational psychology, you may decide to check both *Psychological Abstracts* and one of the education preliminary sources, such as *CIJE, Education Index,* or *RIE,* to be assured that you have fully covered the field. You should work from different copies of the Manual Search Record Form to search preliminary sources that use different descriptor terms for the problem you are investigating.

**Searching *RIE* and *CIJE.*** Once you have selected your key descriptor terms from the *Thesaurus of ERIC Descriptors,* the procedure for searching *RIE* and *CIJE* is similar to that used in searching *Psychological Abstracts.*

In searching *RIE,* first check your descriptors in the subject index of the monthly issues for the current year and then in the semiannual index volumes for previous years. When you locate a reference in the subject index that relates to your topic, copy the ED (Education Document) number at the end of the bibliographical data. Then look up each ED number in the Document Resumes section, where you will find a description of the reference, like the sample entry shown in Figure 2.4. Notice in this figure that the Document Resume contains a great deal of useful information in addition to the usual brief abstract.

If you wish to obtain the full document that is abstracted in the entry, you can order it through the ERIC Document Reproduction Service. A price code for each document is listed in the Document Resume. Current prices are listed in the section How to Order ERIC Documents in the most recent issue of *RIE.* The document can be ordered on microfiches, which are small sheets of microfilm, each containing up to 60 pages of text. It can also be ordered in printed form, reproduced at about 70 percent of the document's original size. The advantage of microfiches is their low cost. For example, in 1990 a microfiche copy of an article up to 480 pages was 85 cents, whereas a printed copy of a 480-page article was $40. However, reading a microfiche requires a special machine, which enlarges the image to normal page size. Nearly all libraries now have these special machines. Most university libraries also maintain a collection of ERIC microfiches, so it is not necessary to order them through the Reproduction Service unless you want a personal copy.

Like *RIE, CIJE* is published monthly and cumulated semiannually. The monthly numbers contain a subject index, author index, and main entry section. Using the descriptors related to your topic selected from the *Thesaurus of ERIC Descriptors,* search the subject index, and note the EJ (Education Journal) numbers of relevant references. Then look up these EJ numbers in the main entry section, which provides approximately the same information as that in the Document Resumes in *RIE.* For

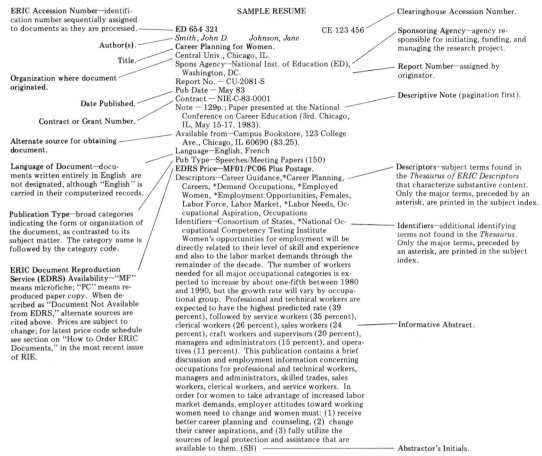

Figure 2.4 Sample Entry from *Resources in Education,* "Document Resume" Section, with Identifying Characteristics (From *RIE, 25,* 1, January 1990, viii.)

example, the article by Leyser that we located in *Psychological Abstracts* is also listed in the July–December 1989 volume of *CIJE*. This entry is shown in Figure 2.5.

You will note that the *CIJE* abstract for this article is much briefer than that found in *Psychological Abstracts*. As a general rule, the abstracts in *RIE* and *Psychological Abstracts* give more detail than those in *CIJE* and are therefore more useful in helping you decide which publications are related to your problem. However, *CIJE* has some advantages compared with *Education Index*. It has a more comprehensive index (based on the *Thesaurus of ERIC Descriptors*), multidisciplinary journal coverage, and abstracts for many of the articles indexed.

In general, the most productive strategy for making a thorough search is to search *RIE* and *CIJE* for the years from 1969 to the present, search *RIE* and *Education Index* for the years 1966 to 1968, and search *Education Index* from 1965 back as far as you wish to extend your review.

## STEP 7: PREPARE BIBLIOGRAPHIC RECORDS

One of the biggest problems in researching the literature is keeping track of the document you are reviewing. You can avoid this problem by using a consistent procedure to record bibliographic information on each document you identify. We recommend that you prepare your bibliographic records on either index cards all of the same size or on standard 8-½- × -11-inch sheets of paper. Put the bibliographic record for each book, article, or other document on a separate card or sheet so that you can sort them easily.

Many people find index cards handy to carry and sort, so you may want to keep your bibliographic records on index cards. By using the 8- × 5-inch card, you will have room below the bibliographic information to take some notes on each reference. (Taking notes on your sources will be discussed in Chapter 4.) Or if you do a computer search and get a printout of information concerning each reference, you can cut the printout apart and paste the information obtained for that reference on the corresponding bibliographic index card.

If you do not wish to use index cards, we recommend that you put the bibliographic information for each reference on a separate sheet of standard three-hole-punched 8-½- × -11-inch paper. This size will give you room for taking notes below the bibliographic information or for pasting the computer printout for that reference on the same sheet that contains the bibliographic information. In addition, you can keep all your bibliographic records in a three-ring binder, and you can easily rearrange or remove records whenever you wish.

Bibliographic data can be recorded in many different formats. If you are writing a review-of-the-literature paper for your master's degree, you should check the rules at

EJ **388 824**          EC 212 448

**The Impact of Training in Mainstreaming on Teacher Attitudes, Management Techniques, and the Behaviour of Disabled Students.**    Leyser, Yona *Exceptional Child;*
v35 n2 p85-96 Jul 1988
*Descriptors* *Mild Disabilities; *Mainstreaming; *Teacher Attitudes; *Student Behavior; *Classroom
   Techniques; Elementary Education; Comparative Analysis; Training; Outcomes of Education; *Teacher
   Student Relationship; Interaction; Attitude Change.
Fifteen elementary education teachers received training in mainstreaming; the experimental teachers and
15 controls were subsequently observed interacting with mainstreamed and matched comparison pupils.
Findings revealed that: training modified attitudes toward mainstreaming by experimental teachers; and
experimental and control teachers did not differ significantly in management techniques employed.
(Author/JDD)

Figure 2.5 Sample Entry from *CIJE,* Main Entry Section (July–December 1989). (Source: Reprinted from *Current Index to Journals in Education* [*CIJE*], Vol. 23, number 10 and Vol. 21, Number 9. Copyright 1989 and 1991 by The Oryx Press, 4041 N. Central at Indian School Rd., Phoenix, AZ 85012. Used by permission of the Oryx Press.)

your college concerning the acceptable format for the bibliography section. Some schools permit any format generally acceptable in your field of study, whereas other schools have a specific format that all graduate students must follow. If your school permits any format acceptable in your field, the easiest approach will be for you to use the format of the preliminary source from which you expect to obtain most of your references.

Because *CIJE* is often the most productive source for educators, its format is advantageous to use when permitted. Most of the references will come from the subject index, and articles listed in this section give the bibliographical data but not the author's name. Therefore, you must get the bibliographic data from the main entry section, not the subject index. In the main entry section the title of the book or article is given before the author's name. For your bibliographic record, the author's name (last name first) should be listed before the title. This change is necessary because it is much more convenient for you to maintain your card file in alphabetical order by author. Also, the bibliography for a thesis or term paper normally will be listed in this order.

If you use *CIJE* format, the bibliographic data from articles found in other preliminary sources such as *Education Index* and *Psychological Abstracts* should be converted to the *CIJE* format. Let us compare bibliographical data for the same article as it appears in *CIJE, Education Index,* and *Psychological Abstracts.*

### Current Index to Journals in Education (CIJE)

**EJ 391 807**                          CG 535 885
**The Effect of School Entrance Age on Academic
Achievement and Social-Emotional Adjustment of
Children: Follow-up Study of Fourth Graders.**
Breznitz, Zvia; Teltsch, Tamar *Psychology in the
Schools;* v26 n1 p62-68 Jan 1989 (Reprint: UMI)

### Education Index

**Breznitz, Zvia, and Teltsch, Tamar**
   The effect of school entrance age on academic achievement and social-emotional adjustment of children:
   follow-up study of fourth graders. bibl *Psychol Sch*
   26:62-8 Ja '89

### Psychological Abstracts

**Breznitz, Zvia** & *Teltsch, Tamar.* The effect of school entrance age on academic achievement and social-emotional
adjustment of children: Follow-up study of fourth graders.
*Psychology in the Schools, 1989(Jan), Vol 26(1), 62–68.*
                                                  24035

Although these formats are similar, note that the journal *Psychology in the Schools* is abbreviated in *Education Index* and not in the other two sources and that the volume number, pages, and year are given in a different format. Notice also that all main words in the title are capitalized in *CIJE,* whereas only the first word is capitalized in the other sources. If a reprint of the article is available from University Microfilms International (UMI), the *CIJE* citation will indicate this, but the other preliminary sources do not provide this information. Finally, note that the *Education Index* format includes the notation "bibl," indicating that there is a bibliography with the article. Obviously, many errors and inconsistencies can be avoided by selecting one format and converting all references to that format when making up bibliography cards. If you are reviewing the literature in one of the areas of educational psychology, you will normally obtain the majority of your references from *Psychological Abstracts,* and in this case that format may be preferred.

If your college has specified a format for the bibliography that differs from the one used by your preliminary source, the easiest procedure is to copy the bibliographic data from the preliminary source in whatever form they are found. Then, when checking the document to determine whether it contains anything pertinent to your problem, you can recopy the bibliographic information in the format required by your institution on the other side of your bibliographic record. You need to do this only for documents that contain pertinent information. In our experience, only one out of every three or four references for which you prepare bibliographic records will contain material that you wish to use in your review of the literature.

Accuracy and thoroughness are extremely important in preparing bibliographic records. A mistake made in copying the data can cause a great deal of extra work later on. For example, if you skip or incorrectly copy the name of the journal, date, volume number, or page numbers, you may not be able to find the article. Then you are faced with the problem of trying to determine which portion of your bibliographic information is incorrect. Unless you take special care, it is easy to make such mistakes, and then you must go back to the preliminary source to find the reference. Thus, if you reviewed several preliminary sources, this search can take much longer than it should have.

Although some mistakes in recording bibliographic data do not interfere with finding documents, for example, misspelling the author's name, the mistake is still serious because it will be repeated in your report. Nothing reflects more unfavorably on a person's scholarship than frequent errors in bibliographic data.

## STEP 8: WRITE NOTES ON PERTINENT PRIMARY SOURCES AND ORGANIZE THE NOTES; AND STEP 9: WRITE A REPORT

If you wanted merely to learn about educational research, you could carry out only the first seven steps described above. However, when educators carry out an extensive search of the research literature it is because they need to *apply* the findings—that is, answer a question, or solve a problem of practical concern. In order to apply educational research, you also need to summarize the findings that pertain to your problem or question and formulate recommendations for action. The most efficient way to do this is to carry out two final steps in reviewing the educational research literature: (8) write notes on pertinent primary sources and organize the notes, and (9) write a report based on your notes.

Chapters 4 and 5 discuss how to carry out these steps. Chapter 4 describes procedures for taking notes on relevant primary sources and ways to classify documents that you have read. It also provides suggestions for organizing your notes and writing a report of your findings. In Chapter 5 we discuss how to evaluate the research studies that you will cite in your report.

# Recommended Reading

BUREK, D. M., ed. (1992) *Encyclopedia of Associations,* 26th ed. Detroit: Gale.

This annual encyclopedia contains over 2,000 entries under key words related to education. Each entry provides the name, address, and telephone number of the organization. It also lists officers, a contact person, the date the organization was established, the organization's aims or purposes, and the names of any publications.

BUTTLAR, L. J. (1989). *Education: A guide to reference and information sources.* Englewood, CO: Libraries Unlimited.

This reference book indexes general preliminary and secondary sources relevant to education as well as sources in 14 specific areas of education, for example, elementary and secondary education, special education, and career and vocational education. Over 900 titles are included.

DURNIN, R. G. (1982). *American education—a guide to information sources.* Detroit: Gale.

The purpose of this volume is to provide a brief guide to a sample of important and definitive books on American education. The first section, "Bibliographic Essay," describes important work in chronological order from the seventeenth century to 1981. The remainder of the book is an annotated bibliography organized by subject, starting with "academic freedom" and ending with "women, education of." It is a good source for gaining historical perspective on your problem and is also useful for locating important older books in your field.

GOVER, H. R. (1981). *Keys to library research on the graduate level: A guide to guides.* Washington, DC: University Press of America.

Designed to give graduate students the skills they need to use fully the library resources at their disposal, this book covers the card catalog, basic periodicals indexes, computer-prepared indexes and abstracts, and the Library of Congress classification system.

WOODBURY, M. L. (1985). *Childhood information resources.* Arlington, VA: Information Resources Press.

In this comprehensive reference, the author describes over 1,100 sources of information on children, pulling together in one volume sources that have been compiled by many agencies and organizations in recent years. Although international sources are annotated, the primary emphasis is on current sources concerned with American children from conception through age 12.

# Application Problems

1. Suppose you are an elementary school principal. The new superintendent of your school district wants to reassess the district's use of ability grouping in classrooms. He asks you to check the recent educational literature and try to find information on the benefits and drawbacks of ability grouping as perceived by elementary schoolteachers. The following activities will help you to learn how to use educational literature when faced with problems of this kind.

   a. Check the most recent issue of *Books in Print* and list bibliographic data for one book that deals with ability grouping published in 1990 or later.

   b. Check the *Yearbooks of the National Society for the Study of Education* from 1988 to date. Do any of these volumes deal with the problem? If so, list bibliographic data for the volume, check the chapters in the selected volume, and give the author and title of one chapter that appears to be most relevant.

   **c.** Check the five most recent annual volumes of the *Review of Educational Research*. Do any of the articles relate to ability grouping? If so, list bibliographic data for one relevant article.

   **d.** Check the five most recent monthly volumes of *CIJE, RIE, Education Index,* and *Psychological Abstracts*. List bibliographic data for one relevant article from each of these four preliminary sources. You will find that different key terms are appropriate for different sources. Check the appropriate thesaurus for *CIJE, RIE,* and *Psychological Abstracts* to define your key terms.

**2.** Write or select five problem statements or questions related to education in areas that interest you. Following are some sample questions. You may select some of your problems from this list, but be sure to write at least two problem statements or questions of your own.

   **a.** What strategies can a teacher use to improve the classroom climate in the elementary grades?

   **b.** What classroom management procedures are effective in reducing disruptive student behavior in secondary schools?

   **c.** What can the teacher do to increase the amount of school time in which students are academically engaged?

   **d.** What can the teacher do to manage retarded children who are placed in regular classrooms?

   **e.** How can social skills be taught in elementary school?

   **f.** What is the impact of teacher anxiety on the educational process? What effect does team teaching have on science achievement at the secondary school level?

   **g.** What has been the effect of special educational programs for gifted secondary school students?

   **h.** Should teachers write behavioral objectives? In other words, what effect do these objectives have on student learning?

   **i.** How effective is the values clarification approach in improving pupil self-concept and achievement?

   **j.** How should parents be involved in the education of their gifted children?

   **k.** What educational approaches have been found effective in stimulating moral development?

   **l.** What factors in the school can increase or decrease cheating?

   **m.** What are the characteristics of teachers who are successful in working with gifted children?

   **n.** How can classroom rewards be used to improve pupil performance?

   **o.** What effect has desegregation had on the academic achievement of black students?

   **p.** What are other countries doing to provide educational programs for gifted students?

   **q.** How can feedback be used to improve learning in the elementary school?

   **r.** How can pupils be taught self-control that will improve their classroom behavior?

   **s.** What methods are effective for early identification of gifted children?

**3.** Review your five problems and select the one that seems most interesting, photocopy the Manual Search Record form from Appendix 1, and enter your purpose and problem definition.

**4.** Check the table of contents of the *NSSE Yearbooks* and the *Review of Educational Research* for the past five years for an article or chapter that relates to your problem statement. If you find a reference, enter the bibliographic data in your copy of the Manual Search Record Form (Appendix 1).

5. Check the subject volume of *Books in Print* for the most recent year available and try to locate at least three books published since 1975 that appear to relate to your problem statement. Enter the bibliographic data under secondary sources in the record form. If you need more space, use the back of the form.

6. Check your library card catalog, locate an additional book related to the problem you have selected, and enter the bibliographic data under secondary sources in the record form.

7. Select one of the secondary sources you located in steps 4, 5, and 6; read the section most relevant to your problem; and write a brief summary of what you learned.

8. Rewrite your problem definition, based on what you have read.

9. Select the preliminary source you believe is most relevant to your problem and enter it in the record form.

10. Make up a list of key words related to your problem and enter it in the record form.

11. Check your key words in one volume of your preliminary source. Make up bibliography cards for three references that appear relevant to your problem. (If you can't find three references, check a second year of your preliminary source.) Keep these cards, as you will use them in an application problem in a later chapter.

# CHAPTER 3

# COMPUTER SEARCHES
# OF PRELIMINARY SOURCES

*In collaboration with Kathleen Lenn, education reference librarian at the University of Oregon*

## Overview

The use of computer technology to locate relevant references in preliminary sources has significant advantages over a manual search. Many university libraries have terminals on which you can conduct computer searches at low or no cost. If you decide to use this service, you will need to follow six major steps: (1) Define the problem to be searched, (2) state the purpose of the search, (3) select a data base, (4) select descriptors, (5) plan the search strategies, and (6) conduct the search.

## Objectives

1. Briefly describe four advantages of conducting a computer search of preliminary sources in education.
2. Name and describe three data bases related to education that are available for computer searches.
3. Describe each of the six main steps you should carry out in planning and conducting a computer search of the ERIC data base.
4. Using the Computer Search Record Form, select a problem and plan a search.

The increased availability of preliminary sources has made the task of locating literature related to an educational problem much easier. Before 1929, when *Education Index* was first published, a reader had to check the table of contents of each journal, month by month, to locate articles related to an area of interest. Until 1966 there still was no easy way to locate educational documents such as unpublished research reports and papers presented at professional meetings. Most researchers simply ignored these works or checked them in a hit-or-miss way by trying to locate the programs of professional meetings. The problem of finding educational documents was largely solved with the start of *Research in Education* (later to become *Resources in Education, or RIE*) in 1966. It is designed specifically to provide access to the thousands of important educational documents that emerge each year but are never published. Detailed abstracts as well as microfiches containing the complete text of most of the documents covered in *RIE* are available in research libraries throughout the world. As a result, various types of educational documents that were almost impossible to search systematically before 1966 are now readily available.

In 1969, ERIC began publishing the *Current Index to Journals in Education (CIJE),* thus providing a very thorough coverage of journals related to education. ERIC also provides abstracts, which are lacking in *Education Index.* The development of the *Thesaurus of ERIC Descriptors* made the researcher's task still easier by providing standard terminology and by linking relevant descriptors to every article cited in *RIE* and *CIJE.*

You may have wondered how the vast number of primary sources are referenced in preliminary sources. Reviewers read journal articles or documents and then prepare entries that appear in preliminary sources such as *RIE, CIJE,* or *Psychological Abstracts.* The reviewer decides which descriptors (referred to in some indexes as subject headings) apply to the primary source, writes a brief abstract, and prepares all information that must be included in the preliminary source. Entries like those in Figures 2.3 and 2.4 are the final result of this process.

Each document entered into a preliminary source is assigned a set of descriptors. Therefore, the computer can be instructed to locate information on items for which there is a combination of descriptors. The availability of data bases on computer now makes it possible to conduct a more detailed search in 10 minutes than could be done manually in 10 weeks.

In this chapter we will give you examples and instructions for conducting an effective computer search of a preliminary source.

# Advantages of a Computer Search

A manual search of preliminary sources, which was described in Chapter 2, is not too difficult if you need only a few references related to a simple problem. However, if you are planning to conduct a major review of the literature to make an important educational decision or to write a master's thesis or other major report, you will find the manual search process time-consuming and tiresome. A computer search of the appropriate preliminary sources has several important advantages.

*1. Low cost.* Many university libraries now have a variety of CD-ROM (compact disk-read only memory) terminals, which run compact disks. These disks store data from indexes. You can conduct your own search of these data bases without cost or for a very low charge. If CD-ROMs are not readily available or do not cover your topic, consult a librarian. Many libraries also have access to services that allow data bases to be searched for a small fee. An exhaustive search of the ERIC data base, which includes all references that have been listed in *RIE* and *CIJE,* using the fee-based rather than the CD-ROM method, can usually be carried out at a cost of $20 to $40. A comparable manual search would take from 25 to 75 hours. Less comprehensive searches, such as needed for writing a graduate-level term paper, can usually be conducted for about $10.

2. *Printed or downloaded results.* Data bases will provide bibliographical data plus descriptors and an abstract, if available. Usually you can obtain a printout of this information, which saves you the trouble of copying bibliographic data onto cards or sheets. Instead you can cut out the citations you want to check and paste them onto cards. In many cases you will have to make additional notes when you read the reference to supplement the abstract obtained in the computer search, but the savings in time will still be significant. In most cases, you may also download the information to a diskette to be used later with your word-processing software. Typing your bibliography will be easier since it will not be necessary to reenter bibliographic information when developing your bibliography for research papers. You will only have to adjust it so that it is in the correct bibliographic format.

3. *Speed.* The computer will search and print out preliminary source information while you wait, usually in a matter of minutes.

4. *Simultaneous searching.* When doing a manual search, you can look up only one descriptor at a time in the subject index of your preliminary source. Therefore, manual searches are difficult to conduct for problems that involve several different concepts, especially if each concept is large. For example, a problem such as "the effects of television violence on the aggressive behavior of preschool children" involves three major concepts: *television violence, aggression,* and *preschool children.* It would be very time-consuming to locate references that include all three concepts through a manual search. In contrast, the computer can search for references that contain all three of these descriptors. Therefore, if a search is done properly, a high percentage of the references that are accessed in a computer search are likely to be relevant, eliminating much reading and rejecting of unusable references. In addition to several subject headings, many years of publication can also be searched simultaneously.

# Where to Conduct a Computer Search

Many university libraries now have data bases on compact disks. Some of these systems, called CD-ROM, contain only part of their print counterparts, whereas others, like ERIC, include the entire index. Still other data bases have no print counterparts and are available only on compact disk or on-line formats. The ERIC CD-ROM includes all citations from *RIE* and *CIJE* from 1966 to the present. Updated disks are sent to subscribing libraries each quarter.

At some libraries a search of the relevant data bases can be carried out without any charge. The disks are typically loaded on a personal computer. These search systems are relatively easy to use, containing step-by-step instructions for your search. Most systems also have "help" keys, which offer assistance when search questions arise.

Many libraries today have computerized catalogs, and some have loaded data bases on the same computer system that operates the catalog. Consult a librarian to see if data bases are available on your library's on-line catalog.

If the computerized index you need to consult is not available in either of these ways, most universities can access one of the information retrieval systems such as DIALOG or BRS. These systems have a great many data bases that can be searched by an on-line computer. Currently, more data bases are available through this method than through CD-ROMs, but there usually is some fee for on-line searches. Check with your school district, state department of education, or media specialist in your school to see if you have access to data bases through other sources or if an office or agency, such as the school district, will provide a search for you.

The cost of an on-line computer search varies with the service, the data base, and the length of the search. On-line computer time ranges from about $35 to $120 per hour, and the cost of printouts of the selected citations ranges from 25 cents to $25 for each citation.

These searches are usually conducted by a librarian who is trained to use the system. Careful planning is essential to keep on-line computer time to a minimum. It is advisable to go over your search strategy with the person who will conduct the search *before* going on-line. A typical ERIC search, including a printout of 25 abstracts, will cost about $30.

In addition to ERIC, a number of other data bases provide information that can be very useful for research problems. The following is a description of several data bases that are commonly used by educators as a supplement to or substitute for ERIC. Some are available both in CD-ROM and on-line formats, and others are available only in on-line format.

PsycINFO, the computer equivalent of *Psychological Abstracts,* contains citations to psychological literature from 1967 to the present. It is available in CD-ROM and on-line formats. The references are indexed from the *Thesaurus of Psychological Index Terms.* Many of the descriptors in this thesaurus differ from the ERIC descriptors, so check to see which descriptors best fit your problem. If thorough coverage is necessary, it is usually desirable to search both the ERIC and PsycINFO data bases.

*Dissertation Abstracts* is a data base of references to documents in *Dissertation Abstracts International* and *American Doctoral Dissertations.* It contains bibliographic citations to doctoral dissertations completed at many North American universities since 1861. Abstracts, however, are available only for dissertations completed since 1980. Citations to master's theses since 1966 and European dissertations since 1988 are also available. It is available in CD-ROM and on-line formats.

*Exceptional Child Education Resources (ECER)* is a data base of journal and document abstracts dealing with the education of handicapped and gifted children. It uses the same descriptors as the ERIC system and includes more than 70,000 citations dating back to 1966. Approximately half the citations in *ECER* are duplicated in the ERIC data base. It is available in on-line format.

*Sociological Abstracts* includes approximately 300,000 citations from around the world in sociology and related disciplines, from 1963 to the present. More than 1,600 journals are searched for relevant articles. This computer data base, which contains all the information included in the printed copy of *Sociological Abstracts,* is available in CD-ROM and on-line format.

*Magazine Index* and *Readers' Guide* are indexes to popular magazines. These indexes, available in a variety of formats, cover educational topics in general news magazines such as *Time* and *Newsweek.*

*Education Index* is available in CD-ROM and on-line formats. The coverage of education journals is similar to that of the *CIJE* portion of ERIC.

New data bases are appearing all the time. Consult a librarian to determine if there is a data base not mentioned here that may be better suited to your topic.

# Steps in Conducting a Computer Search

The steps involved in conducting a computer search are explained below. These steps can be applied to a variety of data bases, with changes to the search protocol and descriptors, as necessary. Figure 3.1 shows a completed Computer Search Record Form for planning and executing a computer search. A blank copy of this form is included in Appendix 2 and may be photocopied.

### STEP 1: DEFINE THE RESEARCH PROBLEM

The key to a successful search is to write a short but precise statement of your research problem. If your description is too general, your search will probably produce a great many items that are not closely related to your problem. This will make reading through the results of the search more laborious and more expensive, if you are being charged for it. If you have difficulty stating your problem in specific terms, first read two or three secondary sources to get a quick overview of the subject area.

You may find it easiest to state your problem in the form of the specific question that you want to answer. For example, suppose you are interested in the problem of how to help learning-disabled students with reading. This problem can be stated in question form: "What teaching methods can be used to improve the reading comprehension of elementary students who have learning disabilities?" The question describes the problem succinctly and uses terms that will help focus the search: *teaching methods, reading comprehension, elementary students,* and *learning disabilities*. By contrast, a question such as "What is the best way to teach elementary reading?" is not precise enough to describe the specific problem. We have entered this problem definition into the Computer Search Record Form (Figure 3.1) and will use it as an example.

### STEP 2: STATE THE SPECIFIC PURPOSE OF THE SEARCH

Educators conduct literature searches for a variety of reasons, including the following:
1. To learn what is known about a problem before conducting research on it.
2. To update an earlier review. It is not uncommon for graduate students to take two or three years after completing the review of literature to complete their research project and write the thesis or dissertation. By this time the review will be somewhat out of date. Using the same descriptors employed in their initial computer search, they can update their review of literature by instructing the computer to select only those references published since the initial search was conducted.
3. To update someone else's review. You may locate a review of the literature that is relevant to your problem but was published some years previously. You have the option of.updating this review, rather than starting from scratch, by instructing the

# COMPUTER SEARCH RECORD FORM

_____Mary Jones_____
**Your Name**

**Purpose of Search:** *To get information for an inservice teacher education program*
*for elementary teachers in mainstream classrooms*

**Problem Definition:**

*What teaching methods can be used to improve the reading comprehension of elementary students*

*who have learning disabilities?*

**Secondary Sources Reviewed:** *Leed, D.F. (1984) The Intuitive Approach to Reading*
*and Learning Disabilities. A Practical Alternative New York; C.C. Thomas*

**Data Base to be Searched:**

*ERIC using the DIALOG SYSTEM*

**ERIC Descriptors or Psychological Index Terms:**

1. *LEARNING DISABILITIES (8354)*
2. *COMMUNICATION DISORDERS (401)*
3. *LANGUAGE HANDICAPS (1872)*
4. *READING COMPREHENSION (8047)*
5. *REMEDIAL READING (2833)*
6. *READING SKILLS (7916)*
7. *READING ACHIEVEMENT (4179)*
8. *TEACHING METHODS (56,579)*
9. *READING INSTRUCTION (14,060)*
10. *CLASSROOM TECHNIQUES (7411)*
11. *ELEMENTARY EDUCATION*
12. *PRIMARY EDUCATION*
13. *ELEMENTARY SECONDARY EDUCATION*
14. 
15. 
16. 

**Search 1:** *1 AND 4 AND 8*

**Search 2:** *1 AND 4 AND 8 AND 11*

**Search 3:** *(1 OR 2) AND (4 OR 5) AND (8 OR 9)*

**Search 4:** *(1 OR 2 OR 3) AND (4 OR 5 OR 6 OR 7) AND (8 OR 9 OR 10)*

**Search 5:** *(1 OR 2 OR 3) AND (4 OR 5 OR 6) AND (8 OR 9 OR 10) AND (11 OR 12 OR 13)*

**Search 6:**

Figure 3.1 Computer Search Record Form Filled Out with a Complete Plan for Search of a Preliminary Source

computer to select only those references that were published after you think the reviewer completed the review. If the cutoff point of the review is not clear, you can estimate it and then go back a few years further to be sure that you don't miss any relevant references.

4. To prepare a master's paper or term paper that reviews research related to a particular topic.
5. To assemble research evidence that can help your school or other organization make an important decision, for example, "Should our school district adopt minimum competency examinations for high school graduation?"
6. To help locate or develop a new program for adoption in your school. The example given in Figure 3.1 fits this category.
7. To help solve a specific problem in your own classroom or work situation, for example, "What techniques can I use to stop John from hitting other children?"

You should think through the precise purpose of your search because you will use different approaches for different kinds of searches. Knowing the purpose will help you decide how many items you need to retrieve, how exhaustive your list of descriptors should be, and what type of material you need. The purpose of our sample search is stated in Figure 3.1.

## STEP 3: SELECT THE DATA BASE

The next step in a computer search is to select one or more data bases that are most relevant to your problem. A search of the ERIC data base, which includes *RIE* and *CIJE,* will produce much of the relevant literature for educational problems.

For our problem on teaching reading to learning-disabled children, a search of *ECER* and *Psychological Abstracts* could be added to ERIC for more complete coverage. However, at this point we will limit our sample search to the ERIC data base.

## STEP 4: SELECT DESCRIPTORS

Data bases can be searched in a variety of ways. For example, in ERIC some fields or areas that can be searched include author name, journal name, words that appear in the abstract, and descriptors. Since most researchers are searching for references about a subject, the two most common ways to search are by descriptor or by words in the abstract. As your research progresses and you identify specialists in your field, you can return to a data base and find material written by these individuals by doing an author search.

It is possible to search for words that appear anywhere in the title, abstract, or descriptor fields. Although this method is very broad and usually results in too many references, it is useful in several circumstances. If you are searching for a unique term that is not a descriptor, such as a place name (e.g., Oregon), an acronym (e.g., ITIP) or a test name (e.g., LASSI), this may be the method you will have to use.

Another method is to conduct a word search similar to the one described above but to stipulate that the words must appear next to or in close proximity to each other. We can also search for both words in the same field (e.g., both words must be somewhere in the title). This method, called proximity searching, is useful when you want to search a sharply defined topic or when there are no descriptor terms for the topic.

This type of searching involves phrases, or several words that appear in close proximity. These words do not have to be descriptor terms; any combination of words can be used. To illustrate, suppose we were interested in studies on the use of forced busing to achieve school desegregation. We find that "forced busing" is not a descriptor. However, we can still search for forced busing by carrying out a proximity search of the two words "forced" and "busing."

The most productive method of searching is by descriptor. Select the descriptors that best describe your problem. As we explained in Chapter 2, these descriptors must be terms that are appropriate for the preliminary source (in this case, ERIC) that you have selected. Also the terms must be entered *exactly* as they appear in the thesaurus. If you spell a descriptor incorrectly or modify it (e.g., by adding an *s*), the computer will not recognize the descriptor and will not find any references.

Using the *Thesaurus of ERIC Descriptors,* let's locate the descriptors that are relevant to our search for teaching methods to improve the reading comprehension of learning-disabled elementary students. First we would take the four main concepts from our problem statement and put them in order of importance: "Learning disabilities," "Reading comprehension," "Teaching methods," and "Elementary students."

Although the order of the terms is not critical, it is necessary to identify the least important concept because we may want to drop it if our initial search produces too few references. We have decided that "Elementary students" is the least important term because nearly all studies of reading are carried out in the elementary grades, so we will probably get relevant studies whether we specify elementary level or not. Also, studies not carried out in the elementary grades may still provide useful information if related to our other three main concepts.

The next step is to look up each of the three terms in the ERIC *Thesaurus* to identify the correct descriptors. You will find that a considerable amount of information is provided for each descriptor in the *Thesaurus.* For example, Figure 3.2 shows the information given for the descriptor "Competency based education." You will need to select the descriptor that most closely fits each of the terms you used in your problem. You can also broaden your search by selecting related terms (RT) for similar concepts. List the selected descriptors and related terms on the record form exactly as they appear in the *Thesaurus.*

When checking descriptors in the *Thesaurus,* you will see the number of items that have been assigned to that descriptor in *CIJE* and *RIE* from the date the descriptor was first used to the publication date of the *Thesaurus.* This information can be useful in helping you set up your search plans, as you will know how many items you will be dealing with before you do your search. You may want to make a note of this information for future reference.

Notice in Figure 3.1 that we listed 13 descriptor terms. In looking at the other descriptors under the subject heading "Learning disabilities," we find the related terms "Communication disorders" and "Language handicaps." We also find that dyslexia, aphasia, and other specific learning disabilities are mentioned. If we want everything

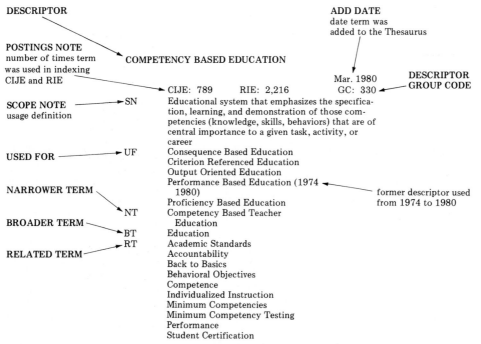

Figure 3.2  Sample Entry from the *Thesaurus of ERIC Descriptors,* Alphabetical Descriptor Display

on learning disabilities, including articles that deal only with the disability identified as dyslexia, "Dyslexia" would have to be entered along with "Learning disabilities." It is useful to make note of these more specific terms because persons who prepare abstracts and select descriptors for ERIC references follow the rule of using the most specific descriptors possible. For example, a study of children with the learning disability dyslexia would be classified by the descriptor "Dyslexia" rather than by the descriptor "Learning Disabilities" because the former is more specific. We may want to make a note of these descriptors and add them later.

In addition to "Reading comprehension," we have also listed "Remedial reading," "Reading skills," and "Reading achievement." For our next term, "Teaching methods," we listed two related terms, "Reading instruction" and "Classroom techniques." Our last term is "Elementary students." Each reference in ERIC is assigned a "mandatory educational level" descriptor. The introductory pages of the *Thesaurus of ERIC Descriptors* contain a list of these descriptors. By examining the list we determine that "Elementary education" is the most appropriate educational level descriptor for our search. If this term produces too few citations, we can remove it. But if after removing it the number of citations is too large, we can reenter "Elementary education" and similar terms. "Primary education" and "Elementary secondary education" may produce additional relevant items. The second term may produce studies that are not carried out in the elementary grades but are related to our other three main concepts. Because "Elementary education" is the least important of our four concepts, we may not need to add it at all.

## STEP 5: PLAN THE COMPUTER SEARCH

Computer data bases of preliminary sources enable us to conduct as broad or as narrow a literature search as we wish. A narrow search plan is desired when the problem is sharply focused or when one is not concerned with identifying all possible references related to the problem. A broad search plan is desired when it is not possible to define the problem precisely or when one wishes to do an exhaustive search for all possibly relevant references.

The search plan is put into action by instructing the computer to search for references that are classified by a particular *combination* of descriptors. Descriptors may be combined by using *and* and *or*. As we plan alternate searches, you will see that *or* connectors increase the number of references selected by the computer because there are more references that have one descriptor *or* the other than there are references that have either by itself. *And* connectors tend to reduce or limit the number of references because only references that have all of the descriptors connected by *and* will be selected.

In planning your searches, you also should note the number of *CIJE* and *RIE* references for each descriptor. If one of your key descriptors has been assigned to only a few references, you may want to retrieve all of these references. As a rule, such a descriptor should not be linked with other descriptors by an *and* connector because doing so will probably reduce the number of references reported by the computer to near zero. For example, if we were interested in the use of "indemnity bonds" by school districts, we would find in the *Thesaurus* that the system contains only four *CIJE* and eight *RIE* references with this descriptor.

You will note in Figure 3.1 that each of the 13 descriptors we have chosen has been assigned to large numbers of references (these are the numbers in parentheses adjacent to each subject descriptor). Therefore even if we link several of the concepts in our problem statement, using *and* connectors, the computer probably will yield some references. For example, we could plan a search of our four most relevant descriptors connected with *and* as follows:

> Learning disabilities (1) *and* Reading comprehension (4) *and* Teaching methods (8) *and* Elementary education (11)

This information is shown as Search 2 in Figure 3.1. We would expect this search to locate only a few references, but those located should be mostly on target since all four of our most relevant descriptors are used. It is planned as our second search because when three or more *and* connectors are used, the search often yields too few references to meet our needs.

The first search plan in Figure 3.1 has a broader focus. It includes three broad descriptors, and it omits "Elementary education," which we earlier identified as our least important concept. Thus, Search 1 consists of

Learning disabilities (1) *and* Reading comprehension (4) *and* Teaching methods (8)

This search plan tells the computer to locate only references that have all three of these descriptors because we have connected the descriptors with *and*. This search should produce more references than Search 2 and would probably retrieve enough references for our sample problem as defined on our Computer Search Record Form.

If we wanted a more thorough search, we could include some or all of our related terms. Related terms are usually joined by *or* connectors because we are interested in references that are classified by one of these terms or the other. It is very unlikely that a reference would be classified by both terms.

In our third search plan we will use one related term with each of our three most important descriptors. This will give us the following, which is listed as Search 3 in Figure 3.1:

(1 or 2) *and* (4 or 5) *and* (8 or 9)

This search plan tells the computer to locate references that have either descriptor 1 *or* 2 (Learning disabilities *or* Communication disorders) *and* either descriptor 4 *or* 5 (Reading comprehension *or* Remedial reading) *and* either 8 *or* 9 (Teaching methods *or* Reading instruction). This instruction will broaden the search related to our three most important concepts and will therefore produce more references than Search 1 or 2.

You may have noted that we used the *and* connector in these first three searches to link descriptors that referred to different concepts. We did so because we are interested in a reference only if it involves *all* the concepts in the search. Thus if a reference has been classified by only one of two descriptors that you have linked by the *and* connector, it will not be selected by the computer. As a general principle, the *and* connector is used to link descriptors for different concepts, whereas the *or* connector is used to link similar descriptors (also called related terms) for the same concept.

In Search 4 we broaden our search to include all of the related descriptors for our first three concepts:

(1 or 2 or 3) *and* (4 or 5 or 6 or 7) *and* (8 or 9 or 10)

This search would produce more references than any of our other searches because we included a large number of terms related to our three main concepts, with many of them linked by an *or* connector. This search has a broad focus, and so it probably will yield many references that are not closely related to our problem. It will take a great deal of time to read all these references and to select those that are most relevant. Therefore, a broad search plan should be designed only if you wish to do an exhaustive literature search.

We can reduce the number of references in Search 4 by adding our least important concept, "Elementary education," and other related level descriptors (Search 5). This search, like Search 2, would be restricted by using three *and* connectors, but it would probably produce more references than Search 2.

The Computer Search Record Form now contains all the information important to planning our search. We have stated the problem, described the purpose of the search, selected a data base, listed the descriptors, and planned several alternative searches.

## STEP 6: CONDUCT THE SEARCH

It is important to plan your search carefully before you actually begin. A well-planned search decreases your chances of missing relevant material or burying yourself in too much material.

The following searches were run on DIALOG's ERIC CD-ROM data base. The disk included the years 1980 through September 1991. Exact instructions for entering information in the computer is not given here since methods differ among data-base producers. In addition, search software and technology are constantly evolving. Therefore, check with your librarian to confirm what data bases are available in your area and for instructions on the correct method of entering information in the data base you plan to use.

Figure 3.3 shows the retrieval information for 10 subject descriptors, 3 educational level descriptors, and their combination. The computer will indicate how many references exist in the data base for each descriptor. For example, the system contained 5,692 references that have "Learning disabilities" as a descriptor at the time this search was conducted. (If you repeat the search, you probably will obtain more references because new references are added each month.)

As discussed earlier, the purpose of our search determines how broad it should be. If we need only a few references to prepare a brief report for the school board, the 16 references produced by Search 2 probably would be sufficient because all of them are likely to be relevant to our problem. However, if the purpose of our search is to get information that would help us set up an in-service teacher-training program, the 23 references located by Search 5 probably would be sufficient. If we want a broader coverage as a starting point for developing a district-wide or state-wide program, probably Search 1 would be our best choice because it produced 79 references.

If we need a very thorough review as part of a major research funding proposal, Search 3 probably would be our best choice. It would include many references that are only peripherally related to our problem, but it would give us a much broader understanding of the context into which our problem fits and would also reduce the chances of missing an important reference.

Search 4, which produced 216 references, would be inappropriate for anything other than an exhaustive search in which you must reduce the chances of missing an important source as much as possible. It is also appropriate if you require good coverage of peripheral material that will help you place your problem into a broad context of research and theory. However, it is unlikely that you will want to print all 216 references. You should look through the references and print or download only those that will be useful.

```
  1.  Learning disabilities
         Number retrieved                          5,692

  2.  Communication disorders
         Number retrieved                            436

  3.  Language handicaps
         Number retrieved                          1,037

  4.  Reading comprehension
         Number retrieved                          5,375

  5.  Remedial reading
         Number retrieved                          1,371

  6.  Reading skills
         Number retrieved                          4,075

  7.  Reading achievement
         Number retrieved                          2,235

  8.  Teaching methods
         Number retrieved                         30,840

  9.  Reading instruction
         Number retrieved                          8,090

 10.  Classroom techniques
         Number retrieved                          6,589

 11.  Elementary education
         Number retrieved                         25,397

 12.  Primary education
         Number retrieved                          5,572

 13.  Elementary secondary education
         Number retrieved                         65,394

SEARCHES

  1.  1 and 4 and 8
         Number retrieved                             79

  2.  1 and 4 and 8 and 11
         Number retrieved                             16

  3.  (1 or 2) and (4 or 5) and (8 or 9)
         Number retrieved                            159

  4.  (1 or 2 or 3) and (4 or 5 or 6 or 7) and
      (8 or 9 or 10)
         Number retrieved                            216

  5.  (1 or 2 or 3) and (4 or 5 or 6 or 7) and
      (8 or 9 or 10) and (11 or 12 or 13)
         Number retrieved                             23
```

Figure 3.3 Selected Descriptors, Number of References for Each Descriptor, and Five Searches

Once you have decided which search best meets your needs, it often is helpful to look at the bibliographical information on 10 to 15 of the references. This procedure will give you an idea of the kinds of references that have been selected. If none of the references appear relevant, you should restudy your search plans to determine whether they accurately reflect your problem.

# Focusing the Scope of Your Search

You may think it desirable to follow a search plan that yields many potentially useful references. Search 4, for example, yielded 216 potentially useful references. Keep in mind, though, that you will need to obtain and read the abstracts for all these references; then read the actual documents for at least some of them; and, finally, organize and report all the information you have gathered.

This process can far exceed the time you have available for a literature search. Therefore, you need to use search strategies that yield the most benefit for the time expended. We discussed above one such strategy, namely, to use only your key descriptors and combine them by *and* connectors. This is the strategy used in the first two search plans shown in Figure 3.1. In this section we describe other strategies you can use to save time by restricting the number of references yielded by a computer search.

## ASKING FOR MOST RECENT REFERENCES

Most data bases arrange citations in a definite order. Items are retrieved in reverse chronological order, that is, with the most recent material at the top of the list. You can limit your search by date, by looking only at those items at the top of your list. Most data bases allow you to limit your search by date. Some are naturally limited, in that only 5 years of an index appears on the whole data base. In others you can usually specify a range of years or ask for the last 5 or 10 years.

Date commands are also useful when you want to study documents published in specific years. For example, suppose a researcher is conducting a historical study that compares the content of articles dealing with school segregation at five-year intervals starting in 1968. This researcher could limit the literature search to documents published in 1968, 1973, 1978, 1983, and 1988 having the descriptor "School segregation."

## LIMITING THE SEARCH TO MAJOR DESCRIPTORS

Have you wondered how descriptors are applied to each document that is entered into the ERIC system? This activity is carried out by persons called "abstractors" at the ERIC clearinghouses. Abstractors read each document, write an abstract or use the abstract provided, and assign descriptors to the article. Descriptors are selected to identify the subject content of the document, the age levels and educational levels addressed by the content, the research methodology, tests used if any, and other pertinent information.

In addition to assigning these descriptors to a document, the abstractors classify them as major descriptors and minor descriptors. Up to six major descriptors are assigned to each document in order to cover its main focus. Minor descriptors are used to indicate less important aspects of the subject covered as well as to describe nonsubject features, such as the educational levels addressed by the document and research methods that were used.

An effective way to reduce the number of references produced by a search is to instruct the computer to select only documents for which your key descriptors have been classified as major descriptors. When Search 3 is conducted with only major descriptors, the number of references drops from 159 to 44. Although this procedure may result in the elimination of some references of peripheral relevance to your problem, you are unlikely to lose any key references and you will save a great deal of time.

The practice of assigning major and minor descriptors is not used by all data bases and therefore cannot be used as a search technique in every data base.

## DEFINING SPECIFIC TYPES OF DOCUMENTS TO BE ACCESSED IN YOUR SEARCH

When doing a computer search, you have an advantage in being able to specify descriptors not only for the topics you want to search but also for certain types of documents dealing with those topics. For example, you can add a descriptor for terms such as "Bibliography," "Meta-analysis," "Literature review," or "Literature search." Adding these terms as descriptors will limit your search to documents that have been classified under these descriptors.

For example, we recently did a brief search on an ERIC CD-ROM to find resources that have identified and described a variety of parent education programs. We used three search terms: "Parents" *and* "Literature review" *or* "Meta-analysis." The search turned up 28 references, all of which had been classified under both the descriptor "Parents" and the descriptor "Literature review." (No meta-analytic studies concerning parents were found.) Thus, we were able to limit our search to documents that provided an extensive listing of references in the area of parent education.

You will find these terms listed in the *Thesaurus of ERIC Descriptors,* but reviewers assign them as minor descriptors. Talk to your librarian about specific types of documents that are most likely to give you the type of information you need. You can also experiment with descriptors to pinpoint studies that utilized a particular research method, such as "Experimental research" or "Qualitative research."

## SPECIFYING THE FORM OF THE REFERENCES

After finalizing your search plan, you need to decide (1) the amount of detail you want about each reference and (2) the form in which you want to receive this information. The data bases offer various options concerning the level of detail. The following are three of the most popular.

*1. One option provides the title.* If your search involves more than 20 references, you may choose to select this option first. Rather than waste paper and your time by printing all citations, relevant and nonrelevant, you can first read through the titles to decide which citations you really want printed. If you are being charged for your search it is wise to read through the titles first, since there is no charge for them, and then pay only for the abstracts of the titles you want.

The title is often useful in helping you decide whether you should read the document, but it is much less useful than an abstract. In some cases the title tells you almost nothing. For example, our search for references on teaching reading to learning-disabled elementary students produced these titles: "A Corner on Reading," "The Reluctant Reader," and "Case Studies in Reading."

*2. Another option includes complete bibliographic data and an accession number.* For example,

> EJ188759      EC111239
> Learning Word Meanings: A
> Comparison of Instructional Procedures
> Pany, Darlene; Jenkins, Joseph R.
> Learning Disability Quarterly, 1, 2, 21-
> 32 Spr 78

This option gives you a slightly better basis than the first option for judging the content of the document. The accession number in ERIC will begin with ED (document) or EJ (journal article). The ED number is important for retrieving ERIC documents on microfiche because they are filed that way in most libraries. This option also provides enough information to find the item without further information from the data base.

*3. A third option includes all the data from the second option plus descriptors and an abstract, if one is available.* Here is an example from another computer search we conducted that dealt with teacher use of educational research:

> ED246023 SP024890
> On Getting from Here (Research) to There (Practice).
> Fenstermacher, Gary D.
> Mar 1984 7p.; In: Egbert, Robert L., Ed., and Kluender, Mary M., Ed.
> Using Research to Improve Teacher Education: The Nebraska Consortium.
> Teacher Monograph No. 1. (SP 024 888), p22–27.
>
> There is no easy way to get from research on teaching to teaching practice; moreover, trying to make teaching practices directly out of research can have destructive effects for teaching. Research can be extremely beneficial when results are linked with teachers' goals, and when teachers are aware that a specific occasion is appropriate for realization of the goal. This awareness enables them to engage in actions appropriate to fulfilling the goal. Research results can be brought to bear on teaching practices through careful, considered incorporation into the practical arguments in the minds of teachers. If research is presented to teachers in a manner that shows regard for their prior beliefs and experience, teachers will be encouraged to consider the research and its impact on practice. (CJB)
>
> Descriptors: *Adoption (Ideas); Behavior Change; Educational Research; Elementary School Teachers; Elementary Secondary Education; *Research Utilization; Secondary School Teachers; *Teacher Attitudes; *Teacher Behavior; *Teacher Improvement
> Identifiers: *Research Practice Relationship

This information is probably sufficient to decide whether the document is relevant to your problem. Also, the abstract may provide sufficient detail about its content, so that it will not be necessary to locate and read the actual document. Descriptors are printed to provide alternative descriptors that may not have occurred to you. The "Identifiers" that follow the descriptors are used for key concepts for which descriptors do not exist. These include program names, place names, tests, or procedures.

After deciding which of the above three options is best for you, you will need to decide how you wish to capture the information. You can either print the selected references or download them to a disk.

## CHECKING YOUR PRINTOUT

After completing your search, you should read all the abstracts and rate them for relevance. The purpose of the ratings is to help you decide which references to read first. The rating system also can be used to classify the aspect of your problem to which each reference is relevant. Here, for example, is a rating system that we have used:

> + +   a very important and relevant reference
> +   relevant reference, should be read
> −   check this reference, it may be relevant
> 0   not relevant, do not check

After you have read the abstracts and rated them, you may find it helpful to cut out all references you plan to read or check and paste each on a 5- × -8-inch note card or sheet of binder paper. Start your reading with the most recent of your most important (i.e., + +) articles. After reading and making whatever supplementary notes are needed for all of your + + references, follow the same procedure for your + references and then for your − references. You will find many helpful suggestions on how to read and take notes on primary source references in the next chapter.

Some researchers are suspicious of computer searches because they carried out a search that omitted references that they knew were relevant to their topic. This problem can occur if the researcher failed to use a sufficient number of related terms with *or* connectors. Another possibility is reviewer differences in assigning descriptors. This type of error can occur because of the process employed in preparing abstracts and selecting descriptors for a given article. Each indexing service assigns items to staff, and someone who is knowledgeable about the subject reads the article, prepares the abstract (in most cases), and selects the descriptors. Unfortunately both the preparation of the abstract and the selection of descriptors are quite subjective. Therefore, if the same document were assigned to a group of reviewers, it is unlikely that any two would include exactly the same material in their abstract or list exactly the same descriptors.

This subjectivity is clearly illustrated by the two journal citations from the ERIC system shown in Figure 3.4. In this unusual case the same article has been indexed twice in the same index. It is clear that they are two reviews of the same article. However, if you read the two abstracts, you will see that they have little in common. A look at the descriptors is even more surprising. The first review lists nine descriptors, whereas the second review lists only six. Note furthermore that only four of the descriptors, "Autism," "Middle schools," "Peer teaching," and "Program descriptions," are common to the two reviews.

This example clearly illustrates the fallibility of preliminary sources. Remember that

---

EJ282648 EC152054

Peer Tutors Help Autistic Students Enter the Mainstream.

Campbell, Ann: And Others

Teaching Exceptional Children. v15 n2 p64–69 Win     1983

Available from: Reprint: UMI

Language: English

Document Type: JOURNAL ARTICLE (080): PROJECT DESCRIPTION (141)

A peer tutoring program in which tutors were taught behavioral techniques as well as background information through a broad game format was successful in promoting integration of a class of autistic adolescents in a middle school. Peer tutors helped to promote positive attitudes among students and teachers.

(CL)

Descriptors: *Attitude Change: *Autism: Behavior Modification; Middle

Schools; *Peer Influence; *Peer Teaching; Program Descriptions; Student

Attitudes; Teacher Attitudes

---

EJ274446 EC151160

Peer Tutors Help Autistic Students Enter the Mainstream.

Campbell, Ann; And Others

Teaching Exceptional Children. v15 n2 p64–69 Win     1983

Available from: Reprint: UMI

Language: English

Document Type: JOURNAL ARTICLE (080); PROJECT DESCRIPTION

(141)

The peer tutoring program was initiated at the Belle Vue (Florida) Middle School as an effective way of bringing autistic students into contact with the mainstream. (SW)

Descriptors: *Autism; Mainstreaming; Middle Schools; *Peer Relationship;

*Peer Teaching; Program Descriptions

---

Figure 3.4 Two Citations of the Same Article in the ERIC System

these problems are found in the paper form of the indexes as well as in the computer versions. However, they should not stop you from using indexes since the alternative of checking every journal, issue by issue, is just not feasible.

Remember, too, that computer searching is much faster and better than manual searching. Of course, it is still possible to miss a relevant reference when you do a computer search. The chances of missing important references are even greater, however, when you conduct a manual search because of the amount of time required to do an exhaustive search manually. It also takes time to develop skills in using a computer to carry out a literature search. However, once you have these skills, you will save a great deal of time by conducting literature searches on computer, compared to that involved in carrying out manual searches.

# Developing Computer Search Skills

You should not expect your first attempt at computer searching to be a complete success. Most people have to plan and carry out three or four searches before they are sufficiently familiar and feel comfortable with the process. Therefore, it is advisable to conduct a few small-scale searches on topics needed for term papers or topics related to specific classroom problems that interest you. Such searches will give you valuable experience. Another method that helps reduce anxiety and increases your knowledge of search systems is to sit at the computer with a friend, classmate, or colleague as you work through the system. Choose someone with as much or more knowledge about the system as you. You both will probably learn more about the system than if you tried to work through it yourself. There is usually a reference librarian or other person in the vicinity of the CD-ROMs who knows a great deal about the system, so be sure to ask for assistance when you need it. Also, most libraries produce handouts on how to use the system and/or offer training sessions; be sure to take advantage of them.

# Recommended Reading

BATT, F. (1988). *Online searching for end users: An information sourcebook*. Phoenix, AZ: Oryx Press.

This book provides a brief discussion of major topics relating to on-line searching, for example, searching by using intermediaries and searching by end users, various data bases and vendors, and search strategies. Following each overview is an extensive annotated bibliography.

FUSTUKJIAN, S., & TAHERI, B., eds. (1990). *Directory of ERIC information service providers*. Washington, DC: Educational Resources Information Center.

This document lists organizations that provide access to the ERIC data base and its related resources. This list includes organizations that provide computer searches of ERIC, hold collections of ERIC microfiches, and collect various ERIC publications. Entries include the name and address of each organization, population served, data bases available, cost, and other information.

HARTLEY, F. J., KEEN, E. M., LARGE, J. A., & TEDD, L. A. (1990). *Online searching: Principles and practice*. London: Bowker-Saur.

This book contains chapters on basic searching, search strategies, and Boolean logic. Examples are used to illustrate techniques discussed. A bibliography follows each chapter.

LI, T. C. (1985). *An introduction to online searching*. Westport, CT: Greenwood Press.

This book is designed to introduce readers to on-line searching with an emphasis on the basics of bibliographic searching. The first seven chapters deal with important reference sources, thesauri, and types of data bases. The remaining chapters cover basic procedures for on-line searching, as well as specific procedures for searching DIALOG, BRS, and other data-base vendors.

# Application Problems

**1.** List the library or libraries near you at which you can carry out a literature search.

---

---

**2.** For each of the libraries you listed in problem 1, answer the following questions:
  **a.** Which of the following data bases are available?

| On-line | On CD-ROM | |
|---------|-----------|---|
| _____ | _____ | (1) ERIC |
| _____ | _____ | (2) *Psychological Abstracts* |
| _____ | _____ | (3) *Exceptional Child* |
| _____ | _____ | (4) *Dissertation Abstracts Online* |

  **b.** What other data bases are available that may be useful for your topic?

---

**3. a.** If they are not available at your library, list the location of the nearest available CD-ROM.

---

  **b.** If CD-ROMs are not available at your library, list the closest location that will provide an online search for you.

---

**4.** Suppose you are planning to set up a program of individualized instruction in your elementary school for children with learning disabilities and want to locate research related to this topic. Carry out the following steps.
  **a.** Photocopy the Computer Search Record Form (Appendix 1).
  **b.** Enter the Purpose of Search and the Program Definition on the form.
  **c.** Check the library card catalog for books related to this problem and list two books under Secondary Sources.
  **d.** Write *Psychological Abstracts* under data base to be searched.
  **e.** Underline key words in problem definition.
  **f.** Look up key words in the *Thesaurus of Psychological Index Terms* and enter these words. Which is the least important of your key terms?
  **g.** Enter broader, narrower, or related terms that might be useful.
  **h.** Develop three possible search plans and enter on the record form: a brief search using key terms only, a broader search with two *or* connectors, and an exhaustive search.

5. Make a photocopy of the Computer Search Record Form (Appendix 1).
   a. Select one of the problem statements or questions you wrote for Application Problem 2 in Chapter 2 and write it in the Problem Definition section of the record form.
   b. Underline the key words in your problem definition and use the *Thesaurus of ERIC Descriptors* to list one descriptor and two related terms for each key word. Enter these descriptors in your record form.
   c. Plan the following complete searches, and for each one write down the search plan on your record form, including descriptor numbers, *and* connectors, and *or* connectors.
      (1) A search that would be likely to produce a few references that are closely related to your problem or question, using not more than two *and* connectors.
      (2) A search that would be likely to produce a large number of references, many of which are not closely on target.

# CHAPTER 4

# REVIEWING PRIMARY SOURCES AND WRITING A REPORT

## Overview

After completing your search of preliminary sources, you will need to locate, read, and take notes on the references that you found. Many of these references will be primary sources, that is, reports of research studies by the researchers who conducted them. This chapter describes the four main types of publications in which primary sources appear: professional journals, reports, scholarly books and monographs, and dissertations. You will learn how to locate primary sources and take notes on them. You also will learn how to organize your notes and use them in writing a report of your findings.

*[handwritten margin note: 4 Types of Pubs For Primary Sources]*

## Objectives

1. Name and briefly describe the four major types of primary source references.
2. Explain the advantages of reports over professional journals.
3. Describe *Dissertation Abstracts International*.
4. Describe how you can obtain references not available in your local library.
5. Describe an effective strategy for reading and making notes on journal articles and longer references such as reports, books, or dissertations.
6. Explain how your note cards can be classified to facilitate writing a report of your findings.
7. Describe what should be covered in each of the main sections of your report.
8. State 12 rules that you should follow in writing the body of your report.

## Types of Primary Sources

The end product of your search for references in preliminary sources will be a set of bibliographic citations, each on an index card or sheet of paper. The next steps in carrying out your review are to use the citation information to locate the document, read it, and take notes. Before explaining this process, we will describe the four types of publications in which most primary sources appear: (1) professional journals, (2) reports, (3) scholarly books and monographs, and (4) dissertations.

### PROFESSIONAL JOURNALS

Many journals publish reports of research in education and in related social sciences. Some are general in focus, publishing articles on a wide range of educational topics.

Others are specialized journals dedicated to a single field such as teacher education, mathematics education, or learning disabilities.

The *American Educational Research Journal* is a good example of a general journal. Its purpose is to publish what it describes as "original reports of empirical and theoretical studies in education." The journal is published quarterly, and a typical issue contains six to eight articles ranging from about 15 to 30 pages in length. In recent years both qualitative and quantitative studies have appeared regularly.

The *Journal of Staff Development* is an example of a specialized journal. Published bimonthly, each issue has several articles dealing with a particular theme in teacher education (for example, mentoring programs for new teachers) as well as other articles. The articles tend to be short, ranging from four to six pages. Only a few are primary source reports of research; most report the experiences and opinions of experts in staff development.

Both general and specialized journals vary greatly in the types of articles they publish. Some emphasize reports of original research studies, whereas others emphasize theoretical analyses, the opinions of experts, and descriptions of new programs. All make a contribution to our understanding of educational problems. However, you must be aware of the particular type of article you are reading because each type will contribute differently to your understanding of a problem.

## REPORTS

Many important research studies and theories first appear as reports. These reports can take the form of papers read at professional meetings; conference proceedings; or documents prepared by government agencies, commissions, professional associations, foundations, school districts, or universities. Many of these reports are indexed and abstracted in the Documents Resume section of ERIC's *Resources in Education (RIE)*.

Reports have several advantages over professional journals as sources of new ideas and research findings about education. The most important advantage is that research appears sooner in reports than in journal articles. For example, when researchers finish a federally funded project, they must submit a final report within a short time period. Copies of this report typically are sent to ERIC for inclusion in *RIE*. The time lag between completion of the report and inclusion in *RIE* may be only a few months. If the researchers then decide to publish their findings in a professional journal, they must rewrite their report, submit it to a journal, and typically wait a year or more before it is published.

Another advantage of reports over journal articles is that they usually provide more detailed information because they are not subject to the severe space limitations of most journals.

Reports that are included in the ERIC system have special advantages. They are available at any university or school district having an ERIC microfiche collection. Because most ERIC reports are not copyrighted, they usually can be freely copied. By contrast, many journals—especially those of a specialized nature—are not likely to be available at local university or college libraries. Also, copyright restrictions often prohibit copying articles published in a journal.

## SCHOLARLY BOOKS AND MONOGRAPHS

Research studies or theoretical works of major importance often appear initially as reports but are later developed further and published as scholarly books or monographs. Some of these works are published by commercial publishers, but many are published by university presses because the target audience, and hence the market for them, is small. *Teachers for Our Nation's Schools* by John Goodlad, published in 1990, is a good example of a scholarly book that reports important research insights with national implications. Goodlad and a team of researchers did intensive case studies of teacher education programs in 29 colleges and universities and discovered obstacles that keep these programs from full achievement of their mission, including "tyrannical" credentialing requirements and emphasis on research over teacher preparation. Goodlad reviews these research findings and offers recommendations on how teacher education programs can be improved.

## DISSERTATIONS

Most doctoral dissertations in education report on original research and therefore are primary source documents. They are indexed in *Dissertation Abstracts International (DAI)*. This preliminary source is a monthly compilation of abstracts of doctoral dissertations submitted by more than 375 cooperating institutions in the United States and Canada. It has been published in various forms since 1938, when it first appeared as *Microfilm Abstracts*.

The paper version of *DAI* has two sections: Section A, covering dissertations in the humanities and social sciences including education; and Section B, covering the sciences (including psychology) and engineering. The abstracts within each issue of Section A are organized into 32 major content areas, one of which is Education. There are 37 subtopics such as Adult, Art, Higher, Preschool, and Teacher Training under the Education content area. If you are interested in checking dissertations in one of these topic areas, you can examine the table of contents of *DAI* to locate pages containing relevant abstracts.

Each monthly issue of *DAI* contains a Keyword Title Index, in which the bibliographic entries are classified and arranged alphabetically by important key words in the title. To search a specific topic, check the Keyword Title Index to locate relevant abstracts. For example, a person who is interested in the social development of preschool children could check "Social," "Development," and "Preschool" in the Keyword Title Index; read the dissertation titles listed under each key word; copy the page number on which the abstract for each relevant dissertation appears; and then locate and read the selected abstracts. In most cases you can decide from reading the abstract whether a dissertation is sufficiently relevant to your problem to justify ordering and reading it.

By using *Dissertation Abstracts Online,* you can also search *DAI* by computer. (This is one of the preliminary source data bases described in Chapter 3.) To conduct a search, you first enter the key words from your problem statement. The computer will search only the titles of older dissertations for these words. However, for dissertations completed since 1980 the computer will search the entire citation, including the abstract. In effect, you are conducting a proximity search as described in Chapter 3. Unlike the ERIC system, you cannot search *DAI* with standard descriptors. Therefore, to get a complete search, you need to enter a large number of synonymous terms in the hope that one of them will be in the title or abstract.

For example, if you were interested in dissertation studies of learning disabilities, you would enter "Learning (W) Disabilities" into the computer. (The "W" is a connector symbol that tells the computer the two words must be adjacent to each other and in that order.) The computer would retrieve dissertations with this phrase in the title. For dissertations published since 1980, the computer would search the entire reference, including both the title and abstract.

You also can conduct simultaneous searches of the key terms and phrases in your problem statement by using *and* and *or* connectors in the same way they are used in computer searches of ERIC (see Chapter 3). For example, we entered Searches 1 and 2 from our search plan concerning the improvement of reading comprehension of elementary students with learning disabilities (see Figure 3.1). Search 1 produced no dissertations, and Search 2 produced only three. This example illustrates the need to use a large number of related terms to explore the *DAI* data base fully for relevant studies.

Abstracts entered into the system since 1980 can be printed on-line by the terminal in your library. However, it is almost as fast and somewhat less expensive to have the computer print only the bibliographic citation, and for you to look up the abstracts in your library's paper copy of *DAI*.

Any dissertation indexed in *DAI* can be purchased from University Microfilms International, either on microfilm or in hard-copy format. The order number is given at the end of the abstract. The cost of a microfilm copy is currently $20.00, and a hard copy can be obtained for $36.50.

Interlibrary loan is another option for obtaining a dissertation. However, many universities will not loan dissertations, and most are rather slow in mailing them. Often the cost of borrowing a dissertation through interlibrary loan is greater than the cost of buying the microfilm.

Because it helps the reader locate dissertations, which are primary sources, *DAI* can be considered a preliminary source. However, *DAI* also can be considered a primary source because it contains abstracts written by the authors of the dissertations. The abstracts vary in length up to a full page and usually give a good summary of the study.

# Obtaining Primary Sources

### USING THE LIBRARY

The majority of the references you decide to track down probably will be in professional journals because this is the principal type of primary source in which research is reported. If you need to obtain many journal issues, you most likely will need to travel to a university library.

Once at the library, you can save a lot of time locating journal issues if you are systematic. The first step is to study the layout of the library and then to talk with the reference librarian to determine what method of obtaining journal issues will require the least amount of time. In many libraries all the journals are shelved in a central location called the stacks. If study space is available in the stacks, it is usually desirable to set up your work area there. You can bring all your journal issues to your work area, take notes, and put placeholders in pages that you wish to photocopy. When it is time for photocopying, you can do all this work at once.

Some libraries do not permit students and other patrons to enter the stacks. Instead you need to make out a call slip for each journal issue you need, and a library clerk will search the stacks for it. In this case you usually can save time by making out call slips for about 10 journal issues at a time. While waiting for the library clerk to return with these issues, you can make out call slips for your next 10 references. The clerk can look for the second 10 references while you are scanning and making notes on whatever you received from the first 10 call slips. Keep in mind that a certain percentage of the journal issues you want will be lost, checked out, or in the bindery, so it is always advisable to submit call slips for 10 or more at a time.

## OBTAINING DOCUMENTS NOT LOCALLY AVAILABLE

You almost certainly will find that some of the documents you wish to examine are not available at your local library. These documents can be obtained by several methods. The quickest and easiest way to obtain a brief document, such as a journal article or book chapter, is to write directly to the author (or senior author in the case of a multiauthored article) and ask for a reprint of it. Most authors are willing to send a reprint to anyone requesting it.

The main problem encountered in writing for reprints is obtaining the address of the author. If you located the article in *Psychological Abstracts* or *RIE,* the address is usually given. This information, however, is not available in *Education Index* or *Current Index to Journals in Education (CIJE)*. In this case you can search for addresses in various professional directories such as *Who's Who in American Education,* the *Biographical Directory of the American Psychological Association,* and the *American Educational Research Association Biographical Membership Directory.* The reference librarian usually can suggest other directories if an individual is not listed in any of the ones mentioned. If your library does not have the membership directory that you need, check with educators who are likely to belong to the organization that publishes that directory.

If you cannot obtain a reprint from the author, the next step is to see if the needed document is available in other libraries nearby. Large population centers tend to have several colleges or universities within a small geographical area, so you usually can find the document you need at one of their libraries. If there are no other libraries, you might be able to obtain selected journal issues through interlibrary loan. Some libraries place restrictions on who can use this service because it is rather expensive.

Another approach is to try to obtain microfilms or photocopies of documents not locally available. The reference librarian at your local library should be able to locate needed publications and arrange for their reproduction, but you probably will be charged for the cost of reproduction and shipping. The cost varies considerably, usually from 15 to 35 cents per page, so this approach is often practical for short articles but too expensive for books or lengthy documents. Reproduction of copyrighted publications is restricted, so you should check the current regulations with your librarian. As a rule, however, you may make a single copy of most reference material for private study or research without violating copyright laws.

If a needed publication appears to be of major importance to your problem, you should find some method of obtaining it. The satisfaction of knowing you have done a thorough and scholarly review of the literature will more than compensate for the expense.

# Reading and Note Taking

Different reading methods are appropriate for different types of publications in the educational literature. In this section we discuss what those methods are for research publications and for publications that present theories, descriptions, and opinions.

## RESEARCH PUBLICATIONS

In Chapter 3 we recommended that you code your bibliographic citations to indicate their importance to your problem. You should start your review by checking the most recent of the most important documents. The reason for starting with the most recent documents is that they have the earlier research as a foundation and thus are likely to be more valuable. By reading them, you can quickly build up a reasonably deep understanding of what has been learned about your problem. It will then be much easier to see how older publications and publications on peripheral topics relate to your problem.

Many research documents, especially journal articles and technical reports, contain an abstract. If there is no abstract, start by reading the discussion or conclusions section of the document. (Some reports contain an "executive summary" at the front.) In this way you usually can determine quickly whether the publication contains any information that would justify reading it in its entirety.

If you decide the document is relevant to your problem, check the accuracy of the data on your bibliographic citation, in case the source from which you obtained the citation contained errors. Then you are ready to take notes on the document as you read it. These notes should be made on your bibliography card or sheet of paper, so that they do not get separated accidentally from the bibliographic citation.

If you conducted a computer search, you may have pasted a computer printout containing the abstract of the document on the bibliography card or sheet of paper. If this information is available, you should review it so you do not take redundant notes.

Research articles average 5 to 10 pages in length and thus take little time to read. Reports, scholarly books, and dissertations are usually much longer. For these longer documents, scan the entire document and then read carefully only those parts that are directly relevant to your problem. Pay particular attention to tables because they constitute summaries of the main research findings. A brief review of these tables usually is sufficient for you to decide whether the document is worth studying in greater depth.

Most reports of research studies follow a standard format. As you learn this format, you can search more quickly for the information you need. The format typically follows this sequence: (1) an abstract; (2) an introduction that states the problem and discusses important previous research; (3) a statement of the objectives or hypotheses to be tested; (4) a description of the research method, including subjects, measures, and research design; (5) a presentation of statistical and/or qualitative analyses; and (6) a discussion of the research results that includes interpretations and implications for further research and practice.

Taking notes is a time-consuming process. Also, it is very frustrating to take notes on a report at a library only to find later that your notes omitted an important detail. The only alternatives are to continue your review without knowing the detail or to make a time-consuming return trip to the library. Therefore, if you think you will need to take a lot of notes on a particular document, you should consider photocopying it instead. You can save a lot of time by marking relevant information on the photocopy rather than writing notes on a bibliography card or sheet of paper. Also, you can refer back to your photocopies whenever you wish.

If note taking is adequate for your purposes, you can save time and space by abbreviating whenever possible. Among the abbreviations you could use are $N$ for number of subjects, $S$ for subjects, $SIG$ for statistically significant, $NS$ for nonsignificant, $X$ for experimental group, $C$ for control group, $M$ for mean, $SD$ for standard deviation, $r$ for correlation, $ANOVA$ for analysis of variance, $ANCOVA$ for analysis of covariance, and $QL$ for a qualitative study.

The introductory and discussion sections of a research report might mention relevant previous studies that did not emerge in your search of preliminary sources. If this is the case, copy the bibliographic data onto bibliography cards or sheets of paper, code their probable level of importance, and check them when time permits.

You should consider making notes on your own evaluation of the study and its relevance to your problem while it is still fresh in your mind. (Chapters 5–8 explain how to evaluate research reports.) Your notes may include promising or unusual techniques employed in the study, measures that could be of use to you, interesting theoretical points, and any apparent weaknesses that make the results questionable or limit their application to your problem.

Figure 4.1 (p. 74) shows a note card on a published article that illustrates the procedures and principles discussed above.

## THEORETICAL, DESCRIPTIVE, OR OPINION PUBLICATIONS

Many of the references you find in your literature search will not be reports of research projects but will be theoretical formulations, descriptions of a program or method, or the personal opinions of the author. These publications do not follow the format of a research report and are unlikely to contain an abstract or summary.

Theoretical articles are relevant if they help to explain the phenomena that concern

*McFaul, S. A., & Cooper, J. M. Peer clinical supervision in an urban elementary school. Journal of Teacher Education, 1983, 34(5), 34-38.*
*Problem: (1) to document how teachers implemented peer clinical supervision (PCS) in an urban elementary school; (2) to discover contextual factors in the school that are congruent or incongruent with PCS; (3) to analyze the feasibility of implementing PCS.*
*Procedure: 12 teachers (11 female) from same school took semester course in clinical supervision (CS) for credit. In last 3rd of course, they worked in pairs to do CS with each other for 8 cycles (4 as supervisor; 4 as teacher). Data were in form of preobservation agreement forms, data collection instruments, tape recordings of postobservation conferences, ethnographic field notes, interviews, & other self-report data.*
*Findings: (1) All but 1 teacher was able to implement PCS. (2) Teachers who had best clinical skills were rated most helpful by peers. (3) Teacher-supervisor match was important. (4) Videotape recordings helped teachers. (5) Lack of time was a major problem. (6) Primary focus of PCS cycles was kids' on-task behavior, teacher-student interaction, teacher presentation behavior. (7) Teachers accepted validity of peer supervisors' data. (8) Most conferences lacked in-depth problem solving. (9) PCS appears to work best with teachers who are analytic & committed to teaching. (10) 4 context factors worked against PCS: isolation & fragmentation; stratification; standardization; and reactionism.*
*Conclusion: "The reality of some of our schools may be such that they are impervious to change strategies such as peer clinical supervision" (p. 37).*
*Comment: If we are to implement peer coaching in our district using a clinical supervision model, we'd better examine these 4 context factors first. Also, these results are for an elementary school only. Would results be same for middle schools/high schools?*

Figure 4.1  Sample Note Card

you. For example, suppose you are interested in finding effective programs for improving students' reading comprehension. You might find research evidence in your literature search that some programs are more effective than others. You also might find that the effective programs tend to be based on contemporary theories of human information processing. Reading articles about these theories will help you to understand the conceptual underpinnings of successful programs and to defend these programs if you are questioned by school board members, parents, or others.

Articles that describe new educational programs and methods can stimulate your thinking about how to solve the problem that is the subject of your literature search. However, you should be wary of authors' claims for a program or method unless the claims are supported by research evidence. You might be stimulated to plan your own test of the program or method to determine how well it works in your situation. With careful planning, you can do your own action research by using the procedures described in Chapter 15.

It sometimes happens that your literature search identifies certain programs or methods that are highly recommended but are not substantiated by research evidence. Other programs or methods may address the same need, but they have been tested and validated by research. It is important to know about all these programs and methods regardless of whether they have been the subject of research. For example, you may conclude that program X should be implemented because it is best supported by research. However, a policymaker or colleague may argue for program Y. If you have learned about program Y in your literature search, you will be better able to defend your recommendation for program X.

Opinion articles also can be important to your literature search. Suppose, for example, that you are interested in whether your school system should allow more choice for parents and students. It is important to search the literature to determine not only what kinds of choice programs are most effective but also the range of opinions about these programs. People's opinions influence their actions—often more so than research evidence. By knowing the range of existing opinions, you can develop your own opinion on the issue and defend it, if necessary. Furthermore, you will understand better where policymakers and colleagues stand on the issue and thus can do a better job of addressing their concerns.

When checking a theoretical, descriptive, or opinion article, first scan it to get some idea of its content. One method of scanning is to read only the first few sentences under each heading. If you decide that the article is relevant, you can then read it more closely. As with research reports, you should consider whether it is more efficient to photocopy the article or take notes on it.

## QUOTATIONS

As you read, be alert for quotations that will be useful in writing your report. If you find statements that you might want to quote, copy them very carefully onto the bibliography card or sheet of paper. Be sure to enclose each statement in quotation marks to help you remember that it is a quote and not your own paraphrase. Also, record the page number of the quote because most style manuals require the author to include this information when making a direct quotation. Knowing the page number also enables you to check the quotation if necessary.

Some reviewers use far too many quotations in their reports. A good rule of thumb is to quote only statements that are worded particularly well and concisely. For example, one of us began a review of the literature on effective questioning techniques with this sentence: "Teachers have been described as 'professional question-askers' (Aschner, 1961)." The phrase, "professional question-askers" was so pithy and to the point that it merited a direct quote rather than a paraphrase.

After copying a quotation, recheck to be sure that you have copied it exactly. Inaccurate quotations are a serious reflection on the scholarship of the writer and may raise questions about the validity of everything else in the literature review.

## CLASSIFYING THE DOCUMENTS YOU READ

As you read the documents identified in your literature search, think about categories for grouping them. For example, suppose you are reviewing the literature to help your school system plan a staff development program for its administrators. As you read the literature, you may observe that some publications concern school administrators specifically, whereas others concern administrators generally or administrators in business and industry. This observation suggests grouping the publications into three categories: (1) school administrators, (2) administrators in business and industry, and (3) general. You also may find that different documents concern different purposes of staff development, leading you to formulate the following categories: (1) staff development to help administrators improve staff morale, (2) staff development to help administrators lower their stress and maintain a healthy lifestyle, (3) staff development to help administrators improve organizational effectiveness, and (4) staff development for other purposes.

In carrying out your review, you should be alert for natural categories that can be used to group your studies. These categories can provide a framework for reading the documents you have located and also help you to organize your report. As soon as you have developed a set of categories, you should use them to develop codes for indicating what type of information is contained in each publication. The codes can be written on the bibliography card or sheet of paper that you have prepared for each document.

A coding system developed by one of us for a review of the literature on ability grouping illustrates procedures that you can use in developing your own coding system. In this case the following codes were developed:

S  Studies dealing with social interaction
A  Studies describing grouping systems and their relationship to student achievement
G  Studies discussing problems involved in grouping, such as individual variability
B  Studies relating grouping to behavior problems
P  Studies relating grouping to personality adjustment, personality variables, and self-concept

The appropriate code was placed in the upper right-hand corner of each bibliography card. Documents that covered several different topics were assigned multiple codes.

# Writing a Report of Your Findings

Whether you have done a literature review to help solve a local school problem or to meet a requirement for a college or university degree, you probably will need to prepare a report of your findings. The purpose of the report usually is to describe the state of knowledge about the problem you have investigated and to make recommendations based on that knowledge.

Reports of literature reviews usually contain the following sections:

1. *Introduction.* A description of the problem or question you are seeking to answer and your literature search plan.
2. *Body of the report.* The findings of your review, organized into meaningful categories.
3. *Discussion.* Your conclusions about the state of knowledge relating to the problem or question that initiated the literature search and your recommendations for a course of action.
4. *References.* Complete bibliographical data for all primary and secondary sources you have cited.

Each of these sections is described in more detail below.

## THE INTRODUCTION

The introductory section of the report should state your problem or question and explain its importance. Writing this section gives you the opportunity to redefine your problem statement based on what you learned from conducting your literature search. It is almost always desirable to define your problem more specifically than you did originally. Or you may find it useful to discuss various aspects of the problem and how you chose the aspects on which to focus.

As an example of how to narrow a problem statement, a graduate student started her literature search with the goal of examining the relationship between self-esteem and academic achievement. After reading a secondary source on academic achievement, she realized that this was a broad topic and that her specific interest was the effects of self-esteem on keeping students in school. She next carried out a computer search, using the descriptors "self-esteem" and "dropout." When she saw that the search would produce a great many references, she next added "middle school or adolescents" as a descriptor since she had the most experience with and the greatest interest in this age and grade level. The relevant references were now reduced to a manageable number. After reading the references that seemed relevant to her interest, this student defined her topic as "self-enhancement for at-risk middle school students as a factor in attendance behaviors."

Also, you should describe your literature search plan in detail. The description should include the preliminary sources you consulted, the years covered by the review, the descriptors or proximity search terms, and any special situations or problems you encountered. If particular secondary sources were important to the review, these too should be mentioned.

## THE BODY OF THE REPORT

The best way to organize a report is by the major topics that relate to your problem or question. If you coded your bibliographic citations by topic, as suggested above, sort the note cards or sheets of paper containing the citations into piles. Then decide the order in which the various topics should be discussed in your report.

Read the citations and corresponding abstracts and notes in your first pile. Then decide tentatively on the order you will follow in discussing the various research studies, theories, descriptions, and opinions. Major writings should be discussed individually, but if several minor writings make similar points or report similar results, they can be discussed together. By grouping together closely related writings, you can emphasize areas of agreement and disagreement that would be of interest to the reader.

Repeat this process until the citations in each of your piles are arranged in the approximate order you plan to use in your report. Keep in mind that major research studies are likely to contain findings relevant to several of your topics. The citations for these studies should be placed with the topic in which the findings will be discussed and then moved to the piles for later topics as your writing progresses.

You now have all your information in the order that it will be discussed in your report. With the first pile of citations in front of you, you are ready to start writing the body of your report. After reviewing all the citations in the pile to get their information firmly in mind, you can follow this process: Review the first citation briefly, decide whether to write about it alone or with others, write what you want to say about it, include a reference to indicate where the information came from (for example: Jones and Bullock, 1991), and then go on to the next citation.

Your review may include several studies on a particular problem, for example, the relationship between class size and student achievement. Some studies might yield similar results, but others might differ—sometimes dramatically. You will need to synthesize these results in some way. Methods for this purpose are discussed in Chapter 8; they range from simple "vote counting" to a statistically precise method known as meta-analysis. If many studies have been done on your problem, it is possible that someone will have conducted and published a synthesis of the results. In this case your review can provide an overview of this body of research, with a focus on the results of the published synthesis.

The following are other recommendations for writing the body of your paper:

*1.* Discuss major studies in detail, but devote little space to minor studies. This seems obvious, but it is distressing to see how many reports devote the same three or four sentences to each study regardless of its importance.

*2.* If you have located several minor studies having similar results or similar weaknesses, discuss all of them together. One approach is to discuss the best study in the set in some depth and then dispose of the others with a single sentence such as, "Several other studies have reported similar results (Anderson, 1989; Flinders, 1991; Lamon, 1985; Moursund, 1990; Wolcott, 1990)." Another example: "Several one-year studies reported better achievement for students in ability-grouped classrooms (Frank, 1969; Grey & Brown, 1973; Redd & Green, 1980). However, because of their short duration, all of these studies were probably subject to the Hawthorne Effect."

*3.* The body of your report should state what you have found in objective, unbiased language. You can make your own viewpoints and preferences known in the discussion section.

*4.* Describe strengths and weaknesses of methods used in important studies so that readers have enough information to weigh the results and draw their own conclusions.

*5.* Use frequent headings and subheadings to help the reader follow your sequence of thought more easily. If you cannot find subheadings that fit your content, your paper probably is not well organized.

*6.* Include transition sentences to connect the main ideas and topics covered in your report. The reader should feel that each of your sections proceeds logically from what has come before it.

*7.* Use language that clearly expresses whether you are reporting someone's research findings, theories, or opinions. For example, an author may describe a new program and its advantages but report no empirical evidence. In this case you might write, "Jiminez (1991) claims that. . . ." If the author developed a theory or referred to another's theory, you might write, respectively, "Jiminez (1991) theorized that . . ." or "Jiminez (1991) referred to Piaget's theory of. . . ." If the author did a research study, you might write, "Jiminez (1991) found that. . . ."

*8.* Do not fall into a repetitive writing style. One of the more common repetitive patterns is to start a discussion of each study with the author's name. For example, consecutive paragraphs may start "Chou found that . . . , Smith studied . . . , Wychevsky reported that. . . ."

*9.* Avoid repeating the same words in discussing each document. This is difficult, but you should do your best. For example, instead of using the word *study* repeatedly, you can use other words such as *experiment, project, investigation, research,* and so forth.

*10.* Use short, simple sentences when possible. Long, complex sentences may confuse the reader.

*11.* Avoid jargon, little-used words, and pedantic expressions. The purpose of your report is to communicate, not to impress the reader with your vocabulary.

*12.* Use direct quotations only when they convey an idea especially well or when you want to make sure the reader realizes that you are stating someone else's position, which is not necessarily your own. Frequent quotations tend to interfere with the flow of your paper and make it difficult to read.

## THE DISCUSSION SECTION

The body of the report should be as objective as possible. You should be as literal and objective as you can be in representing what the literature states about your problem. In the discussion section, however, you are free to provide your own interpretation and assessment of others' findings, theories, descriptions, and opinions. For example, suppose the reviewer is concerned with the effectiveness of a particular teaching method because the school district is considering whether to have all teachers participate in an in-service program about it. The reviewer should try to state objectively in the body of the report what researchers have found about this method and what experts think about it. In the discussion section the reviewer can make statements such as, "The research evidence is consistently positive, but I think the gains in student learning when teachers use this method are weak relative to the amount of effort required to implement it"; or, "The method has been found to produce good learning gains, but I am concerned about possible side effects that critics of the method claim can occur."

A good procedure for preparing the discussion section is to start by listing the main findings of your review. You can do so by asking yourself, "What did I learn from this review?" Answer this question without looking at the body of your report. By relying on memory, you are more likely to isolate the prominent findings from the myriad of details. You then can read over what you wrote to be sure you did not miss any important finding. List the findings in order or importance, and reflect on what you think about each one. Do you agree with the research evidence, theories, descriptions, and expert opinions? Are alternative interpretations possible? Why do you think there are contradictions in the literature, if any? What is the significance of a particular finding for the problem you need to solve or question you need to answer?

The discussion also should contain your recommendations regarding the problem or question that initiated your research review. The recommendations should be stated clearly and, if possible, without qualification. If you are too tentative or indirect, readers of your report will not know where you stand. They *want* to know your opinions and recommendations because you did the review of the literature, which makes you an expert compared to policymakers and colleagues who do not know the literature. Keep in mind, too, that even if you state your opinions and recommendations forcefully, your readers are unlikely to accept them uncritically. They will use your views as one source of input for making up their own minds about the question or problem.

## THE REFERENCES

All references that you cite in the report should be included in this section. Complete bibliographic information should be given for each reference.

Different institutions use different citation styles, so you will need to check on this matter. They might not have a required style, however. In this case we recommend you follow the citation style of the American Psychological Association because it is the most widely used style in educational and psychological journals. To learn this style, obtain a copy of the third edition of the *Publication Manual of the American Psychological Association* (1983). It is available at most college and university libraries, or it can be ordered by writing to Publication Sales, American Psychological Association, 1200 Seventeenth Street, N.W., Washington, DC 20036.

You should use a consistent citation style throughout the reference list. As we explained in Chapter 2, different preliminary sources use different citation styles. Therefore, if you consulted several of these sources, your bibliographic citations might be written in different styles. Be sure to convert all of them to the same style before typing your reference list. Because typing errors in reference lists are so easy to make, check the reference list once again for accuracy and consistency after it is typed.

# Chapter Reference

GOODLAD, J. (1990). *Teachers for our nation's schools.* San Francisco: Jossey-Bass.

# Recommended Reading

BEASLEY, D. (1988). *How to use a research library.* New York: Oxford University Press.

The author assumes that the reader knows virtually nothing about the use of a research library. Such topics as card catalogs, bibliographies, interlibrary loans, and on-line computer searches are covered. Although the specific procedures in this book refer to the New York Public Library, they apply equally well to most university libraries.

BECKER, H. S. (1986). *Writing for social scientists.* Chicago: University of Chicago Press.

This small book should be of great help to graduate students who are writing a research paper. Most of the common blunders are discussed, such as a pedantic writing style, wooly thinking, and the habit of using 20 words when 10 would communicate better. Although most of the examples are taken from sociology, they are easily related to education. The educational literature would be greatly improved if all writers, regardless of academic level, put the recommendations of this book into practice.

JOLLEY, J. M., MURRAY, J. D., & KELLER, P. A. (1984). *How to write psychology papers.* Sarasota, FL: Professional Resources Exchange.

This readable handbook gives practical guidelines for preparing term papers and research reports. Use of the library is also discussed briefly. Although focused primarily on psychology, most of the content is also applicable to writing papers in education. A sample term paper and research report are included in the appendices.

REED, J. G., & BAXTER, P. M. (1983). *Library use: A handbook for psychology.* Washington, DC: American Psychological Association.

This is an excellent resource for educators planning research in a college or university library. Although written for psychology students, it is equally useful for students of education. The topics include selecting and defining a research topic, locating books, using *Psychological Abstracts,* locating government publications, and searching by computer.

# Application Problems

1. Check all articles in Volume 52 (1983–1984) of the *Journal of Experimental Education:*
   a. Locate an article that would be useful to a high school principal who is considering setting up remedial math classes for low achievers, which may lead to poor self-concept and attitude toward school.
   b. Locate a study concerned with teaching aids to improve the handwriting of first-grade pupils; list bibliographical data.
2. Locate a dissertation in the April 1985 issue of Section A of *Dissertation Abstracts International* that is concerned with the following problem: A junior high school teacher discovers as a result of the district testing program that most of the students in her seventh-grade homeroom have low self-concepts as compared with national norms. She wants to find out if there are any programs available designed to improve the self-concept of junior high school students.
   a. List the bibliographical data for the dissertation.
   b. Briefly describe how you found this reference.
   c. Write a brief review of the abstract on a 5- × -8-inch note card following the format recommended in this chapter.
3. Locate in your library two journals that specialize in each of the following areas, and list their titles:
   a. Adult education
   b. Teaching biology
   c. Educational administration
   d. Special education
   e. Reading
4. Locate the most recent issue of *Resources in Education* and find an example of each of the following types of reports. Provide bibliographical data and an ED number for each report on an 5- × -8-inch note card. Also, locate the microfiche for one of these references in your library's microfiche file, scan the document, and take notes about it on the note card.
   a. Paper presented at a professional meeting
   b. Report by a professional association
   c. Conference or committee report
5. List three of your main interests in education. For each interest try to find a journal that specializes in it, and list the journal's title. Check recent issues of each journal until you locate an article that is closely related to your interests. Prepare a bibliography card for each article.

PART **III**

# EVALUATING
# AND SYNTHESIZING
# RESEARCH EVIDENCE

After you have located research documents, you face the task of evaluating the information contained in these documents for its relevance and applicability to your problem. You must also synthesize and reconcile the various, often inconsistent, findings bearing on your problem. Part III is designed to help you evaluate and synthesize research evidence.

Chapter 5 discusses the typical organization of a research report and provides criteria for evaluating each section. Because the educational measures and statistical tools used in research reports are key to grasping the results of research, we have devoted two chapters to these matters. Chapter 6 discusses the kinds of measures used in educational research and describes ways to obtain and evaluate them. Chapter 7 provides an overview of the common statistical tools that are used to describe and make inferences about research results. Finally, Chapter 8 discusses the value of reading research syntheses relevant to your problem and describes how to obtain and evaluate syntheses of various types.

Chapter 8 also introduces an important feature of this text, namely, the inclusion of actual research articles that exemplify the different types of educational research that we discuss. The reprinted articles have been carefully selected to provide good examples of the research method described. All have direct relevance to educational practice. To help you get the intended value from reading and evaluating each article, we will explain how they are presented.

As indicated in the Table of Contents, 11 articles are reprinted in the text. Each article appears in the chapter dealing with the type of research that is reported in that article. Thus, Chapter 8 includes an article reporting on meta-analysis, which is one form of research synthesis. After the title of each article, the contents page lists four elements: Abstract, Researcher's Comments, The Study, and Critical Review. For each reprinted article, you will be reading these four elements, in that order.

First the *Abstract* of the article is reprinted, to give you a brief overview of the problem that was addressed. The abstract is reprinted directly from the published article.

Next, one or more of the researchers who carried out the research and wrote the article have provided *Researcher's Comments,* written especially for this text. In these comments the researchers place their research in context by explaining how and why they came to carry it out. To give you insight into the researchers as people and a personal flavor of the research process, the researchers tell you some of the experiences they had in designing and conducting the research. They also go beyond the information provided in the article itself by discussing implications of the research and the directions in which it pointed their later work.

Next *The Study* itself is reprinted in full, just as it was published in the original journal article. You will see that research articles follow a fairly standard format, beginning with brief introductory comments and proceeding to describe the method of investigation, how the variables that were investigated were measured, and the procedures used to conduct the research. Then the results are presented, which in the case of quantitative research typically include both descriptive and inferential statistics. A discussion of the results and/or a conclusion follows, and the article concludes with a list of references.

To make your reading easier, we have added *footnotes* to each article that explain some of the measures and statistics referred to in the article. Read the footnotes carefully; they will greatly enhance your understanding of the specific article you are reading. The information in the footnotes will also expand your grasp of the research process generally.

Finally, a *Critical Review,* written by us, concludes the section on each article. The critical reviews cover factors you should consider in interpreting the results and discuss changes that could have strengthened the research. In reading our critical reviews, remember that all the articles included in the text were selected because they are examples of good research. Whenever investigators carry out educational research they confront many practical issues, such as a small budget, a limited number of subjects available, and dependence on cooperation from participating schools. Therefore, virtually no research is conducted in the best way possible. In addition, space and time constraints in publishing research often cause limitations, and occasionally inaccuracies, in the research reports as they appear in journal articles. Any limitations we discuss in our reviews do not imply that the research reported in the articles was weak. They are pointed out to help you identify potential issues that affect the generalizability and validity of the research findings.

As you read each article we recommend that you do your own evaluation of the research. For this purpose you can use Appendix 3, the Form for Evaluating Quantitative Research Reports or, in the case of a qualitative research study, Appendix 4, the Form for Evaluating Qualitative Research Reports. These forms are designed to focus your attention on important aspects of the articles you evaluate. You may then want to compare your own evaluation of the article to our critical review to see if you detected the most significant strengths and potential limitations of the research.

We suggest that you discuss your impressions about each article with a colleague, or with a classmate if you are using the text as part of a class on educational research. The experience of reading and evaluating actual articles, with the help of researchers' comments, critical reviews, and discussion with other educators, will help you develop critical skills in reading and applying research.

# CHAPTER 5

# EVALUATING RESEARCH REPORTS

## Overview

This chapter gives you guidelines for evaluating a report of either a quantitative or qualitative study. These guidelines include four questions you should ask when checking the introductory section of a report for bias and four criteria you can apply to evaluate a research hypothesis. We then consider how to evaluate the researcher's sampling procedures. Next we discuss procedures for evaluating tests and other measures used in research studies. General guidelines for evaluating a study's research design, the statistical results, and the researcher's conclusions are presented here, but these topics are treated in depth in subsequent chapters.

## Objectives

1. Describe several characteristics of researchers that can bias the procedures and outcomes of a study.
2. Describe guidelines for evaluating constructs and variables in quantitative and qualitative research studies.
3. Distinguish among a research hypothesis, question, and objective.
4. State four criteria that can be used to evaluate a hypothesis.
5. Given the description of a population, explain how a simple random sample, a systematic sample, a stratified sample, and a cluster sample would be selected from it.
6. Explain why most educational researchers use volunteer samples and the problems in doing so.
7. Describe population validity, how it is estimated, and how it relates to applying research results to other groups drawn from a target population.
8. Explain how sampling procedures used in qualitative research differ from those used in quantitative research.
9. Explain procedures for evaluating the reliability and validity of educational measures in quantitative and qualitative research.
10. Explain how educational practitioners can judge the applicability of research results to local conditions.

## Sections of a Research Report

In Chapter 4 you learned that the typical research report is organized into the following sections, in the order stated:

1. An *abstract* or *executive summary,* which provides a brief description of the study and its findings.
2. An *introduction,* which states the problem and provides a brief literature review in

*INTRODUCTION*

1. Are the research problem, procedures, or findings unduly influenced by the researchers' institutional affiliation, beliefs, values, or theoretical orientation?
2. Did the researchers express a positive or negative bias in describing the subject of the study (an instructional method, program, curriculum, person, etc.)?
3. Is the literature review section of the report sufficiently comprehensive? And does it include studies that you know to be relevant to the problem?
4. (Quantitative) Is each variable in the study clearly defined?
5. (Quantitative) Is the measure of each variable consistent with how the variable was defined?
6. (Quantitative) Are hypotheses, questions, or objectives explicitly stated, and if so, are they clear?
7. (Quantitative) Did the researchers make a convincing case that a research hypothesis, question, or objective was important to study?

*RESEARCH PROCEDURES*

8. (Quantitative) Did the sampling procedures produce a sample that is representative of an identifiable population or of your local population?
9. (Quantitative) Did the researchers form subgroups that would increase understanding of the phenomena being studied?
10. (Qualitative) Did the sampling procedure result in a case or cases that were particularly interesting and from whom much could be learned about the phenomena of interest?
11. Is each measure in the study sufficiently valid for its intended purpose?
12. Is each measure in the study sufficiently reliable for its intended purpose?
13. Is each measure appropriate for the sample?
14. Were the research procedures appropriate and clearly stated so that others could replicate them if they wished?

*RESEARCH RESULTS*

15. Were appropriate statistical techniques used, and were they used correctly?
16. (Qualitative) Did the report include a "thick" description that brought to life how the individuals responded to interview questions or how they behaved?
17. (Qualitative) Did each variable in the study emerge in a meaningful way from the data?
18. (Qualitative) Are there clearly stated hypotheses or questions? Did they emerge from the data that were collected?

*DISCUSSION OF RESULTS*

19. Do the results of the data analyses support what the researchers conclude are the findings of the study?
20. Did the researchers provide reasonable explanations of the findings?
21. Did the researchers draw reasonable implications for practice from the findings?

*Note:* Questions that apply specifically to quantitative research or to qualitative research are so noted. Otherwise the questions apply to both types of research.

Figure 5.1 Summary List of Questions to Use in Evaluating a Quantitative or Qualitative Research Report

which the problem is related to previous research. The researcher also explains the significance of the problem and may relate it to a theoretical framework.

3. A statement of the specific *hypotheses, questions,* or *objectives* that guided the study. This information typically is included in the introduction, but we list it separately here because of its importance.

4. A description of the *research procedures,* including sampling, measurement, and research design.
5. A report of the *findings.* This section includes statistical analyses of quantitative data or interpretive analyses of qualitative data.
6. A *discussion,* which considers alternative explanations for the results, their significance, limitations of the research procedures, and implications of the study for theory and practice.

Nearly all research reports follow this format. This consistency makes it easy for you to locate quickly the information you need. It also promotes brevity, which helps researchers write within the severe space limitations of most journals. An unfortunate consequence of consistency and brevity in research reports is that they tend to be less interesting to read than popular educational writing. Another consequence is that the reader may have to assume or guess about aspects of the study for which insufficient detail is provided.

The different sections of a research report need to be evaluated separately because each section is subject to different flaws. Therefore, the following discussion is organized by the sections of a research report. (We omitted the abstract or executive summary, because it does not bear directly on the quality of a study.) We will discuss each section, beginning with the introduction, and suggest what you should look for in making your evaluation. However, we cannot discuss here all the factors that affect the soundness of a study. Some of the factors involve elements of research design that are not introduced until Part Three of the book. Therefore, your ability to evaluate the quality of a research study will increase as you progress through the rest of the book.

Appendix 3 provides a Form for Evaluating Quantitative Research Reports, and Appendix 4 provides a Form for Evaluating Qualitative Research Reports. Each form lists questions that can guide your evaluation, the type of information in the report that is relevant to each question, and a sample answer for each question. Figure 5.1 presents a summary list of the questions in each form. You can make copies of it to use in evaluating research reports. We recommend that you examine this figure and both appendixes before proceeding.

# The Introductory Section

## CHARACTERISTICS OF THE RESEARCHERS

The introduction is usually the place in the report in which you learn most about the researcher, or researchers, who did the study. Who are they, and what are their affiliations? Why did they do the study? Why do they think it is important? Do they appear to know about other relevant studies? Do they seem committed to a particular point of view?

These questions are important to ask because knowledge about the researchers and their perspectives can indicate whether a study is biased. For example, some research studies involve experimental tests of the effectiveness of an educational program or product. If we know that the researchers developed the program or product themselves, which is often the case, we need to be especially concerned that the design of the experiment is not slanted in favor of it. Even if the researchers did not develop the experimental program, we should try to find out about them because they may be biased for or against it.

Whenever researchers have reason for wanting their research to support a particular viewpoint, the likelihood of bias is greatly increased. Occasionally, the bias becomes so great that the researchers slant their findings or even structure their research design to produce a predetermined result. A famous case of emotional involvement is the research into intelligence based on studies of twins that was conducted by Sir Cyril Burt. It appears that Burt was so intent on proving that intelligence is inherited that he slanted, or even fabricated, the research data to prove his hypothesis (Evans, 1976).

Personal bias is often easy to detect in the language of the research report. For example, studies that are introduced with remarks such as "This study was conducted to prove . . ." must be considered suspect. Researchers do not conduct their studies to prove a point but to get an answer.

The use of emotionally charged words or intemperate language in the introduction is the most obvious indicator of a biased viewpoint. For example, in reviewing the literature concerned with ability grouping, one of the authors found several articles that referred to ability grouping as "segregation." Inasmuch as this word has strong negative emotional associations for most of us, its use in this context suggests bias. One is not surprised to find that an article entitled "Must We Segregate?" is strongly biased against ability grouping (Tonsor, 1953).

The researchers' professional affiliation also should be noted because it may predispose them toward a particular point of view. For example, a comparison of racial attitudes of children in private and public schools in the South might be biased if conducted by an official in the NAACP (National Association for the Advancement of Colored People). A researcher's affiliations do not necessarily indicate that he or she is biased, but the affiliations should serve as a signal to be alert for possible indications of bias in the report.

The personal characteristics of the researcher must be examined with particular care in qualitative research, in which the researcher is the primary data collection instrument. For example, some qualitative researchers use the ethnographic method, developed originally by anthropologists, to study an individual or an aspect of school culture. The researcher makes intensive observations and may even participate in the individual's activities or the school's rituals.

To assess the personal characteristics of the researchers, look for information concerning their motivation for doing the study, theoretical orientation, personal beliefs and values, and relationship to the individual being studied. This information sometimes is not provided directly, but it can be inferred to some extent from the researchers' description of their procedures and the account of what they observed or heard.

Evaluating the personal characteristics of qualitative researchers poses an interesting dilemma. On the one hand, qualitative researchers are necessarily *subjective* because they use their personal mind-set and powers of observation to investigate how the individuals being studied view their world and how they are affected by their social-cultural context. On the other hand, qualitative researchers also must be *objective* to an extent, so that we have some assurance that if others did the same study, they would observe and hear the same things. If the report appears highly subjective, we will learn more about the researchers than about the phenomena being studied. However, if the report seems very objective, we may miss the richness of perspective that is the hallmark of qualitative research.

You should examine a qualitative research report to determine whether the researchers demonstrated an awareness of this subjectivity-objectivity dilemma and took steps to deal with it. For example, did the researchers check their perceptions against the perceptions of others, including the individuals who were studied? Or did the researchers make an effort to present a balanced account, so that both positive and negative aspects of individuals and their sociocultural context are presented?

## LITERATURE REVIEW

If you are doing a comprehensive review of the research literature on a particular problem, you will soon notice that a few key studies are cited in most subsequent research reports. If these key studies are not reviewed in a particular research report, it might indicate that the researchers were careless in reviewing the literature. If important studies that disagree with the researchers' findings are omitted, bias may be the reason.

Most research journals allow researchers little space for reviewing previous research, so you should not expect detailed reviews. However, the 5 to 10 most relevant previous studies should be cited, if only briefly. Research reports not appearing in journals, such as reports included in *Resources in Education (RIE)*, usually provide much more detailed reviews because they are not subject to space limitations.

## CONSTRUCTS OR VARIABLES

The introductory section of a research report should identify and describe each of the concepts that was studied. Examples of concepts studied in educational research are learning style, aptitude, academic achievement, intrinsic motivation, top-down management, and implicit curriculum. Researchers usually refer to these concepts as *constructs* or *variables*. We will use the latter term here.

In simple terms, a variable is anything that can take on different values in the research study. For example, if the researchers analyzed their data separately for male and female students, gender is a variable in the study. If students' scores on an achievement test were correlated with their level of cooperativeness on a team project, both achievement and cooperativeness are variables. A less obvious example is the comparison of teaching method A with teaching method B in a study. Teaching method is a variable here because it can take on two values: method A or method B.

If a concept is part of the research design but is not varied, it is called a *constant*. For example, suppose an experiment compares the effectiveness of teaching method A and teaching method B for community college students. The educational level of the students (that is, community college) is a constant because no other educational level is included in the research design. Suppose, however, the experiment compares the effectiveness of the two teaching methods to see which is most effective for community college students and which is most effective for high school students. In this case educational level is a variable because it takes on two values: community college and high school.

Researchers can define their variables in one of two ways. The first approach is to define them by referring to other concepts. For example, "attitude toward social studies instruction" might be defined as the tendency to feel or think positively about, or act positively toward, classes in which social studies content is taught. This definition refers to many other concepts (for example, "feel," "think," and "is taught"), each of which needs to be defined so that readers do not find them confusing.

The other approach to defining variables is to refer to the technique that was used to measure them. For example, "attitude toward social studies instruction" can be defined as students' scores on the ABC Attitude Scale. The problem with this approach is that it leaves unanswered what the scores on the scale mean. Thus a good research study will define each variable by including both a conceptual definition and a description of the measure used to assess it. Obviously there should be a meaningful correspondence between the conceptual definition of each variable in a study and its measurement. Also, the researchers should explain whether their definition is consistent with other researchers' definitions, and if not, why not.

In reviewing a research report, you should examine carefully how each of the variables is defined and measured. If definitions are unclear or nonexistent, the significance of the research results is cast into doubt. Similar doubts are created if conceptual definitions of the variables are inconsistent with the methods used to measure them.

These guidelines for evaluating research variables do not apply to qualitative studies because the goal of most qualitative research is to *discover* constructs. For example, suppose a qualitative study is done to discover how high school at-risk students view school and life outside of school. If the researchers started with preconceived constructs, they would defeat their purpose. They would learn how the students respond to measures of these constructs, but these data might be totally irrelevant to how the students actually view the world. In evaluating a qualitative research report, then, you should determine whether the researchers biased what they would find by using preconceived constructs or whether they created a research design that would let pertinent constructs emerge as data collection progressed.

# Research Hypotheses, Questions, and Objectives

## HYPOTHESES COMPARED WITH QUESTIONS AND OBJECTIVES

We often are faced in our professional work with problems that we seek to solve by gathering information. One way to focus this process is by trying to identify possible solutions or explanations and then gathering information to see if they are correct. For example, a school principal may find that there is a drug abuse problem among students at certain grade levels. Initial data gathering may lead a committee to speculate that the problem is limited to a small group of students, and therefore the solution is to intervene only with this group. The committee then intervenes and gathers more data to determine whether the speculations are correct.

The committee's *speculations* about causes of phenomena and interventions that might work are similar to what researchers call *hypotheses*. A hypothesis in a research study is a speculation—an educated guess—about how two or more variables are related to each other or about which of two or more programs or methods is most effective. After formulating a hypothesis, researchers collect data to test it and then examine the data to decide whether or not to reject it. For example, researchers might hypothesize that the reason some teachers emphasize lower-cognitive questions rather than instruction in problem solving when teaching mathematics is that they feel pressured to rely exclusively on the required textbook, which focuses primarily on lower-cognitive objectives. Among the ways researchers could test this hypothesis is by interviewing a sample of mathematics teachers to determine their instructional objectives and why they chose them. The researchers could then analyze the interview data to determine whether the data support their hypothesis.

Hypotheses usually are formulated on the basis of theory and previous research findings. If theory or previous research do not provide an adequate basis for formulating specific hypotheses, however, researchers will formulate questions or objectives to guide their investigation. For example, suppose the researchers in the preceding example were not ready to make an educated guess (i.e., a hypothesis) about the reason for some teachers' overreliance on lower-cognitive learning in mathematics instruction. In this case they could pose a question such as "Why do some teachers not include problem-solving instruction when teaching mathematics?" Or they could state an objective: "The objective of this study is to determine why some teachers do not include problem-solving instruction when teaching mathematics."

The choice of research questions or objectives is generally a matter of personal preference. Both formats guide the study design, but neither expresses a prediction about what the research findings will show. By contrast, a research hypothesis makes a specific prediction before data collection. If the researchers are willing to make predictions about some of the phenomena they are studying but are unwilling to make predictions about other phenomena, they will often specify both hypotheses and questions (or objectives).

To summarize, formulating hypotheses, questions, or objectives is one of the first steps researchers take in planning a study. These formulations guide the rest of the planning process, data collection, and data analysis. Therefore, you should look for hypotheses, questions, or objectives in the introductory section of the report. If none are present, you have reason to be concerned about the quality of the study and the validity of its findings. You should be similarly concerned if hypotheses, questions, or objectives are stated but refer to concepts that are poorly defined.

## CRITERIA FOR GOOD HYPOTHESES, QUESTIONS, AND OBJECTIVES

The following are three criteria for evaluating the hypotheses, questions, and objectives that appear in research reports:

1. *The variables and their relationship to each other should be made explicit.* Consider this hypothesis: "There is a positive relationship between peer-group acceptance and attitude toward school among sixth-grade boys." This is a good hypothesis because the two variables (peer-group acceptance and attitude toward school) are made explicit. Furthermore, the hypothesized relationship between the two variables is made explicit: The researcher expects a positive relationship, meaning that boys who have greater peer-group acceptance will have better attitudes toward school, and boys who have less peer-group acceptance will have more negative attitudes.

This example can be contrasted with the following hypothesis: "The lecture method will have a different effect than the discussion method on students' performance on essay tests." Only one of the variables in this example is explicit: teaching method (lecture versus discussion). The other apparent variable, essay test performance, is actually a measure, but the variable being measured is not identified. Furthermore, the predicted effects of the teaching methods on essay test performance are not made explicit.

Vagueness in research questions and objectives also is possible. For example, consider this research objective: "The purpose of this study is to explore how new principals are socialized into their role." Although this statement provides a general idea of the study's objective, it does not indicate the kinds of variables that will be examined and measured. A more explicit objective might state, "The purpose of this study is to identify the types of individuals who influence new principals' socialization, the types of formal and informal strategies they use in this process, and the principals' perceptions of the value of these strategies." This statement includes the variables that will be examined: (1) types of individuals who influence new principals' socialization, (2) formal influencing strategies, (3) informal influencing strategies, and (4) perceived value of the strategies. Each of these variables could be analyzed into more specific variables, but further specificity is generally not necessary in stating research objectives and questions. Identification of more specific variables can be provided elsewhere in the introductory section or in the research procedures section.

2. *Hypotheses, questions, and objectives should be grounded in theory or previous research.* If researchers have done a good review of the literature, they should be able to formulate a good rationale for each of their hypotheses, questions, or objectives. This rationale should be made explicit. For example, Randall Eberts and Joe Stone (1988) did a research study, the objective of which is included in the following statement: "Using nationally representative data . . . we tested the major conclusions drawn from case studies regarding principal effectiveness" (p. 291). This objective developed from their observation that published case studies of school principals showed that principals having certain characteristics (e.g., setting clear priorities and organizing and participating in staff development programs) had a positive effect on the learning of students in their school. However, Eberts and Stone noted a weakness in the case studies:

Case studies have many advantages in generating hypotheses, in evaluating the implementation of new techniques, and in providing detailed explanations and backgrounds for observed phenomena, but they are not necessarily representative and often suffer from weak controls for individual student and teacher attributes. (p. 291)

These researchers' rationale for their objective, then, was that nationally representative data would provide a stronger test of the principals' influence on student achievement than was provided by previous case studies.

Research hypotheses usually are derived from a theory in education, psychology, or other social science. For example, many current studies of reading comprehension are based on schema theory and metacognition theory. Such theories provide a rationale for the research studies, and at the same time the studies provide a test of the theories. In other words, if the hypothesis is supported by the researchers' findings, the validity of the theory is strengthened. If the hypothesis is not supported, proponents of the theory need to reexamine critically their theoretical constructs and principles.

Hypotheses, questions, and objectives that lack a rationale pose a problem for interpretation. For example, suppose a study is done to identify teachers' testing practices. If there is no rationale for this objective, the readers have no basis for understanding why particular testing practices were studied or whether testing practices identified as important in previous research were ignored in this study. Also, the readers, as well as the researchers who conducted the study, are likely to be at a loss in judging whether the testing practices that were observed are desirable or undesirable.

*3. Hypotheses, questions, and objectives in qualitative research should emerge as data collection progresses.* Qualitative research is largely a process of discovery, bound by as few preconceptions as possible. Narrowly framed hypotheses, questions, and objectives specified during the planning of the study would constrain what could be discovered about the phenomena being studied. Therefore, qualitative research studies tend to be guided initially by broad research questions or theoretical frameworks. For example, a researcher might propose to study administrator-teacher relationships from a feminist perspective. The recent literature on feminist theory might suggest some hypotheses and questions to direct the study initially, but other hypotheses and questions should be free to emerge as the study progresses.

The goal of some qualitative research studies is development of a theory that can explain, at least tentatively, the data that were collected. Glaser and Strauss (1967) developed a method for this type of research inquiry. They called it *grounded theory* to convey the notion that a theory should be developed and refined by continually "grounding" it in data. (A nongrounded theory would be derived from armchair speculation and reasoning.)

If the researchers used the method of grounded theory, or a variant of it, you should evaluate their hypotheses and questions in this context. Did the hypotheses and questions emerge from the data rather than precede the collection of data? Were they refined through successive rounds of data collection, for example, by doing new case studies?

Some qualitative research studies do not employ the grounded theory method. Even in these studies, research hypotheses and questions should emerge from the research results. Otherwise the study is simply a description and personal interpretation of the phenomena that were observed. A good qualitative study is guided by a spirit of inquiry that leads to hypotheses and questions, which in turn stimulate further research. Some researchers believe that quantitative and qualitative research complement each other, in that qualitative research generates research hypotheses and questions that then can be tested (in the case of hypotheses) or answered (in the case of questions) by the rigorous methods of quantitative research.

*4. Hypotheses, questions, and objectives should be stated as briefly and clearly as possible.* Some researchers only indirectly refer to their hypotheses, questions, or objectives in the introductory section of their reports. Readers must infer this information for themselves or search patiently for the relevant information. This is not a weakness in the study itself, only in its reporting. However, it may signal writing problems in other sections of the report. For example, some researchers fail to define key terms or omit important details. When this happens, readers find it difficult to evaluate the quality of the research or the significance of the results because they cannot figure out what happened in the study.

# The Research Procedures

## SAMPLING

In conducting a study, researchers ideally would investigate all persons to whom they wish to generalize their findings. These persons constitute a *population,* meaning that they make up the entire group of persons having the characteristic, or characteristics, that interest the researchers. Because of the great expense involved in studying most populations of interest, researchers must content themselves with studying a *sample* of persons who presumably represent that population. For example, suppose the researchers wish to study the effect of a new reading program on the reading comprehension of visually impaired children in first-grade classrooms in the United States. Because the researchers cannot try out the new reading program with the entire population, they must select a sample from the population to be studied and carry out the research with that sample. The researchers now have solved the problem of making the study feasible to conduct, but they have created a different problem in the process, namely, whether they can generalize the results from their sample to the entire population.

You will need to evaluate research reports carefully to determine the extent to which the researchers' results, obtained from a sample, can be generalized to the population. As we explain below, the size of the sample and the procedure used in selecting it determine how confident you, and the researchers who did the study, can be in making generalizations to a population of interest.

Samples very rarely will have the exact same characteristics as the populations from which they are drawn. For example, if you randomly selected three male students from each class in a large high school and measured their height, it is unlikely that the mean height of this sample would be identical to the mean height of all male students in the school (defined to be the population in this example). The difference between the sample's mean height and the population's mean height is a *random sampling error.* The "error" is the difference between a statistic (e.g., a mean score) for a sample and the same statistic for the population. (The technical term to describe a statistic for the population is *parameter.*)

Sampling errors are likely to occur even when the sample is randomly drawn from the population. The size of the errors tends to become smaller as we select a larger random sample. For this reason we can be more confident in generalizing results from studies with a large random sample than studies with a small random sample. The likelihood of sampling errors for a sample of a given size can be estimated by using a mathematical procedure.

A sampling procedure is *random* if each member of the population has an equal and independent chance of being included in the sample. Researchers often use nonrandom samples, however. In the above example, the sampling procedure would be nonrandom if you asked each teacher to send three boys to be measured for height, and the teachers responded by selecting students who could most easily make up the lost class time— probably the brighter ones. Because there is a relationship between intelligence and physical size, a *systematic sampling error,* or bias, would occur. Systematic errors tend to be in a given direction and cannot be estimated by mathematical procedures. Therefore, these errors are more serious than random sampling errors because they can distort the research findings and lead to false conclusions.

**Types of Sampling.**   One of the most effective sampling procedures is *simple random sampling.* With this sampling procedure, all the individuals in the defined population have an equal and independent chance of being selected as a member of the sample. By "independent" we mean that the selection of one individual does not affect in any way the chances of selection of any other individual.

The usual way to select a simple random sample is to assign a number to each person in the population and use a table of random numbers to select the sample. A table of random numbers lists thousands of numbers in random order. To use it you randomly select a starting point and then list as many numbers as you need for your sample. You then refer to your numbered population list and select the individuals whose numbers you have taken from the table.

Simple random sampling is effective because it yields research data that can be generalized to a larger population within margins of random error that can be determined statistically. The procedure is not used often in educational research, however, because of the difficulties in obtaining resources and permission to select randomly students, teachers, administrators, or other groups to participate in a study.

*Systematic sampling* is similar to simple random sampling except that all individuals in the defined population are on a list, such as a membership directory or a school census. Suppose the researcher wants to select a sample of 100 pupils from a census list of 1,000 pupils. To use systematic sampling, the researcher first divides the population by the number needed for the sample (1,000 ÷ 100 = 10). Next the researcher selects at random a number smaller than the number arrived at by the division (in this example, a number smaller than 10). Then, starting with that number (e.g., 8), the researcher selects every 10th name from a list of the population, thus selecting pupils 8, 18, 28, 38, and so on for a total of 100.

Systematic sampling is easier to use than simple random sampling when there is a list of the population. Because a list is used, however, each member of the population is not chosen independently. Once the first member has been selected, all the other members of the sample are automatically determined. Therefore, systematic sampling should be used only if one is certain that there is no bias in the way that individuals are arranged on the list. For example, suppose a school census list is arranged by classroom, with students in each classroom listed in alphabetical order. If we selected every 23rd name, we might get nothing but children whose names start with *W, X, Y,* or *Z.* If some ethnic groups have a disproportionate number of last names starting with these letters, our systematic sample will have proportionally more students from these groups and proportionally fewer from other groups. Thus, the sample is not representative of the population from which it was drawn.

*Stratified sampling* is a procedure for ensuring that individuals in the population who have certain characteristics are represented in the sample. For example, suppose researchers are interested in whether boys and girls from three different home environments (single parent, mother; single parent, father; both parents together) have different attitudes toward mathematics. If the researchers draw a simple random sample or a systematic sample from the school district list, they may by chance get few or no students in one of these six classifications: (1) boys with single parent, mother; (2) girls with single parent, mother; (3) boys with single parent, father; (4) girls with single parent, father; (5) boys with both parents together; and (6) girls with both parents together.

To ensure that all six groups are represented in the sample, the researchers can use stratified sampling. They would consider each group (called strata in sampling terminology) as a separate population. They then would draw the same size random sample from each group, thereby ensuring that each population is represented adequately in the sample. Another option is to draw random samples of different sizes (but each size being an adequate number) so that the proportion of students in each group in the sample is the same as their proportion in the population. This procedure is called *proportional random sampling.*

In *cluster sampling* the unit of sampling is not the individual but rather a naturally occurring group of individuals. Cluster sampling is used when it is more feasible or convenient to select groups of individuals than to select individuals from a defined population. It is often used in educational research, with the classroom as the unit of sampling. Suppose that one wishes to administer a study habits questionnaire to a random sample of 300 students from a population defined as all sixth-graders in four school districts. The population includes a total of 1,250 sixth-graders in 50 classrooms, with an average of 25 pupils in each classroom. One approach would be to draw a simple random sample of 300 students from a census list of all 1,250 students. By contrast, in cluster sampling one would draw a random sample of 12 classrooms from a census list of all 50 classrooms. Then one would administer the questionnaire to every student in each of the 12 classrooms.

The advantages of cluster sampling in this situation are obvious. It is less disruptive to the school routine than the simple random sampling procedure, which would result in a few students being selected from each class. Also, the researchers need solicit the cooperation of only 12 teachers rather than 50, and they have to travel to only 12 classrooms rather than to 50 classrooms.

**Volunteer Samples.**   Random sampling of large populations generally is possible only in survey research making slight demands on individuals. For example, most public opinion polls can obtain random samples because they typically ask only a few questions and take only a few minutes of each respondent's time. Demands on the individual are much greater in most educational research. Consequently, even if researchers select a random sample, they rarely can obtain the cooperation of all the selected individuals. When some individuals refuse to participate in a study, the remaining individuals no longer constitute a random sample because those who agree to participate are likely to be different from those who do not.

Another reason random sampling is difficult in educational research is that researchers have the legal and ethical requirement to obtain informed consent from human subjects (or their parents in the case of young children) before involving them in a research project. An individual can refuse to participate for any reason. As a result, nearly all educational research is conducted with volunteer samples.

The main difficulty with volunteer samples is that a systematic sampling error can occur so that members of the sample have different characteristics from the population from which the sample was drawn. In fact, research has shown that volunteers tend to be different from nonvolunteers in many ways. For example, studies have found that volunteers tend to be better educated, of higher social class, and more intelligent than nonvolunteers (Rosenthal & Rosnow, 1975).

The amount of sampling bias in a volunteer sample can be estimated by checking the percentage of individuals who are invited to participate who agree to do so. (In a questionnaire study, you would check the percentage of individuals who return the completed questionnaire to the researcher.) The higher this percentage, the less likely is the sample to be biased. Skillful researchers work closely with school personnel, fully explain the research, solicit their ideas and suggestions, and provide benefits to those who participate. These actions tend to increase the percentage of volunteers and thus reduce sampling bias.

**Population Validity.**   The significance of research findings is heavily dependent on their *population validity*. This term refers to the degree to which the sample of individuals in the study is representative of the population from which it was selected.

Population validity is established by showing that the selected sample is similar to the *accessible population,* which is the immediate population from which the researchers drew their sample. The researchers also must demonstrate that the accessible population is similar to the *target population,* which is the population to which the researchers want to generalize or apply their research findings. For example, if you were interested in sexual stereotypes among high school seniors, the target population could be defined as all seniors in U.S. public and private high schools. This of course is a very large population, and so it would be difficult and expensive to draw a national sample from this population and use the selected individuals in your research. If you lived in Denver, let's say, you might find that your resources allow you to draw your sample only from the Denver public high schools. Denver high school seniors would be the accessible population.

It may be that the accessible population (Denver public school seniors) is different in certain ways (for example, achievement level, socioeconomic status, or ethnic composition) from the target population (all U.S. high school seniors). To the degree that such differences exist, the research findings based on a Denver sample might not apply to the target population. Thus, to establish population validity, the researchers must show how the sample, the accessible population, and the target population are similar on variables that appear to be related to the problem they are investigating. Because the research problem involves sexual stereotypes, the researchers may have reason to believe that different ethnic groups may have different cultural beliefs about the roles of women. Thus, the researchers should determine whether (1) their sample, (2) the accessible population, and (3) the target population all have about the same proportion of different ethnic groups. If similar proportions are found, this evidence will help to establish the population validity of their study.

Evidence to establish population validity—especially when the target population is a national population—is difficult to obtain. Census data, statistical abstracts published by the U.S. Department of Education, and national norms reported by publishers of standardized tests sometimes provide relevant evidence.

Data on characteristics of the accessible population are often easier to obtain, especially if the accessible population is at the school district level. For example, a typical school district gathers a good deal of test and demographic data about its students.

**Generalizing to Your Local Situation.** In conducting a critical evaluation of a research report, you should pay close attention to the accessible population and the sample that was used in the study. However, it probably is even more important to determine the degree to which students, teachers, or other groups in the research sample are similar to the groups in your local setting to whom you wish to apply the research findings. As the similarity between the research sample and the local group decreases, the research results are less likely to apply. For example, suppose a teacher works in an upper-middle-class, mostly white, suburban school in California. Results from a study of the reading problems of inner-city, mostly black children in Philadelphia would have to be applied very cautiously and may not be relevant because of the differences between this teacher's students and the research sample. However, some of the Philadelphia findings might apply if the reading problems identified were not related to race, socioeconomic status, or geographic area. Therefore, an educator who is seeking research data to help deal with a local problem must consider carefully not only how the research sample is different from local groups but also how these differences might affect the relevance of the research results.

Making these comparisons is a difficult task for several reasons. First, researchers often include very little information in their reports about the sample and the accessible population from which it was drawn. Second, local educators often have only limited data about the characteristics of children in their school or district. Third, it is difficult to decide what differences between the research sample and the local population actually affect the applicability of the research findings.

The best check of population validity is to try out the course of action suggested by the research findings and see how well it works in your local situation. This approach involves using *action research,* which we discuss in Chapter 15.

**Sampling in Qualitative Research.**    Qualitative researchers typically want to learn as much as possible about the individuals, settings, and events they study. They wish to generate what sometimes is called "thick" descriptions, rather than precise statistics calculated on scores yielded by tests, attitude scales, and other objective measures. For this reason qualitative researchers typically study only a few cases. In fact, some qualitative studies report findings for just one case—one teacher, one child, one school band, and so on.

Because the sample size in qualitative research is so small, the procedures for selecting a sample in a quantitative study are not applicable. For example, the ideal sampling situation in quantitative research is to select a random sample from a target population. In qualitative research, however, the ideal situation might be to select the one individual or setting of most interest to the researcher. A researcher might want to study a particular teacher because she has attained fame or is known for her unique teaching methods. Historians (who primarily are qualitative researchers) do not write biographies at random but instead write biographies of individuals who are important to a particular era or event.

Another sampling method in qualitative research is *purposive sampling.* In this method the researchers select a case, or cases, from which they can learn the most. For example, suppose a qualitative researcher wants to learn how cliques operate in schools and what needs they fill for students. The researcher might designate several criteria for selecting a clique to study, such as the following: (1) the clique has been in existence for at least one school term; (2) it is recognized as a clique by the clique members, other students, and teachers; (3) the clique has at least four members and no more than seven members; (4) clique members attend school regularly; (5) clique members are willing to be interviewed regularly; and (6) clique members are willing to let the researcher attend their out-of-school activities. The researcher selects these criteria because she believes that they will result in the selection of a clique that is manageable for the purposes of data collection and that will exhibit the phenomena of interest.

Random sampling procedures used in quantitative research sometimes are also appropriate in qualitative research. For example, suppose the researcher wants to do an intensive study of the teaching methods of a particular woodworking teacher. The researcher plans to make videotaped recordings of 10 lessons, with each lesson followed by an interview, over the course of a semester. Each lesson can be considered an "event." If she wishes to obtain a representative sample of these events, she can use a random sampling procedure. Each lesson during the semester can be given a number, and a table of random numbers can be used to draw 10 lessons that will be observed.

## EVALUATING MEASURES USED IN RESEARCH

Research results can be no better than the measures used to obtain them. For this reason you should pay special attention to the description of the measures in a research report. The following is a brief summary of the most important factors to consider in evaluating educational measures. In the next chapter we discuss educational measurement in greater depth. This discussion will give you the basic understanding you need to make intelligent evaluations of educational measures.

A thorough check of all measures used in all studies included in your literature review would probably be too time-consuming. We recommend instead that you focus on measures used in studies of major importance in your review.

If a study used standardized measures with which you are not familiar, you should consult the *Mental Measurements Yearbooks,* check other sources of information to be discussed in Chapter 6, and perhaps even study a specimen set. A *specimen set* typically includes a copy of the measure, answer key, and manual containing administration procedures and technical information. Many university libraries, counseling centers, and departments of psychology maintain specimen sets of frequently used tests and other measurement tools.

After obtaining information about the measure, you need to evaluate it critically. The following three questions are helpful for this purpose:

*1. What evidence of validity is available?* A test or other measurement tool is valid to the degree to which it measures what it claims to measure. Therefore, to evaluate the validity of a measure, you need to find out what claims the researcher made for it and what evidence is presented to support those claims. Validity evidence should be studied carefully because the soundness of research results hinges on the validity of the measures used to generate the results.

The usual tools of measurement in quantitative research are tests, questionnaires, attitude scales, and observation checklists. The validity claims that typically are made for such instruments are well understood, as are the types of evidence used to support these claims. For example, *content validity* is important in studies of school achievement because it is concerned with the claim that an achievement test used in a study actually covers the curriculum that was taught. An achievement test that asks many questions about content that students have not been taught and few about content they have been taught has low content validity and thus will not accurately measure what students have learned. You will learn more about content validity and other types of test validity in Chapter 6.

In evaluating reports of quantitative research, you should determine what types of validity claims were made for each measure. Then you should determine whether adequate evidence is presented to support each claim.

The validity of measures used in qualitative research is more difficult to determine than in quantitative research. The difficulty stems in part from the measures typically used—field notes of the researcher's personal observations; notes or audiorecordings of semistructured interviews; and inspection of written records, ranging from historical documents and institutional records to individuals' personal journals. These measures are more subjective than those used in quantitative research. Also, they often are used to record fleeting, difficult-to-define phenomena, such as culture or artistry.

Researchers are still not in agreement about how the validity of measures used in qualitative research should be determined. One procedure is for the researchers to show the participants in the study the data that were generated by a particular qualitative measure. As participants examine the data, the researchers ask questions such as, "Is this what you said?" and "Does this accurately convey what happened?"

Although there are no well-accepted criteria for judging the validity of qualitative measures, you can evaluate a report to determine whether the researchers demonstrated a sensitivity to validity issues in their study and attempted to collect validity evidence that they considered appropriate.

*2. What evidence of reliability is available?* A test or other measurement tool is reliable to the degree that it is free of measurement error. For example, if two individuals score a test and obtain different scores, measurement error has occurred. Less obviously, suppose a student takes the same achievement test on two different days and obtains two different scores. These different results constitute measurement "error," although they are not errors in the usual sense of the word.

It is difficult to develop a measure that is perfectly reliable, meaning that it is completely free of error, because a variety of factors can create error, for example, differences in the accuracy of persons who administer the test or other measure; changes in testing conditions from one day to the next; temporary fluctuations in how individuals respond to the testing situation; and idiosyncrasies in the nature of the test items that affect different individuals differently. It is virtually impossible to eliminate all these sources of error.

Different reliability procedures have been developed to estimate different measurement errors. (You will learn more about them in Chapter 6.) Research reports should include the types of measurement error that were examined for each measure and the reliability evidence that was collected. Reliability evidence is much easier to obtain than validity evidence; therefore, if no reliability coefficients are reported, you should be concerned that the study was not carefully conducted. Another possibility is that the investigator failed to report reliability because it was low.

Tests and other measurement tools with very low reliability will produce large errors of measurement. These errors will obscure the effects of experimental programs or the extent of a relationship between variables. This problem can be understood by considering the case of a completely unreliable test. After the test is administered, the resulting scores will consist entirely of measurement error, meaning that they are essentially random numbers. Random numbers obviously cannot reveal the true effects of experimental programs or the true relationships between variables. For this reason you need to check how reliable a measure is before you reach conclusions about findings based on its use.

The above discussion of reliability applies primarily to measures commonly used in quantitative research. The meaning of measurement reliability and procedures for assessing it are much more difficult to specify in qualitative research. For example, it is feasible to develop a reading test that is reliable in the sense that it produces approximately the same scores for each student if administered on one day and then again a week or so later because reading ability usually changes slowly. The phenomena studied in qualitative research tend to be much less stable. An interviewee may respond one way to a question today and another way tomorrow. We cannot conclude, however, that the interview procedure used to stimulate these responses is unreliable. The inconsistency probably is not measurement error but rather a characteristic of the phenomena being investigated.

Suppose also that in a qualitative study two interviewers ask the same questions of an individual and get different answers. Does this mean the interview procedure is not reliable? Perhaps. But it may also mean that the individual has a different feeling about each interviewer, and this feeling influences the responses. If this is the case, each interviewer and her questions constitute a separate "measure," and the two measures cannot be expected to produce reliably similar responses.

These examples illustrate how difficult it is to evaluate the reliability of measures used in qualitative research. In evaluating a research report, you will need to read how the researchers approached the problem of reliability, if at all, and judge whether the approach was sensible. It is hoped that the researchers considered the reliability of their measures within the total context of the situation that was studied.

*3. Is the measure appropriate for the sample?* Even a measure with good validity and reliability will have little value if administered to an inappropriate sample. For example, a researcher might administer tests that were designed for a particular population of students to a sample of students who represent a different population. The tests consequently might be either too easy or too difficult for the majority of the sample. If the test is too easy, both high-achieving students and moderately achieving students can obtain similar scores even though the former group knows more. If the test is too difficult, some students will earn very low scores, even though they might know a lot about the subject being tested.

Some measures are inappropriate for a particular sample because they are culturally biased. For example, they might contain culture-specific questions that are easier for persons from one culture than for persons from other cultures. This and other types of cultural bias unfortunately can be difficult to determine. You can consult published reviews of measures to see whether they address the problem. Also, you can ask test experts or experts in the cultural setting to which you wish to apply the research findings to inspect the measures. They might be able to detect subtle cultural biases that would not be evident to the test developer or to the typical professional educator.

## RESEARCH DESIGN

Research reports should contain a description of the research design that was used to obtain data to test the research hypotheses, answer the research questions, or achieve the research objectives. Depending on the research design, the description can be brief or quite detailed. Descriptive research designs generally are simple. The researchers might consider it sufficient to mention who administered the measures and how and when they were administered. If descriptive data were collected periodically, as in longitudinal research, the time intervals should be specified.

Other research designs, especially experimental designs, require more detailed explanations. For example, the time line of the experiment needs to be described so that the reader knows when the various measures and treatments were administered. Also, each of the experimental treatments (for example, a new teaching method) needs to be described so that others could try them out as intended if they wished to replicate the study.

You will need a basic understanding of various research designs to evaluate the adequacy of the research design used in a particular study. Part Three is intended to help you develop this understanding. In addition to explaining each design, we present a report of an actual research study that used it. In addition, we provide a critical review of the study to illustrate the aspects of research design that need to be evaluated. If there are flaws or weaknesses in the research design, they will limit the conclusions you can reach from the research results.

# The Research Results and Discussion

Following the description of procedures for selecting a sample, selecting or developing measures, and creating a research design, research reports generally have two sections. First is the *results section*. If a quantitative study was done, the results of the statistical analyses are presented. If a qualitative study was done, some statistical results might be presented, but primarily there will be detailed, "thick" descriptions of the phenomena that were observed. In other words, numbers dominate the results sections of quantitative research reports, and words dominate the results sections of qualitative research reports.

We explain commonly used statistical techniques and conditions for their appropriate use in Chapter 7. Then in Part Three, we explain the various research designs and the statistical techniques generally used with each of them. Also, we analyze and evaluate the statistical analyses in actual research reports included in Part Three. In Chapter 9 we describe the presentation of qualitative results and discuss how to evaluate them.

The final section of a research report is the *discussion section* (sometimes labeled the *conclusions section*). It is here that researchers are free to express their interpretations of the results, draw conclusions about the practical and theoretical significance of the results, and make recommendations for further research. A personal perspective is quite acceptable in the discussion section. By contrast, the results section should focus on an objective account of the statistical analyses. If a qualitative research study was done, the account of what was observed necessarily will be subjective. Still, the emphasis is on description rather than discussion, which is reserved for the last section of the report.

In evaluating the discussion section, you will be deciding whether you agree with the researchers' judgments about how the results should be interpreted and what their implications are for theory and practice. The most critical factor in this evaluation is whether you think the researchers' judgments are supported by their research results and by previous research results. Your ability to make this evaluation will improve as you develop an understanding of research methodology and knowledge of the research literature to which a particular study contributes.

# Chapter References

EBERTS, R. W., & STONE, J. A. (1988). Student achievement in public schools: Do principals make a difference? *Economics of Education Review, 7*(3), 291–299.

EVANS, P. (1976). The Burt affair: Sleuthing in science. *APA Monitor,* no. 12, pp. 1, 4.

GLASER, B. G., & STRAUSS, A. L. (1967). *The discovery of grounded theory.* Chicago: Aldine.

ROSENTHAL, R., & ROSNOW, F. L. (1975). *The volunteer subject.* New York: Wiley.

TONSOR, C. A. (1953). Must we segregate? *National Association of Secondary School Principals' Bulletin, 37,* 75–77.

# Recommended Reading

BORG, W. R., & GALL, M. D. (1989). *Educational research: An introduction,* 5th ed. White Plains, NY: Longman.

This text will be useful for the student who requires more information on critical evaluation and research methodology.

EISNER, E. W., & PESHKIN, A., eds. (1990). *Qualitative inquiry in education: The continuing debate.* New York: Teachers College Press.

This is a collection of papers by leading qualitative researchers on unresolved issues in their field. Among the issues discussed are subjectivity and objectivity in research, the meaning of validity, and whether qualitative findings can be generalized. The book is intriguing because it does not offer pat answers; rather it provokes the reader to question the nature of educational research and what it might contribute to practice.

JAEGER, R. M., ed. (1988). *Complementary methods for research in education.* Washington, DC: American Educational Research Association.

This book gives a readable overview of various research methods written by leading researchers. Their commentaries provide guidelines for the proper use of each type of research, which you can use to help you evaluate studies you locate in your literature search. The book covers these research methods: histories, philosophical inquiries, ethnographies, case study methods, surveys, and experiments.

KATZER, J., COOK, K. H., & CROUCH, W. W. (1982). *Evaluating information—A guide for users of social science research,* 2nd ed. Reading, MA: Addison-Wesley.

This book provides a simple overview of methods for reading and evaluating social science research, including educational research. The authors focus on the various kinds of errors that are found in research studies. An understanding of these errors will help you become a more skillful evaluator of research.

MERRIAM, S. B. (1988). *Case study research in education: A qualitative approach.* San Francisco: Jossey-Bass.

This textbook will be useful for students who wish more information about the qualitative research concepts and procedures discussed in this chapter.

# Application Problems

1. Review the following introductory section of a research article and identify possible indicators of investigator bias.

## TEAM TEACHING IS THE ANSWER

### BY R. B. SMITH

Two years ago the author recommended that the freshman psychology course at Catatonic State University be taught through a team-teaching approach. Each faculty member in the department selected the topics in which he or she had the greatest expertise and developed lessons in these topics. We felt that this approach had many advantages over the timeworn approach that students find so dull in which one instructor lectures predominantly and is responsible for the entire course, including areas in which he or she has had little background. The purpose of this study was to demonstrate objectively that a team-teaching approach produced better achievement and better attitudes among freshman students than a conventional lecture approach carried out by a single instructor.

2. Evaluate the following "hypothesis," using the criteria given in this chapter:

Two experiments were undertaken. The first investigates the use of computer feedback in changing the rate of students' responses to computer-presented questions, and the second deals with the effect of computer feedback on the accuracy of students' responses to these questions.

3. The district reading supervisor wants to investigate students' attitudes toward reading in a large urban school district in the hope that this survey will produce information that can be used to modify the school's reading program. The supervisor has decided to select her sample from all sixth-grade students listed on the district roster. This roster lists students alphabetically by classroom for each of the district's 200 elementary schools. Forty of these schools (having 3,520 sixth-grade students) are classified as serving predominantly upper-middle-class neighborhoods. A total of 54 schools (4,968 students) serve lower-middle-class neighborhoods, 62 schools (6,211 students) serve working-class neighborhoods, and 44 (4,507 students) are inner-city schools serving mainly welfare families. Thus there are a total of 800 sixth-grade classrooms, containing an average of 24 students. Total district enrollment in grade 6 is 19,206. Describe the steps you would take to:
   a. Select a simple random sample of 1,000 students from this population.
   b. Select a systematic sample of 1,000 students.
   c. Select a sample of 1,000 students stratified on the basis of socioeconomic status of the schools.
   d. Select a cluster sample of about 1,000 students.

4. In Application Problem 3, what is the accessible population? To what target populations might the results be generalized?
5. Suppose a group of researchers wishes to study factors that affect students' learning of chemistry. A standardized test of chemistry is used to measure learning. What aspects of the test should you evaluate? Suppose the researchers also use an interview procedure to determine what students have learned. What aspects of the interview procedure should you evaluate?

# CHAPTER 6

# EDUCATIONAL MEASURES

## Overview

Unless researchers use sound measures to collect data, their findings are of little value. For this reason your evaluation of a research study should include a careful inspection of its measures. To perform this task well, you need a basic knowledge of the principles of educational measurement. This chapter aims to provide this knowledge. We describe the use of paper-and-pencil tests, questionnaires, interviews, and direct observation to collect educational data. Next we discuss important characteristics of educational measures such as objectivity, validity, and reliability. Finally, we review sources of information about educational measures.

## Objectives

1. State the advantages and limitations of paper-and-pencil tests and scales.
2. State six questions that a reviewer should ask in evaluating questionnaires used in a research study.
3. State advantages and limitations of the interview as a measurement procedure in educational research.
4. Explain what a response effect is in the context of interviewing.
5. State six questions that a reviewer should ask in evaluating interviews used in a research study.
6. Explain the difference between high-inference and low-inference variables.
7. State five questions that a reviewer should ask in evaluating direct observation measures used in a research study.
8. Define test objectivity, and give examples of more objective and less objective measures.
9. Define five types of test validity, and describe the evidence needed to support each type of validity claim.
10. Describe four procedures that can be used to strengthen the validity of a qualitative measure.
11. Define three types of test reliability, compare them, and describe the conditions under which they are used.
12. Explain how the reliability of a qualitative measure can be determined.
13. Describe at least three reference books and at least three computer data bases for locating and evaluating educational measures.

All research involves measurement. For example, astronomers measure the distance between stars, physicists measure the mass of nuclear particles, ecologists count the

frequency of members of a species in a given area, sociologists measure the socioeconomic status of individuals, and educational researchers measure how much students
have learned in a given period of time.

Measurement in the physical and biological sciences has become very accurate and
sophisticated compared to measurement in education. Educational research is concerned with the most complex of all scientific subjects, the human being, and some
human characteristics that are relevant to the educational process can be better measured at present than others. For example, measures of strength, manual dexterity, and
visual acuity are quite precise and reliable. Measures of academic achievement are
moderately accurate. But when we attempt to measure such complex human characteristics as personality traits or creativity, our measures are subject to large errors.

The research findings of any study are no more accurate than the measures on which
these findings are based. For this reason, if you are interested in applying the findings
of educational research to practical problems, you must know something about the
principles of educational measurement and how to apply them to evaluate research
studies. This chapter is designed to give you the basic knowledge you will need to
make such evaluations.

# Kinds of Measures Used in Educational Research

Educational researchers have developed many types of procedures for measuring
human characteristics and behavior. The following is a review of four of the most
widely used procedures: paper-and-pencil tests and scales, questionnaires, interviews,
and direct observation.

## PAPER-AND-PENCIL TESTS AND SCALES

Tests measure an individual's knowledge, depth of understanding, or skill. Scales
measure an individual's attitudes, personality characteristics, emotional states, interests, values, and related factors. Thousands of paper-and-pencil tests and scales purport to measure variables ranging from the academic aptitude of preschoolers to
interest in working in various occupations. These measures are widely used in educational research projects because of their advantages over other forms of measurement:
First, they are generally cheaper. Second, because of their huge number and variety,
researchers usually can find at least one paper-and-pencil test or scale for virtually any
variable. Third, they generally are easier to use and require less time than other forms
of measurement.

Paper-and-pencil tests and scales also have limitations. First, most of these measures
require the ability to read and write. Thus, students who cannot read or write well will
be unable to show what they really know or think about the variables measured by
tests and scales. For example, because most achievement tests are timed, a slow reader
may complete fewer items and obtain a lower score on a science achievement test than
a fast reader, even though the slow reader may know more science. Therefore, in
evaluating a research study that used paper-and-pencil tests or scales, you should

check the procedures that were used to eliminate reading ability as a factor. These procedures may include: (1) selecting a measure that is easy for the individuals to read, (2) reading all items aloud to the individuals, and (3) giving help to poor readers by explaining directions and difficult words.

Another limitation of paper-and-pencil tests and scales is that they rely on self-report. This is not a serious problem when measuring academic achievement, but an individual can easily give misleading answers on scales that measure attitudes, personality traits, or vocational interests. In attitude measurement, for example, the individual may wish to hide his true attitude in order to get a more socially acceptable score. Some personality and attitude scales are designed to disguise their purpose to reduce this problem. However, the purpose of most paper-and-pencil scales is transparent, and when it is, faking or distortion is possible.

Many paper-and-pencil tests and scales are group-administered. A limitation of this type of measure is that it is difficult for the test administrator to determine the physical and mental state of the persons being tested. If a student is ill, tired, or emotionally upset, he is likely to perform below his capacity on the measure. Even though the student's resulting score is not valid, it is likely to be included with other research data. If there are several invalid scores, they may be sufficient to distort the research findings and lead to unsound recommendations for practice. Individually administered tests and scales are much less susceptible to this problem.

Many educational variables are measured by paper-and-pencil tests and scales because of the advantages stated above. However, more accurate measurement of these variables usually is possible with other measurement techniques. For example, students are more likely to give thoughtful and complete responses in an interview than on a paper-and-pencil measure of study habits. Direct observation is another technique that provides better measurement of many variables. For example, observation of behavior in the classroom usually will provide better information on the degree and types of aggression that students exhibit than scales that purport to measure these variables. Similarly, we can learn more about an educator's counseling skills by watching that person conduct a counseling session than we can by administering a multiple-choice test about counseling.

Later in this chapter we will discuss further how the tests and scales used in a research project can be evaluated.

## QUESTIONNAIRES

Questionnaires are similar to paper-and-pencil tests and scales in appearance and in the fact that they elicit written responses. However, they differ in other respects. Paper-and-pencil tests and scales usually measure one or two variables (e.g., knowledge of vocabulary or attitude toward social studies instruction), whereas questionnaires typically measure many variables. For example, a questionnaire might ask respondents about the type of computer they use, the types of applications they make, the frequency of each application, their previous training in computer use, and their intentions to expand their computer use in the future. Another difference is that the items on tests and scales are summed to yield a total score, whereas questionnaire items typically do not yield a total score. Responses to each item are examined separately.

Questionnaire items can be either the closed form, in which the question permits only certain responses (such as a multiple-choice question), or the open form, in which individuals make any response they wish in their own words. The choice of item form is determined by the objective of the particular question. Generally, though, it is desirable to design the questions in closed form so that the data can be quantified and analyzed efficiently.

In evaluating a questionnaire study, you should consider the following questions:

1. *Was the questionnaire pretested?* It is impossible to predict how the items will be interpreted by respondents unless the researcher tries out the questionnaire and analyzes the responses of a small sample of subjects before starting the main study. The pilot study should include a sample drawn from the same population that will be sampled in the main study. Results of the pilot study should be used to refine the questionnaire and locate potential problems in the interpretation or analysis of the data. If a pilot study was done, you can have more confidence that the data obtained in the main study are valid.

2. *Did the questionnaire include any leading questions?* A copy of the questionnaire usually is included in the research report. You should check it carefully for leading questions. If a question is framed in such a way that individuals are given hints about the kind of response that is expected, they will tend to give this response. The tendency is especially strong when the letter of transmittal that accompanies the questionnaire was signed by someone whom the subject is eager to please. Results obtained from leading questions are likely to be biased, so they should be used cautiously.

3. *Were any psychologically threatening questions included in the questionnaire?* In constructing items, the researcher should avoid questions that may be psychologically threatening to the respondents. For example, a questionnaire sent to school principals concerning the morale of teachers at their schools would be threatening to some principals because low morale suggests that they are failing in part of their job. Many individuals who receive a questionnaire containing threatening items will not return it. If they do return it, little confidence can be placed in the accuracy of their responses because of their ego involvement in the situation.

A good method for evaluating whether a questionnaire is psychologically threatening is to put yourself in the position of the respondent. Then read the questionnaire and judge whether any of the questions are threatening to you. Research results for items that you judge to be threatening should be given little credence.

4. *Were the subjects who received the questionnaire likely to have the information requested?* An obvious factor to consider in selecting a sample for a questionnaire study is to select individuals who will be able to supply the desired information. If the researcher does not have a thorough knowledge of the situation involved, he may send the questionnaire to a group of persons who do not have the desired information. For example, a graduate student seeking data on school financial policies sent questionnaires to a large number of elementary school principals. Many of the questionnaires

returned were incomplete and contained few specific facts of the sort the graduate student wanted. This study failed because the trend in recent years has been for superintendents and their staffs to handle most matters concerning school finance. Because the principals who received the questionnaire had little specific knowledge concerning this topic, they were unable to supply the information requested.

5. *What percentage of subjects responded to the questionnaire?* The most difficult problem in conducting a questionnaire study is to get a sufficient response rate. You should be concerned if the response rate is less than 70 percent. If the percentage is lower, you should place little confidence in the results reported because individuals who respond to a questionnaire tend to be different from those who do not. Therefore, their answers will not accurately represent the results that would have been obtained if everyone in the sample had responded. The problem of a low response rate can be overcome if the researcher collects evidence that the part of the sample that responded to the questionnaire is representative of the population from which the total sample was drawn.

6. *What steps were taken to contact nonrespondents, and how many ultimately responded?* A desirable procedure in a questionnaire study is to conduct at least two follow-up contacts of nonrespondents in order to get a higher percentage of responses. The researcher also should compare the answers of individuals who responded initially with those who responded only after follow-up contacts were made. This comparison helps you estimate what the pattern of responses would have been if all subjects had responded. It also provides some idea of how respondents and nonrespondents differ in their answers to each question. If follow-up contacts and comparisons are not made, you should be concerned about the validity of the reported results.

## INTERVIEWS

The interview is a form of measurement that is being used increasingly as educational researchers do more qualitative studies. Unlike paper-and-pencil tests, scales, and questionnaires, interviews involve the collection of data through direct interaction between the researcher and the individuals being studied. This direct interaction is the source of both the main advantages and the disadvantages of the interview as a research technique.

The principal advantage of interviews is their adaptability. The well-trained interviewer can alter the interview situation at any time in order to obtain the fullest possible responses from the individual. For example, if the individual makes an interesting remark, the interviewer can ask a follow-up question on the spot. Or if the individual becomes nervous, the interviewer can interrupt the questioning sequence to put him at ease.

Another advantage of interviews is that they elicit data of much greater depth than is possible with other measurement techniques. A serious criticism of questionnaire studies, for example, is that they are often shallow; that is, they fail to dig deeply enough to produce a true picture of the respondents' opinions and feelings. By contrast, experienced interviewers can create a climate of rapport and trust that allows them to obtain information that the individual probably would not reveal under other circumstances. Examples of such information are perceptions about negative aspects of the self or negative feelings toward others.

The major disadvantage of the interview method is that the direct interaction between researcher and interviewee makes it easy for subjectivity and bias to occur. The eagerness of the interviewee to please the interviewer, a vague antagonism that sometimes arises between interviewer and interviewee, and the tendency of the interviewer to seek out answers that support his preconceived notions are a few of the factors that may contribute to biasing of interview data. These biasing factors are called response effects by survey researchers. A response effect occurs when there is a difference between the answer given by the respondent and the true answer. For example, a respondent, if asked his annual income, may give an incorrect reply for any of a great many reasons. He may forget some sources of income such as stock dividends, he may be ashamed of or wish to hide some income such as money won gambling, he may want to impress the interviewer and therefore exaggerate his income, and so on.

Another disadvantage of the interview as a measurement technique is that it is costly and time-consuming. Thus the interview method is seldom used in quantitative studies, which typically involve a large sample. It is much more likely to be used in qualitative studies because they typically focus on a few individuals.

The following questions will help you evaluate research studies that use interviews to collect data:

1. *How well were the interviewers trained?* The level of training required for interviewers is directly related to the type of information being collected. Interviewers need extensive training in studies in which they will be called on to draw inferences or make judgments or collect sensitive data. Information on the training of interviewers should be included in the research report.

2. *How was information recorded?* Audiotaping is the most accurate method of recording interview information. If interviewers take notes instead of audiotaping the interview, they may overlook important information. Also, interviewers who take notes get to decide what will be recorded. Consequently their notes may be biased. For example, interviewers may write information that agrees with their preconceived ideas or beliefs and omit information that disagrees with these beliefs.

3. *How much judgment was called for?* Interviews are of three main types: structured, semistructured, and unstructured. In structured interviews, the interviewer asks specific questions from an interview guide and does not deviate from these questions. In a semistructured interview, the interviewer does not employ a detailed interview guide but has a general plan and usually asks questions or makes comments intended to lead the interviewee toward the interviewer's objectives. Unstructured interviews are generally called for when the type of information sought is difficult for the subject to express or is psychologically distressing. Because of the threatening nature of topics covered by unstructured interviews, this procedure must be continually adapted, depending on how the interviewee is responding. Unstructured interviews obviously

require sophisticated judgment on the part of the interviewer concerning what to ask, what responses should be pursued further, and what should be recorded.

Most interviews in educational research are semistructured. The interviewers follow a guide that lists questions covering all essential information needed by the researcher. However, they also have the option to follow up any answer in an effort to get more information or clarify the interviewee's replies.

4. *Were the interview procedures tried out before the study began?* Although the interview can provide valuable data, you should keep in mind that it is a highly subjective method of measurement. The researcher must use many controls and safeguards to obtain reasonably objective and unbiased data. A careful pilot study is necessary to develop these controls and safeguards before data for the main study are collected. The pilot study should be described in the research report. Inclusion of a pilot study indicates to the reviewer that the research project has been carefully conducted.

5. *Were leading questions asked?* A factor that often biases the results of interview studies is the use of leading questions by the interviewer. A leading question is any question whose phrasing leads the respondent to consider one reply more desirable than another. For example, suppose we were interviewing a random sample of voters concerning their attitudes toward federal aid to education. After establishing whether the respondent is familiar with the issue of federal aid to education, a reasonable question might be, "What is your opinion of federal aid to education?" A question that could be classified as moderately leading might be, "Do you favor federal aid to education?" This question is a little easier for the respondent to answer in the affirmative than in the negative. A more serious attempt to lead the respondent would result in a question such as, "In view of the dangers of federal control, do you feel that federal aid to education is advisable?" Here the respondent is strongly motivated to give an unfavorable response. Questions can be slanted even further by the use of emotionally toned words to which the respondent is inclined to react for or against with little thought about the basic issue involved. Such a question might be, "Do you favor federal aid to education as a means of providing each child with an equal educational opportunity?" The phrase "an equal educational opportunity" has an emotional connotation that is likely to elicit favorable replies.

If an interview was a primary measure in a research study, the report should include at least the main questions that were asked. You should study these questions for signs of bias.

6. *How much did the interviewer know about the research?* Ideally interviewers should know as little as possible about the research for which they are collecting data. To accomplish this goal, the researcher should not serve as an interviewer but should employ another individual for this purpose. Even if this procedure is followed, interviewers can infer a great deal from the questions on the interview guide. However, they should not be told anything about the hypotheses or research design. Such information allows for the possibility of bias that could not occur if they had no access to that information.

For example, suppose the researcher wants to study the effectiveness of two different approaches to improve the adjustment of young couples who are having difficulty raising their children. He selects 30 couples who are having serious problems of this type and randomly divides them into two groups. He then gives one group a program of counseling designed to improve overall personal adjustment. The other group receives a program in which they identify specific conflict situations with their children and then role-play until they arrive at mutually acceptable solutions. Three months after the completion of the programs, the researcher trains an interviewer who will interview each couple to determine parent-child problems they have had during the past month; collect data on the seriousness of these problems; and find out if the problems were resolved and if so, how.

It is clearly impossible to keep the interviewer from knowing that the study has something to do with problems involving child rearing. However, he should not be told anything about the treatments, and of course he should not know which couples were given each treatment. If the interviewer has this information, bias can easily occur. If he considers counseling to be the better approach, he may consciously or unconsciously solicit information that supports this bias and overlook information that disagrees with it, he may be more cordial in his relationship with the couples who received counseling, or he may frame some of his questions to these couples in ways that will tend to increase positive responses.

The desirability of keeping the interviewer ignorant about the purposes of the research project does not apply to certain types of qualitative research, especially ethnographic studies (see Chapter 9), because the research questions often emerge from the interview process itself. Therefore, the interviewer must be the researcher directing the project, so that he or she can design each phase of the project based on all the knowledge that has accumulated in preceding phases. Also, the researcher will not be able to interpret the interview data during the data analysis phase of the project unless he knows the complete context in which each interview was conducted. The only way to know the complete context is to conduct the interviews himself.

In summary, the interview is an excellent technique for collecting certain kinds of research information. However, its subjectivity opens the door to many potential types of bias. Thus, in reviewing studies in which interviews have been used, you should carefully consider evidence related to the six questions we have discussed.

## DIRECT OBSERVATION

In recent years educational researchers have increasingly turned to direct observation as a method of collecting data. For example, in one study (Borg & Ascione, 1979), observers were trained to record the frequency of four kinds of teachers' praise in elementary classrooms. Use of praise was then related to student variables such as work involvement and disruptive behavior. Praise in this study would be classified as a _low-inference_ behavior. The reason for this classification is that observers were trained to count the frequency of specific, clearly defined types of praise statements; little or no inference was required to decide whether a behavior was an instance of praise. This approach to direct observation usually produces very reliable and valid measures of the variables being observed.

However, suppose observers are given a general definition of praise and asked to rate each teacher on a scale from 1 to 10 on the degree to which they use praise. In this situation praise is considered a *high-inference* behavior because the observers must form an overall judgment with no specific guidelines. This process requires a high level of inference, which increases the probability of observer bias.

Early observational studies often used untrained observers, such as principals, and asked for general ratings rather than the recording of specific frequencies. In some studies the researcher would ask the principal to rate all teachers in the school on such general variables as dedication or warmth without giving precise definitions of the variables. Such high-inference ratings are usually invalid for several reasons. First, different principals will define these abstract variables differently. Second, the ratings are easily subject to bias, as when the principal's general opinion of the teacher influences the ratings of specific performance. Third, because some principals visit classrooms much more often than others, some ratings are likely to be much more valid than others. If you encounter a study that uses untrained observers to rate individuals on abstract, high-inference variables, you can have little confidence in the validity of the results.

In evaluating the use of observational procedures in a research study, you should consider the following questions:

*1. Were high-inference or low-inference behaviors observed?* Although some high-inference behaviors such as teachers' enthusiasm can be observed reliably, low-inference behaviors are preferable in most research. An important advantage of low-inference variables is that research findings are usually easier to translate into practice. For example, a study that recommends that teachers use verbal praise whenever a child gives a correct response during a discussion lesson is easier for the teacher to adopt than a study that indicates that teachers should be warmer or more enthusiastic.

*2. Were observers trained to identify the variables to be observed?* The researcher should describe the kind and duration of training given to the observers. Most observer training programs approximate the following sequence:

(1) The observers study definitions and examples of the behaviors to be observed.
(2) The observers study the observation form to be used.
(3) All observers watch the kind of activity they are being trained to observe (such as time on task in a first-grade classroom) and independently record what they see on the observation form. The activities are usually recorded on video- or audiotape by the researcher so that they can be replayed.
(4) The recording of the activity is replayed. The correct scoring and differences between observers are discussed.
(5) Steps (3) and (4) are repeated until the observers independently obtain very similar scores on the observed behaviors.

*3. What was the interobserver reliability?* Reliability in this context refers to the level of agreement between the observations of independent observers. The level of interobserver reliability can be determined by computing a correlation coefficient between the scores of different observers or by determining the percentage of events observed in which the two observers agreed. If observers have been adequately trained, the percentage of agreement is usually above 85 percent. If a correlation coefficient was computed instead, a value of .75 or greater is considered acceptable.

*4. How long was the observation period?* The observation period should be long enough to obtain a representative sample of the behaviors being studied. Otherwise the observation data will yield atypical results. The necessary period of observation will depend on such factors as the nature of the behaviors being observed, the circumstances under which the behavior can occur, and its frequency of occurrence. For example, suppose you are observing classroom behavior that occurs very frequently and can occur in a variety of situations, such as the number of times teachers ask fact questions and higher-cognitive questions during a classroom presentation. Because these are high-frequency behaviors in classroom instruction, a one-hour observation period may be sufficient to obtain a reliable score. But if you are measuring low-frequency behavior such as fighting among pupils, a much longer period of observation would be needed. In reviewing observational research, therefore, you must consider the entire observational situation and judge whether the length of the observation period was sufficient.

*5. How conspicuous were the observers?* In the ideal case observers would be stationed behind a one-way screen, and their presence would not be known to the subjects. These conditions are virtually impossible to achieve in practice. Observers need to be visible to the individuals being studied for ethical reasons. Consequently, the observers are likely to have some impact on the persons being observed. For example, an observer entering a classroom for the first time probably will arouse the curiosity of the students and possibly the teacher. The resulting inattentiveness of the students to the teacher may not reflect their usual behavior. Research data based on these observations will not represent typical behavior of the teacher or the students.

This problem can be overcome to a large extent if the researcher asks the observers not to record any observational data for at least the first 5 or 10 minutes that they are in the classroom. It may even be necessary for observers to make several visits to the classroom before students take them for granted and behave as if they were not present. Also, the observers should be as unobtrusive as possible. They should not comment or participate in any way in the ongoing activity, nor should they make nonverbal responses to the situation such as laughing or shaking their heads.

In reviewing studies that rely on observational data, you should estimate the possible effects of the presence of the observer. Because research reports often are brief, sufficient information may not be given for you to make this judgment. You may need to draw on your own experience, and that of others, to imagine the situation that was observed and how likely it was that observer effects occurred.

As we discussed above in the case of interview measures, qualitative research has different purposes from quantitative research. These purposes involve learning the perspectives of the individuals being observed and the context in which their activities occur. This focus on perspectives and context requires a level of researcher rapport with the individuals being observed and participation in their activities that would be considered unacceptable in a quantitative study. Therefore, procedures for ensuring valid, reliable observations do not apply to qualitative research. We have more to say about this matter in the following section of this chapter and in Chapter 9, which focuses on qualitative research designs.

# Characteristics of Educational Measures – OBJECTIVITY, RELIABILITY, VALIDITY

All educational measures share certain characteristics that must be evaluated when reviewing a research study. The most important characteristics are objectivity, reliability, and validity. We will discuss these characteristics in the following sections, with special attention to their relevance to paper-and-pencil tests.

## OBJECTIVITY

The objectivity of a measure reflects the degree to which it is free of influence from the beliefs or biases of the individuals who administer or score it. The degree of objectivity of paper-and-pencil tests usually can be determined by carefully studying the procedures for administering and scoring them. The less judgment required by the tester, the more objective the test is likely to be. For example, most standardized tests, such as the achievement tests that are used so widely in the public schools, are highly objective. The person giving the test reads instructions verbatim from the test manual. The manual also contains information on the time allowed to complete the test, how to respond to students' questions, and other topics related to test administration. Scoring of such measures is also highly objective. If followed carefully, the scoring procedure, which consists of checking answers against a scoring key, eliminates virtually any chance of bias. It is also possible to score many tests by machine. This procedure provides maximum objectivity.

When the test administrator is given more latitude in administering a test or when scoring the test requires making judgments, objectivity is reduced. This is the case with many essay tests. Scorers of these tests must be trained carefully so that they conform to a common set of standards and do not let themselves be influenced by personal biases.

Many tests sacrifice a degree of objectivity in order to achieve other goals. For example, the *Thematic Apperception Test (TAT)* involves showing a series of pictures and asking the individual to tell a story related to each picture. This test and others like it are based on the theory that when presented with an amorphous stimulus and freedom of response, the individual will "project" his inner thoughts, fantasies, and structuring of reality onto the stimulus and this projection will be revealed in his stories. (Because of this phenomenon, the TAT and similar tests are called *projective techniques*.)

Obviously, much judgment is called for in scoring and interpreting an individual's responses to a projective technique. Bias can easily influence these judgments, thus reducing the objectivity of the data. For this reason projective measures usually require extensive training and experience to administer, score, and interpret. Thus, in evaluating research in which such measures are employed, you should pay special attention to the qualifications of the test scorers and the steps taken in the research to reduce the chance of bias. Probably the most effective strategy to reduce bias is to have the tests administered and scored by persons who know nothing about the research being conducted. This is a desirable precaution in any study, but it is especially important for measures that are low in objectivity.

## VALIDITY

1) content Validity
2) Predictive Validity
3) concurrent Validity
4) construct Validity
5) Face (Reliability) Validity

The validity of a test is of utmost importance. A test is valid to the extent to which it lives up to the claims that the researcher has made for it. Different types of claims are appropriate for different measurement situations, and so different types of test validity have been distinguished. The five types of test validity that you should understand in order to evaluate measures used in educational research are content validity, predictive validity, concurrent validity, construct validity, and face validity.

**Content Validity.**    A test has content validity to the extent that its items represent the content that the test is designed to measure. In other words, the researcher's claim is that the test assesses the learner's knowledge, understanding, or ability with respect to a certain body of content. Thus the XYZ Test of Algebra Achievement would have content validity if the researchers can demonstrate that it measures what students were taught in the algebra classes that the researchers are studying.

Content validity should not be confused with *face validity,* which is concerned with the degree to which the test appears to measure what it claims to measure. Face validity is determined by reviewing the test items and making a subjective appraisal of whether they appear to measure what the test claims to measure. For example, we may examine the items of the XYZ Test of Algebra Achievement and conclude that the test has face validity because the items correspond to our view of what students are taught in an algebra course.

By contrast, content validity is determined by systematically comparing the test content with the course content. This means that the XYZ Test of Algebra Achievement may have high content validity for algebra courses in high school A and low content validity for courses taught in high school B. This difference in content validity can occur, for example, if the two schools use textbooks that cover markedly different content.

Content validity is important primarily in achievement testing and various tests of skill and proficiency, such as occupational skill tests. For example, a test of achievement in ninth-grade English will have high content validity if the items covered on the test are representative, in type and proportion, of the content presented in the course. If test items cover topics not taught in the course or ignore or overemphasize certain topics that were taught, the test's content validity will be lower.

Some types of test validity are expressed in numerical terms as a correlation coefficient (sometimes called a validity coefficient). By contrast, content validity usually involves an objective comparison of the test items with curriculum content and/or textbook content. The usual procedure is for the test developers to select several of the most widely used textbooks in the given subject. Then they carefully analyze each book to determine the concepts covered and the proportion of the total book devoted to each. The test developers then construct the test so that the concepts covered and the proportion of items on each concept are as similar as possible to the coverage in the textbooks. The test manual may include a table that demonstrates the degree of similarity.

Content validity is particularly important in selecting tests to use in experiments involving the effects of different instructional methods or programs on student achievement. For example, if a school district wants to determine which of two seventh-grade general science programs results in greater student achievement, they must select an achievement test that is equally appropriate for both programs. If the test fits the content of program A better than the content of program B, program A students may score higher even though program B is superior. When two programs to be evaluated do not cover exactly the same content, the researcher can select a test that fits both programs reasonably well and then score only the test items that deal with the concepts covered in both programs.

**Predictive Validity.**   A test has predictive validity if scores on the test predict individuals' subsequent performance on a criterion measure. For example, it may be that students' scores on the XYZ Test of Algebra Achievement predict well the grades they will earn in courses on geometry and calculus. If so, we can say that the XYZ test has good predictive validity for these two courses. We cannot make the claim, however, that performance on the test has predictive validity for any other mathematics course, unless evidence to support that claim is available.

The usual method of determining a test's predictive validity is to administer the test to a group of individuals, wait until the behavior that the test attempts to predict has occurred, and then determine the degree of relationship between the occurrence of the behavior and the individuals' scores on the test. Using the example given above, the researchers might administer the XYZ Test of Algebra Achievement to a sample of students at the end of, say, a ninth-grade course on algebra. The researchers would follow the sample students for another year, until they completed a course on geometry. They then would administer a test of geometry achievement. At this point the researchers have the data they need to determine predictive validity. They would correlate students' scores on the algebra test with their scores on the geometry test. (The subject  of correlation is discussed in Chapters 7 and 12). The greater the correlation between the two sets of scores, the better the predictive validity of the XYZ Test of Algebra Achievement.

Tests that have good predictive validity are useful in certain kinds of research projects. These tests also have practical significance for the educator. For example, if the XYZ test is found to have good predictive validity, it can be used to counsel students. Students who earn low scores on the test can be informed that they are likely to have difficulty in a subsequent course on geometry. This information may help students to decide between taking an easier or more difficult course on this subject or to get tutorial assistance so that they can cope with the challenge of whatever course is offered.

**Concurrent Validity.**    A test has concurrent validity if it can be shown that individuals' scores on the test correlate with their scores on another test administered at the same time or within a short interval of time. Concurrent validity studies are often carried out in an effort to locate simple, easy-to-use tests that can be administered in place of complex, expensive tests. For example, suppose that research demonstrated that young children's scores on a brief, group-administered test correlated well with their scores on a lengthy, individually administered test of school readiness. We can conclude on the basis of this evidence that the brief test has good concurrent validity with the long test. This information would be of great help to early childhood educators because it means that the brief test can be administered as a substitute for the long test. The savings in time and money involved in testing would be substantial.

Concurrent validity and predictive validity are determined by similar procedures. The main difference is that to determine concurrent validity, researchers calculate the correlation between students' scores on test A and their scores on test B, and both tests are administered within a short time of each other (typically a few days to a week). By contrast, predictive validity involves correlating students' scores on test A with their scores on test B when test B is administered substantially later (typically months or years later). Also, a concurrent validity study usually is done to determine whether an easier-to-administer test can be substituted for a more difficult-to-administer test. By contrast, a predictive validity study is done to determine whether a test predicts performance on an important criterion, such as grade point average or success in a work setting.

**Construct Validity.**    A test has construct validity to the extent that it can be shown to measure a particular hypothetical construct. Psychological concepts such as intelligence, anxiety, and creativity are considered hypothetical constructs because they are not directly observable but rather are inferred on the basis of their observable effects on behavior.

To obtain evidence of construct validity, the test developer often starts by setting up hypotheses about the characteristics of persons who would obtain high scores on the measure as opposed to those who would obtain low scores. Suppose, for example, that the test developers publish a test that they claim is a measure of anxiety. What kind of evidence can they collect to support this claim? One approach might be to draw on the theory that anxiety causes an individual's performance to deteriorate. Assuming the theory is true, we would expect that high-anxious students' performance would deteriorate faster under conditions of stress than would low-anxious students' performance. Our reasoning would proceed to the next step, which is to predict that students who score high on the test that purportedly measures anxiety should demonstrate more deterioration of performance than students who score low on the test. If the results conform to this prediction, we have some evidence that the test indeed measures the hypothetical construct called anxiety. You should keep in mind, though, that if the results do not conform to prediction, it does not mean necessarily that the test is an invalid measure of anxiety. It may mean that the theory used to assess the test's construct validity is unsound.

A good measure of a hypothetical construct will have multiple sources of evidence to support its construct validity. Therefore, in the case of the anxiety measure, the test developers would seek additional ways to check its construct validity besides the method described above. For example, they might hypothesize that if the new test measures anxiety, it should correlate with already validated measures of anxiety. They could test this hypothesis by administering the new test and several validated measures of anxiety to a sample of individuals. If scores on the new test correlate well with scores on these measures, this finding provides additional evidence in support of its construct validity.

**Face Validity.**    As mentioned above, a test has face validity to the extent that it *appears* to measure what it purports to measure. No evidence can be collected to support a test's face validity other than to ask individuals to inspect the items and decide whether the test seems to measure what it claims to measure.

Claims of face validity are rather shallow. Nonetheless it is an important feature of tests intended for practical use because people generally react more favorably to tests that have high face validity. For example, Nevo (1985) suggests that tests with high face validity are more likely to: (1) bring about higher levels of cooperation and motivation while subjects are taking the test; (2) reduce feelings of dissatisfaction or injustice among low scorers; (3) help convince potential users (e.g., teachers and school administrators) to use the test; and (4) improve public relations, because nonexperts can more easily see the relationship between the test and the performance or characteristic it purportedly measures.

Face validity is low for many personality measures. Such measures often contain items that validly differentiate between groups that have and do not have the characteristic being measured even though they do not appear to be related to the characteristic. Persons tested with such measures often reject the results or refuse to cooperate because they cannot perceive any relationship between the test and the characteristic being measured. Thus, face validity can be an important consideration in selecting tests for situations in which subjects' acceptance is essential. However, a test can be face valid yet lack any other substantive type of validity. Therefore, you should keep firmly in mind that face validity can only supplement information about the predictive, concurrent, construct, or content validity of a test and never can take the place of such information.

A single individual, such as the school principal, often makes subjective judgments about the face validity of a test being considered for use in the public schools. Face validity can be better estimated by obtaining objective ratings from a sample of individuals who are drawn from the population for whom the test is intended. The composite of their ratings will provide a much more reliable estimate of face validity than a single subjective judgment. For example, suppose we want to estimate the face validity of a test of vocational interests for high school students. A sample of students could be asked, "How relevant are the items on this test to your level of interest in the vocations stated in the items? Rate each item on the following five-point scale."

    5—extremely relevant
    4—very relevant
    3—somewhat relevant
    2—not very relevant
    1—irrelevant

A mean score could then be computed to estimate the face validity of each item. These item means could in turn be combined to give an estimate of the face validity of the entire test.

## VALIDITY OF QUALITATIVE MEASURES

Qualitative research relies heavily on interviews and observation to collect data. These data collection methods are much less objective than traditional measures such as multiple-choice tests. Therefore, it is more difficult to determine whether they yield valid measurements.

As stated above, a test is valid to the extent to which it lives up to the claims that the researcher has made for it. Given this definition, we need to determine what claims qualitative researchers make for their measures and what types of evidence might support those claims.

In a typical qualitative study, the researcher asks interview questions and makes observations about the phenomena of interest. For example, in a recent qualitative study Ackley (1991) asked mentor teachers and first-year teachers (called protégés in his study) about factors that interfered with the mentoring process. We can look at his interview questions to determine whether they were sensible in light of the information he wanted. In a sense, this is a face-validity test. More important, we would want to determine whether his questions elicited accurate information. The implied validity claim is that the self-reports elicited by the interview questions accurately reflect what the mentor or protégé actually did, said, thought, or felt.

The validity of the information yielded by qualitative measures such as interviews and observation can be checked in four ways.

*1. Multiple sources of evidence.* When asked about problems, several of the mentor teachers studied by Ackley mentioned lack of proximity between mentor and protégé in the school building. The validity of these interview data can be checked by searching for corroborative evidence from other sources. For example, when Ackley also asked protégés this question, several mentioned proximity as a problem, thus corroborating the mentors' interview data. Moreover, Ackley was able to visit the school sites and observe the distance between classrooms of mentor-protégé teams that mentioned proximity as a problem and the distance for teams that did not. These observations provided additional support for the validity of the data.

*2. A chain of evidence.* The validity of qualitative research data can be checked by evaluating links among (1) the interview questions or observation procedures, (2) the data that were collected, and (3) conclusions drawn from the data. Suppose Ackley stated in his research report that his data revealed that lack of proximity between classrooms was a major problem in mentoring because it meant that mentors and protégés did not have sufficient time during the school day to travel between their respective classrooms to share ideas and solve the protégé's problems. Our confidence in this conclusion would be stronger if Ackley described the data and how they led to this conclusion. One way of describing the data is by using selective quotations of interview comments made by the informants.

Our confidence would increase further if we knew how the data resulted from the interviews or observations. The researcher can include the major interview questions and observation procedures in the research report and show the kind of data they generated.

In summary, the chain of evidence provides a validity check by placing the qualitative research data in a total context. The validity of the interview or observational measures is strengthened if all parts of the context are consistent: data collection procedures, analyzed data, and conclusions drawn from the data.

*3. Review of key informants.* Quantitative researchers, as a rule, do not have individuals take an achievement test or other objective measure and then ask them to check their test answers to see if the answers reflect the responses they wanted to make. Instead the accepted research practice is for individuals not to see their tests once they turn them in.

Qualitative researchers, however, often do show their data to the individuals being studied as a way of checking their validity. For example, a qualitative researcher might conduct observations of an individual, type his notes, and then ask the interviewee to check them for accuracy. When the interview data have been analyzed and incorporated into a draft of the research report, the researcher can show the draft report to the interviewee as a further check. The interviewee thus has the opportunity to check on the accuracy of the recording and interpretation of what he said in the interview.

Ackley followed this procedure in his study of mentor teachers by showing each mentor-protégé team a draft copy of his case study report and giving them an opportunity to make changes in it.

*4. Researchers' self-reflection.* Interview and observational data are easily subject to researcher bias, especially in qualitative research. To the extent that bias is present, the validity of the data is threatened. The researchers can check on the validity of their data by engaging in a process of self-examination to determine their biases and whether they attempted to keep any biases from influencing the data. Thus the researchers themselves can control, to an extent, the validity of their qualitative data. Ackley, for example, noted that he chose elementary mentor-protégé teams to study because he had extensive experience in elementary education. He felt that this experience enabled him to understand clearly what he observed and what he was told.

## TEST RELIABILITY

A test is reliable to the extent that it is free of measurement errors. To understand what this means, we can use the everyday example of measuring the length of a room with a tape measure. Let's say the true length of the room we'll be measuring is 12 feet. If the tape measure is accurate but we are careless in using it, we might measure the room as 12 feet, 6 inches. Because of our carelessness, we introduced a measurement error of 6 inches.

Now suppose we are very careful in our use of a tape measure, but it happens that the tape measure is defective, that is, certain sections are elastic and contract unpredictably. When we measure the length of the room, the result is 11 feet, 10 inches. In this case the defect in the tape measure produced a measurement error of 2 inches.

To take this example one step further, suppose that we and the tape measure are accurate but the room is made of materials that react to temperature changes and the room is located in a highly variable climate. Thus when we measure the room on day 1, the length of the room is 12 feet, $\frac{1}{4}$ inch; on day 2 it is 11 feet, $11\frac{3}{4}$ inches; and on day 3 it is 12 feet, $\frac{1}{10}$ inch. In this case the measurement error is caused by unstable building materials combined with an unstable climate.

These three examples illustrate the nature of measurement error and the fact that there are different types. In the first example, the measurement error was caused by our carelessness. The comparable situation in educational testing would be errors in test scores because of careless administration of the test or inaccurate scoring of students' errors. (The problem may not be carelessness; it might be lack of knowledge about how to administer or score the test.)

In the second example, the measurement error was caused by errors in the tape measure. A comparable error in educational testing would be inconsistencies in the items that make up the test. Some of the items might be accurate indicators of what the test is measuring, whereas other items might be measuring something different.

In the third example, the measurement error was caused by instability in the room itself and the climate. A comparable error in educational measurement would be the administration of the test under various conditions. For example, a student might earn a certain score on a test one day and a different score on the same test on a different day because he was sick or distracted by something in the test situation.

Measurement errors in tests are virtually unavoidable. However, test developers and test users can follow certain procedures to minimize them. One of these procedures is to develop tests with many items. To understand this point, suppose we wish to measure students' knowledge of physics. A physics achievement test consisting of one multiple-choice item would be highly unreliable. Some students may know quite a bit about physics but may not happen to know the answer to this particular item; conversely, some students whose overall achievement level in physics is low may happen to know or may guess the correct answer. Thus, a one-item test has a lot of measurement error because it is susceptible to many chance factors.

Suppose we increase the number of items on the test. As the number of items increases, we are sampling more and more of the concepts of physics, and so chance factors have less likelihood of occurring. For example, if the test has 50 multiple-choice items, a student with a poor knowledge of physics may make some lucky guesses, but it is unlikely that he can make enough correct guesses to earn a high total score. Thus, a test with many items is likely to be more reliable (that is, have less measurement error) than a test with few items.

A point to watch for in evaluating test reliability is that many tests yield a number of subscores in addition to a total score. This is the case for some intelligence and achievement tests that provide subscores in order to give a profile of the student's performance in the various areas making up the test. However, reliability is often reported only for the total score. In this case, the subscores must be used cautiously. Because subscores have fewer items than the total score, you can be certain that all or most of the subscores will be less reliable than the total test score.

The reliability of educational measures is usually expressed by a statistical expression known as a correlation coefficient. The nature of correlation coefficients is discussed in Chapters 7 and 12. For present purposes it is sufficient for you to know that reliability coefficients range from 0, which indicates no reliability, to 1.00, which indicates perfect reliability. Or to state it in different words, a reliability coefficient of 0 means that the test scores are meaningless because they consist totally of measurement error; a reliability of 1.00 means that the measure has no measurement error. As a rough rule of thumb, a measure is considered reliable for most research and practical purposes if the reliability coefficients calculated on it are .80 or higher.

In our example of the tape measure, we noted that there are different types of measurement error. Different types of reliability coefficients have been developed to assess these different types of measurement error. The most common reliability coefficients are discussed below.

**Item Consistency.** One type of measurement error is caused by inconsistencies in the items that make up the test. For example, if a test of visual creativity contains some items that measure this construct and other items that measure a somewhat different construct, the total score will be an inaccurate indicator of visual creativity. Therefore, test developers want all the items on the test, or on the subtest, to measure the same construct; in other words, they want the items to be consistent. If the items are consistent, individuals who score one way on an item should score the same way on all the remaining items. (For example, if they answer one item correctly, they should answer all the other items correctly) Similarly, individuals who score another way on the items should score the same way on all the remaining items.

The extent to which the items on a test are consistent with one another usually is determined by one of two methods. In the first method (sometimes called the *split-half method*), the test is administered to an appropriate sample. It is then split into two subtests, usually by placing all odd-numbered items in one subtest and all even-numbered items in another subtest. A reliability coefficient is then computed to determine the extent to which the sample test takers are consistent in their scores on the odd-numbered and even-numbered items. This reliability coefficient is called the *coefficient of internal consistency*.

The other method of determining the consistency of items is called the *method of rational equivalence*. This method is based on an analysis of all the individual items, without grouping them into subtests, as is the case with the split-half method. A well-known set of formulas, called the *Kuder-Richardson formulas,* is used to calculate a reliability coefficient based on this analysis. One desirable aspect of the Kuder-Richardson formulas is that they generally yield a lower reliability coefficient than would be obtained by using the other methods described here. Thus, they can be thought of as providing a minimum estimate of the reliability of a test.

**Test Stability.**   As we observed above, measurement error in a test will occur if the individuals being tested vary in their performance from one testing occasion to the next. These variations can occur for many reasons, for example, if some individuals are fatigued on one occasion and rested on the next and if some individuals have just reviewed relevant test information on one occasion and not on the next.

If a test is free of this type of measurement error, individuals should earn the same score on each testing occasion. To determine the extent to which this is the case, researchers administer the test to a sample of individuals, and then after a delay they administer the same test again to the same sample. Scores obtained from the two administrations are then analyzed to determine their reliability. The resulting reliability coefficient is called the *coefficient of stability*. This type of reliability is called *test-retest reliability* or *test stability*.

The most critical problem in calculating test-retest reliability is to determine an appropriate delay between the two administrations of the measure. On the one hand, if the retest is administered too soon after the initial test, individuals will recall their responses to many of the items, which will tend to produce a spuriously high reliability coefficient. On the other hand, if the retesting is delayed too long, there is a good possibility that the individuals' ability to answer some items will change.

**Consistency of Test Administration and Scoring.**   We started our discussion of reliability with the example of measurement errors caused by carelessness in using a tape measure. Similarly, individuals who administer or score tests can cause measurement errors because of carelessness or for some other reason, such as not knowing the correct procedures. Highly objective measures, such as multiple-choice tests, tend to be free of this type of measurement error. However, even test-scoring machines have been known to make scoring mistakes because of mechanical defects. Less objective measures, such as individually administered intelligence and personality tests, are more subject to administration and scoring errors.

The presence of administration errors can be determined by having several individuals administer the same test—or alternate forms of the same test—to the same sample. Their scores are then correlated with one another to yield a reliability coefficient. The presence of scoring errors can be determined quite simply by having several individuals—or machines—score the same set of tests. A reliability coefficient is calculated on the sets of scores to determine how well they agree.

It is particularly important to check for administration errors when the "test" involves direct observation. For example, in classroom research it is common to have observers calculate the percentage of time that each student in the class is on task. Measurement error will occur if different observers code the same behavior differently. The presence of this type of error is determined by having the observers record observational data on the same set of classrooms (or other situation). Their data are then analyzed to determine what is sometimes called an *interobserver reliability coefficient* or *interrater reliability coefficient*.

We discussed above three types of test reliability: item consistency, test stability, and consistency of test administration and scoring. It is unlikely that researchers will determine all three types of reliability for each measure used in a study. One type of reliability is typically of most concern, depending on the measure involved and the research situation. You will need to determine whether the researcher made the appropriate reliability check, or checks, for each measure. In doing your evaluation, keep in mind that it is much easier to establish the reliability of a test than to establish its validity. Therefore, if no specific information on reliability is provided in a research report, you are probably safe in assuming that the reliability of the test is low.

## RELIABILITY OF QUALITATIVE MEASURES

You will recall that we defined test reliability as the extent to which a test is free of measurement errors. This definition applies well to the objective measures used in quantitative research. However, qualitative researchers do not agree on how, or even whether, the notion of test reliability applies to the subjective measures (primarily, interviews and observation) that they typically use.

There does appear to be agreement among qualitative researchers that measurement error can occur in their studies and that it can be controlled to some extent. Their main method for controlling measurement errors is to keep careful records of their interview and observation procedures. For example, it would not be sufficient for the researcher to write, "I interviewed the mentor teachers about strategies they used to help their protégés," or "I observed the mentor teachers and protégés as they interacted with each other to determine what helping strategies were used." This information would be insufficient for other researchers to replicate the measurement procedure so that they could determine whether they would obtain the same or different results. The measurement procedure would be reliable to the extent that the results obtained by other researchers who used it match those obtained by the original researcher.

What information about their measurement procedures should qualitative researchers include in their research report? The general answer is that they should include enough information so that another researcher would know how to use the same procedure. More specifically, it seems reasonable for the researcher to include the following types of information in the report: The time line for collecting the data, the individuals or events that were measured, the context in which the measurements were  made, the procedures used to gain access to the individuals or events, the interview questions that were asked or the foci of the observations, the methods used to record the data, and whether the data collectors received special training.

In practice, qualitative researchers do not replicate their measurement procedures to check their reliability. The check is more theoretical. The reader of a qualitative research report is expected to read the measurement procedures in the report and then *imagine* whether they would yield the same data if replicated by another researcher. This situation is somewhat analogous to the "audit trails" created by skillful accountants. They keep careful records of the procedures they use in creating a balance sheet for a company or other institution. If auditors, or other individuals, wanted to check the reliability of the financial data sources and calculations, they could do so by following the audit trail. The report of measurement procedures followed in a qualitative research study serves a similar purpose.

In evaluating the measures used in a qualitative study, then, you should note how carefully the measurement procedures are reported. If there is no information of this type, you have good reason to suspect the reliability of the researcher's data. If information is provided, you can do a "thought experiment" in which you form a judgment about the likelihood that the procedures would lead to the type of data reported by the researcher.

# Sources of Information about Measures

In reviewing research reports that are not highly relevant to your question or problem, you usually can rely on the information given in the report. This is desirable because a thorough evaluation of an educational measure requires considerable time and effort. This effort, however, is justified if you plan to use the research report as a basis for making an important decision.

We present below the main sources of information about educational measures in common use. You can consult these sources to obtain information about the rationale for particular tests and their validity and reliability. Also, there may be situations in which you are not evaluating published research but instead want to search for a particular kind of test to solve a local measurement problem. The sources described below are useful for this purpose, too.

## THE *MENTAL MEASUREMENTS YEARBOOKS*

The *Mental Measurements Yearbooks (MMYB)* are an important source of information on standardized tests. The most recent of the series is the *Tenth Mental Measurements Yearbook* (Conoley & Kramer, 1989). This is a completely new work that supplements the earlier editions. The Tests and Reviews section of the current edition lists 396 tests that are new or revised since publication of the *Ninth MMYB* in 1985. The *Tenth MMYB* includes 569 critical test reviews and approximately 1,880 references on the construction, use, and limitations of tests included in this edition.

Because there is virtually no overlap between the *Ninth MMYB* and the *Tenth MMYB,* it is advisable to check both editions when searching for a suitable test. The *Ninth MMYB* covers 1,409 commercially published tests and provides reviews of most of them. Because many educational tests have been in use for 10 years or longer, you also can find useful information in even earlier editions.

You can use the *MMYB* to obtain specific information about tests used in research projects you are evaluating. The *MMYB* can also be used to locate and compare tests that are available in a particular field to help you decide which test is most appropriate for your situation.

To use the *MMYB,* you look up the test in the Index of Titles. The entry number of the test is given after the title. Turn to this number in the Tests and Reviews section, where you will find the following information about the test: the age range for which the test is appropriate, the year the test was published, the variables measured by the test, the cost of the test, the availability of a manual and other materials, the name of the author and publisher, and other useful information. Also, references are given to reports of research that has been done to check the test's validity and reliability and to reports in which it has been used as a measure in a research project. Finally, critical reviews written by experts in the field are provided for many of the tests. These reviews are especially valuable to the person who has limited training in educational measurement.

The above procedure is appropriate if you are searching the *MMYB* for information about a particular test that you have identified. However, suppose you wish to know what tests are available to measure a particular construct such as vocational interests or Spanish-language achievement. Your first step is to refer to the Classified Subject Index. Here the tests are classified under a number of broad categories such as Achievement, Personality, Foreign Language, and Reading. Under each category is a list of pertinent tests. Upon locating tests that interest you in the index, note their entry numbers, check each number in the Tests and Reviews section, and read the reviews to help decide which test best meets your needs.

The *Tenth MMYB* includes several other useful indexes:

1. The Score Index lists all the scores, in alphabetical order, for all tests included in the *Tenth MMYB*. Thus, if you want to identify a measure of self-esteem, for example, you would look up this term in the Score Index, where you would find two *ask* measures cited, numbers 128 and 357. In the Tests and Reviews section, the description of test number 128, Gordon Personal Profile–Inventory, indicates that it provides five scores, including one for self-esteem. The description of test number 357, Taylor-Johnson Temperament Analysis, indicates that one of the four supplemental scales for this measure is self-esteem. A check of some items in the Score Index and in the Classified Subject Index indicates discrepancies; thus, both indexes should be searched.

2. Many tests are commonly referred to in the literature by their acronyms rather than by their full titles (for example, *CAT* is the acronym for the *California Achievement Tests.*) The Index of Acronyms gives the full title and entry number for each acronym.

3. The Index of Names lists the names of all test authors, reviewers, and authors of selected references. This index is useful if you know the test author's name but not the title.

4. The Publishers Directory and Index gives the names and addresses of the publishers of all tests included in the *MMYB*. You can write to publishers for their catalogs or for additional information on tests that you are reviewing.

The greatest strength of the *Mental Measurements Yearbook* is the evaluative information given in the test reviews. Their greatest limitation is that they include only commercially published tests, thus overlooking many useful measures. Also, the Classified Subject Index categories tend to be too broad, and the indexes are not adequately cross-referenced.

## ETS *TEST COLLECTION BIBLIOGRAPHIES*

If you fail to locate the measures you need in one of the *Mental Measurements Yearbooks,* the next step is to search the *Test Collection Bibliographies* published by the Educational Testing Service (ETS). More than 200 of these bibliographies are currently in print. They include more than 11,000 measures, which is by far the most comprehensive compilation of tests available.

The ETS bibliographies cover both published and unpublished tests and are frequently updated, thus overcoming a limitation of other published sources such as *MMYB,* which are updated at infrequent intervals. However, the bibliographies provide much less information on the tests listed than do the yearbooks. The information usually given includes the name of the test, author, date published, age or grade levels for which the test is appropriate, name and address of publisher, and a brief description of the variables the test is designed to measure. For experimental measures having no commercial publisher, the author frequently is listed as publisher. Many such measures, which are not available from commercial publishers, can be obtained from ETS on microfiche for individual measures or in sets of 50 measures. Many universities have purchased these sets, so you should check with the reference librarians of institutions in your area before purchasing microfiches.

To use these bibliographies, you should use the following procedure:

1. Check the list of *Test Collection Bibliographies* available from ETS and decide which ones are most likely to list tests that cover the variables you want to measure.
2. Check whether the *Test Collection Bibliographies* you need are available in any of the reference libraries in your vicinity. Other places to check are university departments of psychology and counseling centers. If not locally available, order the bibliographies you need from ETS Test Collection, Educational Testing Service, Princeton, NJ 08541.
3. Read the selected bibliographies and identify measures that fit your needs.
4. Obtain single copies of the measures you have identified from ETS or the test publishers.

You will now be ready to evaluate the measures you have obtained and make your final selection.

## TESTS: A COMPREHENSIVE REFERENCE FOR ASSESSMENTS IN PSYCHOLOGY, EDUCATION, AND BUSINESS

*Tests* (Sweetland & Keyser, 1988) is currently in its second edition. The first edition was published in 1983, and a supplement appeared in 1984. It provides information on more than 3,000 tests, including a statement of the test's purpose, cost, and publisher and a description of the content, administration time, grade range, and scoring information.

Tests are listed under three major headings: Psychology, Education, and Business and Industry. Each of the sections is divided into several subsections. For example, the subsections under Education include such topics as academic subjects, achievement and aptitude, intelligence, reading, and special education.

To use *Tests: A Comprehensive Reference* to locate tests on a particular topic, check the table of contents and locate the relevant subsection. Then turn to this subsection and scan the information given. For example, if you were looking for measures to identify first-grade children with learning disabilities, you would check "Learning disabilities" in the table of contents. Tests on this topic are described on pages 546–555 of the first edition, pages 147–151 of the Supplement, and pages 576–589 of the second edition. You would search for specific measures that met your needs by scanning the information provided on these pages.

*Tests: A Comprehensive Reference* is an excellent source for locating tests relevant to your needs. It is not highly useful in evaluating tests, however, because no information on reliability, validity, or norms is included.

## TEST CRITIQUES

*Test Critiques* (Keyser & Sweetland, 1984–1990) was compiled by the same authors who compiled *Tests: A Comprehensive Reference.* Its eight volumes were published during 1984–1990, and future volumes are likely to appear. *Test Critiques* contains reviews of tests by specialists.

Each review includes five sections: an introduction, which contains a detailed description of the measure as well as useful background information; a practical application/uses section, which provides information on administration, scoring, and interpretation; a section on technical aspects, which is concerned primarily with reliability and validity; an overall critique, which is very useful in helping the potential user evaluate the test; and a brief list of references dealing with the measure and related topics. On the average, seven to eight pages are devoted to each test, and a great deal of information is provided to help you evaluate the test.

The eight volumes currently available cover over 800 measures, and subsequent volumes are planned to appear at six- to nine-month intervals. The best approach to using *Test Critiques* is to check the most recent volume because it contains cumulative indexes that cover all previous volumes. If you are looking for evaluation data on a particular test, use the Index of Test Titles. If you are trying to locate tests in a particular subject, use the Subject Index.

These volumes, together with the *Mental Measurements Yearbooks,* are the best sources of evaluations of available tests. The main advantage of *Test Critiques* is the thoroughness of the information provided for each test. The main limitation is the small number of tests covered thus far. As new volumes become available, this limitation will be largely overcome.

There are several other references that can assist you in locating and evaluating tests. Although most of them are over 10 years old, many of the tests they cover are still in use. Descriptions of several of these references are provided in this chapter's Recommended Reading.

## THE TEST DEVELOPER

The best source of recent information on a test is often the test developer. Because there is a considerable lag between the completion of research and its publication, the developer often will have information on the test that has not yet been printed. Also, the developer is likely to know of other persons who have recently used the test. Contacting the developer is especially useful in getting the latest data on recently developed tests. There may be very little published data on the test's validity and reliability but much unpublished data. Thus, it is advisable to ask the test developer for any information that has not appeared in print. If you explain the purposes for which you want to use the test, the test developer probably will be cooperative. Current addresses for persons who have developed tests can often be found in the latest volumes of *The Consolidated Roster for Psychology* or the *Membership Directory* of the American Educational Research Association.

## THE TEST MANUAL

Some tests undergo extensive development and standardization. A test is considered *standardized* if it has explicit procedures for administration and scoring as well as norms, so that an individual's score can be compared to the scores of a specified population. The publishers of these tests usually sell a specimen set, which typically includes a sample copy of the test, scoring key, and test manual.

The test manual provides much of the information that is needed to evaluate a standardized test. Among the questions that the manual usually helps to answer are these: What types of validity have been studied, and what validity data are available? What types of reliability have been studied, and what reliability data are available? For what types of subjects is the test appropriate? What conditions of administration are necessary to use the test? Is special training needed to administer the test or interpret the results? Is a shorter form of the test available that will yield substantially the same results? Are there norms for the test? A limitation of the test manual is that it may be biased because it is written by persons in the employ of the publisher. Thus, the test manual should not be your sole source of information about a test.

## THE TEST ITSELF

One of the best sources of information about a test is a copy of the test itself, particularly if you are concerned about content validity or the appropriateness of the test for your students. For example, the test manual may claim that the test is appropriate for fifth-grade students. Your examination of the test may reveal that the reading level is beyond that of the fifth-graders whom you are planning to test. Or suppose that your school district wants to conduct an evaluation of two methods for teaching reading. In selecting a test of reading achievement to evaluate the effectiveness of the two methods, you may find that the test manual and other sources such as the *Mental Measurements Yearbooks* do not provide enough information about the reading content covered by the test. To determine whether the reading content is representative of that included in your district's reading program, your best source of information will be a copy of the test itself. The various reference books described above typically provide the publisher's address for each test so that you can write to obtain a copy.

# Computer Searches for Test Information

Reference books such as the *Mental Measurements Yearbook* are excellent sources of information about tests. However, they obviously cannot include test information that becomes available after their publication. If you wish up-to-date information on a particular test, you are advised to conduct a computer search. The search procedures are similar to those described in Chapter 3. (You may find it helpful to review that chapter before reading the following section.)

## PROXIMITY SEARCH

Several different computer search options are available for locating information about tests. The best option probably is to conduct a proximity search by the name of the test with (W) limiters. For example, a proximity search of ERIC for the term "Graduate (W) Record (W) Examination" located 146 references. Because this examination usually is referred to as the "GRE," we also searched that term and located 189 references. There were 248 references that used either or both terms some place in the citation. To eliminate references that would not help in evaluating the GRE, we next searched

> (Graduate (W) Record (W) Examination or GRE) and (Test Reviews or Test Reliability or Test Validity).

This search produced 47 references. A check of the abstracts of these references indicated that most would be useful to an educator who wanted to evaluate the GRE.

Other descriptors in the *Thesaurus of ERIC Descriptors* can be searched along with the test name if you are interested in only certain kinds of information. For example, the descriptor "Foreign students" could be added to the above search if you were interested only in the validity and reliability of the GRE when administered to foreign students.

## SEARCH OF IDENTIFIERS

Another computer search option is to use the name of the test as an identifier. In the ERIC system identifiers are key words or concepts that are not descriptors but that supplement the descriptors to add depth to the search. Identifiers are used to enter such information as geographical location, personal names, and test names. Thus, if you are interested in a specific test, you can ask the computer to locate references that have the test name as an identifier. Again using the GRE as an example, we entered

Graduate (W) Record (W) Examinations/ID.

This search produced 205 references. Note that we used the plural, "Examinations," in this search. There is a tendency for reviewers to enter identifiers as plural, probably because most descriptors in the ERIC *Thesaurus* are plural.

## SEARCHING PsycINFO

PsycINFO is useful for getting up-to-date information on well-known tests such as the GRE, the Stanford Achievement Test, and the California Test of Personality. The names of many widely used tests are included as index terms in the *Thesaurus of Psychological Index Terms*. Thus you could conduct the following search to locate data to help evaluate the GRE:

Graduate Record Examination and (Test Reliability or Test Validity)

A proximity search of PsycINFO also can be conducted, using essentially the same procedures described for the ERIC data base. If you plan to include index terms such as "Test validity" in your PsycINFO search, be sure to check the Thesaurus because PsycINFO index terms sometimes differ from ERIC descriptors.

## *MENTAL MEASUREMENTS YEARBOOK* DATA BASE

The *MMYB* data base contains all the information covered in the *Mental Measurements Yearbooks* from 1972 to the present, including monthly updates on measures that will be included in the next yearbook to be published. If a test you wish to evaluate is covered in this data base, the updated reviews and other information may be useful.

## ETS TEST COLLECTION DATA BASE

The ETS Test Collection data base currently contains approximately 9,400 test records available from Bibliographic Retrieval Services (BRS). You can enter the name of the test for which you desire information. Another option is that you can enter a question describing the kind of test you need. The computer will search the data base and provide descriptions of measures that meet your needs.

# Chapter References

ACKLEY, B. C. (1991). The role of mentor teachers in Oregon's Beginning Teacher Support Program. Doctoral dissertation, University of Oregon, Eugene.

BORG, W. R., & ASCIONE, F. R. (1979). Changing on-task, off-task, and disruptive pupil behavior in elementary mainstreaming classrooms. *Journal of Educational Research, 72*(5), 243–252.

CONOLEY, J. C., & KRAMER, J. J., eds. (1989). *The tenth mental measurements yearbook.* Lincoln, NE: Buros Institute of Mental Measurement.

KEYSER, D. J., & SWEETLAND, R. C. (1984–1990). *Test critiques* (8 vols.). Kansas City, MO: Test Corporation of America.

NEVO, B. (1985). Face validity revisited. *Journal of Educational Measurement, 22*(4), 287–293.

SWEETLAND, R. C., & KEYSER, D. J. (1988). *Tests: A comprehensive reference for assessments in psychology, education, and business,* 2nd ed. Kansas City, MO: Test Corporation of America.

# Recommended Reading

The following books provide a good coverage of educational and psychological measurement and are recommended for students who want to develop their understanding of this field.

## GENERAL

COMMITTEE TO DEVELOP STANDARDS FOR EDUCATIONAL AND PSYCHOLOGICAL TESTING. (1985). *Standards for educational and psychological testing.* Washington, DC: American Psychological Association.

This long-awaited volume was prepared by a committee of measurement experts representing the three most important national organizations that are directly concerned with testing standards. Several sections of the book are especially useful for educators who must select and use tests and interpret test results. These include the sections on validity, reliability, educational and psychological testing in the schools, and testing people who have handicapping conditions.

## MEASUREMENT INFORMATION

These are introductory texts that will provide a good foundation in educational measurement.

EBEL, R. L., & FRISBIE, D. A. (1986). *Essentials of educational measurement,* 4th ed. Englewood Cliffs, NJ: Prentice-Hall.

GRONLUND, N. E., & LINN, R. L. (1990). *Measurement and evaluation in teaching.* New York: Macmillan.

SAX, G. (1988). *Principles of educational psychological measurement and evaluation,* 3rd ed. Belmont, CA: Wadsworth.

## TESTS

The following are additional references that will help you locate and evaluate tests in your area of interest. However, the sources discussed in the body of Chapter 6 generally are more useful than those listed below.

ANTTONEN, J. (1980). *An annotated bibliography of practical tests for young children,* (ERIC Microfiche ED 198 162). 3rd rev. ed. Harrisburg, PA: State Department of Education.

This bibliography covers 109 tests for children aged two to six. Tests related to most of the areas covered in early childhood programs are included. The measures listed do not require subjective judgment in scoring or specialized training for administration.

CHUN, K. T., COBB, S., & FRENCH, J. R. P., JR. (1974). *Measures for psychological assessment: A guide to 3,000 original sources.* Ann Arbor: Institute for Social Research, University of Michigan.

Contains experimental measures for the most part. Although no measures developed since 1970 are included, many of those listed are still currently in use.

HAMMILL, D. D., BROWN, L., & BRYANT, B. R. (1989). *A consumer's guide to tests in print*. Austin, TX: PRO-ED.

The first part of the book discusses evaluation of the technical and nontechnical characteristics of standardized tests. For each test listed, technical characteristics such as reliability are rated on a three-point scale. Nontechnical characteristics such as administration and scoring procedures are summarized on a Reviewer Evaluation Form.

JOHNSON, O. G. (1976). *Tests and measurements in child development: Handbook II*. San Francisco: Jossey-Bass.

JOHNSON, O. G., & BOMMARITO, J. W. (1971). *Tests and measurements in child development: Handbook I*. San Francisco: Jossey-Bass.

These handbooks cover over 1,200 unpublished measures, that is, measures not published by regular test publishers or included in the *Mental Measurements Yearbooks*. The authors searched 148 journals for the period 1956 through 1965 for *Handbook I* and 1966 through 1974 for *Handbook II* to locate measures that can be administered to subjects from birth to age 18.

LEVY, P., & GOLDSTEIN, H. (1984). *Tests in education: A book of critical reviews*. New York: Academic Press.

The measures reviewed in this reference are for the most part British in origin, although a few measures developed in the United States are reviewed. The book will be most useful to American users when a suitable measure cannot be located in American sources such as the *Mental Measurements Yearbooks*. The test reviews are organized into seven broad content areas. Each review provides a great deal of useful information. All in all, this is an excellent source of information on British measures.

REDICK, R. L. (1975, October). A compilation of measurement devices compendia. *Measurement and Evaluation in Guidance, 8*(3), 193–202.

This article describes 30 sources of information on measures in the behavioral sciences. Bibliographic data and a brief description are given for each compendium (i.e., source of information). Most of the sources described were published between 1967 and 1975. However, because many tests currently in use were developed more than 100 years ago, reviews and evaluations from these sources can still be useful.

## OBSERVATION

BOEHM, A. E., & WEINBERG, R. A. (1987). *The classroom observer,* 2nd ed. New York: Teachers College Press.

The authors discuss the entire process of classroom observation. Separate chapters are concerned with defining the problem, categorizing behavior, making reliable observations, and sampling and recording behavior. Of special interest is their discussion of the teacher as an observer.

BORICH, G. D., & MADDEN, S. K. (1977). *Evaluating classroom instruction: A sourcebook of instruments*. Reading, MA: Addison-Wesley.

This book reviews a large number of instruments that can be used to evaluate teachers' and students' behavior. Many are observation forms. Most of the information that a researcher needs to select an instrument is provided.

HERBERT, J., & ALTRIDGE, C. (1975). A guide for developers and users of observation systems and manuals. *American Educational Research Journal, 12*(1), 1–20.

The authors developed 33 criteria that can help you evaluate observation instruments. Each criterion is discussed, and many examples are given.

## INTERVIEWS

FOWLER, F. J., JR. (1984). *Survey research methods.* Beverly Hills, CA: Sage.

The book discusses survey research methodology, including sampling, data collection, and analysis. It contains useful chapters on both questionnaires and interview procedures.

TOLOR, A. ed. (1985). *Effective interviewing.* Springfield, IL: Thomas.

Several of the chapters in this book contain useful information for persons who plan to conduct interviews in an educational setting.

## QUESTIONNAIRES

BERDIE, D. R., ANDERSON, J. F., & NIEBUHR, M. A. (1986). *Questionnaires: Design and use,* 2nd ed. Metuchen, NJ: Scarecrow Press.

This short book is filled with useful information on designing and carrying out a questionnaire study. The sections on item construction and procedures to stimulate responses are especially valuable. The appendixes contain four sample questionnaires, follow-up letters, and a case history of a questionnaire study. Finally, an extensive annotated bibliography includes most important references on questionnaires published during the past 30 years.

CONVERSE, J. M., & PRESSER, S. (1986). *Survey questions: Handcrafting the standardized questionnaire.* Beverly Hills, CA: Sage.

This monograph contains a wealth of practical information about questions and questionnaires. The authors have drawn from the experience of questionnaire developers and the research evidence that has emerged from the many experimental studies of questionnaire effectiveness. If you plan to develop a questionnaire, make this the first book you read.

# Application Problems

1. Review the following items taken from a questionnaire to be sent to a sample of high school teachers and indicate those that are nonbiased (N), leading (L), or psychologically threatening (T).

   _____ **a.** In what college did you complete your teacher training?
   _____ **b.** Have you found that much of what you learned in teacher training cannot be applied in your classroom?
   _____ **c.** How successful are you in maintaining order in your classroom?
   _____ **d.** What was your college major?
   _____ **e.** How good a student were you in college?

2. A researcher develops a program designed to increase teachers' empathy with minority group children. Sixty teachers volunteer to take the program, for which they will receive credit at the local university. The researcher randomly assigns the 60 teachers to two groups of 30 and trains one group in the program. The researcher then interviews all 60 teachers to determine if the teachers who completed the program have more empathy with minority children. Is there a possibility of bias in this study? If so, explain.

3. Which of the following observation approaches is likely to produce the most reliable information about teachers' use of thought questions? Why?

   **a.** Observer A observes in each classroom one hour per day for five days. At the end of each hour the observer checks each teacher's performance on the following scale, and at the end of the week, averages the scale scores for each teacher for the five days.

    _____ **(1)** Uses a large number of thought questions.

    _____ **(2)** Uses more thought questions than the average teacher.

    _____ **(3)** Uses an average number of thought questions.

    _____ **(4)** Uses fewer thought questions than the average teacher.

    _____ **(5)** Uses no thought questions.

**b.** Observer B who uses a checklist that defines thought and fact questions and gives examples, observes in each classroom one hour per day for four days. Each time the teacher asks a question, the observer tallies it as either a thought question or a fact question. At the end of four days the observer computes for each teacher

    _____ **(1)** The average number of thought questions per hour

    _____ **(2)** The average number of fact questions per hour

    _____ **(3)** The percentage of thought questions, that is, the number of thought questions divided by the total number of questions.

**4.** Identify the type of test validity that is most critical in each of the following research studies.

    _____ **a.** The researcher selects a test to determine how well students have mastered a new state-adopted textbook on mathematics.

    _____ **b.** The researcher wants to determine whether a measure with 10 items drawn from a 50-item measure is an adequate substitute for the 50-item measure.

    _____ **c.** The researcher wants to determine whether a new scale is a good measure of students' boredom with instruction.

    _____ **d.** The researcher is searching for a test that can be given to high school freshmen to determine which of them are most likely to leave school before graduating.

**5.** A group of researchers is planning a qualitative study to determine effective teaching strategies for gifted and talented students. Their primary measure will be a semistructured interview schedule, and they will collect data from teachers of gifted and talented students, the teachers' supervisors, and the students' parents.

**a.** How should the researchers establish the validity of the interview schedule?

**b.** How should they establish the reliability of the interview schedule?

**6.** Suppose you are given the task of selecting a new social studies achievement test for grades 4 through 6 in your school district. All teachers in the district follow the state curriculum guide in social studies and use the same social studies textbook.

**a.** Name two sources you could use to locate standardized social studies achievement tests.

**b.** Name two sources you could use in searching for evaluative data on the tests you have located.

**c.** What kind of validity would be most important in selecting a test?

**d.** How would you determine this validity for your school district?

**7.** Locate the following in the *Tenth Mental Measurements Yearbook:*

**a.** A test that could be used to measure the health knowledge of high school students.

**b.** A test to measure computer anxiety of college freshmen.

**8.** Locate the following in *Tests: A Comprehensive Reference* (2nd ed.), and enter the title of the test and the page where it is found.

    **a.** A test of musical aptitude that can be administered to second-grade children.

    **b.** A group-administered test of library skills suitable for fifth-grade students. Two forms are needed because you want to test your students before and after they are given the library skills curriculum unit.

**9.** Locate a measure in *Test Critiques* (Vol. 7) that can be used to measure the decoding skills of third-grade students.

    **a.** Give the name of the test and the pages where the review is found.

    **b.** How many subtests are included in this measure?

    **c.** What range of test-retest reliability is reported for the subtests?

# CHAPTER 7

# STATISTICAL ANALYSIS

## Overview

Most research reports include statistical analyses. The purpose of this chapter is to help you develop a basic understanding of these analyses. Three major topics are discussed: the different types of scores yielded by tests and other measures; descriptive statistics, which summarize how the research sample performed on a measure; and inferential statistics, used to make inferences from the sample's scores to the population represented by the sample.

## Objectives

1. Explain the role of statistics in educational research.
2. Describe four types of scores yielded by tests and measures.
3. Explain the purpose of descriptive statistics, and describe the most commonly used statistical tools of this type.
4. Explain the purpose of inferential statistics, and describe the most commonly used statistical tools of this type.
5. Explain the difference between parametric and nonparametric tests of statistical significance.
6. Given a research report, determine whether an appropriate statistical tool has been used.

Most research studies, whether quantitative or qualitative, generate data that can be expressed in numerical form. For example, if the researchers administered an aptitude test to their sample, the analysis of the sample's performance on the test will generate numerical scores. There may be a total test score for each individual in the sample, as well as scores for subsections of the test (e.g., verbal aptitude and mathematical aptitude). In addition, the researchers may have collected numerical data on each individual's personal background (e.g., age and number of years of professional experience).

Qualitative research studies usually yield verbal data (e.g., transcripts of interviews) or visual data (e.g., videorecordings of events). These data are analyzed in their original state by the researchers. However, this method of analysis sometimes is supplemented by transforming the data into numerical form. For example, suppose that the researchers made transcripts of a set of interviews. The transcripts can be analyzed by counting the frequency with which certain words or themes are mentioned. The frequency counts constitute numerical data.

The numerical data in a research study are subjected to various statistical analyses.

Statistics is a branch of mathematics, and therefore you need to have some understanding of mathematics in order to understand the assumptions and computational procedures for the various statistical procedures used in educational research. Development of this understanding typically requires taking one or more courses in statistics as applied in educational research. Coursework is also advised if you wish to make expert judgments about the statistics used in published research or use some of the more complex statistical techniques in your own research.

Because you may not have taken such courses, we minimize the mathematical basis for statistical analysis in the following presentation. Each statistical procedure is described in nontechnical rather than in mathematical terms. We focus on the purpose of each statistical procedure, its appropriate use in research studies, and the information that it yields. You may follow the discussion better if you have scratch paper handy as you read, so that you can see for yourself how we did certain calculations with data presented in tables.

# Types of Scores

The first level of numerical data analysis is to determine the numerical score of each individual in the research sample on each variable that was measured. These scores will be of different types, depending on the type of variable that was measured. For example, a student's raw score on a typical achievement test is of a different type from, say, the student's "score" on the variable of gender.

Four types of numerical data are commonly collected in educational research studies: (1) continuous scores, (2) gain scores, (3) rank scores, and (4) categorical scores. You need to understand these different types of numerical data because different statistical analyses are appropriate for each type.

## CONTINUOUS SCORES

Continuous scores are values of a measure that has an indefinite number of ordered points. Most achievement and aptitude tests, attitude scales, and personality measures yield scores of this type. For example, suppose a test has 50 items, with a score of 1 point for each item answered correctly. Thus, scores on this test have 51 continuous points, ranging from 0 to 50. The points are ordered so that each value is greater than the value preceding it. The points are not truly indefinite in number but only approximately so, because, like most standardized tests, the continuous scores are limited to whole numbers. To be truly indefinite, the test should yield fractional values such as 41.25.

One type of continuous score is the raw score, which is simply the total score obtained by following the test developers' scoring procedures. Raw scores by themselves are difficult to interpret. For example, a score of 30 on the 50-item test mentioned above may be high or low, depending on how difficult the test is and on how well other individuals in the research sample performed on it. Therefore, researchers often report derived scores in addition to raw scores. Derived scores provide a quantitative comparison of each individual's performance relative to a comparison group. Four types of derived scores are commonly reported: age equivalents, grade equivalents, percentiles, and standard scores.

**Age Equivalents.**    This type of derived score is commonly used with academic achievement tests. A student's age equivalent score is the age level of other students who typically earn the same raw score that the student did. The other students usually are a large sample representing a national population. This sample sometimes is called a norming sample. The average score obtained by students at each age level in the norming sample is determined and reported in a table of norms. Thus, the raw score of each student in the research sample can be found in the table of norms, which will report the age of students in the norming sample who earned that score, on the average. For example, if the age equivalent for a student who earned a raw score of 30 is 12.0, it means that this student performed at the average level of students in the norming sample who were 12 years old.

**Grade Equivalents.**    These derived scores are similar in meaning to age equivalents. The only difference is that the table of norms reports the average raw score earned by students at each grade level in the norming sample. For example, if the grade equivalent for a student who earned a raw score of 20 is 3.5, it means that this student performed at the average level of students who were in the middle of the third grade in the norming sample.

**Percentile Scores.**    These derived scores represent the percentage of individuals whose raw score falls at or below the raw scores of other individuals in a sample. For example, suppose that 40 percent of students in a research sample earn a raw score of 27 or below. In this case a raw score of 27 would represent a percentile score of 40; more commonly, we would state that the student scored at the 40th percentile.

Test developers often construct a table of norms in percentile form. If this table is available, researchers can use percentile scores, in addition to or instead of age and grade equivalents, to express how well individuals in their sample performed relative to the norming sample. In the above example, a raw score of 27 may be at the 40th percentile with respect to other students in the research sample but at, say, the 35th percentile with respect to the norming sample.

**Standard Scores.**    These derived scores are similar in meaning to percentiles. However, they have mathematical advantages over percentile scores and therefore are commonly used in statistical computations. An individual's standard score is derived by subtracting his or her raw score from the mean score earned by the research sample and then dividing that result by the standard deviation of the scores of research sample. (Mean scores and standard deviations are explained later in the chapter.) Some test manuals include a table of norms in which the sample's raw scores can be converted to standard scores derived from a norming sample.

Intelligence test scores are a common example of standard scores. For example, the mean score on the Stanford-Binet Intelligence Scale is set at 100, meaning that half of the norming sample obtained a score that is at or below this standard score. The standard deviation is set at 16. By referring to the normal probability curve (discussed later in this chapter), you can determine the percentage of individuals in the sample who earned at or below a particular IQ score.

## GAIN SCORES

Learning and development are the focus of much educational research. Both processes involve change from one time to another. These changes can be detected by administering the same measure to individuals at two or more time intervals. A *gain score* is  simply the difference in an individual's score on the measure from one time interval to the next. Gain scores are often positive, but they can also be negative, as when an individual forgets information learned earlier. Although gain scores probably can be calculated from rank scores, they make most sense when calculated from continuous scores.

Gain scores are sometimes reported by researchers, but you should view them with caution. For example, they are subject to a ceiling effect caused by the measure used to assess change. Suppose a student scores 95 out of 100 possible points on initial testing. The student can only improve by a maximum of 5 points on this test when it is readministered. These 5 points may be inadequate (the ceiling is too low) to measure all the new information or skills that the student learned during the intervening time interval.

Another limitation of gain scores is that most tests tend to have unequal intervals. For example, suppose a test has 50 items, and each item answered correctly earns a score of 1. Also suppose the items vary in difficulty. Now consider the case of two students who earn the same gain score of 5, but one goes from a raw score of 10 to a raw score of 15, whereas the other goes from a raw score of 40 to a raw score of 45. It probably is more difficult for the second student to make a gain score of 5 than it is for the first student because he or she will need to answer more difficult items on the test. If so, the gain score does not have the same meaning for both students.

Still another problem is that most tests contain different types of items. For example, suppose that a test contains different types of subtraction items. Two students, then, may earn the same gain score but do it by making gains on different types of subtraction items. Once again, the gain score is the same, but it does not mean the same thing for the two students.

Despite these problems and others not mentioned here, gain scores continue to be used in educational research and practice. To determine whether they provide meaningful information, you need to check for possible ceiling effects and whether similar gain scores for different individuals reflect similar learning or development.

## RANK SCORES

Rank scores are used by educators for various purposes. For example, a school may rank the students at a particular grade level with respect to academic achievement, or athletes may be ranked with respect to performance in a sports contest (e.g., first place, second place, and third place). These examples illustrate the educational or social significance of some measures that yield rank scores. Because of their significance, rank scores sometimes are collected and analyzed by educational researchers.

Rank scores typically have unequal intervals. For example, in one classroom there may be very little difference in academic achievement between the first-ranked and second-ranked student. In another classroom, however, these two ranks may reflect substantial differences in academic achievement. This limitation of rank scores should be kept in mind when interpreting statistical results based on this type of numerical data.

## CATEGORIES

Categories are variables that yield values that are discrete and nonordered when measured. An example would be students' parental status. We could develop categories to classify different types of parental status, such as two parents together, mother only, father only, and other. These categories are discrete in that each student would be assigned to only one category; the categories do not overlap. Note, too, that the categories do not form an ordered continuum. For example, it would not make sense to say that a father-only family is "more" or "less" than a mother-only family or that either is "more" or "less" than a family categorized as "other." Because categories cannot be ordered, categorical data must be analyzed by different statistical techniques from continuous or rank scores.

A dichotomy is a special type of categorical variable, which when measured yields only two values. Gender, for example, is a dichotomous variable because only two values are possible: male and female. Gender is a natural dichotomy, but other dichotomies are artificial; that is, the values are defined by the researchers or by other individuals. For example, researchers may classify school districts as having a centralized or a decentralized administration, or students may classify themselves as college bound or not college bound.

## USE OF SCORES IN STATISTICAL ANALYSIS

In reviewing statistical analyses in a research report, you should start by determining what type of score was used in each analysis. This information will help you understand the meaning of the statistical analyses. If your understanding is sufficiently sophisticated, you can use this information to determine whether the researchers selected an appropriate statistical procedure for analyzing the data.

# Descriptive Statistics

Research studies often yield a large amount of numerical data. Descriptive statistics serve a useful purpose by summarizing all the data in the form of a few simple numerical expressions, called statistics. To illustrate, we created data for a hypothetical research study and present it in Table 7.1. The main purpose of this study was to determine whether there is a relationship between students' interest in history and their final grade in a history course.

The ID column in this table is simply an identification code to distinguish each individual in the sample from the others. The ID numbers are in consecutive order, beginning with 01. We see, then, that the sample includes 20 individuals.

The first data column of Table 7.1 shows each student's score on the interest measure; higher scores indicate greater interest. The second data column shows the course grade (A = 4; B = 3; C = 2; D = 1; F = 0). The students were classified as having part-time jobs or not employed, and the scores of these groups are shown separately. The data in Table 7.1 constitute the raw data of the study.

Raw data seldom are included in a research report. Journals, the main publication source for research reports, lack space to include raw data. Even if they had space, however, they would not use it for this purpose because conclusions drawn from raw data tend to be imprecise. For example, one would be limited to statements such as, "It appears that students who are more interested in history tend to do better in a course on this subject," or, "Employed students tend to be less interested in history than nonemployed students." These statements do not tell us exactly how strong the tendency to do better is or exactly how much less interested employed students are than nonemployed students. Therefore, descriptive statistics are reported instead. They lead to mathematically precise statements such as, "There is a strong positive correlation

Table 7.1   Interest in history and history course grade for employed and nonemployed students

| Employed students | | | Nonemployed students | | |
|---|---|---|---|---|---|
| ID | Interest in history | Course grade | ID | Interest in history | Course grade |
| 01 | 31 | 2 | 11 | 25 | 2 |
| 02 | 30 | 3 | 12 | 37 | 3 |
| 03 | 27 | 0 | 13 | 41 | 3 |
| 04 | 38 | 2 | 14 | 42 | 3 |
| 05 | 18 | 1 | 15 | 32 | 3 |
| 06 | 34 | 3 | 16 | 47 | 4 |
| 07 | 29 | 3 | 17 | 33 | 3 |
| 08 | 25 | 2 | 18 | 38 | 4 |
| 09 | 33 | 1 | 19 | 44 | 1 |
| 10 | 42 | 4 | 20 | 37 | 2 |
| | $M = 30.70$ | $M = 2.10$ | | $M = 37.60$ | $M = 2.80$ |
| | $SD = 6.73$ | $SD = 1.20$ | | $SD = 6.43$ | $SD = .92$ |

Total Sample ($N = 20$)

| Interest in history | Course grade |
|---|---|
| $M = 34.15$ | $M = 2.45$ |
| $SD = 7.32$ | $SD = 1.10$ |

of .XX between students' interest in history and their grades in a course on this subject" or "Employed students scored an average of YY points less than nonemployed students on a ZZ-item measure of interest in history."

The following is an explanation of the descriptive statistics that are commonly used in educational research.

## MEAN, MEDIAN, AND MODE

Researchers are interested in the individuals who make up their sample, but they also are interested in the sample as a whole. In our hypothetical study, they would want to know the typical, or average, interest level of the sample and whether the average interest level of employed students differs from that of nonemployed students. A statistic known as the *mean* is often used to determine what the average is. The mean is calculated by summing the individual scores of the sample and then dividing the total sum by the number of individuals in the sample. Table 7.1 reports the mean (represented by the symbol *M*) for the total sample and separately for employed students and nonemployed students for the two variables (interest in history and course grade).

The *median* is another statistic that describes a sample's typical score on a measure. The median is the middle score in the distribution of scores. Half the individuals in the sample will score at or above the median score, and half the individuals will score at or below it. The median for the total sample on the interest measure is 33.5, and the median course grade is 2.5. (Where there is an even number of individuals in a sample, the median is the score halfway between the scores of the two middle individuals.) You will note that the medians are similar to the corresponding means. If the distribution of scores deviates substantially from the normal curve (see Figure 7.1), the median will provide a better representation of the "average" score than will the mean.

The *mode* is simply the most frequently occurring score among the scores for the sample. It is seldom calculated, except when each score on a measure has a common meaning. This would be the case for the course grade measure in our hypothetical study. The mode for course grades is 3, which corresponds to a grade of B.

The mean is most often included in research reports because it is more stable than the median or mode. In other words, if one selected many samples at random from a population with scores on a certain test, the means for the samples would be more similar to one another than would the medians or the modes. The mode is the least stable statistic, and so it seldom is included in research reports.

The mean, median, and mode are appropriate descriptive statistics for continuous scores and rank scores.

## FREQUENCY COUNTS AND PERCENTAGES

Suppose that the data for our hypothetical sample include the variable of type of employment. The three categories are (1) food service worker, (2) gas station attendant, and (3) store clerk. The mean, median, and mode are inappropriate statistics for data of this type. Instead, the frequency or percentage of individuals in each category is

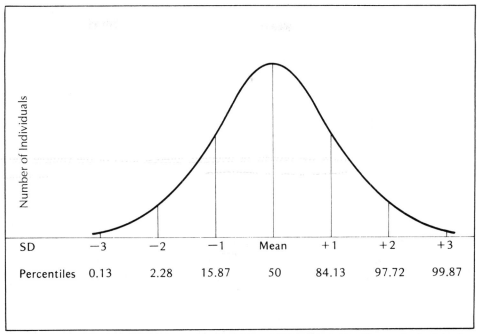

Figure 7.1 Normal Curve Distribution of Scores [*Source:* From *Educational Research: An Introduction,* Fifth Edition (p. 345) by Walter R. Borg and Meredith D. Gall, 1989, White Plains, NY: Longman. Copyright © 1989 by Longman Publishing Group. Adapted by permission.]

determined. Table 7.2 reports these statistics for the employed students in our hypothetical sample. The frequency is simply the total number of individuals in the sample who fit into a particular category. The percentage is the frequency in a particular category divided by the total number of individuals in the sample. Some research reports include only the frequency or only the percentage, rather than reporting both, because the other statistic can be calculated by readers if they wish to know it.

## RANGE AND STANDARD DEVIATION

The mean provides a mathematically precise and succinct description of the sample's average performance on a measure. This information, however, is not sufficient. We

Table 7.2   Type of employment for employed students

| Type of employment | Frequency | Percentage |
| --- | --- | --- |
| Food service worker | 5 | 50 |
| Store clerk | 4 | 40 |
| Gas station attendant | 1 | 10 |

also want to know how much variation is present in the individual scores. Did most of the individuals in the sample obtain scores at or near the mean, or did they vary widely from the mean?

One way to answer this question is to determine the range of scores. The range is calculated as the difference between the lowest and highest score plus 1 in the distribution of scores for a measure. Referring to Table 7.1, we see that the range for the interest measure is 30 (47 − 18 + 1), and the range of course grades is 5 (4 − 0 + 1).

Some research studies include the range of scores for each measure, but most report the standard deviation of scores because it is more stable and mathematically meaningful. The standard deviation is a statistical expression of how much individual scores vary around the mean score. Table 7.1 reports the standard deviation (abbreviated as *SD*) for each mean that was calculated.

A simple way to understand the standard deviation is to imagine taking each individual score and subtracting it from the mean score of the sample. Following this procedure for the first student (ID = 01), we calculate a variation of 4.15 points from the total sample mean (34.15 − 31.00). Suppose we followed this procedure for the entire sample, ignoring whether the subtraction process yielded a negative or positive score. We then could sum these difference scores and divide the total sum by the number of individuals in the sample. The result is called the *average variation,* that is, the average amount by which individual scores deviated from the mean score. This is approximately what a standard deviation means. (The actual formula for calculating the standard deviation involves squaring the individual difference scores and a few other procedures.)

The *standard deviation* is a particularly useful statistic if the individual scores on the measure form a normal distribution. A normal distribution of scores, known more commonly as a *normal curve,* is shown in Figure 7.1. To understand this figure, suppose that a large number of individuals were measured on a particular variable. The height of the curve at any point along the horizontal line would indicate the number of individuals who obtained the score represented by that point. You will note that the mean of the sample's scores is indicated on the horizontal line. If the sample's scores are normally distributed, more individuals will obtain the mean score than any other score in the distribution of scores.

You will note, too, that actual scores for a measure are not shown in Figure 7.1. Instead, the scores are represented as standard deviation units. In the hypothetical data set shown in Table 7.1, the standard deviation for the total sample on the interest measure is 7.32. Individuals who score 1 standard deviation unit above the mean (34.15) would obtain a score of 41 (34.15 + 7.32 = 41.47, rounded to the whole number of 41). This score corresponds to the +1 in Figure 7.1. Individuals who score 1 standard deviation unit below the mean score would obtain a score of 27 (34.15 − 7.32). This score corresponds to the −1 in Figure 7.1.

Now consider the case of an individual who scores 2 standard deviations (7.32 × 2 = 14.64) above the mean. That individual's score would be 49 (34.15 + 14.64). This score corresponds to the +2 in Figure 7.1. No individual in the sample actually obtained that score because the distribution of scores does not follow the normal curve perfectly.

The advantage of standard deviation units in constructing the normal curve shown in Figure 7.1 is that scores for *any* measure can be represented on it, assuming the scores are normally distributed. It does not matter whether one measure has 100 possible points and another 20 possible points. The standard deviation of scores for each measure has the same meaning with respect to the normal curve.

The normal curve has practical value in interpreting the results of research studies. If you know the mean and standard deviation for the scores on a measure, you can use these two bits of information to determine the amount of variability in the scores (assuming the scores are normally distributed). Referring to Figure 7.1, you will see that scores 1 standard deviation below the mean are at approximately the sixteenth percentile, and scores 1 standard deviation above the mean are at approximately the eighty-fourth percentile. Thus, approximately 68 percent of the sample (84 − 16) will earn scores between +1 and −1 standard deviations. By a similar procedure, we can determine that approximately 96 percent of the sample (99 − 2) will earn scores between +2 and −2 standard deviations.

Suppose that for a particular sample the mean of the scores on a measure that has 50 possible points is 25 and the standard deviation is 2. Assuming the scores form a normal curve, we can conclude that most of the sample (approximately 96 percent) earned scores between 23 (− 2 *SD* units) and 27 (+ 2 *SD* units). In other words, the scores are clustered tightly around the mean score, and so the mean is a good representation of the performance of the entire sample.

Suppose that for another sample, the mean is again 25 but the standard deviation is 10. The variation in scores is quite large. If we consider only those individuals who scored within the range of +1 and −1 standard deviation units (approximately 68 percent of the sample), their scores are expected to vary from 15 (25 − 10) to 35 (25 + 10) if the distribution of scores follows the normal curve perfectly. In this case the mean does not represent closely the performance of the sample. In interpreting the research results, we need to keep in mind that the individuals in the research sample are more different than alike with respect to the variable that was measured.

The mathematical elegance of the mean and standard deviation is that these two statistics provide a succinct summary of the raw data. Even if the sample includes 1,000 individuals, we can tell much about how they performed on a measure just by knowing the mean and standard deviation.

Keep in mind, however, that the standard deviation is interpretable only if the scores are normally distributed (as shown in Figure 7.1) or approximately so. If the distribution of scores deviates substantially from normality, the standard deviation cannot be interpreted in terms of the normal curve. For this reason researchers should state in their reports whether scores for any measure deviate substantially from the normal curve. Fortunately, it seems to be a law of nature that most variables of educational significance are normally distributed.

The range and standard deviation are meaningful descriptive statistics for continuous scores and gain scores. They are not appropriate for categorical scores. The variability in distribution of these scores can be determined simply by looking at the frequency counts or percentages in each category. For example, if the variable being measured has five categories, you need only inspect the frequency counts or percentages to determine whether individuals are evenly distributed across the categories or whether a disproportionate number are distributed in a few of the categories.

## BIVARIATE CORRELATIONAL STATISTICS

A major purpose of research is to explore the relationship between variables. In the case of our hypothetical research study, the purpose is to determine the relationship between high school students' interest in history and their final grade in a history course. *Correlational statistics* can be used to describe the extent of this relationship in mathematically precise terms. If only two variables are involved, a *bivariate* correlational statistic is calculated. This type of statistic is discussed at length in Chapter 12, which is concerned with the correlational research method. Therefore, we provide only a brief description of this topic here.

Correlational statistics involve the calculation of a correlation coefficient, which is represented by the symbol $r$. Larger values of this coefficient indicate greater magnitudes of relationship between the variables that have been measured. Different types of correlation coefficients can be calculated, depending on whether continuous scores, rank scores, dichotomous scores, or categorical scores are involved. These types include

1. Pearson product-moment coefficient
2. Rank-difference coefficient
3. Kendall's tau
4. Biserial coefficient
5. Widespread coefficient
6. Point-biserial coefficient
7. Tetrachoric coefficient
8. Phi coefficient
9. Contingency coefficient
10. Correlation ratio

These correlational coefficients are explained in Chapter 12.

The two variables in Table 7.1 both involve continuous scores, so we selected the product-moment coefficient to describe the magnitude of their relationship. Positive values of this coefficient can vary between 0 and 1.00. The obtained coefficient ($r = .49$) indicates a moderately positive relationship, meaning that students with more interest in history tend to earn somewhat higher grades in a history course than students with less interest. For example, the student with ID 05 had an interest score of 18 and a course grade of D (numerical value = 1), whereas the student with ID 10 had a higher interest score of 42 and a higher course grade of A (numerical value = 4). The relationship between the two variables is less than perfect, however, as illustrated by the student with ID 19, who had a high interest score (44) but a course grade of D.

## MULTIVARIATE CORRELATIONAL STATISTICS

As research studies have become more sophisticated, researchers have explored the relationship between more than two variables at the same time. In our hypothetical study, students' scores on a measure of interest in history were used to predict their grade in a history course. Suppose we included several more measures to make this prediction, for example, measures of students' verbal aptitude and study habits. It may be that a combination of the three measures (interest in history, verbal aptitude, and study habits) yields a better prediction of course grades than any one measure alone. A correlational procedure known as multiple linear regression can be used for this purpose. It determines which measure, or combination of measures, to use and how to weight students' scores on each measure to produce the best prediction of the criterion variable (in this case, students' course grades).

Multiple linear regression is the most commonly used of the multivariate correlational techniques. Discriminant function analysis and canonical correlation are similar to multiple linear regression but are used for slightly different functions. These multivariate correlational techniques and others are discussed in Chapter 12.

# Inferential Statistics

In Chapter 5 we discussed procedures for selecting samples for quantitative research. We explained that samples ideally are selected at random from defined populations. If random selection is not possible, the researcher still should attempt to select a sample that represents a population of interest. Sampling procedures are important because the researcher's goal is to generalize from the sample to the population, that is, to make *inferences* about the population from the results obtained with the sample. Inferential statistics are statistical procedures that enable researchers to make inferences about the population based on the descriptive statistics calculated on data from a sample.

The mathematical basis for inferential statistics is complex. Therefore, we will provide a nontechnical explanation here by considering one of the results of the hypothetical study in Table 7.1.

If you examine this table, you will see that the mean of employed students on the measure of interest in history ($M = 30.70$) is lower than the mean of nonemployed students ($M = 37.60$). The question we must answer is whether a similar difference would be found if we studied the entire population of students taking this type of history course. In other words, can we generalize the results from our small sample to the population of students that it represents? (Let's assume the population is all U.S. high school students, and this sample is representative of that population.)

To conclude that the results are generalizable, we first must reject the possible explanation that the results are a chance finding. One way to reject this explanation would be to do the study repeatedly with different samples representing the same population. If these replications consistently yielded roughly the same direction and degree of difference between employed and nonemployed students, this would constitute strong evidence of generalizability.

Replication studies, in fact, are commonly carried out for important findings. In medicine, for example, positive findings about a new drug obtained by one group of researchers rarely are accepted. Other laboratories around the world will also test the drug to confirm or disconfirm the original results. The consequences of using a drug claimed to be effective but actually not so are far too serious to rely on the results of

Table 7.3  Hypothetical populations of employed students and nonemployed students with identical mean scores on a measure of interest in history

Population of employed students ($N$ = 100; $M$ = 32.28)

| | | | |
|---|---|---|---|
| 27 | 32 | 30 | 28 |
| 26 | 34 | 28 | 23 |
| 31 | 29 | 36 | 28 |
| 28 | 39 | 33 | 25 |
| 28 | 31 | 26 | 34 |
| 35 | 37 | 32 | 38 |
| 30 | 36 | 24 | 36 |
| 45 | 34 | 27 | 28 |
| 29 | 41 | 29 | 27 |
| 38 | 29 | 31 | 42 |
| 22 | 37 | 34 | 21 |
| 35 | 38 | 39 | 39 |
| 37 | 31 | 23 | 32 |
| 38 | 43 | 29 | 36 |
| 34 | 37 | 38 | 33 |
| 35 | 26 | 33 | 35 |
| 20 | 37 | 26 | 30 |
| 31 | 40 | 30 | 19 |
| 32 | 32 | 40 | 25 |
| 29 | 40 | 39 | 28 |
| 36 | 35 | 26 | 42 |
| 30 | 41 | 27 | 41 |
| 37 | 21 | 40 | 33 |
| 29 | 35 | 24 | 25 |
| 36 | 32 | 27 | 44 |

Population of nonemployed students ($N$ = 100; $M$ = 32.28)

| | | | |
|---|---|---|---|
| 27 | 32 | 30 | 28 |
| 26 | 34 | 28 | 23 |
| 31 | 29 | 36 | 28 |
| 28 | 39 | 33 | 25 |
| 28 | 31 | 26 | 34 |
| 35 | 37 | 32 | 38 |
| 30 | 36 | 24 | 36 |
| 45 | 34 | 27 | 28 |
| 29 | 41 | 29 | 27 |
| 38 | 29 | 31 | 42 |
| 22 | 37 | 34 | 21 |
| 35 | 38 | 39 | 39 |
| 37 | 31 | 23 | 32 |
| 38 | 43 | 29 | 36 |
| 34 | 37 | 38 | 33 |
| 35 | 26 | 33 | 35 |
| 20 | 37 | 26 | 30 |
| 31 | 40 | 30 | 19 |

*(continued)*

Table 7.3 *(continued)*

| Population of nonemployed students ($N$ = 100; $M$ = 32.28) | | | |
|---|---|---|---|
| 32 | 32 | 40 | 25 |
| 29 | 40 | 39 | 28 |
| 36 | 35 | 26 | 42 |
| 30 | 41 | 27 | 41 |
| 37 | 21 | 40 | 33 |
| 29 | 35 | 24 | 25 |
| 36 | 32 | 27 | 44 |

Results of taking random samples of size 10 from populations of employed and nonemployed students having identical scores on a measure of interest in history

| Employed $M$ | Nonemployed $M$ | Difference |
|---|---|---|
| 33.2 | 31.4 | + 1.8 |
| 32.0 | 35.4 | − 3.4 |
| 34.0 | 29.8 | + 4.2 |
| 32.3 | 32.3 | .0 |
| 34.4 | 30.3 | + 4.1 |
| 30.4 | 35.0 | − 4.6 |
| 31.8 | 32.9 | − 1.1 |
| 29.2 | 31.1 | − 1.9 |
| 32.0 | 31.1 | + .9 |
| 31.3 | 29.6 | + 1.7 |

a single research study. In education, too, important findings are replicated across many studies. For example, hundreds of research studies on the effects of class size have been done because class size is an important factor in educational policy and finance.

Inferential statistics are not as strong a test of generalizability as replication studies. However, they require only a tiny fraction of the effort required for a single replication study. As with replications, inferential statistics test the possible explanation that an observed result for a sample is a chance finding. What do we mean by chance finding? To answer this question, imagine that we have two populations whose members have identical sets of scores on the measure of interest in history. These sets of scores are shown in Table 7.3. We labeled one population "Employed Students" and the other, "Nonemployed Students." Because the populations are identical with respect to interest in history, the mean of the scores for each population must be identical.

Now let's draw a random sample of 10 individuals' scores from one population and then do the same with the other population. Having done so, we compute the mean score of each sample and determine the difference. The results of these computations are shown on the first data line under the heading that describes the random sampling results in Table 7.3. Note that even though the population means are identical, the two sample means differ from each other. In this case the mean score of the employed students, by chance, is greater than the mean score of the nonemployed students.

Table 7.3 shows the results of repeatedly drawing new samples of size 10 from each population and computing their mean scores. In some samples the employed students score higher, and in other samples the nonemployed students score higher; in one sample there is no difference. The important thing to note is that whenever a difference between employed and nonemployed students is obtained, it is a *chance* difference. Even though the population means are identical, differences between samples drawn from the two populations occur simply by chance.

We see, then, the possibility that the difference between the mean scores of employed and nonemployed students shown in Table 7.1 could have occurred by chance. Now the question arises, just how likely is it that the result occurred by chance? The answer to this question is obtained by using inferential statistics. In nonmathematical terms, inferential statistics are the equivalent of creating identical populations and then drawing thousands of pairs of samples of a given size—just as we did in Table 7.3—and computing the difference between the mean scores. These difference scores will form a normal distribution, also known as a normal curve (an example is shown in Figure 7.1).

Researchers can determine how often the difference they obtained in their sample occurs in the normal distribution. Suppose we calculated this number for our hypothetical study and found that our obtained difference of 6.90 points (employed students' $M$ minus nonemployed students' $M$) occurs only once in 100 times when we draw samples of the same size as our samples from two identical populations. In this case, we can conclude that it is possible that our obtained difference in mean scores is a chance finding but not very likely. Therefore, we reject the explanation that our obtained result occurred by chance. Instead, we accept the alternative explanation that our obtained result came about because the two samples (employed students and nonemployed students) represent different populations, and the population mean of nonemployed students is greater than the population mean of employed students.

In reflecting on this deductive process, you may come to the realization that it is not perfect by any means. Even though our obtained difference between employed and nonemployed students would occur only once in 100 times by chance if the populations were identical, our samples may constitute that once-in-a-100-times occurrence. Also, even if we are correct in concluding that the obtained difference reflects real population differences, our sample means may not reflect the actual population means. For example, the mean score of the employed students in our sample may not be the actual population mean score. The actual mean score may be somewhat higher or lower than the obtained mean score. (A particular inferential statistic, not discussed here, can be used to determine the range of mean scores within which the population mean score is likely to fall.)

The above explanation of inferential statistics should be sufficient to help you understand several technical terms you are likely to encounter in research reports. One term is *null hypothesis,* which simply is the explanation that an observed result for a sample is a chance finding. The basic purpose of any inferential statistic is to test the null hypothesis. The findings of this test are used to accept the null hypothesis (that is, attribute the obtained result to chance) or to reject the null hypothesis (that is, conclude that the obtained result can be generalized to the population).

Other technical terms you are likely to see in research reports are $p$ and statistical significance. A $p$ *value* refers to the percentage of occasions that a chance difference between mean scores of a certain magnitude will occur when the population means are identical (see the above discussion). The lower the $p$ value, the less often it is that a chance difference of a given magnitude will occur; therefore, the more likely it is that the null hypothesis is false. For example, a $p$ value of .001 indicates that it is much more likely that the null hypothesis is false than would a $p$ value of .01. A $p$ value of .001 indicates that a mean score difference as large as the obtained mean score difference would occur only once in 1,000 drawings of two samples from identical populations. A $p$ value of .01 indicates that a mean score difference as large as the obtained mean score difference would occur only once in 100 drawings.

In educational research, a $p$ value of .05 generally is considered sufficient to reject the null hypothesis. This high a $p$ value makes it fairly easy to reject the null hypothesis because the researcher's obtained difference between mean scores only would need to exceed the difference that would occur once in 20 times in samples drawn from identical populations. Therefore, some obtained results with $p = .05$ are likely to be chance findings. Therefore, you should be cautious about generalizing them. You have less need for caution, though, if other research studies in the literature reported similar findings, that is, replicated the study results.

Some researchers will report $p$ as $<.05$ rather than $=.05$. The symbol $<$ means "less than." Usually the $p$ value is not exactly .05 but rather some value less than that. The $<$ symbol is a mathematical statement that this is the case.

When the null hypothesis is rejected, the obtained result is said to be statistically significant. For this reason the various inferential statistics sometimes are called tests of statistical significance. In reading research reports, you should be careful not to confuse statistical significance with practical significance. A statistically significant result only means that it is likely to be generalizable beyond the sample, or in other words, that it is not a chance finding. Although generalizable, the obtained result may reflect such a small difference between groups that it has little practical significance.

Inferential statistics are appropriate for quantitative research studies but not for qualitative studies. Qualitative studies, almost without exception, do not involve the selection of a sufficiently large sample to allow the use of inferential statistics. Inferences may be made about generalizability from the few cases that were studied, but these inferences involve a subjective reasoning process rather than the mathematical process described above.

We describe below the main types of inferential statistics used in educational research. Different types are necessary to test the generalizability of the different types of results obtained in research studies. In the above example, we considered only one of many obtained results, that is, the difference between two mean scores.

## THE *t* TEST

The *t* test is used to determine whether the observed difference between the mean scores of two groups on a measure is likely to have occurred by chance or whether it reflects a true difference in the mean scores of the populations represented by the two groups. In our hypothetical study of high school history instruction, the *t* test would be used to determine whether the mean score of employed students on the interest measure is truly different from the mean score of nonemployed students. Similarly, the *t* test could be used to determine whether the mean course grade of these two groups is truly different.

The computations involved in a *t* test yield a *t value*. Researchers look for this value in a table of the *t* distribution. A *t* value of 2.10 is statistically significant at the .05 level for a sample of 20 individuals, meaning that only once in 20 times ($1 \div 20 = .05$) will a difference in mean scores as large as or larger than the observed difference occur when drawing samples of a given size from identical populations. Researchers generally agree that *t* values yielding a *p* of .05 or lower are sufficient to conclude that a difference in mean scores of two groups can be generalized to the populations represented by the samples used in the study.

In our hypothetical study, the *t* value for the difference in mean scores on the interest measure for employed students ($M = 30.70$) and nonemployed students ($M = 37.60$) is 2.35. Because our obtained *t* of 2.35 exceeds the *t* (2.10) required for statistical significance at the .05 level, we would reject the null hypothesis that this is a chance finding. Instead, we would conclude that nonemployed students in other settings with characteristics similar to those of the research sample would demonstrate more interest in history than employed students.

The distribution of scores for one or the other group being compared sometimes deviates substantially from the normal curve (see Figure 7.1). The *t* test cannot be used under this set of conditions. Alternative tests of statistical significance can be used instead: the Mann-Whitney *U* test or the Wilcoxon signed-rank test. They do not require the same assumptions about score distribution as the *t* test.

The *t* test also can be used to determine whether observed correlation coefficients occurred by chance. For example, we could determine whether the correlation coefficient value of .49, representing the level of relationship between interest in history and history course grade in Table 7.1, occurred by chance. The null hypothesis to be tested is that the true relationship between interest and course grade in the population represented by the sample is 0.00 and that the observed coefficient of .49 is a chance deviation from that value. The test of this null hypothesis yields a *t* value of 2.39 (*p* < .05), and therefore we conclude that the relationship between interest and course grade would be found in other groups similar to the research sample.

## ANALYSIS OF VARIANCE AND ANALYSIS OF COVARIANCE

In our hypothetical study the students were classified as having part-time jobs or as nonemployed. Suppose instead that we had three classifications: nonemployed, part-time job of 10 hours a week or less, or part-time job of 11 hours a week or more. This situation would yield three mean scores on the measure of interest in history, one for each of the three groups. The *t* test can compare only two means at a time. Therefore, another test of statistical significance, known as analysis of variance, must be used. This test determines the likelihood that the three mean scores occurred by chance, in other words, that they are chance values generated by drawing repeated samples from three populations having identical scores.

Analysis of variance yields an inferential statistic known as *F*. If the *F* value exceeds a certain value determined by examining a particular statistical table (a table of the *F* distribution), we would reject the null hypothesis and conclude that the difference between the three mean scores is generalizable. However, analysis of variance does not tell us which of the differences between the three mean scores is generalizable. If we represent the three mean scores by the symbols A, B, and C, we see that three comparisons are possible: A versus B, A versus C, and B versus C. One or more of these comparisons may be generalizable. To make these comparisons, a special form of the *t* test is applied to each comparison. The most common of these special tests is Tukey's test and Scheffé's test.

Another application of analysis of variance is the determination of the likelihood that differences in the standard deviations of two or more groups occurred by chance. For example, we could use analysis of variance to test whether the standard deviations of the interest scores for the two groups of employed students (*SD* = 6.73) and nonemployed students (*SD* = 6.43) differ by chance. More accurately, we would be testing whether the variances in the two sets of scores differ by chance. The variance of a set of scores is the square of the standard deviation.

Analysis of variance plays an important role in drawing conclusions from data yielded by experiments. To understand its role in this context, we constructed data for a hypothetical experiment comparing two types of text. Two groups of students were formed prior to the experiment: students with high reading ability and students with low reading ability. Students in each group were randomly assigned to the experimental and control treatments. Students in the experimental treatment read a text passage with inserted questions inviting them to relate the information being presented to something they already know. Students in the control treatment read the same text passage but with no inserted questions. A multiple-choice test covering the content of the text passage was administered a day before students read the passage (the pretest) and a day after (the posttest).

Table 7.4 shows the students' mean scores on the posttest. Note that the mean scores of the experimental and control groups are presented separately, as are the scores of high- and low-reading-ability students within each treatment group. Also, mean scores for all students in a particular row or column are shown. For example, the bottom row of the first data column shows the mean score for all experimental-group students, ignoring whether they have high or low reading ability.

Many comparisons are possible for the mean scores shown in Table 7.4, for example, all experimental-group students versus all control-group students; high-ability students versus low-ability students in the experimental group; high-ability students in the experimental group versus high-ability students in the control group. One could do

Table 7.4   Posttest scores for students classified by reading ability and experimental or control-group assignment

| Experimental group | | Control group | |
| --- | --- | --- | --- |
| High reading ability | Low reading ability | High reading ability | Low reading ability |
| 23 | 18 | 19 | 3 |
| 14 | 17 | 12 | 7 |
| 16 | 9 | 16 | 1 |
| 18 | 10 | 14 | 6 |
| 16 | 17 | 7 | 4 |
| 17 | 19 | 8 | 7 |
| 19 | 8 | 13 | 6 |
| 20 | 20 | 10 | 5 |
| 17 | 15 | 19 | 3 |
| 17 | 16 | 9 | 2 |
| $M$ = 17.70 | $M$ = 14.90 | $M$ = 12.70 | $M$ = 4.40 |
| $SD$ = 2.50 | $SD$ = 4.33 | $SD$ = 4.32 | $SD$ = 2.12 |

| Subgroup | Subgroup statistics | | |
| --- | --- | --- | --- |
|  | $N$ | $M$ | $SD$ |
| Experimental group | 20 | 16.30 | 3.73 |
| Control group | 20 | 8.55 | 5.39 |
| High-reading-ability group | 20 | 15.20 | 4.29 |
| Low-reading-ability group | 20 | 9.65 | 6.33 |

$t$ tests for all these comparisons, but this method is tedious and increases the likelihood of false conclusions because of the number of comparisons made. (It can be shown mathematically that as the frequency of inferential statistics calculated for a set of data increases, so does the likelihood of falsely rejecting the null hypothesis.) Analysis of variance is a more elegant and accurate method of making all the comparisons at once to determine which ones are likely to be chance differences.

Table 7.5 shows a summary of the $F$ values generated by the analysis of variance of the data presented in Table 7.4, and whether each $F$ value is statistically significant ($p$ = .05 or less). The first line of results shows the $F$ value (49.88) for the comparison of all experimental-group students ($M$ = 16.30) and all control-group students ($M$ = 8.55) on the posttest, ignoring whether the students have high or low reading ability. This $F$ value is statistically significant ($p$ < .001), meaning that the difference is generalizable. The second line shows the $F$ value (25.58) for the comparison of all high-reading-ability students ($M$ = 15.20) and all low-reading-ability students ($M$ = 9.65) on the posttest. This $F$ value, too, is statistically significant ($p$ < .001).

The next line shows an $F$ value of 6.28 ($p$ < .05) for the interaction effect. In educational practice, an interaction effect is implied when we claim that different

Table 7.5 Summary of analysis of variance for posttest scores in hypothetical experiment on inserted questions in text

| Source | $F$ | $p$ |
|---|---|---|
| Treatment ($T$) | 49.88 | $< .001$ |
| Reading ability ($R$) | 25.58 | $< .001$ |
| $T \times R$ interaction | 6.28 | $< .05$ |

instructional methods are effective for different types of students. In technical terms, an interaction effect is said to have occurred when the difference between two groups on variable B varies according to the value of variable A. To understand what this means, consider the research results shown in Table 7.4. The difference in posttest mean score between the experimental and control groups (variable A) is substantial (14.9 − 4.4 = 10.5 points) for students with low reading ability (one level of variable B); however, the difference in posttest mean scores between the experimental- and control- treatment students (variable A) is small (17.7 − 12.7 = 5 points) for students with high reading ability (the other level of treatment variable B). Thus, it seems that the experimental text passage helps poor readers much more than it helps good readers. The inclusion of both variables in the experimental design yielded a better understanding of the experimental treatment's effectiveness than if the design had involved only an experimental group versus control group comparison.

The experiment described above is fairly simple. There are two levels of each variable (sometimes called a factor). The first factor is the type of reading passage, and it has two levels: inserted questions versus no inserted questions. The other factor is reading ability, and it also has two levels: high versus low. Some experiments reported in the research literature have more complex designs, for example, three factors with three or more levels of one or more of the factors. Analysis of variance is capable of testing the statistical significance of group differences on each factor and also the statistical significance of the various interaction effects.

Analysis of variance is widely used in educational research because of its versatility. However, it can produce inaccurate results if the distribution of scores for any of the measures deviates substantially from the normal curve. Another condition that can produce inaccurate results is large differences in the size of the groups being compared.

We have ignored up to this point the pretest results for our hypothetical experiment. The pretest mean scores for each group are shown in Table 7.6. These results complicate our interpretation of the posttest results because they show that the experimental group had higher scores on the pretest than did the control group. The experimental group's superior knowledge of the subject beforehand may be responsible for its higher score on the posttest rather than the inserted questions in the text passage.

We can eliminate superior preknowledge as an explanation for the results by doing another experiment so that students selected for the experimental and control groups are equivalent on the pretest. This solution, however, is time consuming and expensive.

Table 7.6   Pretest means for students in hypothetical experiment on inserted questions in text

|  | Experimental group $M$ | Control group $M$ |
|---|---|---|
| High-ability readers | 10.10 | 7.70 |
| Low-ability readers | 4.30 | 2.90 |

Another solution is to use gain scores, which are computed by subtracting the pretest score from the posttest score for each student in the experiment. As we discussed above, however, gain scores have several limitations, and so they are rarely used to analyze experimental data.

The best solution to the problem is to make the groups equivalent on the pretest by applying a statistical technique known as analysis of covariance. In this method, each student's posttest score is adjusted up or down to take into account the pretest performance. Statistical tables in research reports sometimes show both the actual posttest means and the adjusted posttest means after analysis of covariance has been applied. There is no need to do an analysis of variance if an analysis of covariance has been conducted. Analysis of covariance yields $F$ values similar in meaning to those described above.

The procedure used in analysis of covariance is somewhat similar to the handicapping procedure used in some sports such as golf. Poor golf players can compete with good golf players by being assigned a handicap based on their past performance. Each golf player's score in a tournament is determined by how much better or worse she does than her handicap (that is, her previous performance).

Analysis of covariance requires certain conditions and mathematical assumptions to yield valid results. If the research data do not satisfy these assumptions, the results of the analysis of covariance are likely to be invalid. In reading a research report, you should look for a statement by the researchers that they checked at least the key assumptions before using this statistical method. If there is no such statement, you should view the $F$ values and $p$ values associated with them with caution.

## THE CHI-SQUARE TEST

The $t$ test, analysis of variance, and analysis of covariance are appropriate inferential statistics for data that are in continuous or rank score form. They are not appropriate for categorical data. The chi-square test is the appropriate test of statistical significance in this case.

To illustrate the use of this test, suppose that we want to determine whether urban school districts are more likely to employ female school superintendents than are rural school districts. A random sample of 100 urban school districts and 100 rural school districts is drawn from a population of school districts. The gender of each district's superintendent is determined.

The two variables involved in this study are gender (male vs. female) and type of school district (urban vs. rural). Both variables are categorical because they cannot be ordered on a continuum. For example, a rural district is neither "more" nor "less" than an urban district.

Table 7.7 shows hypothetical data relating to our research question. The descriptive statistics are in the form of frequencies, each frequency being the number of superintendents in each gender category for a particular type of district. Table 7.7 shows that the distributions of male and female superintendents vary across districts. We need to determine whether these differences occurred by chance or are characteristic of other districts similar to those used in the study.

The chi-square test is used to make this determination. It yields an inferential statistic known as chi and is represented by the symbol $\chi^2$. The $\chi^2$ value for the distributions shown in Table 7.7 is 7.42. This value is associated with a $p$ value that is less than .01. Therefore, we reject the null hypothesis that these results occurred by chance, and instead we conclude that they can be generalized to other districts having similar characteristics to those in the study.

## PARAMETRIC VERSUS NONPARAMETRIC TESTS

All the tests of statistical significance described above, with the exception of the chi-square test, are parametric tests. These tests make several assumptions about the measures being used and the populations that are represented by the research samples. For example, one of the assumptions is that the scores form an interval scale, meaning that there is an even interval between each point on the scale.

Suppose the assumptions underlying parametric tests, especially the assumption of equal intervals, cannot be satisfied. In this case, researchers may use a parametric test anyway if the assumptions are not violated seriously. Otherwise they will use a nonparametric test of statistical significance. The chi-square test is the most commonly used nonparametric test because many variables are in the form of categories, which do not form an interval scale.

Other nonparametric tests sometimes found in the research literature are the Mann-Whitney $U$ test and the Wilcoxon signed-rank test. These are nonparametric counterparts of the $t$ test. Another nonparametric test is the Kruskal-Wallis test, which is the nonparametric counterpart of the analysis of variance.

## PRACTICAL SIGNIFICANCE AND EFFECT SIZE

As we stated above, statistical significance should not be confused with practical significance. If a result is statistically significant, it means only that the result probably

Table 7.7    Distribution of male and female superintendents in urban and rural school districts

|  | Urban | Rural |
|---|---|---|
| Males | 65 | 82 |
| Females | 35 | 18 |

did not occur by chance and so one can generalize from the sample to the population that it represents. Even a trivial result can be statistically significant if the sample is sufficiently large because the calculation of inferential statistics is affected by the sample size. The larger the sample, the smaller the observed result required for statistical significance.

The practical significance of statistical results is a matter of judgment. For example, an experimental treatment may have only a small effect on learning relative to conventional instruction, but the type of learning may be so important that even small increments are considered worthwhile.

Researchers have developed a statistical approach to determining practical significance. This approach involves the calculation of a statistic known as effect size. It is discussed in Chapter 8, which concerns procedures for synthesizing research findings. For present purposes, we will note only that the effect size statistic is most commonly used as an aid in determining the practical significance of the results yielded by experiments. It provides a numerical expression of how well the experimental group learned or otherwise performed relative to the control group. Effect sizes of .33 or larger generally are considered to have practical significance.

Although the effect size statistic provides useful information, it should not be the sole basis for making judgments about the practical significance of statistical results. You should examine the total context of the research study, especially the measures that were used and the scores they generated, in judging whether an observed result is sufficiently large to have implications for practice.

# Recommended Reading

BRUNING, J. L., & KINTZ, B. L. (1987). *Computational handbook of statistics,* 3rd ed. Glenview, IL: Scott, Foresman.

   This book provides easy-to-follow computational procedures for most of the statistical techniques presented in this chapter.

LINN, R. L. (1986). Quantitative methods in research on teaching. In *Handbook of research on teaching,* 3rd ed., ed. M. C. Wittrock, pp. 92–118. New York: Macmillan.

   The author provides a mathematical discussion of the statistical techniques covered in this chapter and also of more sophisticated aspects of statistical analysis. The relationship among research design, causal inference, and statistical analysis is discussed.

SHAVER, J. P. (1985). Chance and nonsense. *Phi Delta Kappan,* Part 1, *67*(1), 57–60; Part 2, *67*(2), 138–141.

   This is an interesting and easily understood series of two articles written as a conversation between two teachers. Such concepts as statistical significance, practical significance, statistical power, and effect size are discussed in the context of one teacher's thesis study.

# Application Problems

1. What types of scores are each of the following?
    a. Teachers are divided into two types: middle-school teachers with elementary school training and middle-school teachers with secondary school training.

b. The years of teaching experience of each teacher are recorded.

c. Each teacher takes a test that measures professional knowledge.

d. The school principal is asked to rank the teachers from high to low based on a judgment of their overall teaching competence.

e. Each teacher is interviewed, and on the basis of this interview, each teacher is classified as having one of four teaching philosophies.

2. Identify an appropriate statistical technique if a researcher wishes to determine

a. How well the sample performed, on the average, on a test

b. Whether there is a significant difference among the mean scores of music educators, English educators, and science educators on a measure of satisfaction with an in-service program

c. Whether a correlation coefficient is statistically significant

d. The amount of variation in the sample's scores on a test

e. Whether the distribution of males and females is significantly different in an early childhood education program and an elementary teacher education program

f. Whether a computer software program is more effective for students with good keyboarding skills than for students with poor keyboarding skills

3. Decide whether the researcher used the appropriate statistical technique in each of the following situations:

a. A test of teaching competency was administered to a sample of 15 education students applying for a teaching certificate. Their scores on the test were as follows: 30, 41, 47, 59, 62, 65, 66, 84, 84, 84, 86, 87, 89, 92, 92. The researcher determined the average score earned by this sample by computing a statistic known as the mean.

b. The researcher administered a measure of study skills and a test of English to a sample of foreign students beginning college in the United States. After students completed their first term of coursework, the researcher computed three statistics: (1) a correlation coefficient to determine how well students' scores on the study skills measure predicted their first-term grade point average; (2) a correlation coefficient to determine how well their scores on the English test predicted their grade point average; and (3) a multiple regression coefficient to determine how well the study skills test scores and English test scores together predicted students' grade point average.

c. The researcher selected three first-grade classrooms to participate in an experiment on reading programs. In one classroom students participated in a whole-language program. In another classroom students participated in a basal reader program. In the third classroom students participated in a program that combined whole-language and basal reader approaches. The researcher found that the three classes of students differed substantially on a beginning-of-year reading test and an end-of-year reading test. The data were analyzed by an analysis of variance on the end-of-year reading test scores.

# CHAPTER 8

# SYNTHESIS OF RESEARCH FINDINGS

## Overview

This chapter discusses the value of using published syntheses of research findings to guide you in making educational decisions. We will explain three types of research syntheses that are commonly found in educational literature: primary source analyses, conceptual-methodological critiques, and professional reviews. Suggestions are provided to help you locate research syntheses that are relevant to your needs. We also provide guidelines for evaluating research syntheses to ensure that they are giving you valid and reliable information.

## Objectives

1. Understand the value of reading syntheses of the research literature when searching secondary sources.
2. Describe the common and unique features of three kinds of research syntheses: primary source analyses, conceptual-methodological critiques, and professional reviews.
3. Apply six criteria in evaluating research syntheses.
4. Describe strategies for finding research syntheses that address your questions and problems.

## Characteristics of a Research Synthesis

One of the biggest challenges in applying educational research is dealing with the vast number of research studies that have made their way into the literature. Some scholars have devoted themselves to helping educators by doing literature reviews in which the research findings relating to a particular problem or topic area are synthesized.

You will recall from Chapter 2 that the research literature is of three types: preliminary sources, primary sources, and secondary sources. Preliminary sources are indexes that help you locate books, articles, and other educational documents relevant to your problem. Some of these indexes also include abstracts of the documents. Primary sources are documents in which a research study is reported by the researchers who actually conducted it. Secondary sources are publications in which the author reports on research that someone else conducted. A research synthesis is a type of secondary source because the author is reporting on the research of others.

In a research synthesis, the reviewer identifies, interprets, and draws conclusions from a set of research studies that have some relation to a particular problem or topic. If the reviewer has carried out his own research on the problem or topic being investigated, a summary of this work probably will be included in the synthesis too.

Research syntheses vary in their scope, that is, the number of studies reviewed; the period of time covered; and the range of subjects, settings, populations, and disciplines included. The scope of a research synthesis depends both on the amount of research that has been carried out concerning a particular question and on how exhaustive the author's search was for documents reporting that research. An ideal research synthesis covers the findings of research conducted by a variety of researchers with different theoretical and practical perspectives and probes various aspects of a problem. The research reviewed may be based on various research methodologies. Other types of syntheses can also be found in the educational literature. For example, in a synthesis of opinions, various experts present their views on an educational issue, such as the pros and cons of whole-language instruction, but do not cite research as the basis for their opinions. In a synthesis of educational practices, the author might identify the different meanings of an educational concept in practice, such as cooperative learning, by describing examples of the practice in operation. However, little or no research concerning the practice is cited. By contrast, this chapter concerns *research* syntheses, in which the findings of scientific research on an educational problem or topic are summarized and implications from those findings are drawn.

# Advantages of Reading Research Syntheses

Carrying out your own literature review obviously has some benefits. Searching the literature will give you in-depth familiarity with the research findings that bear on your problem and a better understanding of the educational research process. If you are in a graduate degree program, you may be expected to conduct a thorough literature search as part of the requirements for your degree.

There are numerous disadvantages, however, to conducting your own literature search from scratch. The biggest problem is the time it takes to do a thorough literature review, especially when you are seeking an immediate answer to a pressing educational concern. As we described in preceding chapters, you must spend time defining your problem, selecting appropriate preliminary sources, and using them to identify references to primary and secondary sources. Next you must judge the relevance of each reference by reading abstracts and some actual documents after you have finished the time-consuming process of locating them. Then you must organize, evaluate, and interpret what each study has found. Finally, you must synthesize the various findings, formulate conclusions, and prepare a report.

The time and effort involved in this type of literature search are simply beyond the resources of many practitioners. Nonetheless, most educators, policymakers, and the public believe that practitioners should inform their educational decision making with the results of research. Reading research syntheses enables them to do so with much less effort. Even if you find a research synthesis that was published some years ago, you can save yourself a great deal of time and effort by carrying out only a search of more recent sources to update the information contained in the synthesis, rather than starting from scratch.

A published research synthesis has a special advantage if its authors are well informed and experienced in the area they are investigating. You reap the benefits of their expertise in finding, organizing, evaluating, and interpreting research relevant to your problem. It is difficult for most practitioners to develop the same level of skill as expert reviewers in comprehending the entire range of methodologies, measures, and statistical tests that are reflected in the educational research literature.

Still another advantage of reading a well-done, published research synthesis is that it is authoritative, and so may carry more weight with policymakers than your own search. If you can cite well-documented research syntheses as the basis for your opinions, policymakers and colleagues are likely to give your opinions more weight. These potential advantages of reading a good research synthesis do not mean that you can fully rely on such a research synthesis in forming your opinions. You still need to exercise independent judgment about the literature cited and use your own reasoning to determine whether the conclusions reached are justified by the body of research findings reviewed. It is wise to track down selected studies and read them yourself. Reading primary sources selectively will give you more detailed information than is contained in a synthesis and will deepen your understanding of the research process.

# Criteria for Evaluating Research Syntheses

The following criteria are intended to help you search for the most useful research syntheses for your purpose. If a specific synthesis is recommended to you by someone, or if in examining the literature you happen to find a research synthesis, you can use these guidelines to determine its potential usefulness.

1. *The reviewer's credentials.* The author's reputation and experience with the topic are factors to consider when reading a research synthesis. One way to make this determination is to examine the reference list at the end of the review to see whether the author has done research on the topic himself and, if so, where and when it was published. You can also check whether information about the author's affiliation, title, and experience is part of the abstract or article itself.

2. *The search procedures used.* In older published reviews, it was not customary for reviewers to specify their search procedures. Thus it was difficult for readers to determine whether the research cited in the review resulted from an exhaustive search or whether it was haphazardly selected. It is now common practice for reviewers to identify the preliminary sources examined, the descriptors used, and the years covered.

3. *The breadth of the search.* Research syntheses vary widely in their breadth, from an exhaustive search of all primary sources on a topic to a highly selective search. The advantage of an exhaustive search is that the reviewer has done the job for you of finding, selecting, reading, evaluating, and summarizing a large number of references. A narrower search may be just as useful for your purposes, but in this case it is even more important to know how the reviewer selected the documents included in his review. The following dimensions reflect how broad or narrow the reviewer's search of the literature was:

a. The period of time covered by the search. The publication dates of the most recent and oldest sources provide an indication of this time period. Keep in mind, though, that the time period may extend beyond these dates although the search did not yield older or more recent references that were relevant to the topic.

b. The types of documents reviewed. For example, does the synthesis include only published journal articles or does it also include dissertations and unpublished documents?

c. The geographical scope of the search. Did the reviewer only examine studies carried out in the United States, or were foreign sources also included?

d. The range of grade levels and types of students, teachers, and schools that were studied in the reviewed research.

e. Whether the sources reflect varied perspectives on the research topic, including different theoretical orientations, or whether just one view of the topic is presented.

f. Whether criteria were applied to exclude from the review certain documents that were initially examined, for example, documents not reporting results of statistical significance tests. This information about breadth may be provided by the reviewer. If not, you may be able to infer it from an examination of the documents included in the review.

4. *The amount of information provided about the studies reviewed.* The writer of a research synthesis has a challenging task: to summarize findings of a large number of studies briefly so as to be readable, yet in enough detail that the basis of his conclusions and interpretations is reasonably clear. Simply citing a reference or two in parentheses following a sweeping generalization by the reviewer does not accomplish this goal. A better approach is for the reviewer to describe briefly the relevant information from a research study that led him to cite it in his synthesis. For example, the reviewer might describe how the different phenomena that were studied, such as school achievement or aggressiveness, were defined and measured. If the results varied because of characteristics of the subjects, the length of the experimental treatment, or some other factor, the reviewer should mention these factors.

5. *The extent to which the reviewer exercised critical judgment.* Research syntheses range from those that reflect uncritical acceptance of research findings to those in which the reviewer finds flaws in every research study and asserts that no conclusions can be drawn from them. Neither extreme is justified for topics that have been extensively researched.

Another aspect of critical judgment is whether the reviewer tended to lump studies together or pointed out important differences among studies that appeared to deal with the same question but were actually quite different in design or purpose. The latter approach generally reflects better critical judgment.

6. *How inconsistent findings were resolved.* Nearly every research synthesis will reveal that the results obtained in some studies do not agree with those found in other studies. You should examine carefully how the reviewer dealt with these inconsistencies. Several quantitative approaches, including meta-analysis and vote counting, can be used. These approaches are most common in primary source analyses and are

described below. Another approach is to make more holistic judgments. This approach, common in conceptual-methodological critiques and professional reviews, also is described below.

# Three Types of Research Synthesis

Research syntheses in the educational literature are generally of three types: primary source analyses, conceptual-methodological critiques, and professional reviews. We will now explain each of these types, citing examples from the current educational literature.

## PRIMARY SOURCE ANALYSES

Primary source analysis has a very limited scope, involves an exhaustive search process, and focuses on primary sources. The purpose of the analysis is to draw diverse findings together into a consistent picture of the state of research knowledge related to a particular question. The article reproduced in this chapter by Haller, Child, and Walberg (1988) is an example of a primary source analysis.

Quantitative techniques have been developed to enable reviewers who do primary source analyses to synthesize research findings resulting from diverse measures and statistical techniques. A simple approach is vote counting, which was recommended by Gregg Jackson (1980). First studies are identified in which the effect of one variable on another variable or the relationship between two variables has been measured. Then all these studies are classified into four categories, depending on the significance and direction of the results obtained. Studies with significant positive results, that is, in the direction hypothesized, are coded $+ +$; studies with nonsignificant positive results are coded $+$; studies with significant results in the direction opposite the direction hypothesized are coded $- -$; and studies with nonsignificant results in the direction opposite the direction hypothesized are coded $-$.

One problem with vote counting is that many studies show a mixture of positive and negative results at various levels of significance. Barak Rosenshine (1971) used a form of vote counting combined with conceptual analysis in his review of the relationship between specific teaching behaviors and student achievement. His analysis makes it clear that vote counting is not a mechanical procedure; the reviewer must make careful judgments about which studies are relevant to a particular variable. Once this determination was made, Rosenshine made up tables showing significant results and nonsignificant results from each relevant study. He then discussed the overall trend found in the results and drew conclusions. For example, Rosenshine examined nine studies that concerned teachers' use of student ideas and found that

> . . . not one yielded a significant linear correlation between the use of this variable and student achievement. However, there was a positive trend . . . in eight of the nine studies. . . . Although a great deal has been written about the importance of teacher use of student ideas . . . the significance of this variable alone is not as strong as has been claimed. (p. 71)

Other approaches to quantitative synthesis are more mathematically precise than vote counting. N. L. Gage (1978) describes a procedure for testing the statistical significance of two or more results across studies of a particular program or method. (If a result is statistically significant, it means that the result is probably true of the population, not just the sample used in the study.) Gage reviewed individual studies of how teaching techniques such as teachers' praise, criticism, and acceptance of students' ideas affect learning. Gage demonstrated that although individual studies tend to show weak, nonsignificant effects for these techniques, combining the results across studies by using his quantitative synthesis method leads to strong, generalizable conclusions about the effectiveness of these techniques.

Meta-analysis has become the most widely used method for quantitatively combining research results from different studies in recent years. Most meta-analyses in education follow the procedures developed by Gene Glass (1976). Meta-analysis involves translating the findings of a set of related studies into effect sizes. The studies typically are experiments that test the effectiveness of a particular program or method. The "effect size" indicates how well the group that received the experimental program or method does relative to a comparison group (called the control group) that receives either no treatment or an alternative program or method.

The effect size is computed by taking the difference between the mean score of the experimental treatment and the mean score of the control treatment on a criterion measure (for example, an achievement test) and dividing this difference by the standard deviation of the scores for the control group. For example, say that a study concerns the effect of small cash rewards on the achievement of students in an inner-city high school. For one school year, experimental students received cash rewards for passing weekly quizzes, and control students received no rewards. At the end of the year the experimental students made a mean score of 46.2 on the XYZ Mathematics Test, which is the criterion measure. The control group mean was 41.2, with a standard deviation of 4.0. The effect size would be 46.2 minus 41.2 divided by 4.0, or 1.25. An effect size of .33 or larger is generally considered to indicate a difference that has practical significance. Thus one can conclude that giving students cash rewards for passing quizzes improved their academic achievement substantially.

Calculating an effect size for every relevant study in a primary source analysis transforms the results from various studies into a comparable unit of measure. It does not matter that one study used the XYZ Mathematics Test, on which scores can vary from 0 to 70, and another study used the ABC History Test, on which scores can vary from 0 to 100. An effect size can be calculated for the results of both studies, and these effect sizes can be directly compared. An effect size of 1.00 is twice as large as an effect size of .50, regardless of the measures and scoring systems that were used. The mean of the effect sizes from different studies can be calculated to yield an estimate of the effect that the experimental program or method produces relative to a comparison intervention.

Not all studies in the research literature report the necessary means and standard deviations for calculating effect size. Procedures have been developed, however, for estimating effect size from virtually any statistical data reported in the primary sources included in the meta-analysis.

Meta-analysis has gained much popularity, and an increasing number of primary source analyses using this method of research synthesis can be found in the research literature. You should be aware of the issues involving this technique, however. One of the key issues is the reviewer's basis for selecting studies. In the article reproduced in this chapter, for example, Eileen Haller and her colleagues (1988) state that they examined 150 references but limited their analysis to 20 studies. These 20 studies met certain criteria: use of metacognitive intervention, employment of a control group for comparison, and provision of statistical information necessary to compute effect sizes.

Gene Glass (1976), the developer of contemporary meta-analysis procedure, would argue that Haller and her colleagues should have included as many of the 150 original studies as possible in the analysis, even though some are methodologically sounder than others. Glass asserts that either weaker studies will show the same results as stronger studies, and thus should be included, or that a truer picture will emerge if weak studies are also analyzed. By contrast, Robert Slavin (1986) would argue against including every possible study in a meta-analysis. Slavin examined eight meta-analyses conducted by six independent sets of investigators and compared their procedures and conclusions against the studies they analyzed. He reported that he found errors in all eight meta-analyses that were serious enough to invalidate or call into question one or more major conclusions. Slavin therefore recommends including only studies providing "best evidence," that is, those that meet criteria such as methodological adequacy and relevance to the issue at hand. He also makes a strong case for not merely relying on overall mean effect size but examining results separately for subsets of studies, for example, those using different measures of the dependent variable or those studying different ethnic groups.

Whatever method is used to summarize results, a good primary source analysis offers you certain benefits as a reader. It allows you to see the general trend of the findings on a particular topic. For example, in the meta-analysis by Haller and her colleagues, the effects of metacognitive instruction (the independent variable) on reading comprehension (the dependent variable) was found to be substantial, as indicated by a mean effect size of .71. Because this finding was derived from 20 studies, we can be fairly confident that the effectiveness of metacognitive instruction is real rather than an artifact of an atypical experiment. By comparing the effect of metacognitive instruction as determined in one research synthesis to the effect of other instructional interventions as determined in other research syntheses, you can see which methods hold the most promise for improving student learning. As a practitioner you can try to implement or increase your use of the most promising methods. In addition, if the primary source analysis includes references to the individual studies included in the analysis, it provides a comprehensive list of documents that you can use in searching the literature for studies of specific interest.

 You also need to remember the limitations of this approach. While looking at the forest, you lose a great amount of information about the specific trees, that is, characteristics of the individual studies in the research synthesis. You may thus be assuming similarity among different studies that in fact had important differences, as Slavin (1986) cautioned.

To find primary source reviews in the research literature, various approaches can be used. One approach is to include "Meta analysis" as an *and* descriptor when doing a computerized ERIC search of your research topic. This procedure will indicate whether any of the documents that cover your topic involve a meta-analysis. Another approach is to check preliminary sources for particular authors who have conducted meta-analyses. For example, Walberg conducted a classic meta-analysis in 1984, and in recent years he and his colleagues have continued carrying out meta-analyses on different instructional methods (such as the one reproduced in this chapter). Also examine the reference list of documents you are reviewing for titles involving such terms as *effect size* and *meta-analysis*.

## CONCEPTUAL-METHODOLOGICAL CRITIQUES

In conceptual-methodological critiques, the reviewer's purpose is to clarify conceptual, theoretical, or methodological issues relating to a body of research. The focus of the synthesis is thus on defining such issues and determining how research findings bear on them. In a good critique, research studies are cited. However, there is no intention to do an exhaustive review of studies related to the topic being addressed. Instead, the reviewer focuses on studies that are definitive or that illustrate key conceptual and methodological issues.

A recent article by Lynn Curry (1990) is a good example of what we mean by a conceptual-methodological critique. Entitled "A Critique of the Research on Learning Styles," the study was published in a theme issue of *Educational Leadership* called "Learning Styles and the Brain." In this issue, all 22 articles had to do with the topic of learning styles. Curry's article stands out in that it reflects on the entire body of research concerning this topic. Curry asks how good the claims are for the effect of adaptations to students' learning styles on four major aspects of teaching and learning in schools: curriculum design, instructional methods, assessment methods, and student guidance. The critique begins with the identification of three pervasive problems in the operationalization of learning style theory: confusion in definitions of learning style, weakness of evidence for the validity and reliability of measures of learning style, and difficulty in identifying what specific adaptations within educational settings are effective in interaction with which range of learning styles.

Curry is selective in citing research on learning styles. Many primary sources are cited, but she also refers to a number of definitive secondary sources. For example, two articles included in the reference list are "Cognitive Styles: Some Conceptual, Methodological, and Applied Issues" (Shipman & Shipman, 1985) and "Field Dependent and Field Independent Cognitive Styles and Their Educational Implications" (Witkin, Moore, Goodenough, & Cox, 1977). Thus the author's own research synthesis builds on previous research syntheses that also are conceptual-methodological critiques.

In dealing with the topic, Curry not only summarizes research bearing on the problems identified earlier but also highlights problems in the research on learning styles and draws conclusions and implications. For example, four problems are noted that threaten the external validity of research designs presently used in learning style research. In addition, three alternate explanations are posed for the positive results that have been attributed to supposed learning style effects: general intelligence effects, principles of adaptive education, and instructional alignment.

Thus, Curry's purpose was to examine critically research methodology and theoretical assumptions in learning style research. This is far different from the purpose of a meta-analysis, which in this case would be to determine the average effect size produced by instructional programs that use a learning style approach.

In most conceptual-methodological critiques, research findings are synthesized in what is commonly called the narrative or traditional form. That is, rather than using a quantitative formula, the author uses logic, analysis, speculation, and reasoned judgment to form impressions and draw conclusions from the specific studies examined. A major benefit of reading conceptual-methodological critiques is that they help to explain inconsistent findings in the research literature. More broadly, they help educators explore different conceptual and theoretical perspectives and thus deepen their understanding of the state of knowledge relating to the problem. A good critique also helps specify needed directions for further research.

There are some limitations on this type of research synthesis. It usually does not provide an exhaustive, or even a comprehensive, review of the research studies that have been conducted on a given topic. The quality of the review is heavily dependent on the reviewer's judgment and expertise. Therefore, you need to ask whether the reviewer's language or the procedures used to examine research appear to reflect bias. Also, some conceptual-methodological reviews are rather technical and thus difficult for practitioners to understand. Because they are written primarily for researchers, conceptual-methodological critiques often do not draw clear implications for practice.

Despite these limitations, we urge you to read one or more conceptual-methodological critiques bearing on your question. You can use several strategies to find them in the literature. One approach is to include the descriptor "*and* Literature Review" when searching the ERIC data base (that is, *RIE* and *CIJE*). Some references that are classified under this descriptor are likely to be conceptual-methodological critiques. For example, we mentioned in Chapter 2 a computer search we conducted with the descriptors "Parents" *and* "Literature Review." One of the 28 references resulting from this search was an article entitled "Research in Review: Parent Education and Support Programs" (Powell, 1986). The abstract of this article suggests that it provides a conceptual framework for examining research on parent involvement in education and a critique of such research:

> Discusses the impact of parent education programs, describing the effects on child and parent of such interventions and summarizing research on different types of programs. Differences in parent participation and outcomes, the problem of sustaining program involvement, and directions for the future are also outlined. (p. 47)

Our reading of the article confirmed that it is a good conceptual-methodological critique of research on parent education. It describes many characteristics differentiating particular parent education and support programs; summarizes findings of numerous studies of the effects on children and parents of parental participation in such programs; describes factors that affect parental participation in, retention in, and satisfaction with such programs; and concludes with a section detailing unanswered questions and future directions for program designers and researchers.

Another approach for identifying conceptual-methodological critiques is to examine the secondary sources in which these types of research syntheses often appear. For example, the two earlier research syntheses cited in Curry's (1990) article on learning styles were published in the *Review of Research in Education* and *Review of Educational Research,* respectively. See Chapter 2 for a description of these and other secondary sources that contain reviews of research on significant topics in education and related fields. Most of these reviews are conceptual-methodological critiques.

## PROFESSIONAL REVIEWS

Both primary source analyses and conceptual-methodological critiques often draw implications for educational practice. However, this is not their main purpose, and they generally are not written for the educational practitioner. By contrast, professional reviews are intended for practitioners and policymakers and use nontechnical language to describe research findings relevant to educational practice. Many of them are geared toward a particular audience of practitioners, such as elementary school teachers. Professional reviews tend to focus on recent studies. They provide a synthesis of research findings as reported in selected primary sources, but they also use primary source analyses and conceptual-methodological critiques as data sources to arrive at implications for practice. The value of these implications for practice depends almost entirely on the judgment and experience of the reviewer and his understanding of conditions in the field.

In a professional review, the author selects studies for review primarily on the basis of their relevance to the intended target audience. Professional reviews tend to be brief and selective in the references that are cited. For example, the *Encyclopedia of Educational Research* primarily consists of professional reviews, which average about four pages in length, with a list of about 10 to 15 references. Because of these space limitations, the scope and depth of a professional review tend to be limited. Unless the professional review is recent, it may not be useful because new advances in research and changing conditions of educational practice are likely to invalidate the reviewer's recommendations.

A recent article in *Phi Delta Kappan* is a good example of a professional review. The article, entitled, "The Evolving Effort to Improve Schools: Pseudo-reform, Incremental Reform, and Restructuring," by Mary Anne Raywid (1990), is about four pages long and cites 14 references. The author focuses on recent school improvement efforts in Kentucky; in the Chicago public schools; and in the state of Hawaii, where she was a visiting professor recently. She identifies three fairly distinct types of school reform proposals.

The first type of school reform, pseudo-reform, involves spending funds to make superficial changes, or "symbolic politics," in which policymakers broadcast that significant reform efforts are needed or are underway. These efforts represent pseudo-reform, however, because no fundamental changes are made in the actual teaching-learning process. The second type, incremental reform, involves serious efforts to change classrooms for one group of children or within one sphere of educational activity. However, the "interconnectedness" of schools makes it "impossible to modify any one piece without also altering those pieces connected to it" (p. 141). As a result, such reform efforts tend to fade away because they do not pay sufficent attention to the fundamental arrangements that render schools resistant to major change.

The third type is school restructuring, which is described as involving either "fundamental and pervasive alterations in the way we organize and institutionalize education" (p. 142) or "alterations in the way in which public schools are governed and held accountable to the public" (p. 142). Raywid describes site-based management and choice as two of the most prevalent recent strategies for school restructuring. She briefly reviews research findings on the effectiveness of these two strategies and provides an interpretation of why site-based management has met with far less success than choice, that is, "officials' freeing and supporting teachers to design and implement distinctive programs among which families can choose" (p. 142). Raywid concludes her review with a prediction of one of three possible outcomes of the United States' current quest for excellence: that reform efforts will be limited to pseudo-reform; that school governance will be radically transformed, as has occurred recently in Kentucky and the Chicago schools; or that "genuine restructuring will begin in a less extreme and less roughshod fashion" (p. 143).

Raywid's article represents a brief yet thoughtful effort to tie together several educational phenomena that are treated separately in the research literature. By comparing these phenomena under the rubric of school improvement, the author draws important implications for school practitioners who may be engaged in, or considering undertaking, school improvement efforts.

A good professional review is beneficial to you because it contains both research evidence and explicit implications and recommendations for practice. It also tends to be brief and easy to understand. Furthermore, if the review was carried out by an organization or individual dealing with the specific topic or question that concerns you, the review may suggest guidelines or directions that are directly applicable to the educational decision with which you are faced.

The limitations of a professional review also need to be taken into account. They generally lack the rigor of a good primary source analysis, and therefore the reviewer's conclusions and recommendations may not be warranted. Also, some of these reviews are done by practitioners whose experience in the conduct or interpretation of educational research is limited. Thus you are advised to read for yourself some of the primary and secondary sources cited in a professional review before basing important educational decisions on its conclusions.

A good way to find professional reviews in the educational literature is to examine the types of journals that are intended for education professionals. For example, *The Reading Teacher* periodically publishes reviews that synthesize research findings relevant to schoolteachers. *Phi Delta Kappan,* the journal in which Raywid's article appears, contains articles citing research and drawing practical implications for many important educational issues, such as cooperative learning, educational technology, and recent trends in national assessments of student achievement.

Another strategy for identifying professional reviews is to scan the titles and abstracts of documents identified in your manual or computer search of preliminary sources. An example of a book that you might find in this way is entitled *Tools for Learning: A Guide to Teaching Study Skills,* in which we (Gall, Gall, Jacobsen, & Bullock, 1990) and our colleagues synthesized research findings concerning the effects of various study skills on student achievement. As suggested by the title, the book also provides explicit guidelines for teaching study skills. Thus it is an example of a comprehensive professional review in the area of study skills instruction.

As a practitioner you may be a regular or a casual reader of educational literature. Or perhaps you read research studies only when conducting a search of the literature to collect information bearing on a current question or problem. Whatever your situation, we recommend that you look for research syntheses like those described in this chapter when facing an important educational decision.

# Sample Research Synthesis:
# CAN COMPREHENSION BE TAUGHT?
# QUANTITATIVE SYNTHESIS OF
# "METACOGNITIVE" STUDIES

## Abstract[1]

To assess the effect of "metacognitive" instruction on reading comprehension, 20 studies, with a total student population of 1,553, were compiled and quantitatively synthesized. For 115 effect sizes, or contrasts of experimental and control groups' performance, the mean effect size was .71, which indicates a substantial effect. In this compilation of studies, metacognitive instruction was found particularly effective for junior high students (seventh and eighth grades). Among the metacognitive skills, awareness of textual inconsistency and the use of self-questioning as both a monitoring and a regulating strategy were most effective. Reinforcement was the most effective teaching strategy.

## Researchers' Comments[2]

Our study is an example of how three people with complementary interests and backgrounds can collaborate on research. Herb Walberg had led several groups of students and faculty who investigated nine factors that make learning productive. These teams eventually compared about 134 quantitative syntheses of 8,000 comparative studies and large-scale national surveys (Walberg, 1990).

Eileen Haller has a background in psychology and the teaching of reading. Having an interest in gaining further research experience beyond her Ph.D. dissertation, she discussed with Walberg the possibility of spending a year at the University of Illinois at Chicago to study new developments in the field of reading. It appeared to us that the most exciting research front was "meta-cognition." In reading research, the term emphasizes the child's evolving executive capacity to marshall knowledge and skills—not merely to exercise separate skills, but to choose which combinations to use to ask and answer questions of the text. The term also suggests the capacity to monitor progress and to replan if necessary.

Since it appeared that at least a dozen studies of metacognition had already been published, we chose not to do yet another. Rather we decided to conduct a meta-analysis of the accumulating work. As elaborated in the article, this means employing computer searches for relevant studies, "coding" (characterizing and recording) the features of each study, calculating "effect sizes" that indicate the magnitude of each study's effects, and evaluating the overall results.

Having collaborated on many previous syntheses, Walberg specified the procedures for coding of student samples, research methodology, and other study characteristics. Haller set forth the psychological aspects of reading methods for coding, conducted the search for studies, and coded them.

As the coding was completed, doctoral student David Child asked Walberg about the possibility of gaining research experience. Walberg recognized that David's statistical and word processing skills could contribute to the remaining work.

As the mounds of computer output and our written account of it grew, we began to realize the significance of the work. Meta-cognition is one of the hottest topics in psychological research and has a growing significance in educational practice. Our results showed strong and consistent effects of metacognitive instruction on students' reading comprehension.

We thought of trying to get the work published in the *Educational Researcher,* perhaps the most widely circulated and influential journal of educational research. Unfortunately, *ER* prefers short articles of wide interest rather than the 80-page highly technical document we had drafted. We struggled painfully through five revisions to reduce our findings to a 15-page manuscript, which *ER* published as the lead article with a picture of our office building on the front cover.

Haller presented the paper at the annual meeting of the American Educational Research Association and also in Madrid, Spain, at the European Association for Research in Learning and Instruction. At latest count, she has received 76 requests for reprints and the extended bibliography of the article. We are now writing another article aimed at reading teachers to point out the practical implications of the results, although they are treated briefly in a recent summary of similar syntheses (Walberg, 1990). We are also thinking of doing a similar synthesis of meta-cognitive instructional research in mathematics and science.

# Reference

WALBERG, H. J. (1990). Productive teaching and instruction: Assessing the knowledge base. *Phi Delta Kappan, 73,* 470–478.

# CAN COMPREHENSION BE TAUGHT? QUANTITATIVE SYNTHESIS OF "METACOGNITIVE" STUDIES

Eileen P. Haller
READING CONSULTANT
EVANSTON, ILLINOIS

David A. Child
GRADUATE STUDENT
UNIVERSITY OF ILLINOIS AT CHICAGO

Herbert J. Walberg
RESEARCH PROFESSOR OF EDUCATION
UNIVERSITY OF ILLINOIS AT CHICAGO

Psychologists have done considerable research on thinking and learning skills (Segal, Chipman, & Glaser, 1985). They have focused recently on "metacognitive" strategies aimed at facilitating reading comprehension. The purpose of this paper is to use quantitative synthesis or meta-analysis[3]* (Glass, McGaw, & Smith, 1981; Hedges & Olkin, 1985; Light & Pillemer, 1984) to examine the body of accumulated literature concerned with the effect of instruction of metacognitive skills on reading comprehension.

## Metacognition

While studying memory in young children, Flavell (1971) coined the term "metamemory," and soon the terms "metacognition" and "metacomprehension" came into use. The term metacognition is generally used to refer to the awareness, monitoring, and regulating of one's cognitive processes.

Recognition of the importance of these mental activities in the learning process contributed to the growing influence of a cognitive approach in research that began to displace the behaviorist orientation of the 1940s,

Haller, Eileen P., Child, David A., and Walberg, Herbert J. "Can Comprehension Be Taught: Quantitative Synthesis of 'Metacognitive' Studies." *Educational Researcher*, 1988, 17(9), 5–8. Copyright © 1988 by the American Educational Research Association. Reprinted by permission of the publisher.

* Numbered notes to articles are supplied by the authors of this text.

1950s, and 1960s. One consequence of this shift was a new focus on the mental activity of the learner. This interest was buttressed by the work of Piaget in Switzerland and Luria and Yudovich in the USSR. During the 1950s and 1960s, Piaget (Flavell, 1963) studied the maturation of the cognitive system; Luria and Yudovich (1959) investigated the interaction of language and verbal thinking in the cognitive development of young children; and Vygotsky's (1962) work was translated into English.

Behaviorism seemed insufficient for the development of effective instructional planning for comprehension of written materials. In an effort to understand comprehension better, Smith (1967) examined the reading strategies of eighth-grade students. She found that skilled comprehenders described planful interaction with the written content such as establishing goals or formulating questions, whereas less skilled readers relied mainly on rereading. Her investigation anticipated research in metacognition during the middle and late 1970s.

Another influence was computer science: Descriptions of higher cognitive functioning or metacognition as "higher order control processing . . . used in executing planning and decision making" (Sternberg, 1985, p. 226) and "the management of one's processing resources" (Chipman, 1985, p. 27) are similar to the earlier descriptions of the executor role in computer science (Miller, Galanter, & Pribram, 1960). The recognition of the learner as "an active problem-solver and processor of information" (Reeve & Brown, 1985, p. 344) directed attention toward mental activities such as awareness, monitoring, and regulating strategies.

Several writers have distinguished between the cognitive and metacognitive functions: Meichenbaum (1985) referred to cognition as the ongoing operations, such as memorizing, and described metacognition as the learner's overseeing of these cognitive operations. In a similar vein, Forrest-Pressley and Waller (1984) wrote, "Cognition refers to the actual processes and strategies that are used by the reader" and "metacognition is a construct that refers, first, to what a person knows about his or her cognitions and second, to the ability to control these cognitions" (p. 6).

## Metacognition and Reading Research

Because reading is a learned skill, metacognitive development can be studied as comprehension grows. Studies of instructional features and informational components in texts for instruction have contributed insight into metacognitive functioning. Such efforts to facilitate comprehension not only extend understanding of the metacognitive process but also can guide instructional planning.

Although the essence of metacognition is still being debated, there seems to be more agreement about the mental activities it comprises: awareness, monitoring, and regulating functions to aid faltering understanding. A description of the three clusters of mental activity follows.

### Awareness

Monitoring and adjusting of cognitive processing are facilitated by awareness of one's cognitive activities. For example, awareness of insufficient comprehension prompts the skilled reader to search for the source of the difficulty. Is the difficulty due mainly to the reader's lack of sufficient vocabulary or relevant background information, or is it due to the author's logic or presentation of the content?

Awareness also involves recognition of implicit as well as explicit information. In the current synthesis, awareness included responsiveness to the various textual components, to level of comprehension, to text dissonance or inaccuracies, and to explicit and implicit ideas.

### Monitoring

Monitoring checks comprehension during reading. Monitoring includes goal-directed reading to provide a meaningful framework in which to digest new information. Its importance was recognized by Betts (1954), who wrote, "The purpose of the reading controls comprehension" (p. 95). As noted above, Smith (1967) found that more-skilled readers initiated their own goal setting to facilitate comprehension.

Monitoring also includes self-questioning, paraphrasing, and summarizing. Text-related questions stimulate understanding and may reveal nuances missed by more passive readers whose minds are only vaguely engaged. Self-questioning may alert the reader to insufficient comprehension (Wong, 1985).

Other types of monitoring include integrating prior knowledge with content information; comparing main ideas; relating details to main ideas; and evaluating activities, such as confirming assumptions and making predictions.

### Regulating

Regulating consists of compensatory strategies to redirect and bolster faltering comprehension. When faltering ensues, rereading, backward and forward search strategies, self-questioning, contrasting textual information with prior knowledge, and comparing main ideas with each other and with details may restore comprehension.

Awareness, monitoring, and regulating improve with maturation and instruction (Baker & Brown, 1984; Chipman, 1985). They have practical utility because they suggest specific alterable practices. They deserve the research effort of the past decade as well as the present effort to synthesize the findings.

## Method
### Search Procedure

Five resources were used to search the literature for articles and reports concerning the effect of instruction of metacognitive skills on reading comprehension. Three data banks—the Educational Resource Information Center (ERIC), *Psychological Abstracts,* and *Dissertation Abstracts*—were searched by computer for 1975–86.[4] The descriptors used for these searches included metacognition with the following: reading comprehension, reading instruction, teaching methods, instructional psychology, and instruction.[5] *Reading Research Quarterly* was searched manually for relevant studies for 1975–87. All bibliographies of articles selected for inclusion were also searched. The searches identified 150 references for possible inclusion in the meta-analysis. Only 20 studies used metacognitive intervention, employed a control group for comparison, and provided statistical information necessary to compute effect sizes.[6] The remaining 130 sources either discussed metacognitive theory, reported correlations of metacognitive skills and comprehension scores, or reviewed the literature. Although they contained many useful insights, they did not meet the selection criteria. The majority seemed to be in agreement with our conclusion, although neither a measure of consensus nor a synthesis of views was the purpose of our work.

## Variables

A coding manual was devised to ensure consistency in the definition and description of each item.[7] The coding sheet was divided into 11 areas. The initial coding was the study identification, which included the author, year, and source. This was followed by characteristics of the setting, such as study sample size, comparison sample size, type of instructor (classroom teacher, other teaching personnel, experimenter, other), and location (urban, suburban, rural). Next came subject characteristics for ability level (most able, less able, or on grade level) and grade (2nd through 12th grade).

Treatment characteristics followed next. These included class length, number of treatments, difficulty levels of the reading materials, source of the reading selections (school instructional materials, experimenter-composed materials, other), and type of reading selection (expository or narrative). Another coding area was procedural threats to validity; this pertains to whether the control group was aware of a treatment group and whether there was compensation for possible Hawthorne effects.[8]

The instructional coding included the three clusters of metacognitive skills—awareness, monitoring, and adjusting. The first included awareness of text organization, level of comprehension during reading, text dissonance and inaccuracies, and explicit and implicit ideas. Monitoring skills included intentionality (instruction preplan-

ning, formulation of purpose, or a goal-directed activity), monitoring activities (checking of understanding through self-questioning, summarizing, synthesizing, or paraphrasing), self-directing activities (comparing main ideas, relating details to main ideas, integrating textual information with prior knowledge), and evaluating activities (testing prediction or assumptions confirming hypothesis). Adjusting strategies included rereading, backward-forward search, self-questioning, and main idea-details comparison. The instructional coding also included a description of the method of instruction (direct instruction, such as lecture, demonstration modeling, discussion, reinforcement feedback, practice, handouts, other).

Information also was included on follow-up (whether one was done and if so, how long after the posttest;[9] whether the outcome measure was the same as the posttest), design characteristics (such as random assignment of subjects to treatment and control groups), and other threats to validity (based on Campbell & Stanley, 1963).[10]

## Analysis

Glass et al.'s (1981) meta-analytic approach was used to transform findings to effect sizes.[11] A general linear model using the Statistical Analysis System (SAS) was used to assess the distributions of effect sizes.[12]

The number of effect sizes in each study ranged from 1 to 20. To avoid having a few studies with a large number of effect sizes bias the statistical results, each study was assigned a weight of 1. For example, if a study had only one effect size, that effect size would have a weight of 1, but if a study had 20 effect sizes, each individual effect size would have a weight of $1/20$. This not only gives each study equal weight but also complies with the statistical requirement for inference by allowing one degree of freedom for each piece of independent information.[13]

One outlier effect size, 4.80, was found to be extreme in comparison to the others.[14] This effect size was one of two effect sizes in one study (Duffy et al., 1987). The comparisons were based on standardized tests, the Michigan Educational Assessment Program (MEAP) and the Stanford Achievement Test. The difference between the effect sizes (4.80 and .245, respectively) was large. This discrepancy may be due, in part, to the difference in test features, such as administration (the MEAP is given over a number of days), norming (the MEAP is normed statewide, whereas the Stanford Achievement Test is nationally normed), and purpose (the Stanford Achievement Test provides a means for comparing classes, whereas the MEAP generally is used to identify schools and educational districts that may need state assistance). Also, the MEAP is given yearly, so familiarity with the instrument and its reputation may influence instructional approaches. Because of this large difference, it was decided to "winsorize" or set this effect size equal to the next lower effect size (3.80) to offset the possibility of this large effect size's biasing the total results (Dixon & Massey, 1983, p. 380).[15]

## Results

Figure 1 shows the results from 1,553 students in the 20 studies.[16] The mean effect size for the 20 studies was .71, with a standard deviation of .81; the median effect size was .57. The average effect size of .71 is among the larger ones that have been uncovered in educational research. Among 26 effects of instructional techniques that have been estimated, it is exceeded only by the estimated effects of reinforcement, acceleration, instruction of students to vary their reading pace, instructional cues and feedback, and cooperative learning (Walberg, 1984).[17]

Of 115 comparisons, 87% were positive.[18] The stem and leaf distribution in Figure 1 shows the typical positive skew with outliers (Walberg, 1986).

We selected $p = .05$ as the minimum significance level.[19] The year of publication is significant, and the results suggest that earlier studies had lower effect sizes than more recent ones. Study size was also significant; studies with smaller sample sizes produced larger effects. Neither instructor nor setting, major characteristics of the natural classroom situation, was significant; but location was. The results show that urban students benefited more from instruction than rural or suburban students.

Although the analysis showed that the Hawthorne effects were not significant,[20] a caveat should be kept in mind: "The increased energy and attention devoted to tasks by teachers in experimental groups rather than the nominal treatments themselves may partly account for superior results of treatment over control groups in teaching methods and other educational studies" (Walberg, 1986, p. 220; also see Pflaum, Walberg, Karegianes, & Rasher, 1980).

The lack of significance between the means of the outcome measures suggests that the various types of measures, including standardized tests, were equally effective measures of the impact of the metacognitive interventions, a surprising result, as there has been con-

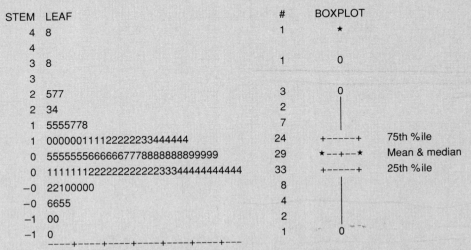

Figure 1  Stem and Leaf Distribution and Boxplot of Effect Sizes of the Unwinsorized Sample

cern (Paris, Cross, & Lipson, 1984) that gains in comprehension, evident on experimenter-designed measures, were not reflected on nationally standardized tests.

## Age Effects

Effects were largest for the seventh and eighth grades, close to the age when Piaget described formal logical operations as reaching full maturity (Flavell, 1963). The next highest effects were for the second and third grades; however, the second-grade results were based on only one study (Duffy et al., 1987; possible reasons for this high score were discussed above). Metacognitive instruction seems to have had the least influence on students in the fourth, fifth, and sixth grades. Chall (1983) suggested that fourth grade is a transition point when the conceptual demands of instruction significantly increase. She noted that even students able to read stories may inadequately comprehend content selections. This may be due, in part, to a shifting curriculum emphasis from learning to read to reading to learn and, as classroom observations have shown (Durkin, 1978–79), little instruction time is allotted to comprehension.

## Instructional Variations

Although class length, number of treatments, and duration of instruction were significant time variables, inconsistencies in these findings suggest additional research could provide further clarification. The patterns of findings, however, show that 10 minutes or less of instruction per lesson is insufficient.

Analysis of awareness, monitoring, and regulating suggests that some metacognitive activities were more effective than others. These include the textual-dissonance approach in awareness, the self-questioning strategy in monitoring, and the backward-forward and self-questioning approaches in regulating.

Among instructional approaches, reinforcement stood out as significantly greater in its effect. The results suggest, however, that the more instructional features involved, the more effective the results. Because students may respond differently to different instructional features, the more varied the approach, the more students may be positively affected.

## Conclusions

"Can comprehension be taught?" Results from this body of research suggest a strongly affirmative answer, for the average effect is substantial. Although metacognitive instruction was helpful at all grade levels, it seemed particularly effective for seventh and eighth graders.

The findings are relevant for optimal conditions of instruction, because several metacognitive skills are particularly effective. These include awareness of textual inconsistency and the use of self-questioning as both a monitoring and a regulating strategy. In addition, the findings of this study suggest that the use of reinforcement and several, rather than a few, instructional modes increases comprehension.

Finally, several areas of research seem in order: Because metacognition facilitates reading comprehension, it may be applicable not only across content areas but also across skill areas such as creative writing, composing, and artistic endeavors. Moreover, because the differential effects of metacognitive components were unclear, further theoretical and operational clarification is required. None of this, however, should obscure the main message of the existing literature: The average effect of metacognitive instruction on reading comprehension is substantial.

## References

BAKER, L., & BROWN, A. L. (1984). Metacognitive skills and reading. In P. D. Pearson (Ed.) & R. Barr, M. L. Kamil, & P. Mosenthal (Section Eds.), *Handbook of reading research* (pp. 353–394). New York: Longman.

BETTS, E. A. (1954). *Foundations of reading instruction.* New York: American Book Company.

CAMPBELL, D. T., & STANLEY, J. C. (1963). *Experimental and quasi-experimental designs for research.* Boston: Houghton Mifflin.

CHALL, J. (1983). *Stages of reading development.* New York: McGraw-Hill.

CHIPMAN, S. F. (1985). Introduction. In J. W. Segal, S. F. Chipman, & R. Glaser (Eds.), *Thinking and learning skills: Vol. 2. Research and open questions* (pp. 19–35). Hillsdale, NJ: Erlbaum.

DIXON, W. J., & MASSEY, F. J., JR. (1983). *Introduction to statistical analysis* (4th ed.). New York: McGraw-Hill.

DUFFY, G. G., ROEHLER, L. R., SIVAN, E., RACKLIFFE, G., BOOK, C., MELOTH, M., VAVRUS, L., WESSELMAN, R., PUTNAM, J., & BASSIRI, D. (1987). Effects of explaining the mental processing associated with using reading strategies on the awareness and achievement of low group third graders. *Reading Research Quarterly, 22,* 347–368.

DURKIN, D. (1978–79). What classroom observations reveal about reading comprehension instruction. *Reading Research Quarterly, 14*, 481–533.

FLAVELL, J. H. (1963). *The developmental psychology of Jean Piaget.* New York: Van Nostrand.

FLAVELL, J. H. (1971). First discussant's comments: What is memory development the development of? *Human Development, 14*, 272–278.

FORREST-PRESSLEY, D.-L., & WALLER, T. G. (1984). *Cognition, metacognition, and reading.* New York: Springer-Verlag.

GLASS, G. V., MCGAW, B., & SMITH, M. L. (1981). *Meta-analysis in social research.* Beverly Hills, CA: Sage.

HEDGES, L. V., & OLKIN, I. (1985). *Statistical methods for meta-analysis.* Orlando, FL: Academic Press.

LIGHT, R. J., & PILLEMER, D. B. (1984). *Summing up: The science of reviewing research.* Cambridge, MA: Harvard University Press.

LURIA, A. R., & YUDOVICH, F. I. (1959). *Speech and the development of mental processes in the child: An experimental investigation.* (J. Simon, Ed.; O. Kovasc & J. Simon, Trans.) London: Staples.

MEICHENBAUM, D. (1985). Teaching thinking: A cognitive-behavioral perspective. In J. W. Segal, S. F. Chipman, & R. Glaser (Eds.), *Thinking and learning skills: Vol. 2. Research and open questions* (pp. 407–426). Hillsdale, NJ: Erlbaum.

MILLER, G. A., GALANTER, E., & PRIBRAM, K. H. (1960). *Plans and the structure of behavior.* New York: Holt.

PARIS, S., CROSS, R. D., & LIPSON, M. Y. (1984). Informed strategies for learning: A program to improve children's reading awareness and comprehension. *Journal of Educational Psychology, 76*, 1239–1252.

PFLAUM, S. W., WALBERG, H. J., KAREGIANES, M. L., & RASHER, S. P. (1980). Reading instruction: A quantitative analysis. *Educational Researcher, 9*(7), 12–18.

REEVE, R. A., & BROWN, A. L. (1985). Metacognition reconsidered: Implications for intervention research. *Journal of Abnormal Child Psychology, 13*, 343–356.

SEGAL, J. W., CHIPMAN, S. F., & GLASER, R. (1985). *Thinking and learning skills: Vol. 1. Relating instruction to research.* Hillsdale, NJ: Erlbaum.

SMITH, H. K. (1967). The responses of good and poor readers when asked to read for different purposes. *Reading Research Quarterly, 3*, 56–83.

STERNBERG, R. J. (1985). Instrumental and componential approaches to the nature and training of intelligence. In J. W. Segal, S. F. Chipman, & R. Glaser (Eds.), *Thinking and learning skills: Vol. 2. Research and open questions* (pp. 215–244). Hillsdale, NJ: Erlbaum.

VYGOTSKY, L. S. (1962). *Thought and language* (E. Hanfmann & G. Vakar, Eds. & Trans.). Cambridge, MA: MIT Press.

WALBERG, H. J. (1984). Improving the productivity of America's schools. *Educational Leadership, 41*(8), 19–30.

WALBERG, H. J. (1986). Synthesis of research on teaching. In M. C. Wittrock (Ed.), *Handbook of research on teaching* (3rd ed., pp. 214–229). Washington, DC: American Educational Research Association.

WONG, B. Y. L. (1985). Self-questioning instructional research: A review. *Review of Educational Research, 55*, 227–268.

# Critical Review

The researchers' purpose was to review the body of accumulated research to determine whether teaching metacognitive skills to students improves their reading comprehension. Few teachers probably provide this type of instruction, so a massive amount of in-service effort would be needed to help teachers learn and implement it. If policymakers recommend this investment of effort, they would want to be certain that research findings support this type of instruction. The researchers concluded from their review that metacognitive skills instruction does improve reading comprehension.

The researchers used a thorough search procedure, and so the 150 references they found were probably a fairly complete selection of the literature on metacognition available at that time. Had they checked the 20 selected studies in the *Social Science Citation Index,* however, they might have found some additional studies because researchers who cite a study often report work related to it.

The fact that the reviewers identified 150 relevant studies demonstrates the value of seeking published meta-analyses in one's own literature search. Finding and reviewing all studies on popular research topics would be extremely time-consuming for a busy educator conducting a literature search.

It is important for reviewers to make their criteria for study selection explicit so that readers can decide whether the criteria were unbiased. Reviewers conceivably could include only studies whose results support their views about what is effective. In this review, the criteria for study selection were rigorous, focusing on evidence from experimental and quasi-experimental research designs. Although some potentially useful correlational studies were thus omitted, the selection of 20 studies is sufficient to give us considerable confidence in the meta-analysis results.

The coding of characteristics of the 20 studies was important in this review because metacognitive skills instruction appears to be effective only in certain situations. For example, the reviewers report that metacognitive instruction seems to have the most influence on students in seventh and eighth grades and the least influence on students in fourth, fifth, and sixth grades.

More information about the outcome measures in the reviewed studies would have been helpful. Reading comprehension can be measured in various ways, each way reflecting a different view of what reading comprehension is. For example, comprehension can mean the ability to understand the literal message of a text, or it can mean the ability to make appropriate inferences from the text. Furthermore, comprehension can vary for different types of text (e.g., fiction vs. nonfiction or historical vs. scientific). Because the reviewers did not describe the outcome measures in detail, we do not know what types of reading comprehension are improved by instruction in metacognitive skills.

We think that the reviewers made a good decision in considering the largest effect size to be an outlier and to reduce it to the next largest value. It is good review procedure to tell readers why they consider a certain person, sample, or effect size to be an outlier and how it was handled in the review. Readers thus are in a position to make their own judgment about whether the treatment of outliers was appropriate.

The reviewers reported that the mean effect size for the 115 comparisons included in their meta-analysis was .71, among the larger ones that have been uncovered in educational research. However, Figure 1 shows that some of the effect sizes were quite small or even negative. (A negative effect size means that metacognitive skills instruction was less effective than the instruction given to the control group.) The reviewers might have gained additional insights by examining closely these small or negative effect sizes. They could have prepared a table listing the variables measured and effect sizes found in each study, a feature often included in published meta-analyses. To the reviewers' credit, they included a note indicating how interested readers could obtain this information by mail.

# Chapter References

CURRY, L. (1990). A critique of the research on learning styles. *Educational Leadership, 48*(2), 50–55.

GAGE, N. L. (1978) *The scientific basis of the art of teaching.* New York: Teachers College Press.

GALL, M. D., GALL, J. P., JACOBSEN, D. R., & BULLOCK, T. L. (1990). *Tools for learning: A guide to teaching study skills.* Alexandria, VA: Association for Supervision and Curriculum Development.

GLASS, G. V (1976). Primary, secondary, and meta-analysis of research. *Educational Researcher, 5,* 3–8.

HALLER, E. P., CHILD, D. A., & WALBERG, H. J. (1988). Can comprehension be taught? A quantitative synthesis of "metacognitive" studies. *Educational Researcher, 17*(9), 5–8.

JACKSON, G. B. (1980). Methods for integrative reviews. *Review of Educational Research, 50,* 438–460.

POWELL, D. R. (1986). Research in review: Parent education and support programs. *Young Children, 41*(3), 47–52.

RAYWID, M. A. (1990). The evolving effort to improve schools: Pseudo-reform, incremental reform, and restructuring. *Phi Delta Kappan, 72*(2), 139–143.

ROSENSHINE, B. (1971). *Teaching behaviors and student achievement.* London: National Foundation for Educational Research in England and Wales.

SHIPMAN, S., & SHIPMAN, V. C. (1985). Cognitive styles: Some conceptual, methodological, and applied issues. In *Review of research in education,* ed. E. W. Gordon. Washington, DC: American Educational Research Association.

SLAVIN, R. E. (1986). Best-evidence synthesis: An alternative to meta-analytic and traditional reviews. *Educational Researcher, 15*(9), 5–11.

WITKIN, H. A., MOORE, C. A., GOODENOUGH, D. R., & COX, P. W. (1977). Field dependent and field independent cognitive styles and their educational implications. *Review of Educational Research, 47,* 1–64.

# Recommended Reading

COOPER, H. M. (1989) *Integrating research.* Newbury Park, CA: Sage.

This book emphasizes the importance of using rigorous methodology in reviewing and integrating previous research findings. Each stage of the research review process is discussed in depth.

HUNTER, J. E., & SCHMIDT, F. L. (1990). *Methods of meta-analysis.* Newbury Park, CA: Sage.

The authors provide an overview of various methods that can be used to obtain average results across studies. Much of the book focuses on psychometric meta-analysis, an approach developed by the authors to integrate research findings. This approach is unique in that it provides a means of estimating how much variance across studies is due to various artifacts. Their approach appears to overcome most of the problems that have been raised about meta-analytic procedures by providing methods to adjust for the effects of these artifacts.

LIGHT, R., & PILLEMER, D. B. (1984). *Summing up: The science of reviewing research.* Cambridge, MA: Harvard University Press.

In this classic book, the authors discuss typical weaknesses of narrative reviews and present guidelines for conducting quantitative reviews. The book includes a detailed 10-item checklist for evaluating one's own or others' research reviews.

TYLER, R. W. (1984). A guide to educational trouble-shooting. *Educational Leadership, 41*(8), 27–30.

This article appeared in the same issue as Walberg's meta-analytic synthesis of factors influencing student learning. Tyler praises Walberg's work as an example of a "macro study" and argues that education needs both macro and micro studies to progress. Tyler discusses the practical use of the results of research for trouble-shooting and notes the importance of shedding more light on two major problems of school learning, that is, the problems of transfer and retention.

WALBERG, H. J. (1984). Improving the productivity of America's schools. *Educational Leadership, 41*(8), 19–27.

In this classic article Walberg discusses results from several meta-analytic studies carried out by him and his colleagues to synthesize the findings from 3000 studies about student learning. Nine factors are identified that require optimization to increase affective, behavioral, and cognitive learning. The article includes a table summarizing effect sizes on learning for 26 different instructional methods.

# Application Problems

1. Based on the descriptions, indicate whether each of the following research syntheses represents a primary source analysis, a conceptual-methodological critique, or a professional review.

   **a.** "The Character of Discussion: A Focus on Students" (Bridges, 1990). The reviewer synthesizes the research literature to determine whether classroom activity meets the criteria of a true discussion and proposes that the best way for the teacher to foster a true discussion is not to lead it but to help students lead it.

   **b.** "Parent-Teacher Conferences" (Epstein, 1988). The reviewer distinguishes between group and individual parent-teacher conferences and reviews the research literature to identify effective procedures to use before the conference, during the conference, and after the conference.

   **c.** "Studying" (Anderson & Armbruster, 1984). The reviewers define studying as a form of reading associated with the requirement to perform identifiable cognitive and/or procedural tasks. They summarize research on the *state variables* (e.g., knowledge of the criterion task) and *processing variables* (e.g., focusing attention) involved in studying and recommend that future research focus not on a quest to find the perfect studying strategy but rather on ways to make the studying techniques identified compatible with the demands of different instructional programs, disciplines, and student backgrounds.

   **d.** "Effects of Practice on Aptitude and Achievement Test Scores" (Kulik, Kulik, & Bangert, 1984). The reviewers synthesize the results of 40 studies examining the relationship between practice tests and achievement on a subsequent criterion measure by calculating the difference between the initial average score on a test and the final average, divided by the standard deviation of the initial scores.

2. In a meta-analysis of the effect of practice tests on students' achievement test scores (Kulik, Kulik, & Bangert, 1984), the reviewers report that the average effect size for treatments involving one practice test was .42 when students took an identical form of the test and .23 when students took a parallel test. The average effect size for treatments involving seven

practice trials was 1.89 when students took an identical test and .74 when students took a parallel test. Which of the following statements is/are true, based on these results?

  **a.** Taking one practice test before taking an achievement test has an effect on students' scores on the achievement test that is practically significant.

  **b.** The more practice students had before taking the achievement test, the greater the improvement in their scores on the achievement test.

  **c.** Practice on an identical form of the test improves performance on the achievement test more than practice on a parallel form of the test.

**3.** Check the most recent five years of *Education Index, CIJE, RIE,* and *Psychological Abstracts* at your university library and identify a research synthesis relating to a problem of interest to you. Specify two or more descriptors that you can include in your search to find research syntheses.

**4.** Using the six criteria for evaluating research syntheses discussed in this chapter, read and evaluate the research synthesis you identified in problem 3 above.

# Chapter Notes

1. The abstract from the article is reprinted here to help you understand the researchers' comments.
2. This commentary was written by Dr. Herbert J. Walberg and Eileen P. Haller.
3. Meta-analysis is a statistical method used to determine the general trend of findings in a set of research studies on the same topic.
4. Data banks (also called preliminary sources) are regularly updated indexes to journal articles, conference papers, doctoral dissertations, and other documents. The data banks are available in bound volumes or computer files.
5. Descriptors are labels used to categorize topics discussed in a publication. The use of descriptors helps a reviewer find all studies on the same topic in a data bank.
6. A metacognitive intervention is an effort by the researcher to train or stimulate students to use metacognitive processes. The control group is a sample of students who do not receive the intervention; this group is compared to an experimental group, which does receive the intervention. Effect sizes are explained in note 11.
7. A coding manual is used so that different reviewers will code the characteristics of a study in the same way. Several reviewers are used to help prevent the biases of a single reviewer from affecting how a study is coded.
8. A procedural threat to validity is a flaw in the design of the study that allows a factor other than the intended intervention (in this case, metacognitive training) to affect the behavior of the experimental and control groups. The flaw threatens the study because the reviewer cannot determine whether the intended intervention or some other factor is causing observed differences in the learning of the two groups. Hawthorne effects are explained in note 20.
9. A posttest is a test given right after the training period in an experiment to measure immediate learning. A follow-up test may be given at a later time to measure retention of learning.
10. Threats to validity were explained in footnote 8. Campbell and Stanley (1963) classified the common flaws (threats to validity) that can make it difficult to interpret the results of an experiment. The reviewers used this classification system to identify flaws in the metacognitive studies.

11. An effect size indicates the difference between the mean scores of the experimental and control groups on a posttest. The difference score is adjusted so that experimental-control group differences on different posttests can be compared. For example, the experimental group may differ from the control group by 10 points on a 50-item posttest and by 3 points on a 20-item test. The calculation of effect sizes allows the reviewer to determine whether one difference is greater than the other regardless of the length and other characteristics of the posttests.

12. Statistical Analysis System is a computer software program used to perform various statistical analyses on data.

13. A test of statistical inference (also called a test of statistical significance) allows the researcher to determine whether the results for a sample can be generalized to the population that it represents. For this test to be valid, each person (or in this review, each effect size) cannot be influenced by others in the sample (hence, "independent"). Each effect size in the sample contributes a degree of freedom, which is part of the test of statistical inference. More degrees of freedom allow one to make more certain generalizations from the sample to the population.

14. An outlier in this context is an effect size that is much larger or smaller than others in the sample. The magnitude of the difference is substantial enough to cause concern that the effect size is not a normal variation in the population of effect sizes that it presumably represents.

15. Winsorizing, as explained by the authors, is a procedure used to adjust an unusually large or small effect size so that it does not distort a statistical analysis.

16. The stem-and-leaf distribution is shown in the left half of Figure 1. This display allows the reader to see graphically all the effect sizes that were reviewed. For example, look at the first line of numerals under Stem Leaf, that is, 4 8. The 4 is the effect size's stem, and the 8 is its leaf, for an effect size of 4.8. Now examine the line of numerals 2 577 further down in the column. This line represents three effect sizes: 2.5, 2.7, and 2.7. If you count all the numerals under Leaf, you will find that there are 115. When you combine each of these numerals with its corresponding stem, you get 115 effect sizes. Thus the 20 studies included in the review involved 115 posttest comparisons between an experimental and a control group.

    The next column in Figure 1 is labeled #. Each number under this heading is the number of effect sizes for a particular stem and its leaves. If you add the numbers under #, you will find that the total is 115.

    The column labeled Boxplot shows how the effect sizes are clustered. It is apparent that most of the effect sizes (the twenty-fifth to the seventy-fifth percentiles) ranged between 0.1 and 1.4. The mean effect size was somewhere between 0.5 and 0.9, as shown in Figure 1, and the text states that the exact mean was .71.

17. In another study the reviewers computed the effect size for many instructional techniques (26, to be exact) that have been researched. The effect size for metacognitive instruction (.71) is relatively large, indicating that it is one of the more powerful techniques known to improve student learning.

18. Four of the stems in Figure 1 are negative ($-0$, $-0$, $-1$, $-1$). These negative effect sizes mean that the difference between the experimental and control groups' mean scores on a posttest favored the control group.

19. A significance level is a measure yielded by doing a particular kind of statistical test on a set of data. In this study the test was done to decide whether an observed difference (for example, the difference between the average effect size for all studies that involved urban schools and the average effect size for all studies that involved rural schools) can be

generalized from the sample studied to the population from which it was drawn. A significance level (represented by the symbol $p$) of .05 or less is considered sufficient by most researchers to conclude that a result can be generalized from the sample to the population.

20. A Hawthorne effect results when participants in a study work harder because the experimenters are present and paying attention to them. If a Hawthorne effect occurred in these metacognitive studies, it would mean that experimental students learned more than control students not because of the metacognitive intervention but simply because the teachers put more effort into the instruction or because the students worked harder due to the presence of the experimenters.

# PART IV

# TYPES OF EDUCATIONAL RESEARCH

Part Four includes seven chapters, each describing a different type of educational research. We begin with a chapter on qualitative research, followed by chapters on four types of quantitative research: descriptive, causal-comparative, correlational, and experimental. The last two chapters cover evaluation and action research, both of which are especially useful to practitioners. Complete reports of published research studies that illustrate these research methods are presented in each chapter.

Chapter 9 is about qualitative research, a distinctly different approach from quantitative research, which until recently dominated the field of educational research. We describe how qualitative researchers define their purpose, approach the tasks of sampling and making generalizations, relate to the individuals being studied, deal with the issues of values and context, and collect and analyze data. Three major types of qualitative research (case study, historical, and ethnographic) are described, as well as criteria for evaluating such studies. We also compare qualitative research methods with those of quantitative research. Therefore, by reading this chapter first, you will have a better understanding of the subsequent chapters on quantitative research.

Chapter 10 explains the important contribution that descriptive research makes to education. As its name implies, the purpose of this type of research is to produce quantitatively based descriptions of educational phenomena. Two common forms of descriptive research—survey and observation—are discussed.

Chapter 11 is about causal-comparative research. Like experimental research, this method explores possible cause-and-effect relationships between variables. However, causal-comparative research uses simpler design and data analysis procedures than those required by experimental research. We explain the conditions under which causal-comparative research is preferable and how to interpret the findings.

Chapter 12 concerns the correlational research method, which enables researchers to investigate the precise degree of relationship between two or more variables. One type of correlational research is relationship research, in which possible cause-and-effect relationships between variables are examined. It is similar to causal-comparative research except for the statistical procedures used to analyze

191

the data. The other type is prediction research, in which particular variables are measured at one time and used to predict the performance of individuals on a criterion variable at a later time.

Our discussion of quantitative research methods concludes in Chapter 13, which describes various experimental research designs. We explain the advantages of experiments for determining true cause-and-effect relationships between variables. We explain internal validity, which involves the extent to which observed effects are due to the experimental treatment rather than to nontreatment factors called extraneous variables. We also explain external validity, which involves the extent to which experimental results can be generalized to other persons, settings, and times from those in the research. We distinguish true experiments, in which individuals are randomly assigned to treatment and control groups, from quasi-experiments, which do not involve random assignment. The last section of the chapter is about a special type of experiment, the single-subject experiment, which involves interventions administered to a single individual or group.

In Chapter 14 we discuss the advantages of using evaluation research findings to make important decisions about educational practice. The major characteristics and uses of evaluation research in education are described, and six criteria for judging an educational evaluation study are presented. We briefly compare quantitative and qualitative models of evaluation research and conclude the chapter by presenting a sample evaluation study based on the quantitative model.

Chapter 15 provides a shift from the perspective of the educational practitioner as primarily a consumer of research findings. It explains the value of conducting your own action research to solve educational problems that arise in practice. We discuss how action research differs from formal research and illustrate the steps in a typical action research project.

As mentioned, Part Four includes actual reports of research studies to illustrate the various types of educational research that are discussed. Comments written by the primary author-researcher precede each report, and our critical review follows the report. We recommend that you refer back to the introduction to Part Three, where we described more thoroughly the format in which the sample studies are presented and a strategy for reading them to maximize your understanding of educational research.

# CHAPTER 9

# QUALITATIVE RESEARCH

## Overview

Qualitative research in education employs methods originally developed in the social sciences, especially anthropology, sociology, history, and psychology. The major advantage of these methods is that they allow the researcher to study an individual instance of a phenomenon in great depth. In this chapter we describe qualitative methods of inquiry and how they differ from quantitative research methods, which you will study in subsequent chapters. We also describe the main types of qualitative research: case studies, historical studies, and ethnographic studies. The chapter concludes with a description of a form in Appendix 4 for evaluating qualitative research reports.

## Objectives

1. Explain the purpose of qualitative research.
2. Describe the typical approach of qualitative researchers to sampling and making generalizations.
3. Explain how qualitative researchers relate to the individuals they study.
4. Explain how qualitative researchers deal with values and context in interpreting their findings.
5. Explain how qualitative researchers collect and analyze data.
6. Describe the strengths and weaknesses of qualitative research.
7. Describe the distinguishing characteristics of case studies, historical studies, and ethnographic studies.
8. Explain how the personal characteristics of the researcher can affect the overall quality of a qualitative research study.
9. Compare qualitative and quantitative research in their general approach to issues of research design and interpretation.

## Introduction

In the preceding chapters, you learned that educational researchers do not use one method of investigation exclusively. Rather, their sampling procedures, measurement tools, and research designs vary greatly, depending on the problem being investigated.

The various methods used in educational research can be grouped into two classifications: quantitative research and qualitative research. Quantitative research methods in education are adapted in large part from the physical and biological sciences. Measurement procedures used in these scientific disciplines typically yield statistical

*Physical + Biological* (handwritten margin note)

analyses of numerical data; hence the label "quantitative research." Until the past decade, most educational research was of this type.

*Qualitative Research* (handwritten margin note)

In recent years educational researchers have turned their attention to investigative methods used in the social and behavioral sciences, especially anthropology, sociology, history, psychology, and linguistics. Humanistic disciplines such as philosophy and aesthetic criticism also have provided useful methods. Studies that employ these various methods of inquiry are called "qualitative research" because their measurement procedures usually involve verbal descriptions and interpretations rather than statistical analysis of numerical data.

*Verbal descriptions + Interpretation* (handwritten margin note)

Chapters 6 and 7 explain how quantitative and qualitative research differ in their approach to sampling and measurement, respectively. In this part of the book we explain the different types of research designs that they employ. This chapter describes qualitative research designs, and the next four chapters (10–13) describe quantitative research designs. Two other chapters (14 and 15) describe types of research that can involve either quantitative or qualitative designs.

# How Qualitative Research
# Differs from Quantitative Research

To explain the characteristics of qualitative research and how it differs from quantitative research, we will use examples of published research. The qualitative research report, entitled "Giving Voice to High School Students: Pressure and Boredom, Ya Know What I'm Saying?" was written by Edwin Farrell, George Peguero, Rasheed Lindsey, and Ronald White (1988). The study was designed to identify the problems of students at risk of dropping out of high school. The quantitative research report, entitled "Modifying School Attendance of Special Education High School Students," was written by Barbara Licht, Tracy Gard, and Chet Guardino (1991). It was designed to evaluate the effectiveness of an experimental program to improve the school attendance of students classified as learning disabled, emotionally handicapped, physically handicapped, or mildly retarded.

**PURPOSE**

The purpose of qualitative research is to develop an understanding of individuals and events in their natural state, taking into account the relevant context. For example, many qualitative researchers try to understand the phenomenological reality of particular individuals or groups and the cultural settings within which they function. (By "phenomenological reality," we mean an individual's perceptions of inner experiences and the world around her.) These researchers have a keen interest in the methods used by anthropologists, historians, artists, and other groups who seek to understand a time and place from the perspective of the participants.

By contrast, the purpose of quantitative research is to make objective descriptions of a limited set of phenomena and also to determine whether the phenomena can be controlled through certain interventions. Thus, initial quantitative studies of a research problem typically involve a precise description of the phenomena and a search for pertinent variables and their interrelationships. Subsequently, experiments are undertaken to determine whether the manipulation of certain variables produces effects on other variables. Ultimately, a theory is formulated to account for the empirical findings. These purposes and methods of quantitative researchers in education also characterize the inquiries of other scientists, for example, physicists, biologists, and economists.

The contrasting purposes of qualitative and quantitative research can be found in our two research examples. In the qualitative study, Farrell and his collaborators were concerned about solving the dropout problem of at-risk students. They felt that any solutions must be "based on the perceptions of students rather than on educational theory" (p. 489). Accordingly, the purpose of their study was to learn "what the lives of the students were like and how school fitted into those lives" (p. 489). In the quantitative study, Licht and her colleagues sought to test the effectiveness of an experimental program intended to improve school attendance of special education students. The design of the program was based not on perceptions of students about their condition but rather on findings of previous research and the researchers' own ideas about how to solve the problem.

## GENERALIZABILITY AND SAMPLING

Qualitative research is predicated on the assumption that each individual, each culture, and each setting is unique. Furthermore, qualitative researchers consider it important to study and appreciate this uniqueness. Thus, they carry out case studies of individuals, and they may replicate their findings by doing additional case studies. If replication occurs, they may propose tentative generalizations. Their tentativeness reflects the researchers' awareness that such generalizations are context-dependent, meaning that they may lose their validity from one setting to the next or from one time period to another.

Quantitative researchers make a different assumption, namely, that they can discover "laws" that lead to reliable prediction and control of educational phenomena. They view their task as the discovery of these laws by searching for regularities in the behavior of samples of individuals. This search is aided by statistical analysis, which reveals trends in the sample's behavior. Quantitative researchers believe that such trends or laws are sufficiently strong to have practical value, even though they do not allow for perfect prediction or control.

In the qualitative study, the primary researcher recruited at-risk students as collaborators to interview other at-risk students about their concerns. The collaborators conducted 77 interviews of 61 different individuals (an unusually large sample for a qualitative study). Although the data were analyzed for group trends, atypical cases were noted. Furthermore, excerpts from individual interviews were included to give the flavor of the individual case. For example: "A young woman in a dialogue that turned to sexual attitudes complained to one of my (male) collaborators of the sexual pressures she felt, 'Y'all have to sit there and say, 'Yeah, I did this with this girl. I had sex.' Why y'all think sex made you all men?' " (Farrell et al., 1988, p. 493).

In our example of quantitative research, the investigators selected a sample of 20 special education students and randomly assigned them to the experimental program (involving tangible rewards for good attendance and individualized parental contact whenever students were absent) or to the control condition (involving no rewards or individualized parental contact). The research data were analyzed to determine whether the experimental program was generally more effective in improving class attendance than the control condition. Data for individual students were not analyzed or reported.

## RELATIONSHIP OF RESEARCHER TO SUBJECT

In qualitative research, the researcher deliberately interacts in a personal way with each individual in the study. Thus, the researcher's data collection procedures are open to modification depending on how the individual acts. Furthermore, the researcher is free to use her intuition and judgment as a basis for deciding how to frame questions or how to make observations. Similarly, the individual being studied may be given opportunities to volunteer ideas and perceptions and even to participate in the analysis of the data.

In quantitative research, the investigators' goal is objectivity. That is, they seek to keep their personal values, beliefs, and biases from influencing the data collection and analysis process. Thus, they typically administer tests and other paper-and-pencil measures that involve minimal personal interaction between them and the research sample. If interaction is necessary, as when conducting an interview, they try to standardize the interaction process so that it is identical for every individual in the sample. Conversely, the sample's role in the study is relatively passive. Their function is to react to the researcher's questions and interventions. They are not asked to interpret the research data or to offer any opinions other than those requested by the measuring instruments.

In the qualitative study, the primary researcher was concerned about his status as a "white, middle class, middle-aged academic entering a social setting made up, for the most part, of low-income black and Hispanic adolescents" (Farrell et al., 1988, p. 490). The researcher solved this problem by using collaborators drawn from the student population he wished to study. The collaborators both conducted the interviews and participated in analyzing and interpreting the resulting interview data. The rationale for this procedure was that student-collaborators would have the same frame of reference as the individuals being studied. Thus, they would have better rapport with those individuals, and would be able to interpret the meaning of their responses. In contrast to the quantitative research example, described below, this researcher had a subjective perspective in his data collection and analysis procedures.

In our example of quantitative research, data were collected on three variables during and after the experimental program period: (1) the percentage of special education class sessions that the students attended, (2) the percentage of special education class sessions for which the students were on time, and (3) the percentage of regular class sessions that the students attended. These data are objective because they require no judgment or intuition by either the researchers or the individuals being studied. In fact, most of the data were obtained from the data base compiled by the attendance office computer.

## VALUE ORIENTATION

*Look at all aspects of issue*

Qualitative researchers believe that all research is value-laden. Rather than avoiding the issue of values, they make explicit their personal values and try to expose the values that are embedded in the context being studied. Quantitative researchers, however, attempt to keep their personal values from influencing the design of their investigations. They also strive to avoid making value judgments about the individuals whom they study. Our example of quantitative research is value-laden, but the researchers did not explicate these values. For example, consider the purpose of the experiment, which was to improve the attendance record of special education students. The researchers take it for granted that this is a desirable goal, and in fact most people would agree that regular, on-time attendance at classes is important. Yet questions can be raised about this goal, for example, whether the students themselves value attending their classes. Suppose they have sound reasons for not attending certain classes, such as the desire to avoid the taunts of classmates or to avoid feelings of frustration at not being able to understand the teacher's instruction. If these conditions exist, the experimental program could do more harm than good for the individuals it purports to help. Qualitative researchers would argue that the value of attendance should not be taken for granted but should be investigated as part of the experiment.

Values also are involved in the researchers' procedure of awarding points to students for attending class and then allowing students to trade their points each week for tangible rewards such as fast-food coupons and movie tickets. Critics might argue that this reward system is a form of bribery and that it hinders the development of students' intrinsic motivation to learn. These criticisms may or may not have merit, but the significant point is that the researchers, as is typical in quantitative research, did not make explicit the values inherent in their program, nor did they question them.

In contrast to the quantitative study, the qualitative research is almost entirely about values. The primary researcher (the white, middle-class professor) shows concern throughout the report for understanding the values of the students who were interviewed. He also expresses concern about his own values and the values of the teachers in the dropout prevention program in which these students were enrolled. For example, at one point in the report, he observed a class that he thought was particularly interesting and was surprised to hear a collaborator say, "Now that was the most boringest class I have" (Farrell et al., 1988, p. 498). Rather than questioning the judgment of the collaborator, he viewed it as data that needed to be understood.

One of the main conclusions of this study (Farrell et al., 1988) is that the values of at-risk students and their teachers are in conflict:

> What is happening is that realities or "meaning systems" . . . are constructed by teachers and administrators for the students. They presume enough overlap in cultural perspectives for common values and understandings between the students

and themselves. These meaning systems, however, have very little relationship to the meaning systems constructed by the students who have to function in their daily lives within a larger and, compared with the teachers, less secure world context. (Farrell et al., 1988, p. 500)

This insight into students' values and worldview is not a solution to the problem of helping at-risk students, but it may point the way to a solution. The solution is likely to be more effective because the values of students and their teachers have been made explicit rather than taken for granted.

## STUDY OF CONTEXT

Qualitative researchers seek to understand a complex phenomenon by examining it in its totality, in context. Thus, they may not know what to focus on until the research is underway. As they conduct interviews and observations, they begin identifying relevant themes and patterns in the total context, which then become the focus of more intensive observation or interviewing in later stages of data collection. Thus data collection tends to be much more intensive and continuous than in quantitative research.

Quantitative researchers take the opposite approach. They seek to understand a complex phenomenon like instruction by analyzing it into its component parts (called variables). Each of their investigations typically examines only a few of the possible variables that could be studied and only some of the interrelationships among these variables. The situational context is either ignored or controlled by creating a laboratorylike setting. Also, data are collected at just a few intervals, such as just before and just after an experimental program. This focus on a few points in time makes it possible to measure each variable precisely. If the phenomenon were measured continuously over a long interval, the researcher would need resources not usually available or would have to revert to imprecise measurement procedures.

As we might expect, our example of quantitative research focused on a few precisely defined variables: the treatment variable (experimental program versus control condition), and the three outcome variables having to do with class attendance and being on time. We are told little about the students other than their special education classification (learning disabled, emotionally handicapped, etc.) Similarly we are told little about the individuals who administered the point system and made phone calls to parents other than that they were "undergraduate students who are seeking participation in research or clinical work" (Licht et al., 1991, p. 369).

An exception to these superficial descriptions is the researchers' discussion of the feelings of students in the control group, specifically their possible resentment of the rewards earned by the experimental group students for good attendance. The researchers were concerned that if these feelings occurred, the experimental design would be weakened because the control group might attend school less often than normal because of resentment about not receiving rewards. Thus, the experimental group would have a better attendance record than the control group not because the intervention worked, but because attendance of the latter was artificially depressed. The researchers dealt with this problem by telling the control group students that they could participate in the experimental program the following semester.

Unlike the quantitative study, in the qualitative study all aspects of the students' lives were of interest to the researchers, as reflected in their statements that the interviews with students were "unstructured" and "on the general topic of what life is like for a young person in New York City" (Farrell et al., 1988, pp. 491–492). The researchers gathered additional data about the context by interviewing the students' teachers and tape-recording some of their classes.

The focus on the context in qualitative research is also reflected in the data analysis. The researchers identified broad themes and patterns rather than narrow, precisely defined variables. In the discussion of findings, we learn much about various kinds of social pressures on the students: sexual, familial, peer and street culture, and occupational. We also learn about various school pressures, including the oppressive boredom that they experienced in class and their ways of dealing with it. This study, as is typical of qualitative research, has a broad sweep in order to learn everything of relevance to the individuals being studied.

*People - not a commodity - manuales*

## MEASUREMENT AND DATA ANALYSIS

Procedures for collecting and analyzing data in qualitative research are somewhat subjective because qualitative researchers collect data by drawing on their capacities to observe and interact with other humans and the environment. They believe that only these capacities are sufficient for the complex tasks of collecting data on the total context and adapting to the varied, ever-changing conditions found in natural field settings.

The goal of the measurement procedures used in quantitative research is objectivity, meaning that the collection and scoring of data are not influenced by the researcher's values, biases, and idiosyncratic perceptions. Hence there is heavy reliance on tests, scales, and structured questionnaires that can be administered under standardized conditions to all individuals in the sample. Also, procedures for scoring data yielded by these measures are specified precisely to increase the likelihood that any two scorers will obtain the same results.

Differences in the data collection procedures are paralleled by differences in the procedures for analyzing the data. Qualitative research typically yields verbal descriptions, largely derived from interview and observational notes. These notes are analyzed for themes and patterns, which are described and illustrated with examples, including quotations and excerpts from documents (e.g., official records, memoranda, and diaries) when possible.

Quantitative research yields primarily numerical data, which are susceptible to analysis by statistical procedures. In our example of quantitative research, data on students' class attendance were collected primarily by school staff members responsible for maintaining attendance records. They entered this information into the school's computer, and it was then made available to the researchers. As a check on the computer data, the researchers also asked the students' teachers to fill out attendance forms while the experiment was in progress.

*Qualitative*

Interviews and tape recordings were the data collection procedures used in the qualitative research. The primary researcher expressed no concern about the validity and reliability of the data collected by these methods. For example, he stated that interviewer reliability was not an issue because the interviewer's comments were part of the data. In other words, the interviewers were deliberately subjective in their structuring of their interviews, presumably adjusting their questions in response to the situation and the individual being interviewed. The only statement dealing with the data's validity was a comment that in the opinion of the interviewers, the students trusted them.

No statistical analyses are included in the qualitative research report. Instead, the collaborators analyzed the interview transcripts by underlining comments that they felt were particularly "telling" about a student's life. Comments underlined by all three collaborators became the subject of more intensive analysis to identify recurrent themes. These themes are described in the report and illustrated with quotations from the transcripts. For example, one of the identified themes was loyalty to and support of friends. Several quotes are used to illustrate this theme, including the following:

> Brenda: I mean actually yesterday. I was so upset. I was so depressed that I felt my life was useless; I was worthless. I was so sad I really didn't know what to do really. And my friends, like my boyfriend, they really hang onto me. Well, you understand, they really helped me, it was like a help. And that love and that charm I received from them, you know, like, "Wow, there's no need for me to die." (Farrell et al., 1988, p. 495)

This type of quotation provides a direct description of the individual's phenomenological reality, which is one of the primary goals of most qualitative research.

By contrast, descriptive and inferential statistics were used to analyze the data from the quantitative study. (Chapter 7 provides an explanation of these statistical procedures.) The descriptive statistics are shown in Table 9.1, which is reproduced from the journal article about the study. The table shows students' attendance and on-time record averaged across three-week periods. The researchers predicted that there would be little or no difference between the experimental group and control group for the first three weeks because this time interval was near the start of the school year, when attendance is generally good. They also predicted that the control group's attendance would get progressively worse, whereas the experimental group's attendance would remain high or decline at a much slower rate. The descriptive statistics generally support the researchers' predictions.

The researchers also examined their data through analysis of variance, an inferential statistical procedure. The purpose of this analysis was to determine the likelihood that the observed differences between the two groups occurred by chance and so did not represent differences that would be found if the experiment were repeated with other students similar to those in the study. The analysis of variance revealed that it was very unlikely that the observed differences between the experimental group and control group on the three attendance variables was due to chance.

Table 9.1   Means and standard deviations for SE attendance, SE on-time, and regular class attendance

| Group | First 3 weeks | | Second 3 weeks | | Third 3 weeks | | Fourth 3 weeks | |
|---|---|---|---|---|---|---|---|---|
| | M | SD | M | SD | M | SD | M | SD |
| | SE attendance | | | | | | | |
| Control | 92.27 | 6.98 | 79.10 | 25.53 | 80.80 | 22.03 | 68.57 | 33.09 |
| Treatment | 88.37 | 11.79 | 92.80 | 8.80 | 89.53 | 11.63 | 82.57 | 20.68 |
| | SE on-time | | | | | | | |
| Control | 88.72 | 9.02 | 76.58 | 26.82 | 76.53 | 22.32 | 64.47 | 32.20 |
| Treatment | 85.13 | 11.76 | 89.38 | 10.38 | 84.68 | 10.61 | 79.33 | 20.90 |
| | Regular class attendance | | | | | | | |
| Control | 89.27 | 18.01 | 71.83 | 30.69 | 73.50 | 24.06 | 63.83 | 32.12 |
| Treatment | 87.27 | 13.45 | 91.27 | 10.76 | 87.73 | 12.04 | 83.10 | 17.38 |

Source: From B. G. Licht, T. Gard, & C. Guardino, "Modifying School Attendance of Special Education High School Students," *Journal of Educational Research, 84*(6), 1991, 368–373. Reprinted with permission of the Helen Dwight Reid Educational Foundation. Published by Heldref Publications, 4000 Albemarle Street NW, Washington, DC 20016. Copyright © 1991.
SE is an abbreviation for "special education students."

## WHICH IS BETTER: QUALITATIVE OR QUANTITATIVE RESEARCH?

Both qualitative and quantitative research have their advocates and critics. Advocates of the latter argue that it has led to remarkable discoveries in the physical and biological sciences and in allied professions such as engineering and medicine. Quantitative research in education has had a briefer history than in these fields, but it already has yielded much useful knowledge. Over longer periods of time, it may yield even greater breakthroughs in our understanding of education. However, critics of quantitative research claim that it is inappropriate for the study of human behavior and that it has yielded little knowledge of practical use to educators.

Advocates of qualitative research argue that its methods are particularly appropriate for the study of education because they are derived from the social sciences. Both education and the social sciences are concerned with the study of human behavior and thinking in various settings. Advocates observe, too, that educational practitioners find it easy to read reports of qualitative research and to relate the findings to their own situation. Critics of qualitative research, however, claim that its methods are so subjective that one cannot judge whether the findings have any validity or generalizability.

We take the position that both qualitative and quantitative research have much to offer education if they are used with sensitivity and discipline. It is important to support both approaches because each addresses different questions about education. For example, the methods of qualitative research are more appropriate if we wish in-depth information about such matters as how students feel about their science instruction or why a particular teacher is highly regarded as a mentor for new teachers. Conversely, the methods of quantitative research are more appropriate if we wish to know about such matters as the number of students who are classified as learning disabled in the United States or whether teaching method A produces better student achievement on a particular test than teaching method B.

Some researchers (e.g., Reichardt & Cook, 1979) believe that many educational phenomena are best studied through a combination of quantitative and qualitative research designs. For example, a quantitative research study can be done to determine *how well* a particular instructional program works, whereas a concurrent qualitative study can be done to discover *why* it works or does not work and how it is perceived by educators, students, and the community.

Qualitative and quantitative research can complement each other in still another way. Some research methodologists (e.g., Biddle & Anderson, 1986) believe that qualitative research is best suited for initial investigations of a problem. For example, qualitative studies can produce thick descriptions of an interesting phenomenon, discover relevant variables, and generate hypotheses about cause-and-effect relationships between them. Quantitative research then can make rigorous measurements of these variables and test for the presence of the hypothesized relationships.

For example, in the qualitative investigation of at-risk students that we have been discussing, the researchers found themes in their interview data that might explain why these students do so poorly in school. These themes concern the overwhelming social pressures that the students experience outside of school and the boredom they experience in school as a consequence of a long history of academic failure. These insights suggest the need for a school program that provides intensive counseling to help students deal with their social pressures and that also provides learning experiences with a high probability of success. Once such a program is designed, quantitative research methods can be employed to provide a rigorous experimental test of the program's effectiveness and whether the effects are likely to generalize across schools.

In summary, we believe that both qualitative and quantitative research can make important contributions to the improvement of educational practice. Neither approach is better than the other. However, some qualitative studies are better designed and more important than others. The same is true of quantitative research.

We now proceed to a discussion of the major types of qualitative research and the criteria for judging the soundness of a qualitative study. Criteria for judging quantitative research studies are described in the following chapters.

# Types of Qualitative Research

## CASE STUDY METHOD

Case study investigations are conducted in many fields, including psychology, sociology, political science, economics, and business management. They are being conducted increasingly in education as researchers have become more interested in studying complex educational phenomena in their natural context.

A recent research report, "Change in Teaching Mathematics: A Case Study," by Terry Wood, Paul Cobb, and Erna Yackel (1991) illustrates the essential features of this method. The purpose of the study was to identify and describe the conflicts that an experienced second-grade teacher encountered as she switched from the traditional approach to teaching mathematics to a constructivist-sociological approach. The constructivist approach considers the student to be an active constructor of knowledge rather than a passive recipient of knowledge transmitted by the teacher, textbook, or other source. The sociological approach is based on the view that students find meaning in mathematics through their interactions with fellow students and with the teacher, who represents the wider society's conceptions of mathematics. In addition to determining the conflicts that the teacher encountered in switching to this approach, the researchers wished to learn how the teacher resolved these conflicts in her daily mathematics lessons.

Case studies are well suited to developing detailed descriptions of the type desired in this research project. The researcher can collaborate with subjects in the study and can interview them intensively to learn their phenomenological perspectives. Case studies also can be done for explanatory purposes, that is, when the researcher wishes to understand the causes or effects of events or interventions.

Case studies focus on *contemporary* phenomena by studying a single instance of the phenomenon. (Some research investigations include several case studies in order to determine whether findings replicate across cases.) This focus on contemporary phenomena distinguishes the case study method from historical research, which focuses on *past* phenomena. In other words, in a case study, the researcher can observe events as they occur and can interview participants in the events. In historical research, the investigator must rely on others' observations and records of the events.

Another characteristic of case studies is that phenomena are studied in their total context. In the mathematics study, the phenomena of interest were the teacher's conflicts experienced in changing her instruction to a constructivist-sociological approach and her resolution of these conflicts. The researchers took the context into account by observing every mathematics lesson taught by this teacher for an entire school year. Thus the context included the totality of the teacher's instruction over a meaningfully long period of time. When they interviewed the teacher about her conflicts and resolutions, both the researchers and the teacher were aware of the specific instructional contexts in which the conflicts arose and of the contexts in which she tried new teaching methods to bring her instruction in line with constructivist-sociological principles.

Another characteristic of the case study method is that it typically involves multiple data sources. In the mathematics study, data were collected in several contexts: whole-class discussions between the teacher and students, interactions between pairs of students as they worked on activities designed to develop their conceptual understanding of mathematics, and project meetings between the researchers and the teacher. Data on whole-class discussions and pair interactions were collected by videorecordings and direct observations recorded as field notes. In addition, students' completed mathematics worksheets were collected, and notes were taken at the project meetings. Thus the researchers had multiple data sources for understanding the phenomena of interest. For many of the phenomena, one data source could be used as a check on another data source about what actually happened during a specific instructional event.

In case studies researchers develop a conceptual framework to understand the data that are collected. If there were no conceptual framework, the result would be a chronicle, not a research study. In the mathematics case study, concepts from constructivist and sociological theories of learning were used to help the researchers understand the children's behavior during mathematics instruction. Furthermore, these concepts helped the researchers understand the teacher as a learner struggling to resolve conflicts between how she had learned to teach mathematics and her new learnings as she participated in the researchers' project.

Other case studies, of course, involve different conceptual frameworks. Many of them are drawn from theories developed by psychologists and sociologists, but they can be drawn from theories in other disciplines as well. For example, the case study that you will read in its entirety later in this chapter involves a conceptual framework derived from an aesthetic theory of teaching developed by Elliott Eisner. In reading case study reports, you should focus not only on the researchers' findings but also on the conceptual framework used to interpret their findings.

## HISTORICAL RESEARCH

Historical research can be defined as the systematic search for and interpretation of facts about past events to answer research questions about the past. Historians of education study such subjects as changes in educational policies, legislation, curriculum, and instructional methods over time; the lives of prominent educators; and the development of educational institutions (e.g., kindergartens). Like other types of qualitative research, historical studies emphasize the study of phenomena in their natural context.

Historians occasionally use the method of oral history, that is, interviewing individuals who experienced events or knew individuals relevant to the research project. Historians also use the method of document analysis, examining documents such as official records (e.g., censuses and birth records) and papers (e.g., contracts, commission reports, newspapers, manuscripts, memoranda, diaries, and transcripts of speeches). Document analysis also may be used in case studies, ethnographies, and various types of quantitative research, but it is not used as commonly as in historical research.

Documents need to be examined for their authenticity and accuracy before they are used as a data source. This process of examination is called *historical criticism*, which is of two types: external and internal.

In external criticism, the researcher raises questions about the nature of the historical document: Is it genuine? Is it the original copy? Who wrote it? Where? When? Under what conditions? It is important to ask these questions because some historical documents have been found to be forgeries. Others have a listed author but in fact were ghostwritten by another individual. Prior to the introduction of the typewriter (circa

1880), many documents were written longhand. Different copies of the document might vary because of errors in transcription.

Internal criticism involves evaluating the accuracy and worth of the statements in a document. The researcher asks such questions as these: Is it probable that the events occurred in the way described by the author? Do the numerical data in the census records seem reasonable? Does the author appear biased or prejudiced? Most documents used in historical research are not research reports written for the scientific community but those written for private use or for the general public or members of an organization. Therefore, they are especially prone to bias. People often exaggerate their own role in events, or they distort events to conform to the values and prejudices of a group, such as a political party whom they represent.

The characteristics of historical research in education are illustrated in the report "Reforming Again, Again, and Again," by Larry Cuban (1990). Like many other historical studies, its purpose is to help us understand a present condition or issue by examining the past. The reasoning is that if we develop an understanding of the past, we can avoid repeating its mistakes, or reinventing the wheel. In Cuban's study the purpose was to help us "understand why reforms return but seldom substantially alter the regularities of schooling. The risks involved with a lack of understanding include pursuing problems with mismatched solutions, spending energies needlessly, and accumulating despair" (Cuban, 1990, p. 11).

Part of the study involves documentation of several types of reforms that have been tried repeatedly in the past. One of these reforms concerns the school curriculum. At one phase of the reform cycle, reformers call for a core academic curriculum for all students; in the next phase, reformers call for a diversified curriculum that meets the needs of diverse types of learners. Cuban demonstrated that this cycle has repeated itself several times in the past hundred years. For example, in the recent past, reformers in the 1970s brought about a diversified curriculum through alternative schools, vocational programs, and curricula that blended the academic and the practical. By the early 1980s, however, another group of reformers called for a traditional academic curriculum.

Cuban documented these repetitive cycles of reform by using multiple data sources, a typical procedure in qualitative research. He referred to other historians' accounts of particular eras in American education; reform-oriented books published at certain points in the reform cycle; and the actions, writings, and speeches of influential educators and commissions. For example, to document the recent reform aimed at restoring a traditional academic curriculum, he cited a speech in which California's state superintendent, Bill Honig (1985), said, "a traditional education worked for us, why shouldn't we give at least as good a shot at the common culture to today's children" (p. 5). In quoting from this speech, Cuban noted that Honig was a graduate of an academically selective high school. This is an example of internal criticism because it involved an analysis of how the speech possibly reflected Honig's personal value system and the values of an elite group of constituents, rather than the values of the general public.

Much of Cuban's report involves an effort to develop conceptual frameworks to interpret these repeated cycles of reform and their apparent lack of impact on teachers. This emphasis on interpretation is characteristic of historical research. As the British historian Edward Carr (1967) put it, "History means interpretation" (p. 26). Among the frameworks considered by Cuban are a rational model of organizational behavior, a political perspective on value conflicts in American society, and an institutional perspective that emphasizes the decoupling of classroom instruction from administration and policy-making. He concludes that none of these frameworks provides a fully satisfactory explanation for the persistent reappearance of reforms and their minimal impact on classroom instruction. Therefore, he ends his report with a call for further research on "particular reforms and tracing their life history in particular classrooms, schools, districts, and regions" (Cuban, 1990, p. 12).

## ETHNOGRAPHIC RESEARCH

Educators have become increasingly sensitive to the cultural diversity of students in the nation's schools and appreciative of the role it plays in students' performance. Thus, cultural aspects of the educational process have become frequent topics of study by educational researchers. Their investigations often use the ethnographic method, which was developed by anthropologists specifically for the study of culture.

Like other types of qualitative research, the ethnographic method focuses on the study of the phenomenological reality of individuals, their behavior in naturally occurring settings, and the total context affecting them. Ethnographic studies use the same data collection methods as other types of qualitative research: interviews, observations, and document analysis. The distinctive characteristic of ethnographic research is its focus on culture. According to the educational anthropologist Harry Wolcott (1980):

> Specific ethnographic techniques are freely available to any researcher who wants to approach a problem or setting descriptively. It is the essential anthropological concern for cultural context that distinguishes ethnographic method from fieldwork techniques and makes genuine ethnography distinct from other "on-site-observer" approaches. And when cultural interpretation is the goal, the ethnographer must be thinking like an anthropologist, not just looking like one. (p. 59)

Wolcott's perspective suggests that an educator should have had at least some formal training in anthropology to undertake ethnographic research or to appreciate fully a completed ethnography.

Anthropologists typically spend a great deal of time in the field—a year or two is not unusual—to develop an understanding of a culture or cultural process. They also rely extensively on a method of data collection known as *participant observation.* In this method the researcher becomes actively involved in the situation being observed in order to develop an understanding of the phenomenological reality of members of the culture. It is unlike observation in quantitative research, in which the researcher strives for objectivity by remaining uninvolved with the situation being observed.

Participant observation can occur to varying degrees. In complete participant observation, the researcher becomes a full member of the culture, and her role as an observer is concealed. At the other end of the spectrum, the researcher functions primarily as an observer but participates sufficiently in the culture to gain rapport and information from its members.

Use of the ethnographic method in educational research is illustrated in the report "Trauma of Sioux Indian High School Students" by Peggy Wilson (1991). The purpose of the study was to identify cultural factors that might explain why many Indian students in Canada do well in elementary schools located on reservations but perform poorly when they transfer to off-reservation schools for their high school education. In the high school that Wilson studied, 18 of the 23 Indian students dropped out during the school year. Of the 5 remaining students, none were enrolled in college-preparatory classes.

Wilson (1991) described her use of the ethnographic method as follows:

> Observations were contextualized, with constant interaction between observation and interviews. This was a study of human behavior within a social context. I was present in the situation, and the students being observed and interviewed were deemed best equipped with the emic knowledge that I was looking for in its most natural form. (p. 370)

She also noted her qualifications as an experienced teacher in both public and reservation schools, as an experienced high school administrator, and as a member of an Indian tribe (called brand in Canada). Interestingly, she did not reveal her tribal affiliation to the teachers. She believed that the fact that they viewed her as a white teacher "helped them to open up and express their deeper thoughts and feelings" (p. 371).

In interpreting her data, Wilson characterized the Indian students' phenomenological reality in high school as a confrontation with racism, alien cultural norms, and economic stress. She argued that this reality was extremely difficult for them because their phenomenological experience of elementary school on the reservation was positive. They had enjoyed academic success and affirmations of their self-worth. For this reason Wilson used the concept of trauma to characterize their transition from a reservation elementary school to a mainstream high school.

Wilson considered alternative explanations of her research findings. One of them was Ogbu's theory of cultural ambivalence, which states that minority students do not succeed in mainstream schools because they oppose, or feel ambivalent toward, the expression of majority culture in these schools. Wilson concluded that some of the data fit this theory, but other data did not. For example, the Indian students attributed some of their failure to the fact that they were not treated well and did not know how to change this situation. Also, they attributed some of their truancy from class to their felt obligation to lend support to fellow students in need, even when this meant not attending class.

Wilson drew several implications of her findings for the improvement of educational practice. Specifically, she identified the need for minority group students to have a say in their education and for school personnel to be trained to understand and be more sensitive to students' culture.

# Evaluation of Qualitative Research

Appendix 4 provides a form that you can use to evaluate qualitative research studies. It is sufficiently general to apply to most types of qualitative research, including case studies, histories, and ethnographies. In examining the form, note that it consists of a series of questions. Also provided is information needed to answer each question and a sample answer.

Some research reports unfortunately do not provide the information needed to evaluate every aspect of the research design or findings. The omissions may be minor and therefore will not affect your judgments about the overall quality of the study or its usefulness for your purposes. Other omissions are so serious that they call into doubt the entire study.

Qualitative studies that appear in journals published by major professional associations generally have been evaluated by a board of consulting editors before publication. These studies may still have minor design flaws, and the report may fail to include certain details. It is unlikely, however, that the problems are serious. If a study has been published in a journal, you may find it useful to see if the journal is sponsored by a professional association and who the members of the editorial board are.

The questions in Appendix 4 refer to specific features of qualitative studies. An overriding consideration is your evaluation of the researcher's qualifications for this type of investigation. Qualitative studies are necessarily subjective because the researcher is the main "instrument" for data collection and analysis. Subjectivity, however, is not a license to observe and write whatever one wishes. The researcher needs to be sensitive to the nuances in what is observed, interpersonally skillful so that the individuals being observed do not distort or mask their behavior, and capable of absorbing the entire context in which the events of interest occur. The researcher also needs to be sensitive to her own biases and to take care that she does not distort the process of data collection and analysis. You will need to read between the lines of a research report to get a sense of whether the researcher possesses these qualities.

You now have an opportunity to read a complete qualitative research report, illustrating the use of the case study method. Although the report does not include an abstract, the Researcher's Comments provide the background information needed to understand the study.

# Sample Case Study:
# DOES THE "ART OF TEACHING" HAVE A FUTURE?

## Researcher's Comments[1]

### Background

The study described in the following article is based on my doctoral dissertation. As a graduate student, I initially expected that my dissertation would stem either from theory or from reviews of the research literature within some academic area of concentration. Both of these sources contributed to my study. In the end, however, I did not find my inspiration by poring over books and research journals in the library. Rather, I found it by going "back to school." Let me explain how this happened.

My doctoral program advisor was Elliot Eisner, an art educator and qualitative researcher. While I was finishing up my graduate coursework, Dr. Eisner asked me to serve as his research assistant on a project to collect information about high school curriculum and instruction. As part of that work, I visited several local schools to observe and interview a small number of teachers. I was enthusiastic about this opportunity to gain practical experience doing classroom research. I discovered that talking with teachers and watching them work raised some compelling questions: What do we know about the day-to-day professional lives of teachers? How do they experience their work? What are their strongest concerns? From what sources do they derive their everyday satisfactions? These questions became the initial focus of the study reported here.

### The Study

Having decided that I wanted to learn more about classroom teachers, I designed my research as a series of qualitative case studies. Each case study focused on one of six high school English teachers. I focused on English because my own training is in this area, and I wanted to bring to the study as much subject-matter knowledge as possible. Focusing at the high school level was also an attempt to capitalize on my previous teaching and research experience.

After talking with the English department chairs at two schools, I selected six teachers from a pool of volunteers. I aimed at selecting a sample that represented the typical range of high school English teachers in terms of experience, gender, educational background, and type of teaching assignment. Three teachers worked at a public school that serves an upper-middle class professional community, and the other three worked at a school that serves primarily a working class community. At the time of the study, both schools had enrollments of about 1,500 students.

My fieldwork involved both observations and interviews. Observations took the form of "shadowing" each teacher for one full week. I would simply meet one of the teachers when he or she arrived at school each morning, and follow that teacher throughout the day until he or she left school each afternoon. During this time I took extensive field notes, which I reviewed and summarized at the end of each day. I also collected written documents from each teacher, including course syllabi, class handouts, curriculum guidelines, and sample text materials.

In addition to classroom observations, I tape-recorded interviews with each teacher on three separate occasions. Interview questions focused on the teachers' routine experiences and conditions of their work. On the one hand, I was careful not to impose upon the teachers' time, recognizing that teachers are generally quite busy with the demands of their daily work. On the other hand, the teachers often enjoyed talking about their experiences in the classroom. At the end of one long interview, the teacher jokingly suggested that I charge him for "this professional therapy." Of course, all I had done was listen to him talk.

The information I collected through interviews, observations, and written documents was analyzed and written up using an approach known as *educational criticism*. This genre of qualitative inquiry takes its lead from the arts and humanities rather than from the social sciences. For this reason it is not surprising that my case studies give particular attention to the artistic dimensions of the teaching that I observed. Yet, this was not my guiding purpose initially. As already explained, I set out with only broad interests in how teachers experience their work. The focused themes (communication, perception, cooperation, and appreciation) emerged gradually over the course of the study, as did my express interest in the artistry of teaching. They emerged in part because I found them to be salient features of the teachers' day-to-day work. I also recognized that the artistic side of teaching is often neglected. The professional and academic community rarely stops to scrutinize what makes for a beautiful lesson or a well-orchestrated class discussion.

# Aftermath

The study had several positive outcomes. As my doctoral research, it received the Association for Supervision and Curriculum Development's Outstanding Dissertation of the Year award for 1987. An abridged version of the dissertation was published as a monograph by the ERIC Clearinghouse on Educational Management (Flinders, 1989). This monograph is now being used in pre-service and graduate teacher education. Several professors have told me that they assign the monograph as a reading in their courses on qualitative research methods, and I know of at least one professor who uses it as a basis for class discussion with his teacher certification students. I have also published two journal articles and presented papers describing the study at several national conferences.

More recently, the study has contributed to development of an approach to classroom instruction that Dr. C. A. Bowers and I call "responsive teaching" (Bowers & Flinders, 1990). This approach looks at the context in which teaching and learning occur. It views the classroom as an ecology of language, culture, and thought. We have used examples and several narrative vignettes from my study to illustrate various features of the responsive teaching approach.

# Implications

Of course no single study can provide solutions to the complex problems that teachers face in the course of their work. Nevertheless, my study does have modest implications, some of which are stated in the article. I hope that the study will help educators more fully recognize the intricate skills that good teaching demands. In making them explicit, we open the door for teachers to use these skills more deliberately, and to share their expertise more often with their colleagues. In this way, we can stay in close touch with our own professional lives.

In a broader context, I believe that my study is a small example of the type of research that can bridge the work of universities with that of public schools, theory with practice, and disciplined inquiry with imagination.

# References

BOWERS, C. A., & FLINDERS, D. J. (1990). *Responsive teaching.* New York: Teachers College Press.

FLINDERS, D. J. (1989). *Voices from the classroom.* Eugene, OR: ERIC Clearinghouse on Educational Management.

# DOES THE "ART OF TEACHING" HAVE A FUTURE?

## David J. Flinders
### UNIVERSITY OF OREGON

Penelope Harper quickly takes roll, steps out from behind her desk, and glances around the classroom. Her eyes meet those of her students. Standing with her back to the chalkboard, she clasps her hands close in front of her, a ballpoint pen intertwined between her fingers. She holds her arms close to her sides and shifts her weight onto the heels of her shoes. This posture signals the beginning of class.

The students quiet down. Harper shakes back her dark hair and then addresses the class: "OK, today we need to discuss chapter two. Who would like to share something from your reading notes?" Silence. Harper breathes out, assuming a more casual and relaxed attitude. She is smiling softly now, confident that her students have read the assignment and that the silent classroom alone will motivate someone to risk putting forth an idea. Someone does. Harper listens intently and nods her head. "Good," she replies. "I really hadn't thought of it that way, but it tells us something, doesn't it? What's the author getting at here?" Harper steps forward, closer to her students, as their discussion begins to unfold.

## Artistry in Professional Life

Penelope Harper (the name is a pseudonym) is good at what she does. She's a professional. But in Harper's line of work, what exactly does it mean to be a professional?

Does it mean simply possessing a body of expert knowledge and a repertoire of technical skills? Climbing a career ladder toward greater autonomy and increased occupational rewards? Or, for classroom teachers, does professionalism mean something more?

These questions were the focus of a qualitative study I conducted on the nature of professional life in schools (Flinders 1987). Penelope Harper was one of six high school English teachers I observed and interviewed as part of this study. My purpose was to identify what Harper and her colleagues regard as the salient concerns of their day-to-day work experience. I hoped to view professional life through the eyes of classroom teachers.

I began my research with an understanding of professional life strongly influenced by the "new reform" (Shulman 1987). Two prominent examples of this reform are the reports by the Carnegie Task Force (1986) and the Holmes Group (1986). These reports share a common theme: the need to increase the professional status of teaching. In particular, they call for strengthening the career advancement opportunities, the subject-matter knowledge, and the technical expertise of all classroom teachers.

This focus on career development and expert knowledge reflects a widely shared and commonsense image of professionalism (Schon 1983). However, in listening to teachers talk about their work and in observing their teaching day after day, I soon realized that this image did not match their daily routines and their concerns. This image of professionalism failed to capture the artistry that these teachers often spoke of and demonstrated as central to their work.

Perhaps I can clarify this point by referring to my description of Penelope Harper. Consider, for example, her ability to signal the beginning of class through body language or her use of silence to motivate student participation. These skills reveal something of the grace, subtlety, and drama of Harper's day-to-day teaching. Granted, these deft moves cannot be evaluated solely by conventional testing procedures or through the use of systematic rating scales. Yet they are no less important than Harper's technical expertise or subject-matter knowledge. As my study progressed, the challenge became to understand this other side of teaching—the artistic side.

## The Arts of Teaching

Elliot Eisner (1983) has examined at a theoretical level various ways in which teaching can be regarded as art and craft. He calls attention, for example, to the dynamic and emergent qualities of classroom life, as well as to the intricate skill and grace that can characterize the teacher's classroom performance. In this context, Eisner uses the term *art* in its broad sense to signify engaging, complex, and expressive human activity. It is this sense that allows us to speak of a beautiful lesson or of a well-orchestrated class discussion.

If we want to observe artistry in teaching, where might we look in order to find it? My research suggests several possible locations. The first I have already touched on in my brief description of Harper's work: the art of communication.

### Communication

On a day-to-day basis, classroom teachers rely heavily on interpersonal forms of communication. Philip Jackson's (1965) early research, for example, suggests that teachers engage in as many as a thousand interpersonal interactions each day. This is an impressive number, particularly if we consider the intricate nature of even the most routine instances of face-to-face communication. Such communication, as Harper's teaching reveals, goes far beyond the spoken and written word—it also encompasses the use of space (what sociolinguists call *proxemics*), body language, and paralinguistics (voice tone and rhythm). One teacher I observed, for example, consistently demonstrated uncanny responsiveness toward her students. When a student asked a question or made a comment, that student could feel the teacher's undivided attention. In talking with students, the teacher would face them directly, lean or step in their direction, and maintain eye contact. At appropriate moments she would raise her eyebrows, nod her head, smile, and bring the index finger of her right hand up to her lips in a gesture of serious concentration. All of these nonverbal cues were coordinated to signal a coherent message: *I care about what you have to say.* This unspoken message was often as important to the students as the substantive meaning of her verbal responses.

Nonverbal cues serve primarily as a form of metalanguage (Tannen 1986). That is, they help teachers establish a context for communication. Consider yet another, somewhat different example. During a literature class, one teacher I observed lighted a kerosene lamp, asked his students to sit in a circle, turned on a recording of the sound effects of a storm, and read passages from Dickens' *Bleak House*, just as a Victorian father might have read the novel to his family. This teacher's well-calculated nonverbal cues provided a context for his students to gain insight into the novel that could not be "explained to them" using words alone. Creating a setting—this too is part of communication.

### Perception

It would be difficult to imagine good teachers who could not communicate well with their students. Yet effective communication does not begin with formulating a message or selecting a medium, but rather with the processes of learning to see and to hear. This notion suggests another, perhaps more fundamental art relevant to classroom teaching: the art of perception.

The teachers in my study often alluded to this art in describing their work. During an interview, for example, one teacher casually mentioned that she adapts her daily lesson plans depending on "how the group comes in at the beginning of the period." Such a comment underscores her ability to read those subtle cues in student behavior that signal the changing mood and tone of a class. Another teacher, when I asked how he evaluates his work, replied: "The real test in teaching is how the kids feel about you, and it's the vibrations that you pick up from them that tell you the most." Again, this comment suggests that perceptiveness—the ability to pick up on student attitudes, motives, beliefs, and so forth—lies at the heart of this teacher's professional expertise.

The type of perceptiveness and sensitivity to which these examples refer is a largely tacit dimension of social life. It depends on the ability to make complex and fine-grained distinctions between, for example, a wink and a blink, or between a sigh of relief and a sigh of frustration. All of us learn to make such discernments, at varying levels of sophistication, through social interaction. The point, however, is that this learning reflects an intuitive receptivity that Noddings (1984) has identified as critical to sound pedagogy. At a practical level, learning to operate in a receptive mode is basic to getting to know the students, and I was not surprised to find that all of the teachers in my study mentioned this process as central to their work.

## Cooperation

Knowledge of students, of "what they are like as people," as one teacher described perception, serves as the foundation for a third art that is salient in the professional lives of teachers: cooperation. For classroom teachers this means negotiating an alliance with their students. As one teacher commented, "You have to get the students on your side with honesty and a certain amount of candor, so they understand you, and you understand them." This teacher continued, "I'm here to work *with* the kids; I'm not here just to shovel out stuff and let them grab it." The other teachers were also quick to stress the practical value of student-teacher cooperation. One teacher summed it up simply: "You can't force students to do what you want them to do, but if they know you're working hard and care about 'em, from there on it's gravy."

The teachers I observed displayed various strategies for negotiating a cooperative relationship with their students. Some of these strategies include: (1) using humor and self-disclosure to promote teacher-student solidarity, (2) allowing students to choose activities, (3) occasionally bending school and classroom rules in the students' interest, (4) providing opportunities for individual recognition, and (5) creating pockets of time that allow teachers to interact one-to-one with students.

An example of this last strategy, creating pockets of time, is illustrated by a teacher who set aside every Thursday for mini-conferences. On this day, while his students worked independently, he went around the classroom to speak individually with as many students as possible. He justified this routine by insisting that "it helps break the mannequin-like image of me standing up in front of the room. It pays tremendous dividends. It allows the students to ask questions, and I find out a lot."

## Appreciation

The final art of teaching is appreciation. Unlike communication, perception, and cooperation, the art of appreciation is not primarily something that teachers *do*. Instead, it is a product of their artistry and, thus, cannot always be directly observed. Nevertheless, I found it readily apparent in how teachers describe the types of satisfaction they derive from their teaching. As Harper explained: "In almost any job you do, if you do it well, you get a certain ego-satisfaction from it. It's really a good feeling—when I run a discussion—to know that I did it well." Eisner (1983) describes the same idea in another way: "The aesthetic in teaching is the experience secured from being able to put your own signature on your own work—to look at it and say it was good (p. 13)." Both the classroom teacher and the scholar are describing the intrinsic sense of worth that comes from having done a difficult job well. This idea is central to the daily work of classroom teachers.

## A Challenge to Educational Leaders

The artistic dimensions that teachers recognize as basic to their profession stand in sharp contrast to the priorities of the new reform movement. Of course, professionalism is about opportunities for career advancement, the expert knowledge teachers possess, and the types of learning that can be easily tested. Yet the day-to-day experience of teachers reminds us that teaching is also about much more. It is about subtle interpersonal skills, discernment, caring, and "ego-satisfaction." These artistic aspects reflect highly complex forms of human expression that may well influence teacher effectiveness more than career ladders and fifth-year preparation programs.

If the art of teaching is to have a future, we must enlarge our understanding of professionalism to include the artistic skills and judgment that good teaching demands. This task presents a challenge to educational leaders for at least two reasons. First, artistry cannot be mandated by the central office. Neither can it be fostered by an afternoon of inservice training once or twice a year. Therefore, we have to think more deeply about the conditions under which teachers work, their opportunities for interacting with each other, the amount of discretionary time in their daily schedules, the number of students they see each day, and the resources with which they have to work. Second, the art of teaching is simply less well understood than technical aspects of instruction. We know more, for example, about the mechanics of lesson planning, test construction, and curriculum development than we do about how Penelope Harper is able to gracefully orchestrate a class discussion.

The profession can learn much about the complexity and artistry of teaching from colleagues like Penelope Harper. We might begin by cultivating our own abilities to engage teachers in genuine dialogue. Basic to this dialogue is our perceptiveness—learning to see and hear teachers in ways that take us beyond stereotypical images. Like teachers, we must operate in a receptive mode. We might also promote a cooperative alliance both with and between classroom teachers, for example, by occasionally bending rules for their professional well-being and by involving them in decision making. Finally, we might strive to fully appreciate the multifaceted nature of this collaborative effort as an art and craft in its own right.

## References

CARNEGIE TASK FORCE ON TEACHING AS A PROFESSION. (1986). *A Nation Prepared: Teachers for the 21st Century.* Washington, D.C.: Carnegie Forum on Education and the Economy.

EISNER, E. W. (January 1983). "The Art and Craft of Teaching." *Educational Leadership* 40: 4–13.

FLINDERS, D. J. (June 1987). "What Teachers Learn from Teaching: Educational Criticisms of Instructional Adaptation." Doctoral dissertation submitted to the Graduate School of Education, Stanford University.

THE HOLMES GROUP. (1986). "Tomorrow's Teachers, A Report of the Holmes Group." East Lansing, Mich.: The Holmes Group, Inc.

JACKSON, P. W. (1965). "Teacher-Pupil Communication in the Elementary Classroom: An Observational Study." Paper presented at the American Educational Research Association Annual Meeting. Chicago.

NODDINGS, N. (1984). *Caring: A Feminine Approach to Ethics and Moral Education.* Berkeley: University of California Press.

SCHON, D. A. (1983). *The Reflective Practitioner.* New York: Basic Books.

SHULMAN, L. S. (February 1987). "Knowledge and Teaching: Foundations of the New Reform." *Harvard Educational Review* 57, 1: 1–22.

TANNEN, D. (1986). *That's Not What I Meant!* New York: Ballantine Books.

# Critical Review

Flinders's study differs in several respects from the other studies in this book because it used qualitative research methods instead of quantitative research methods. In quantitative research, the researcher typically states hypotheses or questions in advance of data collection. Flinders instead allowed his questions and interests to develop as the study progressed. For example, he stated that his research purpose shifted from a focus on career development and expert knowledge to an effort "to understand this other side of teaching—the artistic side."

Flinders's study also differs from quantitative research in how data were collected and interpreted. In quantitative research, objective instruments (for example, tests) are used to collect data, and the data are then analyzed by statistical techniques. In Flinders's study the researcher was the primary instrument of data collection. He personally observed and interviewed the sample of high school teachers. His data consisted of his detailed field notes during this phase of the study. (An example of these notes is presented at the beginning of his report.) He then analyzed the data in a personal, impressionistic manner to discover prominent themes. His analysis revealed four themes—actually four dimensions of teachers' artistry. Flinders documented these themes by quoting the teachers' remarks and selecting illustrative events recorded in his field notes. His description and documentation of each dimension (communication, perception, cooperation, and appreciation) suggests that he did, in fact, succeed in identifying some important qualities of effective teaching.

Additional information in the research report would have been helpful. For example, readers would benefit from knowing more about what educational criticism involves. We wonder also what types of questions Flinders asked the teachers during the interviews and whether there was any attempt to standardize them, that is, ask the same questions of each teacher.

The report appears to be written to stimulate readers to examine and ponder their own values and beliefs regarding the concepts and generalizations that were discovered in the study. Qualitative research may be particularly effective in this regard because the significance of findings is based not on statistical tests but rather on a trained expert's ability to find meaning in complex phenomena through observation and analysis. The possibility of researcher bias, however, may affect the validity of the findings. Therefore, the reader needs to know something about the researcher in order to judge whether his values, role, and experience biased the results.

By reading the research report we learn that Flinders was a former English teacher and that in graduate school he studied under Elliot Eisner, an art educator. As a result, Flinders is probably more likely to see teaching as involving artistic elements than would a researcher with a different background. Thus one can question whether a researcher effect compromised the validity of the findings.

The reader can weigh the possibility of researcher bias by determining whether the researcher used multiple sources of evidence to support the findings. If multiple sources of evidence are present, we can be more confident that the findings are valid. Flinders used interview data as well as his own perceptions of what the teachers did. One way to strengthen his findings would be to make videotapes of the teachers' instruction and then have expert judges watch the videotapes to determine whether they saw the same artistic elements that Flinders saw.

Flinders's comments demonstrate an effort to choose a representative sample of high school English teachers, in terms of experience, gender, educational background, type of teaching assignment, and the social class of the community served by their schools. There is thus some evidence of population validity, that is, information to indicate that the findings can be generalized beyond this sample of six teachers to other teachers similar to them.

One of the hallmarks of scientific research is the replication of important findings by other researchers. If the findings hold up under replication, we can be more certain that they are valid. In this case, other researchers can study new samples of teachers to determine whether they can discern in their teaching styles the same artistic elements identified by Flinders. Another possibility is to use quantitative research methods to extend Flinders's research findings. For example, researchers could develop an objective measure of each of the four dimensions of artistic teaching. They then could assess a sample of teachers on each measure to determine how often, and to what degree, they expressed each dimension of teacher artistry.

Flinders ends his report in a provocative manner by posing challenges and questions to educators rather than stating practical implications of his findings. You might think about which approach you prefer researchers to take with their findings—to spell out the implications, or to guide readers in formulating the implications themselves.

# Chapter References

BIDDLE, B. J., & ANDERSON, D. S. (1986). Theory, methods, knowledge, and research on teaching. In *Handbook of research on teaching,* 3rd ed., ed. M. C. Wittrock. New York: Macmillan.

CARR, E. H. (1967). *What is history?* New York: Random House.

CUBAN, L. (1990). Reforming again, again, and again. *Educational Researcher, 19*(1), 3–13.

FARRELL, E., PEGUERO, G., LINDSEY, R., & WHITE, R. (1988). Giving voice to high school students: Pressure and boredom, ya know what I'm sayin'? *American Educational Research Journal, 25*(4), 489–502.

HONIG, B. (1985). *Last chance for our children.* Reading, MA: Addison-Wesley.

LICHT, B. G., GARD, T., & GUARDINO, C. (1991). Modifying school attendance of special education high school students. *Journal of Educational Research, 84*(6), 368–373.

REICHARDT, C. S., & COOK, T. D. (1979). Beyond qualitative versus quantitative methods. In *Qualitative and quantitative methods in evaluation research,* eds. T. D. Cook & C. S. Reichardt. Beverly Hills, CA: Sage.

WILSON, P. (1991). Trauma of Sioux Indian high school students. *Anthropology & Education Quarterly, 22*(4), 367–383.

WOLCOTT, H. (1980). How to look like an anthropologist without really being one. *Practicing Anthropology, 3*(2), 6–7, 56–59.

WOOD, T., COBB, P., & YACKEL, E. (1991). Change in teaching mathematics: A case study. *American Educational Research Journal, 28*(3), 587–616.

# Recommended Reading

BOGDAN, R. C., & BIKLEN, S. K. (1992). *Qualitative research for education: An introduction to theory and methods,* 2nd ed. Needham Heights, MA: Allyn & Bacon.

This a comprehensive introduction to current methods used in qualitative research in education. The authors provide a history of the development of this approach; a detailed description of qualitative research methods; and a discussion of their uses in evaluation, action research, and educational practice.

BUTTON, H. W. (1986). Why and when history doesn't work: The case of Miss Purington. *American Behavioral Scientist, 30,* 28–41.

The author provides an entertaining discussion of various flaws that can occur in historical research. An understanding of these flaws will improve your ability to evaluate historical studies in education.

GLESNE, C., & PESHKIN, A. (1992). *Becoming qualitative researchers: An introduction.* White Plains, NY: Longman.

The field of qualitative research is undergoing rapid change and development. The authors describe the most current methods of qualitative research and discuss such issues as how history and culture shape the researcher's perspective and how the researcher and researched affect each other.

YIN, R. K. (1991). *Case study research: Design and methods.*, rev. ed. Newbury Park, CA: Sage.

This is a highly readable introduction to the procedures used in case study research in education and other applied social science disciplines. Many examples of actual case studies are used to illustrate the research procedures.

# Application Problems

1.  The following are brief descriptions of research procedures. State and justify your opinion of whether each procedure is more likely to be part of a qualitative study or a quantitative study.
    a.  The homework completed by the students in the sample was collected and analyzed at three points in the school year: the second week of school, the fifteenth week, and the thirtieth week.
    b.  The researcher visited the principal's home on several occasions, even though the principal's school life, rather than her home life, was the focus of the study.
    c.  The purpose of the study was to determine the effects of a new distance education program. The researchers interviewed the program administrators, instructors, technicians, and students to identify what effects they hoped to achieve and why.
    d.  The researcher administered an attitude scale twice to the sample to check the reliability of students' responses across time. Also, each completed attitude scale was scored twice to check for scoring errors.
2.  Theories have been developed in recent years to explain how and why adults learn differently from young students. Suppose funds were available for research on whether principles derived from adult learning theory could be used to improve staff development programs for teachers. How could qualitative and quantitative researchers work together to explore this question?
3.  A state department of education wishes to commission an in-depth study of how policies about the education of migrant workers' children have changed over time. What type of research specialist should they commission to do the study?

# Chapter Note

1.  This commentary was written by David Flinders.

# CHAPTER 10

# DESCRIPTIVE RESEARCH

## Overview

This chapter shows how descriptive research contributes to education and describes two common forms—survey and observational research. A published descriptive study of students' learning of reading and writing skills is presented. Comments by the researchers who conducted the study and our critical review are included to help you understand descriptive research reports that you may come across in a literature review.

## Objectives

1. Distinguish between descriptive, relationship, and experimental research.
2. Explain the purpose and methods of survey and observational research.
3. Explain three situations in which self-report evidence is likely to be distorted.
4. State a major advantage of direct observation as a means of gathering descriptive information.
5. Describe three errors in observational research that are likely to reduce the validity of the research results.

## The Importance of Descriptive Research

Most research studies can be placed in one of three broad categories that form a continuum from lesser to greater complexity: (1) descriptive, (2) relationship, and (3) experimental research. Descriptive research, as its name implies, aims to describe the characteristics of the phenomena being studied. For example, descriptive research might identify how reading teachers plan their lessons and how much time they spend in planning. Relationship research, which includes both correlational and causal-comparative research, is more complex in that it explores relationships between variables. An example would be a study to determine whether the students of reading teachers who spend more time planning their lessons (variable 1) have higher achievement (variable 2). Finally, experimental research is the most complex because the researchers manipulate one or more variables and measure the effect on another set of variables. For example, an experiment might be done in which one group of teachers is trained in effective lesson planning techniques (the manipulated variable) and another group is not trained. Then the effects on students' reading achievement (the dependent variable) are measured.

Before the complex research questions that are characteristic of relationship research and experimental research can be answered, it is necessary to know a good deal about the characteristics of the individuals and situations involved, so much of the research in education to date has been descriptive in nature. Even so, there is still much that we do not know about students, teachers, administrators, curriculum, instructional methods, and learning processes—the usual subjects of educational research.

Most descriptive research in education can be classified as either survey or observational research. These two types of research, conducted through quantitative methods, are discussed in the following section. Qualitative descriptive research is discussed in Chapter 9.

# Survey Research

Survey research typically employs questionnaires and interviews to determine the opinions, attitudes, preferences, and perceptions of persons of interest to the researcher. Perhaps the best-known surveys are public-opinion polls. Surveys in education can be used to explore many topics, for example, the extent to which cooperative learning is being used in elementary schools, the perceptions of teachers and principals about various school reform proposals, the related work experience of high school business education teachers, parents' preferences for different schooling choices, procedures being used to teach learning-disabled children, and problems encountered by first-year special education teachers.

Survey studies that deal with highly sensitive topics, such as students' attitudes about sexuality, or that attempt to elicit deeper responses that cannot be easily measured by questionnaires, frequently employ interviews. Some survey studies use both questionnaires and interviews, the former to collect basic descriptive information from a large sample and the latter to follow up the questionnaire responses in depth with a smaller sample.

You will recall from Chapter 6 that the way a question is asked can affect the responses. Thus, both questionnaires and interviews are subject to bias. For example, leading questions or questions that give the respondent a clue to what answer is desirable will yield biased responses.

In evaluating survey research, pay special attention to the procedure that was used to select the sample. For example, if survey researchers draw their sample from the telephone directory to predict the outcomes of a bond election, the resulting sample is biased because many citizens do not have telephones or have unlisted telephone numbers. Sampling biases are sometimes quite subtle, but they can result in erroneous and misleading conclusions. Sampling bias also occurs when the response rate is low because nonrespondents tend to differ from respondents, as discussed in Chapter 5.

It is also possible to describe the characteristics of a sample of individuals by making observations. The term *observation* refers to any objective procedure for recording the characteristics or behavior of the subjects. Observations are more objective than surveys because they do not depend on subjects' self-report.

In many descriptive studies in education, tests are administered to the subjects. Tests that measure students' ability, for example, their performance of a task or their knowledge of vocabulary, can be considered a form of observation because they provide objective information about the characteristics or behavior of the subjects. However, some tests, like many measures of personality or interest, involve self-report and thus are subject to distortion, as discussed above. For convenience, we will treat the use of tests to describe subjects' characteristics as a form of observation. However, in reading descriptive research, you should evaluate how likely it is that the information based on test scores is objective.

Suppose you were interested in doing a descriptive study of the personality characteristics of successful high school counselors. You would first need to establish a method for selecting successful counselors, such as obtaining ratings of each counselor from high school students who had received counseling. Once you had selected your sample of successful counselors, you could collect descriptive personality data on them in several ways: (1) administering a battery of personality tests to the counselors; (2) administering an adjective checklist to close associates of each counselor to obtain a measure of perceived personality traits; and (3) making direct observations of each counselor to record behaviors that indicate certain personality characteristics such as assertiveness, anxiety, or self-confidence. Regardless of your method of observation, the end result of your study would be a set of characteristics that successful high school counselors tend to have in common.

The procedures used to analyze descriptive research data are usually simple and easily understood. Table 10.1 summarizes common statistics that are often presented in descriptive research reports. You will note that most of the statistics are measures

Table 10.1    Statistical techniques often used to analyze descriptive research data

| Procedure | Purpose |
| --- | --- |
| Mean ($M$ or $X$) | Gives an indication of the central tendency of the group on the score in question. Equals the sum of the scores divided by $N$. Means are reported in virtually all descriptive studies. |
| Median (Med) | Also indicates central tendency. Used when extreme scores are present that would distort the mean. The median is the middle score in the score distribution. |
| Mode | Also indicates central tendency. Equals the most frequently obtained score. This is a crude measure, seldom used. |
| Standard deviation $(SD)$ | Most widely used measure of the variability of the group. A large $SD$ indicates a heterogeneous group. Based on the sum of the squares of the deviations of scores from the mean. |
| Average deviation $(AD)$ | Also measures variability. Equals the sum of the deviations of scores from the mean, divided by $N$. Used when extreme scores would unduly influence $SD$. Seldom used. |
| Quartile deviation $(Q)$ | Used in conjunction with the median, when a simple estimate of variability is sufficient. Equals the difference between the score at $Q_3$ (75th percentile) and the score at $Q_1$ (25th percentile), divided by 2. |
| Percentage $(P)$ | Often used to report the group's responses to multiple-choice questionnaire items. |

of central tendency, measures of variability, or percentages. These same three types of descriptive statistics also are used in relationship and experimental research, along with the special inferential statistics that were described in Chapter 7.

Suppose researchers had carried out a descriptive study of the characteristics of bilingual students in grades 4, 5, and 6 whose achievement was in the top 15 percent on a standardized achievement test. Their measurement procedures might include questionnaires answered by teachers and parents and interviews with the students themselves. Questions might focus on the students' characteristics, such as study habits, socioeconomic status, attitudes toward school, and level of parental involvement, that they hypothesize to be related to school success. Students could receive scores for general traits such as study habits, which would be based on several questions, as well as scores for their response to single items, such as "How many hours did you spend on homework during the past week?"

Statistical measures of central tendency could be used to describe the typical characteristics of the students being studied. For study habits, students could be assigned a total score based on their responses to all the items concerning the ways in which the students study. In turn the mean score for the sample of students could be calculated by adding all the students' total scores and dividing by the number of students.

Statistical measures of variability help researchers estimate how closely the scores of the sample cluster around the mean score. Do most of the individuals in the sample earn about the same score, or do their scores vary widely? For example, suppose the researchers wanted to determine the socioeconomic status of high-achieving bilingual students. They might assign an SES (socioeconomic status) score of 1 for students from working-class backgrounds, 2 for students from middle-class backgrounds, and 3 for students from upper-class backgrounds. Say that nearly all the high-achieving bilingual students came from the middle class. In this case, the standard deviation, a measure of the variability of individual subjects' SES scores around the mean, would be low. The researchers would conclude that middle-class socioeconomic status is characteristic of this group. However, if a substantial number of students came from each social class, the standard deviation would be high, reflecting a great deal of variability in students' SES scores.

Much descriptive research is based on self-report; that is, the subject tells you about himself. This is the case for questionnaires, interviews, and some paper-and-pencil tests. A serious potential weakness of self-report measures is that the subject may tell you only what he wants you to know. Thus, the information may be distorted or incomplete. When evaluating research based on self-report, be alert to any aspects of the study that might cause the subject to provide inaccurate information.

Even if subjects want to give accurate information, they may lack the insight to do so. For example, research has shown that self-ratings on many variables differ considerably from ratings of the individual by others on the same variables. Also, if the study is in any way threatening to the subjects, if they feel that honest answers can harm them, or if the questions call for a level of insight that the subjects do not possess, you can assume that many subjects will lie or give inaccurate answers. Self-report data on topics such as cheating in school, sexual orientation, or attitudes toward one's teachers are especially prone to this problem. If good rapport is established between the subjects and those conducting the research, and if the subjects believe that the investigator has used a foolproof system to ensure the confidentiality of their responses, self-report data will produce more accurate results.

# Direct Observation

Because of the weakness of self-report evidence, educational researchers have increasingly used direct observation of behavior by trained observers. You were introduced to direct observation as a measurement procedure in Chapter 6.

Direct observation is essentially a technique for gathering "live" data about the individuals and events being studied. The data are "live" in that behavior and events are recorded as they are occurring. Descriptive data would be less immediate and more subject to distortion if they were collected by other measurement techniques such as paper-and-pencil tests. For example, we probably can learn much more about interracial attitudes by observing children of different races in their actual interactions with one another than we can by asking questions about typical racial interactions in a paper-and-pencil test.

Direct observation is especially effective when the researcher wishes to study specific aspects of human behavior in detail. For example, the following questions are well suited for study by observation: (1) How do severely retarded children respond to specific strategies for teaching basic number facts? (2) How do preschool children behave after watching a television program that contains a large number of violent acts? (3) How do parents interact with their children when discussing homework assignments?

In reviewing studies that employ direct observation, you should pay particular attention to the potential for observer bias and any procedures used by the researchers to avoid it. For example, if observers are involved in a descriptive study of the social behavior of kindergarten children during free play, they may tend to see a higher level of social behavior in the children who they know have higher verbal aptitude. The solution to this observer bias is to design the observational procedures so that observers do not have knowledge about the children's background and school performance.

Other errors in observational research that reduce its validity include using broad, general definitions of the behavior to be observed rather than narrow, specific definitions; observing high-inference behaviors, such as rating the subject's sports performance from poor to excellent rather than counting the number of times a specific behavior occurs; and requiring the observer to record more aspects of behavior than can be attended to effectively.

To collect reliable observational data, it is usually necessary to train observers carefully. The procedures used to train observers are described in most good reports of observational research. Statistical information on the reliability of the observational data also should be included, and you should look for it when you review research reports. A typical sequence for training observers was described in Chapter 6.

In the rest of this chapter you will read a study that illustrates descriptive research.

As you will see, the study also used correlational statistics to examine the relationship between the variables that were investigated. Thus you may want to refer to Chapter 12 for a preview of correlational research before reading the article.

# Sample Descriptive Study:
# LEARNING TO READ AND WRITE:
# A LONGITUDINAL STUDY OF 54 CHILDREN
# FROM FIRST THROUGH FOURTH GRADES

## Abstract[1]

My research focused on literacy development in children through fourth grade and followed an earlier study (Juel, Griffith, & Gough, 1986). The Simple View of reading and writing received support in this earlier study and was examined in my current research. Of particular concern were these questions: Do the same children remain poor readers year after year? Do the same children remain poor writers year after year? What skills do the poor readers lack? What skills do the poor writers lack? What factors seem to keep poor readers from improving? What factors seem to keep poor writers from improving? The probability that a child would remain a poor reader at the end of fourth grade if the child was a poor reader at the end of first grade was .88. Early writing skill did not predict later writing skill as well as early reading ability predicted later reading ability. Children who became poor readers entered first grade with little phonemic awareness. By the end of fourth grade, the poor readers had still not achieved the level of decoding skill that the good readers had achieved at the beginning of second grade. Good readers read considerably more than the poor readers both in and out of school, which appeared to contribute to the good readers' growth in some reading and writing skills (e.g., in ideas for stories). Poor readers tended to become poor writers. The Simple View received support in accounting for reading and writing development through fourth grade.

## Researcher's Comments[2]

## Background

When I was a child I had a terrible time learning to read. I couldn't understand how my first-grade peers did it. I couldn't figure out how they knew what the print in the book said, or what words were on the cards our teacher flashed in front of us. I was frustrated and embarrassed.

When I was an elementary school teacher I saw children struggle, as I had, trying to read and write. I wasn't sure how to facilitate their passage into literacy. I wasn't sure why some children caught on and others faltered. I did a lot of observing and a lot of listening to my elementary students. I found some hypotheses about the insights and skills a child needed to possess in order to decipher print.

I decided to take a short break from teaching and go back to graduate school for a master's degree. I wanted to see what others would say about my hypotheses. I got caught up in the excitement of research, of testing one's hypotheses, of forming new ones. I was hooked. What was intended to be a one-year respite from elementary school teaching ended up in a doctoral degree and a new twist to my teaching career: I became a university professor.

My initial research tested cognitive models of the processes involved in learning to identify printed words. After several years my research yielded a developmental model of word recognition that satisfied me (Juel, 1983). I then became concerned with how the factors identified in this model would be affected by the type of words children saw in their instructional reading texts in first grade. I spent a year in first-grade classrooms studying the relationship between type of basal text (e.g., whether they were phonics or nonphonics texts) and the development of particular cognitive insights or skills such as the ability to decode (Juel & Roper/Schneider, 1985). During this year I again noted that some children learned to read with relative ease while others failed. I began to wonder whether those factors that seemed to contribute to difficulty in first grade would be overcome by certain experiences and skill developments in subsequent grades. The idea of the current longitudinal study was born.

I had been trained in graduate school to consider *all* the factors that could affect a phenomenon, and to develop and test models that included as many of these factors as possible. For me this meant that when investigating how a child learns to read at school, it is necessary to consider the myriad of factors associated with the child, the textbooks, the instruction, the setting for instruction, and so forth. I've examined a *lot* of factors in my studies.

I now have a colleague, Philip Gough, who shares my interest in initial reading and with whom I have collaborated on many studies. He holds a quite different philosophy from the one I learned in graduate school. His approach is to take the simplest view possible, take the fewest number of factors that you think can be responsible for a phenomenon, test those factors, and add or change factors only when the data force one to do so. His "Simple View" of reading, which was part of the initial study (Juel, Griffith, & Gough, 1986), illustrates this philosophy.

Clearly both research approaches have merit. At times trying to consider everything leaves one in the proverbial "Can't see the forest for the trees" position. At times trying to see everything leads to discovering something that might be the "missing piece" in the puzzle.

The study you are about to read tests the Simple View of reading and writing. Those factors thought to be responsible for literacy development within this view were examined. You will no doubt think of some other "trees" that could have been examined. I could not ignore instructional setting, for instance, and have written about the effects of reading groups on the literacy growth of these children elsewhere (Juel, in press).

# Experiences

There are many problems associated with doing lengthy field-based research. Our study was not exempt. Our first problem was securing the various and required permissions to do a four-year study. We needed permission from the human subjects committee at my university and from the school district, school principal, teachers, and the students' parents. One problem we encountered was that different requirements were imposed by the school district and the university over such things as the wording of permission slips, and whether both parents needed to sign them (many of our children were from single-parent homes). The university committee also wanted the children themselves to sign permission slips. Since our entering first-grade children were nonreaders, this requirement obviously was impossible.

We had planned to start our study at the very beginning of first grade, but the time required to present our case to the university committee delayed our starting the study until late in the school year. Once in the school, we spent considerable time meeting with the teachers and administrators. It was critical to keep on good terms with everyone and to have their support and interest in the study. If any teacher had decided not to have his or her class participate, our longitudinal design would have been greatly hampered. To have children removed from a class is understandably disruptive. Thus, to agree to such disruption for an entire year, the teachers needed to value the study.

We met with the teachers fairly often, communicated our findings, and solicited their input. We also accommodated our testing schedule to the teachers' schedules. Sometimes our tests would sit for long periods of time until a convenient testing opportunity arose. Some days such opportunities never arose. Flexibility, patience, and communication are critical in sustaining a longitudinal school-based study. (Then there was the time a fifth-grade student—not one of our subjects—brought a homemade bomb to school, that exploded. No data were collected on that day.)

Another problem with longitudinal research is attrition of subjects. We had requested that the school district select a research school that: (1) was large, (2) was located in a low-income area of town, (3) was attended by many minority students, and (4) had a low attrition rate. We got all but the last request. We began the study with 129 first-grade children; only 54 remained at the school through fourth grade (63 of the 9 who were retained at the end of first grade are counted).

The high attrition rate was partly due to studying a school in a low-income housing area. Many of our children lived in rental houses or apartments, with parents who frequently moved in search of better jobs. Many of the parents of our children were enlisted military personnel at an Air Force base, which has a built-in attrition factor. The attrition rate was compounded by the crash of the Austin economy that occurred during the course of the study. This increased the number of children whose parents moved out of Austin in search of jobs.

# Aftermath

In a typical journal format, each individual child's development gets lost. I am working on a book that describes this longitudinal study and includes a number of case studies.[3]

A very sobering finding in the current study was that a child who was a poor reader at the end of first grade almost invariably remained a poor reader at the end of fourth grade. This finding led me to my current research project, which involves developing and testing a first-grade intervention program (Juel, 1991).

# References

JUEL, C. (1983). The development and use of mediated word identification. *Reading Research Quarterly, 18,* 306–327.

JUEL, C. (1990). Effects of reading group assignment on reading development in first and second grade. *Journal of Reading Behavior, 22*(3), 233–254.

JUEL, C. (1991). Cross-age tutoring between student athletes and at-risk children. *The Reading Teacher, 45*(3), 178–179.

JUEL, C., & ROPER/SCHNEIDER, D. (1985). The influence of basal readers on first grade reading. *Reading Research Quarterly, 20,* 134–152.

JUEL, C., GRIFFITH, P. L., & GOUGH, P. B. (1986). Acquisition of literacy: A longitudinal study of children in first and second grade. *Journal of Educational Psychology, 78,* 243–255.

# LEARNING TO READ AND WRITE: A LONGITUDINAL STUDY OF 54 CHILDREN FROM FIRST THROUGH FOURTH GRADES

Connie Juel
**UNIVERSITY OF TEXAS AT AUSTIN**

This study examined the development of literacy in one elementary school with a large minority, low socioeconomic status population. The reading and writing development of 54 children was followed as they progressed from first through fourth grade. This in-depth examination of literacy acquisition in a microcosm of at-risk children attempted to answer the following questions: Do the same children remain poor readers year after year? Do the same children remain poor writers year after year? What skills do the poor readers lack? What skills do the poor writers lack? What factors seem to keep poor readers from improving? What factors seem to keep poor writers from improving?

I began my study by conceptualizing reading and writing from the Simple View (Gough & Tunmer, 1986; Juel, Griffith, & Gough, 1986). The development of those cognitive factors that are thought most responsible for literacy development within this view were closely followed in children who came to school with few reading and writing skills.

In the Simple View, reading ability is composed of two factors, decoding and comprehension. Decoding is the process that leads to word recognition. Learning to break the code of written text is partly dependent on being aware that words are composed of sequences of mean-

ingless and somewhat distinct sounds (i.e., phonemes). This is often referred to as phonemic awareness. This realization is not necessary for understanding or producing speech. In speech production there is no clear distinction between phonemes, because one phoneme overlaps another. But phonemic awareness is necessary in learning to decode an alphabetic language, as print decoding depends on mapping phonemes to graphemes (i.e., letters in English). In school, phonics instruction attempts to make these correspondences explicit. Juel et al. (1986) found that phonics instruction is not effective unless children have (or quickly develop) some phonemic awareness at the beginning of first grade.

Phonemic awareness is not a unitary, indivisible insight or ability. Rather there are various phonemic insights (e.g., being able to judge which is a longer word in acoustic duration or being able to rhyme words, knowing that *toad* is composed of three distinctive—albeit overlapping and abstract—sounds, being able to say *cat* without the /t/). Some phonemic abilities (such as phoneme blending) appear prerequisite to learning to read, whereas other abilities (such as phoneme deletion) may be outcomes of learning to read (Perfetti, Beck, Bell, & Hughes, 1987). There is converging evidence from both experimental and longitudinal studies conducted in several countries that some form of phonemic awareness is necessary to successfully learn to read alphabetic languages (Blachman & James, 1985; Bradley & Bryant, 1983; Elkonin, 1963, 1973; Fox &

Routh, 1975; Juel et al., 1986; Lundberg, Oloffson, & Wall, 1980; Share, Jorm, Maclean, & Matthews, 1984; Tornéus, 1984; Tunmer & Nesdale, 1985; Williams, 1984).

Low socioeconomic status Black and Hispanic children are more likely than low socioeconomic status Anglo children to have poor phonemic awareness of school English, which hinders the development of decoding skill (Juel et al., 1986; Juel & Leavell, in press). This may be a result of greater differences between school and home language for Black and Hispanic students, as well as cultural differences (which include such variables as time spent at home with word play, experience with nursery or Dr. Seuss rhymes, and general print exposure in storybook sharing). In a 15-month longitudinal study of British children from the age of 3 years, 4 months, Maclean, Bryant, and Bradley (1987) found (a) that there is a strong relation between children's early knowledge of nursery rhymes and the later development of phonological skill and (b) that phonological skill predicted early reading ability. Both relations were found after controlling for the effects of IQ and socioeconomic status.

The second component in the Simple View of reading is comprehension. Comprehension is the process by which the meanings of words are integrated into sentences and text structures. In spite of certain differences in form between speech and written text (cf. Rubin, 1980), in the Simple View a single underlying process is seen as producing both reading and listening comprehension. This implies that, given perfect word recognition, a child will read and comprehend a written text exactly as well as he or she would comprehend the text if it is spoken.

Children who come from homes in which language is used almost exclusively for direct (i.e., instrumental) communication may have difficulty with the decontextualized nature of communication in books and in school. On the other hand, children who have experienced decontextualized language by having been read to, by hearing language used for purely conceptual discussions, or in other abstract contexts are better prepared for the language used in classrooms. Such children are also likely to be familiar with story structures and complex syntax and have richer vocabularies and developed concepts that will foster reading (as well as listening)

comprehension of books. There is evidence that suggests minority and low socioeconomic status children are more likely to lack extensive experience with decontextualized language (Heath, 1983; Snow, 1983). As measured by standardized tests, the children in my research were below average in school language and listening comprehension at both the beginning and end of first grade.

The Simple View also considers writing to be composed of two basic factors, spelling and ideation. Just as learning to read words appears to require a degree of phonemic awareness, so does spelling (Bradley & Bryant, 1983; Juel et al., 1986; Lundberg et al., 1980). Children's invented spellings are created from letter name knowledge coupled with some degree of phonemic awareness. Read (1971, 1975, 1986) showed that there is a phonetic reason for certain nonstandard spellings frequently produced by young children. Schreiber and Read (1980) state that

> children's spelling is phonetic, not merely in the expected sense that it represents each phoneme of English more or less consistently, but also in the sense that it represents details of pronunciation that adults are unaware of. A spelling such as "SIK" for "sink" is phonetically accurate in that for many, if not most pronunciations, "sink" does have only three phonetically distinct segments: [sɪk]. Any trace of a velar nasal that does occur is typically so short that it is by no means obvious that it is the "same sound" (same phoneme) as the one that occurs at the end of "sing" [sñ]. (p. 212)

In comparison with such sophisticated spelling, Juel, Griffith, and Gough (1985) found that first-grade children who lacked phonemic awareness (as well as spelling-sound knowledge) made spelling errors that often seemed unrelated to phonetic elements (e.g., spelled *rain* as *yes* or *wnishire*). The children in their study lived in a low socioeconomic status area and may represent a different population of children than Read's subjects (who are usually not lower socioeconomic status children). It may be fairly hypothesized that the child who spells *rain* as *yes* has not engaged in writing activities as frequently as the child who spells *rain* as *rane*.

The second component of the Simple View of writing

is ideation. Ideation is the ability to generate and organize ideas. The term is used broadly to encompass both the generation of creative thoughts and their organization into sentence and text structures. The lower socioeconomic status child, who may not have been read to as much as the higher socioeconomic status child, is likely to come to school with less knowledge of stories and fewer ideas for their creation.

Our models of reading and writing may seem somewhat simplistic at first. It should be recognized that each component (e.g., ideation) is complex in its own right and may be broken down into many subcomponents. But only two components of each model (i.e., spelling and ideation for writing, word recognition and comprehension for reading) seem necessary to characterize both the primary lower level skill (i.e., spelling or word recognition) and the primary higher level skill (i.e., ideation or comprehension) that form the central components of writing or reading.

Poor lower order processes may impede the development of higher order processes. Until the lower order process of spelling is somewhat automatic—at least for a corpus of high frequency words—the attention of the writer may be diverted from higher order composing processes (Bereiter, 1980; Gundlach, 1981; Scardamalia, 1981). The development of automatic lower level processing of words may also be required for attention to be fully focused on comprehension when reading (LaBerge & Samuels, 1974). It seems clear that early efficient word recognition leads to better comprehension than does the reverse order (Calfee & Piontkowski, 1981; Lesgold, Resnick, & Hammond, 1985).

In the model called the Simple View, if someone is a poor reader, then he or she must be either a poor decoder, a poor listener, or both. If someone is a poor writer, then he or she must be either a poor speller, a poor generator of ideas, or both. In this study I investigated whether the sample of children who were poor readers and writers fit these models, and if so, where their problems began.

# Method
## Subjects

The children attended one large, neighborhood elementary school and lived in a low socioeconomic status area of small houses, duplexes, and apartments in Austin, Texas. Many of the children's parents were either en-

listed military personnel or other nonmilitary employees of a nearby Air Force base. As a result of the transient nature of this population, the study began with 129 children in first grade and ended with 54 children at the end of fourth grade. Data are presented in this study on the 54 children who remained in the school from first through fourth grade. The children were 26% Anglo, 31% Black, and 43% Hispanic Americans. There were 31 girls and 23 boys.

The children were in eight different classrooms in first grade, seven classrooms in second grade, and six classrooms in the third and fourth grades. The children were instructed with basal series that were eclectic in nature, blending sight word, phonics, and use of context approaches to word identification. The basal program was supplemented in first and second grade with a synthetic phonics program developed by the local school district.

## Procedure

The measures and interviews given to the children are detailed below.

### Phonemic Awareness Test

In October and April of each grade except the fourth, we administered the Phonemic Awareness Test developed by Roper/Schneider (1984). By the end of third grade, the children had reached ceiling on the test.[4]* This oral test has six subtests, each with seven items, and is individually administered. The subtests measure skill in phonemic segmentation, blending, deletion of first phoneme, deletion of last phoneme, substitution of first phoneme, and substitution of last phoneme. The seven alpha coefficients, representing the average of all possible split-half reliabilities, are greater than .7 for all subtests.[5] Details on test development can be found in Roper/Schneider (1984).

### Decoding

In October/November and April of each grade the Bryant Test of Basic Decoding Skill (BTBDS; Bryant, 1975) was individually administered. The Bryant test consists of 50 pseudowords, which children read aloud. The first 20 pseudowords are CVCs (consonant-vowel-consonants, e.g., *buf, dit, nuv*). The next 20 items are more complex

---

* Numbered notes to articles are supplied by the authors of this text.

single syllable pseudowords (e.g., *yode, shi, fler, cleef*). Only the last 10 items have more than one syllable (e.g., *cosnuv, uncabeness*). The test reliabilities (Cronbach's alpha) were between .96 and .90 in each grade.[6]

## Word Recognition
At the beginning of first grade, we had each child read a list of 10 words that would appear in their first pre-primer. Only one child could read more than five of these words; most children could not read any. Several times each year each child was asked to read a list of the core vocabulary words from each book in their basal reading series. Each child was tested only on those words that the individual had actually covered in the basal series; in other words, a child was not asked to read words from the first third-grade reader until the child had read the text. The percentage of words each child correctly read aloud from each reader list was calculated.

In April/May of each grade the Iowa Test of Basic Skills (ITBS; Hieronymous, Lindquist, & Hoover, 1980) was administered by the school. The vocabulary subtest requires the child to find which of four printed words labels a picture. It measures word recognition as well as vocabulary. The composite test-retest reliability on the ITBS is .98.[7]

The Wide Range Achievement Test reading subtest was administered in April of each grade (WRAT; Jastak, Bijou, & Jastak, 1978). The WRAT reading subtest consists of 75 words (e.g., *cat* to *aborigines*). Children were individually asked to read the words aloud. The test-retest reliability is .96.

## Listening Comprehension
The Metropolitan Readiness Test (MRT; Nurse & McGauvran, 1976) was administered by the school in September of first grade. The MRT language subtest assesses school language and listening comprehension. The child marks pictures that correctly illustrate the meaning of orally presented short passages. The test-retest reliability of this subtest is .72. Similar to this subtest is the listening comprehension subtest of the ITBS. It was used as a year-end measure of listening comprehension in each grade.

## Reading Comprehension
The reading comprehension subtest of the ITBS was used to assess reading comprehension of both sentences and passages.

## Place in Series
Each child's place in his or her basal reader was determined. This measure represents the number of words the child had seen in running text in the readers.

## Home Reading
Each year the children were asked about their reading behaviors at home. The testers inquired about what (if anything) they read at home. They were asked about titles, authors, and plots of books they read. The children were also asked, over a period of several weeks, how many days or nights they read at home.

## Attitude toward Reading
Each year the children were asked a series of questions about their attitude toward reading. Some questions focused on which of two activities they would rather do. For example: Would you rather watch television or read? Would you rather play with friends or read? Would you rather clean your room or read? The children were also asked, Do you like to read? Why?

## IQ
At the beginning of second grade the Vocabulary and Block Design subtests from the Wechsler Intelligence Scale for Children-Revised (WISC-R; Wechsler, 1974) were administered. Results of these two subtests were summed to form an estimated IQ score. The test-retest reliability is .86 on the WISC-R Vocabulary subtest and .85 on the Block Design subtest.

## Spelling
In April of each grade the WRAT spelling subtest was administered. The spelling subtest requires a child to write words pronounced orally by the tester. The maximum number of words to be spelled, depending on performance, is 45. The test-retest reliability for the spelling subtest is .97. The ITBS spelling subtest was used as another measure of spelling. This subtest requires recognition of words that are incorrectly spelled.

## Writing
In February and April of first grade, November and April of second grade, and January in third and fourth grades, each child was shown the same colorful picture of animals in a schoolroom setting and asked to write a story about what might be going on in the picture. In Novem-

ber of fourth grade, the children were asked to write a story about "The Friendly Ghost." Before beginning the story, each child was encouraged to talk about what a ghost is.

In both the animal and the ghost stories the children were told to spell words as best they could, but not to worry about spelling. After they wrote the story they read it back to the testers to resolve any possible discrepancies about words they had used. (These rereadings were later used by the raters to resolve ambiguities resulting from inadequate spelling.)

A score was assigned to each sample on the basis of the judgments of two raters. A representative writing sample for each rating was used as a guide for assigning these scores.

In second, third, and fourth grade, the same scoring guidelines were used. These scores ranged from 1 (low) to 9 (high). A score of 1 was assigned when the child wrote either a series of isolated words or text devoid of sentence structure. A score of 2 was assigned when the child had attempted to write complete sentences, but the sentences were not interrelated. A score of 3 indicated an attempt to write complete sentences to describe characters (i.e., the ghost or animals) or objects in the picture. A score of 4 was assigned when the child wrote a higher level, coherent description of characters or objects. A score of 5 indicated the child brought in background knowledge to create an elaborated description of characters or objects. A score of 6 was assigned when the child wrote an incomplete (or somewhat incoherent) episode. A score of 7 was given when the child wrote a complete episode that included several story grammar components (i.e., setting, initiating event, attempt, reaction, consequence). A score of 8 indicated a story containing more than one episode, with at least one episode containing several components of story grammar. A score of 9 was assigned if a story contained several fairly complete episodes, with a storyline or bridge to connect the episodes.

In first grade there were few children who wrote anything higher level than simple descriptions of the animal picture, and thus different scoring criteria had to be used than that used in the other grades. In first grade a score of 1 indicated that the child had produced either drawings in lieu of text, meaningless tangles of letters, or lists of words that were either not related or only tangentially related to the picture. A score of 2 was assigned to samples that contained occasional groups of related words, lists of words related to the picture, or barely comprehensible language. Scores of 3 through 7 were assigned to the remaining samples on the basis of relatedness or completeness of parts of the produced text.

Raters were instructed to disregard spelling but instead to consider level of story development, syntactic maturity, and richness of vocabulary when assigning a score. On occasion, a written sample would not quite fit any of the guidelines for the above categories and was assigned a score whose criteria it most resembled. The average interrater reliability was .86 (Pearson's r).[8]

### Ideas

A week or two after the children had written their last animal story in a grade, we asked each to orally tell a story about the picture. The oral stories were tape recorded and later transcribed and rated according to the same 1 to 9 criteria described above for writing in second through fourth grade.

## Results and Discussion

### Do the Same Children Remain Poor Readers Year after Year?

The reading development of the bottom quartile of children in reading comprehension at the end of first grade was examined. This bottom quartile consisted of 29 children who scored no better than a 1.2 grade equivalent on the ITBS Reading Comprehension subtest.[9] The mean of these children's scores on the subtest was K6 at the end of first grade.[10]

Of these 29 children, 24 remained in the school at the end of fourth grade. Two had been retained at the end of first grade, and three had left the school. Of the 24 remaining, all but 3 were still poor readers in fourth grade. Twenty-one were still reading at least 6 months below an appropriate grade equivalent at the end of fourth grade. These children were reading at no greater than a 4.2 grade equivalent on the ITBS Reading Comprehension subtest, with a mean for the group of grade equivalent 3.5.

Of the 86 children who were average or good readers at the end of first grade, 30 remained at the end of fourth grade. Of these 30, 26 were still average or good readers, and 4 had slipped to below a 4.3 grade equivalent on the ITBS.

The probability that a child would remain a poor reader at the end of fourth grade, if the child was a poor reader at the end of first grade was .88; the probability that a child would become a poor reader in fourth grade if he or she had at least average reading skills in first grade was .12. The probability that a child would remain an average reader in fourth grade if the child had average reading ability in first grade was .87; the probability that a child would become an average reader in fourth grade if he or she was a poor reader in first grade was only .13. The evidence in this sample of children indicates that the poor first-grade reader almost invariably remains a poor reader by the end of fourth grade.

## Do the Same Children Remain Poor Writers Year after Year?

Early writing skill did not predict later writing skill as well as early reading ability predicted later reading ability. This may be attributed in part to the curricular emphasis at our research school on reading, as opposed to writing, in first grade.

The correlation between writing at the end of first grade and writing in fourth grade was .38, $p > .01$,[11] but the correlation increased with each subsequent grade level. The correlation between end-of-year second grade writing and fourth grade writing was .53, $p < .001$. The correlation between third and fourth grade writing was .60, $p < .001$.

## What Skills Do the Poor Readers Lack?

The children who became poor readers entered first grade with little phonemic awareness. The modal score for this group on the phonemic awareness test administered at the beginning of first grade was 0. The mean score on this test for the children who became good readers (21.7) was considerably higher than that of the poor readers (4.2). By the end of first grade, the good readers had a mean score on the phonemic awareness test that approached ceiling (37.5). The poor readers made considerable gains in phonemic awareness in first grade, ending the year with a mean score of 18.6. The poor readers did not approach ceiling on the phonemic awareness test until the end of third grade, when their mean score was 36.2.

Growth in spelling-sound knowledge was initially slow for the poor readers, and they never reached the level of the average and good readers. Nine of the poor readers could not read a single pseudoword on the BTBDS at the end of first grade, despite a year of phonics instruction. (These 9 children had little or no entering phonemic awareness.)

At the end of fourth grade, all but 2 poor readers were at least one standard deviation below the good readers on the BTBDS.[12] The majority of the poor readers still could not decode all the monosyllabic pseudowords (e.g., *buf*) on the test by the end of fourth grade (see Table 1).

If the 2 poor readers in fourth grade who were good decoders had good listening comprehension, they would contradict the Simple View of reading. But this was not the case; both children had poor listening comprehension, one standard deviation below that of the good readers. Although there are many references in the literature to poor readers who are "word-callers," they were not found within this sample. The 2 poor readers who were good decoders could not comprehend well whether the input was oral or written.

There were 3 children who were poor decoders but had average listening comprehension. This is exactly the pattern that so-called dyslexic children should exhibit. But all the rest of the poor readers were also poor listeners.

Poor fourth-grade readers were mainly children who were neither competent at decoding nor competent listeners (see Table 1). For each grade, word recognition on the WRAT was more predictive of ITBS reading comprehension than was listening comprehension on the ITBS. The impact of listening comprehension steadily rose with each grade level. In first grade, word recognition accounted for 44% of the variance in a *hierarchical regression* predicting reading comprehension (after controlling for the influence of listening comprehension), whereas listening comprehension had no unique influence.[13] By fourth grade, word recognition still made a unique contribution of 25%, but listening comprehension also made a unique contribution of 12%.

## What Skills Do the Poor Writers Lack?

The mean score on "The Friendly Ghost" story was 4.8 (SD = 2.0). The mean score on the animal picture story in fourth grade was 5.0 (SD = 2.3). The correlation

Table 1   Means and standard deviations for reading variables for good and poor readers

| Variable | Poor readers | | Good readers | |
|---|---|---|---|---|
| | M | SD | M | SD |
| ITBS reading comprehension | | | | |
| Grade 1 | K6 | .4 | 2.4 | .4 |
| Grade 2 | 1.7 | .5 | 3.8 | .7 |
| Grade 3 | 2.6 | .4 | 4.8 | .8 |
| Grade 4 | 3.5 | .3 | 5.9 | .8 |
| ITBS listening comprehension | | | | |
| Grade 1 | 1.4 | .5 | 1.5 | .5 |
| Grade 2 | 2.5 | .6 | 3.2 | .5 |
| Grade 3 | 2.5 | .8 | 4.9 | .9 |
| Grade 4 | 2.6 | .8 | 5.2 | .9 |
| BTBDS (End of year) | | | | |
| Grade 1 | 8.3 | 9.2 | 24.9 | 11.9 |
| Grade 2 | 19.6 | 5.9 | 36.0 | 7.8 |
| Grade 3 | 28.7 | 11.7 | 41.4 | 6.4 |
| Grade 4 | 28.4 | 9.2 | 42.6 | 7.2 |
| WRAT word recognition | | | | |
| Grade 1 | 12.9 | 5.2 | 26.4 | 7.5 |
| Grade 2 | 26.7 | 8.7 | 44.6 | 10.3 |
| Grade 3 | 35.6 | 7.3 | 45.5 | 9.2 |
| Grade 4 | 39.1 | 6.4 | 54.7 | 7.1 |
| ITBS vocabulary (word recognition) | | | | |
| Grade 1 | 1.5 | .4 | 2.4 | .6 |
| Grade 2 | 2.1 | .6 | 3.2 | .4 |
| Grade 3 | 3.1 | .4 | 4.2 | .5 |
| Grade 4 | 3.5 | .7 | 5.8 | .7 |

*Note.* ITBS = Iowa Test of Basic Skills; BTBDS = Bryant Test of Basic Decoding Skills; WRAT = Wide Range Achievement Test. ITBS score grade equivalents are presented here for convenience of interpretation. Raw scores were used in data analysis.

between the two writing samples in fourth grade was .83, *p* < .001. In fourth grade, 21 children had a mean of 3.5 or below on the combined writing scores. None of these children scored above a 5 on either writing sample. That is, 21 children were still writing descriptions rather than stories at the end of fourth grade.

Fourth-grade students with scores one standard deviation below the average WRAT spelling of the entire sample were labeled poor spellers. Fourth-grade students with an oral story production score of not more than 3.0 were defined as poor generators of story ideas. Using these criteria, 7 of the 21 poor writers had good spelling but poor ideas. Seven poor writers had good ideas but poor spelling. Seven poor writers had both poor ideas and poor spelling. As the Simple View would predict, no poor writers who had good spelling and good ideas were found in my study.

Although written samples were not evaluated in terms of spelling, this lower level skill seems to control to some degree the act of writing. This seems especially likely in the first grade, when children in a school setting may have been unwilling to try to write words that they could not spell—even though they were encouraged to do so in my study. It may also be just too difficult to write a story when one has to struggle with how to write the words. Spelling had more of an impact on first-grade writing than it did on fourth-grade writing. In a hierarchical regression predicting[14] written animal stories in first grade, spelling accounted for 29% of the variance (after controlling for the influence of ideas), whereas in fourth grade spelling accounted for 10% of the variance. The influence of the higher level skill (i.e., ideas) on the written stories was apparent in each grade level's writing, however. The influence of ideas on the written stories also increased in impact with each grade. In first grade ideas accounted for 8% of the variance (after controlling for the influence of spelling); by fourth grade the impact of ideas had increased to account for 30% of the variance.

## What Factors Seem to Keep Poor Readers from Improving?

A primary factor that seemed to keep the poor readers from improving was their poor decoding skill. The poor readers at the end of fourth grade had not achieved the level of decoding on the BTBDS that the good readers had achieved by the beginning of second grade. This lack of decoding skill prevented the poor readers from being able to read as much text—both in and out of school—as the good readers, which appeared to create further problems, as will be described later.

By the end of first grade, the good readers had seen, on average, 18,681 words in running text in their basal readers. In contrast, the poor readers had seen, on average, 9,975 words, about half as many. After first grade, differences in exposure to print in school became more complex to estimate because some poor readers were asked to reread basals previously covered. By simply counting words children were exposed to in readers (whether read or reread), it appeared in my study that the difference in exposure to print between good and poor readers grew larger with each grade. Many poor readers were still in beginning third-grade readers at the end of fourth grade. By contrast, the good readers had finished the fourth-grade reader. The good readers, on average, had read about 178,000 words in running text in their basal readers by the end of fourth grade, whereas the poor reader had read less than half of that—about 80,000 words.

After second grade there also appeared to be wide differences in the amount of reading done out of school. The children were asked several questions about their reading habits at home. Although such data are not always reliable, a very close rapport developed between the children and the testers, and I believe that these self-reports are reasonably accurate. One of the questions the children were asked (over the course of several weeks each year) concerned the number of nights they read at home each week. The average number of nights reported per week by each group of readers is shown in Figure 1. Neither group of readers indicated they read much after school in first or second grade; but in third and fourth grade reading after school became quite frequent for the good readers. The good readers also could

tell us the authors or titles or plots of many of the books they were reading, whereas few poor readers could supply such information.

The more frequent reading experiences—both in and out of school—of the children who learned to read well early in school likely contributed to the steadily widening gulf in listening comprehension (i.e., knowledge of vocabulary, concepts, text structures, syntax, and pragmatics) between the good and poor readers (see Table 1). The means of both the group of children who would become good readers and those who would become poor readers were in the 4th stanine (i.e., below the 39th percentile) on the MRT Language subtest (School Language and Listening Comprehension) at the beginning of first grade. At the end of first grade, both groups were still low average in listening comprehension on the ITBS. But unlike good readers, poor readers made almost no progress in listening comprehension after second grade. Poor readers ended fourth grade with a mean grade equivalent of 2.6 on the ITBS Listening Comprehension subtest compared with the good reader's mean score of 5.2.

It seems apparent that poor readers read little voluntarily, partly because reading was so difficult for them, and reading experiences in school must have been rather aversive. Throughout the grades each child in the study read a list of core vocabulary words from his or her basal reader. This list was individualized for each child and included only words already seen in the basal. Usually reading educators recommended that students be given textbooks in which they can read at least 90–95% of the words in order to allow easy comprehension. In Figure 2 is shown a bar-graph comparison between the basal word reading of average/good readers and poor readers in each grade level book (no matter what grade level they were at when they read the book). The poor readers rarely correctly read even 80% of the words. For these children, reading each year in school was at best difficult and certainly not a successful experience.

We used a variety of questions to ascertain the children's attitudes toward reading. We asked them to select which of two activities they would rather do and why. For example, when asked whether they would rather watch television or read, about 70% of both good and poor readers said they would prefer to watch television; when asked whether they would rather play with friends

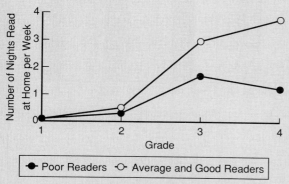

Figure 1  Mean Number of Nights per Week Poor and Average to Good Readers Read at Home by Themselves.

or read, about 70% of each group said they would rather play. When asked whether they would rather clean their room or read, only 5% of the good readers said they would clean, whereas 40% of the poor readers preferred to clean—one child stated, "I'd rather clean the mold around the bathtub than read."

The fourth-grade children were also asked, "Do you like to read? Why?" Whereas 26 good readers answered with an unqualified *yes* to liking to read, only five poor readers responded yes.

Some typical reasons that good readers gave for liking to read were "You get neat ideas," "You get to picture things in your mind and use your imagination," "You learn new things from books," "I learn new words," "You know what happens in the story and you might learn from the mistakes of people in the stories," "It's fun to pretend like you're the one in the book," and "It keeps you going to see what happens next."

Poor fourth-grade readers seemed to read little because they hated reading (which several children said) or because of the failure experiences associated with reading. The most common response of the poor readers to why they did not like to read was that it was boring.

## What Factors Seem to Keep the Poor Writers from Improving?

Poor readers appear to become poor writers. The correlation between writing and reading comprehension was .27, $p < .05$ in first grade, .39, $p < .01$ in second grade, .43, $p < .01$ in third grade, and .52, $p < .001$ in fourth grade. By fourth grade 17 of the 25 poor readers were poor writers, whereas only 4 of the 29 good readers were poor writers.

Of the 4 good readers who were poor writers, 3 were good spellers but produced as poor oral stories as their written stories. The other child had good story ideas but was a poor speller.

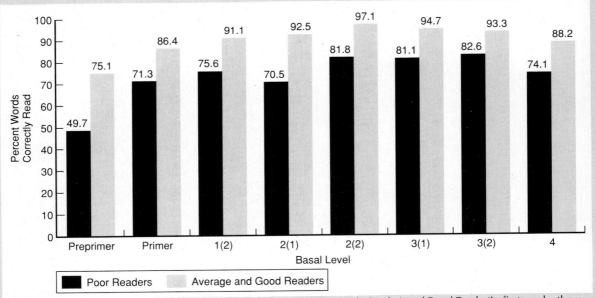

Figure 2  Mean Percentage of Words Correctly Read after Reading Each Grade Level Basal Book. (In first grade, there are three book lists: Preprimer (combining words in the three preprimers), Primer, and the 1[2] reader. In second and third grade, there are two basal readers. In fourth grade there is only one basal reader. Each child was tested only on the books that he or she covered in class. Several poor readers never got to the 3[2] or fourth-grade basal.)

Of the 17 poor writers who were also poor readers, 11 could neither write nor tell a good story. They lacked what I called story ideas (i.e., knowledge of story structures and the delivery of interesting story episodes). Of these 11 children, 7 were also poor spellers. The 6 poor readers who had good ideas were all poor spellers.

Through the years the good readers' proficiency in producing ideas steadily grew, whereas poor readers made no apparent progress in their ability to tell an oral story from first to fourth grade (see Table 2). Most poor readers were still telling and writing descriptions rather than stories in the fourth grade. These descriptions usually amounted to little more than an expanded list of what was seen in the animal picture (e.g., "It is a big classroom. They have seven desk in there classroom. They have five pictures in it . . .") or a simple description of "The Friendly Ghost" (e.g., "There was a ghost but he was a friendly ghost. He will help other people . . .")

By at least fourth grade most good readers were writing stories that included some elements of story grammar (i.e., setting, elaborated description of characters, and at least one episode). Their animal stories sometimes involved real classroom situations (e.g., "Once upon a time there was a teacher who was talking to Roger. She asked him if he did his homework . . ."). Their animal stories often involved quite imaginative story lines. An example of the latter is the following excerpt from a very long story about the "animal class" on a field trip:

They went hiking up a very, very, . . . very long trail. They hiked for hours and hours. Then they got lost a sand storm came and covered up the trail. Everyone got very scared.

It was finally dawn then Lisa ground squirrel found a cave. The class stayed there overnight thank god they brought their lunches and had that for dinner . . ."

The good readers' use of imaginative story lines, more story grammar elements, and interesting vocabulary was also evident in their "Friendly Ghost" stories. These elements are illustrated in the opening line of a story by a good reader: "One day a girl name Magi walked down a chilly street on the way home. . . ."

Table 2    Means and standard deviations for writing variables for good and poor readers

| Variable | Poor readers | | Good readers | |
|---|---|---|---|---|
| | M | SD | M | SD |
| Writing (animal story)[a] | | | | |
| Grade 1 | 2.8 | 1.5 | 4.2 | 1.4 |
| Grade 2 | 2.9 | 1.3 | 4.9 | 2.6 |
| Grade 3 | 3.5 | 2.5 | 5.8 | 2.6 |
| Grade 4 | 3.8 | 2.2 | 6.2 | 1.8 |
| Ideas (oral animal story) | | | | |
| Grade 1 | 3.8 | 2.4 | 4.0 | 2.6 |
| Grade 2 | 3.3 | 2.0 | 4.5 | 2.6 |
| Grade 3 | 3.9 | 2.1 | 5.2 | 2.3 |
| Grade 4 | 3.8 | 2.0 | 6.0 | 1.9 |
| WRAT Spelling | | | | |
| Grade 1 | 4.9 | 2.6 | 12.5 | 2.7 |
| Grade 2 | 12.7 | 3.5 | 19.1 | 3.3 |
| Grade 3 | 19.5 | 4.4 | 23.6 | 3.3 |
| Grade 4 | 20.5 | 3.4 | 27.5 | 3.8 |
| ITBS Spelling[b] | | | | |
| Grade 1 | 1.4 | .4 | 2.7 | .7 |
| Grade 2 | 2.2 | .4 | 3.5 | .9 |
| Grade 3 | 3.3 | .4 | 4.6 | .9 |
| Grade 4 | 4.2 | .6 | 5.7 | 1.0 |

*Note.* WRAT = Wide Range Achievement Test; ITBS = Iowa Test of Basic Skills.
[a]Writing means are from the end-of-year stories in first and second grade. Means for first grade are based on different scoring criteria than the means for the other grades.    [b]ITBS score grade equivalents are presented here for convenience of interpretation. Raw scores were used in data analysis.

The more frequent reading experiences of the good readers probably led to better story ideas (as well as knowledge of story structures and vocabulary with which to express those ideas). A hierarchical regression predicting[15] the children's oral stories in each grade supported this notion. IQ was entered first in the regression, accounting for from 16% of the variance in first grade to 10% of the variance in fourth grade. Place in series (the number of words read in the basal) was then entered. After controlling for IQ, place in series still accounted for a significant amount of variance in each grade. Place in series contributed 6% to the variance in first grade, but its contribution rose with each subsequent grade—accounting for 30% of the variance in fourth grade.

## General Discussion

In this study, the poor first-grade reader was almost invariably still a poor reader by the end of fourth grade. The good first-grade reader almost invariably remained a good reader at the end of fourth grade. Other studies have found similar trends. Clay (1979) discusses results of a study of children learning to read in New Zealand, where reading instruction begins at age five:

> There is an unbounded optimism among teachers that children who are late in starting will indeed catch up. Given time, something will happen! In particular, there is a belief that the intelligent child who fails to learn to read will catch up to his classmates once he has made a start. Do we have any evidence of accelerated progress in late starters? There may be isolated examples which support this hope, but correlations from a follow-up study of 100 children two and three years after school entry lead me to state rather dogmatically that where a child stood in relation to his age-mates at the end of his first year at school was roughly where one could expect to find him at 7:0 or 8:0. (p. 13)

It is interesting to note that in Sweden, where formal schooling does not start until age 7, Lundberg (1984) found similar results. Of 46 Swedish children with low linguistic awareness and low reading achievement in first grade, 40 were still poor readers in sixth grade. Lundberg, as in our study, linked the poor readers' problem to poor entering phonemic awareness. Lundberg found that linguistic awareness of words and phonemes in first grade correlated .70 with reading achievement in sixth grade.

In comparing the findings of Clay (1979), Lundberg (1984), and my study, it appears that age of entry into formal school reading instruction (whether age 5, 6, or 7) is not the critical variable. It may be that method of reading instruction also does not affect this trend. Certainly reading instruction in Clay's New Zealand study, with its emphasis on reading for meaning, use of context

for word identification, and early emphasis on writing, contrasts with the synthetic phonics program and lack of substantial writing in first grade in my research school's curriculum. The same finding appears whether reading occurs in Swedish or English. Although certainly not definitive, these three studies suggest that despite age of school entry, method of instruction, or language, a child who does poorly in reading in the first year is likely to continue to do poorly.

It is unlikely that as poor readers get older they will change. The most recent National Assessment of Educational Progress report found that good 9-year-old readers from previous assessments were likely to remain good readers through secondary school (National Assessment of Educational Progress, 1985, p. 33). Early success with reading appears critical.

There are many variables that need to be explored further in order to determine how early pedagogic practice can be improved. Home, preschool, and kindergarten influences on first-grade reading as well as teacher and curriculum influences in first grade should be studied. As I indicated earlier in this article, many studies in several countries have shown that skill in entering phonemic awareness has a powerful influence on reading and spelling acquisition, and this was a factor of particular interest to me in this study.

In my research the children who became poor readers entered first grade with little phonemic awareness. Although their phonemic awareness steadily increased in first grade, they left this grade with a little less phonemic awareness than that which the children who became average or good readers possessed upon entering first grade.

Tunmer and Nesdale (1985) showed that in first grade phonemic awareness affects reading comprehension indirectly, through phonological recoding (as measured by pseudoword naming). Juel et al. (1986) found the same relation. They further found, in a hierarchical regression predicting word recognition at the end of first grade, that phonemic awareness accounted for 49% of the variance after accounting for the influence of IQ (WISC-R block design and vocabulary subtests) and listening comprehension.

In my study, poor entering phonemic awareness appeared to contribute to a very slow start in learning spelling-sound correspondences. Nine of the poor readers could not read a single pseudoword on the BTBDS (e.g., *buf*) at the end of first grade—despite a year of phonics instruction. By the end of fourth grade the poor decoders had still not achieved the level of decoding that the average to good readers had achieved by the beginning of second grade.

Although in my research the poor decoder appeared doomed, Calfee and Piontkowski (1981) offer some hope that a school's program may change the outcome. They studied the reading development of 50 first-grade children from 10 classrooms in four schools. They compared end-of-year first-grade development with end-of-year reading achievement in second grade. They found a moderately strong correlation between decoding skill in first grade and reading achievement in second grade ($r = .65$), but there was considerable variation in this relation among the four schools. In one school the relation was virtually impossible to measure because so few children learned to decode; in another school, the ranking on the decoding test was almost identical to that on the reading achievement test. The exceptional case was a school in which the reading program in second grade appeared to promote a uniformly high level of reading achievement by the end of the year, despite students' success or lack of success in learning letter-sound correspondences in first grade (pp. 369–370). Unfortunately, the specific processes that made the second grade program at this school so successful remain unknown.

There is a need to develop ways to remediate quickly poor decoding, because poor early decoding appears to lead to additional problems in both reading and writing. Faulty decoding skill prevents poor decoders from reading as much as good decoders. By the end of first grade, the good readers in my study had seen about twice as many words in running text as the poor readers (18,681 vs. 9,975). These findings are remarkably similar to those of Clay (1967). She estimated that a child who made superior progress in the first year of instruction and was in the high reading group read about 20,000 words, whereas the low middle reading group child read 10,000 words and the low group child only 5,000 words. Allington (1984) and Biemiller (1977–1978) have found similar differences among ability groups in exposure to print.

In my study the difference in exposure to print in school only increased with each grade. These in-school differences in exposure to print were further compounded by out-of-school differences in reading behaviors. The average good reader in fourth grade reported reading at home almost four nights per week; the average poor reader reported reading at home about once a week.

Nagy and Anderson (1984) postulate that "beginning in about third grade, the major determinant of vocabulary growth is amount of free reading" (p. 327). Stanovich (1986) states,

> The effect of reading volume on vocabulary growth, combined with the large skill difference in reading volume, could mean a "rich get richer" or cumulative advantage phenomenon is almost inextricably embedded within the developmental course of reading progress. The very children who are reading well and who have good vocabularies will read more, learn more word meanings, and hence read even better. Children with inadequate vocabularies—who read slowly and without enjoyment—read less, and as a result have slower development of vocabulary knowledge, which inhibits further growth in reading ability. (p. 381)

Findings from my study are consistent with these statements. I did my research in a low socioeconomic status neighborhood school with a racially mixed population of children. Whether a result of the predominant (i.e., home) language being Spanish, or dialect differences, or other factors associated with low socioeconomic status, entering school language and listening comprehension was somewhat low both for those children who became good readers and those who became poor readers. By the end of second grade, the good readers had made substantial gains in listening comprehension. The poor readers made some gains in listening comprehension between first and second grade but made little gain thereafter (see Table 1).

The correlational nature of the data collected in my longitudinal study, however, precludes making a causal connection between the increased reading experiences of the good readers and their increased listening comprehension. Certainly an intervention study is called for to further test this hypothesis, as it seems particularly relevant to the understanding of the low socioeconomic status child.

Chall and Jacobs (1983), in a cross-sectional study of low socioeconomic status children, report that poor readers begin their reading deceleration first in word meanings, beginning around fourth grade. Because their study did not start until the children were in second grade and involves a cross-sectional comparison, it is difficult to directly equate their results with those of my study. Whether poor general listening comprehension (e.g., oral vocabulary, knowledge of syntax) is brought to school at the beginning of first grade or does not appear in low socioeconomic status children until fourth grade, it remains a matter of deep concern because it eventually affects reading comprehension.

According to the Simple View, reading is the product of decoding and comprehension (i.e., listening comprehension). Indeed, by the end of fourth grade the poor readers appeared deficient in at least one and usually two areas, decoding and listening comprehension. Although in each grade word recognition was more predictive of reading comprehension than was listening comprehension, the impact of listening comprehension steadily rose with each grade level. It seems likely that this trend would continue into higher grades. Because there is less variation in decoding skill among students in each grade (i.e., they can all read words fairly well), reading comprehension will come to approximate their ability to comprehend text as if it were spoken to them (i.e., depend on their skill in reasoning, on their knowledge of vocabulary, syntax, pragmatics, and so on) (Curtis, 1980; Singer, 1976).

Similar to Chall and Jacobs (1983), my study found that poor readers tend to become poor writers. Whereas Chall and Jacobs did not observe this trend until after third grade, I found it somewhat earlier. It is not too surprising that poor readers are poor spellers. As previously indicated, poor readers tend to be exposed to less print than good readers, both in and out of school. Spelling depends to a great extent on word specific knowledge (Juel et al., 1986). Such knowledge can only be acquired through print exposure (e.g., knowledge that *green* is spelled with "ee" rather than *grean* or *grene*).

It may be surprising that poor readers do not grow as much as good readers in their ability to generate an oral story. As one good reader explained, however, he liked to read because "you get neat ideas." Children who do not read much likely do not gain as much in vocabulary as prolific readers (Nagy & Anderson, 1984; Stanovich, 1986), and also they may not develop in knowledge of what constitutes a good story. In my study, this notion received support through a hierarchical regression predicting oral story ideas. After accounting for IQ in the regression, place in series (the number of words read in the basal) accounted for a rising portion of the variance with each grade—accounting for 30% by fourth grade.

My study supported the Simple View of writing; poor writers were either deficient in spelling, in the generation of ideas for stories, or in both.

In my research, a vicious cycle seemed evident. Children who did not develop good word-recognition skill in first grade began to dislike reading and read considerably less than good readers, both in and out of school. They thus lost the avenue to develop vocabulary, concepts, ideas, and so on that is fostered by wide reading. This in turn may have contributed to the steadily widening gulf between the good and poor readers in reading comprehension and written stories. This cycle seems to illustrate the "Matthew Effect" described by Stanovich (1986).[16]

One may speculate on what the findings suggest to prevent the low socioeconomic status or minority child from becoming a poor reader. First, the study once again illustrates the criticality of phonemic awareness in learning to decode words. Juel et al. (1986) showed both that the low socioeconomic status or minority child frequently needs more phonemic awareness and also that children will not benefit from phonics instruction until they gain some phonemic awareness. My study suggests that low phonemic awareness contributes to slow acquisition of decoding and is one of the early contributors to the vicious cycle. It would appear that more phonemic awareness training should occur in preschools and kindergarten, and, if needed, even in first grade.

Clay (1979) found that many 6-year old children who were not making good progress learning to read could not hear the sound sequences in words. She proceeded to adapt a phonemic awareness training program developed by the Russian psychologist D. B. Elkonin to train these children (cf. Elkonin, 1973). She found that the children could learn and apply the strategy of analyzing the sound sequence of words. Such phonemic analysis training is now part of her Reading Recovery program, where it is particularly connected to sounding out and writing words.

It seems clear that instructors should not wait to build phonemic awareness until after the child has already experienced failure learning to read. A recent study by Lundberg, Frost, and Petersen (1988) showed that pre-school children can be successfully trained to discover and manipulate the phonological elements in words. Their 8-month training program involved a variety of games, nursery rhymes, and rhymed stories. Danish children who went through the training program showed dramatic gains in certain phonemic awareness skills, such as phoneme segmentation skill, compared with children who did not go through the program. The pre-school training had a facilitating effect on reading and spelling acquisition through second grade.

Second, educators must make certain that children learn to decode in first grade. Clay (1979) writes,

A strategy of analysing spoken words into sounds, and then going *from sounds to letters* may be a critical precursor of the ability to utilize the heuristic tricks of phonics. And many children may not need phonic instruction once they acquire and use a sound sequence analysis strategy. (p. 66; emphasis added)

Whether this strategy would eliminate a need for phonics instruction is intriguing but unclear; certainly children should learn to decode in first grade. If decoding skill arrives much later, it may be very hard to change the direction that reading achievement will take: Poor decoding skill leads to little reading and little opportunity to increase one's basic vocabulary and knowledge through reading, leaving a shaky foundation for later reading comprehension.

There is currently great attention in the literature to increasing the reading comprehension skills of older students. However, a recent review by Carver (1987) of studies that have attempted to teach comprehension found little evidence that such efforts have much payoff. Many studies that have attempted to improve students' reading comprehension through development of vocab-ulary or metacognitive comprehension strategies show very little effect. It seems intuitively obvious that it would be very hard to make up for years of lost experiences with the words and concepts found in print with relatively short-term treatments. Although there is no doubt the higher order comprehension skills of older students need to be improved, the most straightforward way to achieve this goal in the future may be to concentrate on the rapid and early attainment of the lower level skills.

Third, for children who are not learning to decode and who are not reading much, every effort must be made both to keep them motivated to read and to keep up their listening comprehension so they do not fall so far behind in vocabulary, concepts, and so on. The age-old technique of reading to children often seems to fit the requirement nicely and should not be forgotten in the elementary grades.

Fourth, it appears likely that extensive reading (or listening to a lot of stories) is important to acquiring ideas with which to write one's own stories. The observed moderate correlation between good reading ability and good writing ability—which has been found in this and other studies—does not require an elaborate explanation, such as the currently popular view that this relation is the result of the similarity of the two thinking processes involved. Rather the correlation can be more parsimoniously explained by the fact that good readers simply read more and over time have experienced more ideas and vocabulary that can be incorporated into their writing. In the words of Steven Spielberg at the 1987 Academy Awards, "Only a generation of readers will spawn a generation of writers."

## References

ALLINGTON, R. L. (1984). Content coverage and contextual reading in reading groups. *Journal of Reading Behavior, 16,* 85–96.

BEREITER, C. (1980). Development in writing. In L. W. Gregg & E. R. Steinberg (Eds.), *Cognitive processes in writing* (pp. 73–96). Hillsdale, NJ: Erlbaum.

BIEMILLER, A. (1977–1978). Relationships between oral reading rates for letters, words, and simple text in the development of reading achievement. *Reading Research Quarterly, 13,* 223–253.

BLACHMAN, B. A., & JAMES, S. L. (1985). Metalinguistic abilities and reading achievement in first-grade children. In J. Niles & R. Lalik (Eds.), *Issues in literacy: A research perspective* (pp. 280–286). Rochester, NY: National Reading Conference.

BRADLEY, L., & BRYANT, P. E. (1983). Categorizing sounds and learning to read—a causal connection. *Nature, 301*, 419–421.

BRYANT, N. D. (1975). *Diagnostic test of basic decoding skills.* New York: Columbia University, Teachers College.

CALFEE, R. C., & PIONTKOWSKI, D. C. (1981). The reading diary: Acquisition of decoding. *Reading Research Quarterly, 16*, 346–373.

CARVER, R. P. (1987). Should reading comprehension skills be taught? In J. E. Readance & R. S. Baldwin (Eds.), *Research in literacy: Merging perspectives* (pp. 115–126). Rochester, NY: National Reading Conference.

CHALL, J. S., & JACOBS, V. A. (1983). Writing and reading in the elementary grades: Developmental trends among low SES children. *Language Arts, 60*, 617–626, 660.

CLAY, M. M. (1967). The reading behaviour of five year old children: A research report. *New Zealand Journal of Educational Studies, 2*, 11–31.

CLAY, M. M. (1979). *Reading: The patterning of complex behaviour.* Auckland, New Zealand: Heinemann.

CURTIS, M. (1980). Development of components of reading skill. *Journal of Educational Psychology, 72*, 656–669.

ELKONIN, D. B. (1963). The psychology of mastering the elements of reading. In B. Simon & J. Simon (Eds.), *Educational psychology in the U.S.S.R.* (pp. 165–179). London: Routledge & Kegan Paul.

ELKONIN, D. B. (1973). U.S.S.R. In J. Downing (Ed.), *Comparative reading* (pp. 551–579). New York: Macmillan.

FOX, B., & ROUTH, D. K. (1975). Analyzing spoken language into words, syllables, and phonemes: A developmental study. *Journal of Psycholinguistic Research, 4*, 331–342.

GOUGH, P. B., & TUNMER, W. E. (1986). Decoding, reading, and reading disability. *Remedial and Special Education, 7*, 6–10.

GUNDLACH, R. A. (1981). On the nature and development of children's writing. In C. H. Frederiksen & J. F. Dominic (Eds.), *Writing: The nature, development, and teaching of written communication. Vol. 2: Writing: Process, development and communication* (pp. 133–152). Hillsdale, NJ: Erlbaum.

HEATH, S. B. (1983). *Ways with words.* Cambridge, England: Cambridge University Press.

HIERONYMOUS, A. N., LINDQUIST, E. F., & HOOVER, H. D. (1980). *IOWA Test of Basic Skills.* New York: Houghton Mifflin.

JASTAK, J., BIJOU, S., & JASTAK, S. (1978). *Wide Range Achievement Test.* Wilmington, DE: Jastak Associates.

JUEL, C., GRIFFITH, P. L., & GOUGH, P. B. (1985). Reading and spelling strategies of first grade children. In J. A. Niles & R. Lalik (Eds.), *Issues in literacy: A research perspective* (pp. 306–309). Rochester, NY: National Reading Conference.

JUEL, C., GRIFFITH, P. L., & GOUGH, P. B. (1986). Acquisition of literacy: A longitudinal study of children in first and second grade. *Journal of Educational Psychology, 78*, 243–255.

JUEL, C., & LEAVELL, J. A. (in press). Retention and nonretention of "at risk" readers in first grade and their subsequent reading achievement. *Journal of Learning Disabilities.*

LABERGE, D., & SAMUELS, S. J. (1974). Toward a theory of automatic information processing in reading. *Cognitive Psychology, 6*, 293–323.

LESGOLD, A., RESNICK, L. B., & HAMMOND, K. (1985). Learning to read: A longitudinal study of word skill development in two curricula. In G. E. MacKinnon & T. G. Waller (Eds.), *Reading research: Advances in theory and practice* (Vol. 4, pp. 107–138). New York: Academic Press.

LUNDBERG, I., (1984, August). Learning to read. *School Research Newsletter.* National Board of Education, Sweden.

LUNDBERG, I., FROST, J., & PETERSEN, O. (1988). Effects of an extensive program for stimulating phonological awareness in preschool children. *Reading Research Quarterly, 23*, 263–284.

LUNDBERG, I., OLOFFSON, A., & WALL, S. (1980). Reading and spelling skills in the first school years predicted from phonemic awareness skills in kindergarten. *Scandinavian Journal of Psychology, 21*, 628–636.

MACLEAN, M., BRYANT, P., & BRADLEY, L. (1987). Rhymes, nursery rhymes, and reading in early childhood. *Merrill-Palmer Quarterly, 33*, 255–281.

*National Assessment of Educational Progress.* (1985). The reading report card, progress toward excellence in our schools: Trends in reading over four national assessments, 1971–1984 (Report No. 15-R-01). Princeton, NJ: Educational Testing Service.

NAGY, W. E., & ANDERSON, R. C. (1984). How many words are there in printed school English? *Reading Research Quarterly, 19,* 304–330.

NURSE, J., & MCGAUVRAN, M. (1976). *Metropolitan Readiness Tests, Level II.* New York: Harcourt Brace Jovanovich.

PERFETTI, C. A., BECK, I., BELL, L. C., & HUGHES, C. (1987). Phonemic knowledge and learning to read are reciprocal: A longitudinal study of first grade children. *Merrill-Palmer Quarterly, 33,* 283–319.

READ, C. (1971). Pre-school children's knowledge of English phonology. *Harvard Educational Review, 41,* 1–34.

READ, C. (1975). *Children's categorization of speech sounds in English.* Urbana, IL: National Council of Teachers of English.

READ, C. (1986). *Children's creative spelling.* London: Routledge & Kegan Paul.

ROPER/SCHNEIDER, H. D. W. (1984). *Spelling, word recognition, and phonemic awareness among first grade children.* Unpublished doctoral dissertation, University of Texas at Austin.

RUBIN, A. (1980). A theoretical taxonomy of the differences between oral and written language. In R. J. Spiro, B. C. Bruce, & W. F. Brewer (Eds.), *Theoretical issues in reading comprehension* (pp. 411–438). Hillsdale, NJ: Erlbaum.

SCARDAMALIA, M. (1981). How children cope with the cognitive demands of writing. In C. H. Fredericksen & J. F. Dominic (Eds.), *Writing: The nature, development, and teaching of written communication. Vol. 2: Writing: Process, development, and communication* (pp. 81–104). Hillsdale, NJ: Erlbaum.

SCHREIBER, P., & READ, C. (1980). Children's use of phonetic cues in spelling, parsing, and—maybe—reading. *Bulletin of the Orton Society, 30,* 209–224.

SHARE, D. L., JORM, A. F., MACLEAN, R., & MATTHEWS, R. (1984). Sources of individual differences in reading achievement. *Journal of Educational Psychology, 76,* 1309–1324.

SINGER, H. (1976). Substrata-factor theory of reading: Theoretical design for teaching reading. In H. Singer & R. Ruddell (Eds.), *Theoretical models and processes of reading* (2nd ed.). Newark, DE: International Reading Association.

SNOW, C. (1983). Literacy and language: Relationships during the preschool years. *Harvard Educational Review, 53,* 165–189.

STANOVICH, K. E. (1986). Matthew effects in reading: Some consequences of individual differences in the acquisition of literacy. *Reading Research Quarterly, 21,* 360–406.

TORNÉUS, M. (1984). Phonological awareness and reading: A chicken and egg problem? *Journal of Educational Psychology, 76,* 1346–1358.

TUNMER, W. E., & NESDALE, A. R. (1985). Phonemic segmentation skill and beginning reading. *Journal of Educational Psychology, 77,* 417–427.

WECHSLER, D. (1974). *Manual for the Wechsler Intelligence Scale for Children-Revised.* New York: The Psychological Corporation.

WILLIAMS, J. P. (1984). Phonemic analysis and how it relates to reading. *Journal of Learning Disabilities, 17,* 240–245.

# Critical Review

**INTRODUCTION**

The author has stated her objectives in the form of questions, a format often used in descriptive studies. It has the advantage of focusing the reader on the answers to these questions as they emerge in the statistical analyses. In this study the author further helps the reader by organizing her results section around these questions.

A strength of this study is that the author designed it to test the "simple view" theory of reading and writing ability, that is, that each consists of two factors. Studies that test theories generally provide more valuable information than those that do not. When evidence related to a theory is gathered, it supports, fails to support, or leads to revision of the theory. Over time such studies accumulate and theories evolve that can be accepted with greater and greater confidence.

The previous studies covered in the literature review are relevant, and many recent articles are cited. A careful literature review is essential because it provides a theoretical and research foundation on which to build.

## PROCEDURE

This study is an excellent example of the value of descriptive research in helping us understand educational problems. The extensive descriptive data provided on good and poor readers and writers over a four-year period suggest many possible experiments that could test the effectiveness of strategies for breaking the described pattern of poor reading and writing. In fact, having completed a series of descriptive studies, Juel is now working on a program of intervention designed to help children break out of the poor reading–poor writing rut in which so many are caught. Such programs are typically evaluated through an experimental design, illustrating that experimental research follows the leads provided by descriptive research.

This is a longitudinal study, which means that the same children were followed and compared over the four-year period. In a cross-sectional study, a sample of children from each grade level would be tested at the same time and compared. The main advantage of a cross-sectional study is that the children are all measured at the same time. As a result, the study may be completed in a short time, and there is little or no attrition. The main disadvantage of a cross-sectional study is that we must assume that the children selected at the different grade levels are comparable. Differences between children at different grade levels introduce errors in cross-sectional studies that can lead to misinterpretation of the findings. Thus, most investigators consider the longitudinal study to be superior in design.

## SAMPLE

As is true of most longitudinal studies, the problem of attrition raises some questions about the findings of this study. The study began with 129 children and ended with 54. Are the 54 remaining children a representative or biased sample of the original 129 children? Note that a much higher proportion of average to good readers were lost (30 of 86 were retained) than was the case for poor readers (24 of 29 were retained).

A larger $N$ would have permitted the comparative analysis of the reading and writing ability of students from the three ethnic groups (Anglo, Black, and Hispanic), as well as comparisons between boys and girls. This kind of subgroup analysis in descriptive studies often provides insights that help the investigator better understand the phenomena being studied.

With studies in schools that draw their students from lower socioeconomic levels, a high rate of attrition almost always occurs. Thus it is desirable to compensate for the anticipated attrition by increasing the initial sample size if possible. However, as sample size increases the study becomes more costly. For example, it is much more difficult to use expensive data-gathering techniques, such as one-on-one interviews.

Because investigators have limited budgets, they must make hard decisions concerning tradeoffs among sample size, types of measures used, and other considerations.

## MEASURES

Note that the author made extensive use of interview and individually administered measures. These methods, although more costly than group-administered tests, should be used when necessary for the collection of valid data. An investigator who conducts a small-sample study that uses interview and individual tests often learns more than one who conducts a large-scale study using group-administered paper-and-pencil tests only.

The data on reading done out of school were collected by interviews, and their validity depends on the accuracy of student self-reports. This procedure raises questions: How important is rapport in getting accurate self-report data? What factors could lead to students giving inaccurate information in a study of this kind? What aspects of Figure 1 suggest that the self-report data are probably accurate?

Having children keep a reading log on a daily basis probably would have been desirable. A log would provide more accurate data (such as book titles) and would rely less on the child's memory. The interviewers could then have focused on the accuracy of the self-report data by asking about a sample of the books listed in the log.

# Recommended Reading

BERDIE, D. R., ANDERSON, J. F., & NIEBUHR, M. A. (1986). *Questionnaires: Design and use,* 2nd ed. Metuchen, NJ: Scarecrow Press.

This book is filled with useful information for designing and carrying out a questionnaire study. The sections on item construction and procedures to stimulate responses are especially valuable. The appendices contain sample questionnaires, follow-up letters, and a case history of a questionnaire study. An extensive annotated bibliography includes the most important references on questionnaires published in the past 30 years.

CROLL, P. (1986). *Systematic classroom observation.* Philadelphia: Falmer Press.

This is a good source for the student who wants to learn more about observational research. Discusses the design and conduct of observational research and the analysis of observational data and provides useful examples. The final chapter discusses criticisms of systematic observation.

DEVAUS, D. A. (1986). *Surveys in social research.* Boston: Allen & Unwin.

This text covers all the major steps in survey research from formulating a research question to conducting the data analysis. The chapters on analysis are recommended since they deal with analysis procedures in clear, nontechnical language and provide frequent examples.

EVERTSON, C. M., & GREEN, J. L. (1986). Observation as inquiry and method. In *Handbook of research on teaching,* 3d ed., M. C. Wittrock. New York: Macmillan.

This text is recommended to anyone who is considering an observational study for a thesis or dissertation. After a brief historical orientation, the authors explore the observation process. Four broad systems of recording observational data are then discussed in detail. The authors are especially skillful in using tables to summarize and figures to illustrate important processes. An extensive reference list is included.

FOWLER, F. J., JR. (1988). *Survey research methods,* 2nd ed. Beverly Hills, CA: Sage.
   This is an excellent source for students who want to know more about survey research. Covers topics such as sampling, nonresponse bias, data collection, questionnaire design, interviewing, and data analysis.

STEWART, C. J., & CASH, W. B., JR. (1982) *Interviewing: Principles and practices,* 3rd ed. Dubuque, IA: Brown.
   The first four chapters introduce the reader to the interview process and structure and the phrasing of questions. The remaining chapters deal with various kinds of interviews. Most relevant for educational researchers is the discussion of the survey interview.

SUDMAN, S., & BRADBURN, N. M. (1982). *Asking questions: A practical guide to questionnaire design.* San Francisco: Jossey-Bass.
   The authors have conducted extensive research in this area, which they combine with the research of others to develop a comprehensive guide to the design of questionnaires. Examples are given from actual surveys, and three complete questionnaires are included to illustrate the principles of questionnaire design. Different chapters focus on different kinds of questions such as knowledge questions, attitude questions, and threatening questions. The final chapter provides a checklist covering all of the steps in constructing a questionnaire.

TOLOR, A., ed. (1985). *Effective interviewing.* Springfield, IL: Thomas, 1985.
   Each chapter discusses a different type of interview. Most of the types described can be employed in educational research, such as the behavioral interview, the oral history interview, and the research interview.

# Application Problems

1. Decide whether an interview, questionnaire, direct observation, or test would be most appropriate for each of the following research problems and explain why.
   a. The study concerns parents' level of monitoring of their eighth-grade child's completion of homework assignments.
   b. The researcher wants to determine whether first-grade male students who are only children are less aggressive on the playground than male students with younger siblings.
   c. The researchers are investigating the relationship between teachers' sexual history and their attitudes toward teaching sex education.
   d. An investigator wants to classify kindergarten students as having high, medium, or low prereading skills.
2. Using the evaluation form in Appendix 3, evaluate the article by Juel that is reprinted in this chapter.

# Chapter Notes

1. The abstract of the article is reprinted here to help you understand the researcher's comments.
2. This commentary was written by Connie Juel.
3. The book in preparation is tentatively entitled *Learning to Read and Write in One Elementary School* and is to be published by Springer-Verlag.
4. "Ceiling" on a test refers to the highest possible score on the test, or it may be considered to be the top range of scores, for example, scores between 35 and 40 on a measure on which the highest possible score is 40.

5. An alpha coefficient is a statistical measure of whether the items of an instrument consistent-ly measure the same ability, attitude, or other construct. If a test has a high alpha coefficient (typically, .60 or higher, the highest possible coefficient being 1.00), it means that students who do well on one part of the test are likely to do well on another part. A split-half reliability coefficient is a similar statistical measure but less precise than an alpha coefficient because it may be affected by the order in which items appear on the test.

6. Cronbach's alpha is another name for an alpha coefficient. Lee Cronbach developed this statistical measure.

7. Test-retest reliability is a statistical measure of the extent to which the sample's scores on a test administered at one time are consistent with their scores on the same test at a later time. If test-retest reliability is high, students with high scores at time 1 will earn high scores at time 2, and students with low scores at time 1 will earn low scores at time 2. You will note that the alpha coefficient (see note 5) also is a measure of reliability, but it measures a different type of consistency in students' test performance. The composite reliability is the reliability for the total ITBS, which includes several subtests.

8. An interrater reliability coefficient is a statistical measure of how well the ratings of two or more independent raters who score a test or other measure agree. The coefficient can range in value between $-1.00$ and $+1.00$. The closer the coefficient is to $+1.00$, the better the agreement. The letter $r$ is a symbol for correlation coefficient. Correlation coefficients can be calculated by different procedures, one of which is a procedure developed by Karl Pearson.

9. The bottom quartile comprises the 25 percent of the sample that scored lowest on the test. The highest score earned by a student in this subgroup was a 1.2 grade equivalent, which is the average score earned by a sample of students who took the ITBS shortly after starting first grade. The sample was probably representative of a national sample of students.

10. The score of K6 indicates that when the bottom quartile of students took the ITBS reading comprehension subtest at the end of first grade, their mean score was equivalent to the mean score of a national sample of students who took the same test in the sixth month of kindergarten.

11. A correlation coefficient is a statistical measure of how well two sets of scores agree. A coefficient of .38 means that there is only a moderate probability that students who got high ratings on their writing in first grade would receive high ratings on their writing in fourth grade. As the coefficient gets closer to the maximum value of 1.00, the degree of agreement between two sets of scores increases. A $p$ value is a statistical measure of the likelihood that the obtained coefficient for this sample represents what would be found if the entire popula-tion of similar students had been tested. A $p$ value of .01 means that the result obtained for the sample tested is probably representative of the result that would be obtained if one tested the entire population from which the sample was drawn. The symbol $<$ in the expression $p < .01$ means that the value is not .01 but a value less than that.

12. A standard deviation $(SD)$ is a statistical measure of the spread of scores that students earn on a test. The statement "at least one standard deviation below" means that all but two of the poor readers had lower scores on the BTDS than the score earned by students who were at the sixteenth percentile of the distribution of scores earned by good readers. In other words, almost all poor readers in the first grade had poor reading ability in the fourth grade relative to students who had been good readers in the first grade.

13. Hierarchical regression is a sophisticated statistical technique for determining how well each of several variables that were measured predicts performance on a test or other measure. In this instance, the researchers stated the conclusion from the hierarchical regression that for first-grade students, ability to recognize words is a good predictor of reading comprehension,

whereas listening comprehension has no predictive value at all. For fourth-grade students, however, both word recognition and listening comprehension predict reading comprehension. Word recognition is a somewhat better predictor (25 percent) than listening comprehension (12 percent). These percentages have a special statistical meaning in the context of the hierarchical regression procedure. If the measured factors, when combined, predicted performance on a measure perfectly, the percentages would total to 100.

14. According to Juel, the hierarchical regression being referred to here was predicting writing scores on the written animal stories in first grade.

15. According to Juel, the hierarchical regression being referred to here was predicting scores for ideas in the children's oral stories in each grade.

16. Stanovich found that students who have good vocabulary knowledge read a lot and with good comprehension, which stimulates further vocabulary growth; and this vocabulary growth stimulates even more reading and improved comprehension. The opposite is true of students who have poor vocabulary knowledge. Stanovich labeled this "rich-get-richer" phenomenon the Matthew effect, after the Gospel according to Matthew: "For unto every one that hath shall be given, and he shall have abundance: but from him that hath not shall be taken away even that which he hath."

# CHAPTER 11

# CAUSAL-COMPARATIVE RESEARCH

## Overview

This chapter describes the causal-comparative method of research, which enables researchers to explore possible cause-and-effect relationships between variables without carrying out an experiment. Two or more groups are formed on the basis of one variable (for example, first-career and second-career teachers). If the samples are found to differ with respect to another variable (for example, teaching ability), a causal relationship between the two variables is hypothesized (in this example, that teachers' career patterns influence their teaching ability). However, causal relationships cannot be firmly established except by experimental research. Thus causal-comparative research is a useful method of exploring possible causal relationships prior to conducting experiments to determine definitive causal connections.

## Objectives

1. Describe the conditions under which causal-comparative research is more appropriate than experimental research to examine the causal effect of one variable on another.
2. Explain why the selection of comparable groups is important in causal-comparative research.
3. Describe three possible interpretations that can be made when causal-comparative research finds a positive relationship between two variables.
4. Describe the conditions under which inferences about cause-and-effect relationships from causal-comparative results are nearly as sound as those from experimental results.
5. Describe the similarities and differences between causal-comparative and correlational research.

## The Purpose of Causal-Comparative Research

In many research projects the investigator would like to examine the possible effects of variables that are difficult or impossible to manipulate experimentally. A study by Gary Green and Sue Jaquess (1987) illustrates this point. These researchers were interested in the effect of part-time employment of high school students on their academic achievement. The sample included 477 high school juniors, some of whom were unemployed and some of whom were employed at least 10 hours a week. The researchers obviously could not experimentally manipulate student employment, asking some students to work part time and others not to work. Instead, through careful

247

sampling, the researchers were able to select two comparable groups of students and then assess the effects of natural variations in their employment. The variation was natural because it did not involve any artificial arrangement such as experimental manipulation by the researchers.

In causal-comparative research, the variable thought to be the cause is called the *independent* variable. The variable thought to be affected is called the *dependent* variable. In the study described above, employment is the independent variable because it is hypothesized to affect students' academic achievement (the dependent variable).

In reviewing causal-comparative studies you should evaluate whether the two groups are similar except for the independent variable on which they are being compared. If two groups are formed because they differ on independent variable $X$ but they also differ on variable $Y,$ the researchers will not know whether group differences on the dependent variable are caused by $X$ or $Y$. For example, in the study by Green and Jaquess (1987), employed students had lower scores on a measure of scholastic aptitude. Thus we do not know whether their lower academic achievement (the dependent variable) is the result of their employment (independent variable $X$) or their lower academic aptitude (independent variable $Y$). To rule out independent variable $Y,$ the researchers would have to select groups of employed and nonemployed students that have similar aptitude. Another possibility is to use a sophisticated statistical technique that can sort out the relative effects of independent variable $X$ and independent variable $Y$ on the dependent variable.

Examples of other problems amenable to causal-comparative research are: (1) a study of the personality characteristics of delinquent and nondelinquent adolescent boys, (2) a study of the physical development of bottle-fed and breast-fed infants, and (3) a study of the academic performance of sixth-grade students who have had nutritionally deficient diets and similar students who have had nutritionally adequate diets over the previous three years. You will note that in all these examples causal-comparative research permits us to study the possible effects of variables that are difficult to manipulate experimentally with human subjects. Even if it were possible to manipulate these variables it would be unethical to do so, because one condition clearly is more desirable than the other. For example, researchers could not ethically withhold adequate nutrition or parental nurturing from one group of subjects to compare them to a group who were exposed to these desirable conditions.

Sometimes the independent variable used to form comparison groups is naturally present in one group and absent in the other group. In example 1 above, once a definition of delinquency is established it is either present or absent in each subject, and thus two samples can be formed on that basis. In some cases, however, the samples are chosen on the basis of being either at the high or the low extreme of a particular characteristic or occurrence. For example, in example 2, suppose that the researchers hypothesize that breast-fed babies develop faster physically than bottle-fed babies. First they would obtain a sample of babies who are consistently breast-fed. Next, for a comparison group, they would obtain a sample of babies who are never breast-fed. Many babies experience a combination of being breast- and bottle-fed, however, so they fall between the extremes of breast-fed and bottle-fed babies. The researchers would try to limit their sample to babies who are consistently breast-fed and compare them to a sample of babies who are consistently bottle-fed. They would seek to eliminate from either sample babies who received a combination of breast and bottle feeding.

In example 3 above, the researchers might obtain a measure of the nutritional adequacy of the diets of all students in one or more classrooms. The scores would probably range along a continuum of high to low, with many students falling between the extremes. The researchers in this case could compare students at either end of the continuum or they could form multiple comparison groups, for example, students with excellent nutrition, students with adequate nutrition, and students with poor nutrition.

Once the two (or more) samples to be compared have been selected, the next step in causal-comparative research is to collect data on the dependent variable. In example 2, they would obtain a measure of the rate of physical development of babies in both the breast-fed and bottle-fed group. Finally, they would analyze the data to see whether the breast-fed babies showed faster physical development than the bottle-fed babies. If so, they would conclude that their hypothesis that breast-fed babies show faster physical development than bottle-fed babies was confirmed.

Analysis of data obtained in causal-comparative research involves the same statistical tools used in analyzing data from experimental research. Specifically, mean scores of each group are computed on the dependent variable, and the mean scores are compared to determine whether any differences obtained are statistically significant. The statistical tools used to make these comparisons are called *inferential statistics* because they help researchers draw inferences about the meaning of their findings. You will recall from Chapter 7 that inferential statistics can be classified as either parametric or nonparametric, depending on the assumptions made about characteristics of the population from which the research subjects were drawn. Table 11.1 briefly summarizes the inferential statistics that are most widely used in causal-comparative research. These statistics can also be used to analyze data from experimental and quasi-experimental research, which are discussed in Chapter 13.

The causal-comparative method is valuable in identifying possible causes or effects, but it cannot provide incontrovertible evidence that one of the variables studied actually caused the other. When we find that variable A is related to variable B, three possible interpretations can be made: that differences in variable A caused the observed differences in variable B; that differences in variable B caused the observed differences in variable A; or that the differences in both variables A and B were caused by differences in a third variable, C. Considering example 1 above, for example, if we found that delinquent boys had much less interest in school than comparable nondelinquent boys, it could be that lack of interest in school (variable A) caused the delinquent behavior (variable B). It is also possible, however, that participation in delinquent behavior (variable B) caused the lack of interest in school (variable A). Finally, it is possible that some third variable, such as a highly frustrating or unstable home environment (variable C), caused both the delinquent behavior and lack of interest in school.

As you can see, causal-comparative research can identify possible causes, but it is necessary to carry out experimental research to establish conclusive evidence of a cause-and-effect relationship. Therefore, the two types of research frequently go hand

Table 11.1    Inferential statistics often used to analyze causal-comparative, experimental, and quasi-experimental research data

| Test of statistical significance | Purpose |
| --- | --- |
| Parametric | |
| *t* test, or critical ratio *(z)* | Used primarily to determine whether two means differ significantly from each other; also used to determine whether a single mean differs significantly from a specified population value. |
| Analysis of variance | Used to determine whether mean scores on one or more variables differ significantly from each other and whether the variables interact significantly with each other. |
| Analysis of covariance | Used primarily in studies in which the mean scores of groups exposed to different independent variables are compared on one or more dependent variables. Similar to analysis of variance but permits adjustments to the posttreatment mean scores of different groups on the dependent variable to compensate for initial group differences on variables related to the dependent variable. |
| Nonparametric | |
| Mann-Whitney *U* test | Used to determine whether two uncorrelated means differ significantly from each other. |
| Wilcoxon signed-rank test | Used to determine whether two correlated means differ significantly from each other. |
| Kruskal-Wallis test | Used to determine whether three or more mean scores on a single factor differ significantly from one another. |
| Chi-square test | Used to determine whether two frequency distributions or sets of categorical data differ significantly from each other. |

in hand. There are, however, conditions under which the evidence from causal-comparative research can produce cause-and-effect findings that can be accepted with nearly the same level of confidence as experimental findings. These conditions are:

*1.* When the sequence of events is such that although variable A could cause variable B, it is impossible for variable B to have caused variable A. For example, in studies of the relationship between cigarette smoking and lung cancer, the smoking occurs before the incidence of lung cancer, so it is impossible for lung cancer to cause smoking. Thus, we can conclude that if a causal relationship exists, it can occur in only one direction.

*2.* When many causal-comparative studies have been conducted by different researchers working with different samples in different settings and when consistent results emerge from these studies. Again, this is the case with causal-comparative research on smoking and lung cancer. When the combined evidence from these studies is considered, the probability that these results could occur if smoking does not cause lung cancer is so slight that most scientists who have worked in the area have accepted the combined results as tantamount to conclusive proof.

# Similarities between Causal-Comparative and Correlational Research

Like correlational research, which you will study in the next chapter, causal-comparative research is a method of examining relationships between two or more variables. In fact, the main difference between these methods is not how the research itself is carried out but how the data that are obtained are statistically analyzed. We suggest you review Chapter 7 for a discussion of the statistical tools used to analyze data in causal-comparative research. Another difference between causal-comparative and correlational research is the types of variables that are easier to study with each method. In general, causal-comparative research is more often used to examine relationships involving dichotomous groups (such as comparing boys and girls) or categorical groups (such as administrators of elementary, middle, and high schools). Correlational research is better for examining relationships between continuous variables that can vary on a dimension from high to low (such as most measures of personality traits or aptitude measures). In addition, correlational statistics are generally more powerful and are useful for studying relationships among three or more variables at a time.

# Sample Causal-Comparative Study:
# CLASSROOM BEHAVIOR OF GOOD AND POOR READERS

## Abstract[1]

The purpose of this study was to investigate objectively observable categories of behavior for good and poor readers in classroom settings. Seven specific observable behaviors of 3 good and 3 poor readers from each of three regular classrooms at each of six grade levels were viewed under natural classroom conditions. Trained observers recorded student behavior for 30 minutes a day for 10 days. A two-way analysis of variance procedure was used in data analysis. Results indicated that poor readers did not differ from good readers in starting to work on assignments, having necessary materials available, making unacceptable noise, being out of place, or making unacceptable contact with other persons or their property. Poor readers, however, were off task more and volunteered less than good readers did. The results were interpreted to suggest that poor readers could be viewed as uninvolved students. Instructional suggestions are given.

# Researcher's Comments[2]

## Background

Experts in remedial reading have reported for more than forty years that students with reading problems behave differently than do their agemates who do not have difficulty with reading. These reports usually have been based on general impressions of the behavior of poor readers who were receiving special help in reading, most often at university clinics. More recently, observational research has been conducted to compare specific behaviors of good and poor readers in classroom settings. This research generally has been limited to observation of a narrow range of grade levels. Some researchers have found that poor readers exhibit maladaptive behavior, whereas others have found that poor readers behave the same as good readers.

In 1987 Lance Gentile and Merna McMillan reported research in the monograph *Stress and Reading Difficulties* linking student behaviors to reading problems. They proposed that the stress caused by reading difficulties would predispose students to a "fight or flight" reaction. That is, students with reading problems would tend to avoid reading either by confrontation (fight) or by withdrawal (flight). Their proposal helped guide our specification of the behaviors observed in the present study.

Our research team (Dr. Barbara Wasson, specialist in remedial reading; Dr. Paul Beare, specialist in behavioral disorders; and Dr. John Wasson, specialist in learning disabilities) shared an interest in investigating the classroom behavior of poor readers from the primary grades through high school. We also shared the desire to examine a set of specific behaviors that students demonstrate in natural classroom settings. We wanted to investigate whether poor readers in fact do behave differently from good readers, and also whether the behavior of poor readers and good readers changes from grade to grade or if it stays constant.

## Experiences

Although most of our experiences are mentioned in the article, three of importance are not.

First, in order to complete the research, we needed the permission of the school district research director and the three building principals and 18 classroom teachers who would be directly involved. When we explained the purpose of our research and the method we wished to use to collect data, we received the complete support of all these people. We were able to examine district standardized test scores in reading achievement to choose our subjects. In addition, we received permission to observe student behavior in each of the 18 classrooms for 30 minutes a day for 10 days.

Second, all parents of children in the selected classrooms were informed that observations would be conducted, whether their child was going to be observed or not. Parents were informed that although no student's identity would be revealed as part of the research, if they objected to their child being observed, it would not be done. Of the more than 500 parents who were contacted, none objected.

Third, because we wanted an objective fourth person to make the experimental observations, we submitted a proposal for a research grant from Moorhead State University to fund the hiring of a graduate student for that purpose. The grant was funded. The graduate student was trained to make reliable observations of student behavior, but remained unaware of the exact nature of the study. She was told which six students to observe in each classroom, but did not know the reading achievement status of any student.

# Findings

The research team was surprised to find that in regular classroom situations involving reading, but not direct instruction in reading, the behavior of good and poor readers was remarkably similar. We had expected to find more differences in behavior than we did. In addition, we were surprised that the behavioral differences that did occur were consistent across all the grade levels we studied: 1, 3, 5, 7, 9 and 11. We were interested in results that might have indicated whether certain patterns of behavior preceded reading problems or whether they followed the reading problems. Our results did not shed light on this issue.

We did find significant differences between good and poor readers in attending to instructional tasks and in volunteering in class, with poor readers attending less and volunteering less. The decreased levels of on-task and volunteering behavior among poor readers can be viewed as giving partial support to Gentile and McMillan's hypothesis about "flight" or withdrawal behavior as characteristic of poor readers. If one views time to start a task and having missing materials as other aspects of a "flight" reaction, however, Gentile and McMillan's hypothesis was not completely supported, because there were no significant differences between good and poor readers in these behaviors. Furthermore, the similarity between good and poor readers in incidents involving noise, being out of place, and physical contact or destruction does not support their hypothesis about "fight" or confrontational behavior as characteristic of poor readers.

Our results suggest that poor readers may need more prompts and cues to respond in educational settings than do good readers. Also, they probably need a learning environment in which participation is rewarded by success. Furthermore, they are likely to require a teacher who supports their efforts and specifically commends their successes. Without this type of focused, supportive instruction, poor reading skills and educational withdrawal may work in combination to hamper learning throughout the poor reader's educational career.

# Questions for Further Research

If poor readers in fact are less involved in educational tasks than good readers, several questions arise that will need to be answered through further research.

One set of questions concerns how poor readers became less involved. Were they less involved before reading was first taught to them? Did they become less involved because they experienced stress while learning to read; because reading difficulties interfered with their success in almost all school tasks; or because their teachers did not provide an environment where they could be successful?

Another set of questions concerns how poor readers can become more involved. What can teachers realistically accomplish in a classroom situation if they target poor readers for involvement? How would poor readers behave if they had genuine success experiences in academic tasks? How should teachers provide emotional support for poor readers, and how might this support change from grade level to grade level? How could teachers organize instruction so that when poor readers tried harder, it would be possible for them to do better?

# Reference

GENTILE, L. M., & MCMILLAN, M. M. (1987). *Stress and reading difficulties: Research, assessment, intervention.* Newark, DE: International Reading Association.

# CLASSROOM BEHAVIOR
# OF GOOD AND POOR READERS

Barbara B. Wasson, Paul L. Beare, and John B. Wasson
MOORHEAD STATE UNIVERSITY

Researchers have written that poor readers and good readers behave differently. In an early review of clinically observed characteristics of poor readers, Robinson (1946) included restlessness, introversive or withdrawal tendencies, inadequate school relations, and conscious self-control bordering on rigidity. Harris and Sipay (1985) cited expressed hostility, negative emotional response to reading, lack of effort, passivity, distractibility or restlessness, and lack of attentive concentration as characteristics of poor readers.

Poor readers, in general, although not in every case, have been characterized as tending to demonstrate maladaptive behavior (Gentile & McMillan, 1987; Jorm, Share, Matthews, & MacClean, 1985). Based on a substantial review of research, Gentile and McMillan characterized the behavior of poor readers as ranging from anger and aggression to avoidance and apprehension.

Classroom behavior has been shown to be highly related to reading achievement among first- and second-grade children (Jorm et al., 1985; McMichael, 1979; Swanson, 1984). On the other hand, Zigmond, Kerr, and Schaeffer (1988) found that the classroom behavior of learning-disabled adolescents enrolled in Grades 1 through 11 is not significantly different from the behavior of their non-learning-disabled peers. Among the behaviors studied were on-task behavior, disruptive behavior, and volunteering comments.

Confusion arises about behavioral characteristics of good and poor readers when clinically derived subjective descriptions are compared with objectively measured classroom behavior and when the behavior of primary children is compared with that of adolescents.

The present research attempts to provide consistency

B. Wasson, P. L. Beare, J. B. Wasson, "Classroom Behavior of Good and Poor Readers," *Journal of Educational Research*, 83(3), 1990, 162–165. Reprinted with permission of the Helen Dwight Reid Educational Foundation. Published by Heldref Publications, 4000 Albermarle St., N.W., Washington, DC 20016. Copyright © 1990.

by investigating a single set of objectively observable behaviors of both good and poor readers in classroom settings from Grades 1 through 11.

## Method

### Subjects

The subjects were 108 students enrolled in regular classes from Grades 1, 3, 5, 7, 9, and 11. Classrooms were selected from public schools in a midsized (population 65,000) city in the north central United States.

We chose subjects who were the 3 best and the 3 worst readers in each of three classrooms at each of six grade levels. The relative standing of students was determined by examining the latest standardized reading achievement test scores for each student in each class, except for first-grade students, for whom kindergarten teachers' ratings were used as the basis for selection. The 3 students with the highest and the 3 students with the lowest reading achievement scores became subjects. The fourth highest and the fourth lowest students became alternates if any of the original choices were absent on the first day of observation.

At each of six grade levels, we chose a total of 9 good readers and 9 poor readers from three classrooms. Selection thus resulted in the total of 108 students from 18 classrooms, 54 categorized as good and 54 categorized as poor readers. The final sample was composed of 106 originally chosen subjects and 2 alternates.

### Procedure

Based on a review of literature that specified classroom behaviors associated with good as opposed to poor readers (Gentile & McMillan, 1987; Jorm et al., 1985; McMichael, 1979; Zigmond, Kerr, & Schaeffer, 1988), discussion with classroom teachers, and review of methods for objectively observing student behavior in classroom settings (Deno, 1980; Grambrell, Wilson, & Gantt, 1981; Hoge, 1985; Hoge & Luce, 1979), we chose specific behaviors that seemed likely to differentiate good from poor readers. We observed these specific behaviors in classrooms on a trial basis to ensure that they could be consistently identified. From the original set of specific behaviors, we chose seven that could be consistently identified and precisely defined. Behavioral definitions were refined through pilot sessions performed in classrooms not used in the actual research. Pilot sessions continued until a reliability of 90% was attained by independent observers recording the behavior of the same students at the same time.[3]* The behaviors and definitions used in the research follow:

1. *Seconds to start*—number of seconds from the beginning of an activity, as indicated by the teacher, until the student is first on task. Duration recording, 5-min maximum. *First on task*—materials are out and the student is in place, listening to the teacher, making eye contact with the appropriate stimuli, and writing, or has pencil poised, ready to write. The student is not on task when looking for materials.

2. *Materials missing*—number of materials needed for instruction that a student is missing, based on a list obtained from the teacher prior to the observation.

The following five behaviors were recorded using an interval method—one mark for 20-s interval during which the behavior occurred.[4]

3. *Noise*—any sounds created by the student that may distract either another student (or students) or the teacher from the business at hand. The noise may be generated vocally (including talk outs or unintelligible sounds) or nonvocally (tapping a pencil or snapping fingers). Incidentally produced noises (chair squeaks, etc.) are excluded.

4. *Out of place*—any movement beyond the either explicitly or implicitly defined boundaries in which the student is allowed movement. If the student is doing desk work, then movement of any sort out of the seat is out of place. If the student is working with a group, then leaving the group is out of place.

5. *Physical contact or destruction*—any unacceptable contact with another person or another person's property. Kicking, hitting, pushing, tearing, breaking, and taking are categorized as physical contact or destruction.

6. *Off task*—any movement off a prescribed activity that does not fall into one of the three previously defined

categories. Looking around, staring into space, doodling, or any observable movement off the task at hand is included.

7. *Volunteering*—deliberately volunteering to answer questions or verbally participate in class, including raising a hand to answer or speaking out to answer, even without permission.

We gathered research data by observing each classroom for 30 min a day for 10 days. To prevent experimenter bias, we were not told which students were poor readers, but only which 6 students to observe.

We did not observe reading classes because of a lack of secondary-level reading classes and because the behavior that characterizes poor readers, according to the literature, is more general than a simple reaction to a reading class. Instead, social studies classes, which require students to apply reading skills, were selected for observation. When certain elementary classroom teachers did not teach clearly defined social studies lessons, we substituted language arts lessons.

Behavioral observation began at the start of each day's lesson. Prior to the start of the lesson, the classroom teacher supplied the trained observer with a list of materials that the children needed for the lesson. The teacher also indicated to the observer when the lesson began. The observer then measured the length of time until each student was first on task. The maximum time allotted was 5 min. After 5 min elapsed, the observer recorded materials missing, that is, materials the student did not have that were required for the lesson. Length of time until each student was first on task and materials missing were recorded for each student each day.

The remaining five categories of behavior listed above as numbers 3 through 7 were measured on a rotating interval basis. We observed each student, in turn, for 20 s, and he or she could receive a mark any time during the 20-s interval. Following this procedure, we observed each student for 20 s every 2 min, and he or she could receive a score of from 0 to 15 for noise, out of place, physical contact, off task, or volunteering each day.

## Results

We analyzed the data by using a two-way analysis of variance (ANOVA) procedure.[5] Rate of behavior was the dependent variable, and good versus poor reader

---

* Numbered notes to articles are supplied by the authors of this text.

groups and grade level were the two independent variables.[6]

The mean scores for each of the seven measured behaviors are reported by reader group in Table 1 and by grade level in Table 2. Table 2 does not break down grade level by good and poor readers because no significant interactions were found by grade level and reading achievement.[7] Analysis of variance for each of the behaviors yielded the following results:

1. *Seconds to start*—No difference was found between good and poor readers. Although significant differences were found between grade levels, $F(5, 107) = 6.337, p < .05$, they made little practical difference, because most students at every grade level started from $1/2$ to 1 min after the beginning of the lesson.[8]

2. *Materials missing*—No differences were found between good and poor readers or between grade levels. There were almost no missing materials throughout the duration of the study.

3. *Noise*—Incidents of unacceptable distracting noise were infrequent. No difference was found between good and poor readers or between grade levels.

4. *Out of place*—No difference was found between good and poor readers. There were significant grade level differences, $F(5, 107) = 5.851, p < .05$. Post hoc analysis indicated that 1st- and 3rd-grade children were out of place significantly more often than were 5th-, 7th-, 9th-, and 11th-grade students.[9]

5. *Physical contact or destruction*—Incidents of physical contact or destruction were infrequent. No difference was found between good and poor readers or between grade levels.

Table 1    Mean scores for seven behaviors exhibited by 54 good and 54 poor readers over 10 days of observation

| | Behavior | | | | | | |
|---|---|---|---|---|---|---|---|
| Group | Seconds to start | Materials missing[a] | Noise[b] | Out of place[b] | Physical contact[b] | Off task[b] | Volunteers[b] |
| Poor reader | 51 | .00 | 1.67 | .31 | .02 | 6.63 | 1.45 |
| Good reader | 43 | .02 | 1.50 | .32 | .00 | 5.51 | 2.47 |

*Note.* $p < .05$ pertains to both off-task and volunteering behavior.
[a]Number of missing objects.    [b]Number of intervals during which behavior occurs (out of 15 possible).

Table 2.    Mean scores for seven behaviors exhibited by 18 subjects at each of six grade levels over 10 days of observation

| | Behavior totals | | | | | | |
|---|---|---|---|---|---|---|---|
| Grade | Seconds to start | Materials missing[a] | Noise[b] | Out of place[b] | Physical contact[b] | Off task[b] | Volunteers[b] |
| 1 | 42 | .0 | 2.1 | .7 | 0 | 4.8 | 3.6 |
| 3 | 63 | .0 | 0.9 | .7 | 0 | 7.3 | 2.8 |
| 5 | 68 | .0 | 1.3 | .1 | 0 | 8.5 | 1.7 |
| 7 | 26 | .0 | 1.0 | .1 | 0 | 2.8 | 1.9 |
| 9 | 25 | .1 | 1.9 | .3 | 0 | 5.8 | 1.0 |
| 11 | 59 | .0 | 2.3 | .1 | 0 | 7.3 | 0.8 |

[a]Number of missing objects.    [b]Number of intervals during which behavior occurs (out of 15 possible).

6. *Off task*—Much off-task behavior was observed, almost 6 min (median) for the entire group of 108 students per 30-min observation. Poor readers were off task significantly more often than good readers, $F(1, 107) = 7.925$, $p < .05$.[10] Seventh-grade students were significantly less off task, $F(5, 107) = 18.01$, $p < .05$, than were students from other grades.[11]

7. *Volunteering*—Significant differences were found between good and poor readers in deliberately volunteering information, $F(1, 107) = 14.99$, $p < .05$.[12] Students from Grade 5 and above volunteered less than did those from Grades 1 and 3.[13]

## Discussion

We found no differences between good and poor readers in starting to work on assignments, having necessary materials available, making unacceptable noise, being out of place, or making unacceptable contact with other persons or their property. In these respects, poor readers did not differ from good readers when they were systematically observed in regular classroom situations that involved application of reading, but not direct instruction in reading.

On the other hand, we found significant differences between good and poor readers in attending to instructional tasks. Similar to findings reported by Grambrell, Wilson, and Gantt (1981), poor readers attended less. Significant differences also were found in volunteering to participate verbally in class. Poor readers volunteered less.

This research suggests that in the regular classroom, at all grade levels observed, poor readers did not demonstrate disruptive or noncompliant behaviors that interfered with learning any more than did good readers. In terms of active participation in learning, however, a difference did appear to exist. The poor readers were less engaged and involved than good readers and also inferior in responsiveness and attentive learning.

Gentile and McMillan (1987) made suggestions specifically for poor readers who are uninvolved in learning. The authors suggested that the teachers should emphasize drawing these students out and focusing them on instructional tasks. The teachers should directly prompt and cue unengaged, inattentive learners, guiding them back to academic tasks. Unresponsive learners should be, in a supportive manner, directly requested to respond. The teachers should provide emotional and instructional support designed to generate students' willingness to try.

Students will be more willing to respond when teachers do not embarrass them over incorrect responses and do not give them text materials that are too difficult (Wilson, 1985, pp. 183–198). Bristow (1985) recommended that, to encourage active participation, poor readers must encounter instructional situations in which their efforts can make a difference. In addition, because poor readers tend to perceive themselves as less successful than they are, teachers should honestly and accurately expose the readers' successes.

Teachers who want to help poor readers participate more actively in the classroom should directly, but supportively, ask them to respond, ensure that the classroom learning environment permits participation to result in success, and commend poor readers directly and specifically for their responses and for their successes.

## References

BRISTOW, P. S. (1985). Are poor readers passive readers? Some evidence, possible explanations, and potential solutions. *The Reading Teacher, 39,* 318–325.

DENO, S. L. (1980). Direct observation approach to measuring classroom behavior. *Exceptional Children, 47,* 396–399.

GENTILE, L. M., & MCMILLAN, M. M. (1987). *Stress and reading difficulties: Research, assessment, intervention.* Newark, DE: International Reading Association.

GRAMBRELL, L. B., WILSON, R. M., & GANTT, W. N. (1981). Classroom observations of task-attending behaviors of good and poor readers. *Journal of Educational Research, 74,* 400–404.

HARRIS, A. J., & SIPAY, E. R. (1985). *How to increase reading ability* (8th ed.). New York: Longman.

HOGE, R. D. (1985). The validity of direct observation measures of pupil classroom behavior. *Review of Educational Research, 55,* 469–483.

HOGE, R. D., & LUCE, S. (1979). Predicting academic achievement from classroom behavior. *Review of Educational Research, 49,* 479–496.

JORM, A. F., SHARE, D. L., MATTHEWS, R., & MACCLEAN, R. (1985). Behavior problems in specific reading retarded and general reading backward children: A longitudinal study. *Journal of Child Psychology & Psychiatry & Allied Disciplines, 27,* 33–43.

MCMICHAEL, P. (1979). The hen or the egg? Which comes first—Antisocial emotional disorders or reading ability? *British Journal of Educational Psychology, 49,* 226–238.

ROBINSON, H. M. (1946). *Why pupils fail in reading.* Chicago: University of Chicago Press.

SWANSON, B. B. (1984). The relationship of first graders' self-report and direct observational attitude scores to reading achievement. *Reading Improvement, 21,* 170.

WILSON, R. M. (1985). *Diagnostic reading for classroom and clinic* (5th ed.). Columbus, OH: Merrill.

ZIGMOND, N., KERR, M. M., & SCHAEFFER, A. (1988). Behavior patterns of learning disabled and non-learning-disabled adolescents in high school academic classes. *Remedial and Special Education, 9*(2), 6–11.

# Critical Review

The researchers used careful sampling procedures to obtain groups of good and poor readers from six grade levels. Therefore they were able to examine not only whether good and poor readers exhibit different behaviors in class but also whether observed differences are consistent across grade levels. If different behavior patterns are found to distinguish good and poor readers at different grade levels, teachers can use this knowledge to design interventions appropriate for the particular grades they teach.

The sample was selected to include only students at the extremes of reading achievement in each class. That is, the three students in each class who received the highest scores on a standardized test of reading achievement and the three students in each class who received the lowest scores on the test were selected for the sample (except for the first-grade sample, which was selected on the basis of teachers' ratings).

By comparing students at the extremes of reading achievement, the researchers increased the likelihood of finding differences in their classroom behavior. They further increased the likelihood of finding differences by basing their selection of behaviors to observe on the findings of previous research on good and poor readers.

The behaviors selected for observation appear to be objective. That is, they are easily identified, measurable behaviors rather than characteristics that require a high level of inference by the observer. The use of a pilot study in classrooms not included in the actual research was a good approach for developing their classroom observation procedures.

The researchers extensively trained the classroom observer, shown by the fact that an interrater reliability of 90 percent was achieved in the pilot study. This percentage means that in the pilot study independent observers were able to classify student behavior into the same categories 90 percent of the time. Thus, we can be reasonably confident that the data reported in the study reflect objective observation rather than the biases of the individual observer.

Besides training the observer, the researchers controlled for observer bias by not telling the observer which students were good readers and which were poor readers. If the observer had been given this information, it might have led the observer to expect more desirable behaviors from good readers and less desirable behaviors from poor readers. If so, the observer would record greater differences between good and poor readers than would an observer who did not know the students' reading ability.

Social studies classes were chosen for observation presumably because they require students to apply reading skills. More information on the specific classroom activities that were occurring during the observation periods would be helpful. This information could help teachers determine whether the findings would generalize to their own classrooms. For example, it would help to know how much of the time students were expected to be reading, whether reading was silent or oral, what types of specific tasks students were expected to carry out, and whether students were expected to work independently. These variations in classroom activities might affect the behaviors of good and poor readers in different ways.

Providing additional information about the classroom activities during observation would be helpful for another reason as well. In her comments Wasson referred to a monograph by Gentile and McMillan (1987) in which the authors hypothesized that the stress caused by reading difficulties would predispose poor readers to a "fight or flight reaction." If the present study were intended to test this hypothesis, it would be important to specify further the nature of the classroom activities occurring when behavioral observations were made. For example, we would predict that calling on specific students to read would activate the fight-flight stress reaction. Conversely, if the teacher was engaging the students in a simple nonreading activity, we would predict that poor readers would not have a fight-flight reaction and so their behavior would not differ from that of good readers.

In reading the study, we wondered whether the observations were unobtrusive. That is, did students know that certain students were being observed and that other students were not being observed? If so, this knowledge could have caused changes in the behaviors of the observed students. For example, if poor readers knew they were being observed, they might have been stimulated to become more alert or to participate more than they normally would, thinking that such behaviors might lead the observer to give a favorable report to their teacher. If so, the research results would reveal less difference between the behaviors of good and poor readers than would occur under normal conditions.

The significant findings on which researchers base their discussion should be examined closely. In the procedures section of this study, the researchers indicate that each student in the sample was observed for 15 intervals (20 seconds every 2 minutes during the 30-minute observation period), resulting in a possible score range of 0 to 15 for being off task each day. Table 1 shows that poor readers were off task about one time more on average (6.63 times) than good readers (5.51 times). This difference is statistically significant, meaning that it is probably characteristic of other similar classes, not just this sample. However, the difference seems small in absolute terms.

Now consider the different frequency with which students volunteered answers or information in class. Table 1 shows that poor readers volunteered an average of 1.45 times, whereas good readers volunteered an average of 2.47 times. (There were 15 possible observed intervals during which a student could respond.) How are we to interpret this difference? On the one hand, we could conclude that good readers volunteer roughly twice as often as poor readers, given that poor readers volunteered only once and good readers volunteered twice on the average. This sounds like a substantial, practical difference. On the other hand, we could say that good readers volunteer only one more time on average than poor readers. In fact, one could argue that both good and poor readers exhibited a rather low level of volunteering. We would need to know more about the instructional context of the classroom to determine whether the observed difference in volunteering is of practical value and how it affects students' learning.

The most important conclusion that the researchers drew from their analyses is that poor readers are not "disruptive" and "noncompliant," but rather they are "less engaged and involved" in instruction than good readers. If this conclusion is correct, an implication is that classroom management techniques are not likely to improve the learning of poor readers. A further implication is that techniques that increase poor readers' involvement in learning, like those recommended by the researchers, are more likely to be effective.

Although these implications are reasonable, we should be careful not to accept them as fact. Further research is necessary to validate the instructional techniques suggested by the researchers. Generally many studies must be done over a long period of time before trustworthy guidelines for practice are established. The contribution of the study reviewed here is not that it provides "answers" but rather that it points investigators in a promising direction for future research.

# Chapter Reference

GREEN, G., & JAQUESS, S. N. (1987). The effect of part-time employment on academic achievement. *Journal of Educational Research, 80,* 325–329.

# Recommended Reading

BRUNING, J. L., & KINTZ, B. L. (1987). *Computational handbook of statistics,* 3rd ed. Glenview, IL: Scott, Foresman.
    This book provides a step-by-step computational guide for the various statistical tests frequently used in causal-comparative studies.

SIEGEL, S. (1956). *Nonparametric statistics for the behavioral sciences.* New York: McGraw-Hill.
    This text presents nonparametric techniques useful for analyzing data from causal-comparative research, with many examples taken from the behavioral sciences. The average educator who lacks advanced mathematical training will find the book understandable.

# Application Problems

1. Say that a researcher wanted to study the effects of damage in a certain region of the brain on the problem-solving performance of young adults. Why would causal-comparative research be the best approach for investigating this problem?
2. Put the following steps of the causal-comparative research method in the correct sequence:
   Data analysis
   Data collection

Selecting a comparison group
Selecting a defined group
Stating the research problem

3. A researcher selected two groups of fourth-grade children: those who were rated by observers as highly active on the playground during recess and those who were rated as exhibiting a low level of activity. The researcher then obtained teachers' ratings of each child's level of participation during classroom activity. Students rated as highly active on the playground were found to have significantly higher ratings in classroom participation than students rated low in playground activity. What is a causal interpretation of these findings that could be correct?

4. Using the evaluation form in Appendix 1, evaluate the article by Wasson, Beare, and Wasson that is reprinted in this chapter.

# Chapter Notes

1. The abstract of the article is reprinted here to help you understand the researcher's comments.

2. This commentary was written by Barbara Wasson.

3. A reliability of 90 percent means that 90 percent of the data recorded by two people would be identical or very similar. For example, if two observers independently recorded the number of seconds that it took each of 100 students to get on task, their recordings for at least 90 of the 100 students would be identical or very similar.

4. *20-s* is an abbreviation for *20-second.*

5. ANOVA is a statistical procedure to determine the likelihood that a difference found between two or more groups in a sample would also be found if the researcher studied the entire population. For example, the sample included 54 good readers and 54 poor readers in one city. If the ANOVA found that the good readers differed significantly from the poor readers in some behavior, it means we probably can generalize beyond this sample and conclude that good readers differ from poor readers in this behavior in other, similar cities.

6. Independent and dependent variables usually can be thought of as "cause" and "effect," respectively. In this study, grade level and reading ability (good vs. poor readers) are described as the independent variables because each is hypothesized to cause students to get off task, be noisy, and so on. Getting off task and being noisy are described as the dependent variables because they are hypothesized to be at least partly the effects of reading ability and grade level.

7. "No significant interactions" means that the ANOVA technique revealed that observed differences between good and poor readers did not vary by grade level. In other words, if good readers differed in some behavior from poor readers at one grade level, a similar difference is likely to be found at the other grade levels in this sample and in the more general population.

8. The $F$ value and $p$ value are statistical quantities that are the end result of doing an ANOVA. When $p$ is $<$ ($<$ = less than) .05, it means that the difference is significant (see note 5).

9. Post hoc analysis means that after the researchers found significant grade-level differences in students being out of place, they did later (i.e., post hoc) statistical analyses to determine which specific grade levels differed from the others. They found that first- and third-grade students were more often out of place than students at the other grade levels. The fact that

these differences were significant means that these specific differences between grade levels probably would be found in other cities as well.

10. This difference is shown in Table 1. The off-task column shows that poor readers were off task more often (6.63 intervals out of 15 possible intervals) than were good readers (5.51 intervals). The fact that they were off task significantly more often means that a difference between good and poor readers on this behavior probably would be found in cities other than the one studied.

11. This difference is shown in Table 2. The seventh-graders were off task significantly less often (2.8 intervals out of 15 possible intervals) than were students at other grade levels.

12. This difference is shown in Table 1. Good readers volunteered significantly more often (2.47 intervals out of 15 possible intervals) than poor readers (1.45 intervals).

13. This difference is shown in Table 2. Fifth-graders volunteered significantly less often (1.7 intervals out of 15 possible intervals) than did first-graders (3.6 intervals) and third-graders (2.8 intervals). The fifth-graders did not differ significantly in volunteering from students at higher grade levels.

# CHAPTER 12

# CORRELATIONAL RESEARCH

## Overview

Correlational research permits researchers to investigate the precise degree of relationship between two or more variables. Some researchers use the correlational method to examine possible cause-and-effect *relationships* between variables, such as whether parents' educational level affects their children's success in school. Other researchers use the correlational method to *predict* an important criterion from other variables that are correlated with the criterion, such as whether eighth-grade students' scores on a study habits questionnaire predict their first-term grades in high school. In this chapter you will read and evaluate correlational studies of both types.

## Objectives

1. Describe the advantages of correlational research compared to causal-comparative research or experimental research.
2. Explain how characteristics of the research data affect the researcher's choice of a correlational technique for analyzing the data.
3. Explain the possible interpretations of a significant correlation between variable A and variable B.
4. Describe two potential problems in research studies in which correlations are calculated among a large number of variables.
5. Describe what correlation coefficients of various sizes and directions tell you about the relationship between variables.
6. Describe the two major types of correlational research and explain how a research problem of interest to you could be explored through each type.

## Purpose of Correlational Research

Both correlational research and causal-comparative research investigate relationships between different variables. As you learned in Chapter 11, causal-comparative studies determine relationships by examining differences between groups on a specific characteristic (the independent variable). For example, a group of brain-damaged adults is compared with a comparable group of adults who are not brain-damaged, or a group scoring high on a variable such as popularity with peers is compared with a group scoring low on the variable. Having selected groups that differ on the critical independent variable, the researcher then determines whether these groups also differ on other variables.

263

By contrast, correlational research examines all the levels of the variable that were measured. For example, when students take a test of verbal aptitude, their scores typically range on a continuum from high to low, with many students falling between the extremes. In correlational research, all these scores (not just high versus low) are related to students' scores on other variables. The statistical procedure used for this purpose is *correlation*.

Correlational research has an advantage over causal-comparative research because it allows researchers to measure the *degree* of relationship between two or more variables rather than simply whether or not a relationship exists. An additional advantage is that it allows researchers to analyze how several variables, either singly or in combination, might affect a particular pattern of behavior. The experimental method, in contrast, is not well suited to studying the effects of more than a few variables at a time.

To determine the degree of the relationship between two variables with the correlational method, researchers calculate a statistic called a *correlation coefficient*. To understand the correlation coefficient, it is helpful to think about individual differences. For example, students differ in their level of artistic ability. If everyone had the same level of artistic ability, there would be little interest in studying its determinants, predicting it, or measuring it. Yet people do differ in this attribute, and the variations can have important personal and social consequences. If researchers could discover the causes of individual differences in artistic ability, this knowledge might prove useful in helping both highly able and less able individuals.

Let us consider now the role of the correlation coefficient in this kind of investigation. Imagine that a group of students earned scores varying from 40 to 100 on a measure of artistic ability. We want to determine whether students' scores on another variable, such as an intelligence (IQ) test, are related to their scores on the measure of artistic ability. Suppose that all students who received a score of 40 on artistic ability had an IQ score of 85, whereas those with an artistic ability score of 41 had an IQ of 86. Imagine that this pattern continued through the entire range of scores, so that students with an artistic ability score of 100 had IQs of 145. In this case there is a perfect relationship between the two variables of artistic ability and intelligence. On the basis of this finding, we would have reason to believe that artistic ability and intelligence are causally related in some way.

Suppose, by contrast, that students obtaining a particular artistic ability score had widely varying IQ scores: For example, students with scores of 40 on the artistic ability measure had IQs ranging from 85 to 145, and students with scores of 100 on the artistic ability measure also had IQs across the same range. Thus there is no relationship between the two variables. Still another possibility is that students with progressively higher artistic ability scores could earn progressively lower IQ scores. In this case, there is a negative relationship between artistic ability and intelligence.

A correlation coefficient is a precise mathematical expression of the extent to which one variable is related to another. In other words, the coefficient indicates the extent to which scores on one variable *covary* with scores on another variable. The magnitude of the relationship between two variables also can be pictorially represented by a

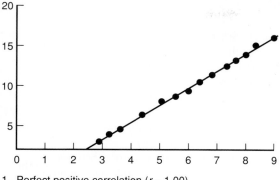

1. Perfect positive correlation ($r = 1.00$).

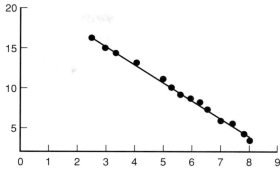

2. Perfect negative correlation ($r = -1.00$).

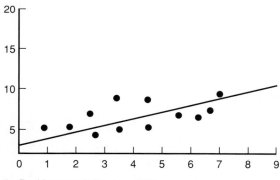

3. Positive correlation ($r = +.70$).

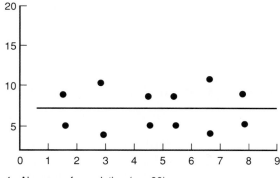

4. Absense of correlation ($r = .00$).

Figure 12.1 Examples of Scattergrams (Adapted from W. R. Borg and M. D. Gall, *Educational Research: An Introduction,* 5th ed. [White Plains, NY: Longman, 1989]. Reprinted by permission of Longman Publishing Group).

*scattergram.* A scattergram plots each individual's scores on one variable on the horizontal, or *X,* axis of a chart and plots each individual's scores on another variable on the vertical, or *Y,* axis. The two scores of each individual in the sample are thus represented by a single point on the scattergram, the point where that individual's scores on the two variables intersect.

Figure 12.1 presents several scattergrams. The first shows a perfect positive correlation. Each point marks one individual's scores on the two variables. As you can see, all the points fall on a straight diagonal line. The line starts at the low end of both the *X* axis and the *Y* axis, and it moves up at a 45-degree angle to the high end of both the *X* axis and the *Y* axis. This graph indicates that each unit of increment, or increase, in the *X*-axis variable is accompanied by a unit of increment in the *Y*-axis variable. The correlation coefficient is 1.00 because if we know the individual's score on one variable we can predict perfectly his score on the other variable.

The second scattergram indicates a perfect negative correlation. Here again, as in scattergram 1, all the points fall on a straight diagonal line. In this case, however, the line starts at the high end on the $Y$ axis and the low end on the $X$ axis and moves down at a 45-degree angle to the low end of the $Y$ axis and the high end of the $X$ axis. This scattergram corresponds to a correlation coefficient of $-1.00$, indicating that each unit of increment on the $Y$ axis is accompanied by a decrement, or decrease, of one unit on the $X$ axis. As with a perfect positive correlation, we can predict perfectly an individual's score on one variable if we know his score on the other.

The third scattergram indicates a fairly high positive correlation between the two variables. If we know an individual's score on the $X$-axis variable, we cannot predict his score on the $Y$-axis variable perfectly, but we can make a fairly accurate prediction. A mathematical formula can be used to calculate the *line of best fit,* which is shown on the scattergram. If we know the individual's score on one variable, we can use the line of best fit to estimate the individual's score on the other variable.

The fourth scattergram is a graphic representation of a complete lack of relationship between two variables. Knowing a person's score on the $X$-axis variable is of no value at all in predicting his score on the $Y$-axis variable. This relationship is graphically depicted by a line of best fit that is parallel to the $X$ axis. The correlation coefficient for this relationship would be .00, or close to it.

# Bivariate and Multivariate Correlation

If only two variables are being investigated, *bivariate* correlational techniques are used to determine the degree of relationship between them. The specific technique that is used depends mainly on the form of the scores that are to be correlated. Many educational data are available in the form of *continuous scores,* such as a total score on an achievement test containing many items. Sometimes data are in the form of *ranks,* such as ordering students according to their overall grade point average in high school. Some data are available in the form of a *dichotomy,* meaning that subjects are classified into two categories based on the presence or absence of a particular characteristic. For example, students can be classified as passing or failing a course, which is an *artificial dichotomy* because selection of the cutoff point for passing is arbitrary. Students can be classified as boys or girls, which is a *true dichotomy* because it is based on a naturally occurring difference. Finally, some data are available in the form of *categories*. For example, students may be classified by the sport they most like to play: volleyball, football, soccer, tennis, and so on. These sports cannot be placed on a scale from high to low or less to more; rather, each sport is a separate, discrete category.

Table 12.1 briefly describes the most widely used types of bivariate correlational techniques. Although the correlation coefficient theoretically can vary only from $-1.00$ to $+1.00$, you will note that for certain types of correlations it can be somewhat greater than 1. In reading correlational research, you can use this table to understand the specific techniques that the researchers used to analyze the data.

We stated earlier that one advantage of correlational research is that it enables researchers to measure the degree of relationship between more than two variables. If this is the purpose, multivariate correlational statistics are used. Table 12.2 provides a brief summary of various correlational statistics of this type.

Multiple regression is probably the most commonly used of the multivariate correla-

Table 12.1    Bivariate correlational techniques for different forms of variables

| Technique | Symbol | Variable 1 | Variable 2 | Remarks |
|---|---|---|---|---|
| Product-moment correlation | $r$ | Continuous | Continuous | The most stable technique, i.e., with the smallest standard error of measurement |
| Rank-difference correlation *(rho)* | $\rho$ | Ranks | Ranks | Often used instead of product-moment correlation when the number of cases is under 30 |
| Kendall's *tau* | $\tau$ | Ranks | Ranks | Preferable to *rho* for samples under 10 |
| Biserial correlation | $r/_{bis}$ | Artificial dichotomy | Continuous | Sometimes exceeds 1 and has a larger standard error of measurement than $r$; commonly used in item analysis |
| Widespread biserial correlation | $r/_{wbis}$ | Widespread artificial dichotomy | Continuous | Used when you are especially interested in persons at the extremes on the dichotomized variable |
| Point-biserial correlation | $r/_{pbis}$ | True dichotomy | Continuous | Yields a lower correlation than $r/_{bis}$ |
| Tetrachoric correlation | $r/_t$ | Artificial dichotomy | Artificial dichotomy | Used when both variables can be split at critical points |
| *Phi* coefficient | $\phi$ | True dichotomy | True dichotomy | Used in calculating interitem correlations |
| Contingency coefficient | $C$ | 2 or more categories | 2 or more categories | Comparable to $r/_t$ under certain conditions; closely related to chi-square |
| Correlation ratio, *eta* | $\eta$ | Continuous | Continuous | Used to detect nonlinear relationships |

Source: Adapted from *Educational Research: An Introduction,* 5th ed. (p. 590) by W. R. Borg and M. D. Gall, 1988, White Plains, NY: Longman. Reprinted by permission of Longman Publishing Group.

Table 12.2    Multivariate correlational statistics

| | |
|---|---|
| Multiple regression | Used to determine the correlation *(R)* between a criterion variable and a combination of two or more predictor variables |
| Discriminant analysis | Used to determine the correlation between two or more predictor variables and a dichotomous criterion variable |
| Canonical correlation | Used to predict a combination of several criterion variables from a combination of several predictor variables |
| Path analysis | Used to test theories about hypothesized causal links between variables that are correlated |
| Structural equation modeling | Used to test theories about hypothesized causal links between variables that are correlated; yields more valid and reliable measures of the variables to be analyzed than does path analysis |
| Factor analysis | Used to reduce a large number of variables to a few factors by combining variables that are moderately or highly correlated with one another |
| Differential analysis | Used to examine correlations between variables among homogeneous subgroups within a sample; can be used to identify moderator variables that improve a measure's predictive validity |

tional statistics shown in Table 12.2. It is used when researchers have scores on two or more measures for a group of individuals and want to determine how well the scores on these measures predict their performance on an outcome or criterion measure. For example, suppose the researchers have scores on three measures for a group of teachers working overseas: (1) their years of experience as a teacher, (2) their extent of travel while growing up, and (3) their tolerance for ambiguity. The researchers wish to know whether these measures predict the teachers' scores on a measure of adaptation to the overseas culture in which they are working. One approach to this question is to compute a separate correlation coefficient for each of the three predictor variables and the outcome measure. Another approach is to do a multiple regression analysis, to determine whether some combination of the three predictor measures correlates better with the outcome measure than any one predictor variable alone.

Discriminant analysis and canonical correlation are specialized forms of multiple regression. Suppose the outcome measure in the above example was a dichotomous variable (i.e., adapted well to the overseas culture versus adapted poorly) rather than a continuous variable (i.e., degrees of adaptation to the overseas culture). In this case the researchers would use discriminant analysis rather than multiple regression.

Canonical correlation would be used if there were multiple measures of the outcome variable. For example, the researchers might administer several different measures of adaptation, each assessing a different aspect (e.g., adaptation to the food, adaptation to the climate, or adaptation to local customs). Canonical correlation would be used to determine which combination of predictor measures best correlates with a composite factor represented by the various outcome measures.

Path analysis and structural equation modeling are sophisticated multivariate techniques for testing causal links among the different variables that have been measured. For example, suppose the researchers hypothesize that among teachers (1) childhood travel experiences lead to (2) tolerance for ambiguity and (3) desire for travel as an adult, and that (2) and (3) make it more likely that a teacher will (4) seek an overseas teaching experience and (5) adapt well to the experience. Path analysis and structural equation modeling are methods for testing the validity of the hypothesized links involving these five factors.

Researchers sometimes wish to determine whether the variables they have measured reflect a smaller number of underlying factors. For example, suppose the researchers have developed measures of eight study skills: (1) organizing one's study materials, (2) time management, (3) classroom listening, (4) classroom notetaking, (5) planning for assigned papers, (6) writing assigned papers, (7) preparing for tests, and (8) taking tests. We are likely to wonder whether these are related skills, so that students who are high on one skill are likely to be high on all the other skills or some subset of the skills. Perhaps the skills reflect three factors: (1) skills that involve writing, (2) skills that involve planning, and (3) skills that involve recall of learned information. Factor analysis is a correlational technique that can examine all eight measures and determine whether they cluster into these three factors or some other set of factors.

The final multivariate technique shown in Table 12.2 is differential analysis. It is sometimes used in prediction research. For example, suppose that we compute a bivariate correlation coefficient to determine how well (1) self-esteem predicts (2) school performance in a sample of high school students. Suppose, too, that we have reason to believe that self-esteem has more effect on school performance for students of lower socioeconomic status than for students of higher socioeconomic status. Socioeconomic status, then, is a third variable—called a moderator variable—that is thought to mediate the relationship between the first two variables. The technique of using moderator variables to form subgroups for examining the relationship between two other variables is called differential analysis.

# Interpreting Correlation Coefficients

In interpreting correlational research, the same limitations apply in making inferences about cause-and-effect relationships as in causal-comparative research (see Chapter 11). Suppose we find a significant positive relationship—say, an $r$ of .63—between students' popularity with peers (variable A) and their scholastic achievement as measured by grade point average (GPA, which is variable B). This correlation coefficient indicates that the more popular students are with peers, the higher their GPA is likely to be. Note that the correlation is not perfect, however; that is, sometimes a student has higher or lower popularity than we would expect based on his GPA.

Now let's speculate about the causal relationship between these two variables. Because the finding is based on a correlation coefficient, we cannot conclusively determine whether peer popularity causes higher achievement (A causes B), whether higher achievement causes students to be more popular (B causes A), or whether both peer popularity and scholastic achievement are caused by a third variable (C causes both A and B). An experiment is necessary to determine which of the explanations is valid. For example, we could test the first explanation (popularity causes achievement) by working with a group of students to teach them social skills designed to increase their popularity with peers. We would then follow them over time to see whether their grades improved.

A major advantage of correlational research is that researchers can explore a wide variety of different relationships in the same study. Suppose we are interested in studying the relationship between specific teaching behaviors and students' achievement in elementary school mathematics. A correlational study could be carried out in which observers recorded the degree to which a sample of elementary teachers used 20 different teaching strategies while teaching mathematics over a period of several weeks. At the end of the observation period, each teacher would have a score on each of the 20 specific strategies that had been observed. Achievement tests would be administered to the students in each of these teachers' classrooms before and after the observation period, and the degree of achievement gain would be calculated for each student. Correlation coefficients would then be computed between each predictor variable (the 20 measures of teacher strategies) and students' achievement gain (the criterion variable) to estimate the degree to which each strategy predicted, that is, contributed to, students' achievement in mathematics.

In reading correlational research, you should pay careful attention to the researchers' rationale for selecting the variables to be measured and correlated. Correlations are easy to compute and can be used to study the relationship between several variables in combination. As a result, researchers sometimes administer a large number of measures to a sample, and they may correlate 20 or more variables with one another or with a single criterion variable.

The problem with calculating correlations among a large number of variables in a single study is twofold. First, it is difficult to interpret the results unless the selection of variables to be correlated is guided by a theoretical or practical rationale. If we find, for example, that students' weight is correlated with GPA, how do we explain this result? Does higher weight cause students to get better grades? Do students with higher grades eat more or get less exercise, and weigh more as a result? Or are weight and grades both caused by some other variable, such as family socioeconomic status? After the fact, most researchers can give several plausible explanations for correlational results. Unless their rationale for examining the variables was sound to begin with, you have reason to suspect such explanations. If researchers concluded from this finding that students should eat more in order to get better grades, many educators would question the value of educational research!

The second problem with measuring and correlating many variables is statistical in nature. When a large number of measures are administered, some will correlate with one another by chance alone. If the study were repeated, these chance findings would not be replicated, that is, confirmed. In the example above of a correlation between weight and GPA, perhaps the correlation is a chance finding that would be unlikely to recur if another sample were measured. Or the correlation may be the result of an artifact, such as teacher bias. For example, perhaps teachers in this study unconsciously gave better grades (and perhaps better instruction) to overweight students.

# Statistical and Practical Significance of Correlation Coefficients

A correlation coefficient expresses the degree of relationship between two or more variables. As we said earlier, the correlation coefficient can vary from $-1.00$ to $+1.00$. Let us say that two variables, students' liking for school (variable A) and students' GPA (variable B) are correlated .50. To determine the amount of variance that the two measures have in common, you simply square the correlation coefficient. In this case, variables A and B have 25 percent of their variance in common because .50 squared $= .25$. As a statement of prediction, we can say that the variance in variable A predicts 25 percent of the variance in variable B, or vice versa.

A correlation coefficient can be tested to determine whether it is statistically significant. If it is statistically significant, we can conclude that a correlation this great is unlikely to have occurred by chance if there is in fact no relationship between variable A and variable B in the population from which the sample was drawn. Whether or not a correlation coefficient is statistically significant depends on several factors: the size of the correlation coefficient, the variability of scores, the significance level selected, the number of subjects, and whether the researchers used a one-tailed significance test in which they predicted the (positive or negative) direction of the relationship.

The goal of many correlational studies is to understand the relationship between two or more variables. Research studies with this purpose are sometimes called *relationship* studies. A relationship study is meaningful whether the correlation coefficient obtained is low or high, positive or negative. Any size correlation coefficient contributes to our understanding of the educational phenomena involved. Therefore, the practical significance of the correlation coefficient is not important.

By contrast, *prediction* studies are concerned with forecasting future behavior. Therefore, the goal is to search for variables that correlate highly with the criterion variable. Variables that are good predictors of an important criterion variable, such as likelihood of completing an academic program, are important even if we do not understand why they predict well. Thus, in prediction studies we are concerned not only with the statistical significance of the correlation coefficient but also with its practical significance. If the coefficient is sufficiently large to achieve statistical significance, we can be fairly confident that this is not a chance result. If the coefficient is sufficiently large to have practical significance, it means that the measure, or measures, used to predict an outcome may be useful for improving educational practice.

# Relationship Studies and Prediction Studies in Correlational Research

As stated above, correlational studies focus either on examining relationships between variables or on using one or more prediction variables to predict a criterion variable. We will briefly describe the characteristics of each type of study to introduce the articles illustrating each type.

## RELATIONSHIP STUDIES

Relationship studies usually explore the relationships between measures of different variables obtained from the same (or similar) individuals at approximately the same time. The purpose of many relationship studies is to gain a better understanding of factors that contribute to a more complex characteristic, such as artistic ability. For example, if we were to find that observational skills, visual acuity, small-muscle dexterity, and creative imagination are all related to artistic ability, we have gained some insight into the nature of this complex characteristic.

Descriptive studies aimed at describing the characteristics of a specific group of individuals often use correlations to explore relevant relationships. For example, researchers might be interested in studying the characteristics of teachers judged by students, peers, and administrators to be effective. First they would obtain ratings of the effectiveness of a sample of teachers, which could range from high to low. Then they might measure each teacher's classroom behaviors, attitudes toward different types of students, age, educational background, and other variables that presumably affect effectiveness. Correlations could then be computed between each of these measures and the measure of teaching effectiveness.

# Sample Relationship Study:
# RELATION BETWEEN TYPES OF AGGRESSION
# AND SOCIOMETRIC STATUS:
# PEER AND TEACHER PERCEPTIONS

## Abstract[1]

The purpose of this study was to identify the relation between five subtypes of aggressive behavior and sociometric status in third and fourth graders as assessed by peer and teacher ratings. The relation between aggressive behavior and sociometric status (the extent to which a child is liked by his or her peers) in third and fourth graders was examined. Forty-seven boys and 51 girls from a northern New England elementary school were given a group-administered peer rating of social status and a peer nomination measure assessing five types of aggressive behavior. Teachers of the same children were given modified versions of these measures. Significant negative correlations were found between social status and all categories of aggressive behavior for both sexes except provoked physical aggression in boys, for which the correlation was not significant. Indirect aggression (tattling, stealing, or breaking others' property) was the type of aggressive behavior that correlated most highly with low peer ratings. There were significant differences between boys and girls on all five categories of aggressive behavior. Teachers' ratings of peer social status correlated more highly with boys' ratings than with girls' ratings, and teacher perceptions of aggressive behavior correlated significantly and positively with peers' ratings on only two categories, unprovoked physical aggression and indirect aggression.

# Researcher's Comments[2]

## Background

This study was based on a thesis that Gary Lancelotta did as part of his Master of Science degree program at the University of New Hampshire. I supervised the study. Both of us had worked in school settings, and as a result of this experience we viewed aggression and peer acceptance as two of the more powerful influences on children's present and future success.

Aggression in general has been frequently studied, but not specific types of aggression and their effect on peer acceptance. We wanted to do research on this problem to test our notion that some types of aggression would affect peer acceptance more than others. For example, we thought that children who use aggression to defend themselves would not be perceived negatively by peers, whereas those who use aggression to get their own way or to "bully" other children would be perceived negatively.

We also were interested in whether teachers' perceptions of a student's aggression and popularity corresponded with their same-sex classmates' perceptions. This question particularly interested us, because school staff often use information from teachers or parents to identify students who are "at risk" for behavior problems or emotional difficulties. They do not use peers as informants, even though research has shown that peer acceptance or rejection is a good predictor of other student problems, such as depression. These research findings supported our own observations that peers can provide information about classmates' behavior that is overlooked by teachers, or not performed in the presence of teachers.

Another of our research interests was whether students' perceptions of a classmate's acceptance corresponded to the teacher's perceptions. We wanted to know whether teachers were "with it" in identifying which students were popular and not popular among their classmates.

G. S. Lesser reported a study in 1959 about the relationship between types of aggression and popularity in lower-class children. He developed a "Guess Who" technique for identifying children who displayed five subtypes of aggression. When Gary Lancelotta suggested using Lesser's technique, my first response was, "Why do you want to use a procedure that was established in 1959?" I suppose that many researchers feel that if something is 30 years old, surely better procedures have been developed since then. After combing the literature, though, we both concluded that Lesser's technique, with minor revisions, was the best instrument available for assessing different types of aggressive behavior.

# Experiences

We sought permission from a school principal and guidance counselor to implement this project in their school. They suggested that the research be conducted as part of the general counseling services curriculum to be provided to all third and fourth graders that school year. Having the project be "part of the school program" encouraged both parents and teachers to cooperate. I will no longer conduct research projects in the public schools unless the school principal decides the project is valuable enough to be part of the school program. The study was successful largely because of the principal's support.

Our research was supported by a small grant to the second author from the research council at the University of New Hampshire. A larger sample would have been desirable, but this would have necessitated hiring personnel to assist with data collection and analysis. Because no financial support was available for such assistance, the study had to be limited to the third and fourth graders in one school.

Accurate reporting on the part of the teachers and students was essential to the project's success. Therefore, with the principal's cooperation, we scheduled a meeting for all the third and fourth grade teachers. At this meeting we explained the purpose of the research and the importance of their role. We then explained the measures and how scales would be completed. We also indicated that we would analyze the aggression and peer acceptance scores separately for each class, and would meet with each teacher individually to interpret them.

We conducted a group activity in each classroom prior to data collection to ensure that students completed the measures accurately. The concepts of "liking" and "disliking" were introduced, and students were taught how to use a five-point Likert scale. The children found this activity fun and asked us to play it again. We did so after the data were collected.

# Aftermath

Numerous requests for copies of this study have been received, both nationally and internationally. It is too soon to know the extent to which it will influence others' research, but we do know that it has had a considerable influence on our own work. Gary Lancelotta examined the relationship between sociometric status and students' behavior problems in his doctoral dissertation research. He also has applied the results of the study in his clinical work with emotionally disturbed children in a day treatment setting. Gary's increased understanding of the subtypes of aggressive behavior has enabled him to develop more effective treatment plans, and to help parents and teachers better understand their children's behavior.

The study's findings also have influenced the research of other graduate students. For example, several studies have been conducted in which attempts were made to increase the peer acceptance of elementary students through a contextualist model of social intervention. The initial findings of this research suggest that children whose difficulties with peers are associated with aggressive behavior require a different type of intervention than children whose difficulties are not associated with aggressive behavior.

# Future Research

Further research is needed to determine whether the Lesser typology of children's aggression is exhaustive, or whether it leaves out significant forms of aggressive behavior. A related question is whether the types of aggressive behavior identified by Lesser cluster together. For example, it may be that children who engage in outburst aggression are also likely to engage in unprovoked physical aggression and verbal aggression. On the other hand, it may be that these are discrete behaviors, such that a child who engages in outburst aggression would be no more likely than any other child to engage in physical or verbal aggression.

An interesting finding of our study is that some children were identified as aggressive by their peers but not by their teachers. Research is needed to determine the reason for this discrepancy. It might yield significant new knowledge about how teachers gather information about their students and form impressions of them. We also would like to investigate the characteristics of children who are identified as aggressive by their peers but not identified as aggressive by their teachers.

We found, as many other researchers have, that girls are less aggressive than boys. This is only a trend, however, for our study did identify some extremely aggressive girls. We would like to know more about the characteristics of these girls, and whether their aggressive behavior changes as they develop.

# RELATION BETWEEN TYPES OF AGGRESSION AND SOCIOMETRIC STATUS: PEER AND TEACHER PERCEPTIONS

Gary X. Lancelotta and Sharon Vaughn
UNIVERSITY OF MIAMI

Aggressive behavior significantly influences the social development of children. Aggression is associated with such negative outcomes as deficiencies in social cognitive processes (Asarnow & Callan, 1985), delinquency (Eron, Walder, Toigo, & Lefkowitz, 1979), and social and mental health problems later in life (Cowen, Pederson, Babigian, Izzo, & Trost, 1973; Roff, Sells, & Golden, 1972). These negative correlates often lead researchers and educators to conclude that aggressive behaviors in children should be discouraged.

However, there may be subtypes of aggression that are associated with positive peer acceptance or at least not related to "rejection" by peers (Lesser, 1959; Olweus, 1986). For example, a student may display aggressive behaviors, but only in self-defense or to ward off the

G. X. Lancelotta and S. Vaughn, "Relation Between Types of Aggression and Sociometric Status: Peer and Teacher Perceptions," *Journal of Educational Psychology*, 81(1), 1989, 86–90.

aggressive behavior of another. It is conceivable that children who use aggressive behavior in this way may not be perceived negatively by peers. Thus, there may be a relation between subtypes of aggression (e.g., provoked and unprovoked aggression) and peer acceptance. Because the role of aggression in peer and teacher relations is complex and its relation to acceptance and rejection is not entirely clear (Hartup, 1983), further information on the subject is needed.

An important aspect of assessing aggression is the extent to which teachers can identify the aggressive behaviors of their students. The complexity and importance of being able to accurately evaluate the extent to which children are engaging in aggressive behaviors that hinder positive social development becomes clear when we consider the fact that many children are misidentified or not identified as having behavior problems (Schachar, Sandberg, & Rutter, 1986). Many behaviors children engage in have antecedents and contexts to which teachers may not be exposed. Thus, although teachers are often responsible for identifying and referring children with behavior disorders, they may have incomplete or inaccurate information. Similarly, the impact of teachers' perceptions of students, both negative and positive, has been shown to have an enormous effect on their own treatment of students as well as on peers' treatment of those students (Brophy & Good, 1986; Siperstein & Goding, 1985). Additionally, teachers may not be able to accurately evaluate the aggressive behaviors of some students who either do not display aggressive behaviors around their teachers or are sufficiently low in social impact that teachers are unaware of the problems (Virtue & French, 1984). Thus, further understanding of subtypes of aggressive behavior requires evaluating teacher perceptions of students' social status and aggressive behavior and the extent to which teacher ratings relate to peers' ratings.

From a growing interest in early peer social interactions has come increased development and use of peer-rating methods as a means of evaluating a child's social status (Dodge, Coie, & Brakke, 1982). These sociometric methods have provided useful information on how students are accepted by peers and others. Previous research has repeatedly demonstrated the relation between aggressive behavior and low ratings of peer acceptance (Dodge, 1983; French, 1987). Kupersmidt and Trejos (1987) reported that boys with low ratings more frequently engage in antisocial and aggressive behaviors. Cantrel and Prinz (1985) found rejected boys and girls to be more aggressive, disruptive, and less prosocial than others. Similar findings demonstrated that rejected boys engage in physical aggression more than do their non-rejected peers (Dodge, 1983). More specifically, Dodge et al. (1982) found that peer descriptions consistently included "starting fights" as a characteristic of poorly accepted children. Some forms of aggressive behavior are more tolerated by peers than other forms of aggressive behavior (Lesser, 1959). Perhaps the types of aggressive behavior are what influence the extent to which children are accepted in the peer group.

The purpose of this study was twofold. First, we examined the relation between five subtypes of aggressive behaviors and peer social status ratings in third and fourth graders. Second, we assessed the relation between teachers' perceptions and peers' perceptions of students' aggressive behavior and social status. Many of the studies attempting to identify aggressive behaviors

that contribute to acceptance in the peer group have used only boys or have used a more homogeneous population (e.g., only lower-class children), thus limiting the generalizability of findings (Lesser, 1959; Solomon & Wahler, 1973). This study involves boys and girls from a relatively heterogeneous sample.

It was expected that boys would be perceived by peers to be more aggressive than girls across all categories of aggressive behavior, that social status in both boys and girls would be negatively correlated with all types of aggressive behavior, and that some forms of aggressive behavior would be viewed by peers as being less tolerated than others.[3]* It was further expected that teacher ratings of students' aggressive behavior and social status would correlate significantly and positively with peer ratings of aggressive behavior and social status.[4]

## Method
### Subjects
Subjects were 98 children (47 male, 51 female) ranging in age from 8 years and 1 month to 10 years and 9 months with a mean age of 9 years and 5 months. Subjects participating in this study were third- and fourth-grade students in a public school located on a U.S. military installation and included students from a wide range of family backgrounds, including children of high-ranking officers and those of enlisted personnel. The student sample was approximately 65% White, 30% Black, and 5% Asian or Hispanic. Eight teachers participated in this study, four from the third grade and four from the fourth grade.

### Procedure
Students were administered in their classroom a peer-rating scale of social acceptance (Roistacher, 1974) and a peer nomination measure of aggressive behavior based on the "Guess Who" technique (Lesser, 1959). The measures were presented as a "fun class activity about friendships" and were administered in the same order to each class. Teachers completed both the sociometric rating scale and the measure of aggressive behavior for each participating student in their classes.

* Numbered notes to articles are supplied by the authors of this text.

## Social Status: Peer and Teacher Ratings of Acceptance

The social status measures were administered to assess each student's popularity as perceived by classmates and teacher. The social status rating scale was administered by giving each participating student a sheet of paper with the names of all of his or her same-sex classmates on the sheet. Next to each classmate's name were the numbers 1 through 5. Children were asked to circle the number that described how much they would like to be friends with that classmate (1 = not at all, 2 = not much, 3 = don't know, 4 = pretty much, 5 = very much). Same-sex ratings have been found to provide a more valid assessment of social status in young elementary school children than do cross-sex ratings (Bukowski & Newcomb, 1984; Coie, Dodge, & Coppotelli, 1982). The scores on the social status measure for peers were standardized and summed, which yielded a composite social status score that would be comparable across classrooms.[5] Teachers were provided with the same protocol as the children but with different directions. They were instructed to circle one number next to each child's name that described how well-liked by same-sex peers that child seemed to be.

## The Nomination Measure of Aggression

The measurement of perceived aggression was obtained through a modified version of the sociometric device referred to as the "Guess Who" technique developed by Lesser (1959). In this sociometric device there are five categories of aggressive behavior: (a) provoked physical aggression: responding aggressively in order to attack or injure following provocation from another; (b) outburst aggression: responding aggressively in an uncontrollable, outburst manner with no apparent provocation, not directed at another person; (c) unprovoked physical aggression: responding aggressively in order to attack or injure another person without provocation; (d) verbal aggression: responding by being verbally aggressive toward another person in order to attack or intimidate; and (e) indirect aggression: responding to attack or injure indirectly through another person or object.

There are a total of 17 items on the nomination measure of aggression; 11 items that pertain to the five categories of aggression and six positive nomination items

that are unrelated to the measure of aggression and not used for data analysis but served as distractors for the aggressive items.[6] A list of all items used in the measure is presented in Table 1.

Children were given a booklet entitled "The Guess Who Game" with sentence descriptions based on those

Table 1    Aggression nomination scale items

### Provoked physical aggression

This boy or girl will fight, but only if someone picks on him or her.
This classmate will always fight back if you hit him or her first.

### Outburst aggression

This classmate gets very, very mad at times all of a sudden.
This classmate gets so mad at times that he or she doesn't know what they are doing.

### Unprovoked physical aggression

This classmate starts a fight for no reason.
This classmate gets mad while he or she is playing and ends up in a fight.
This classmate is always looking for a fight.

### Verbal aggression

This boy or girl often threatens other kids.
This classmate always puts others down when playing a game with other kids.

### Indirect aggression

This boy or girl tattles to the teacher about what other kids do.
This classmate breaks things on purpose that belong to others.

### Distractor items

This classmate is very helpful to others in class.
This classmate seems to be friendly to everyone.
This boy or girl is fun to be with.
This classmate cares about you when you get hurt on the playground.
I would like this classmate as my best friend.
This classmate will always share their lunch or snack.

presented in Table 1, (e.g., This classmate starts a fight for no reason) and the names of each same-sex child in the class printed under each description. Children were asked to read the description and to circle the names of their classmates whom they felt fit the description.

A total score for each category of aggressive behavior as well as for total aggression across categories was obtained for each student and then standardized by class. Teachers were also given the same protocol and were asked to identify students in the room they felt fit each description.

## Results

Scores from the social status measure by sex and scores from the sociometric measure of aggression by category were submitted to a Pearson product-moment correlational analysis.[7] Controlling for sex allowed for the comparison of sex differences among the variables. A Fisher r-to-Z' transformation was used to assess the extent to which boys and girls correlations between peer acceptance and categories of aggressive behavior differed significantly.[8] This same procedure was used to assess sex

Table 2   Correlations between peer acceptance and categories of perceived aggressive behavior

| Peer acceptance versus: | All | Boys[a] | Girls[b] |
|---|---|---|---|
| Provoked physical aggression | − .31*** | − .13 | − .51*** |
| Outburst aggression | − .50*** | − .30* | − .62*** |
| Unprovoked physical aggression | − .48*** | − .35** | − .65*** |
| Verbal aggression | − .50*** | − .39** | − .60*** |
| Indirect aggression | − .59*** | − .44*** | − .71*** |
| Total aggression | − .53*** | − .37** | − .73*** |

[a]$n = 47$.   [b]$n = 51$.
*$p < .05$.   **$p < .01$.   ***$p < .001$.

differences between teachers' and peers' measures of social acceptance and all aggressive categories.

### Peer Ratings of Aggression and Social Status

Significant negative correlations were found (see Table 2) between social status and all categories of aggressive behavior except for one category in boys, provoked physical aggression, for which the correlation was not significant.[9]

There were significant differences between boys and girls on correlations between social status and categories of aggression in all categories except between peer acceptance and verbal aggression. The relation between the following categories of aggression and peer acceptance for girls was significantly more negative than for boys: provoked physical aggression, outburst aggression, unprovoked physical aggression, indirect aggression, and total aggression. Indirect aggression was the type of aggression most rejected by peers. Provoked physical aggression was the type of behavior least rejected and most tolerated by peers of this age group.

### Teacher and Peer Perceptions

Examination of the intercorrelations between teacher and peer measures of social status shows mixed results across the various categories of aggression and social status (see Table 3).[10]

Teachers' perceptions of aggressive behavior correlated positively with students' perceptions on two categories: unprovoked physical aggression and indirect aggression. There was no significant correlation between teachers' perceptions and boys' perceptions of provoked physical aggression, outburst aggression, and verbal aggression. There was no significant correlation between teachers' perceptions and girls' perceptions of provoked physical aggression, outburst aggression, and verbal aggression. Teachers' and boys' ratings of social acceptance correlated significantly, whereas teachers' and girls' ratings were not significantly correlated.

### Aggression Ratings by Type and Sex

To determine if significant differences existed between types of aggression a repeated measures analysis of variance (ANOVA) was performed.[11] There were significant differences among the five aggression scores, $F =$

Table 3    Intercorrelation between teachers' and peers' measures of social acceptance and aggression

| Teacher versus peer rating of: | All | Boys[a] | Girls[b] |
|---|---|---|---|
| Social acceptance | .24** | .43** | .09 |
| Provoked physical aggression | .10 | −.01 | −.17 |
| Outburst aggression | −.06 | −.24 | .08 |
| Unprovoked physical aggression | .58*** | .62*** | .46*** |
| Verbal aggression | .17* | .23 | −.03 |
| Indirect aggression | .26** | .26* | .32* |
| Total aggression | .41*** | .39** | .29 |

[a] $n = 47$.   [b] $n = 51$.
*$p < .05$.   **$p < .01$.   ***$p < .001$.

36.88, $p < .001$.[12] Post hoc analysis, Tukey's honestly significant difference (HSD) test showed significant differences ($p < .05$) for unprovoked physical aggression ($M = 2.95$, $SD = 3.34$) and provoked physical aggression ($M = 3.83$, $SD = 3.42$).[13] No significant differences were found for three types of aggression, indirect ($M = 1.84$, $SD = 2.02$), verbal ($M = 1.84$, $SD = 1.98$), and outburst ($M = 2.00$, $SD = 2.02$).

Multivariate and univariate $F$ tests were performed to determine if there were significant differences by sex on each of the five subtests of aggression.[14] There were significant differences between boys and girls for each of the five subtests with levels of significance for each of the following: provoked physical aggression ($p = .0005$); outburst aggression ($p = .008$); unprovoked physical aggression ($p = .001$); verbal aggression ($p = .04$); and indirect aggression ($p = .0005$).

## Discussion

This study investigated two characteristics in childhood that are thought to have an important impact on later social and emotional functioning: aggressive behavior and social status. It also examined the extent to which peers' and teachers' perceptions of subtypes of aggressive behavior and social status are related.

With the exception of provoked physical aggression with boys, the results of this study do not support the hypothesis that there are types of aggression acceptable to peers, at least in terms of how these subtypes of aggression relate to peer acceptance. The overall findings indicate inverse relations between peers' perceptions of social status with their same sex peers and all categories of aggressive behavior. With the exception of verbal aggression, negative correlations between social status and aggressive behavior were stronger across all categories of aggressive behavior for girls than for boys. This finding that girls are less tolerant of aggressive behavior than are boys is consistent with previous research (Dodge et al., 1982; Hyde, 1984; Maccoby & Jacklin, 1974), which has identified sex differences in tolerance of aggressive behavior.

Indirect aggression had the strongest negative correlation with social status for both boys and girls. Thus, behaviors such as taking things that belong to others and tattling appeared less tolerated and accepted than provoked physical aggression. It is surprising that indirect aggression had a stronger negative correlation with peer acceptance than did all other forms of aggressive behavior. Perhaps it is the furtive behavior associated with indirect aggression that is disagreeable to others. It could also be that students who frequently use indirect aggressive behavior were perceived by their classmates as less desirable because they lacked the "courage" to confront others directly and fight. Because the subjects in this study were children of military personnel, they may have been taught it is more desirable to directly confront others rather than to behave aggressively in an indirect way.

Provoked physical aggression is the category of aggression that had the lowest negative correlation with peers' perceptions of social status for both boys and girls. Although girls' ratings of provoked physical aggression were significantly negatively correlated with peers' perceptions of social status, boys' ratings were not. This suggests that aggressive behaviors, such as fighting in response to provocation by another, is less likely to have a negative effect on boys' social status than on girls'. This is not surprising, because responding to invitations for fighting and defending oneself are considered by many as appropriate male behavior.

Teachers' perceptions of boys' social status correlated positively and significantly with peers' perceptions, whereas teachers' perceptions of girls' social status were low and not significantly correlated. There are several possible explanations for this finding. Perhaps boys' behavior around their same-sex peers was more obvious and easier for teachers to interpret, whereas girls' behavior was more subtle and teachers less able to discern their friendship preferences. It could also be that the friendship patterns of boys this age are more stable than the friendship patterns of girls, and teachers are unable to keep up with which girls are good friends.

Teachers' ratings did not relate with peers' ratings in the categories of provoked physical aggression, outburst aggression, and verbal aggression. This suggests there is little relation between teachers' and peers' perceptions of children who fight back when attacked by another, children who display uncontrolled aggressive behavior, and children who swear and call names. Teachers' ratings were well matched with peer ratings in the category of unprovoked physical aggression; both teachers and students agree when identifying "bullies."

The lack of a significant relation between peer and teacher ratings on three categories of aggression warrants further investigation. Were teachers less aware of which students in the classroom display what types of aggressive behaviors? Validation studies in the area of childhood depression have found that child self-ratings significantly correlate with clinical diagnostic ratings (Birleson, 1981; Carlson & Cantwell, 1980; Kovacs, 1983) but do not correspond well with parent ratings (Lefkowitz & Tesiny, 1984) or teacher ratings (Sacco & Graves, 1985). Sacco and Graves suggested that there is little evidence that teachers are valid assessors of childhood depression, even when teachers display an adequate understanding and knowledge of depression. This study raises questions about the accuracy of teachers as identifiers of several subtypes of aggressive behavior in their students. Consistent with this finding, teachers from this study stated that many of the subtypes of aggressive behavior assessed were not viewed often enough to be accurately evaluated. With the additional emphasis on increased academic time in the classroom, teachers may have had few opportunities to observe students interacting socially and thus may not have been exposed to the aggressive behaviors displayed by their students. It is also possible that students did not display the same disturbing behaviors in front of teachers that they performed for their peers.

Of particular interest is the low relation between teachers' and peers' perceptions in the category outburst aggression. This category measures uncontrolled acting-out behaviors, such as students getting so angry they act as if they do not know what they are doing. It is surprising there was so little correspondence between student and teacher ratings of children who displayed these behaviors. It may be that students who behaved in this way were more likely to display the behavior in environments where teachers have little involvement, such as on the playground and during after-school sports, rather than within the classroom. This suggests that when identifying students who have behavior problems, it may be important to obtain both peer and teacher ratings in order to form a more complete picture of how the student's behavior is perceived.

Additional research is needed that further examines the relation between aggression and teachers' and peers' perceptions of social status, as well as other factors such as friendship patterns and social acceptance outside the classroom.

# References

ASARNOW, J., & CALLAN, J. (1985). Boys with peer adjustment problems: Social cognitive problems. *Journal of Consulting and Clinical Psychology, 52,* 80–87.

BIRLESON, P. (1981). The validity of depressive disorder in childhood and the development of a self-rating scale: A research project. *Journal of Child Psychology and Psychiatry, 22,* 73–88.

BROPHY, J., & GOOD, T. (1986). Teacher behavior and student achievement. In M. C. Wittrock (Ed.), *Handbook of research on teaching* (3rd ed.) (pp. 328–375). New York: Macmillan.

BUKOWSKI, W. M., & NEWCOMB, A. F. (1984). Stability and determinants of sociometric status and friendship choice: A longitudinal perspective. *Developmental Psychology, 20,* 941–952.

CANTREL, V. L., & PRINZ, R. J. (1985). Multiple perspectives of rejected, neglected, and accepted children. Relation between sociometric status and behavioral characteristics. *Journal of Consulting and Clinical Psychology, 53,* 884–889.

CARLSON, G. A., & CANTWELL, D. P. (1980). Unmasking masked depression in children and adolescents. *American Journal of Psychiatry, 137,* 445–559.

COIE, J. D., DODGE, K. A., & COPPOTELLI, H. (1982). Dimensions and the types of social status: A cross-age perspective. *Developmental Psychology, 18,* 557–570.

COWEN, E. L., PEDERSON, A., BABIGIAN, H., IZZO, L., & TROST, M. A. (1973). Long-term follow-up of early detected vulnerable children. *Journal of Consulting and Clinical Psychology, 41,* 438–446.

DODGE, K. (1983). Behavioral antecedents of peer social status. *Child Development, 54,* 1386–1399.

DODGE, K., COIE, J., & BRAKKE, N. (1982). Behavior patterns of socially rejected and neglected preadolescents: The roles of social approach and aggression. *Journal of Abnormal Child Psychology, 10,* 389–410.

ERON, L. D., WALDER, L. O., TOIGO, R., & LEFKOWITZ, M. M. (1979). Social class, parental punishment for aggression, and child aggression. *Child Development, 34,* 849–867.

FRENCH, D. C. (1987, April). *Heterogeneity of peer rejected boys: Aggressive and non-aggressive subgroups.* Paper presented at the biennial meeting of the Society for Research in Child Development, Baltimore, MD.

HARTUP, W. W. (1983). Peer relations. In E. M. Hetherington (Ed.) & P. H. Mussen (Series Ed.), *Handbook of child psychology: Vol. 4. Socialization, personality, and social development* (4th ed.) (pp. 103–196). New York: Wiley.

HYDE, J. (1984). How large are gender differences in aggression? A developmental meta analysis. *Developmental Psychology, 20,* 4, 722–736.

KOVACS, M. (1983). *The children's depression inventory: A self-rated depression scale for school-aged youngsters.* Unpublished manuscript, University of Pittsburgh School of Medicine, Pittsburgh, PA.

KUPERSMIDT, J. B., & TREJOS, L. (1987, April). *Behavioral corre-* lates of sociometric status among Costa Rican children. Paper presented at the biennial meeting of the Society for Research in Child Development, Baltimore, MD.

LEFKOWITZ, M. M., & TESINY, E. P. (1984). Rejection and depression: Prospective and contemporary analysis. *Developmental Psychology, 20,* 776–785.

LESSER, G. S. (1959). The relationship between various forms of aggression and popularity among lower class children. *Journal of Educational Psychology, 50,* 20–25.

MACCOBY, E., & JACKLIN, C. (1974). *The psychology of sex differences.* Stanford, CA: Stanford University Press.

OLWEUS, D. (1986). Aggression and hormones: Behavioral relationship with testosterone and adrenaline. In D. Olweus, J. Block, & M. Radke-Yarro, *Development of antisocial and prosocial behavior* (pp. 51–72). New York: Academic Press, Inc.

ROFF, M. SELLS, B., & GOLDEN, M. (1972). *Social adjustment and personality development in children.* Minneapolis: University of Minnesota Press.

ROISTACHER, R. C. (1974). A microeconomic model of sociometric status. *Sociometry, 37,* 219–238.

SACCO, W. P., & GRAVES, D. J. (1985). Correspondence between teacher ratings of childhood depression and child self-ratings. *Journal of Clinical Child Psychology, 14,* 353–355.

SCHACHAR, R., SANDBERG, S., & RUTTER, M. (1986). Agreement between teachers' ratings and observations of hyperactivity, inattentiveness, and defiance. *Journal of Abnormal Child Psychology, 14,* 331–345.

SIPERSTEIN, G. N., & GODING, M. J. (1985). Teachers' behavior toward LD and non-LD children: A strategy for change. *Journal of Learning Disability, 18,* 129–144.

SOLOMON, R., & WAHLER, R. (1973). Peer reinforcement control of classroom problem behavior. *Journal of Applied Behavioral Analysis, 6,* 49–56.

VIRTUE, M., & FRENCH, D. (1984). Peer and teacher ratings of socially neglected and rejected fourth and fifth graders. *Journal of Applied Developmental Psychology, 5,* 13–22.

# Critical Review

The researchers provide a clear rationale for why educators need to understand aggressive behavior in children. Rather than starting from scratch in their own investigation of this problem, they carefully reviewed previous research to find out what is already known. Then they developed a set of predictions, called hypotheses, based on these findings and tested them.

Hypotheses can be stated in directional or nondirectional form. In this study, the researchers simply could have predicted that the sociometric status of more aggressive and less aggressive children would differ (a nondirectional hypothesis). Instead they predicted specifically that the sociometric status of more aggressive children would be lower than that of less aggressive children (a directional hypothesis). Stating directional hypotheses allowed the researchers to use one-tailed tests of statistical significance. A one-tailed test makes it easier to obtain findings that are statistically significant, meaning that they can be generalized from the research sample to the population of students whom they are presumed to represent.

The researchers suggest that the findings of their study may be more generalizable than previous research because the sample included both boys and girls from a wide range of family backgrounds. They also describe the ethnic characteristics of the sample, which supports their description of the sample as "relatively heterogeneous." A heterogeneous sample helps make the results more generalizable. It also increases the likelihood that correlations between variables (e.g., sociometric status and outburst aggression) will be significant because increased variability in the scores on each variable raises the correlation coefficient.

Two characteristics of the sample may limit the generalizability of the study's findings. First, the number of students in the classrooms apparently was low. Although the researchers do not specify the size of each class, we were able to reach this conclusion on the basis of other information given in the article. The 98 children in the sample appear to have been all the students in the eight classrooms that were studied. If we assume the classes were similar in size and divide 98 students by 8 teachers, we find that the mean class size was about 12 or 13 students. By contrast, most elementary teachers have classes of 20 to 30 students or more. Therefore, the findings of the researchers' study may not generalize to the typical teacher's classroom.

A second difference between this sample and students in general is that the public school that these students attended was located on a U.S. military installation. Furthermore, most, if not all, of the students were children of military personnel. As the researchers note, the children may have been taught views about the expression of aggression that are not typical. They also may spend a shorter time at one school because of family moves. This factor could affect their aggression and social status scores.

Each student in the sample was given a list of same-sex peers and asked to rate the social status of each peer. Students then received a similar list of same-sex peers to nominate those classmates they perceived to be exhibiting various types of aggressive behavior. Data obtained in this manner are subject to a halo effect, that is, a tendency for a rater's overall impression of the individual being judged to influence all of his or her ratings of that individual. For example, a classmate may not like a student and therefore would rate him high in all types of aggressive behavior for that reason, rather than making an independent judgment about each type. The fact that the measures of sociometric status and aggression were apparently presented together as a "fun class activity about friendships" increases the likelihood that a halo effect contributed to the apparent relationship between these two variables. A halo effect might have been less likely if the researchers had separated the two activities by a week or more and introduced them in different contexts.

The measure of aggressive behavior was based on the "Guess Who" technique described in a previously published study. It is good procedure to use measures that have been previously tested because they are more likely to produce reliable data. The researchers should have done their own check of the reliability of the measures, however, because reliability can distort the magnitude of correlation coefficients. Specifically, the correlation coefficient for two measures having low reliability may be much lower than the coefficient for two measures that have high reliability. This phenomenon might explain the nonsignificant correlation coefficient between social status and the provoked physical aggression score. Testing reliability would have been especially wise in this study because modifications were made to the original "Guess Who" technique.

A test of the validity of the "Guess Who" measure would have been desirable, especially because it relies on self-report. A good validity test would be to have an independent observer make observations of students' behavior in class and on the playground, using a checklist of aggressive behaviors. Students' scores on this observation checklist would be correlated with scores on the modified "Guess Who" device to assess its validity.

Another test of validity could have been done by using data already collected in the study. The researchers could have correlated scores on the five distractor items of the "Guess Who" measure, particularly the item "I would like this classmate as my best friend," with students' social status score (how much they would like to be friends with that classmate, rated from 1 = not at all to 5 = very much).

The article indicates that there were significant sex differences on each of the five subtests of aggression, but it does not state whether boys or girls were higher. Our personal communication with Vaughn confirmed our prediction that the boys would be higher in all categories of aggression than girls. She also told us that the original report of this research study was much longer, but it was cut several times to fit page guidelines specified by the journal. At one point, a table presenting mean scores and standard deviations by sex was included, but it was deleted during the editing process.

In our communication with Vaughn, she advised us of the desirability of having someone carefully review the final draft of a research article before publication, to check carefully correspondence between statements made and the reporting of data on which those statements are based. Readers of research articles cannot always assume that this process has been carried out, and thus they should themselves carefully examine whether the findings and claims are supported by the data presented.

The researchers' discussion of findings did not consider why aggression and peer rejection are correlated. Several causal explanations can be hypothesized. For example, it is possible that students who are unpopular react with frustration, which in turn leads to anger and aggressive behavior. Alternately, students who act aggressively may experience peer rejection, leading to anger and further aggression, followed by greater peer rejection, in a vicious cycle that puts students at risk for other difficulties. Still another explanation is that both peer rejection and aggressive behavior are caused by a third variable. For example, some children may have limited ability to interpret social cues of peers. Their misperceptions could lead them to assume that they are not liked. They might remain distant from peers as a result and then receive low social status ratings. Another result could be that they become angry at imagined slights or insults from peers and then exhibit aggressive behavior toward those peers.

When reading a correlational study, you should check whether the researchers considered alternative causal explanations of the findings and what evidence they considered to help them determine the most likely direction of causality.

## PREDICTION STUDIES

Prediction studies differ from relationship studies in that they are concerned with measuring one or more variables (called predictor variables) to predict a future event (called the criterion variable). For example, the U.S. Air Force has developed a battery of tests that can be given to applicants for pilot training. Prediction studies have shown that each of these tests is correlated with later success in pilot training. By administering this battery of tests and studying the correlations obtained in previous research, the researcher can predict the likelihood of any given individual successfully completing the pilot-training program.

In the public schools, prediction studies often are carried out to develop various kinds of aptitude measures, such as reading comprehension or algebra aptitude. An aptitude measure that has been shown to relate to later performance can be used for various practical purposes. For example, counselors can use students' scores on the aptitude measure to counsel students about what subjects to take or what careers they are likely to be successful in. Scores also can be used to assign students to remedial or advanced classes or to identify children who need special education opportunities.

# Sample Prediction Study:
# PREDICTIVE VALIDITY OF AN ABBREVIATED VERSION OF THE PRINTING PERFORMANCE SCHOOL READINESS TEST

## Abstract[15]

This investigation was undertaken to evaluate the effectiveness of an abbreviated version of the Printing Performance School Readiness Test in identifying at-risk or failure-prone children at the start of prekindergarten. Two samples totaling 171 children were tested in October/November of prekindergarten and followed for 3 years. The evidence showed, first, that scores on this test produced an average correlation of − .50

with the children's academic performances in first grade and, second, that the cutoff point on this test correctly identified 70–78% of those prekindergarten children whose subsequent school work placed them at or near the bottom of the class (true positives) whereas the average false-positive rate was 19%.

# Researcher's Comments[16]

Every beginning kindergarten class contains a few children whose spontaneous name printing looks like the examples in Figure 12.2. For many children, "form errors" such as these are merely bothersome mistakes that occur from time to time and interfere with the legibility of the children's printing. The research described in my article indicates, however, that children who produce an excessive number of form errors are at high risk of experiencing serious learning problems when they enter school.

I discovered the relationship between form errors and school achievement when, in a study of the development of printing skills, I asked beginning kindergarten children to reproduce a series of letters from slides shown one at a time on a screen. Standing behind the children as they copied this material, I was struck by the odd mistakes that some of them made. I wondered why, for example, a child who seemed to be looking directly at the letter *E* would a moment later use four, five, or even six horizontal lines when attempting to reproduce it. I also was curious as to why a few children continued to make errors of this type for almost every one of the letters shown on the screen. I

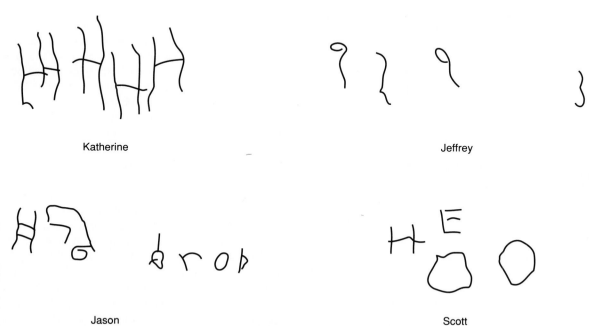

Katherine

Jeffrey

Jason

Scott

Figure 12.2. Examples of Kindergarten Children's Name Printing

wondered whether this persistence of form errors revealed anything of importance about these children, so I asked permission to obtain the teachers' evaluations of the children's command of the kindergarten curriculum.

By comparing the teachers' evaluations with the children's protocols (that is, the papers on which they printed their letters), I found that the children who had produced the largest number of form errors were those who seemed to be having the greatest difficulty learning. After replicating this finding with additional kindergarten children followed through the end of first grade, I launched an extensive study that eventually involved more than 850 kindergarten children, many of whom were followed for periods of up to three years. This longitudinal work culminated in the development of the Printing Performance School Readiness Test (PPSRT; Simner, 1990). The PPSRT appears to have considerable value in predicting those children who are at risk for later school failure.

It eventually became apparent to me that a shorter version of this test would be desirable, for two reasons. First, a shorter version would be easier for younger children to complete. Second, it could be administered at the start of prekindergarten, giving an earlier indicator of possible problems in later school performance.

As the research report indicates, the Abbreviated Printing Performance School Readiness Test (APPSRT) proved to be as effective as the longer version of the test in predicting those students whom teachers would later judge to be poor performers in first or second grade. Three questions, however, remain unanswered: (1) why do these errors occur, (2) why do they predict future school performance, and (3) how can we help children who produce an excessive number of form errors avoid failure?

Previous accounts of similar drawing errors (e.g., Berry & Buktenicka, 1967; Koppitz, 1963) suggest that these printing errors may be due to perceptual/motor difficulties. If this is true, perhaps children who habitually exhibit form errors should be placed in perceptual/motor training intervention programs such as those described by McCarthy and McCarthy (1976). However, my other studies (Simner, 1979; 1986) showed that when children print while looking directly at the letters rather than from memory, or when they are asked to trace the letters rather than copy them, they reduce their error rate considerably. Thus it seems that form errors do not occur because children are suffering from a perceptual deficit (being unable to see the letters as they actually appear), nor from a motor deficit (being unable to execute the fine muscle movements required to reproduce the letters), nor from a visual/motor integration problem (being unable to combine the visual information they receive from the letters with the motor output required to make a correct reproduction of the letters).

I thus was led to consider two alternative explanations for why form errors occur and why they are related to poor school performance. (See Simner, 1986; Simner, in press.) The first explanation is that form errors reflect a problem with short-term memory and attention. Possible evidence for this explanation is that the letters and numbers having curved features in Figure 1 of the article tend to generate form errors that are largely curved, while those with linear features tend to produce mostly linear form errors. This error pattern suggests that children might start printing a letter with the proper visual memory image in mind, but that the memory image fades as printing continues, leaving them without an appropriate model to follow. I also found that children who produce many form errors tend to have short attention spans (Simner, 1982).

A second explanation for excessive form errors is that they reflect difficulty in planning and organizing the sequence of pencil movements that are needed to generate proper renditions of the letters. This difficulty may be indicative of a more general deficit in problem solving or strategy planning, which affects subsequent school performance.

Both of these explanations are supported by research findings that many young children who are unable to master the school curriculum have memory as well as planning problems (Hughes, 1988; Smith, 1981). These children often benefit by placement in structured, academically oriented preschool programs such as those based on the Direct Instruction Model (Gersten, Darch, & Gleason, 1988) or the Cognitively Based Curriculum (Schweinhart & Weikart, 1988).

My prediction, then, is that children who produce high scores on the PPSRT or APPSRT are more likely to avoid school failure if they are placed in academically oriented preschool programs rather than in perceptual/motor training programs. Although this prediction is supported by the research discussed above, the evidence is indirect. Further research is needed to test the prediction directly.

# References

BERRY, K. E., & BUKTEKNICA, N. 1967. *Developmental test of visual-motor integration.* Chicago: Follett.

GERSTEN, R., DARCH, C., & GLEASON, M. 1988. Effectiveness of a direct instruction academic kindergarten for low-income students. *The Elementary School Journal, 89,* 227–240.

HUGHES, J. N. 1988. *Cognitive behavior therapy with children in schools.* New York: Pergamon Press.

KOPPITZ, E. M. 1963. *The Bender Gestalt Test for young children.* New York: Grune & Stratton.

MCCARTHY, J. J. & MCCARTHY, J. F. 1976. *Learning disabilities.* Boston: Allyn & Bacon.

SCHWEINHART, L. J. & WEIKART, D. P. 1988. Early childhood education for at-risk four-year-olds? Yes. *American Psychologist, 43,* 665–667.

SIMNER, M. L. 1979. Mirror-image reversals in children's printing: Preliminary findings. *ERIC Document Collection* (ED 174 354).

SIMNER, M. L. 1982. Printing errors in kindergarten and the prediction of academic performance. *Journal of Learning Disabilities, 15,* 155–159.

SIMNER, M. L. 1986. Further evidence on the relationship between form errors in preschool printing and early school achievement. In H. S. R. Kao, G. P. van Galen, and R. Hoosain (Eds.), *Graphonomics: Contemporary research in handwriting.* Amsterdam: North-Holland.

SIMNER, M. L. 1990. *Printing performance school readiness test.* London, Ont., Canada: Phylmar.

SIMNER, M. L. (in press). Estimating a child's learning potential from form errors in a child's printing. In J. Wann, A. M. Wing, and N. Sovik (Eds.), *Development of graphic skills: Research perspectives and educational implications.* London: Academic Press.

SMITH, D. D. 1981. *Teaching the learning disabled.* Englewood Cliffs, NJ: Prentice-Hall.

# PREDICTIVE VALIDITY OF AN ABBREVIATED VERSION OF THE PRINTING PERFORMANCE SCHOOL READINESS TEST

## Marvin L. Simner
UNIVERSITY OF WESTERN ONTARIO

When preschool children print, it is not unusual to find a letter such as the capital *E* containing four or more horizontal lines, an *S* drawn in the shape of a backward three, or *Q* appearing without a diagonal. These errors are known as form errors because they involve the addition, deletion, or misalignment of parts, thereby producing a distortion in the overall shape or form of the intended letter or number (see Figure 1, page 289, for other examples).

In the past, errors of this nature generated very little interest among educators and psychologists except for those concerned with developing instructional procedures to improve legibility. Recently, though, we discovered that an excessive number of form errors in a kindergarten child's printing can be an important early warning sign of later school failure (Simner, 1982). Incorporating procedures derived from this work, we then developed the Printing Performance School Readiness Test (PPSRT) to provide a standardized means for identifying kindergarten children who exhibit this warning sign (Simner, 1985). Although the PPSRT is quite appropriate for use at the kindergarten level, the task is unfortunately too long and too demanding to employ with younger children. Hence, the present longitudinal investigation was undertaken to determine if form errors, measured with a shorter, less taxing version of the PPSRT, can be employed as effectively at the start of prekindergarten as they can during the kindergarten year to help identify children at risk for school failure.

M. L. Simner, "Predictive Validity of an Abbreviated Version of the Printing Performance School Readiness Test." Reprinted with permission from *Journal of School Psychology*, 27, 1989, 189–195. Pergamon Press.

## Methods

### Subjects

Two samples of children were employed. Sample 1 contained 104 prekindergarten children (60 male, 44 female) tested in October/November, 1983. Sample 2 consisted of 67 prekindergarten children (38 male, 29 female) tested in October/November, 1984. Detailed information describing the procedure used to obtain the children and the population from which both samples were drawn can be found in Simner (1987). The mean age of the children at the time testing took place was 52 months ($SD = 2.9$).[17*]

### Test Instrument

To select as few letters and numbers as possible with which to construct an effective yet shorter, or abbreviated, PPSRT (APPSRT), we followed recommendations by Anastasi (1982, pp. 203–210) and performed an item analysis on results from our earlier investigations at the kindergarten level, in which all 41 letters and numbers in the PPSRT were employed.[18] The aim of this analysis was to determine which letters and numbers were most predictive of later school failure. On the basis of the outcome of this work, 18 letters and numbers were chosen and presented to the prekindergarten children on two 22-cm × 28-cm response sheets using the fixed but random order illustrated in Figure 2 (p. 290).

---

* Numbered notes to articles are supplied by the authors of this text. Original notes appear as endnotes to the article.

| Letter | FORM ERRORS | Letter Number | FORM ERRORS |
|--------|-------------|---------------|-------------|
| B | (figure) | s | (figure) |
| C | (figure) | u | (figure) |
| D | (figure) | y | (figure) |
| E | (figure) | z | (figure) |
| F | (figure) | 2 | (figure) |
| G | (figure) | 3 | (figure) |
| J | (figure) | 4 | (figure) |
| K | (figure) | 5 | (figure) |
| L | (figure) | 6 | (figure) |
| N | (figure) | 7 | (figure) |

Figure 1  Examples of Form Errors in Children's Printing. (From "Printing errors in kindergarten and the prediction of academic performance" by M. L. Simner, 1982, *Journal of Learning Disabilities, 15,* p. 156. Copyright 1982 by Pro-Ed, Inc. Reprinted by permission.)

## Procedure

The children, tested one at a time, were asked to copy each letter and number in the spaces provided below the letters and numbers on the response sheets. No time limit was employed; however, all of the children completed the task without difficulty in less than 3 min. The resulting protocols were scored for the presence of form errors according to the instructions in the PPSRT manual. Because each of the children's attempts at reproducing a letter or number received a score of 0 (form error absent) or 1 (form error present), total scores ranged from 0 through 18.

As in our earlier work, all of the children in both samples were followed for 3 years. To assess the children's aca-

demic achievements at the end of this period and to permit a direct comparison between the present findings and our previous results, we employed the same sets of criteria as those used in our earlier investigations. The first set made use of the children's report card marks in reading and arithmetic issued in June of first grade. These marks ranged on a 12-point scale from $D-$ to $A+$ and reflected the teacher's judgments of the children's command of the core curriculum established by the board of education.[a] The second set of criteria consisted of the children's raw scores at the end of first grade on two standardized achievement tests. Here we employed, as before, the word identification subtest from the Woodcock Reading Mastery Test (WRMT) by Woodcock

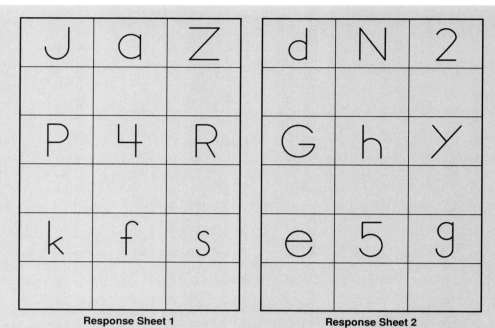

Response Sheet 1          Response Sheet 2

Figure 2 Response Sheets Making Up the APPSRT.

(1974) along with the addition, subtraction, numerical reasoning, word problem, and time subtests from the Keymath Diagnostic Arithmetic Test (KDAT) by Connolly, Nachtman, and Pritchett (1971). Both tests were administered to 93% of the children who completed first grade by a tester who was unaware of the children's classroom performance evaluations.

## Results

### Interrater and Test-Retest Reliability

To evaluate interrater reliability, all of the protocols from Sample 1 were scored independently by two people.[19] The results yielded a product-moment correlation of .95 ($p < .001$).[20] Furthermore, the total scores generated by both raters differed by three points or less in 90% of the cases.

Test-retest reliability was evaluated by a different tester, who was unaware of the scores the children obtained the first time they were given the APPSRT.[21] Because of budget restrictions, however, it was not possible to retest all of the children. Therefore, 44 of the 67

children in Sample 2 were selected at random and tested on a second occasion 1 month later. Here the product-moment correlation was .87 ($p < .001$) and the total scores on each occasion differed by three points or less in 78% of the cases. Together, these findings agree with the evidence we obtained with the PPSRT.

### Follow-up Results

Table 1 contains, for Sample 1 and Sample 2, the product-moment correlations between the children's total scores on the APPSRT and the children's performances, 3 years later, on the two criteria. As the evidence in Table 1 shows, when in-class performance was the criterion the correlations ranged from $-.42$ through $-.58$, and when the criterion was achievement test performance the correlations extended from $-.40$ through $-.60$.[b22] Hence, the predictive validity correlations obtained from both samples are also in line with the predictive validity correlations that we obtained earlier with the PPSRT. In that work, the samples of kindergarten children followed through the end of first grade produced scores on the

Table 1   Product-moment correlations ($p < .001$) between children's scores on the APPSRT administered in the fall of prekindergarten and children's subsequent academic performances at the end of first grade

|  | June report card marks | | Achievement test performance | |
|---|---|---|---|---|
|  | Reading | Arithmetic | WRMT[a] | KDAT[b] |
| Sample 1 | −.42 | −.44 | −.40 | −.49 |
| Sample 2 | −.58 | −.51 | −.57 | −.60 |

[a]Woodcock Reading Mastery Test.   [b]Keymath Diagnostic Arithmetic Test.

PPSRT that correlated from −.40 to −.70 with the two achievement tests and from −.43 to −.56 with the two measures of classroom performance (see Table 1 in Simner, 1986).

Next we asked if scores on the APPSRT could be used with the same accuracy as scores on the PPSRT to identify children who later had serious learning problems. In our previous work the cutoff on the PPSRT correctly identified, on average, 81% of those kindergarten children who subsequently experienced considerable difficulty mastering the curriculum (true positives) while, at the same time, achieving an average false-positive rate of 23%.[23]

To compare these previous findings with the present data, we adhered to our earlier procedure and chose as a cutoff on the APPSRT a score that corresponded to somewhat less than 1 SD above the mean for Sample 1 ($M = 11.80$, $SD = 5.33$) and Sample 2 ($M = 11.80$, $SD = 5.27$). This procedure resulted in a score of 16 form errors as the cutoff. Also as before, the children were divided into two categories reflecting the teachers' end-of-year overall evaluations of the children's command of the curriculum. Children whom we placed in the *Poor performance* category were the ones who either failed, were promoted to a slower or junior section of the next grade, or were recommended for some type of special education class. The second category, labeled *Good performance*, contained children who received an overall rating of $B-$ to $A+$ on their report cards at the end of first grade. According to the children's teachers, these ratings were awarded only to children who were not experiencing any major problem with the core curricu-

lum. The remaining children who received C ratings were not included in the present analysis, because these ratings were assigned when there was some uncertainty with regard to the child's mastery of the curriculum. In other words, this uncertainty prevented us from applying the true-positive/false-positive, true-negative/false-negative designations to this group of children in an unambiguous fashion.[24]

Table 2 contains the number and percentage of prekindergarten children in Sample 1 and Sample 2 who were placed either in the Poor performance or in the Good performance category and whose scores on the APPSRT were either above or below the cutoff of 16 form errors. For the sake of completeness, Table 2 also contains the number of children who were given C ratings. Once again the findings were similar in the two samples and were nearly identical to the results we obtained previously. Specifically, with this cutoff we correctly identified 70–78% of the children in the Poor performance category (true-positives) while achieving, on average, a false-positive rate of 19%.

## Conclusions

In short, the outcome of this 3-year longitudinal investigation demonstrates that form errors in children's printing, even as early as the start of prekindergarten, can be scored reliably, and that they remain stable over time and are tied to children's performances in first grade. Hence, the present findings not only agree with the results we obtained in our previous work at the kindegarten level, they also extend this work by suggesting

Table 2    Prediction of children's classroom performance evaluations from the cutoff score on the APPSRT administered in the fall of prekindergarten

| | Poor performance | C ratings | Good performance |
|---|---|---|---|
| **Sample 1** | | | |
| Poor prognosis (16 errors or more) | (True-positive) 14 (70%) | 13 | (False-positive) 8 (18%) |
| Good prognosis (15 errors or less) | (False-negative) 6 (30%) | 26 | (True-negative) 37 (82%) |
| **Sample 2** | | | |
| Poor prognosis (16 errors or more) | (True-positive) 7 (78%) | 9 | (False-positive) 9 (20%) |
| Good prognosis (15 errors or less) | (False-negative) 2 (22%) | 5 | (True-negative) 35 (80%) |

that form errors can provide a useful source of additional information to consider when deciding which prekindergarten children may require special academic assistance before school entry.[c]

## Notes

[a]This information was not available for seven children who either failed or were placed in special education classes prior to entering first grade.

[b]Separate correlations were calculated for males and females in each sample, but no reliable sex differences were found.

[c]Some possible reasons for the relationship between form errors and school achievement are given in Simner, 1982, 1985, and 1986. Recommendations for assisting children who produce an excessive number of form errors also can be found in these sources.

## References

ANASTASI, A. (1982). *Psychological testing* (5th ed.). New York: MacMillan.

CONNOLLY, A. J., NACHTMAN, W., & PRITCHETT, E. M. (1971). *Keymath Diagnostic Arithmetic Test.* Circle Pines, MN: American Guidance Service.

SIMNER, M. L. (1982). Printing errors in kindergarten and the prediction of academic performance. *Journal of Learning Disabilities, 15,* 155–159.

SIMNER, M. L. (1985). *Printing Performance School Readiness Test.* Toronto, Ontario: University of Toronto, Guidance Centre, Faculty of Education. A revised version of the Printing Performance School Readiness Test is available from Phylmar Associates, 191 Iroquois Avenue, London, Ontario, Canada N6C 2K9.

SIMNER, M. L. (1986). Further evidence on the relationship between form errors in preschool printing and early school achievement. In H. S. R. Kao, G. Van Galen, & R. Hoosian (Eds.), *Graphonomics: Contemporary research in handwriting* (pp. 107–119). Amsterdam: North-Holland.

SIMNER, M. L. (1987). Predictive validity of the Teacher's School Readiness Inventory. *Canadian Journal of School Psychology, 3,* 21–32.

WOODCOCK, R. W. (1974). *Woodcock Reading Mastery Tests.* Circle Pines, MN: American Guidance Service.

# Critical Review

This study assessed the validity of a shortened version of a test of prekindergarten children's printing performance in predicting later school failure. The study is a good example of the use of correlational research to develop a test that can predict an important criterion of student performance. It further demonstrates how a researcher's continuing investigation in a focused topic contributes to the refinement and application of test instruments over time.

Item analysis is an effective technique for refining a test. In this case, the researcher was able to reduce the 41 items in the original Printing Performance School Readiness Test (PPSRT) to the 18 items that best predicted later school failure. These 18 items became the abbreviated version of the test (APPSRT).

In validating the PPSRT, Simner was careful to duplicate as closely as possible the procedure that was used in his earlier investigations of the longer test. He followed the sample for three years, as in his previous studies, and obtained similar outcome measures (grades in reading and arithmetic and raw scores on two standardized achievement tests) at the end of first grade. This attempt to match procedures with those used earlier is an example of replication. Replication helps us determine whether the findings obtained in one situation are a chance result or whether they hold up across situations.

The use of two raters to score the children's test protocols allowed Simner to calculate an interrater reliability coefficient. For Sample 1 the correlation of .95, and the fact that total scores generated by both raters differed by three points or less in 90 percent of the cases, shows that the APPSRT can be scored reliably.

Table 1 shows that scores on the APPSRT correlated significantly, in the expected negative direction, with all four grade and achievement test criteria. The measures of school success (teacher's grades, the Woodcock Reading Mastery Test, and the Keymath Diagnostic Arithmetic Test) appear to have good face validity.

The chosen cutoff score on the APPSRT of 16 form errors is quite high, considering that the maximum possible score is 18. Thus the APPSRT is valid for identifying only children at the extreme high end of producing printing errors as likely to experience school failure. With this cutoff, however, the APPSRT was able to identify correctly 70 to 78 percent of the children in the poor performance category.

The false-positive rate of 19 percent means that about one of every five students who actually performed well in school was incorrectly identified by the APPSRT as having a poor prognosis for school performance. This does not seem a serious problem: there is probably little harm in treating a child as potentially at risk when he is not at risk. A potentially more serious problem is the false-negative rate of 30 percent (Sample 1) and 22 percent (Sample 2). This is the percentage of children who would not be classified as at risk by the APPSRT but who actually performed poorly in school. These children may not receive the special assistance that could help them succeed. The false-negative rate can perhaps be lowered by using other measures, including expert ratings of other behaviors, to supplement APPSRT scores.

The curious reader might wonder why there is a relationship between high APPSRT scores and later school failure. Simner offered several possible explanations in his comments written for this book. These explanations can help teachers identify promising directions for remediation for students scoring high on the test.

# Recommended Reading

BORG, W. R., & GALL, M. D. (1989). *Educational research: An introduction,* 5th ed. White Plains, NY: Longman.

See Chapter 14 for a nontechnical discussion of correlational research that will supplement the topics covered in this chapter.

BRUNING, J. L., & KINTZ, B. L. (1987). *Computational handbook of statistics,* 3rd ed. Glenview, IL: Scott, Foresman.

This book provides easy-to-follow computational procedures for these correlational techniques: product-moment correlation, Spearman rank-order correlation, Kendall rank-order correlation, point biserial correlation, correlation ratio, *phi* coefficient, contingency coefficient, partial correlation, multiple regression, and the test for difference between independent/dependent correlations.

COHEN, J., & COHEN, P. (1983). *Applied multiple correlation/correlation analysis for the behavioral sciences,* 2nd ed. Hillsdale, NJ: Erlbaum.

This book presents research applications and computational procedures for many of the statistical techniques in this chapter. The authors also discuss procedures for handling missing data, computer analysis of data, and the relationship between analysis of variance and multiple regression.

JACKSON, D. N., & MESSICK, S., eds. (1967). *Problems in human assessment.* New York: McGraw-Hill.

Many of the articles reprinted in this book will be helpful to the student planning a prediction study. Among them are Robert L. Thorndike, "The Analysis and Selection of Test Items"; J. P. Guilford, "Some Lessons from Aviation Psychology"; David R. Saunders, "Moderator Variables in Prediction"; and Edward E. Cureton, "Validity, Reliability, and Baloney."

# Application Problems

1. The following are examples of relationships that can be investigated through correlational research: (1) physical strength and peer-group popularity of sixth-grade boys, (2) algebra aptitude scores obtained in the eighth grade and subsequent measures of algebra achievement obtained in the ninth grade, (3) racial attitudes of first-grade children and the attitudes of their parents, (4) the amount that students can remember from a series of photographs viewed for one minute each and their ability in graphic art as measured by evaluations of pencil sketches, and (5) high school GPA and college GPA for students from ghetto environments.

   a. Note with *S-D* the correlations that can be computed based on measures of the same individuals on two or more different variables, with *D-S* the correlations that can be computed based on measures of different individuals on the same variable, and with *S-S* the correlations that can be computed based on measures of the same individuals on the same variable taken at different times.

   b. Note with an *R* the studies that illustrate relationship studies and with a *P* the studies that illustrate prediction studies.

2. A researcher wants to learn more about the nature of mathematical aptitude. He hypothesizes that verbal IQ, logical reasoning, and creativity are all related to mathematical aptitude. He selects 200 high school students who have enrolled in trigonometry, an elective mathematics

course, and administers tests of mathematics aptitude (MA), verbal IQ (VIQ), logical reasoning (LR), and creativity (C) to this group. The following correlations were obtained:

MA and VIQ = .54
MA and logical reasoning = .40
MA and creativity = .30

**a.** Indicate whether this is a relationship study or a prediction study.
**b.** Identify a limitation that needs to be considered in interpreting the results.
**c.** Indicate the amount of common variance between the variables that were correlated.

3. A researcher wants to estimate which entering college freshmen will earn the highest grades during their first year of college. He collects the following data on 500 entering freshmen: (1) high school GPA; (2) scores on the California Test of Mental Maturity (CTMM); (3) scores on the Education Skills Test, college edition (EST). At the end of the year, 266 freshmen are still enrolled. The researcher computes correlations between their GPA during the first year of college and high school GPA, CTMM scores, and EST scores. He obtains the following correlations:

First-year GPA and H.S. GPA = .68
First-year GPA and CTMM = .61
First-year GPA and EST = .48

**a.** Indicate whether this is a relationship study or a prediction study.
**b.** Identify a limitation that needs to be considered in interpreting the results.
**c.** Indicate the amount of common variance between the variables that were correlated.

4. A researcher correlates a number of measures that he has collected on a sample of college seniors. He finds a correlation of +.65 between (1) the amount of time a student has been employed during his college years and (2) a paper-and-pencil measure of the student's personal maturity. On the basis of this finding, would the researcher be justified in concluding that

**a.** The college should institute a work-study program to increase the maturity level of its students? Explain your answer.
**b.** It is probable that the longer a student has worked during college, the higher will be his score on the personal maturity measure? Explain your answer.
**c.** More mature students are better able to obtain jobs while in college than their less mature peers? Explain your answer.

5. Using the evaluation form given in Appendix 1, evaluate the article by Lancelotta and Vaughn reprinted in this chapter.

6. Using the evaluation form given in Appendix 1, evaluate the article by Simner reprinted in this chapter.

# Chapter Notes

1. The abstract of the article is reprinted here to help you understand the researcher's comments.
2. This commentary was written by Sharon Vaughn.
3. An expected negative correlation in this context means that the researchers predicted that children with higher status would show less aggressive behavior. In other words, a negative correlation means that as scores on one variable (social status) increase, scores on the other variable (aggression) decrease.
4. A prediction of a positive correlation means that the researchers expect that as scores on one variable (e.g., teachers' nominations of students' aggressive behavior) increase, scores on another variable (e.g., students' ratings of their peers' aggressive behavior) will also increase.

5. To understand standardizing of scores, suppose that students in classroom A tended to give one another high ratings on the 5-point rating scale. By contrast, students in classroom B tended to give one another low ratings. A rating of 4 in classroom A, then, would have a different meaning than a rating of 4 in classroom B. Standardizing scores is a statistical procedure for adjusting students' ratings so that a given rating has the same meaning across classrooms. A composite social status score for a particular student is the sum of the ratings that his peers gave him on the 5-point social status measure.

6. A distractor is an item designed to conceal the real purpose of a measure from the student who is responding to it.

7. A correlational analysis is a statistical procedure to determine whether variations in one set of scores (for example, social status ratings) are related to variations in another set of scores (for example, aggression ratings). The Pearson product-moment procedure is a particular method for calculating the exact extent of the relationship between the two variables. The calculation results in a mathematical expression called a correlation coefficient.

8. The Fisher $r$-to-$Z'$ transformation is a statistical procedure for determining whether two correlation coefficients differ significantly from each other. If the difference is significant, it means that a similar difference is also likely to be found if one compared other groups similar to those compared in this study.

9. The numbers shown in the main part of Table 2 are correlation coefficients. The coefficients can range in value from $-1.00$ to $1.00$. All coefficients in the table are negative, meaning that high scores on one variable are associated with low scores on the other variable. For example, the coefficient $-.31$ means that for the total sample (All), higher ratings of peer acceptance tend to be associated with lower ratings of provoked physical aggression. The asterisks after the coefficients indicate how statistically significant each coefficient is. More asterisks mean that one can conclude with more confidence that a similar relationship between peer acceptance and aggression would be found in other samples of students like those in this research project. You will note that more asterisks are associated with lower $p$ values ($<$ means "less than"). A $p$ value of .05 or less usually is considered statistically significant. You will note that the coefficient $-.39$ in the Boys column has two asterisks, but the smaller coefficient $-.31$ in the All column has three asterisks and is therefore significant at a higher level of confidence because the statistical significance of a coefficient depends on the size of the sample. In this case, the All sample includes 98 students (47 boys and 51 girls), whereas the Boys sample includes 47 students.

10. Most of the coefficients shown in Table 3 are positive, meaning that high scores on one measure tend to be associated with high scores on another measure. Positive coefficients can vary between .01 and 1.00. Coefficients that are nearer in value to 1.00 indicate a closer relationship between the two variables.

11. Analysis of variance (ANOVA) is a statistical procedure for determining whether mean scores on three or more measures differ significantly from one another. In this instance, the researchers calculated students' mean rating on each of the five aggression scales. The ANOVA told the researchers whether the mean scores differed significantly, that is, whether similar differences would be found if one studied other samples of students like this one. A repeated measures ANOVA is a variant of the ANOVA procedure. It is used when the measures being compared are similar in certain ways. In this instance, the measures (ratings of five types of aggression) are similar in that each student completed all five measures.

12. The $F$ value is a statistical quantity that results from doing an ANOVA. The $p$ value indicates whether the $F$ value is statistically significant (see also note 9).

13. ANOVA indicates that students' mean scores on the five aggression scales differ significantly. It does not indicate which pair(s) of mean scores differ significantly. A post hoc

analysis is done for this purpose. Various types of post hoc analyses are available, including Tukey's test. *M* stands for mean score. *SD* is a symbol for standard deviation, which is a statistical measure of how tightly students' scores are distributed around the mean score.

14. A multivariate *F* test is a broadscale ANOVA. It is used in this context to determine whether boys and girls generally differ to a statistically significant degree across all five measures of aggression. If the multivariate *F* value is significant, univariate *F* tests are done next to determine the specific measures of aggression on which boys and girls differ to a statistically significant degree.

15. The abstract of the article is reprinted here to help you understand the researcher's comments.

16. This commentary was written by Marvin Simner.

17. *SD* is an abbreviation for *standard deviation,* which is a statistical measure of how much the obtained test scores vary around the mean score. An *SD* of 2.9 means that approximately two-thirds of the children in the sample are between 49 months (mean score of 52 minus 1 *SD* of 2.9) and 55 months (mean score of 52 plus 1 *SD* of 2.9) of age.

18. An item analysis, as its name implies, involves the analysis of individual test items for various purposes. In this case, the purpose was to determine which items best predicted school failure. These items were selected for the abbreviated version of the test.

19. The scoring of children's errors in printing requires some judgment. Interrater reliability is the extent to which two raters exercise the same kind of judgment in scoring. If the reliability is low, it means that the raters are using different or inconsistent criteria, and so the children's scores have little meaning.

20. A product-moment correlation is a statistical measure of how well two sets of scores agree. Perfect agreement would yield a correlation of 1.00, so a correlation of .95 in this situation means that the two raters were in near-perfect agreement in their scoring of children's printing errors. The expression "$p < .001$" is a way of showing the results of a test of statistical significance. In this case, the obtained *p* value of less than ($<$) .001 means that we can generalize with confidence beyond these two raters and conclude that other, similar raters would agree highly in their scoring of children's printing errors.

21. Test-retest reliability is an analysis of how consistently students perform on a test from one administration of it to another. If test-retest reliability is low, interpretation of a student's score is difficult because the student's score on the same test at a different point might be quite different. In fact, students' performance on the abbreviated test is quite stable (the correlation is .87).

22. A negative correlation means that as students' scores on one measure increase, their scores on another measure decrease. Negative correlations in this instance make sense because it means that students who have few printing errors (yielding low scores on the APPSRT) are likely to have high grades and achievement test scores. Conversely, students who have many printing errors (yielding high APPSRT scores) are likely to have low grades and achievement test scores. Correlations in the range between $-.40$ and $-.60$ mean that we can make moderately good predictions about a student's grades and achievement test scores from knowing his score on the APPSRT.

23. A true positive is a student who the APPSRT predicts will experience difficulty in school and who in fact experiences difficulty. A false positive is a student who the APPSRT predicts will experience difficulty in school but who in fact experiences success.

24. A true negative is a student who the APPSRT predicts will not experience difficulty in school and who in fact does not experience difficulty. A false negative is a student who the APPSRT predicts will not experience difficulty in school but who in fact experiences difficulty.

# CHAPTER 13

# EXPERIMENTAL RESEARCH

## Overview

In this chapter we discuss the characteristics of experimental research. We examine three types of experiments conducted by educational researchers—"true" experiments, quasi-experiments, and single-subject experiments—illustrated by three studies. We also discuss how to evaluate an experiment's internal validity (that is, the extent to which one can be confident that the observed effects are due to the experimental treatment rather than to confounding variables) and its external validity (that is, the extent to which the experimental conditions approximate those of regular educational settings, so that the research results can be more easily generalized to a target population).

## Objectives

1. State the two essential characteristics of an experiment.
2. Describe some of the extraneous variables that can threaten the internal validity of experimental results.
3. Describe three factors that affect the external validity of experimental results.
4. Describe the main differences among three common designs used in experimental research.
5. Describe the main differences among three common designs used in quasi-experimental research.
6. Describe two single-subject designs that can be used in educational research.

## The Characteristics of Experimental Research

Many people associate the term *research* with experiments. Many experiments are conducted to test the effectiveness of new instructional methods and curricula. Experiments utilize more standard, rigorous design characteristics than other types of research. As a result, researchers can control many of the variables that normally operate in regular educational settings, and thus are able to demonstrate cause-and-effect relationships. In other words, experiments lead to conclusions, such as "If you implement teaching method $X$, student learning of $Y$ will improve."

The typical experimental design in education involves (1) selection of a sample of subjects (students, teachers, administrators, etc.), (2) random assignment of subjects to experimental and control groups, and (3) exposure of the experimental group to an intervention (also called a treatment). In some studies the control group is exposed to an alternate treatment, whereas in others the treatment simply is withheld from the control group. Finally, (4) the two groups are evaluated by comparing their performance on the variable that the researcher is trying to affect. If subjects in the experimental group receive a higher or lower average score on this variable than subjects in the control group, the researchers can conclude that changes in the treatment *caused* the changes observed in the variable being measured.

A "true" experiment has three essential characteristics. First, there must be an intervention, that is, a treatment that is administered to subjects in the experimental group. This intervention or treatment is called the *independent variable*. Second, subjects must be randomly assigned to the treatment and control groups. *Random assignment* means that each subject has an equal chance of being in either group. Use of random assignment permits the researchers to generalize the findings of an experiment to a larger population within margins of error that can be determined statistically. Third, the presumed effect, or effects, of the treatment must be measured. These effects are called *dependent variables* because they are presumed to be dependent on the treatment introduced by the experimenter.

Quasi-experiments, which we shall discuss later in the chapter, are just like true experiments except that random assignment of subjects to the experimental and control groups is lacking.

Let us consider an example of a simple educational experiment. (When we use the term *experiment,* assume it to mean a true experiment.) Suppose that a special program has been developed to improve the racial tolerance of children in racially mixed first-grade classrooms. This program is the experimental treatment, and so the independent variable is exposure or nonexposure to the treatment.

The first step in carrying out the experiment would be to assign randomly a group of, say, 200 children to 10 racially mixed classrooms. The researchers would then randomly select 5 of these classrooms and introduce the program on racial tolerance into their curriculum. Students in the other 5 classrooms would receive the control treatment, which could be either an alternative program dealing with racial tolerance, or no program.

At the end of first grade, a measure of racial attitudes would be administered to children in all 10 classrooms. This measure is the dependent variable, that is, the variable that the researchers expect will be affected by the experimental treatment. Statistical analyses would be done to determine whether children in the experimental classes obtained more favorable scores on the racial attitudes measure than children in the control classes. Assume that at the conclusion of the experiment, the scores of the experimental students and those of the control students were different at a previously selected level of statistical significance. Then the researchers could *generalize* their findings. That is, they could conclude, with some certainty, that administering the same special program to improve children's racial tolerance to other students, who are similar to those who participated in the experiment, would result in improved racial attitudes of those students.

Researchers have created many variations on this basic experimental design. For example, in some studies a pretest is administered before a program starts, and a posttest (the measure of the dependent variable) is administered at the end of the experimental program. The pretest data can be analyzed to check whether the experimental and control groups were similar at the outset of the experiment and to measure pretest-to-posttest gains. In some studies, several programs may be compared in a single experiment. For example, a school district could conduct an experiment to compare the effectiveness of five different reading programs for first grade. Each reading program would be considered a separate treatment, and so students would need to be randomly assigned to five treatment groups.

In some experimental studies the research is designed so that more than one independent variable is manipulated. In the aforementioned study of racial tolerance, the researchers could randomly assign children to classrooms so that some classrooms contained 80 percent Caucasian and 20 percent Afro-American students, others contained half Caucasian and half Afro-American students, and still others contained 80 percent Afro-American and 20 percent Caucasian students.

In this example the racial tolerance program is the first independent variable. However, the experiment has been designed so that the racial composition of the classroom also differs for different groups of students. Racial composition thus constitutes a second independent variable—sometimes called a *moderator variable*. In analyzing the results, the researchers would not only evaluate the overall effects of the racial tolerance program but also determine whether racial composition *moderates* the effects of the program, by investigating its differential effects in classrooms of different racial composition.

Analysis of experimental research data typically involves computing the mean scores of each group on the dependent variable and then comparing the mean scores to determine whether the differences obtained are statistically significant. See Table 11.1 for a summary of the inferential statistics commonly used in causal-comparative, experimental, and quasi-experimental research.

## INTERNAL VALIDITY OF EXPERIMENTS

The observed effects in any experiment are partly due to the treatment variable and partly to *extraneous variables* that operate during the study. Extraneous variables are nontreatment factors that are present while the experiment is in progress. If extraneous variables are present in a particular experiment, the researchers will be unable to determine whether the observed effects on the dependent variable are caused by the treatment or by the extraneous variables. The practical implication is that you may implement the treatment in your local situation with the expectation that you will obtain the same positive effects as were observed in the experiment. However, you may be surprised and not get these effects because they were caused by extraneous factors rather than by the treatment.

To demonstrate the importance of controlling for extraneous variables, we will consider a research problem that can be studied through a simple experimental design. Suppose the researchers wish to evaluate the effectiveness of a newly developed program in whole-language instruction for slow learners. At the beginning of the school year, they select 100 students for participation in the program. All the students meet the selection criterion of scoring at least two grades below the age norm on a standard test of reading achievement. After participation in the program for a school year, the students are once again given a reading achievement test.

Suppose the researchers find a large, statistically significant gain in achievement (as determined by the *t* test for correlated means). Can they conclude that this achievement gain was caused by the experimental treatment, that is, the whole-language program? The answer depends on how well extraneous variables have been controlled.

Campbell and Stanley (1963) identified eight types of extraneous variables that can affect the internal validity of an experiment. We will describe each of these threats to internal validity and discuss how each might have affected the results of the aforementioned experiment.

*1. History.* Experimental treatments extend over a period of time, providing opportunity for other events besides the experimental treatment to cause changes in the experimental group. The students in our example participated in the whole-language program over the period of a school year. Therefore, other factors, such as the students' regular instruction from teachers, could have accounted for all or part of their achievement gain in reading.

*2. Maturation.* While the experimental treatment is in progress, certain biological or psychological processes are occurring within the students. For example, research subjects may become older, stronger, fatigued, elated, or discouraged, all of which are defined as "maturation" by Campbell and Stanley (1963). During the year of the experimental program, students were developing physically, socially, and intellectually. Possibly maturation in one of these areas, rather than the whole-language program itself, enabled students to overcome their reading deficiency.

*3. Testing.* In many educational experiments a pretest is administered, followed by the experimental and control treatments, and concluding with a posttest. If the pretest and posttest are similar, students may show an improvement on the posttest simply as a result of their experience with the pretest; that is, they have become "test-wise." It is unlikely that this extraneous variable was operating in our hypothetical experiment. Because of the long period of time between the pretest and posttest, students are not likely to remember enough about the pretest for it to affect their posttest performance. However, a testing effect is a possibility in experiments in which the interval between pretest and posttest measures is short or if the nature of the pretest makes it easy to remember. In these situations the researchers cannot clearly determine how much of the subjects' posttest performance is due to the treatment and how much to exposure to the pretest.

*4. Instrumentation.* An apparent learning gain may be observed from pretest to posttest because the nature of the measuring instrument has changed. This situation often occurs in experiments in which the researchers use alternate forms of the same standardized test that are supposed to be equivalent but are not. Suppose that the students in our example had been administered a posttest of reading achievement that was actually easier than the pretest they had taken. The gain in achievement then would be caused by differences in the testing instruments rather than by the experimental treatment.

5. *Statistical regression.* Whenever a test-retest procedure is used to assess learning in an experiment, the possibility exists that statistical regression accounts for observed gains in learning. We will not present the mathematical basis for the phenomenon of statistical regression but will briefly describe its effects on test scores.

Upon retesting, statistical regression tends to move extreme scores toward the mean. Suppose that the students in our example fell below the fifteenth percentile on a pretest of reading achievement. When this group of students is tested again on the same or a similar test, they are likely to earn a higher mean score because of statistical regression, with or without an intervening experimental treatment. Say that another group of students was selected who earned very high scores on the first test, that is, above the 85th percentile. These students are likely to earn a lower mean score when retested on a similar measure, again as a result of statistical regression.

The researcher should be alert to the confounding effects of statistical regression whenever students have been selected for their extreme scores on a pretest and are retested later on a posttest measure that is correlated with the pretest. The probable amount of regression can be estimated through statistical formulas and taken into account in the results.

6. *Differential selection.* In quasi-experimental designs, subjects are selected for the experimental and control groups by some procedure other than random selection. As a result, the effect of the treatment may be distorted because of differential selection of students for the two groups. Suppose that the students in our example had two characteristics: They fell below the 15th percentile in reading achievement, and they also volunteered to participate in the program. Further, suppose that their learning was compared with that of a control group of students who had equivalent reading deficiencies but who did not volunteer for the program. If the experimental group shows greater achievement gains than the control group, the effect could be attributed to their "volunteer" characteristics rather than to the experimental treatment itself. To avoid this confounding effect, the researchers need to select experimental and control groups that do not differ except for exposure to the experimental treatment. In other words, the same criteria should be applied to selecting subjects for both the experimental and control groups. The best way to accomplish this goal is to assign subjects randomly to the two groups, which is one of the basic requirements of a true experiment.

7. *Selection-maturation interaction.* This extraneous variable is similar to differential selection, except that maturation is the specific confounding variable. Suppose that first-grade students from a single school district are selected for the whole-language program in our example. The control group is drawn from the population of first-grade students in another school district. Because of different admissions policies in the two school districts, the average age of the control group is six months older than that of the experimental group. Now, suppose the experiment shows that the treatment group made significantly greater achievement gains than the control group. Do these results reflect the effectiveness of the experimental treatment, or do they show that reading gains are more influenced by maturational factors in younger students than in slightly

older students? Because of differential assignment of students varying in maturation to the experimental and control groups, it is not clear which of these alternative explanations is correct.

*8. Experimental mortality* (sometimes called *attrition*). Experimental mortality is the loss of subjects during the period of the experiment. This extraneous variable can bias the results because the subjects who drop out are usually different in important ways from the subjects who remain. Furthermore, a larger number of subjects is often lost from the experimental group than from the control group. Differential attrition from these groups can distort the results when the posttreatment scores of the remaining subjects are compared.

Suppose that in our research example there was a systematic bias in the type of students who dropped out of the whole-language program during the school year. For example, some students might leave the school district, and they happened to be the lowest-achieving students. If the researchers measured the achievement gains of only the students who completed the program, the effectiveness of the experimental treatment would be exaggerated.

When you evaluate an experimental or quasi-experimental study, it is helpful to keep these eight threats to internal validity in mind and try to estimate how well the study was designed to deal with them.

## EXTERNAL VALIDITY OF EXPERIMENTS

Experiments are externally valid to the degree that their results can be generalized to persons, settings, and times different from those involved in the research. The results may have high external validity for some local settings and low external validity for others, depending on the similarity between the research conditions and local conditions. Thus, potential users must compare the experimental conditions with the local conditions to which they want to generalize the results and make a decision about how well the findings are likely to apply. Bracht and Glass (1968) described specific aspects of external validity that you should consider when reviewing an experimental study.

*1. Population validity.* You will recall from our discussion of sampling in Chapter 5 that population validity is the degree to which the results of a research study can be generalized from the specific sample that was studied to the population from which this sample was drawn. Population validity is determined by examining evidence of the similarity among the *sample* used in the study, the *accessible population* from which the research sample was drawn, and the *target population* to which the research results are to be generalized. The more evidence the researcher provides to establish links among the sample, the accessible population, and the target population, the more confident you can be in applying the research findings to the target population.

However, educators wishing to apply research findings to their own setting are interested in the similarity between the research sample and the *local* population rather than the target population. To determine this type of similarity, you should note all information that the researchers provide about the research sample, such as age, gender, scholastic aptitude, racial composition, achievement, socioeconomic status, and the communities from which subjects were drawn. You then should gather the same data for the local population to which you want to apply the research findings. Comparing these two sets of data will give you a basis for estimating the degree to which the research findings are likely to apply to your local setting.

*2. Personological variables.* Another type of external validity that you should consider is the degree to which personological variables are likely to *interact* with the research findings. An interaction is present if the experimental results apply to subjects with certain characteristics but not to subjects with other characteristics. For example, the Beginning Teacher Evaluation Study sought to relate specific teaching procedures and strategies to the achievement of second- and fifth-grade pupils in mathematics and reading (Fisher et al., 1978). The researchers found that some strategies were significantly related to academic achievement at both grade levels and in both subject areas, but the majority were not. For example, academic monitoring was negatively correlated with achievement in grade 2 reading but was positively correlated with achievement in grade 2 mathematics. At grade 5, correlations between academic monitoring and achievement in both subject areas were virtually zero. However, academic feedback was positively related to achievement at both grade levels and for both subject areas. Thus, even though a teaching procedure may have general merit, it may vary greatly in its effectiveness at different grade levels, in different subject areas, or for students with different characteristics. You need to be cautious, therefore, in generalizing from the results of a specific experiment except when the subjects are similar to the individuals with whom you are working.

*3. Ecological validity.* Ecological validity involves the extent to which the situational conditions that existed during the experiment affect the generalizability of the experimental results to other situational conditions. When applying the experimental results to your local situation, you should ask two questions: (1) How similar is the environment in which this experiment was conducted to the local environment to which I want to generalize the results? (2) If major differences exist between the two environments, how are these differences likely to affect the generalizability of the experimental results?

As a rule, you can assume that the larger the difference between the experimental environment and the local environment to which you want to apply the experimental results, the less confidence you can have that the results will apply. Keep in mind, however, that not all experimental results are situation-specific. Thus, the results of a study of the effects of a new whole-language program conducted with first-grade children in a small town in the South may generalize very well to other small towns, rural communities, and medium-sized cities. In other words, the size of the community may have nothing to do with the program's effectiveness. However, suppose the first-grade children in the research sample were in classrooms of 20 students and their teachers had two part-time aides to help with instruction. If your classroom has 28 students and no aides, the generalizability of the experimental results is questionable.

## RESEARCH TRADEOFFS

You may have noted that the very kinds of control of the research situation that lead to high levels of internal validity tend to make the research environment different from the environment of the typical classroom. For example, one of the best methods of ensuring internal validity is random assignment of students to classrooms that will receive different treatments. In practice, however, students are seldom randomly assigned to classrooms, especially when the classrooms used in the experiment are in more than one school. Therefore controls like random assignment reduce the external validity of the research results. No completely satisfactory solution to this dilemma is possible. All that researchers can do is weigh the advantages of rigorous control of extraneous variables against the advantages of doing research in natural educational environments. They then need to make a compromise that provides acceptable levels of both internal and external validity.

# Experimental Designs

We will now consider one preexperimental and two true experimental designs often used in educational research and discuss the threats to internal validity that are typically present in each. Before doing so, however, we need to explain some symbols often used to describe experimental designs. $R$ means that the subjects were randomly assigned, $X$ is used to represent the experimental treatment, and $O$ means observation of the dependent variable by administering either a pretest or posttest.

## ONE-GROUP PRETEST-POSTTEST DESIGN

Using the symbols explained above, we can describe the one-group pretest-posttest design as follows:

$$O \quad X \quad O$$

This indicates that

$O$ = A pretest is given to all subjects.
$X$ = All subjects receive the experimental treatment.
$O$ = The posttest is administered to all subjects.

In this design there is no control group, so most of the internal validity threats are present. For example, consider the internal validity threat of history. Any change from pretest to posttest can be explained by other events occurring during the experimental period rather than by the treatment variable. Suppose that the experiment involved measuring teachers' morale (the pretest), giving them a pay raise (the treatment variable), and measuring their morale a month later (the posttest). If an improvement in morale is observed, the effect could be attributed to the pay raise. But suppose during the treatment period a national commission released a highly publicized report arguing for the importance of teachers to the economic and social well-being of the country. We would not know whether the improvement in morale was due to the pay raise, to the national commission's report, or to both. The fact that the results of a one-group pretest-posttest experiment can be attributed easily to extraneous effects rather than to treatment effects makes it a weak design. Cook and Campbell (1979) called it a preexperimental design because it lacks crucial elements of a true experimental design.

## PRETEST-POSTTEST CONTROL GROUP DESIGN

The pretest-posttest control group design is written

$$R \quad O \quad X \quad O$$
$$R \quad O \qquad O$$

The top line represents the experimental group; the second line represents the control group. These symbols mean that

$R$ = Subjects are randomly assigned to experimental and control groups.
$O$ = Both groups are given the pretest.
$X$ = The experimental group is given the treatment and the control group gets no treatment or an alternative treatment.
$O$ = Both groups are given the posttest.

This is an excellent design for controlling the eight internal validity threats described above.

The power of this design can be illustrated by the teacher morale experiment described in connection with the one-group pretest-posttest design. Suppose that this experiment had included a group of teachers randomly assigned to a control group (no pay raise). The design then would be a pretest-posttest control group design. The addition of the control group is an effective method for ruling out extraneous variables such as history. For example, suppose the national commission's report, which was released at the same time that the pay raise occurred, had a positive effect on teachers' morale. The control group, then, would have a pretest-posttest gain in morale as a result of the report. If the treatment group had the same amount of gain, we could conclude that the pay raise had no effect. However, if the treatment group had a *greater* gain than the control group, we could conclude that the pay raise had an effect on morale independent of the effect created by the national commission's report.

The same logic would apply to other extraneous variables such as testing, instrumentation, and statistical regression. To the extent that these variables have an effect, they will affect the experimental and control groups equally. Thus, if the gain of the experimental group exceeds that of the control group, the differential gain can be attributed unequivocally to the treatment variable.

The only exception to this principle is the extraneous variable of experimental mortality. Even though the experimental and control groups are initially comparable in the pretest-posttest control group design, differences in the demands made on the subjects in the two groups can lead to large differences in the number of subjects lost during the course of the experiment. Thus, posttreatment differences on the dependent variable may be due to differences in such characteristics as motivation and ability between the remaining experimental group and control group members rather than to the experimental treatment.

## POSTTEST-ONLY CONTROL GROUP DESIGN

The posttest-only control group design is written

$$R \quad X \quad O$$
$$R \quad \quad \phantom{X} O$$

where

$R$ = Subjects are randomly assigned to the experimental and control groups.
$X$ = The experimental group is given the experimental treatment.
$O$ = Both groups are given a posttest that measures the dependent variable.

This design is useful in studies in which the administration of a pretest may influence the subjects' behavior during the experiment and on the posttest. For example, suppose the pretest is a measure of subjects' attitude toward people with a certain handicap. After completing the pretest, the subjects view a film about this handicapping condition. It is possible that the pretest would dispose the subjects to view the film in a certain way. If so, any differential change between the experimental and control groups can be attributed to *both* the film and the pretest. By using the posttest-only control group design, the researchers can determine the effect of the film by itself.

# Sample Experimental Study: MODIFIED RECIPROCAL TEACHING IN A REGULAR CLASSROOM

## Abstract[1]

This study was designed to increase reading comprehension and academic achievement of students through the use of a modified reciprocal teaching program. Modified reciprocal teaching involved small groups of students working together to read and comprehend a portion of text. The students took turns "teaching" these groups by assisting the rest of the group in selecting key words and phrases, summarizing, questioning, clarifying, and predicting. Students were randomly assigned to one of three seventh-grade regular education social studies classes. One class used modified reciprocal teaching twice a week for 8 weeks. The other two classes received a traditional instructional program. All classes were taught by the same teacher. Significant differences included higher scores on comprehension tests and writing samples, improvement in second-quarter social studies grades, and better conduct records for students who participated in modified reciprocal teaching. Several explanations for the superior performance of the modified reciprocal teaching group are hypothesized.

# Researcher's Comments[2]

## Background

One of the researchers had been tutoring two mornings a week in seventh-grade and eighth-grade functional (lower-track) geography and English classes. Many of the students were bored and frustrated. Teachers were frustrated and dreaded meeting the functional classes. Most of the students were low achievers and/or high-risk adolescents. Another of the researchers, a school psychologist, reported that approximately 60 percent of the referrals in this building were for low achievement. Most of the time these students were not eligible for special education classes.

With encouragement from the principal and dean of students, we began an extensive literature search on low-achieving students and on programs that improved their achievement. The search revealed lots of ideas and programs but very little empirical data.

The knowledge base that did exist suggested to us that the students would need to be actively engaged in the learning process and would need help in reading and comprehending text material. It happened that Ann Marie Palincsar had presented a paper at a national conference that supported our views. We wrote and obtained a copy of her report, which contained a lot of research results demonstrating positive effects of her instructional method on the academic achievement of low-performing students. Subsequently she sent us copies of the training materials and a videotape of reciprocal teaching in process. Her interest and support played an important role in our decision to continue with the project.

The senior author attended a workshop on cooperative learning led by David and Roger Johnson and spoke to them about our ideas. They were very supportive and offered helpful suggestions. The Johnsons encouraged us to use regular classrooms rather than pullout programs.

We decided finally to do our research on the reciprocal teaching model for several reasons: (1) it was supported by empirical data reflecting generally positive outcomes; (2) it addressed students' motivation, particularly that of low achievers, by making the reading of text material a meaningful task; and (3) the cooperative learning format provided opportunities for students to help their peers and also be helped by them.

## Experiences

As educational researchers, we have always been puzzled by the seeming absence of concern of most educators about whether instructional activities and programs have been empirically evaluated. Our interest in random assignment of students to classes and random selection of the experimental class and two control classes seemed both foreign and unnecessary to the educators with whom we were working. It took most of an academic year to develop the relationships that enabled us to do the study.

We wish we had anticipated a number of unpredicted problems that arose. Shortened assembly schedules on some days did not allow enough time for teaching and assessing outcomes. Unexpected changes in classroom activities and materials on a few occasions made it impossible to conduct the research. Some of the brightest students became impatient with and openly critical of their slower classmates. Approximately 75 percent of the students, however, were enjoying reciprocal teaching. They were telling others about it, which led to inquiries about why students in other classes weren't allowed to participate as well.

One of the more difficult issues evolved out of the marked improvement of the experimental class. The teacher felt that its superior performance was making her look bad in the other two classes. We tried hard to make the project "theirs" and not just "ours," but we were never completely successful.

## Aftermath

Reciprocal teaching is not being used in our community at present, and we have had very few requests for information about the program. Our impression is that teaching continues to be equated with dispensing information and having students work independently. Encouraging and implementing effective instructional strategies to improve students' achievement has not been incorporated widely in classrooms, although its importance is being acknowledged more.

## Implications and Future Directions

The original intent of reciprocal teaching was to develop reading skills and strategies that students could use on their own to become more effective and independent learners. To use reciprocal teaching on a regular basis for an entire school year may be neither necessary nor desirable. It may be that brief, intense instruction in this method—perhaps twice a week, as was the case in the present study, or perhaps more than twice a week—would be most effective. Further research is needed to explore these issues.

The senior author has continued to use this research experience to enhance his own teaching. He finds that teaching students more effective learning strategies, including those embodied in modified reciprocal teaching, helps them interact meaningfully with course content and learn more. For example, he has developed a comprehension paper assignment for each unit that is studied in the course. Completion of the comprehension papers requires a great deal of reading, thinking, and writing. Extensive use of several reading comprehension strategies, organizational strategies (matrix schema, concept/semantic maps, hierarchical schema, and event schema), and summarizing and integrating strategies are both encouraged and modeled by the instructor.

In one class of 60 students, 60 percent opted to complete 15 or more comprehension papers and not take any classroom examinations. Students were encouraged to consult with one another, the instructors, and other people to obtain reactions and suggestions for improving their thinking, reading, and writing skills. Modified reciprocal teaching played an important role in assisting this instructor to modify greatly his approach to instructional planning, teaching, and evaluation of students' progress and understanding.

It appears to us that modified reciprocal teaching is quite compatible with cooperative learning approaches and could be incorporated into the cooperative learning groups that are increasingly being utilized in classrooms. However, the need for additional adults (or slightly older students) to model and supervise the small-group activities appears to be a serious obstacle.

One of the researchers with experience in peer counseling and peer tutoring believes that with proper training and supervision, mature ninth-graders could do an excellent job as modified reciprocal teaching group leaders. Thus far, however, most teachers have found it difficult to open up their classrooms to include volunteers in a significant role such as that involved in modified reciprocal teaching. However, one of our local high schools is now in the third year of training juniors to work as math tutors in some of the regular Algebra I classes. As many as four of the specially trained tutors work in the same classroom at the same time, with from one to five students. The teacher is doing the same thing and presents information only when it appears that it will benefit several students. Tutors work in the classroom for two to three days a week and are also available at other times.

Very few teachers have ever experienced or observed the use of adult volunteers or peers in regular classrooms on a regular basis. Not many teachers are encouraged and strongly supported to try to use adult volunteers or peers in a planned, purposeful way to enhance students' achievement.

We recommend further research on modified reciprocal teaching to help educators better understand its potential role in helping students acquire reading strategies for identifying and summarizing main ideas and supporting details in text material and for using different knowledge structures to construct meaning and integrate subject information. Possibilities include using modified reciprocal teaching to encourage students to experiment with various learning strategies to improve their comprehension and to teach them these learning strategies. The research questions might focus on how to increase students' involvement in learning the course content as well as on the effects of assisting one another in self-concept and efficacy as learners.

# MODIFIED RECIPROCAL TEACHING IN A REGULAR CLASSROOM

**C. Dean Miller**
COLORADO STATE UNIVERSITY

**Larry F. Miller**
POUDRE R-1 SCHOOL DISTRICT
FORT COLLINS, COLORADO

**Lee A. Rosen**
COLORADO STATE UNIVERSITY

Fostering and enhancing reading comprehension continues to be of interest and concern to many educators.

C. D. Miller, L. F. Miller, and L. A. Rosen, "Modified Reciprocal Teaching in a Regular Classroom," *Journal of Experimental Education*, 56(4), 1988, 183–186. Reprinted with permission of the Helen Dwight Reid Educational Foundation. Published by Heldref Publications, 4000 Albermarle St. N.W., Washington, DC 20016. Copyright © 1988.

Palincsar and Brown (1984) recently reported two innovative studies that were designed to facilitate and enhance comprehension-fostering and comprehension-monitoring skills of low-achieving seventh graders. The two studies were formulated and based on several functions they believed were common to strategies that could be used for instruction of comprehension skills. They selected four activities that embodied these functions: (a) summarizing, (b) questioning, (c) clarifying, and (d) predicting. Palincsar and Brown believed that these four activities would serve a dual function of enhancing comprehension as well as providing opportunities to monitor whether or not comprehension was occurring. Palincsar and Brown's two studies involved a total of 27 students. The results were impressive. For both regular and special education children sizable gains were found on tests of comprehension and the gains were maintained over time. In addition, the comprehension-fostering and comprehension-monitoring skills generalized to other classroom comprehension tests.

Palincsar and Brown called their approach "reciprocal teaching." Reciprocal teaching involved a teacher and student(s) taking turns leading a dialogue based on sections of a text. The teacher modeled and demonstrated the four activities the students were to use when they read—summarizing, questioning, clarifying, and predicting. Students were encouraged to participate at whatever level they could. The teacher provided guidance, feedback, and encouragement at the appropriate level for each student.

At this time, there were no other studies examining the effects of reciprocal teaching. Thus, the present study sought to expand our knowledge base in this important area. Reciprocal teaching was modified for the present study based on the premise that regular education students—and not just the low-achieving students previously studied—could benefit from an approach to learning that focused on the four activities identified by Palincsar and Brown: summarizing, questioning, clarifying, and predicting. Brown, Campione, and Day (1981) reported that summarizing can facilitate learning by helping readers clarify the meaning and significance of discourse. In addition, identification of the key words and phrases contained in the material to be learned was added as a component (Winograd, 1984). Support for this comes from theory and research that suggest that comprehension involves the construction of knowledge rather than the storage of knowledge (Brown & Smiley, 1978; Glaser, 1979). For example, Eylon and Reif (1984) stress the importance of knowledge organization, particularly a hierarchical organization of knowledge that the learner must actively construct. A hierarchical organization must include knowledge at each level such as a main idea (high level) supported by more specific knowl-

edge at a lower level in the hierarchy. Thus, summarizing or constructing the main idea based on the key words or phrases can be used to help the student comprehend the information (Harris & Sipay, 1980; Pearson & Johnson, 1978).

## Method

### Subjects

A seventh-grade social studies teacher allowed the study to be conducted with her three social studies classes. Students were randomly assigned to the three classes, and the three classes were randomly assigned to one of three conditions: modified reciprocal teaching (MRT) ($n = 26$); control group I ($n = 20$); and control group II ($n = 18$). All three classes covered the same academic material and completed the same projects and classroom tests, which were graded and recorded by the same classroom teacher. The three groups did not differ significantly on the vocabulary score on the Metropolitan Achievement Test, $F(2, 63) = .95$, $p > .05$, which was administered 3 weeks before the study began.[3*]

### Group Leaders

Five persons served as group leaders. Three were graduate students in school psychology, one was an undergraduate psychology major, and one had received a bachelor's degree in psychology. Four worked as group leaders with the fifth person acting as an alternate. An alternate was used on two occasions.

Each group leader and the alternate received approximately 4 hours of training that included rehearsing and practicing reciprocal teaching. The training included viewing a videotape of a reciprocal teaching session. The tape was provided by Palincsar, author of the original reciprocal teaching research (Palincsar & Brown, 1984). In addition, some of the training materials from the original studies were used in training the group leaders.

* Numbered notes to articles are supplied by the authors of this text.

## Procedure

### Modified Reciprocal Teaching

MRT was conducted 1 hour on Tuesdays and Thursdays for 8 weeks. The class of 26 students was divided into two groups of 6 students each and two groups of 7 students each. Students were randomly assigned to the four groups. All the students participated in MRT, not just the low achievers. Leaders were randomly assigned to the groups. The group leaders introduced MRT to their groups by explaining the purpose and the activities that they would be using when each person took her or his turn being the "teacher." The study activities included (a) questioning, (b) clarifying, (c) summarizing, (d) predicting, and (e) identifying the key words and phrases. The group leaders began the first few sessions by being the "teacher," which enabled the leaders to model the behaviors they wanted the students to imitate. Following all MRT teaching sessions the students completed a 10-item comprehension test and produced a writing sample.

### Control Group I

This social studies class did not receive MRT but did complete the 10-item comprehension tests and the writing samples.

### Control Group II

The students in this social studies class did not receive MRT and they did not take the comprehension tests or do the 3-minute writing samples. These students completed only pre- and postmeasures. This group was included to act as a control/comparison group for the frequent testing conducted in both the MRT group and control group I.

## Measures

Data were collected on the following measures for 11 of 16 sessions. Interruptions such as pep assemblies, vacations, and class projects prevented collection of data at every session.

### Comprehension Test

A 10-question multiple-choice test was prepared for each session of MRT. The test was administered to the MRT group and control group I during the last 10 min-

utes of each class period. The teacher had no knowledge of what the tests contained until after they had been completed by the students. Two types of questions were used for the comprehension test: (a) text-explicit questions, which meant the answer was explicitly mentioned in the text (e.g., In what year did Columbus discover America?), and (b) text-implicit questions, which meant the answer had to be inferred across adjacent segments of the text (e.g., What was the primary purpose of Columbus' voyage?). All of the questions were either written or selected by two of the authors.

### Writing Sample

A 3-minute writing sample was completed in both groups. A story starter (e.g., Last weekend, I . . .) was written on the board and students began writing when instructed to do so. The writing sample was scored by counting the number of words written. Numbers, dates, and addresses were not counted.

### Other Measures

Grades were collected for all students at the end of both the first and second quarters of the school year. Data were also collected regarding each student's conduct. Conduct consisted of absences (excused and unexcused), tardies (excused and unexcused), and suspensions (in school and out of school). This information was obtained directly from the attendance officer and not from the students.

## Results and Discussion

The comprehension test scores of the MRT group and control group I were significantly different, $F(1, 44) = 15.38$, $p < .001$.[4] Students receiving MRT did significantly better than students who were taught in a traditional manner. The overall means on the comprehension tests were 6.40 ($SD = 1.61$) and 5.16 ($SD = 2.22$) for the MRT group and control group I, respectively.[5]

In addition, students in the MRT group wrote an average of 13 more words per 3-minute writing sample than the students in control group I. The overall means were 61.58 ($SD = 17.84$) words per 3 minutes for the MRT group and 48.59 ($SD = 17.95$) for control group I. The difference between the two groups was significant, $F(1, 44) = 14.32$, $p < .001$.

Grades for the first quarter were not significantly different among the three groups. However, using analysis of covariance, with the first-quarter grades as covariate, second-quarter grades were significantly different, $F(2, 59) = 3.84, p < .05$.[6] The means for the second-quarter grades, with 4.0 equalling an A, were as follows: control group I, $M = 2.17$ ($SD = 1.07$); control group II, $M = 2.28$ ($SD = 1.36$); and MRT group, $M = 2.80$ ($SD = 1.21$). Tukey post hoc analyses indicated that the MRT group had significantly better grades than control group I ($p < .05$).[7] No other differences were significant.

Information regarding students' conduct was also analyzed. There was a significant difference among the three groups in the total number of conduct incidents, $\chi^2 (2, N = 64) = 32.35, p < .001$.[8] Control group I had a total of 132 incidents reported, followed by control group II with 83 incidents, and the MRT group with 61.

All of the significant differences among the three groups resulted from the MRT group's superior performance. The MRT group had an overall superior performance on the comprehension tests and writing samples. Grades were considerably higher during the second quarter for students in the MRT group relative to the students in the control groups. In addition, conduct was better for students in the MRT group than for students in the two control groups. These outcomes strongly favor the use of modified reciprocal teaching in a regular classroom.

Several hypotheses explain the superior performance of students who participated in modified reciprocal teaching. First, reading was goal directed, the goals being to select key words or phrases, summarize the main idea, and formulate questions to test the other students' understanding of what had been read. Second, students were actively involved in reading to either ask the questions when they were the "teacher," and answer the questions asked by the "teacher." Taking turns being the teacher appeared to be very motivating for many of the students. Student involvement in summarizing, identifying key words and phrases, asking questions, and answering questions required more encoding effort than is required in passive reading and outlining. Third, paraphrasing was evident in students' statements about the main ideas. Perhaps paraphrasing enabled the students to encode the information in a way that had more meaning for them than they could obtain through passive

reading or rote memorization. Fourth, modified reciprocal teaching provided opportunities for clarifying misunderstandings as well as defining words or concepts that were not understood by everyone in the group. Fifth, simply participating in a small group focused on the facilitation of learning may have impacted the students' performance. In addition, the students were also affected at least somewhat by the approach being fun, the challenge of being the "teacher," being given a chance to participate actively in discussion, and the variety and change in daily routine. Further research will have to be conducted before the individual contribution of the various factors involved in modified reciprocal teaching can be analyzed.

It should be noted that the application of reciprocal teaching in this study was slightly different than that used in the original studies reported by Palincsar and Brown (1984). The present research was conducted with an entire regular classroom as opposed to pulling out low-achieving students, reciprocal teaching was modified to include identification of key words and phrases, and reciprocal teaching was conducted only 2 days a week as opposed to intensive daily intervention. Even with these differences, however, the benefits and improved performance were substantial.

In conclusion, the data consistently favored the students in the modified reciprocal teaching class, and a majority of the students indicated they enjoyed MRT and would like to have it continued. In fact, we believe the strongest evidence and support for MRT was in the improved grades of students in the MRT class. Thus, we would not hesitate to recommend modified reciprocal teaching as a promising approach to increase student interest, involvement, and achievement in regular education classrooms.

## Acknowledgment

We gratefully acknowledge the assistance of Sherry Ritch, principal; Rich Kruetzer, dean of students; Lori Gutierrez, social studies teacher; Lisa Gabardi-Bianchi, Dan Doyle, Doug Strachan, Lisa Strassburger, and Greg Thwaites, group leaders; as well as students of the Poudre R-1 Schools for their help with this research.

## References

BROWN, A. L., CAMPIONE, J. C., & DAY, J. D. (1981). Learning to learn: On training students to learn from texts. *Educational Researcher, 10,* 14–21.

BROWN, A. L., & SMILEY, S. S. (1978). The development of strategies for studying texts. *Child Development, 49,* 1076–1088.

EYLON, B-S., & REIF, F. (1984). Effects of knowledge organization on task performance. *Cognition and Instruction, 1*(1).

GLASER, R. (1979). Trends and research questions in psychological research on learning and schooling. *Educational Researcher, 8,* 6–13.

HARRIS, A., & SIPAY, E. (1980). *How to increase reading ability.* New York: Longman.

PALINCSAR, A. S., & BROWN, A. L. (1984). Reciprocal teaching of comprehension-monitoring activities. *Cognition and Instruction, 1*(2), 117–175.

PEARSON, P. D., & JOHNSON, D. D. (1978). *Teaching reading comprehension.* New York: Holt, Rinehart & Winston.

WINOGRAD, P. N. (1984). Strategic difficulties in summarizing texts. *Reading Research Quarterly, 19,* 404–425.

# Critical Review

The researchers did extensive planning to assign students randomly to the experimental and control groups in this study. The advantage of random assignment is that we can be fairly confident that students in each group were comparable before the study began and that differences in achievement following the experimental treatment (modified reciprocal teaching) were due to the treatment itself.

The researchers described three main differences between reciprocal teaching and the modified version used in their study. In this study, the treatment was conducted with an entire classroom rather than with only low achievers, identifying key words and phrases was part of the treatment, and reciprocal teaching was conducted two days a week rather than daily.

There was still another major difference between reciprocal teaching as implemented in the original two studies described in Palincsar and Brown (1984) and the modified version used in this study. In the first study Palincsar served as the teacher, and in her second study the students' actual teachers served as the teachers for the groups. In this study, by contrast, five college students were brought in especially to serve as group leaders. Because of the importance of the adult "expert" in delivering the experimental intervention, this change in procedure deserves some discussion. Clearly it affected the actual classroom teacher's role in, and feelings about, the experiment. Information about the regular classroom teacher's role, if any, in the experiment; the rationale for training special group leaders; and the effects of their use on the classroom environment would have been helpful.

Teacher bias might have affected the positive results obtained. The teacher gave students their course grades and apparently graded their comprehension tests as well. Although she did not directly participate in the intervention, she was aware of which of her classes comprised the experimental group and which comprised the two control groups. Her knowledge of the group to which each student belonged may have affected her evaluations. The researchers could have reduced the possibility of teacher bias somewhat by having a "blind" associate (for example, a social studies teacher from a different school) grade the comprehension tests. Obtaining course grades and data on student conduct without the teacher's involvement would have been more difficult. The researchers could have indicated in the article, however, whether any precautions were taken to reduce teacher bias.

The researchers reported that the three groups did not differ significantly on the vocabulary subtest of the Metropolitan Achievement Test, administered before the study began. They did not explain why they considered it important for the groups to be equal in vocabulary knowledge. However, we can surmise that they expected vocabulary knowledge to affect student performance on the comprehension tests and on the measure of writing fluency (number of words in a three-minute writing sample) administered to the experimental group and control group I. If this is true, it would be important to establish that the groups had similar vocabulary knowledge at the outset of the experiment. Otherwise, if on any of the postexperiment measures one group had superior performance and superior vocabulary knowledge, we could attribute the group's superiority to its vocabulary knowledge rather than to the particular instruction received during the experiment.

To understand fully the modified reciprocal teaching treatment, the reader would benefit from an expanded description of the study activities of questioning, clarifying, summarizing, predicting, and identifying key words and phrases. It also would be helpful to know more about what a student was doing when serving as the "teacher" for her group. Because of page-length restrictions, researchers must carefully judge how much information to include about variables and treatments when writing a research report. This study is clearly based on the earlier work of other researchers, and that work is cited in the references. Readers wishing to understand fully the experimental treatment used in this report would be well advised to read the study by Palincsar and Brown (1984), as we did before writing our review.

It appears that students in control group II did not take the comprehension tests or produce three-minute writing samples. (The only postexperiment measures available for them were course grades and conduct records.) We do not know, therefore, whether modified reciprocal teaching is more effective than the instruction received by control group II in improving students' reading comprehension and writing. Relevant information could have been obtained by administering the same reading comprehension and writing tests to all three groups at the conclusion of the experiment. Perhaps this was not done because some teachers object to what they perceive as excessive testing of students by researchers. Educators need to consider the tradeoffs between subjecting particular students to unusual procedures and obtaining research knowledge that could benefit large numbers of students.

One of the main outcome measures was a 10-item comprehension test administered at the end of each of 11 sessions of modified reciprocal teaching and at the end of the comparable class periods for control group I. Although the mean difference between the experimental and control groups on this measure is statistically significant, readers must judge for themselves whether a difference of 1.24 on a 10-item test has practical significance. It is noteworthy, of course, that the experimental group also outperformed the control group in the number of words produced in the three-minute writing sample and in having better conduct records during the term in which the experiment was conducted. These measures all appear to be outcomes that practicing teachers would find desirable.

It is especially remarkable that students' conduct (absences, tardies, and suspensions) was so much more positive for the experimental group than for either control group after a 16-hour treatment spread out over 8 weeks. It is difficult to imagine that this difference could be solely the result of teacher bias. We would expect that most teachers would respond positively to an instructional method that resulted in this degree of improvement in students' conduct. They also would appreciate that the experimental group's course grades were significantly higher and showed less variability than those of either control group.

Reciprocal teaching focused on low achievers, whereas the modification in this experiment was designed for application with students at all levels of achievement. It would be interesting to know whether the treatment was equally effective for students at these various achievement levels. The researchers might have been able to obtain this information by classifying students in each group as low, middle, and high achievers on the basis of their vocabulary test scores or school grades before the experiment began. Next, they could have analyzed the data to determine whether modified reciprocal teaching was more effective than the control conditions for each of these achievement groups.

This study demonstrates the problem that sometimes arises in experimental research about the ethics of withholding treatment from control groups. Remember that experimental research requires that some students receive the treatment while others do not. The control groups were not subjected to intentional harm but merely received standard instruction. Therefore, it was not unethical to have withheld treatment from the control groups, even though some students in those groups may have felt that they were at a disadvantage. Because positive outcomes were obtained, the researchers probably hoped to see modified reciprocal teaching continued, and implemented in the control classrooms as well. However, implementing modified reciprocal teaching in regular classrooms involves overcoming certain obstacles, as Miller indicated in his comments. Perhaps it would have been possible for the researchers to do some follow-up work with the classroom teacher whose classes participated in the experiment, and with her colleagues, both to help the teachers overcome these obstacles and to define questions for future research.

# Quasi-experimental Research

In a true experiment subjects are randomly assigned to the different treatments, whereas in a quasi-experiment subjects are not randomly assigned. Researchers do not intentionally avoid random assignment but often are unable to assign subjects randomly because of circumstances beyond their control. For example, suppose that the researchers are allowed to carry out their experiment in two classrooms. Administrators generally will not allow the students to be randomly assigned to treatment and control groups, especially if the experiment will last for an appreciable period of time. Therefore, the researchers must deal with each class as an intact group. The two classrooms can be randomly assigned, so that one class is the treatment group and the other is the control group. This hardly qualifies as random assignment, however, because each student does not have an equal chance of being in either group.

Another common situation is that researchers must form their treatment group in one school and their control group in another school. Administrators often favor this arrangement because the control group is unlikely to know what the treatment group is doing; hence, there are no complaints from teachers or parents about why students are not getting the presumed benefits of the experimental treatment. The drawback of this arrangement, though, is that subjects are not randomly assigned to the treatment or control group. Consequently there is a risk that the two groups differ on some important variable at the outset of the experiment. If the groups are found to differ on the posttest, we do not know whether this difference was caused by the treatment or by another variable on which they differed initially.

We will now discuss three common designs used in quasi-experimental research: posttest-only with nonequivalent groups, pretest-posttest with nonequivalent groups, and the time series design.

## POSTTEST-ONLY DESIGN WITH NONEQUIVALENT GROUPS

The posttest-only design with nonequivalent groups is similar to the posttest-only control group design that we discussed earlier as an example of an experimental design, except in the way that subjects are assigned to groups. Assignment of subjects to experimental and control groups is random in the former design but not in the nonequivalent group design. The steps involved in applying the posttest-only design with nonequivalent groups are as follows: (1) two groups of subjects are selected from the same population, (2) one group of subjects is given the experimental treatment and is then posttested, and (3) another group of subjects is given the posttest only. These steps are represented by the following diagram:

$$X \qquad O$$
-------------
$$O$$

where

$X$ = The experimental group is given the experimental treatment.
---- = The broken line indicates that the experimental and control groups were not formed randomly.
$O$ = Both groups are given a posttest that measures the dependent variable.

The main threat to internal validity in this design is differential selection. That is, posttest differences between groups can be attributed to characteristics of the groups as well as to the experimental treatment. For example, suppose teachers in one school are given an experimental treatment and posttest, and teachers in another school are given only the posttest. If differences on the posttest are found, it can be argued that they are due to differences between teachers in the two schools rather than to the effect of the experimental treatment. When random assignment cannot be used, it is preferable to use the pretest-posttest design with nonequivalent groups that is described below.

Another threat to internal validity in this design is experimental mortality. To illustrate this problem, consider a hypothetical experiment comparing career aspirations of first- and fourth-year college women. Let us define the experimental "treatment" as completion of a college education. This experiment can be considered a posttest-only design with nonequivalent groups because the fourth-year women have received the experimental treatment but the first-year women have not. Moreover, the two groups have not been formed randomly. Suppose it was found that the first-year women had significantly higher career aspirations than fourth-year women. Would we conclude from these results that college education lowers women's career goals? The finding can be explained more plausibly in terms of differential mortality. Although the first-year women are an intact group, many women have dropped out of college by the fourth year of the treatment. We could argue, then, that the differences between groups are caused by women with unrealistically high career aspirations leaving college. Thus, the findings are explained more plausibly in terms of mortality in the experimental group rather than in terms of effects of the experimental treatment. The posttest-only nonequivalent group design is thus a relatively weak quasi-experimental design.

## PRETEST-POSTTEST DESIGN WITH NONEQUIVALENT GROUPS

The pretest-posttest design with nonequivalent groups is represented by the following diagram:

$$O \quad X \quad O$$
-------------------------------
$$O \qquad\quad O$$

where

$O$ = Both groups are given a pretest.
$X$ = The experimental group is given the experimental treatment.
--- = The broken line indicates that the experimental and control groups were not formed randomly.
$O$ = Both groups are given a posttest that measures the dependent variable.

This design is probably the most widely used quasi-experimental design in educational research. It is similar to the posttest-only design with nonequivalent groups, except that in this design both groups are given a pretest. The pretest scores can thus be used to determine whether the two groups were initially equivalent on the pretest variable, even though the groups were not formed by random assignment. Therefore, differential selection is less of a threat in this design than in the posttest-only design with nonequivalent groups. However, we have no evidence that the groups are initially comparable on other unmeasured variables that could influence the results of the study, because some systematic bias of which we are unaware might lead subjects high on variable $X$ to be placed in one group whereas those low in variable $X$ would be placed in another group.

For example, suppose we are using this quasi-experimental design to compare the effectiveness of two methods of teaching Spanish. Students who take Spanish during third period are taught with method A, and those in the sixth-period class are taught with method B. Both classes are given a foreign language aptitude test at the beginning of the term and obtain very similar mean scores. The sixth-period class has a higher mean score on the posttest of Spanish language achievement given at the end of the term, so we conclude that method B is more effective than method A.

Now suppose that the basketball team practices sixth period. As a result, boys who want to be on the basketball team and who also want to take Spanish have to take Spanish third period. Because basketball practice runs for two hours every afternoon, the students in the third-period Spanish class have less time to study and also are more tired in the evenings than students taking sixth-period Spanish. Thus, the achievement difference might well be due to the reduced study time and higher level of fatigue for students taking Spanish during third period rather than to a less effective teaching method.

Let us consider a common situation in educational research that makes necessary this quasi-experimental design rather than a true experimental design. Suppose a researcher is interested in testing the effect of a new educational strategy or curriculum product in the public schools. This strategy or product is so designed that it must be administered to an entire classroom or not at all. For example, the researcher might be interested in whether a series of instructional films in social studies has an effect on students' achievement. To answer this question, the researcher sets up two groups: an experimental group that receives the treatment (the instructional films) in addition to conventional instruction in social studies, and a control group that receives only conventional instruction.

It is difficult to imagine how the researcher could assign students randomly to these two conditions. Once the term has started, the teacher cannot easily arrange to have half the students in her classroom view the films and the other half not view them. Although the researcher might ask to have the control students leave the classroom while the films are being shown, this procedure probably would not be approved because it would have a disruptive effect on the teacher's classroom. In addition, the researcher would need to arrange a special learning situation to occupy the time of the control students while they were out of the classroom. Faced with such problems, the researcher would probably opt to assign all the students in a given classroom to either the experimental or the control group. Of course, this procedure constitutes nonrandom assignment because each student does not have an equal chance of being placed in either the experimental or the control group.

Faced with this situation, the researcher should report as much descriptive data as possible about the experimental and control groups, such as the location of the participating schools, experience level of teachers, socioeconomic levels of the schools, and average achievement scores of students in the different classrooms or schools. This kind of information can help you decide how similar the experimental and control groups are. If researchers must use a quasi-experimental design, they should attempt to draw their experimental and control groups from very similar classrooms or schools. If the treatment and control groups are demonstrated to be similar, results of a pretest-posttest design with nonequivalent groups can be given nearly as much weight as the results of a true experimental design.

## TIME-SERIES DESIGN

In the time-series design a single group of subjects is measured at periodic intervals. The treatment is administered between two of these time intervals. This design can be represented as follows:

$$O \quad O \quad O \quad X \quad O \quad O \quad O$$

where the symbols indicate that

| | | |
|---|---|---|
| $O$ | $O$ | $O$ = three observations (or pretests) were made. |
| $X$ | | = the treatment was introduced. |
| $O$ | $O$ | $O$ = three additional observations (or posttests) were made. |

The effect of the experimental treatment would be indicated by a discrepancy in the measurements before and after its introduction. For example, a researcher might count the attendance of college students at six consecutive lectures in a course. Suppose the attendance at the first three lectures is 100, 115, and 104 (out of the total enrollment of 175 students). At the end of the third class, all enrolled students are informed that the professor will conduct a question-and-answer session during the fourth class. Attendance for this class increases to a mean of 160 students. For the fifth and sixth class sessions the professor again conducts a question-and-answer period, and the attendance is maintained at 152 and 154 students, respectively. These results suggest quite strongly that use of a question-and-answer session (the experimental treatment) leads to increased attendance.

The time-series design is similar to the one-group pretest-posttest design described earlier as a preexperimental design. Both designs involve the study of a single group and measurement before and after the experimental treatment. The use of additional measurements preceding and following the experimental treatment makes the time-series design more powerful than the one-group pretest-posttest design, however. The additional measurements enable the researcher to rule out maturation and testing effects as sources of influence on shifts from pretest to posttest.

# Sample Quasi-experimental Study:
# TEACHER CLARIFYING BEHAVIORS: EFFECTS ON STUDENT ACHIEVEMENT AND PERCEPTIONS

## Abstract[9]

High school social studies students ($N = 448$) were each assigned to one of 16 groups defined by possible combinations of two teacher uncertainty conditions (uncertainty vs. no uncertainty), two teacher "bluffing" conditions (bluffing vs. no bluffing), two lesson discontinuity conditions (discontinuity vs. no discontinuity), and two lecture notes conditions (notes handouts vs. no notes handouts). Each group was presented a lesson about the geography, politics, history, and economy of Botswana. The lessons were the same except for variations in the four conditions stated above. After the lesson, each group was tested on comprehension of the material, and then each group completed a lesson evaluation. Teacher uncertainty negatively affected achievement, and notes handouts positively affected achievement. Both teacher bluffing and lesson discontinuity negatively affected student evaluation of the lesson. Several significant interactions were obtained. These findings are discussed in relation to previous research on low-inference behaviors related to teacher clarity.

## Researcher's Comments[10]

My inspiration for this research came from reading an article by Jack Hiller and others (1969). The authors reported a negative correlation between students' achievement and teachers' communications involving certain phrases that teachers use in attempting to explain concepts. I was skeptical about these results, so I conducted a study that was a replication of Hiller's study (Smith, 1977). My study yielded results similar to Hiller's, even though it involved mathematics classes of experienced teachers whereas Hiller studied social studies classrooms of teacher trainees.

Since that time, I've been hooked by the idea that teachers can improve their clarity of explanation by modifying some of their verbal behaviors in the classroom. I have done research to determine how teachers' verbal behaviors affect students' achievement, independent of the effects of subject matter, grade level, and intelligence.

My research also builds on the work of Jacob Kounin, who, like Hiller, identified teachers' verbal behaviors that have a negative effect on students' task involvement and in turn on students' achievement. In addition, I included ideas from other research about the effectiveness of teachers' use of lecture notes as handouts. I wanted to see if the use of lecture notes could counteract the negative effects that specific verbal behaviors of teachers have on students' achievement and on their perceptions of the quality of the teaching they receive.

Research of the type reported in this study must satisfy two conditions. First, the content or skills that students are required to learn should be neither so difficult that all or most students will fail nor so easy that all or most students have complete success. The second condition is similar: the test that is used to measure achievement should be neither too difficult nor too easy. If these conditions are not met, the research analysis will not be able to detect real differences in the effectiveness of the treatments being compared.

In an attempt to satisfy the conditions described above, I searched recent issues of the *Atlantic Monthly* to find topics that would be interesting to students but that most students would know little about. I decided to use an article about the Baltic States and another article about Botswana. Interestingly, because of subsequent political happenings these areas received much more news attention than they were receiving when the research was conducted.

I then developed tape-recorded lessons on the content of each of the articles I had selected. The lessons were to be the treatment, and so they were designed to demonstrate different combinations of important classroom behaviors of teachers. After students received the lessons, their achievement and perceptions were measured.

Development of the lessons was a tedious process because the taped lessons were intended to be representations of natural classroom instruction. Some of the lessons had to be taped several times before they seemed genuine and unstilted.

Next to developing the lessons, my greatest difficulty was getting an appropriate student sample. Because the research design required 16 groups of students, I was not able to get enough students from one high school to enable me to assign students randomly to each group. To obtain a sufficient sample, I needed to receive permission to work with students from eight high schools.

It was necessary to meet with students at each school on two different days. On the first day, I presented the taped lesson on the Baltic States and tested students on the content. On the second visit to each school, I presented 1 of the 16 recorded Botswana lessons, and then gave students a test on the Botswana content. Because I had to make so many visits to different schools in a brief time, I had to devote several days to little else but this project.

The results of my research were rewarding. I found evidence that lessons in which the teachers' communication contained certain negative behaviors identified by Hiller and his colleagues have an impact on students' achievement and perception. Also, I found that some teaching behaviors affect one another in interesting ways. For example, if a teacher uses many phrases reflecting uncertainty and discontinuity, the use of lecture notes as handouts appears to compensate for the negative effects of these behaviors.

I am currently doing more research on teachers' verbal behaviors. I would like to find the threshold levels at which such behaviors inhibit students' achievement. I also would like to see teacher-training institutions develop teacher-training programs that give more attention to modification of these behaviors.

lesson discontinuity, and use of lecture notes handouts on student achievement and student perception.

## Method

### Subjects

Subjects were 448 students enrolled in high school history, government, or social studies classes in Richmond County, Columbia County, and McDuffie County (Georgia) public schools. Eight high schools participated in the experiment. The students participated by virtue of their teachers' willingness to release them from regularly scheduled class time for one hour on each of two days. Each student was assigned to one of sixteen groups ($n$ = 28 each), which were defined by the possible combinations of two "bluffing" and recovery conditions (bluffing, no bluffing) two uncertainty conditions (uncertainty, no uncertainty), two discontinuity conditions (discontinuity, no discontinuity), and two notes handouts conditions (notes, no notes).[12] The classroom teachers confirmed that none of the 448 students had been presented previous information in class concerning the topics to be covered during the experiment.

### Procedure

Since students were drawn from eight high schools, it was not feasible to randomly assign students to the sixteen groups. In an attempt to equate the groups in terms of ability, a 10-minute tape recorded lesson on the Baltic States, based on an article by Atwood (1980) in the *Atlantic Monthly,* was presented to all 448 students in their regularly scheduled history, government, or social studies classrooms. After the lesson, the students were administered a 16-item test on the historical, geographic, and demographic characteristics of the Baltic States. This test had a reliability of .80, based on the Kuder-Richardson formula 20.[13] The Baltic States test scores were used as baseline data to equate students in terms of ability to comprehend social studies material presented in tape recorded lessons.

Five to eight days after the Baltic States presentation, each of the 16 groups was presented a 12-minute tape recorded lesson based on an article by Dippel (1978) in the *Atlantic Monthly,* which focused on the history, geography, and economy of Botswana. A transparency of a map of South Africa that included Botswana's location

was shown during the lesson presentations. To effect maximum control over teacher behavior variables, the 16 lessons were scripted and were presented by the same instructor. The lessons were constructed so that such factors as rate of speech, tone of voice, and variance of voice pitch were virtually the same for all 16 presentations. The only difference in the 16 lessons was the presence or absence of bluffing phrases, uncertainty phrases, instances of discontinuity, and lecture notes handouts.

The recorded lessons were essential to ensure desired levels of bluffing, uncertainty, and discontinuity. "Live" lessons are more natural and allow more generalizability for research findings, but they do not allow classroom variables to be well controlled. The recorded lessons were constructed to represent natural instruction and it is reasonable to assume that the results of this study can be generalized to secondary school social studies classrooms.

Student comprehension of the lessons on Botswana was determined by administering a 20-item test immediately after each lesson was completed. Students were not allowed to use notes handouts or personal notes during the test. The Kuder-Richardson 20 test reliability was .76. The Botswana test scores then were adjusted by using the Baltic States test scores as a covariate.[14] The covariance-adjusted Botswana test scores were used as one criterion of lesson effectiveness.[15]

Immediately after the students completed the test on Botswana, they were administered an 11-item lesson evaluation (Table 1), which was used as a second criterion of lesson effectiveness. These items were reported by Smith and Land (1980) to be indicators of the presence or absence of teacher clarity, and it was hypothesized that bluffing, uncertainty, discontinuity, and use of lecture notes handouts would be reflected in student ratings for those items.

Eight of the recorded lessons contained bluffing phrases (40 phrases) and eight of the lessons contained no bluffing phrases. Eight of the lessons contained uncertainty (40 phrases) and eight lessons contained no uncertainty phrases. Eight lessons contained eighteen instances of discontinuity (nine irrelevant remarks, nine relevant remarks at inappropriate points of the lesson), and eight lessons had no discontinuity. Based on research by Smith and Land (1981) and Smith (1977),

Table 1    Lesson evaluation form

**What did you think of the teaching?**

| | | | | | | |
|---|---|---|---|---|---|---|
| A. precise | 5 | 4 | 3 | 2 | 1 | imprecise |
| B. decisive | 5 | 4 | 3 | 2 | 1 | indecisive |
| C. explains fully | 5 | 4 | 3 | 2 | 1 | does not explain fully |
| D. coherent | 5 | 4 | 3 | 2 | 1 | incoherent |
| E. well prepared | 5 | 4 | 3 | 2 | 1 | not well prepared |
| F. confident | 5 | 4 | 3 | 2 | 1 | not confident |
| G. well organized | 5 | 4 | 3 | 2 | 1 | not well organized |
| H. speech easy to understand | 5 | 4 | 3 | 2 | 1 | speech not easy to understand |
| I. speech soothing | 5 | 4 | 3 | 2 | 1 | speech irritating |
| J. very clear lesson | 5 | 4 | 3 | 2 | 1 | lesson not clear at all |
| K. clear and understandable explanations | 5 | 4 | 3 | 2 | 1 | confusing explanations |

teachers who were observed in natural classroom settings used an average of 35 to 40 vagueness terms and 8 to 10 instances of irrelevant remarks per 12 minutes of teacher talk. As mentioned previously, vagueness terms have not been studied in terms of separate categories in prior research, but an analysis of data examined by Smith (1977) indicated that one-third to one-fifth of the total number of vagueness terms used by teachers were from the "bluffing" and recovery category, and three-fifths to two-thirds of the vagueness terms used were from the uncertainty categories of vagueness. Therefore, the frequency of bluffing phrases used in the present study (40 per 12 minutes) appears to be higher than one would expect in the average classroom, whereas the frequency of uncertainty phrases used (40 per 12 minutes) appears to be representative of communication in some social studies classes. Similarly, 18 instances of discontinuity per 12 minutes is a realistic frequency in the light of the previous research that reported an average of 8 to 10 irrelevant remarks per 12 minutes. As mentioned previously, discontinuity in the present study was examined in terms of irrelevant remarks as well as relevant information stated at inappropriate spots in the lesson.

The following excerpt is from the lessons containing no bluffing phrases, no uncertainty phrases, and no instances of discontinuity.

South Africans invest heavily in Botswana. They buy cattle from Botswanans in need of cash, fatten the cattle, and then sell the cattle for a profit. But most significant of all is the role the country of South Africa plays in Botswana's mineral industry. The two largest diamond mines are owned by a South African mining

company. The company gets half of the money made by the Botswana mines. In addition to the diamond mines, large copper and nickel mines in Botswana are owned by South African companies.

South African dominance also extends to tourist trade in Botswana. South Africans own the hotels, restaurants, and casinos that attract vacationers from Europe.

The government of the country of South Africa is based on the philosophy that the 19 million blacks of South Africa are to live and work separate from the five million whites of South Africa. Life in Botswana is more calm and stable than life in South Africa. However, signs of bitterness can be detected in the Botswanans. Only 6,000 whites live in Botswana, but they hold 60% of the important government jobs. The Botswana government is trying to reduce the number of whites employed by the government, but this will take years to accomplish.

The following excerpt is from the lessons containing bluffing phrases, but no uncertainty phrases and no instances of discontinuity. The bluffing phrases are italicized.

South Africans invest heavily in Botswana. *Actually,* they buy cattle from Botswanans in need of cash, fatten the cattle, and then sell the cattle for a profit. But, *as you know,* most significant of all is the role the country of South Africa plays in Botswana's mineral industry. *In fact,* the two largest diamond mines are owned by a South African mining company. The company gets half of the money made by the Botswana mines. In addition to the diamond mines, large copper and nickel mines in Botswana are owned by South African companies.

*Of course,* South African dominance also extends to tourist trade in Botswana. South Africans own the hotels, restaurants, casinos, *and so on,* that attract vacationers from Europe.

*Frankly,* the government of the country of South Africa is based on the philosophy that the 19 million blacks of South Africa are to live and work separate from the five million whites of South Africa. Life in Botswana is more calm and stable than life in South Africa. However, signs of bitterness can be detected in the Botswanans, *you know.* Only 6,000 whites live in Botswana, but they hold 60% of the important government jobs. The Botswana government is trying to reduce the number of whites employed by the government, but, *of course,* this will take years to accomplish.

The following excerpt is from the lessons containing uncertainty phrases, but no bluffing phrases and no instances of discontinuity. The uncertainty phrases are italicized.

South Africans invest heavily in Botswana. They *may* buy cattle from Botswanans in need of cash, fatten the cattle, and then sell the cattle for a profit. But *perhaps* most significant of all is the role the country of South Africa plays in Botswana's mineral industry. The two largest diamond mines are owned by a South African mining company. The company gets half of the money made by the Botswana mines. In addition to the *various* diamond mines, large copper and nickel mines in Botswana are owned by South African companies.

South African dominance also extends to tourist trade in Botswana. South Africans own the hotels, restaurants, and casinos that *often* attract vacationers from Europe.

The government of the country of South Africa is based on the philosophy that the 19 million blacks of South Africa are to live and work *someplace* separate from the five million whites of South Africa. Life in Botswana is *fairly much* more calm and stable than life in South Africa. However, signs of bitterness can *sort of* be detected in the Botswanans. Only 6,000 whites live in Botswana, but they hold 60% of the important government jobs. The Botswana government is *somehow* trying to reduce the number of whites employed

by the government, but this will take years to accomplish.

The following excerpt is from the lessons containing instances of discontinuity, but no bluffing and no uncertainty phrases. In this excerpt, there is one instance that is an irrelevant remark and one instance of relevant information interjected at an inappropriate point of the lesson. Both instances are italicized.

South Africans invest heavily in Botswana. They buy cattle from Botswanans in need of cash, fatten the cattle, and then sell the cattle for a profit. But most significant of all is the role the country of South Africa plays in Botswana's mineral industry. The two largest diamond mines are owned by a South African mining company. The company gets half of the money made by the Botswana mines. In addition to the diamond mines, large copper and nickel mines in Botswana are owned by South African companies. *Refugees from fighting in Rhodesia and Angola have come to Botswana.*

South African dominance also extends to tourist trade in Botswana. South Africans own the hotels, restaurants, and casinos that attract vacationers from Europe. *Investment firms from the rich middle east have invested heavily in resort areas of the United States.*

The government of the country of South Africa is based on the philosophy that the 19 million blacks of South Africa are to live and work separate from the five million whites of South Africa. Life in Botswana is more calm and stable than life in South Africa. However, signs of bitterness can be detected in the Botswanans. Only 6,000 whites live in Botswana, but they hold 60% of the important government jobs. The Botswana government is trying to reduce the number of whites employed by the government, but this will take years to accomplish.

Eight of the lessons were accompanied by lecture notes handouts and eight of the lessons did not use handouts. The lecture notes summarized the main topics presented in the lessons and the notes were organized to coincide with the sequence of material as it was covered in the lessons. All of the 20 test questions could be answered by listening to the lessons. Ten of the 20 questions could be answered by reading the notes handouts.

Table 2   Group means and standard deviations

| Uncertainty | No | No | No | No | Yes | No | No | No |
|---|---|---|---|---|---|---|---|---|
| Bluffing | No | No | No | Yes | No | No | Yes | Yes |
| Discontinuity | No | No | Yes | No | No | Yes | Yes | No |
| Notes Handouts | No | Yes | No | No | No | Yes | No | Yes |
| Achievement scores | 9.90 (3.20) | 10.31 (2.57) | 10.32 (2.63) | 10.34 (2.85) | 8.33 (2.01) | 11.36 (2.81) | 8.76 (3.25) | 11.39 (3.49) |
| **Response item** | | | | | | | | |
| A. | 3.21 (1.03) | 3.61 (0.96) | 3.68 (0.86) | 3.50 (0.88) | 3.21 (0.92) | 3.21 (0.96) | 2.82 (0.90) | 3.14 (1.33) |
| B. | 3.39 (0.99) | 3.50 (0.79) | 3.57 (0.74) | 3.36 (0.73) | 3.32 (1.28) | 3.43 (1.14) | 2.71 (0.81) | 3.07 (1.12) |
| C. | 3.64 (1.22) | 4.00 (1.12) | 3.71 (0.94) | 3.50 (1.07) | 3.29 (1.08) | 3.50 (1.23) | 3.29 (1.08) | 3.29 (1.33) |
| D. | 3.04 (1.07) | 3.25 (0.89) | 3.57 (0.92) | 3.04 (0.69) | 3.25 (1.00) | 3.11 (1.10) | 3.11 (0.69) | 3.07 (1.12) |
| E. | 3.96 (1.14) | 4.04 (0.92) | 3.86 (0.71) | 3.57 (0.92) | 3.61 (1.20) | 3.46 (1.10) | 3.46 (1.10) | 3.36 (1.37) |
| F. | 3.78 (1.29) | 3.50 (1.20) | 3.93 (1.02) | 3.36 (1.13) | 3.75 (1.11) | 3.46 (1.35) | 3.25 (0.80) | 3.36 (1.03) |
| G. | 3.57 (1.14) | 3.86 (0.89) | 3.82 (0.90) | 3.61 (1.17) | 3.36 (1.19) | 3.54 (1.17) | 2.93 (1.15) | 3.46 (1.32) |
| H. | 3.25 (1.17) | 3.64 (1.06) | 4.00 (1.05) | 3.54 (1.23) | 3.21 (1.29) | 3.29 (1.21) | 3.54 (1.17) | 3.54 (1.57) |
| I. | 2.86 (1.21) | 3.25 (1.29) | 3.29 (1.01) | 3.07 (1.02) | 2.86 (1.30) | 3.07 (1.30) | 2.89 (1.26) | 2.89 (1.59) |
| J. | 2.89 (1.29) | 3.75 (1.14) | 3.61 (0.83) | 3.46 (1.26) | 3.14 (1.18) | 3.00 (1.05) | 2.89 (1.10) | 3.54 (1.26) |
| K. | 2.75 (1.11) | 3.54 (1.17) | 3.43 (0.79) | 3.29 (0.90) | 3.25 (0.70) | 3.18 (1.09) | 2.96 (0.92) | 3.29 (1.41) |

NOTE: Figures in parentheses are standard deviations.

Students in all 16 treatment groups were advised to take personal notes as they listened to the lesson.

The lessons containing a combined presence of two or three of the bluffing, uncertainty, and discontinuity behaviors were constructed by including all instances of these behaviors from the appropriate bluffing, uncertainty, or discontinuity conditions. All 16 lessons were exactly the same, except for the variations in bluffing, uncertainty, discontinuity, and use of notes.

## Results

A 2 (uncertainty vs. no uncertainty) × 2 (bluffing vs. no bluffing) × 2 (discontinuity vs. no discontinuity) × 2 (notes handouts vs. no notes handouts) analysis of vari-ance was performed on the adjusted Botswana test scores as well as on the scores for each of the 11 lesson evaluation items.[16] The means and standard deviations for all 12 dependent variables are shown for each of the 16 experimental conditions in Table 2.[17] Table 3 shows the F ratios for each of the 2 × 2 × 2 × 2 ANOVAs.[18]

With adjusted Botswana test scores as the dependent variable, students in the uncertainty condition per-formed significantly lower ($p < .01$) than students in the certainty condition.[19] Student scores were higher ($p < .01$) when they were given lecture notes handouts than when they were not given handouts. There were no significant main effects due to the bluffing condition or the discontinuity condition, although there was a signif-

| Yes | Yes | Yes | No | Yes | Yes | Yes | Yes | |
| No | No | Yes | Yes | No | Yes | Yes | Yes | |
| No | Yes | No | Yes | Yes | No | Yes | Yes | |
| Yes | No | No | Yes | Yes | Yes | No | Yes | Totals |
|---|---|---|---|---|---|---|---|---|
| 9.82 | 9.60 | 8.59 | 10.88 | 10.87 | 11.33 | 9.60 | 8.67 | 10.00 |
| (3.47) | (2.99) | (3.56) | (2.78) | (2.70) | (3.22) | (2.81) | (1.80) | (3.04) |
| | | | | | | | | |
| 3.68 | 3.46 | 3.36 | 3.46 | 3.54 | 3.36 | 3.29 | 2.64 | 3.32 |
| (0.94) | (1.48) | (1.03) | (1.23) | (1.10) | (1.06) | (1.15) | (1.10) | (1.09) |
| 3.75 | 3.14 | 3.00 | 3.54 | 3.43 | 3.39 | 3.32 | 2.89 | 3.30 |
| (0.97) | (1.11) | (0.98) | (1.10) | (1.14) | (1.07) | (1.09) | (1.03) | (1.07) |
| 3.57 | 3.54 | 3.36 | 3.68 | 3.46 | 3.82 | 3.54 | 2.96 | 3.51 |
| (1.26) | (1.35) | (1.03) | (1.22) | (1.23) | (1.02) | (1.20) | (0.88) | (1.15) |
| 3.39 | 3.14 | 3.57 | 3.39 | 3.21 | 3.43 | 3.25 | 2.86 | 3.23 |
| (1.07) | (1.27) | (0.88) | (1.03) | (1.10) | (1.03) | (1.11) | (1.30) | (1.03) |
| 3.79 | 3.54 | 3.86 | 3.71 | 3.82 | 4.00 | 3.68 | 2.93 | 3.67 |
| (1.23) | (1.45) | (0.93) | (1.08) | (1.19) | (0.94) | (0.94) | (1.18) | (1.12) |
| 3.39 | 3.54 | 3.36 | 3.64 | 3.50 | 3.36 | 3.64 | 2.57 | 3.46 |
| (1.10) | (0.92) | (1.06) | (1.06) | (1.11) | (1.06) | (1.25) | (1.23) | (1.13) |
| 3.82 | 3.82 | 3.64 | 4.14 | 3.86 | 3.54 | 3.61 | 3.18 | 3.61 |
| (1.19) | (1.31) | (0.83) | (1.24) | (1.08) | (1.10) | (1.17) | (1.02) | (1.14) |
| 3.29 | 3.82 | 3.64 | 3.32 | 3.50 | 3.57 | 3.61 | 2.86 | 3.48 |
| (1.05) | (1.25) | (1.10) | (1.44) | (1.23) | (1.00) | (1.17) | (1.43) | (1.23) |
| 3.14 | 3.00 | 3.11 | 3.25 | 3.11 | 2.79 | 2.75 | 2.46 | 2.99 |
| (1.18) | (1.52) | (1.23) | (1.32) | (1.23) | (1.26) | (1.38) | (1.37) | (1.28) |
| 3.36 | 2.89 | 3.39 | 3.00 | 3.43 | 3.68 | 3.32 | 2.82 | 3.26 |
| (1.03) | (1.47) | (0.96) | (1.25) | (1.29) | (1.12) | (1.12) | (1.16) | (1.19) |
| 3.32 | 3.57 | 3.46 | 3.50 | 3.46 | 3.57 | 3.39 | 2.57 | 3.28 |
| (1.19) | (1.45) | (0.88) | (1.35) | (1.14) | (0.96) | (1.17) | (1.26) | (1.13) |

icant interaction between the bluffing and discontinuity conditions ($p < .01$).[20] Students in the bluffing condition scored higher if they were not in the discontinuity condition. Similarly, students in the discontinuity condition scored higher if they were not in the bluffing condition. This relationship is illustrated in Figure 1. A significant three-way interaction ($p < .05$) between the uncertainty, discontinuity, and notes condition occurred. Students in the no uncertainty, no discontinuity, notes condition and students in the no uncertainty, discontinuity, no notes condition scored high on the test and students in the uncertainty, discontinuity, no notes condition scored low. But students in the uncertainty, no discontinuity, notes condition scored higher than the mean test score for the entire sample. There were no other significant interactions with test scores as the dependent variable.

As shown in Table 3, with perception as the dependent variable, all lesson evaluation items except Item I (speech soothing vs. speech irritating) involved at least one significant main effect or interaction. For Item A (degree of precision), Item B (decisiveness), and Item F (degree of confidence), the no bluffing condition was rated significantly higher than the bluffing condition. For Item F (degree of preparation) and Item J (clarity of lesson), discontinuity resulted in lower evaluation scores. For Item F (degree of confidence), the notes handouts condition produced significantly lower evaluation scores

Table 3   *F* Ratios of ANOVAs

|  | Uncertainty | Bluffing | Discontinuity | Notes |  |  |  |
|---|---|---|---|---|---|---|---|
|  | (A) | (B) | (C) | (D) | AB | AC | AD |
| Achievement scores |  |  |  |  |  |  |  |
|  | 8.46** | <1 | <1 | 17.24** | <1 | <1 | <1 |
| Response item |  |  |  |  |  |  |  |
| A. | <1 | 6.30* | 1.42 | <1 | <1 | <1 | <1 |
| B. | <1 | 8.52** | <1 | 2.34 | <1 | <1 | <1 |
| C. | 1.52 | 2.19 | <1 | <1 | 1.15 | <1 | <1 |
| D. | <1 | <1 | <1 | <1 | <1 | 6.38* | <1 |
| E. | <1 | 3.23 | 4.22* | <1 | 1.24 | 1.05 | <1 |
| F. | 1.96 | 7.60** | <1 | 4.68* | <1 | 1.13 | 1.73 |
| G. | <1 | 3.25 | <1 | 1.48 | <1 | <1 | 1.69 |
| H. | <1 | <1 | <1 | 3.01 | <1 | <1 | <1 |
| I. | 1.94 | 1.94 | <1 | <1 | <1 | 1.05 | <1 |
| J. | <1 | <1 | 6.51* | 1.19 | <1 | <1 | <1 |
| K. | <1 | <1 | <1 | <1 | <1 | 1.02 | 4.68* |

*$p < .05$;  **$p < .01$.

than did the no notes condition. There was no significant main effect due to the uncertainty condition for any of the 11 evaluation items.

Table 3 indicates that 21 significant interactions occurred involving student perception ratings. Item H (understandability of speech), Item J (clarity of lesson), and Item K (degree of clarity of explanations) resulted in interactions between the bluffing condition and the discontinuity condition. As previously noted, these conditions also interacted when achievement was the dependent variable. Graphs of the bluffing × discontinuity interactions for Items H and K are remarkably similar to the graph shown in Figure 1. For Item J, ratings in the bluffing, no discontinuity condition were highest and ratings in the bluffing, discontinuity condition were lowest.

The only other significant interaction that occurred when achievement was the dependent variable was between the uncertainty, discontinuity, and notes conditions. Item B (decisiveness) was the only perception item that produced an interaction between these three conditions. Students in the no uncertainty, discontinuity, notes condition and the uncertainty, no discontinuity, notes condition rated the lesson highest, whereas the uncertainty, no discontinuity, no notes condition and the uncertainty, discontinuity, notes condition were rated the lowest.

Table 3 also shows that, although uncertainty negatively affected achievement, none of the 11 lesson evaluation items involved a main effect due to uncertainty. Similarly, notes handouts positively affected achieve-

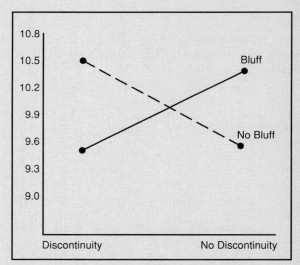

Figure 1  Interaction between Bluffing and Discontinuity for Mean Adjusted Test Scores.

| BC | BD | CD | ABC | ABD | ACD | BCD | ABCD |
|---|---|---|---|---|---|---|---|
| 11.69** | <1 | 1.00 | <1 | 1.45 | 6.33* | 1.88 | 3.07 |
| 2.66 | 1.03 | 1.21 | <1 | 3.59 | 2.12 | 3.93* | 6.76** |
| <1 | <1 | <1 | <1 | 2.93 | 5.58* | <1 | 6.99** |
| <1 | <1 | 2.44 | 2.70 | <1 | 2.70 | <1 | 4.59* |
| <1 | <1 | <1 | <1 | 2.88 | <1 | <1 | 2.04 |
| <1 | <1 | <1 | 6.59** | 2.92 | <1 | <1 | 5.34* |
| <1 | <1 | <1 | <1 | 4.69* | 1.31 | <1 | 5.41* |
| <1 | <1 | <1 | 1.35 | 6.12* | 3.25 | 5.71* | 4.50* |
| 5.54* | <1 | 6.68* | 1.09 | <1 | <1 | <1 | 1.61 |
| <1 | 1.05 | <1 | <1 | 1.05 | <1 | 1.94 | <1 |
| 4.26* | 1.38 | 4.61* | <1 | 1.04 | 1.20 | <1 | 8.72** |
| 5.44* | <1 | 3.65 | 1.66 | <1 | <1 | <1 | 7.67** |

ment, but there was no main effect due to the notes condition for 10 of the 11 lesson evaluation items. On Item F (degree of confidence), students rated the lesson showing less teacher confidence when notes handouts were used.

## Discussion

Cautions should be observed when interpreting these results. First, the lessons were 12 minutes long and may not be representative of longer lessons. The information was presented rapidly with no time allowed for reflection or for class discussion. Second, the Botswana test was administered immediately after the lesson. No time for study or for questions was permitted. It may be that the opportunity to study may partially negate the effects of the behaviors represented in this study. Third, a random assignment to groups was not feasible, so a pretest was used as a covariate to adjust the Botswana test scores. It should be noted that the raw scores for the Botswana test were very similar to the adjusted test scores and that an analysis of variance performed on the raw scores produced almost identical F ratios. However, randomization is preferable whenever possible and lends credibility to research results. A final caution is that, although 31 F ratios indicated significance beyond the .05 level, values of omega squared indicate that no more than 3% of the variance in achievement or student perception can be attributed to any single main effect or interaction.[21] That is, although 31 experimental effects were found to be significant, values of omega squared indicate that these effects are relatively weak.

With these cautions in mind, the following conclusions are made. This research indicates a cause-and-effect relationship between teacher uncertainty and student achievement. Surprisingly, uncertainty had no significant effect on any of the lesson evaluation items. A cause-and-effect relation also was shown between notes handouts and achievement. The results of prior studies (Annis, 1981; Collingwood & Hughes, 1978) are supported in that notes handouts had a positive effect on achievement. However, use of notes handouts caused students to perceive the instructor as being less confident. Although the bluffing condition and the discontinuity condition did not significantly affect achievement, use of bluffing phrases and instances of discontinuity significantly lowered student ratings on certain lesson evaluation items.

For achievement and the 11 evaluation items as dependent variables, a total of 180 main effects and interactions were examined for significance at or beyond the .05 level. Purely by chance, approximately nine of these tests should indicate significance.[22] But 31 of the 180 tests revealed significant main effects or interactions, thus supporting the contention that low-inference teacher behaviors merit further study.[23]

Further research on the differential effects of categories of vagueness terms on student achievement and perception is warranted. The results of this study indicate that different categories of vagueness affect achievement and perception in different ways. The threshold levels at which vagueness categories inhibit learning have not been determined. Preliminary research (Dunkin & Doenau, 1980; Smith & Edmonds, 1980) provides clues to such threshold levels, but such research studied vagueness terms as a single variable rather than as distinct categories.

Teacher trainers should exercise caution in attempting to have trainees avoid excess frequencies of vagueness phrases. Vagueness terms should not be avoided at the expense of distorting the truth. For example, if a rule "generally" or "sometimes" applies, a teacher should not simply state that the rule applies, thus leaving the impression that the rule has no exceptions. Instead, the teacher could state the rule, show instances of the rule, and then state the exceptions to the rule.

A final observation is that this study did not show a direct link between achievement and student perception. For example, uncertainty and notes handouts significantly affected achievement, yet these results were not reflected in the student evaluations of the lesson. Similarly, bluffing and discontinuity did not affect achievement significantly, but student ratings were lower for these conditions. Therefore, although student outcomes in terms of achievement and perception should be used as criteria of teacher effectiveness, care should be exercised in relating perception to achievement.

## References

ANNIS, L. R. (1981). Effect of preference for assigned lecture notes on student achievement. *Journal of Educational Research, 74*, 179–182.

ARLIN, M. (1979). Teacher transitions can disrupt time flow in classrooms. *American Educational Research Journal, 16*, 42–56.

ATWOOD, W. (1980, April). The Baltic States: In custody. *Atlantic Monthly, 244*, 14–20.

BRASKAMP, L. A., CAULLEY, D., & COSTIN, F. (1979). Student ratings and instructor self-ratings and their relationship to student achievement. *American Educational Research Journal, 16*, 295–306.

BUSH, A. J., KENNEDY, J. J., & CRUICKSHANK, D. R. (1977). An empirical investigation of teacher clarity. *Journal of Teacher Education, 28*, 53–58.

COLLINGWOOD, V., & HUGHES, D. C. (1978). Effects of three types of university lecture notes on student achievement. *Journal of Educational Psychology, 70*, 175–179.

DIPPEL, J. V. H. (1978, August). Botswana: In the shadow of Pretoria. *Atlantic Monthly, 242*, 14–20.

DUNKIN, M. J. (1978). Student characteristics, classroom processes, and student achievement. *Journal of Educational Psychology, 70*, 998–1009.

DUNKIN, M. J., & BIDDLE, B. J. (1974). *The study of teaching.* New York: Holt, Rinehart & Winston.

DUNKIN, M. J., & DOENAU, S. J. (1980). A replication study of unique and joint contributions to variance in student achievement. *Journal of Educational Psychology, 72*, 394–403.

FREY, P. W. (1973). Student ratings of teaching: Validity of several rating factors. *Science, 182*, 83–85.

HILLER, J. H. (1971). Verbal response indicators of conceptual vagueness. *American Educational Research Journal, 8*, 151–161.

HILLER, J. H., FISHER, G. A., & KAESS, W. A. (1969). A computer investigation of verbal characteristics of effective classroom lecturing. *American Educational Research Journal, 6*, 661–675.

KENNEDY, J. J., CRUICKSHANK, D. R., BUSH, A. S., & MYERS, B. (1978). Additional investigations into the nature of teacher clarity. *Journal of Educational Research, 72*, 3–10.

KOUNIN, J. S. (1970). *Discipline and group management in classrooms.* New York: Holt, Rinehart & Winston.

KOUNIN, J. S., & DOYLE, P. H. (1975). Degree of continuity of a lesson's signal system and the task involvement of children. *Journal of Educational Psychology, 67*, 159–164.

KOUNIN, J. S., & GUMP, P. V. (1958). The ripple effect in discipline. *Elementary School Journal, 58*, 158–162.

KOUNIN, J. S., & GUMP. P. V. (1974). Signal systems of lesson settings and the task-related behavior of preschool children. *Journal of Educational Psychology, 66*, 554–562.

LAND, M. L., & SMITH, L. R. (1979). The effect of low inference teacher clarity inhibitors on student achievement. *Journal of Teacher Education, 30*, 55–57.

MARSH, H. W., FLEINER, H., & THOMAS, C. S. (1975). Validity and usefulness of student evaluations of instructional quality. *Journal of Educational Psychology, 67,* 833–839.

MARSH, H. W., & OVERALL, J. U. (1980). Validity of students' evaluations of teaching effectiveness: Cognitive and affective criteria. *Journal of Educational Psychology, 72,* 468–475.

MURRAY, H. G. (1983). Low-inference classroom teaching behaviors and student ratings of college teaching effectiveness. *Journal of Educational Psychology, 75,* 138–149.

ROSENSHINE, B. (1971). *Teaching behaviours and student achievement.* London: National Foundation for Educational Research in England and Wales.

ROSENSHINE, B., & FURST, N. (1971). Research in teacher performance criteria. In B. O. Smith (Ed.), *Research in teacher education: A symposium.* Englewood Cliffs, NJ: Prentice-Hall.

ROSENSHINE, B., & FURST, N. (1973). The use of direct observation to study teaching. In R. M. W. Travers (Ed.), *Second handbook of research on teaching.* Chicago: Rand McNally.

SMITH, L. R. (1977). Aspects of teacher discourse and student achievement in mathematics. *Journal for Research in Mathematics Education, 8,* 195–204.

SMITH, L. R. (1982, March). *Training teachers to teach clearly: Theory into practice.* Paper presented at the annual meeting of the American Educational Research Association, New York.

SMITH, L. R., & COTTEN, M. L. (1980). Effect of lesson vagueness and discontinuity on student achievement and attitudes. *Journal of Educational Psychology, 72,* 670–675.

SMITH, L. R., & EDMONDS, E. M. (1980). Teacher vagueness and pupil participation in mathematics learning. *Journal for Research in Mathematics Education, 11,* 137–146.

SMITH, L. R., & LAND, M. L. (1980). Student perception of teacher clarity in mathematics. *Journal for Research in Mathematics Education, 11,* 137–146.

SMITH, L. R., & LAND, M. L. (1981). Low-inference verbal behaviors related to teacher clarity. *Journal of Classroom Interaction, 17,* 37–42.

# Critical Review

In carrying out research in the public schools, researchers often cannot meet the requirement of experimental research that subjects must be randomly assigned to treatment groups. Random assignment provides some assurance that subjects in different experimental and control groups are comparable.

When random assignment is not possible, researchers need to use a quasi-experimental design, like the one in this study. They can compensate for the lack of random assignment by providing other evidence that groups are comparable. One alternative is to employ a pretest, and use students' scores to compensate statistically for initial group differences. Smith's pretest on the Baltic States, administered to all 16 groups under similar conditions, was used for this purpose.

The greatest challenge in this study was setting up 16 experimental treatments to measure the effects of the 4 independent variables. The only way to ensure that each lesson used the precise combination of teachers' verbal behaviors that constituted each treatment was to fully script, tape, and edit each of the 16 lessons.

By giving the researcher greater control over the treatment variables, this procedure reduced the chance that extraneous variables, such as accidental changes in lesson content or teachers' personality differences, could affect the results. The disadvantage of this approach, however, is that taped lessons reduce the generalizability of the findings because they are quite different from the live, teacher-directed lessons that students usually receive.

Another problem is that developing the treatment is a great deal of work. The researcher reduced the workload substantially by keeping the lessons short (12 minutes). The question arises, however, whether a 12-minute lesson is long enough to test the effects of teachers' verbal behaviors on achievement.

You may be surprised, as we were, that the teachers' verbal behaviors defining the independent variables in this study affected students' achievement and perceptions to the extent that they did. The effects would be more interpretable if the researcher had provided a theoretical rationale for this result.

Readers would benefit also from more information about the researcher's rationale for treating bluffing as a separate verbal behavior while lumping together the other six "vagueness" categories that were identified by Hiller. The study indicates that the other six categories measure uncertainty, whereas the bluffing and recovery phrases "do not add to the substantive content of the lesson." More explanation is needed to clarify this distinction. Also, no reason is given for not examining the effects of the other two "vagueness" categories identified by Hiller (error admission and negated intensifiers).

Table 1 gives readers a clear understanding of how students' perception of the teaching was assessed. However, little information is provided about the other dependent variable, students' achievement. It would be helpful to know the types of items included in the test on Botswana and the objectives they were designed to measure. The same comment applies to the achievement tests used in the previous research cited by the researcher.

You might have noted that the test had 20 items and the mean score of all groups was 10.00. The researcher appears to have succeeded in designing an intervention that met the conditions stated in the Researcher's Comments.

To Smith's credit, he carried out a statistical test (omega squared) to determine the strength of the significant effects reported. He noted that although 31 experimental effects were significant, the values of omega squared indicate that these effects were relatively weak. Further research using longer, more natural lessons might yield stronger effects. At this point we can only conclude that teachers' clarifying behaviors are potentially important. Their practical significance for teacher education is not yet clear, however.

In interpreting the results, you should note that according to the researcher, approximately 9 of the 180 main effects and interactions would achieve statistical significance "purely by chance." The study would need careful replication to determine which of the observed differences occurred by chance and which were true differences (that is, differences in the population from which the sample was drawn).

The finding of no relationship between students' achievement and students' perception deserves further consideration. One possible implication of this finding is that teachers sometimes have to make a choice between efforts to keep students happy (which would presumably affect students' perception) and efforts to help them learn (which would presumably affect students' achievement).

# Single-Subject Experiments[24]

Single-subject experiments are favored over group experiments for the study of problems that involve unique characteristics of individual subjects. Using single-subject designs, for example, a researcher can diagnose a student's problem, devise a strategy to solve it, and rigorously test the effectiveness of the strategy through intensive data collection. Counseling is another field in which single-subject experiments are useful because counselors often want to evaluate the effects of a specific counseling strategy on a particular client.

We will explain the value of single-subject research design from the viewpoint of the counseling process. Keep in mind that the application of single-subject designs to counseling is similar to their use in the teaching-learning process and, for that matter, in any process that involves producing changes in individual behavior.

A single-subject experiment makes possible the intensive study of one individual as she progresses through counseling. Because individuals are treated and studied one at a time, it is not necessary to form groups of individuals who have the same concern in order to conduct an experiment. In fact, no matter how unique the client's concern, a single-subject design will permit investigation of the research problem. Also, single-subject designs allow the counselor to function simultaneously as both counselor and researcher. These functions are often handled by different people when group designs are used.

A problem with single-subject experiments is their external validity, that is, the extent to which one can generalize the findings to other, similar subjects in the population of interest. In a single-subject experiment subjects are not randomly selected, and the experiment involves only one or a few subjects. *Replication* can be used to increase the external validity of single-subject experiments, however. Replication involves repeating the experiment with other subjects, perhaps with variations in the investigators, settings, or subject characteristics. Essential to any replication experiment is a careful description of baseline and treatment conditions, subject characteristics, and measurement procedures. This description provides a basis for determining the degree of generalizability of the findings of single-subject research.

We will now describe four common single-subject research designs: the A-B design, the A-B-A-B design, the multiple baseline across behaviors design, and the multiple baseline across individuals design.

## THE A-B DESIGN

The most basic single-subject experiment involves the A-B design. Whenever environmental conditions are constant and a certain behavior is observed to occur at a consistent, stable rate, we have *condition A*. Behavior observed during condition A can be regarded as a *baseline,* that is, the behavior that subjects display under normal, nontreatment conditions. If one of the environmental conditions is changed by the researcher and a concomitant change is observed in the subject's behavior, we have *condition B*.

The A-B design involves making an inference that the change in environmental conditions (that is, the treatment) had something to do with the change in the behavior. This inference is predicated on the assumption that the behavior would have continued at its stable rate (or baseline) as long as condition A remained in effect.

However, in reality environmental conditions tend to keep changing over time. Therefore we cannot be certain that any change observed in a subject's behavior during condition B was due to condition B rather than to some change in the subject's environment other than the treatment. For example, one or more of the extraneous variables discussed earlier in this chapter such as history or maturation, could have caused the observed change.

To explore this problem further, we will use a hypothetical example. A counselor's school-age client seldom studies for her courses and reports having difficulty keeping up with schoolwork. The counselor learns that evenings are the only times the client can study because of an otherwise busy schedule. She also learns that the client usually watches television after supper until bedtime. The counselor asks the client's parent to keep a daily record of her study time.

After several weeks, the parent's record shows that the client has averaged less than 15 minutes of study per night. At this point, the counselor makes her services contingent on the client studying at least five hours during the week prior to the counseling session. The counselor informs the client that upon her arrival at the next session, if her parent's report does not show her to have studied at least five hours during that week, the counseling session will be terminated. This condition, making counseling contingent upon the client having studied at least five hours prior to the session, constitutes the treatment, which is condition B. The client is told that her parent will continue recording her study time. When the client returns the next week, her parent's report indicates that she studied a total of six hours that week.

It seems reasonable to infer that condition B (communicating to the client that counseling would terminate unless the client studied at least five hours before each session) *caused* the increase in study time. However, suppose that the client's first week of treatment occurred early in April, which also happened to be a week in which television was dominated by broadcasts of reruns. Was it the treatment or the fact that mostly reruns were showing on television that caused the decrease in television viewing and the increase in study time?

Reruns on television are an example of how the extraneous variable of *history* might cause changes in the client's behavior. Thus, the A-B design has low internal validity because history, or other extraneous variables rather than the experimental treatment, may cause the changes observed in the subject. The three single-subject designs described below all involve attempts to improve the internal validity of a single-subject experiment, either by using more than one administration of the treatment (A-B-A-B design), by comparing two or more behaviors presumed to be affected by the treatment (multiple baseline across behaviors), or by comparing two or more individuals exposed to the same treatment (multiple baseline across individuals).

## THE A-B-A-B DESIGN

The A-B-A-B single-subject experiment involves several baseline periods (condition A) and several treatment periods (condition B) to establish causality. Using the above example, suppose that when the client returned for the next session, the counselor said that it no longer would be necessary for the client to study five hours per week to "earn" her next counseling session. In other words, the counselor withdrew the treatment procedure, thus reinstating condition A. In the next counseling session, the parent's report indicated a reduced amount of study for the previous week, only one and one-half hours. The counselor then reinstated the five-hour requirement (condition B) and found that the client again increased her study time to more than five hours per week.

Figure 13.1 shows the pattern of study time per day during the six weeks of the study. Note the large differences between the two baseline conditions ($A_1$ and $A_2$) and the two treatment conditions ($B_1$ and $B_2$). This graph is typical of the type used by researchers to report the results of single-subject experiments. The differences obtained in such studies are usually sufficiently clear that no test of statistical significance is needed. Looking at the graph, the counselor is now convinced that the TV reruns had little to do with the client's increased study behavior and that the treatment procedure was effective in producing the desired behavioral change.

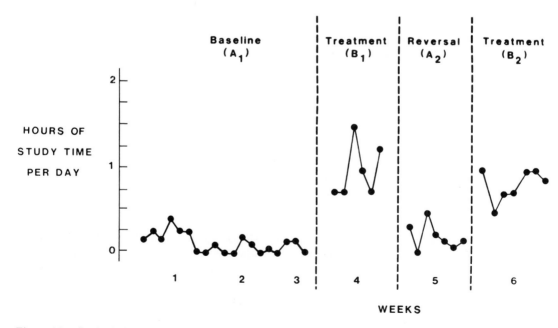

Figure 13.1 Study Time and Treatment: A Typical A-B-A-B Design

The A-B-A-B design is also referred to as a withdrawal, intrasubject replication, equivalent time-samples, or reversal design. This design provides an advantage over the A-B design by returning to condition A or baseline conditions. The purpose of this reversal of conditions is to demonstrate that the client's behavior is not changing by chance but is under the control of the treatment. In this example, the counselor was interested in dealing with the behavior of a single client. Thus this study also could be called an action research project since it was not designed to produce knowledge that can be generalized to other clients. (We will discuss action research in Chapter 15.)

Because research results based on a single subject cannot be generalized to other similar subjects with confidence, single-subject research is weak in external validity. The solution to this weakness is *replication,* that is, repeating the study with other clients. Suppose that the counselor had five clients who did little studying and were failing in school. If she applied the same treatment to each of these students individually and all five made major gains in study time, she could generalize with some confidence that this method would help other students having the same difficulty. A finding that occurs consistently with a number of individuals is much stronger from a scientific standpoint than a finding that occurs only once.

Caution should be exercised in selecting the A-B-A-B design because not all behaviors can be readily reversed during a research study. For example, a teacher's goals for an individual student may include learning various academic or social skills such as table manners, how to take multiple-choice tests, or how to use vocational information materials. Learning such skills is similar to learning to ride a bicycle: although you may get rusty without practice, once you learn how, you never forget. It is important to note that when a behavior does not reverse, control has not been demonstrated. Since the reversal of conditions eliminates explanations for a change in behavior other than the treatment, the failure of a behavior to reverse is tantamount to a failure to eliminate rival hypotheses (such as the television reruns in our example). If the goal for the client includes demonstrating a behavior that appears nonreversible (that is, resistant to extinction) or if the counselor is not sure that the behavior can be readily reversed, multiple-baseline designs are preferable. Two of the most common of these designs are discussed below.

**Multiple Baseline across Behaviors.**    In this single-subject design, baseline measurements are taken on two or more behaviors exhibited by the same subject. After baselines are stable, a treatment condition is applied to one of the behaviors. The treatment is continued until a noticeable change occurs in that behavior. Then the treatment condition is applied to the second behavior until a change is observed.

An important requirement for using the across-behaviors design is the discreteness of the behaviors to be observed. If the occurrence of one behavior is relatively dependent on the occurrence of the other, treatment of one behavior may cause a change in both. If so, explanations that could account for change other than the treatment remain possible.

To understand this design further, suppose that you want to train a teacher in using three behaviors designed to provide reinforcement for correct pupil responses during a question-and-answer lesson. The three behaviors to be learned are as follows:

  A. Teacher smiles at the student who gives a correct response.
  B. Teacher gives the responding student a token that can be exchanged for extra free time.
  C. Teacher praises the responding student.

Here are the steps a researcher would take in conducting this study:

1. She would first collect baseline data on the number of times the teacher emitted each behavior during five half-hour lessons (i.e., one a day for one week) and record the results, as in Figure 13.2.
2. She then would train the teacher to use behavior A.
3. Over the subsequent five days she would record the number of times the teacher used each of the three reinforcement behaviors during half-hour lessons. If her training has been effective, the teacher will increase use of behavior A but will not change noticeably on behaviors B or C (see Figure 13.2).
4. She then would train the teacher to use behavior B.
5. Again she would record the teacher's use of all three behaviors during five half-hour lessons and record the results, as in Figure 13.2. At this point behaviors A and B should be higher than baseline, but behavior C should stay about the same.

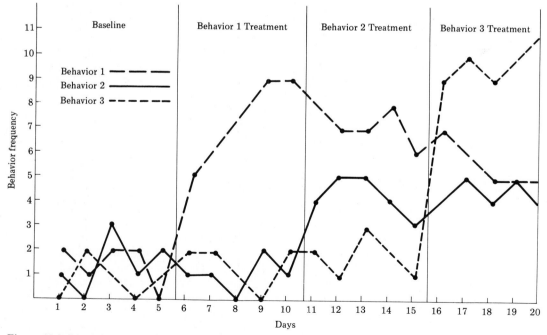

Figure 13.2  Results of a Multiple-Baseline Study across Behaviors

6. She then would train the teacher to use behavior C.
7. She again would record the teacher's use of all three behaviors during five half-hour lessons. If the training has been effective, all three behaviors should occur more frequently than was the case during the baseline condition.

Inspection of Figure 13.2 indicates that the training in all three behaviors was effective. However, notice that behavior A gradually decreased near the end of the study, indicating that the researcher's training program for this behavior is weak and needs to be strengthened or that follow-up instruction may be needed to achieve more permanent results. Notice also that the frequency of behavior B never reaches the levels of behaviors A and C. This result could indicate that (1) more training is needed in behavior B, (2) giving tokens is used less frequently by teachers as a reinforcement strategy than smiles or praise because it takes up more class time, or (3) teachers sense that pupils respond better to smiles and praise than to tokens. Of course, other interpretations, that is, alternate hypotheses, could explain the observed results. In many cases, the researcher will conduct additional research to test alternate hypotheses. As alternate hypotheses are supported or rejected in subsequent studies, the researcher learns more about the phenomenon being studied.

**Multiple Baseline across Individuals.**   In this single-subject design, two or more subjects are selected for whom the behavioral goal of treatment is the same. After baseline rates of behavior have become stable for both subjects, a treatment is applied with one subject. If a change is noted in the treated subject's behavior but the non-treated subject's behavior remains constant, we can conclude that the treatment had an effect. The treatment is then applied to the second subject to see if his behavior changes. If it does change, this result constitutes a replication of the treatment's effect on that behavior.

The across-individuals design is invalidated if the treatment for one subject influences the behavior of the other subjects who are still in the baseline condition. This problem can occur, for example, when treatment is provided to several children in the same classroom, to members of the same family, or to employees in the same work location.

The A-B-A-B design is more powerful than the two multiple-baseline designs discussed above because the reversal phase (the second A condition) demonstrates active control of the behavior by removing the treatment that is hypothesized to have caused the initial change (the initial B condition). Reinstatement of the treatment (the second B condition) provides additional evidence of the effect of the treatment.

Despite the power of the A-B-A-B design, it cannot be used in all situations. For example, in many counseling situations a successful treatment cannot be withdrawn from a client, as when anxiety levels are reduced as a function of treatment. Multiple-baseline designs give counselors the advantage of studying the effects of a treatment without having to withhold it from a distressed client and of allowing the study of treatment-induced behaviors that are not reversible or that have a high resistance to extinction.

# Sample Single-Subject Study:
# A SELF-MONITORING PACKAGE FOR TEACHING SUBTRACTION WITH REGROUPING TO STUDENTS WITH LEARNING DISABILITIES

## Abstract[25]

In this investigation, we evaluated the effectiveness of a self-monitoring package with 3 learning disabled students whose responding to subtraction problems had been highly inconsistent and unsuccessful. Following a two-phase baseline of didactive instruction and special incentives, an error analysis was used to develop individualized self-monitoring checklists that the students then responded to as they completed their subtraction assignments. In the context of a multiple baseline design, the self-monitoring procedures produced immediate gains in correct responding, with more stable levels of successful performance occurring across sessions. In a subsequent maintenance phase, the checklists were removed and the previous incentives condition was reinstated, resulting in continued levels of successful responding. The results are compared to the literature on self-monitoring and learning disabilities and discussed in terms of the continuing need for effective and efficient instructional strategies.

## Researcher's Comments[26]

## Background

This study was conducted when the first author was a special education teacher in a resource program for elementary school students diagnosed with learning disabilities. The three students in the study received mathematics instruction in this program. Although they had mastered a range of mathematics skills, none had been able to complete with consistent success subtraction problems requiring regrouping. Numerous attempts had been made to teach them this skill, mainly in the form of didactic instruction. When given a subtraction worksheet to complete, two of the students (Billy and Carrie) would miss few or no problems on some days and all or almost all problems on other days. The performance of the third student (Casey) was consistently below 50 percent. When given simpler subtraction problems to complete, such as two digits with no regrouping or two digits with one regrouping, all three students did quite well.

The students' ability to do simpler subtraction problems correctly, and their occasionally correct performance on more complex problems, led us to hypothesize that they had the necessary skills in their response repertoires but did not know when to use them. This hypothesis was supported by our observation that often a teacher's simple prompt (e.g., "Remember to regroup if the top number is smaller than the bottom") was sufficient for students to complete the remaining problems correctly. We also noticed that when prompts were given, the students usually seemed to know exactly what the teacher meant, and few additional instructions were needed.

In further support of our hypothesis, Torgesen (cited in our article) found that although students with learning disabilities often demonstrate proficiency with individual skills, they do not know how to determine when to use those skills in sequence to solve a complex problem. Thus our goal became to develop a strategy for teaching students *when* and *in what manner* to apply the various skills needed to complete difficult subtraction problems correctly.

Self-control strategies have not been used extensively with learning-disabled students, even though they have been shown to help a wide range of other students. We decided to try these strategies because didactic instruction, including corrective feedback and prompting, had not been effective in teaching our students to complete subtraction problems with regrouping consistently and independently, perhaps because didactic instruction involves the constant presence and vigilance of the teacher. By contrast, self-monitoring procedures are student-centered, meaning that students are required to monitor their own behavior and make decisions about that behavior. Our intervention would be designed to help learning-disabled students monitor when and in what order (not just how) to apply the necessary procedures during problem completion. We believed that self-monitoring could be cued by a checklist that was individually designed for each student's unique difficulties with complex subtraction problems.

Although we were eager to try this intervention, one important issue remained. Self-monitoring procedures are generally more effective, especially in the initial stages, if performance of the targeted behaviors and successful self-monitoring are accompanied by rewards. We felt that rewards (points that could be exchanged later for prizes) would be particularly reinforcing for these students because they had long histories of failure when requested to perform this type of problem. However, if a self-monitoring package that included rewards was successful, we would not know whether the success resulted from self-monitoring or from the rewards that the students received.

To answer this question, we added a "didactic plus points" condition to the experiment. If the students performed as well in this condition as in the "self-monitoring plus points" condition, we would know that rewards were the critical factor, not self-monitoring. This result would suggest that the students were failing because they just weren't motivated. However, if students performed better in the "self-monitoring plus points" condition than in the "didactic instruction plus points" condition, we would know that self-monitoring, not rewards, was the critical factor. This result would suggest that learning-disabled students are motivated but lack particular skills.

# Experiences

We made several interesting observations while the experiment was in progress. First, the students learned the self-monitoring procedure with striking ease. A brief tutorial session (as short as five minutes for one student) and guided practice on a few problems was all that was necessary for the students to initiate the self-monitoring procedure. This observation supported our hypothesis that these students already possessed the regrouping skills necessary for correct solution of the subtraction problems. If they did not have the skills, it seemed unlikely that the students could learn to self-monitor their use so quickly.

Another anecdotal observation was that students seemed to enjoy self-monitoring. The teacher had not predicted this phenomenon; she thought that students might find the self-monitoring procedure to be cumbersome and too time-consuming. Their enjoyment of self-monitoring probably resulted from the fact that they were experiencing independent success with previously troublesome problems. Indeed, they often commented to the teacher on their success "without any help."

As the students became adept at self-monitoring, very little corrective feedback from the teacher was necessary. If an error was found when checking completed problems, the teacher simply asked the student to "self-monitor number four again." Students generally were able to find their own errors when self-monitoring a second time.

Another interesting observation was that two students began fading their own use of the self-monitoring checklist. Casey was observed completing two or three problems before self-monitoring those two or three, and Billy one day completed almost all the assigned problems when the teacher noticed that he had not used his checklist. At that time the teacher withdrew the checklists (maintenance condition), believing that the students felt confident about completing the problems without the cues provided by the checklists.

The procedures also were very pleasant for the teacher. Aside from the thrill of her students' success, the teacher saved quite a bit of time. As teachers are well aware, this is an important criterion when evaluating an intervention. Because of the high number of students' errors before baseline, during baseline, and during the points condition, the teacher typically spent large portions of the period providing corrective feedback and instruction. Throughout the self-monitoring condition, increasingly less teacher time was necessary. The teacher also enjoyed the change in the type of feedback she was delivering. She made more positive, reinforcing comments and fewer corrective comments (which probably were considered negative by some students).

# Aftermath

Since completing the study, we have continued to use self-monitoring procedures in both academic and nonacademic areas and with other student populations besides those with learning disabilities. The results have been very positive. One of us (Lee, a resource teacher) was able to develop self-monitoring programs that her students could use in their regular classrooms. These programs sometimes reduced or eliminated the need for special education services.

After the study was published, we were contacted by a researcher who replicated these procedures in another public school classroom using a generic checklist, with similarly positive results.

# Implications for Future Research

Self-monitoring procedures have numerous advantages for both teachers and students, as we noted above. Because these procedures are relatively new in the classroom, however, further research is needed to understand the limits of their effectiveness. Preliminary studies show that self-monitoring can be successful with students functioning at a wide range of levels, including students with severe handicaps such as autism. Further research on students with various disabilities and at varying levels of functioning will more firmly establish the range of applicability of these procedures.

Continued research is also needed to explain why such procedures are effective. This knowledge would enable practitioners to determine the necessity of various components, and would facilitate construction of self-monitoring programs.

On a grander scale, the idea that self-monitoring procedures could help reduce the need for specialized student services is exciting to us. Research exploring this possibility should be a high priority.

# A SELF-MONITORING PACKAGE FOR TEACHING SUBTRACTION WITH REGROUPING TO STUDENTS WITH LEARNING DISABILITIES

## Lee Kern Dunlap and Glen Dunlap

FLORIDA MENTAL HEALTH INSTITUTE,
UNIVERSITY OF SOUTH FLORIDA

Research has shown that although students with learning disabilities may demonstrate proficiency with the specific behaviors necessary for successful task completion, they do not always use these skills spontaneously or in the context of complex response chains (Torgesen, 1980). As a result, their performance is often variable, with mastery levels being difficult to interpret and maintain. Thus, a major emphasis of behavioral and educational research has been to identify instructional techniques that serve to increase these students' abilities to learn and perform academic problems in a consistent manner. One set of procedures that has attracted considerable attention is referred to as self-monitoring.

Self-monitoring approaches are derived from the broad area of research on self-control strategies (Rosenbaum & Drabman, 1979). Such strategies have been used with many populations, ranging from normally achieving students (e.g., Ballard & Glynn, 1975) to students with mental retardation (Johnston, Whitman, & Johnson, 1980; Whitman & Johnston, 1983). Studies focusing on self-monitoring processes have shown that these procedures can increase accuracy in many curricular areas, including speech training (Koegel, Koegel, & Ingham, 1986) and writing composition (Ballard & Glynn, 1975). Self-monitoring procedures appear to be particularly promising with learning disabled students (Harris, 1986b) because these procedures provide students with continuously available instructional cues that may produce specific response strategies and self-initiated responding (Kneedler & Hallahan, 1981).

The purpose of the present investigation was to ex-

L. K. Dunlap and G. Dunlap, "A Self-Monitoring Package for Teaching Subtraction with Regrouping to Students with Learning Disabilities," *Journal of Applied Behavior Analysis*, 22, 1989, 309–314. Copyright © 1989 by the Society for the Experimental Analysis of Behavior, Inc.

tend the literature on self-monitoring with learning disabled students by evaluating a self-monitoring package that was applied to subtraction (with regrouping) problems within a multiple baseline format. Prior to implementing the self-monitoring approach, a two-phase baseline was conducted in which each student was instructed with a traditional didactic strategy (baseline) and with a special incentive system (points).[27]* An error analysis was then conducted to develop individualized self-monitoring checklists that the students used to guide their completion of the subtraction problems.[28]

## Method

### Subjects

Three students participated in this study. Although each of the students functioned with some success in many academic areas (e.g., reading), each had been diagnosed as having a learning disability and was enrolled in a public school resource program serving learning disabled students. In the resource room, they received daily instruction in mathematics. Casey was a 10-year-old fifth-grade student who was functioning approximately 1 year below grade level in math. On the Wechsler Intelligence Scale for Children—Revised (WISC-R), his scores reflected a full scale IQ of 79, with a verbal scaled score of 95 and a performance scaled score of 67.[29] Billy was a 12-year-old sixth-grade student who was functioning at approximately a fourth-grade level in math. His WISC-R scores showed a full scale IQ of 94 (verbal, 103; performance, 86). Carrie, a 13-year-old sixth grader, was functioning at approximately a fourth-grade level in math. Her WISC-R scores were: full, 77; verbal, 86; performance, 77. All 3 students had mastered basic opera-

* Numbered notes to articles are supplied by the authors of this text.

tions involving addition, subtraction, and multiplication; however, none of the children were successful consistently with subtraction problems that involved regrouping.[30]

## Task

This study addressed the students' performance in completing subtraction problems. During each daily session, each student was presented with a worksheet containing subtraction problems that he or she was expected to complete independently. Casey's worksheets consisted of 10 to 20 problems with the exact number varying randomly over the duration of the study. The worksheets for Billy always contained 12 problems, and Carrie's worksheets always had 10 problems. The students were provided sufficient time (e.g., 15 min) to complete all of the problems on their worksheets and, in fact, they did complete all of the problems on each day of the study. Each problem on the worksheets contained two to four digits and required up to three instances of regrouping. For example, a typical problem was to subtract the number "257" from the number "314."

## Procedure

### Design

A multiple baseline across students design was used, with a two-phase baseline included for each student.[31] The first phase was traditional baseline instruction consisting of didactic explanation and verbal feedback. The second phase for each student added an incentive of two points per correct response. Together, these phases were implemented for 8 days for Casey, 10 days for Billy, and 25 days for Carrie. Following these two phases, the self-monitoring package was implemented sequentially according to the multiple baseline format. When stability of performance was achieved, the self-monitoring procedures were removed, and the students continued their work under the previous incentive conditions.

### Baseline—Didactic

During the first baseline phase, the students were given verbal instructions on how to perform the subtraction problems and were then given their worksheets. Upon completion of the problems, the teacher provided praise for correct responses and specific verbal feedback and explanations about each error. All feedback was provided on an individual basis.

### Baseline—Didactic plus Points

During this phase, the same conditions were in effect, except that each correct response was reinforced with two points that were part of a classroom incentive system. The system was a part of the regular classroom routine in which points served as reinforcers for desirable social behavior and successful academic performance. The points were exchanged later in the day for an assortment of prizes, such as attractive pencils, notebooks, and other items.

### Self-monitoring Package

Before the self-monitoring procedures were implemented, each student's previous errors were analyzed and, based on the analyses, individualized self-monitoring checklists were developed. The checklists were developed by reviewing each of the student's previous responses and compiling lists of every error for each student. The individualized checklists were then constructed in such a way that each error was represented on the student's list. The types of errors ranged from a failure to copy integers accurately to specific mechanical errors in the regrouping procedure. Thus, the checklists contained specific "reminders," written in a first-person format (Harris, 1986a), that the students would refer to and check off after each problem (e.g., "I regrouped when I needed to"; "I crossed out only the number next to the underlined number and made it one less"). The entries for each student's checklist are shown in Table 1.

As in the previous phases, the students were given worksheets, but in this condition they were also expected to monitor their work on each problem by recording a plus or a minus for each entry on their checklists. If a minus was recorded (acknowledging that the student had failed to perform the specified step), the student was expected to rework the problem without erasing the original attempt. At the end of the session, when the problems were completed, the work was reviewed by the teacher, and the students were awarded one point for each correct response and one additional point for each problem in which all of the steps on the checklist were self-monitored correctly. As in the two

Table 1    Entries on the individual self-monitoring checklists for each of the students

Casey

1) I copied the problem correctly.
2) I regrouped when I needed to (top number is bigger than bottom).
3) I borrowed correctly (number crossed out is one bigger).
4) I subtracted all the numbers.
5) I subtracted correctly.

Billy

1) I underlined all the top numbers that were smaller than the bottom.
2) I crossed out only the number next to the underlined number and made it one less.
3) I put a "1" beside the underlined number.
4) All the numbers on the top are bigger than the numbers on the bottom.

Carrie

Regrouping

1) I underlined all the top numbers that are smaller than the bottom.
2) I started in the one's place and crossed out the number to the left of the underlined number and made it one less. I put a "1" in front of the underlined number.

Regrouping over zero

1) I underlined all the top numbers that are smaller than the bottom.
2) I passed the 0, crossed out the first number to the left of the 0 and made it one less.
3) I put a "1" in front of the 0.
4) I crossed out the "10" and made it a "9."
5) I put a "1" in front of the underlined number.

previous conditions, the students were also provided with praise for correct responses and verbal feedback regarding their errors.

## Maintenance

When the students achieved high levels of stable responding under the self-monitoring condition, the checklists were removed and the students worked for additional days under the preexisting points condition in which two points were given for each correct response. This phase was included to make the procedures more normalized and to assess the students' ability to perform the calculations without the continuing assistance of the checklists.

## Measurement and Interobserver Agreement

The dependent variable throughout the investigation was the percentage of correct responses to the assigned subtraction problems. Because the students' responses were in the form of written answers, all data were collected by the teacher and kept in the form of a permanent record. Interobserver agreement was assessed for all responses by having a second observer count the correct and incorrect answers on the completed worksheets, independently of the teacher, and calculate daily percentages. Agreement was 100% across all phases of the study.

A measure of procedural reliability during the implementation of the self-monitoring package was obtained by reviewing the checklists after they were collected.[32] Two observers independently recorded that each student's checklists were completed for each day of the intervention.

## Results

The results are presented in Figure 1.[33] The data reveal inconsistent and generally low levels of correct responding during the baseline condition for each student. The subsequent points condition produced no change for Casey or Billy. Carrie's data under the points phase show an increasing trend for 11 days followed by a subsequent decline during the final 4 days, with correct responding at the end of this phase being as low as 30%.

Introduction of the self-monitoring package produced immediate and dramatic gains for each student. Although some variability was evident for Casey and Carrie, the results under this instructional strategy were clearly superior to the preceding baseline phases, with each student succeeding on the majority of the problems. When the self-monitoring checklists were withdrawn, the students continued to perform more successfully than they had previously and maintained their improved performance throughout the maintenance condition.

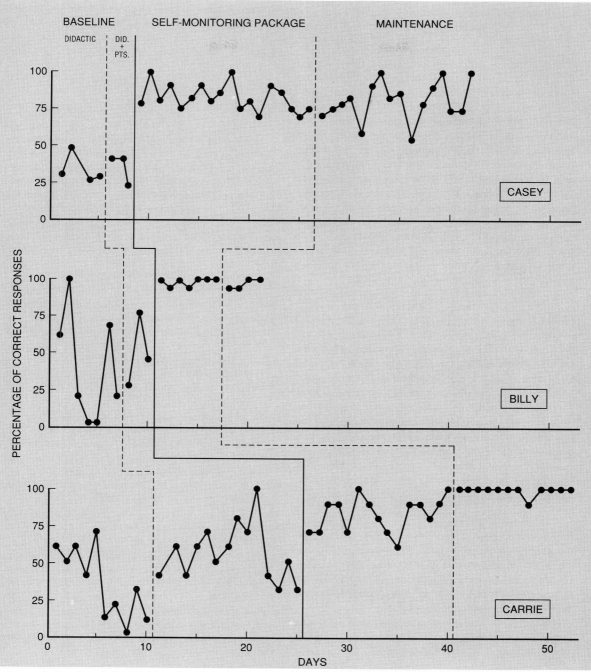

Figure 1 Results of the Multiple Baseline Analysis for the 3 Students. (Percentage of correct responses to the subtraction problems is shown on the ordinate and consecutive school days are plotted on the abscissa.)

## Discussion

The results of this investigation provide support to a considerable amount of previous research on learning disabled students (e.g., O'Leary & Dubey, 1979). A consistent finding has been that the use of self-monitoring checklists helps children to respond correctly and consistently (Kneedler & Hallahan, 1981; Rosenbaum & Drabman, 1979). The present study suggests further that these procedures can be more successful than the use of incentives alone. These findings support Torgesen's (1980) position that students who are learning disabled tend to fail because they do not consistently employ useful task strategies. Thus, the cues for self-checking provided by self-monitoring may enable the students to keep responding in accordance with the successful task strategies. Although the incentives (points) may have been rewarding, they were not sufficient to increase correct responding, perhaps because they did not offer the stimulus control provided by the checklists.

An important aspect of this investigation is that it demonstrates the effectiveness and efficiency of an instructional package that was relatively easy to implement and to fade. Such packages are vital to instructional practice, especially when standard interventions are not successful. The present package included self-monitoring, reinforcement, feedback, and an individualized error analysis of baseline responding. Although the functional impact of the separate components was not delineated in the present design, it is possible that the detailed analysis of baseline responding might be especially important because of the specific, individual task analysis it produced. It is likely that the error analyses enhanced the effects of the self-monitoring checklists by emphasizing the most relevant stimuli in the regrouping process.

A limitation of the present study pertains to the absence of direct observations and procedural reliability on the process of self-monitoring. Future research that includes direct observations of student responding might contribute to an improved understanding of the manner in which self-monitoring approaches facilitate success with various student populations.

From a practical perspective, this study and the results of numerous other articles (Rosenbaum & Drabman, 1979) indicate that self-monitoring procedures have wide applicability in classrooms and other settings. It is apparent that further work in refining and expanding self-monitoring techniques can contribute significantly to improved technologies of instruction for students with learning problems.

## References

BALLARD, K. D., & GLYNN, T. (1975). Behavioral self-management in story writing with elementary school children. *Journal of Applied Behavior Analysis, 8,* 387–398.

HARRIS, K. R. (1986a). The effects of cognitive-behavior modification on private speech and task performance during problem solving among learning-disabled and normally achieving children. *Journal of Abnormal Child Psychology, 14,* 63–76.

HARRIS, K. R. (1986b). Self-monitoring of attentional behavior versus self-monitoring of productivity. Effects on on-task behavior and academic response rate among learning disabled children. *Journal of Applied Behavior Analysis, 19,* 417–423.

JOHNSTON, M. B., WHITMAN, T., & JOHNSON, M. (1980). Teaching addition and subtraction to mentally retarded children: A self-instructional program. *Applied Research in Mental Retardation, 1,* 141–160.

KNEEDLER, R. D., & HALLAHAN, D. P. (1981). Self-monitoring of on-task behavior with learning disabled children. Current studies and directions. *Exceptional Education Quarterly, 1,* 73–82.

KOEGEL, R. I., KOEGEL, I. K., & INGHAM, J. C. (1986). Programming rapid generalization of correct articulation through self-monitoring procedures. *Journal of Speech and Hearing Disorders, 51,* 24–32.

O'LEARY, S. G., & DUBEY, D. B. (1979). Applications of self-control procedures by children: A review. *Journal of Applied Behavior Analysis, 12,* 449–465.

ROSENBAUM, M. S., & DRABMAN, R. S. (1979). Self-control in the classroom: A review and critique. *Journal of Applied Behavior Analysis, 12,* 467–485.

TORGESEN, J. K. (1980). Conceptual and educational implications of the use of efficient task strategies by learning disabled children. *Journal of Learning Disabilities, 13,* 19–26.

WHITMAN, T., & JOHNSTON, M. B. (1983). Teaching addition and subtraction with regrouping to educable mentally retarded children: A group self-instructional training program. *Behavior Therapy, 14,* 127–143.

# Critical Review

The usual instructional model in schools involves three steps: (1) the teacher gives instruction on a topic; (2) the student performs tasks to demonstrate understanding or mastery; and (3) the teacher reviews the student's work and gives praise for correct responses and specific feedback about errors. Although the first two steps can be conducted efficiently with the whole class or in small groups, praise and corrective feedback are usually more effective when the teacher works with one student at a time. Such an individualized approach requires a great deal of time for each student.

Can self-monitoring be used to replace a major part of teachers' feedback and still result in a satisfactory level of learning? This is the general question addressed by the Dunlaps' research. Specifically, the study tested the effectiveness of a self-monitoring package in teaching subtraction to three learning-disabled students.

A major problem in single-subject design is judging the degree to which results can be generalized to the population from which the subjects were drawn. You have two bases for making this judgment. One is the description of the research subjects. The more similar these subjects are to students in another school, the safer it is to generalize the results to that population. The other basis is replication. Single-subject research findings that agree across several replications (that is, across different subjects) can be accepted with far more confidence than findings based on a single individual. In the case of the Dunlaps' study, replication was provided through a multiple-baseline design across individuals.

All three subjects in this study were diagnosed as having learning disabilities. All were functioning at the fourth-grade level, and all scored higher in verbal IQ than in performance IQ. However, the subjects were far from identical, ranging from 10 to 13 in age and from 77 to 94 in full-scale (combined verbal and quantitative) IQ. By replicating their results with subjects who differ on such variables, the researchers can generalize their findings to a broader population.

It would have been desirable for the researchers to give more information about the three subjects, such as their socioeconomic status, their specific performance in other academic areas, and the characteristics of the school they attended. This kind of information helps readers appraise similarities and differences between the research subjects and their own students. The more similar the students are to your own students, the more confidence you can have in using the self-monitoring procedures in your classroom.

The different phases of the research design were introduced to the three subjects at different times. For example, you can see in Figure 1 that on the 15th day Casey was in the self-monitoring phase, Billy was in the maintenance phase, and Carrie was in the second baseline phase. The multiple-baseline design employs staggering of the phases for each subject to check the influence of extraneous variables. If the subjects' performance was influenced by some extraneous variable, such as a special television show about subtraction, its effects would be reflected in the performance of all three subjects, regardless of what phase of the self-monitoring program each was in.

In the self-monitoring phase, one point was rewarded for a correct response, and one point was rewarded for correct self-monitoring of all steps on the checklist. Giving special credit for use of the checklist probably encouraged students to use the checklist initially. It is interesting that once students began self-monitoring their behavior, however, self-monitoring continued even when the checklist was withdrawn. These results suggest that although an extrinsic reward (receiving a point) may help shape a new behavior (self-monitoring), maintenance of the behavior is more dependent on the intrinsic value of the activity to the students. Making these types of inferences when one reads research is important, because it suggests directions for continuing one's literature review and analysis. In this case, for example, a reader might wish to examine literature related to the use of intrinsic and extrinsic rewards to maintain self-monitoring.

The researchers deserve credit for checking and reporting interobserver agreement on measures of the dependent variable, namely, the percentage of correct responses to the assigned subtraction problems. Agreement of 100 percent across all phases of the study demonstrates both that this variable was objectively measured and that the teacher took care to check students' work accurately.

The researchers did not analyze the data to determine their statistical significance but instead graphically illustrated each subject's performance in Figure 1. This procedure is customary in single-subject research, but it raises the question of whether the differences in student performance from one phase of the experiment to the next are only chance fluctuations. The usual criterion for deciding whether the observed differences are real (in the sense that they would appear in other students) is to judge the magnitude of the differences. If the differences appear large to the researcher or reader, they usually are judged to be real. Figure 1 of the article shows a substantial shift in the percentage of correct responses following the introduction of the self-monitoring package. The fact that performance improvement was upheld during the maintenance phase is also noteworthy.

This study illustrates a research procedure that is well suited to action research (see Chapter 15). Trying out a new instructional procedure or package with a small number of students, using a multiple-baseline design like that in this study, is well within the capabilities of most educators.

# Chapter References

BRACHT, G. H., & GLASS, G. V (1968). The external validity of experiments. *American Educational Research Journal, 5,* 437–474.

CAMPBELL, D. T., & STANLEY, J. D. (1963). Experimental and quasi-experimental designs for research on teaching. In *Handbook of research on teaching,* ed. N. L. Gage. Chicago: Rand McNally.

COOK, T. D., & CAMPBELL, D. T. (1979). *Quasi-experimentation design and analysis issues for field settings.* Chicago: Rand McNally.

FISHER, C. W., et al. (1978). *Teaching and learning in the elementary school: A summary of the beginning teacher evaluation study.* San Francisco: Far West Laboratory for Educational Research and Development.

# Recommended Reading

BARLOW, D. E., & HERSEN, M. (1984). *Single case experimental design strategies for studying behavior change,* 2nd ed. New York: Pergamon.

This book provides a comprehensive discussion of the methodology of single-subject research. Examples are selected from education, counseling, and other fields to illustrate basic designs.

BORG, W. R., & GALL, M. D. (1989). *Educational research: An introduction,* 5th ed. White Plains, NY: Longman.

Chapters 15 and 16 cover experimental, quasi-experimental, and single-subject research designs in a nontechnical manner and in greater detail than this chapter.

CAMPBELL, D. T., & STANLEY, J. C. (1963). *Experimental and quasi-experimental designs for research.* Chicago: Rand McNally.

This monograph, although now more than twenty years old, is still a valuable reference for the student who wants to learn more about research design. Many research designs are described and analyzed in terms of internal and external validity.

LINN, R. L. (1986). Quantitative methods in research on teaching. In *Handbook of research on teaching,* 3rd ed., ed. M. C. Wittrock. New York: Macmillan.

This book chapter describes various topics concerning randomization and quasi-experiments. There is a good discussion of the strengths and weaknesses of different procedures for measuring change in subjects' behavior following an experimental treatment.

SHAVER, J. P. (1983). The verification of independent variables in experimental procedure. *Educational Researcher, 12*(8), 3–9.

The article identifies weaknesses in conventional research procedures used to assess whether an experimental treatment was implemented in accordance with the researcher's specifications. Shaver maintains that fidelity of a treatment should be assessed by whether its implementation conforms to prespecified standards rather than by whether its implementation differs from the implementation of the control treatment.

# Application Problems

For each of the brief research descriptions (1–3),

    a. Indicate what kind of research design the researcher is using.

    b. Indicate the major threats to internal validity.

    c. Explain how each threat is likely to affect the results.

**1.** A researcher has developed a remedial spelling program for college freshmen. She administers a spelling test to all students in 20 freshman English classes and identifies 200 students who score less than 50 percent on the test. She then asks these students to volunteer for the 10-hour spelling program. A total of 120 students volunteer, and she randomly assigns 60 to the experimental group and 60 to the control group. She teaches the program one hour per week for 10 weeks to the experimental group. At the end of 10 weeks, 28 students have completed the program. She administers another spelling test to the 28 remaining experimental group subjects and to the 58 subjects remaining in the control group. The mean posttest score is 80 for the experimental group and 66 for the control group. This difference is significant at the .01 level.

2. Two second-grade teachers in Adams School have self-contained classrooms, but they work together in teaching reading. During the reading period Ms. Jones takes all the below-average children from both classes (19 children) and Ms. Smith takes the rest (25 children). They decide to have Ms. Smith evaluate the new *Let's Read* series in her classroom. Ms. Jones agrees to continue to use the *Reading Is Fun* series. They administer the ABC Reading Test to all their students at the start of the school year. The 19 children in Ms. Jones's reading class obtain a mean grade placement score of .8, and Ms. Smith's children obtain a mean score of 1.5. Near the end of the school year in May, all children are tested with another form of the ABC Reading Test. Ms. Jones's group obtains a mean score of 1.5, and Ms. Smith's group mean is 1.8. The national average on this test for second-grade pupils tested in May is 1.7. Since Ms. Jones's pupils gained .7 years (1.5 - .8) and Ms. Smith's pupils gained only .3 years, the teachers conclude that the *Let's Read* series is more effective.

3. The four eighth-grade teachers at Washington Middle School have decided to adopt a new program to teach students to be aware of the dangers of drug and alcohol abuse. They administer a test measuring students' attitudes about the use of drugs and alcohol in September in all four classes (128 students). The mean score for the four classes is 56.2 on an attitude scale ranging from 0 (positive attitude toward use of drugs and alcohol) to 100 (negative attitude toward use of drugs and alcohol). They then teach the program during the school year. In May when the program has been completed, they again test their students' attitudes. The students obtain a mean score of 83.5 on the attitude scale. They conclude that the program has brought about a significant improvement in their students' attitudes against the use of drugs and alcohol.

4. A researcher conducted an experiment in which she administered an arithmetic test before and after students were taught arithmetic skills with a new individualized curriculum. Parallel forms of the test, each with a possible score range of 0 to 100 points, were used as a pretest and posttest. The researcher found that students in the lowest quartile on the pretest ($M = 15.5$) made a good gain on the posttest ($M = 37.6$). Students in the highest quartile on the pretest ($M = 83.7$) declined slightly on the posttest ($M = 80.1$). From the differences in gain scores, the researcher concluded that the new curriculum is more effective for students of low ability than for students of high ability. What are two other interpretations that could be made of the findings?

5. Using the evaluation form in Appendix 3, evaluate the article by Miller, Miller, and Rosen that is reprinted in this chapter.

6. Using the evaluation form in Appendix 3, evaluate the article by Smith that is reprinted in this chapter.

7. Using the evaluation form in Appendix 3, evaluate the article by Dunlap and Dunlap that is reprinted in this chapter.

# Chapter Notes

1. The abstract of the article is reprinted here to help you understand the researcher's comments.

2. This commentary was written by C. Dean Miller.

3. The expression "$F(2, 63) = .95$" represents the results of a statistical test known as analysis of variance. The purpose of the test in this instance was to determine whether differences among the three groups on the vocabulary test were due to chance, or whether the differences mean that the groups represent different populations. If the groups represent different

populations, their score on the final tests might differ because of this fact. Consequently, it would be difficult to determine whether differences among groups on the final tests reflected their initial difference or the effects of modified reciprocal teaching. A $p$ value of $> .05$ ($>$ = greater than) means that we can conclude with confidence that students in the three groups had basically the same vocabulary knowledge.

4. In the previous footnote, $p$ was greater than .05, and so one can conclude that the groups represent the same population. In the comparison of the MRT group and control group I on the comprehension test scores, however, $p$ is less than ($<$) .001, meaning that we can conclude with confidence that the groups represent different populations. Thus, we can generalize beyond this sample and conclude that similar students elsewhere who receive modified reciprocal teaching instruction will develop better reading comprehension than students who get only frequent tests.

5. *SD* is an abbreviation for *standard deviation,* which is a statistical measure of how tightly scores cluster around the mean score. One *SD* above and below the mean typically includes 68 percent of the scores. This means that 68 percent of the MRT group earned comprehension test scores between 4.79 and 8.01.

6. Analysis of covariance is similar to analysis of variance, described in note 3. It is somewhat more sophisticated, however, in that it tests whether two or more groups differ on a posttest after they have been equated on a pretest. For example, suppose group A has a mean score of 1.0 on a pretest and 2.0 on a posttest, whereas group B has a mean score of 1.5 on the pretest and 2.0 on the posttest. If we looked only at posttest scores we would conclude that the two groups benefited equally from instruction. This is not true, though, because group A started at a disadvantage. Analysis of covariance provides a fair test of posttest differences by taking into account initial pretest differences.

7. A Tukey post hoc analysis is a statistical test that is used when an analysis of variance or covariance reveals that the difference among three or more groups on a test can be generalized to a larger population. The Tukey procedure enables the researcher to determine which pairwise comparisons are generalizable. (If there are three groups, A, B, and C, there are three pairwise comparisons: A vs. B, A vs. C, and B vs. C.)

8. $\chi^2$ is a statistical test similar to analysis of variance or analysis of covariance.

9. The abstract of the article is reprinted here to help you understand the researcher's comments.

10. This commentary was written by Lyle R. Smith.

11. A negative correlation signifies that as subjects' scores on one variable increase, their scores on another variable decrease. In this instance, a negative correlation means that teachers who use vagueness terms tend to have lower-achieving classes. The correlation does not prove that teachers' vagueness lowers students' achievement, but it indicates that this is a possibility.

12. You can verify for yourself that it would require 16 different lessons to represent all possible combinations of the 4 factors. For example, one lesson would include bluffing, *uncertainty,* discontinuity, and notes; another lesson would include bluffing, *certainty,* discontinuity, and notes; and so on.

13. Reliability in this context refers to students' consistency in answering the 16 test items. In simple terms, high test reliability means that students who answer most of the first 8 items correctly will be likely to answer the last 8 items correctly; and conversely, students who do poorly on the first 8 items will be likely to do poorly on the last 8 items. The Kuder-Richardson formula 20 is one method of calculating test reliability. The closer the value is

to 1.00, the more reliable the test. A value of .80 indicates good, but not perfect, test reliability.

14. The covariate procedure is a statistical procedure that artificially equates two or more groups on a variable such as academic ability. Suppose, for example, that one group earned a higher mean score on the Botswana test than another group but also had higher initial ability (as measured by the Baltic States test). One could claim that the first group did better on the Botswana test because they were smarter, not because their lesson was more effective. The covariance procedure rules out the "smartness" explanation by equating the two groups on the Baltic States test. (The covariance procedure, however, is tricky, and it does not always work the way it's supposed to.)

15. The covariate procedure described in note 14 equates two groups on initial ability (or another variable) by adjusting their scores on the posttest (in this case, the Botswana test). Typically the posttest scores of the group with higher initial ability will be adjusted downward in this procedure, and the posttest scores of the group with lower initial ability will be adjusted upward.

16. Analysis of variance is a statistical procedure to determine the likelihood that a difference found between two or more groups in a sample would also be found if the researcher studied the entire population. For example, if the ANOVA found that the groups that had notes handouts did better on the posttest than the groups that did not have handouts, we probably could generalize beyond this sample and conclude that notes handouts would help other students similar to those involved in this experiment.

17. A standard deviation is a statistical measure of how much the scores vary around the mean score. One standard deviation above and below the mean score typically includes 68 percent of the scores in the sample.

18. An $F$ ratio is a numerical value yielded by an analysis of variance. If the $F$ ratio exceeds a certain value (indicated by one or two asterisks in Table 3), we can conclude that the result is likely to generalize to other students similar to those included in the experiment (see note 16).

19. A $p$ value of .05 or .01 indicates an $F$ value that permits generalizability from the sample to a wider population. A research finding that yields a $p$ value of .01 is more likely to generalize than one that yields a $p$ value of .05.

20. The main effects in Table 3 are uncertainty, bluffing, discontinuity, and notes. The fact that the main effect of bluffing was not significant means that students whose lessons contained bluffing (see data columns 4, 7, 8, 11, 12, 14, 15, and 16 in Table 2) did not differ on the posttest from students whose lessons contained no bluffing (data columns 1, 2, 3, 5, 6, 9, 10, and 13). The significant interaction between the bluffing and discontinuity conditions is explained by the author in the next sentence and is illustrated in Figure 1. Interaction effects often are difficult to interpret.

21. Omega squared ($\psi^2$) is a statistical measure of the strength of an effect. As $\psi^2$ approaches a value of 100 percent, it indicates that a factor such as bluffing affects every student the same. In other words, every student whose lesson contained bluffing would score less well than every student whose lesson contained no bluffing. A $\psi^2$ value of 3 percent indicates an effect, but a very weak one.

22. To understand what "purely by chance" means, consider the fact that boys and girls do not differ on most measures of verbal ability, but there is considerable variability in verbal ability within each gender. Therefore, by chance one might select a sample of boys who are unusually low in verbal ability and a sample of girls who are unusually high in verbal ability. One could conclude erroneously from this chance finding that girls generally have

greater verbal ability than boys. When a large number of comparisons are made, as in this study, this type of chance finding can occur with a frequency that can be determined rather precisely.

23. The 31 significant differences are well beyond the number that could be expected by chance (see note 22). Therefore, some of the 31 differences may be due to chance, but it is highly unlikely that all of them are due to chance.

24. The authors acknowledge the contributions of John T. Zweig and Kenneth LaFleur, who wrote the section on single-subject research for the second edition.

25. The abstract of the article is reprinted here to help you understand the researcher's comments.

26. This commentary was written by Lee Kern Dunlap and Glen Dunlap.

27. A baseline refers to the period of time in a single-subject experiment before the treatment (in this case, the self-monitoring procedure) is introduced. The purpose of the baseline period was to collect data on how students perform with conventional instruction. This experiment had a two-phase baseline, meaning that learning-disabled students were observed during two types of instruction conventionally used with them: (1) didactic instruction and (2) instruction with a special incentive system.

28. An error analysis is an analysis of the errors that students make in performing a certain task, in this case, solving subtraction problems. This analysis can produce information that is useful in designing instruction to improve task performance.

29. The performance scale of the WISC measures several abilities, including numerical and spatial abilities. A full-scale IQ is the student's intelligence quotient (IQ) based on his or her total performance on the verbal and performance scales.

30. Regrouping in subtraction problems is sometimes called borrowing. An example of this type of problem is 34 minus 19: 9 cannot be subtracted from 4, so the 3 must be regrouped into two 10s and ten 1s.

31. The experimental design in this study involved a multiple baseline across subjects, in that the three subjects controlled for extraneous variables for one another. For example, you will note in Figure 1 that during days 11 to 26, Carrie was still in a baseline condition, while both Billy and Casey were receiving the experimental treatment. If any variable other than the treatment was responsible for Casey's and Billy's improved scores, it should have improved Carrie's scores to the same level, too. Because Carrie's scores were lower, we can conclude that the treatment was responsible for at least some of Casey's and Billy's improvement.

32. *Procedural reliability* is not a standard research term. In this context it refers to an independent check that students followed the directions to complete the self-monitoring checklists each day. This independent inspection of the checklists is more rigorous than, for example, asking the students whether they followed the procedures.

33. The description underneath Figure 1 refers to its *ordinate* and *abscissa*. The ordinate is the vertical dimension of a graph, and the abscissa is its horizontal dimension.

# CHAPTER 14

# EVALUATION RESEARCH

## Overview

This chapter discusses the advantages of using published research findings to evaluate educational phenomena about which you need to make a decision. We explain the difference between formative and summative evaluation and present criteria for determining the usefulness of evaluation studies. We also discuss the main differences between quantitative and qualitative models of evaluation. The chapter includes a sample study that involved evaluation of a classroom management program.

## Objectives

1. Describe the advantages of using published research findings to evaluate educational phenomena about which you need to make a decision.
2. Identify six types of educational phenomena that have been the subject of evaluation research.
3. Describe the major characteristics and uses of evaluation research in education.
4. Describe the difference between formative and summative evaluation and the benefits of each.
5. Describe six criteria that a good evaluation study should satisfy.
6. Describe the main differences between quantitatively oriented and qualitatively oriented models of evaluation.

## Advantages of Using Published Evaluations to Make an Educational Decision

Educators and policymakers are constantly involved in making judgments about the merits of various educational personnel, programs, and materials. Over the past 30 years, evaluation research, both in education and in other fields, has become increasingly sophisticated in its ability to provide information to help decision makers in these judgments. Assessments of the skill of students at different grade levels, public opinion polls on political issues, and comparisons of the recovery rates of medical patients undergoing experimental treatment versus conventional treatment reflect the extent to which evaluation has become part of our everyday culture.

Educators are continually confronted with decisions about such matters as curricula, textbooks, student placement, and instructional programs. As we observed in Chapter 1, many educators rely solely on personal experience or expert advice to make such decisions. Experience and advice can be helpful, but you should keep in mind that these sources of information are subject to bias and error. A well-done evaluation study is a valuable addition because it is more likely to weigh all the factors that affect the decision.

Professional evaluators operate on the assumption that most decisions are complex because they involve diverse perspectives and goals. For example, the relatively minor decision to approve an expenditure for a new filing cabinet for the school office can be considered from the standpoint of its possible relationship to such goals as fostering positive morale among certified staff, maintaining a positive appearance of the school environment, and being environmentally conscious in the purchase of equipment.

When a great deal hinges on a decision, more systematic evaluation that controls for possible bias and the validity of the information is called for. For example, should students be required to take minimal competency examinations as a condition for high school graduation? Which students should be accepted for a talented and gifted educational program? How should the school district allocate limited funds among high-priority programs such as peer counseling, prevention of alcohol and drug abuse, and AIDS education? Reports of evaluation studies will help educators become aware of the issues involved in such questions, less vulnerable to attacks from groups or individuals who are negatively affected by their decisions, and better able to justify the costs associated with the decisions.

# Types of Phenomena That Can Be Evaluated through Evaluation Research

Six types of educational phenomena are commonly the subject of evaluation studies: (1) instructional methods, (2) curriculum materials, (3) educational programs, (4) educational organizations, (5) educators, and (6) students. We explain each type by referring to recent studies involving evaluation of each.

*1. Instructional methods.* Educators want to know which instructional methods are most effective, for example, the lecture versus the discussion method, inquiry teaching, the whole-language approach to reading instruction, or the use of manipulatives in language instruction. The value of one such method, active participation (a key component of Madeline Hunter's program, Instructional Theory into Practice) was evaluated in an experimental study by Jerry Pratton and Loyde Hales (1986). Teachers were trained to deliver a lesson on probability to one fifth-grade class by encouraging active participation (the experimental treatment) and to give the same lesson to another fifth-grade class without encouraging active participation. Active participation involved a deliberate attempt by the teacher to get students to participate overtly in a lesson, for example, by asking students to hold up the correct number of fingers to indicate the number of digits in a dividend in a lesson on division. Students who were taught by the active participation method received significantly higher mean scores on a posttest covering the lesson content.

*2. Curriculum materials.* Educators and students spend large amounts of money each year on textbooks and other instructional materials. Educators count on these materials to help students achieve intended learning objectives, yet research carried out by the Educational Products Information Exchange found that less than 1 percent of the curriculum materials sold by the publishing industry are field-tested with students and revised before publication (American School Board Journal, 1975).

Dale Johnson and Blaine Smith (1987) evaluated a high school algebra textbook developed by John Saxon, a former Air Force Academy engineering instructor. Many claims had been made for the effectiveness of the Saxon text compared to traditional textbooks. These researchers, however, found flaws in previous studies of the text, so they did their own experimental investigation. Their findings showed that the Saxon text was no more effective than a conventional algebra text in improving students' algebra achievement but that students who used Saxon's text had more positive attitudes toward mathematics at the end of the year. However, there was no pretest measure of attitudes toward mathematics. Johnson and Smith posed the possibility that students who had used the Saxon text may have had more positive attitudes toward mathematics at the beginning of the year, in which case the text itself may have had no effect on students' attitudes.

*3. Programs.* An educational program can be defined as a sequence of activities that is guided by a plan and designed to accomplish particular objectives and that provides services on a continuing basis. For example, Head Start, the language arts curriculum in a high school, and the sequence of courses and other activities that preservice teachers must complete in order to be certified are all programs in this sense. Because such programs are complex and operate somewhat differently from one location to another or from year to year, it is important to evaluate them to see if they are operating consistently with their original design and to determine whether they are effective.

In a large-scale evaluation of an educational program, Joann Driggers and Richard Wright (1989) carried out research to determine if the model Life Management Curriculum available at California community colleges since 1987 was meeting its intended goals. The results showed that the program was highly successful in meeting the needs of students of all ages, particularly females. For example, of 200 students participating in the program at one community college, 40 percent rated the degree of change in their life management skills and behavior after one semester as considerable, and another 48 percent rated the degree of change as moderate. Significant changes occurred from pretest to posttest on questions related to defining lifetime goals, decision making, understanding cultural differences, managing change, considering one's energy cycle when planning daily tasks, managing stress, and maintaining balance between career and home responsibilities.

*4. Organizations.* Any school or other educational agency, such as kindergartens, child-care centers, and resource centers, can be evaluated, and its operations can be compared to an ideal, to the operations of other similar organizations, or to the goals of the organization. For example, the Association for Supervision and Curriculum Development (ASCD) is the world's largest professional leadership organization in education. In 1985, the ASCD's Executive Council approved a new five-year plan intended to help educators lead the way into the 1990s. This plan was based on an evaluation design that included "continuous environmental scanning, an internal analysis, and member's ideas . . ." (Berreth, 1988). Based on the evaluation, ASCD's five-year plan identified five areas of focus: (1) education and care of young children, (2) teaching thinking, (3) restructuring the teaching profession, (4) effective leadership and supervision, and (5) technology in the content and process of schooling.

*5. Educators.* Teachers and administrators are continually being evaluated on an informal basis by their students, their supervisors, and to some extent, their colleagues. Formal evaluations also occur in relation to salary reviews and promotions. Another type of evaluation of educators was described by Kenneth Sirotnik (1983), namely, an observational study of over one thousand school teachers by John Goodlad and his colleagues. In presenting the findings, Sirotnik states that the researchers were

> startled by the paucity of variation in the observational results. . . . For example, in the elementary classes observed, we estimate that, on the average, just under 3 percent of the instructional time that the teacher spent interacting with students involved corrective feedback (with or without guidance). At the secondary level, this estimate is less than 2 percent. . . . Thus, one of the most touted pedagogical features of classroom instruction—immediate corrective feedback—rarely occurs. . . . (p. 19)

This finding suggests the need for better supervision and staff development programs for teachers in American school systems.

*6. Students.* Tests, including both classroom tests and standardized tests, are the main methods used to evaluate students. Because so much hinges on students' test performance, it is appropriate that the tests themselves be evaluated. In one such evaluation, Fred Newmann (1990) reported test results from 51 classrooms using a model National Assessment of Educational Progress (NAEP) essay examination developed to evaluate higher-order thinking among high school social studies students. The report concluded that the test assesses higher-order thinking competencies in all subjects.

# Major Characteristics and Uses of Evaluation Research in Education

Educational evaluation is the process of making judgments about the merit, value, or worth of any component of the educational process, such as the six types of educational phenomena described above. The conduct of educational evaluations has greatly expanded in the past 30 years and is continuing to grow. Evidence of its importance include the facts that all educational programs receiving federal funding must undergo formal evaluation, many school districts and state departments of education have evaluation teams, and many universities employ institutional researchers to evaluate their operations.

The findings of evaluation research are used by various groups in their decision-making process, for example, by politicians to create advocacy for specific legislative proposals and budget appropriations and by municipal commissions and agencies to support policy recommendations.

It is important to identify the relevant stakeholders at the outset of an evaluation study. Stakeholders are those individuals, groups, or institutions that are involved in the program being evaluated or may be affected by or interested in the findings of the evaluation. For example, stakeholders in an evaluation of a school career guidance program might include career education teachers, parents whose students are in or might wish to consider taking the program, school counselors, students, administrators, and employers who hire graduates of the program. Stakeholders should have input into the design of the evaluation, the collection and analysis of information, the interpretation of the findings, and the decisions based on the evaluation. Different stakeholders tend to hold conflicting positions on the value of educational phenomena. Thus the evaluator and educators using the findings have a delicate task in reflecting and reconciling the varying views of relevant stakeholders. This task is one of the most important aspects of good evaluation research, but it is not easy to perform. As Ernest House (1990) observed,

> Although the reality of multiple stakeholders who have legitimate and sometimes conflicting interests is recognized, how these interests should be adjudicated remains unresolved. . . . The critical political question remains: Whose interests does the evaluation serve? (p. 27)

As our earlier examples demonstrate, many aspects of a program can be evaluated. For example, Susan Otterbourg (1990) investigated education-business partnerships, a type of educational program that has grown considerably in recent years. She listed the range of questions that participants in these partnerships can consider in evaluating them, for example:

> Are money and other resources given to these programs being distributed efficiently and effectively . . . what happened and what was accomplished—not just in numbers (i.e. how many partners put in what kind of hours or what amount of monies were spent)? Partners are interested in the quality of the effort: did attendance improve? Was substance abuse less prevalent? Did more students pass their courses. . . . Did less [sic] students drop out? Did more students pursue post-high school education and training? (pp. 4–5)

Otterbourg reported that program leaders frequently used information addressing these questions as the basis for decisions concerning such factors as program refinement or expansion, recognition and celebration of program success, documentation of long-term effects of the program on participants, eliciting new resources, strengthening community relations, and redesigning the curriculum.

We will describe three types of evaluation research studies that have been widely used in education: needs assessment, cost-benefit analysis, and educational research and development. These three types reflect the various purposes, stakeholders, and procedures that specific evaluation research projects may involve.

*1. Needs assessment.* Needs assessment is the procedure of identifying and prioritizing needs related to societal, organizational, and human performance (Kaufman &

Thiagarajan, 1987). A *need* is usually defined as a discrepancy between a desired state and an existing state. The assessment of needs may involve both perceptions of needs and controlled observations of actual performance. Rossett (1987) identified five types of questions that can be asked of prospective learners to identify specific needs for which instruction may be a potential solution: (1) questions to identify problems that people are experiencing in a particular domain, (2) questions that ask them to express priorities among possible topics or skills that might be included in a course, (3) questions that ask them to demonstrate particular skills, (4) questions that ask them about their feelings about a particular course or skill, and (5) questions that ask them to identify possible solutions (including noninstructional solutions) to a problem.

When needs are carefully analyzed, proposed solutions are more likely to address the real needs of program participants. For example, one of the authors is coordinating an educational program for parents of middle school students. The students participated in an intensive personal growth course and then were assigned mentors for a year-long follow-through program. Soon after the intensive course, all parents received a telephone call asking about their relationship with their youth since the course and about the kind of support they would like as their youth makes the transition to high school. Parents also were asked to rate their level of interest (high, medium, or low) in several topics that speakers planned to address in subsequent meetings. Based on the results, several aspects of the program were redesigned.

*2. Cost-benefit analysis.* Evaluation research has become an important tool for educational managers who must determine whether programs currently in operation are producing benefits that justify their costs and must make sound decisions about allocating personnel and budget.

In his primer on cost-effectiveness analysis in education, Henry Levin (1983) discusses the steps in a cost-effectiveness analysis of an educational program. First the program objective is determined, and an appropriate measure of effectiveness is selected. Then the alternative solutions that will be evaluated must be specified. One can then design an evaluation of the alternatives on the particular criterion of effectiveness that has been selected and obtain cost information for each alternative. Finally, the cost and effectiveness data can be combined into cost-effectiveness ratios that show the amount of effectiveness that can be obtained for an estimated cost.

Levin presents a hypothetical case in which the costs and benefits of four alternative methods of improving mathematics performance of low-achieving students are compared: (1) small remedial groups working with a special instructor, (2) individually programmed instructional curriculum (IPI) in a special resource room, (3) computer-assisted instruction (CPI) involving a 10-minute drill and practice session, and (4) cross-age peer tutoring for 30 minutes a day. First the cost per student for each alternative is determined. Then the effectiveness of each instructional strategy is determined by comparing the test scores of students compared to those of a control group. By combining the results, a cost-effectiveness ratio is derived that shows the cost per student for an average one-point improvement in test scores. With the hypothetical data provided, peer tutoring was found to be the most cost-effective approach.

Although only half as effective as the small-group approach, peer tutoring achieved a positive effect at only one-sixth the cost.

*3. Educational research and development.* Evaluation is a major component of educational research and development (R&D). We have already discussed needs assessment, which is an important component of the instructional design phase of educational R&D. Once a product or program has been developed, it must be evaluated in terms of its effectiveness, and perhaps in relation to its unintended effects as well.

The systems approach for designing instruction, as presented by Dick and Carey (1985) includes formative evaluation and summative evaluation in its 10-stage model. Michael Scriven (1967) originated the distinction between formative and summative evaluation. Formative evaluation involves collecting data about educational products (such as programs or materials) while they are still under development. These evaluative data are used mainly by the developers to design further and refine the product or to make a decision to discontinue development if appropriate.

Formative evaluation can be done after any of the stages of development until a product is completed. For example, the developers can evaluate the degree to which a need exists for a proposed product, a process that is referred to as needs assessment. They also can carry out evaluations of the product's goals and objectives, examining such issues as the clarity and comprehensiveness of the objectives. Finally, they can evaluate the instructional strategies and materials that the product involves. These evaluations are conducted under field-test conditions, which usually mean a small sample; hands-on involvement of the developers; and a controlled environment, similar to that of a research laboratory, as opposed to the normal operating conditions in which the product eventually will be used.

Summative evaluation is conducted to determine how beneficial the final product is, especially in comparison with competing products. This evaluation is usually carried out by someone other than the developer. However, as the study by Evertson (1989) at the end of this chapter illustrates, summative evaluation can also be done by the development team if appropriate controls are used to reduce researcher bias.

As an educator examining research literature, your goal will be to find an evaluation of a product, program, or method of interest to you and determine whether the approach and findings are useful in reaching your own decision about its value. You probably will be most interested in summative evaluations of educational programs and materials, that is, an evaluation of the program or materials under operational conditions, after development has been completed. Such evaluations will help you determine whether the program or materials are effective under conditions similar to your own situation.

An important source of information about programs that have undergone summative evaluation is the National Diffusion Network (NDN). This national government agency reviews educational programs in various subjects on a periodic basis. Programs are identified for evidence of effectiveness in meeting stated objectives at the original demonstration site and an indication that the program will be successful in similar sites (Office of Educational Research and Improvement, 1991).

Over four hundred programs have been approved by the NDN to date. Many provide instruction in a variety of content areas, and others provide teacher training in instructional methods and classroom management techniques or help administrators solve management problems in the schools. These programs are now available to school systems and other educational institutions for implementation. In the 1988–1989 school year alone, over 29,000 public and private schools adopted NDN programs. (A catalog describing all the projects in the NDN is available by writing to Sopris West, 1140 Boston Avenue, Longmont, CO 80501; telephone 303–651–2829.)

Although programs that have been summatively evaluated may be preferable, you also may wish to examine studies that involve formative evaluations of new products or programs. You may need to implement a solution to your problem before a new product or program is completely developed. The time period from the first appearance of a new product or program, its careful refinement through repeated field tests, and the availability of summative evaluation data on the product's effectiveness under operational conditions is often many years. If you can find out about a promising program while it is still under development, you can get a head start on making decisions regarding its suitability as a solution to your problem. You may even be able to volunteer your work site as a possible field-test site to participate in its formative evaluation.

# Criteria for Judging an Educational Evaluation Study

In reading evaluation research, educators need guidelines for judging quickly the adequacy of the study. In 1981 the Joint Committee on Standards for Educational Evaluation published a set of 30 standards for judging the quality of educational evaluations along with case studies that illustrate each standard. The committee included representatives of 12 important educational organizations, such as the American Association of School Administrators and the American Federation of Teachers.

Below we describe six criteria that synthesize the committee standards. We explain them by referring to a recent evaluation of the Study for Success study skills program, which was developed by two of the authors of this textbook (Gall & Gall, 1991). When you must determine whether a particular evaluation study will be helpful in making an educational decision, we encourage you to apply these criteria. You also should review Chapter 5, which provides guidelines for evaluating research reports in general.

*1. Is the evaluator competent, trustworthy, and unbiased?* In many evaluation studies researchers are evaluating a program that they participated in developing or in which they had some other personal involvement. For example, the study by Evertson (1989) at the end of this chapter involves an evaluation by the author of a program developed by her and her colleagues. Evertson has considerable experience and used well-established methods to carry out the research described in the article. Thus there is evidence that the study meets the criterion of a competent and trustworthy evaluator.

An evaluation was recently conducted by Mona West and Milton West (1992) of the Study for Success study skills program (Gall & Gall, 1991). The evaluators are two educators who have taught study skills to adult learners. Thus they had the necessary competence as well as credibility with the schoolteachers who were the respondents in their evaluation study. They conducted the study and wrote a report on their findings, as part of the requirements for completing a graduate-level course on program evaluation at the University of Oregon. They did not know the program developers and were not familiar with the program beforehand, so their objectivity was assured.

*2. Were fair standards, values, and goals used in interpreting the data?* Typically the purpose of an evaluation study is to see how well a product (such as a program, method, or set of materials) achieves its stated goals. The study should report clearly what goals or objectives of the product were being evaluated. Was the value of the goals taken for granted, or was their worth considered in the evaluation? The study should also indicate how large an effect was found and what guidelines were used to determine whether it does or does not have practical significance.

In their evaluation of Study for Success, West and West reported on how teachers used the teacher's manual, how they incorporated study skills instruction into their teaching, and how well they felt the manual materials addressed the five most highly ranked study concerns of their students. The evaluators also asked the teachers for open-ended comments on what worked, what didn't work, and how they would like to see the materials changed to make them more successful. These evaluation questions, and the evaluators' report of teachers' responses, appear to meet the criterion of using fair standards, values, and goals in interpreting the data.

*3. Were the relevant stakeholders involved in designing the evaluation, collecting data, and reviewing the results?* The study should indicate the various groups or individuals with a stake in the outcome of the evaluation. There needs to be evidence that a sufficient representation of these stakeholders was involved in the evaluation. Also, their willingness to be involved needs to be addressed. For example, if teachers were evaluated in their classrooms, was coercion used or did the teachers voluntarily participate? How was the cooperation of various stakeholders achieved?

In the study by West and West, teachers from two schools who had participated in in-service courses on the Study for Success program were the respondents. Individual interviews were conducted with four teachers at each school. Since the evaluation focused on the teacher's manual, teachers were the most important stakeholders to include in the evaluation. West and West pointed out, however, that the Study for Success program also includes a parent guide, student text, and a book that reviews research and makes recommendations relevant to an overall study skills instructional program, none of which was used by the teachers whom they interviewed. If an evaluation of the entire program were to be conducted, it would be desirable to obtain information from not only teachers but also parents and students about each of these components.

*4. Did the evaluator look for unintended side effects?* Many evaluations are designed to examine specific intended effects of an instructional program. However, it is also important for the evaluators to pay attention to possible unintended effects. In fact, Michael Scriven (1973) argued that evaluators should not know the program goals in advance but instead should examine the actual effects, whether intended or unintended. Most programs have side effects, and these need to be examined in any thorough evaluation. For example, did the evaluator measure several dependent variables and examine the effect of the program on each one?

In addition to evaluating the effectiveness of the Study for Success program in terms of its impact on the students of those teachers who had used it, West and West also discovered that the program was useful as a teacher-training tool. Before using the teacher's manual to teach study skills, the teachers in the study had participated in an in-service course offered by the developers of the manual. "Two teachers, one with many years of experience and one new to teaching, said that the course taught them how and what to teach students" (p. 9). Thus the evaluators investigated not only the usefulness of the program materials but also the value of the training offered to teachers by the program developers.

5. *Did the evaluator take the context into account in interpreting the results?* No matter how complete a product is, it will operate differently depending on the specific location in which and the time at which it is used. Context also includes the extent of familiarity with the product among the users. Was it being adopted for the first time, or had it been in use for a while? Unusual local events or the presence of other interventions made at the same time the program was implemented can affect the outcome and should be examined in the evaluation study. You also need evidence that the participants gave the program a fair trial and that the sample of subjects was appropriate.

The evaluation of Study for Success would have been strengthened if the evaluators had provided more information about the two schools where the participating teachers worked. Because the evaluation report was written primarily for the developers of the program, the authors correctly assumed that we were familiar with the context, and therefore they did not include this information. However, it might have been useful to the evaluators to know more about the context operating within each school, so that they could have considered possible effects of school context on the program's effectiveness.

6. *Were valid and reliable measures used?* The evaluation study should indicate how the independent and dependent variables were measured. If standard or specially developed tests were used, the report should give evidence of their reliability and validity. See Chapter 6 for more information on how to evaluate the educational measures of a research study.

The evaluation of Study for Success was largely qualitative in nature, based on open-ended interview responses. The evaluation report included a copy of the interview form, which listed 13 questions, and a copy of the pages in the teacher's manual that respondents were asked to examine in formulating their responses. An examination of these items helps to establish that the evaluators asked appropriate questions and that they used the same procedures to obtain data from all eight respondents.

# Comparison of Quantitative and Qualitative Models of Evaluation Research

We have shown throughout this book that quantitative and qualitative researchers use different methods in their investigations and that they tend to be interested in different phenomena. Evaluation researchers draw on both of these approaches in their studies. Different models of evaluation have developed over time based on evaluators' preference for one or the other approach. These models are described below.

*1. Quantitative evaluation research models.* Quantitative models of evaluation usually focus on the extent to which an educational product helps students achieve the intended learning objectives associated with it. The National Assessment of Educational Progress (NAEP), for example, is the only representative and continuing assessment of what students in the United States know and can do in various subject areas (National Assessment Governing Board, 1990). The NAEP is a congressionally mandated project of the National Center for Education Statistics of the U.S. Department of Education. It involves quantitative analysis of the percentage of youth at various age levels who are competent in performing tasks that reflect skills that most experts agree are needed to function effectively in society.

Many research studies, particularly those involving an experimental design, involve quantitative evaluation of how well subjects exposed to an innovative program achieve one or more desired objectives compared to how well subjects exposed to a traditional program or no program achieve the same objective or objectives. For example, the experimental study by Miller, Miller, and Rosen (1988), presented in Chapter 13, was a quantitative evaluation of how well students taught by the modified reciprocal teaching method performed on measures of academic achievement and behavior compared to students receiving traditional instruction.

*2. Qualitative evaluation research models.* Qualitative models of evaluation research do not assume that there are objective criteria for judging the worth of an educational program or product. Rather, they assume that judgments of worth depend heavily on the values and perspectives of the individuals doing the judging. Therefore, the selection of the evaluator or evaluation team is critical.

A common model of qualitative evaluation research is expertise-based evaluation. Elliott Eisner (1979) designed a version of this model, called educational connoisseurship and criticism, based on his experience as an art educator. The first aspect, connoisseurship, is the process of appreciating (in the sense of becoming aware of) the qualities of an educational program and their meaning. The evaluator thus must have expert knowledge of the program being evaluated as well as of other comparable or competitive programs. The educational connoisseur is aware of more nuances of the phenomenon being evaluated than a typical educator or layperson. The second aspect, criticism, is the process of describing and evaluating what has been appreciated. The evaluator needs to be sensitive to both the strengths and the weaknesses of the program.

Because the evaluation design is emergent rather than set beforehand, as in quantitative evaluation, educational criticism can illuminate the unique nature and value of a program in ways that are less likely to occur with quantitative research methodology. However, the validity of the evaluator's findings is entirely dependent on the evaluator's expertise. Therefore, in considering the findings of qualitative evaluation studies such as educational connoisseurship and criticism, you should look for other studies, ideally carried out by different experts, to see whether the findings have been replicated. You also should determine how similar the evaluator's experience and values are to your own or to those of the stakeholders you need to satisfy in making your educational decision.

# Sample Evaluation Study: IMPROVING ELEMENTARY CLASSROOM MANAGEMENT: A SCHOOL-BASED TRAINING PROGRAM FOR BEGINNING THE YEAR

## Abstract[1]

In this article I discuss data from a randomized field experiment conducted in 29 classrooms, Grades 1–6. Treatment group teachers were provided with classroom management workshops prior to the beginning of school and again in mid-October. Control group teachers received workshops at the end of the year only. The experiment was designed to evaluate the effectiveness of a research-based classroom management program and to determine if local site personnel could deliver the program. Results showed that the treatment group teachers exceeded the control group in use of key management principles taught in the workshops, had better student task engagement, and had less inappropriate behavior. This study supports similar findings in secondary classrooms.

## Researcher's Comments[2]

My interest in research in classrooms began in the early 1970s when I worked with Jere Brophy at the University of Texas on studies of how teachers affect students' learning. We found that teachers' classroom management techniques have a strong effect on students' learning and behavior.

Stimulated by this finding, we initiated a program of research in the late 1970s at the Research and Development Center for Teacher Education, located at the University of Texas. The research program had two goals: (1) to develop a body of knowledge about techniques that teachers could use from the first day of school to establish a positive learning climate that would continue throughout the school year, and (2) to put this body of knowledge in easily disseminable form.

My colleagues and I began with two descriptive-correlational studies of elementary and secondary classrooms (Emmer, Evertson, & Anderson, 1980; Evertson & Emmer, 1982). The studies sought to determine the relationship between different teachers' beginning-of-the-year classroom management and their students' subsequent cooperation, attention, and task-oriented behavior.

Because the studies were descriptive and correlational in design, they relied on observation of teachers' natural classroom behavior. No training was involved. We subsequently designed two experiments (Emmer, Sanford, Clements, & Martin, 1983; Evertson, Emmer, Sanford, & Clements, 1983) to determine whether a training program on classroom practices based on our descriptive-correlational findings would help teachers in general do what some teachers naturally do to create an effectively managed classroom.

The study that you will read here went beyond these experiments, because it tested the robustness of the findings in real school settings, using local school personnel to carry out the research. It was a program evaluation study used to inform state policymakers about the effectiveness of this teacher-training program and its readiness for statewide dissemination (Evertson, 1985).

The findings supported the viability of developing a group of statewide trainers to work with school districts in Arkansas in implementing the program. The state ultimately did offer the program to school districts and continues to monitor it. By 1989 all school districts in Arkansas had provided training in the program.

Most field studies that involve extensive observation are costly. However, local school districts that wanted to participate in this study were willing to bear the costs of data collection, release time for training teachers, and release time for other school personnel to conduct observations. The Arkansas Department of General Education bore the costs of bringing in school personnel for trainer training and covered other expenses as well.

Gaining the cooperation of teachers was relatively easy. Most were eager to participate because they felt they could learn something that would improve their instruction. However, some school personnel were concerned about the necessity of withholding what might be helpful information from control-group teachers. (The control group did not participate in the training program.) They felt that this feature of the experimental design could be seen as a kind of school-approved inequity.

We countered this concern by explaining the need for a control group to determine whether the workshops really helped. We also scheduled control-group teachers for workshops at the first available time after data collection was complete. It happened that the first available time was spring semester, so training of all teachers was completed in one school year. These accommodations appeared to be satisfactory to all concerned parties.

The only change in the original research plan was to add audiotapes of classroom lessons, at the request of the observers. I originally believed that observers' narrative notes would be sufficient, but they wanted the audiotapes to help them recapture events more accurately. The school personnel were conscientious in conducting the training and making the observations.

We learned as the study progressed that teachers have a tendency to share ideas that they find helpful. Toward the end of data collection we realized that control-group teachers were borrowing techniques from the treatment-group teachers.

This study and three related experimental studies that evaluated our training program on classroom management were submitted to the U.S. Department of Education's Program Effectiveness Panel as evidence of the program's effectiveness. In 1989 the panel granted the program, now called COMP (Classroom Organization and Management Program), formal validation as an "Educational Program That Works." It approved three claims: (1) the program showed evidence of improving teachers' classroom management practices, (2) it improved students' behavior, and (3) it increased students' achievement. This validation made the program eligible for funding from the U.S. Office of Educational Research and Improvement through the National Diffusion Network. Supported with federal funding, the program has been disseminated to school districts and private schools nationwide, in Canada, and overseas.

The findings of our evaluation studies contributed to a major research and development effort for teacher education. A complete set of teachers' manuals and trainers' guides was developed, based on both the experimental studies and subsequent field experience with the training program. Also, two texts on classroom management, one for elementary teachers (Evertson, Emmer, Clements, Sanford, & Worsham, 1989) and one for secondary teachers (Emmer, Evertson, Sanford, Clements, & Worsham, 1989) were developed. In addition, trained staff at Peabody College of Vanderbilt University can assist school districts in implementing the validated training program.

My own research has moved away from designing field studies of the type reported here, although I believe they are important to the improvement of educational practice. I am now examining the effect of classroom social structures and academic task structures on what students have an opportunity to learn. Our recent studies (Evertson & Weade, 1989; Weade & Evertson, 1988) have described the effects of different classroom communication patterns on student outcomes and the relationship between these patterns and teachers' ability to keep classroom task structures in place.

Much of our work has been conducted in self-contained classrooms early in the year when task structures are simple, involving primarily whole-group instruction and seat-work. Future studies will investigate the specific task requirements for carrying out effective instruction in complex, multitask settings. Some important issues to be examined include (1) how teachers sustain effective management and instruction in settings in which students are involved in a wide variety of tasks, (2) how task requirements of teachers vary depending on subject matter, (3) how students can become more involved in developing and maintaining classroom task structure, and (4) what teachers can do to support students' involvement in the classroom social system.

# References

EMMER, E. T., EVERTSON, C. M., & ANDERSON, L. M. (1980). Effective classroom management at the beginning of the school year. *The Elementary School Journal, 80,* 219–231.

EMMER, E. T., EVERTSON, C. M., SANFORD, J. P., CLEMENTS, B. S., & WORSHAM, M. A. (1989). *Class-*

room management for secondary teachers, 2nd ed. Englewood Cliffs, NJ: Prentice-Hall.

EMMER, E. T., SANFORD, J. P., CLEMENTS, B. S., & MARTIN, J. (1983, March). Improving junior high classroom management (ED 234 021). Paper presented at the annual meeting of the American Educational Research Association, Montreal. (ERIC Document Reproduction Service No. ED 234 021.)

EVERTSON, C. M. (1985). Training teachers in classroom management: An experimental study in secondary school classrooms. Journal of Educational Research, 79, 51–58.

EVERTSON, C. M., & EMMER, E. T. (1982). Effective management at the beginning of the year in junior high classes. Journal of Educational Psychology, 74, 485–498.

EVERTSON, C. M., EMMER, E. T., CLEMENTS, B. S., SANFORD, J. P., & WORSHAM, M. A. (1989). Classroom management for elementary teachers, 2nd ed. Englewood Cliffs, NJ: Prentice-Hall.

EVERTSON, C. M., EMMER, E. T., SANFORD, J. P., & CLEMENTS, B. S. (1983). Improving classroom management: An experiment in elementary classrooms. The Elementary School Journal, 84, 173–188.

EVERTSON, C. M., & WEADE, R. (1989). Classroom management and teaching style: Stability and variability of instruction in two junior high English classrooms. The Elementary School Journal, 83, 82–90.

WEADE, R., & EVERTSON, C. M. (1988). The construction of lessons in effective and less effective classrooms. Teaching and Teacher Education, 4, 189–213.

# IMPROVING ELEMENTARY CLASSROOM MANAGEMENT: A SCHOOL-BASED TRAINING PROGRAM FOR BEGINNING THE YEAR

Carolyn M. Evertson
VANDERBILT UNIVERSITY

Research on effective teaching in the past decade has indicated the importance of classroom conditions that depend directly on the ability of teachers to organize and manage their classrooms (Anderson, Evertson, & Brophy, 1979; Brophy & Evertson, 1976; Evertson, Anderson, Anderson, & Brophy, 1980). Some of these conditions include the productive use of time (Frederick & Walberg, 1980; Stallings, 1980), student attention or involvement in focused, goal-directed learning tasks, op-

C. M. Evertson, "Improving Elementary Classroom Management: A School-Based Training Program for Beginning the Year," Journal of Educational Research, 83(2), 1989, 82–90. Reprinted with permission of the Helen Dwight Reid Educational Foundation. Published by Heldref Publications, 4000 Albermarle St. N.W., Washington, DC 20016. Copyright © 1989.

portunities for corrective feedback, and engagement in instructional tasks of appropriate difficulty (Brophy & Good, 1986; Fisher et al., 1980; Medley, 1977).

Research also indicates that the key to organizing and managing classrooms for effective instruction begins with advance preparation and planning from the first day of school (Emmer, Evertson, & Anderson, 1980; Evertson & Emmer, 1982). Even though studies have supported the importance of classroom management as a necessary condition for effective teaching, the problem of translating these principles to practice remains. Interest in using results from classroom studies for the professional development of teachers has prompted investigators to explore ways of making this information more accessible to practitioners.

Experimental studies have shown that teachers can

benefit from systematic exposure to principles of class-room organization and management through specially designed workshops and professional development experiences (Borg & Ascione, 1982; Emmer, Sanford, Clements, & Martin, 1983; Evertson, Emmer, Sanford, & Clements, 1983). Arkansas, in particular, conducted field-based experimental studies to validate a state program on classroom management. Results from one study conducted in secondary school classrooms in Grades 7–9 showed that trained teachers had better student engagement in academic tasks, lower levels of inappropriate behavior, and more efficient and task-oriented classroom environments. For a description of the background and rationale of this study see Evertson (1985).

In this article I report on a replication in the elementary grades of the secondary study mentioned above. I used the same research design; workshop content, materials, activities, and data collection procedures were similar to those used in the secondary classroom study. Procedures were the same, with the exceptions that this study focused on Grades 1–6, and examples used in workshops were geared toward elementary classrooms. Examples and activities in the study in secondary classrooms were more relevant to those grade levels.

## Method

Twenty-nine elementary teachers from two Arkansas school districts participated in this study. I assigned 14 teachers to the treatment group and 15 to the control group. The workshop content for the study was drawn from a teacher manual containing research-based findings on classroom management (Evertson, Emmer, Clements, Sanford, & Worsham, 1981). A content outline is shown in Figure 1. Procedures and activities for the workshops were developed in three 1-day meetings with the principal investigators and district personnel who served as workshop trainers. The trainers spent an additional 2 weeks developing the presentations and activities for the workshops which were held prior to the opening of school.

### Study Design

Participation in this study was not mandatory. Teachers in each school volunteered and were randomly assigned to treatment and control groups within the same school

1. *Planning* (before school starts)
   A. Use of space (readying the classroom)
   B. Rules for general behavior
   C. Rules and procedures for specific areas:
      1. Student use of classroom space and facilities
      2. Student use of out-of-class space
      3. Student participation during whole-class activities/ seatwork
      4. Student participation in daily routines
      5. Student participation during small-group activities
   D. Consequences and incentives for appropriate/ inappropriate behavior
   E. Activities for the first day of school

2. *Implementing rules, procedures, and expectations* (beginning of school)
   A. Teaching rules and procedures using:
      1. Explanation
      2. Rehearsal
      3. Feedback
      4. Reteaching, if necessary
   B. Teaching academic content
   C. Communicating concepts and directions clearly

3. *Maintaining the system* (throughout the year)
   A. Monitoring for behavioral and academic compliance
   B. Acknowledging appropriate behavior
   C. Stopping inappropriate behavior
   D. Using consequences/incentives consistently
   E. Adjusting instruction for individual students/groups
   F. Helping students become accountable for academic work
   G. Coping with special problems

Figure 1. Outline of Workshop Content for Treatment Group

to avoid confounding school effects. Prior to randomization, a step was taken to prevent an imbalance across groups on teaching experience, ability level of classes, and grade level. Teachers were blocked into matched pairs on these demographic variables, then assigned randomly to either treatment or control groups.[3*] Table 1 shows the demographic characteristics of the teachers in each group.

One requirement for participation in the study was that all teachers in both groups had to have had previous

---

* Numbered notes to articles are supplied by the authors of this text.

Table 1    Demographic characteristics of treatment and control group teachers

|  | Treatment | Control |
|---|---|---|
| Teaching experience (years) | | |
| 1–5 | 3 | 3 |
| 6–10 | 3 | 4 |
| 11–15 | 4 | 4 |
| 16–20 | 2 | 2 |
| 20 or more | 2 | 2 |
| Total | 14 | 15 |
| Grade | | |
| 1 | 1 | 0 |
| 2 | 1 | 2 |
| 3 | 5 | 2 |
| 4 | 1 | 4 |
| 5 | 2 | 5 |
| 6 | 4 | 2 |
| Total | 14 | 15 |
| Class achievement level | | |
| High | 5 | 7 |
| Middle | 3 | 4 |
| Low | 6 | 4 |
| Total | 14 | 15 |

training in instructional skills through the state's Program on Effective Teaching (PET) program. This qualification was necessary to hold constant a key background variable related to teachers' previous experience with and instruction in teaching practices.

Treatment group teachers participated in a 1-day, before-school workshop in their respective school districts and were given copies of the manual (Evertson et al., 1981) and workshop materials. Workshop leaders used the training procedures developed in the three 1-day meetings. In mid- to late-October the trainers provided a second 1-day follow-up workshop for all treatment group teachers to reemphasize management principles, to focus on maintaining their management systems already in place, and to address new or persistent problems.

## Data Collection

All teachers in this experiment were observed on six occasions, four times after the first workshop and twice after the second workshop in mid-October. All observations lasted from 30 to 50 min and began on either the first or second day of the school year. Observations were scheduled to include the beginnings and endings of lessons and covered language arts, reading, or math lessons. Approximately the same number of each type lesson was observed for treatment and control groups. Observers were not told the identity of the teachers who participated in the workshops, and observers saw both treatment and control teachers an equal number of times. Treatment group teachers were told the design of the study and asked not to share materials or other information until after the last observation in November. Control group teachers were told the general nature of the study, and they were scheduled for workshops to be conducted in the spring or summer.

## *Description of Data Sources*

Observers from each school district were trained to use a variety of data collection procedures, including narrative descriptions of classroom events, ratings of student task engagement, classroom rating scales, and summary ratings of classrooms. Observers received manuals describing the observation procedures and participated in a 1-day intensive workshop in which they practiced with written scripts of classroom situations and coded videotapes of classroom lessons. I computed reliability by comparing observers' codes and descriptions with a correctly coded criterion videotape.[4] By the end of training, all observers had reached a criterion agreement of 80%.

## Narrative Records

During each procedure, observers recorded descriptions of class activities, as well as teacher and student behaviors. The notes included documentation of the length of activities and transitions. Observers' narrative records preserved the sequence of instructional activities, along with teacher-student dialogue. Information from the narrative records provided an important classroom context that was helpful in interpreting the meanings of the other measures.

## Beginning-of-School Ratings

This set of six ratings used during the first week of school assessed (a) whether teachers presented and discussed rules and procedures, (b) the clarity with which these were explained, (c) the extent of teacher monitoring of the whole class, and (d) the use of rehearsal and feedback in developing the rules and procedures with students.

## Student Engagement

At a randomly determined time during the first 10 min of the observation period, observers scanned the room and categorized each student in one of three categories of task engagement: (a) definitely on task (student is obviously engaged in the current task as defined by the teacher); (b) probably on task (student appears to be engaged, but there is some question); and (c) definitely off task (student is clearly not engaged in the assigned task). Students were categorized as on- or off-task only if no doubt existed; otherwise, students were categorized as "probably on-task."

## Classroom Rating Scales

Five-point Likert scales were completed after each observation. The scales assessed teacher variables related to instructional management, appropriate rules and procedures, meeting student needs and concerns, managing student behavior, and classroom climate. Observers also assessed student variables, such as success in lessons and inappropriate or disruptive behavior.

## Summary Ratings

At the conclusion of the observations in November, a set of summary ratings of each teacher was completed by the observer, who saw a given teacher at least twice. In most instances, two sets of ratings were obtained because at least two observers saw each teacher. These ratings were designed to assess global variables that could be accurately evaluated only after several visits to the classroom. These items included overall time students spent waiting for assignments, decreases or increases in attention from the first of the year, smoothness of transitions, and students' methods of obtaining help. Observer agreement reached 80% or above on most items.

# Results
## Group Differences

I analyzed classroom rating scales, percentages of students engaged, and summary observer ratings, using two-way analyses of variance with group membership (treatment or control) as a between-groups factor, and time of workshop (after the first or second workshops) as a within-groups factor.[5] Descriptive statistics for the two groups after the first and second workshops are shown in Table 2. I found statistically significant differences for 18 of the 31 classroom rating scale items used to assess teachers' management practices.[6] The control group did not outperform the treatment group on any measure.

I assessed the effect of teaching experience and grade level to determine the degree to which the effectiveness of the workshops might be influenced by teaching experience or grade level, but no effects were found.

## Instructional Management

Treatment teachers were rated significantly higher on 5 of the 12 ratings assessing skills in organizing and conducting lessons. Three of these 5 ratings involved teacher clarity in describing lesson objectives, providing explanations, and giving directions for assignments. Lesson objective clarity was demonstrated by either writing objectives on the board or summarizing them in introductions to lessons, and by providing a rationale for material to be learned. Clear explanations were indicated by the teachers' presenting lesson content in a coherent sequence, providing adequate examples, and demonstrating concepts when needed. Clear directions for assignments were indicated by the teachers, who provided step-by-step instructions that were given either verbally (having students repeat them) or by otherwise modeling the steps in completing an assignment. Indirect evidence of lesson clarity was the ease with which students began work and the relative absence of student signs of confusion about what they were to do.

Treatment group teachers also outperformed the control group in lesson pacing and in orchestrating lessons that flowed smoothly from beginning to end. The basic skills needed for the lesson were presented early, before more advanced content was taught. Once students were engaged in the assignment, they were not interrupted frequently by the teacher trying to explain something else. Monitoring student understanding was indi-

Table 2   Means for classroom ratings of teacher behaviors in elementary classrooms

| | Postworkshop 1 | | | | Postworkshop 2 | | | | Main effects[8] | | Interaction[9] |
| | Treatment $n = 14^{7}$ | | Control $n = 15$ | | Treatment $n = 14$ | | Control $n = 15$ | | Grp. | Time | G × T |
| Teacher Behavior | M | SD | M | SD | M | SD | M | SD | | | |
|---|---|---|---|---|---|---|---|---|---|---|---|
| Instructional management | | | | | | | | | | | |
| Describes objectives clearly | 3.99 | 1.25 | 2.94 | 1.22 | 4.02 | 1.13 | 3.03 | 1.09 | ≤.05 | | |
| Variety of materials | 2.05 | 1.17 | 1.74 | .78 | 2.03 | 1.03 | 1.60 | .76 | | | |
| Materials are ready | 4.63 | .49 | 4.20 | 1.09 | 4.50 | .65 | 4.30 | .73 | | | |
| Clear directions for assignments | 4.42 | .63 | 3.90 | .93 | 4.25 | .73 | 3.93 | .62 | ≤.05 | | |
| Waits for attention | 4.32 | .63 | 3.96 | .37 | 4.42 | .49 | 4.00 | .29 | | | |
| Encourages analysis | 3.24 | 1.05 | 2.51 | 1.21 | 3.11 | 1.02 | 2.87 | 1.25 | | | |
| Assignments for different students | 1.48 | 1.07 | 1.35 | .36 | 1.64 | .93 | 1.60 | .85 | | | |
| Appropriate pacing of the lesson | 4.31 | .62 | 3.32 | 1.05 | 4.07 | .87 | 3.67 | .62 | ≤.01 | | |
| Clear explanations | 4.51 | .47 | 3.76 | .79 | 4.25 | .78 | 3.97 | .64 | | ≤.05 | |
| Monitors student understanding | 4.36 | .65 | 3.58 | 1.07 | 4.18 | .70 | 3.97 | .72 | ≤.05 | | |
| Clear standards for academic work | 4.09 | .88 | 3.81 | 1.05 | 4.13 | .79 | 3.69 | .80 | | | |
| Consistently enforces academic work standards | 4.09 | .90 | 3.62 | 1.01 | 4.07 | .81 | 3.80 | .80 | | | |
| Room arrangement | | | | | | | | | | | |
| Suitable traffic patterns | 4.30 | .69 | 4.33 | .64 | 4.04 | .87 | 4.20 | .62 | | | |
| Good visibility | 4.38 | .80 | 4.31 | .63 | 4.29 | .87 | 4.11 | .81 | | | |

| | M | SD | M | SD | M | SD | M | SD | p | |
|---|---|---|---|---|---|---|---|---|---|---|
| **Rules and procedures** | | | | | | | | | | |
| Teacher presents and discusses rules and procedures[a] | 4.11 | 1.05 | 2.38 | 1.51 | — | — | | | ≤.05 | |
| Clear presentations of rules, procedures, and expectations | 4.56 | .88 | 3.00 | 1.58 | — | — | | | ≤.05 | |
| Presentations include statement of rationale for rules and procedures | 3.50 | 2.07 | 2.60 | 1.82 | — | — | | | | |
| Discussion of procedures includes rehearsal and practice | 2.20 | 1.78 | 2.20 | 1.30 | — | — | | | | |
| Teacher provides feedback and review | 2.25 | 1.83 | 1.63 | 1.06 | — | — | | | | |
| Teacher stays in charge of whole class | 5.00 | .00 | 4.72 | .47 | — | — | — | | | |
| Efficient routines | 4.55 | .52 | 3.57 | .92 | 4.45 | .57 | 3.60 | .76 | ≤.05 | |
| Appropriate general procedures | 4.41 | .56 | 3.68 | .72 | 4.45 | .52 | 3.57 | .90 | ≤.001 | |
| Efficient small-group procedures | 4.04 | 1.07 | 2.63 | 1.06 | 4.50 | .76 | 3.50 | 1.04 | ≤.001 | |
| Suitable routines for assigning and checking academic work | 4.20 | .57 | 3.63 | .80 | 4.21 | .51 | 3.97 | .58 | ≤.01 | .07 |
| **Meeting student needs** | | | | | | | | | | |
| Attention spans considered | 4.15 | .59 | 3.43 | .73 | 3.96 | .72 | 3.63 | .77 | ≤.05 | |
| Activities related to students' backgrounds and interests | 3.51 | .72 | 2.96 | .88 | 3.29 | 1.10 | 2.97 | 1.22 | ≤.01 | |

(continued)

Table 2 (continued)

| Teacher Behavior | Postworkshop 1 | | | | Postworkshop 2 | | | | Main effects[8] | | Interaction[9] |
|---|---|---|---|---|---|---|---|---|---|---|---|
| | Treatment n = 14[7] | | Control n = 15 | | Treatment n = 14 | | Control n = 15 | | Grp. | Time | G × T |
| | M | SD | M | SD | M | SD | M | SD | | | |
| Managing student behavior | | | | | | | | | | | |
| Rewards appropriate performance | 3.66 | .97 | 2.77 | .97 | 3.75 | .96 | 3.07 | 1.21 | | ≤.05 | |
| Signals correct behavior | 3.58 | 1.12 | 2.74 | 1.21 | 3.75 | 1.03 | 2.73 | 1.10 | | ≤.01 | |
| Consistency in managing student behavior | 4.40 | .58 | 3.51 | 1.05 | 4.50 | .34 | 3.93 | .68 | | ≤.001 | |
| Effective monitoring | 4.35 | .64 | 3.64 | 1.13 | 4.25 | .47 | 3.77 | .82 | | ≤.05 | |
| Classroom climate | | | | | | | | | | | |
| Task-oriented focus | 4.42 | .56 | 3.83 | .95 | 4.32 | .61 | 4.03 | .79 | | ≤.05 | |
| Relaxed, pleasant atmosphere | 4.46 | .53 | 4.12 | .69 | 4.25 | .83 | 3.97 | 1.01 | | | |
| Teacher uses good listening skills | 4.26 | .63 | 3.82 | .68 | 3.96 | .80 | 3.80 | .94 | | | |
| Expresses feelings | 2.81 | 1.18 | 2.61 | .49 | 2.54 | .46 | 2.57 | .77 | | | |

Note. Means for component ratings are based on 5-point scales: 1 = none, low occurrence, or least characteristic; 5 = high occurrence or most characteristic. Significance levels are based on one-tailed tests.[10]
aThese ratings were made during the 1st week of school only.

cated by the teacher's actively determining how well students were comprehending lesson concepts, directions, or seatwork activities. This procedure could be assessed by frequent questioning during class presentations, quick drills, show of hands with correct answers, patterned turns, or the teacher's circulating widely during seatwork to check students' understanding of the material.

The two groups did not differ in their use or variety of instructional materials or in the degree to which they provided different assignments for various students. Teachers in neither group, however, used a wide variety of instructional materials. They tended instead to rely on a minimum set, such as basal readers, group seatwork assignments copied from the overhead projector, ditto sheets, or commercial workbooks. Under these conditions, the two groups of teachers could have materials ready with little difficulty.

The degree to which teachers waited for student attention was not significantly different between groups, nor was encouraging analyses, reflection, and higher order thinking in their questions. Rather, teachers' questions to students tended to elicit convergent, true-false, or single-word answers. Means for the treatment group were higher for both of these variables, although not significant, indicating that the workshop teachers tended to break this pattern somewhat.

## Room Arrangement

Neither of the items assessing classroom traffic patterns or degree of visibility was significant. These two items require observers to assess the degree to which the arrangement of the desks, chairs, tables, and other furniture in the room did or did not contribute to good traffic flow or helped or hindered students in seeing the instructional displays. The treatment teachers did not differ significantly from the control teachers, possibly because most classes were not crowded and had enough room for students to move about and to recognize their needs.

## Rules and Procedures

Seven of the 10 ratings dealing with the development and implementation of appropriate rules and procedures were significant for the treatment group. These ratings included those that measured implementation and those that measured the maintenance of rules and procedures. I measured the first six items during the first week of school to assess teachers' introduction of rules and procedures and the rehearsal and monitoring of those procedures. The remaining four items were measured throughout the study to assess the effectiveness of the implemented procedures. A large portion of workshop time was devoted to helping teachers plan and outline rules and procedures for the start of school. These data show that the teachers used the experimental management principles to begin their classes more efficiently at the beginning of the year.

The treatment teachers not only began the year with clearer presentations of the rules and procedures, but they also implemented more efficient routines for handling paperwork, keeping records, and checking attendance, which preserved instructional time. General procedures that included restroom use, lining up, coming and going from the room, and using materials and supplies also were more effective in the treatment teachers' classes. These teachers also established efficient means of moving students to and from group areas, attending to students who requested help, minimizing interruptions to group activities, and establishing ways for students outside the reading group to obtain help. Treatment teachers also were rated as having more workable routines for assigning, checking, and collecting student academic work. Their assignments were not only clearer, as was noted in previous ratings, but they had developed efficient procedures for keeping records of assignments, including make-up work for absentees and for collecting, marking, and returning papers.

## Meeting Student Needs

Treatment teachers showed a greater awareness of students' attention levels. The teachers instituted change-of-pace activities rather than allowing activities to continue too long or leaving students with nothing to do. Other evidence of appropriate pacing is shown in one rating in Table 4 [p. 381], indicating less downtime in treatment teachers' classrooms. Consideration of student attention spans was the only one of the four variables that yielded a significant difference between the two groups. There was little or no aggressive student behavior in classes of either group of teachers. Also, levels of student success seemed to be similar in both groups. Observers generally reported difficulty in making this rating. Evidence of students' success was not easy to find. Most students were able to complete assignments and engage in the activities planned by teachers in both groups. The issue was not whether the students were able to do the tasks assigned, but whether they chose to

Table 3 Means for student outcome measures in elementary classrooms

| | Postworkshop 1 | | | | Postworkshop 2 | | | | Main effects | | Interaction |
| | Treatment n = 14 | | Control n = 15 | | Treatment n = 14 | | Control n = 15 | | | | |
| Student outcomes | M | SD | M | SD | M | SD | M | SD | Grp. | Time | G × T |
|---|---|---|---|---|---|---|---|---|---|---|---|
| Student misbehavior | | | | | | | | | | | |
| Amount of disruptive behavior | 1.13 | .29 | 1.32 | .46 | 1.00 | .00 | 1.07 | .26 | | | |
| Amount of inappropriate behavior | 1.69 | .58 | 2.49 | 1.03 | 1.71 | .61 | 1.90 | .60 | ≤.05 | ≤.05 | ≤.05 |
| Stops inappropriate behavior quickly | 3.76 | .87 | 2.85 | 1.00 | 3.89 | 1.38 | 3.00 | 1.39 | ≤.05 | | |
| Ignores inappropriate behavior | 2.19 | 1.03 | 2.74 | .91 | 2.18 | 1.40 | 2.43 | 1.14 | | | |
| Level of student aggression | 1.02 | .08 | 1.03 | .13 | 1.00 | .00 | 1.10 | .28 | | | |
| High degree of student success | 3.82 | .45 | 3.56 | .64 | 3.86 | .82 | 3.57 | .75 | | | |
| Student engagement | | | | | | | | | | | |
| Percentage of students off-task | 3.10 | 2.83 | 12.21 | 14.56 | 3.36 | 4.68 | 6.80 | 7.26 | ≤.05 | .06 | ≤.05 |
| Percentage of students probably on-task | 3.71 | 7.68 | 5.10 | 8.61 | 1.64 | 4.53 | 3.00 | 5.44 | | | |
| Percentage of students on-task | 93.20 | 9.13 | 82.70 | 22.66 | 95.00 | 8.60 | 90.20 | 10.92 | | | |

*Note.* Means for classroom ratings are based on 5-point scales: 1 = none, low occurrence, or least characteristic; 5 = high occurrence or most characteristic. Significance levels are based on one-tailed tests.

engage in them. The degree to which the activities were quality learning experiences for students or just busy work was not always evident to observers.

## Managing Student Behavior

All four variables composing observers' assessments of the teachers' behavior management strategies were significant in favor of the treatment teachers. The teachers rewarded appropriate performance by frequently using praise and encouragement, displaying student work, and allowing privileges more frequently. They also used signals to cue correct behavior, such as a bell to begin an activity, and alerted students as to what was expected of them before beginning an activity. Treatment teachers also were more consistent and predictable in managing student behavior (i.e., they seldom permitted a behavior on one occasion only to disapprove of it on another). They also monitored more frequently and were more aware of what was occurring in class. The teachers avoided becoming so engrossed in helping a particular student that they lost sight of the class.

## Classroom Climate

Treatment group teachers had more task-oriented classrooms. Evidence of this finding is given in Table 3, which shows a lower incidence of inappropriate and off-task behavior.

## Student Outcomes

### Student Misbehavior

Student misbehavior was distinguished in two ways: (a) *disruptive,* meaning that a student's behavior was distracting to others and interfered with class activities, or (b) *inappropriate,* meaning that, although the student did not disturb others, he or she was not engaged in the assigned task (Table 3). Inappropriate behavior could be manifested as inattention, uncooperativeness, wandering around the room, or quiet socializing. Amounts of student disruptive behavior were low for both groups. Average ratings were near 1.00, meaning none. Although disruptive behavior was practically nonexistent, inappropriate behavior occurred in greater amounts in the control group. The inappropriate behavior that occurred in the treatment group classes was stopped quickly. Also, inappropriate behavior diminished in time in the control teachers' classrooms, suggesting that these teachers began to solve the problem

of order and inattention well into the second month of the school year. The workshop teachers had low amounts of inappropriate behavior from the beginning of the year.

## Student Engagement

Treatment group teachers had fewer students off-task during the first weeks of school and had correspondingly more students on-task, although the on-task differences were not significant. Off-task behavior in the control group reached 12.2%, indicating that 3 to 4 students in an average class of 26 students were unengaged at any one observational point in time; whereas in the treatment group classes, 1 student might be off-task during alternate observations. This difference does not suggest that the classrooms of the control group were chaotic. If these conditions persist through the year, however, the teacher will be confronted with a nagging student attentional problem that will eventually take its toll on class climate.

## Differences across Time

I examined these differences, as previously stated, to determine whether the classroom management skills that the teachers learned and implemented during the first weeks of school would sustain from the first of the year to November and to discover if the second workshop was effective in helping to sustain them. Only three of the ratings showed trends across time for the two groups, although none reached significance. Control group teachers improved their procedures for moving students in and out of small groups as the year progressed, and inappropriate behavior decreased in the control group. Additionally, the percentage of students off-task decreased in the control teachers' classroom. On the other hand, the treatment teachers began with less off-task and inappropriate behavior and maintained this level.

There were two interactions between group membership and time: (a) for amount of inappropriate behavior and (b) for percentage of students off-task. There was large variability in the control group in student off-task behavior. This variability decreased after the second workshop, but remained relatively unchanged in the treatment teachers' classrooms from the beginning of school. Mean scores for control teachers ranged from 5% to 58% of students off-task between the first and second workshops, whereas means for the treatment group ranged from 0% to 9%. The improvement in the control group from the first to the second data collection period was chiefly in the classes with the highest off-task rates. For example, the teacher whose class had a mean of 58% students off-task at the beginning of school reduced this number to 20% by the end of data collection.

## Summary Observer Ratings

Summary ratings were filled out after observers had completed all observations in each classroom. Of the 28 rating categories, 14% (4) were significant at $p \leq .05$, and 14%. (4) were significant at $p \leq .10$ (see Table 4).[11] Based on the ratings, treatment teachers and their classrooms were more prepared for the start of school. Teachers who participated in the workshops managed instructional activities more effectively by planning enough work for students, minimizing downtime, orchestrating more efficient transitions, and helping students become accountable for academic work. Observers also rated treatment group teachers as more confident and enthusiastic.

## Discussion

This study investigated three key questions: (a) whether participation in classroom management workshops would enhance teachers' organizational and management skills in comparison with an untrained control group, (b) whether district personnel could be trained to deliver the workshops and conduct observations in classrooms, and (c) whether the training procedures effective in secondary classrooms (Evertson, 1985) also would be effective in elementary classrooms. The answer to all three questions appears to be yes.

Not only did the treatment group exceed the control group on a majority of the observational measures, but this study also supports the earlier finding that school personnel can design and carry out similar professional development workshops effectively. Also, the availability of colleagues who are on-site and available to consult, as well as to provide training, can increase the likelihood that skills are maintained. More important, ongoing professional development can be enhanced by building the capacity for teacher assistance within schools.

The patterns of findings in this study are similar to those obtained in the secondary classrooms (Evertson, 1985). In both studies, treatment teachers had lower off-task rates, less inappropriate behavior, and were able to plan and implement routines that helped the year to begin effectively. Sixteen of the variables measured in both studies were significant for elementary and secondary treatment teachers. Ten of these variables dealt with instructional management, such as describing lesson objectives, appropriate pacing, clear explanations, monitoring students, and suitable routines and procedures. One variable also dealt with consistency in managing behavior. Three variables from the summary ratings (classroom readiness, efficient transitions, and student accountability for work) and two variables measuring student behavior (percentage of students off-task and amount of inappropriate behavior) also were significant in both studies.

A few variables were significant in the secondary but not the elementary study. In secondary classrooms, control of student movement in the class, the teachers' conveying the value of the curriculum, and student avoidance of seatwork were significant. Variables measured in the elementary study, but not the secondary study, were ratings assessing the implementation of rules and procedures during the first week of school and efficiency of small-group procedures. The remaining variables that were significant in one study but not the other do not appear to change the basic pattern of findings.

The efficacy of the workshops most likely lies in two areas. First, none of the concepts or techniques was new to the teachers. However, opportunities to examine their own practices and to apply labels to these practices appeared to serve as a catalyst for change. Second, once teachers could realize the need for critical examination and problem solving, they sought the opportunity to get suggestions from peers to help themselves structure activities and routines. Teachers also reported that these experiences helped them to view their teaching in a new way. On several occasions, trainers reported that treatment teachers commented that they had used many of the techniques and suggestions in the workshops at some time. This use was not systematic, because they

Table 4   Treatment and control group comparisons for summary observer ratings of elementary classrooms

| | Treatment n = 14 | | Control n = 15 | | |
|---|---|---|---|---|---|
| | M | SD | M | SD | p ≤ |
| **Teacher behavior** | | | | | |
| Organizing activities and physical space | | | | | |
| Good use of classroom space | 4.38 | .77 | 4.13 | .92 | |
| Teacher is prepared for school | 4.84 | .38 | 4.33 | .72 | ≤.05 |
| Classroom is prepared for school | 4.54 | .88 | 4.07 | .88 | .09 |
| Handling student problems during seatwork | | | | | |
| Teacher ignores "come-ups" | 1.42 | .79 | 1.60 | .91 | |
| Teacher sends "come-ups" back to seats | 2.08 | 1.31 | 2.00 | 1.20 | |
| Teacher answers "come-ups" questions | 4.83 | .39 | 4.60 | .74 | |
| Managing instructional activities | | | | | |
| Teacher plans enough work for students | 5.00 | .00 | 4.53 | .64 | ≤.01 |
| Teacher allows activities to go on too long; students are bored | 1.92 | .95 | 2.13 | .92 | |
| Assignments are too hard | 1.69 | 1.11 | 1.73 | .96 | |
| Assignments are too short and easy | 1.08 | .28 | 1.20 | .41 | |
| Minimum of down time waiting for next assignment | 4.38 | .96 | 3.73 | .96 | ≤.05 |
| Efficient transitions | 4.58 | .86 | 4.00 | 1.07 | .07 |
| Dealing with misbehavior | | | | | |
| Teacher stops disruptive behavior quickly | 4.84 | .38 | 4.60 | .74 | |
| Monitoring and maintaining accountability | | | | | |
| Teacher checks for understanding | 4.54 | .52 | 4.20 | .86 | |
| Teacher keeps students responsible for academic work | 4.62 | .65 | 3.86 | 1.07 | ≤.05 |
| Teacher leaves room often | 1.08 | .28 | 1.07 | .26 | |
| Personal characteristics | | | | | |
| Teacher is confident | 4.54 | .78 | 4.00 | 1.20 | .10 |
| Teacher is warm and pleasant | 4.38 | .77 | 4.07 | 1.10 | |
| Teacher is enthusiastic | 4.38 | .65 | 3.87 | 1.06 | .07 |
| **Student behavior** | | | | | |
| Engagement in tasks | | | | | |
| Students wander around the room | 1.85 | 1.07 | 2.33 | 1.23 | |
| Students talk during seatwork | 3.00 | .71 | 3.27 | .88 | |
| Class gets out of hand | 1.54 | 1.13 | 1.93 | 1.28 | |
| High noise level | 1.92 | 1.12 | 2.00 | 1.07 | |
| Students begin work quickly without dawdling | 4.54 | .66 | 4.40 | .74 | |
| Obtaining help on assignments | | | | | |
| Students come up for help frequently | 2.00 | 1.00 | 2.47 | 1.25 | |
| Students leave desks to get help | 2.00 | .91 | 2.07 | .80 | |
| Students raise hands to get help | 4.46 | .66 | 4.33 | .72 | |
| Students call out for help | 2.08 | .86 | 1.87 | .92 | |

*Note.* These items were based on 5-point scales: 1 = low occurrence or least characteristic; 5 = high occurrence or most characteristic. Significance levels are based on one-tailed tests.

would try one technique and then another without understanding how they fit into a total organizational framework. The content of the workshops, however, provided the teachers with rationales and a framework that could serve as a guide in setting goals and making the moment-to-moment decisions necessary in daily teaching tasks.

The improvement in the control group bears some discussion. In the final interviews with the observers, I discovered that the control teachers were interacting with the workshop teachers in their schools, looking at their classroom displays (e.g., posted rules), and borrowing techniques to use in their own classrooms. For example, charts and materials that were in the workshop teachers' classrooms began to appear in the control teachers' classrooms. Because these were rural schools, the teachers knew one another fairly well, and although the workshop teachers indicated that they did not share the information directly, some of the new techniques were observable by the other teachers and became part of the talk in the hallways and the teachers' lounge. Control group teachers also learned that inappropriate and off-task behavior were two of the key areas that observers were seeking in class observations. Some control group teachers reported that they told their students to be on their good behavior when the observer was in the room.

By mid-October and early November, the control teachers tended to improve, whereas workshop group teachers tended to stay the same or drop slightly on some of the measures. These findings suggest that at least one advantage of the before-school workshop was that the treatment group teachers achieved an "edge" in getting routines and expectations established and socializing students into the needed procedures. Control group teachers who started out having the greatest problems with off-task and inappropriate behavior were able to maintain control in their classes, but only at the expense of 2½ months of the school year.

This study supports the proposition that giving teachers opportunities to plan and develop academic and administrative routines that keep students productively engaged and keep inappropriate behavior to a minimum results in preserving instructional time. Thus, solving managerial and organizational problems at the beginning of the year is essential in laying the groundwork for quality learning opportunities for students.

# References

ANDERSON, L. M., EVERTSON, C. M., & BROPHY, J. E. (1979). An experimental study of effective teaching in first-grade reading groups. *Elementary School Journal, 79,* 193–223.

BORG, W., & ASCIONE, R. (1982). Classroom management in elementary mainstreaming classrooms. *Journal of Educational Research, 74,* 85–95.

BROPHY, J. E. (1982). Supplemental group management techniques. In D. Duke (Ed.), *Helping teachers manage classrooms.* Alexandria, VA: ASCD.

BROPHY, J. E., & EVERTSON, C. M. (1976). *Learning from teaching: A developmental perspective.* Boston, MA: Allyn & Bacon.

BROPHY, J. E., & GOOD, T. L. (1986). Teacher behavior and student achievement. In M. C. Wittrock (Ed.), *The handbook of research on teaching* (pp. 328–375). New York: Macmillan.

EMMER, E. T., EVERTSON, C. M., & ANDERSON, L. M. (1980). Effective classroom management at the beginning of the school year. *Elementary School Journal, 80,* 219–231.

EMMER, E. T., SANFORD, J. P., CLEMENTS, B. S., & MARTIN, J. (1983, March). *Improving junior high classroom management.* Paper presented at the annual meeting of the American Educational Research Association, Montreal.

EVERTSON, C. M. (1985). Training teachers in classroom management: An experimental study in secondary school classrooms. *Journal of Educational Research, 79,* 51–57.

EVERTSON, C. M., ANDERSON, C. W., ANDERSON, L. M., & BROPHY, J. E. (1980). Relationships between classroom behaviors and student outcomes in junior high mathematics and English classes. *American Educational Research Journal, 17,* 43–60.

EVERTSON, C. M., & EMMER, E. T. (1982). Effective management at the beginning of the school year in junior high classes. *Journal of Educational Psychology, 74,* 485–498.

EVERTSON, C. M., EMMER, E. T., CLEMENTS, B. S., SANFORD, J. P., & WORSHAM, M. E. (1981). *Organizing and managing the elementary school classroom.* Austin, TX: Research and Development Center for Teacher Education, The University of Texas.

EVERTSON, C. M., EMMER, E. T., SANFORD, J. P., & CLEMENTS, B. S. (1983). Improving classroom management: An experiment in elementary school classrooms. *Elementary School Journal, 84,* 173–188.

FISHER, C., BERLINER, D., FILBY, N., MARLIAVE, R., CAHEN, L., & DISHAW, M. (1977). Teaching behaviors, academic learning time, and student achievement: An overview. In C. Denham & A. Lieberman (Eds.), *Time to learn* (pp. 7–32). Washington, DC: National Institute of Education.

FREDERICK, C. W., & WALBERG, H. J. (1980). Learning as a function of time. *Journal of Educational Research, 73,* 183–194.

MEDLEY, D. (1977). *Teacher competence and teacher effectiveness: A review of process-product research.* Washington, DC: American Association of Colleges for Teacher Education.

STALLINGS, J. A. (1980). Allocated academic learning time revisited, or beyond time on task. *Educational Researcher, 9,* 11–16.

# Critical Review

This research report describes one of several studies that evaluated the effectiveness of a training program to improve teachers' classroom management. The program includes two in-service workshops that cover the content of a manual on classroom management written by Carolyn Evertson and her colleagues.

A basic purpose of program evaluation is to generate information that helps educators make decisions about programs. As noted in Evertson's comments, the study was sponsored in part by the Arkansas Department of General Education to help decide whether to disseminate the program throughout the state. For this reason we classify the study as an instance of program evaluation.

Program evaluations can employ a variety of quantitative and qualitative research designs. Evertson chose a quantitative experimental design in which teachers were randomly assigned to an experimental group (training provided) or a control group (no training). This is a powerful research design because it can demonstrate cause-and-effect relationships between variables.

Evertson's experiment demonstrated that the treatment variable (the training program) had an effect on instructional management variables. Because the experiment demonstrated a cause-and-effect relationship between the treatment variable and the other variables, policymakers have reason to be confident that if they sponsor these workshops, improvements in teachers' instructional management will occur.

The validity of Evertson's experiment would have been weakened if certain factors had not been controlled. For example, if the treatment group teachers had had more teaching experience than the control group teachers, policymakers would not know whether the treatment group's superior performance was due to their participation in the training program or to their teaching experience. Evertson avoided this problem by first matching the teachers on critical demographic variables and then randomly assigning them to treatment and control groups.

Table 1 of her article indicates that this procedure succeeded in matching the two groups in years of teaching experience. However, the procedure did not completely equate the groups. For example, more teachers in the treatment group had classrooms with low achievement levels, whereas more teachers in the control group had classrooms with high achievement levels. This imbalance possibly affected the results, but it did not invalidate Evertson's conclusions because it is probably at least as difficult, if not more so, to manage a low-achieving class than to manage a high-achieving class. Thus, the fact that the treatment group teachers had more low-achieving students but also outperformed the control group probably means that the training program is even more effective than the results indicate.

We also need to consider the possible influence of school characteristics. When experimental and control classes are drawn from different schools, differences between the schools in such factors as social climate and the principal's leadership style can influence the research results. The result is that policymakers do not know whether the training program or school factors account for the superior performance of the treatment group.

Evertson avoided this problem by drawing her treatment and control teachers from the same schools. However, this procedure may create another problem. Teachers in the control group may obtain training materials and information from teachers in the experimental group and use them in their own classrooms. The control group teachers consequently may show gains on the outcome measures, and thus make the training program look less effective than it really is.

Communication between experimental and control teachers in the same school is difficult to avoid in experiments, especially if the treatment is perceived by teachers to be good. Evertson reported that this situation occurred in her experiment. Therefore, the difference between experimental and control group teachers on the instructional management measures probably was smaller than if the control group teachers knew nothing about the training program. If policymakers understand this phenomenon, they will realize that the program is even more effective than the results indicate, and consequently they will make better policy decisions about its implementation.

All the teachers who participated in the field study were volunteers. People who volunteer for an experiment are usually different from nonvolunteers. Therefore, we cannot generalize Evertson's results with confidence to all elementary teachers. Her results can be generalized, however, to teachers who volunteer for in-service education. Because many in-service programs are offered on a voluntary basis, using volunteers in this evaluation study seems appropriate.

District personnel served as workshop trainers in the experiment. This procedure has the advantage of representing the usual practice in many school districts. The practice is usual because it is much less expensive than using external trainers. If Evertson had instead used external trainers and found that the program was effective, policymakers would be in a quandary. They either would have to help districts find money to hire external trainers or they could allow districts to use in-house trainers but be uncertain whether instructional outcomes similar to those observed in the experiment would occur.

Evertson's data analyses focused on tests of statistical significance for differences between the treatment and control groups on instructional management measures, shown in Tables 2, 3, and 4. Tests of statistical significance are used frequently by researchers to determine whether results can be generalized from their small sample to the total population represented by the sample. Policymakers, however, are more likely to be interested in the practical significance of program evaluation findings than in statistical significance. Procedures for determining the practical significance of research results are discussed in Chapter 8.

Finally, in judging the merits of this program evaluation, we must consider the fact that the evaluator (Carolyn Evertson) was also one of the principal developers of the program being evaluated. This is customary in education, but in other fields such as medicine and industry, an independent agency often does the evaluation studies.

Education is probably different for two reasons. First, there are virtually no legislative regulations for how educational programs are to be evaluated, or even that they be evaluated. Second, there is little money for evaluation. Most funds are appropriated for development and dissemination. Therefore, if evaluation studies are done at all, they usually are done by persons with a strong vested interest in the program. These persons tend to be members of the development team who also have research expertise. This was true of Evertson.

The results of a program evaluation study are not invalid simply because a developer conducted the study. It just means that the readers of the report need to be alert for signs of bias. For example, the evaluator can show bias by including only measures that will show favorable results for the program. In the case of Evertson's study, this bias seems unlikely because she included a wide range of outcome measures and because her results did not uniformly favor the training program.

# Chapter References

AMERICAN SCHOOL BOARD JOURNAL. (1975). How to tell whether your schools are being gypped. *The American School Board Journal, 162,* 38–40.

BERRETH, D. (1988). Association for Supervision and Curriculum Development. In *Encyclopedia of school administration & supervision,* eds. R. A. Gorton, G. T. Schneider, & J. C. Fisher. Phoenix, AZ: Oryx.

DICK, W., & CAREY, L. (1985). *The systematic design of instruction,* 2nd ed. Glenview, IL: Scott, Foresman.

DRIGGERS, J., & WRIGHT, R. N. (1989). *Impact assessment of Life Management Curriculum* (ED 324 249). Sacramento: California Community Colleges.

EISNER, E. W. (1979). *The educational imagination: On the design and evaluation of school programs.* New York: Macmillan.

EVERTSON, C. M. (1989). Improving elementary classroom management: A school-based training program for beginning the year. *Journal of Educational Research, 83*(2), 82–90.

GALL, M. D., & GALL, J. P. (1991). *Study for success teacher's manual,* 4th ed. Eugene, OR: M. Damien.

HOUSE, E. R. (1990). Trends in evaluation. *Educational Researcher, 19*(3), 24–28.

JOHNSON, D. M., & SMITH, B. (1987). An evaluation of Saxon's algebra text. *Journal of Educational Research, 81,* 97–102.

JOINT COMMITTEE ON STANDARDS FOR EDUCATIONAL EVALUATION. (1981). *Standards for evaluations of educational programs, projects, and materials.* New York: McGraw-Hill.

KAUFMAN, R., & THIAGARAJAN, S. (1987). Identifying and specifying requirements for instruction. In *Instructional technology foundations,* ed. R. M. Gagné. Hillsdale, NJ: Erlbaum.

LEVIN, H. M. (1983) *Cost effectiveness: A primer. Vol. 4, New perspectives in evaluation.* Beverly Hills, CA: Sage, 1983.

MILLER, C. D., MILLER, L. F., & ROSEN, L. A. (1988). Modified reciprocal teaching in a regular classroom. *Journal of Experimental Education, 56*(4), 183–186.

NATIONAL ASSESSMENT GOVERNING BOARD. (1991). *Looking at how well our students read: The 1992 National Assessment of Educational Progress in reading.* Washington, DC: National Assessment Governing Board.

NEWMANN, F. M. (1990). A test of higher-order thinking in social studies: Persuasive writing on constitutional issues using the NAEP approach. *Social Education, 54*(6), 369–373.

OFFICE OF EDUCATIONAL RESEARCH AND IMPROVEMENT. (1991). *Mathematics education programs that work.* Washington, DC: U.S. Department of Education.

OTTERBOURG, S. D. (1990). *Partnerships in education: Measuring their success.* Paper presented at the annual meeting of the American Educational Research Association, Boston, MA.

PRATTON, J., & HALES, L. W. (1986). The effects of active participation on student learning. *Journal of Educational Research, 79,* 210–215.

ROSSETT, A. (1987). *Training needs assessment.* Englewood Cliffs, NJ: Educational Technology Publications.

SCRIVEN, M. (1967). The methodology of evaluation. In *Curriculum evaluation,* ed. R. E. Stake. Chicago: Rand McNally.

SCRIVEN, M. (1973). Goal-free evaluation. In *School evaluation: The politics and process,* ed. E. R. House. Berkeley, CA: McCutchan.

SIROTNIK, K. A. (1983). What you see is what you get: Consistency, persistency, and mediocrity in classrooms. *Harvard Educational Review, 53*(1), 16–31.

WEST, M., & WEST, M. (1992). *Report on the evaluation of the "Study for Success" study skills program.* Unpublished paper for Dr. Kenneth Kempner as part of the requirements for the course on program evaluation, University of Oregon, Fall 1991.

# Recommended Reading

EVALUATION COMMENT AND CRESST LINE NEWSLETTER.

*Evaluation Comment* is a new semiannual publication prepared by the Center for the Study of Evaluation at UCLA and the National Center for Research on Evaluation, Standards and Student Testing (CRESST). Each issue of *CRESST Line* has articles on selected events and topics relating to evaluation theory, procedures, methodologies, and practice. Both publications are available from the UCLA Graduate School of Education, 15 Moore Hall, 405 Hilgard Avenue, Los Angeles, CA 90024–1522.

HOUSE, E. R. (1990). Trends in evaluation. *Educational Researcher, 19*(3), 24–28.

This article provides a historical overview of the issues and trends in educational evaluation over the past 20 years, including the debate between quantitatively and qualitatively oriented evaluation research, the effects of values and politics in evaluation, and the utilization of evaluation findings.

JOHNSON, D. E., MEILLER, L. R., MILLER, L. C., & SUMMERS, G. F., eds. (1987). *Needs assessment: Theory and methods*. Ames: Iowa State University Press.

The papers in this compilation discuss the political and social contexts of needs assessment in education and the social sciences and describe examples of U.S. and international needs assessment studies.

JOINT COMMITTEE ON STANDARDS FOR EDUCATIONAL EVALUATION. (1981). Standards for evaluations of educational programs, projects, and materials. New York: McGraw-Hill.

This book-length report provides 30 standards for judging the quality of educational evaluations and case studies that illustrate each standard. It was developed by representatives of 12 important educational organizations.

LEVIN, H. M. (1983). *Cost-effectiveness: A primer. Vol. 4, New perspectives in evaluation*. Beverly Hills, CA: Sage.

This book provides a systematic introduction to the use of cost analysis in educational evaluation, including a discussion of the nature and use of cost-analytic tools and guidelines for planning and implementing a cost-effectiveness analysis.

LINCOLN, Y. S., & GUBA, E. G. (1985). *Naturalistic inquiry*. Beverly Hills, CA: Sage.

The authors pose a naturalistic research paradigm to replace the positivistic, quantitative research paradigm, which they claim is not appropriate in the social sciences.

OFFICE OF EDUCATIONAL RESEARCH AND IMPROVEMENT. (1991) *Mathematics education programs that work*. Washington, DC: U.S. Department of Education.

This catalog contains descriptions of 18 exemplary mathematics education programs in the National Diffusion Network (NDN). Exemplary programs are programs that have been reviewed and approved by the U.S. Department of Education's Program Effectiveness Panel (which was called the Joint Dissemination Review Panel prior to 1987). The catalog provides a one-page description of each program, including target audience, evidence of program effectiveness, training costs and requirements, services available from program developers, and whom to contact for more information.

PATTON, M. Q. (1987). *How to use qualitative methods in evaluation*. Newbury Park, CA: Sage.

This introduction to qualitative methods of data collection provides guidelines on the design of qualitative studies in education and on the analysis and interpretation of qualitative data. It includes a useful discussion of issues to consider in determining when to use qualitative methods in educational research.

ROSSETT, A. (1987). *Training needs assessment*. Englewood Cliffs, NJ: Educational Technology Publications.

This book provides a description of various needs assessment techniques and supporting tools.

STUFFLEBEAM, D. L., & WELCH, W. L. (1986). Review of research on program evaluation in United States school districts. *Educational Administration Quarterly, 22,* 150–170.

This review of the literature on school district evaluation is a useful guide for answering six questions that an educator needs to consider in utilizing evaluations of an educational program: (1) What gets evaluated? (2) What are the purposes of the evaluation? (3) What methodological approaches are used? (4) Who are the participants? (5) How is the evaluation organized and funded? (6) How are the evaluation findings utilized, and what factors affect their utilization?

WORTHEN, B. R., & SANDERS, J. R. (1987). *Educational evaluation: Alternative approaches and practical guidelines*. White Plains, NY: Longman.

A comprehensive guide to the conduct of project evaluations, this book is also a helpful reference for school administrators responsible for evaluating educational programs. It has matrices explaining different approaches to evaluation as well as checklists, forms, application exercises, and a discussion of situations in which evaluations should and should not be conducted.

# Application Problems

1. A school district curriculum coordinator is preparing a proposal for state funding to start a study skills program. In preparing the budget, he must decide how much money, if any, should be spent on program evaluation. He realizes that the less spent on evaluation, the more money available for program operations. What arguments could you present in favor of allocating at least 10 percent of the total budget for program evaluation?
2. A curriculum developer plans to test a set of self-instructional materials designed to improve the writing skills of college freshmen. List five questions the developer might want the pilot test to answer concerning the materials.
3. An education professor at a nearby university has been asked by an elementary school principal to conduct an evaluation of his school. When the professor asks the principal what it is about the school that he wishes to evaluate, he responds, "I'm not sure; what do you usually evaluate?" If you were the professor, how would you respond to this question?
4. A program has one stated goal—to train high school students who do not know how to swim to swim freestyle two lengths of an Olympic-size pool. Say that you are a "goal-free" evaluator who is called in to evaluate the program's success. How would you approach the task of evaluation?
5. Suppose that you were part of an evaluation team that had been asked to evaluate a classroom management program, similar to the one described in the Evertson study, that was ready to be implemented in the elementary schools of a nearby school district. List four types of stakeholders whom you would seek to include in the evaluation and a possible concern each might have that could be investigated in the evaluation.

# Chapter Notes

1. The abstract of the article is reprinted here to help you understand the researcher's comments.
2. This commentary was written by Carolyn Evertson.
3. The procedure of forming matched pairs and then assigning the members of each pair randomly to treatment and control groups ensured that these two groups were equivalent in the factors of teaching experience, student ability, and grade level. Thus, any observed differences between the two groups could be attributed to the treatment rather than to these factors.
4. Reliability in this context means the degree to which any two trained observers could be expected to make the same ratings of a teacher's behavior.
5. Analysis of variance is a statistical procedure to determine the likelihood that a difference between two or more groups in a sample would also be found if the researcher studied the entire population. In this case the researcher made two comparisons on each measure: (1) treatment group versus control group; (2) all teachers after the first workshop versus all teachers after the second workshop.
6. If a difference between groups is statistically significant, it means that we can generalize

beyond this sample and conclude that a similar difference would be found in other groups that are like this sample.

7.  The symbol $n$ represents the number of teachers; $M$ represents the mean score; and $SD$ represents the standard deviation, which is a measure of how much the scores vary around the mean score.

8.  The main effects are the two comparisons made in the analysis of variance (see note 5): treatment group versus control group and all teachers after the first workshop versus all teachers after the second workshop. Any main effect that has a value of .05 or less is statistically significant.

9.  In addition to identifying main effects, analysis of variance also identifies interaction effects. In this case there would be an interaction effect if the treatment group made a different amount of change from postworkshop 1 to postworkshop 2. The only difference that approached statistical significance (.07 is close to .05, which is the minimal value that is usually considered to reflect a significant difference) is use of efficient small-group procedures. The control group made more change (from 2.63 to 3.50) than did the treatment group (4.04 to 4.50).

10. When using a one-tailed test of statistical significance the researcher predicts that if a difference is found, it will be in a particular direction (e.g., the treatment group will outperform the control group). When using a two-tailed test the researcher does not predict which group will outperform the other. A comparison of two groups on a measure is more likely to yield a statistically significant result if it is subjected to a one-tailed test.

11. A $p$ value usually must be .05 or lower for a research finding to be considered statistically significant. If the researcher is using exploratory measures, however, $p$ values between .10 and .06 sometimes are considered statistically significant. Further research is desirable, though, to determine whether the result represents a real difference in the population or just a chance difference in this particular sample.

# CHAPTER 15

# ACTION RESEARCH

## Overview

This chapter describes the benefits of doing action research to deal with problems or to answer questions that arise in your work. Several examples of actual action research projects are presented as well as procedures for doing your own projects. The chapter includes a published study that demonstrates how this method can benefit not only the practitioners who carry out the research but also their colleagues and the students whom they serve.

## Objectives

1. Describe the advantages of conducting action research as a basis for solving an educational problem.
2. Explain the steps in action research and describe how they might be carried out to solve an educational problem of concern to you.
3. Describe nine differences between formal research and action research.
4. Describe the situations in which action research is appropriate and the conditions necessary for carrying it out.

## Purpose of Action Research

There are two main ways to use research to help you make decisions as an educator. One way is to review the research literature relevant to your needs and then apply the findings. The other way is to do an action research study of your own. Action research has been defined as "research carried out by practitioners with a view to improving their professional practice and understanding it better" (Cameron-Jones, 1983). The purpose of this chapter is to demonstrate the feasibility of doing your own action research. You may discover that you or your colleagues already have carried out action research without necessarily calling it by that name and that it has in fact improved your effectiveness.

The term *action research* can be traced back to the social psychologist Kurt Lewin (1946), who discussed the importance of action research in the social sciences. He emphasized the need to study the conditions for promoting positive social change. For example, in a study conducted during World War II, Lewin brought together groups of housewives to discuss the possible use of organ meats in meal preparation. This was during a time of shortage in normal meat supplies, when the U.S. government wanted to promote cheaper cuts of meat. The study demonstrates the value of group discussion in changing people's attitudes about, and subsequent actions toward, a significant social issue.

Lewin saw action research as a key element in improving methods for solving societal problems. Widely used in the 1940s and 1950s, action research declined in the 1960s as research came to be equated primarily with laboratory-based experimentation and statistical significance testing, and thus became separated from practice. Australia and Great Britain brought action research back to the fore in the 1970s, and they continue to utilize this approach extensively. Today action research has a small but growing foothold in educational practice in the United States.

Action research has at least five advantages for education professionals. First, it contributes to the theory and knowledge base needed for enhancing practice. For example, many schoolteachers seek to supplement the knowledge obtained from their preservice training and their personal teaching experience by attending professional conferences and reading selected education reports. However, the findings from research are often difficult to understand or not directly applicable to practice. As a result, reported research findings generally have little or no direct influence on the everyday work of educators. When educators carry out their own action research, they learn to reconstruct educational theory in terms that are understandable to them and to develop more effective practices in their work settings.

Second, action research supports the professional development of practitioners by helping them become more competent in understanding and utilizing research findings and in carrying out research themselves when appropriate. By carrying out action research, practitioners not only develop needed skills in doing research but also improve their ability to read, interpret, and apply the research of others.

Third, action research builds a collegial networking system. Action research often involves several educators working together; students and parents also may be involved. The communication network that develops during the research project helps reduce the isolation often experienced by individual teachers, administrators, or specialists. The improved communication patterns foster both support and sharing of information among practitioners, and thus continue to benefit both staff and students over time.

Fourth, action research helps practitioners identify problems and seek solutions in a systematic fashion. It requires practitioners to define their problem thoroughly, to identify and try out possible solutions systematically, and to reflect on and share the results of their efforts. Simmons (1984) found that teachers who had participated in a year-long action research experience as part of a graduate degree program reported numerous benefits for their teaching, including changes in their actual classroom practices, in their thinking skills, and in their attitudes toward the need for their own continuing education.

Fifth, action research can be used at all levels and in all areas of education. It can be carried out at the classroom level, schoolwide, throughout a school district, or even statewide. Stevens (1986), for example, describes the benefits of action research as a means of in-service training for principals. Goodlad (1983), arguing that the individual school building is the key unit for educational reform, describes effective schools as those that evaluate programs, examine alternative procedures, and have a faculty willing to try new ideas. The areas that Goodlad describes can all be promoted by action research.

# The Steps in Action Research

Several models for action research, specifying only a few simple steps, have been developed. For example, Perry-Sheldon and Allain (1987) describe four steps (reconnaissance, plan, act, and reflect), and Wood (1988) defines four distinct "moments" of the process (plan, act, observe, and reflect).

In this chapter we use a more comprehensive set of seven steps, for two reasons: (1) to make the description of this research method more comparable to that of the formal research methods covered in earlier chapters of this book and (2) to cover the various aspects of action research that different proponents of this approach have identified. The seven steps of action research are as follows: (1) defining the problem, (2) selecting a design, (3) selecting a sample, (4) selecting measures, (5) analyzing the data, (6) interpreting and applying the findings, and (7) reporting the findings. We will explain the steps by presenting three examples of actual action research projects. The examples illustrate the different contexts in which action research can be used, the various types of educators who do it, and the wide range in the types of problems that can be addressed.

# Examples of Action Research

## EXAMPLE 1. DETERMINING COMMON STUDENT CONCERNS RELATED TO STUDY

**Summary.**    Two of the authors (Joyce and Meredith Gall) asked teachers who participated in our study skills instruction workshops to send us the results of administering a checklist of students' concerns. Responses were tallied for each classroom, and the concerns most commonly checked by elementary, middle/junior high, and high school students were identified.

*1. Define the problem.* We have offered teacher workshops on study skills instruction for several years. In our workshops we had given teachers a 14-item checklist they could use to assess their students' most common concerns about study and schoolwork. We now wished to determine what concerns were most common among elementary, middle, and high school students who responded to the checklist. We thought that it would be useful to include this information when presenting the checklist to teachers in the future and that it would help us decide which aspects of study skills instruction to emphasize in our workshops.

*2. Select a design.* In every workshop or course that we conduct, we administer the checklist to participants (who are primarily teachers) and recommend that they in turn administer the checklist to their own students. We decided to conduct a survey by asking the teachers to send us their results. We promised to compile the results for students at each school level—elementary, middle/junior high, and high school—and to forward them to all teachers who participated in the survey.

*3. Select a sample.* The volunteer sample consisted of all teachers who participated in our courses and workshops over a one-year period and who accepted our invitation to send us the results of their administration of the checklist to their classes. After about eight months we had received usable responses from five classrooms in four elementary schools, nine classrooms in four middle schools, and seven classrooms in three high schools. Most of the schools were in Oregon, where we live, but there were also schools in Canada and Panama.

*4. Select measures.* The primary measuring instrument was the Checklist of Student Concerns, from the Study for Success teacher's manual (Gall & Gall, 1991). Each student who responds to the checklist is asked to check the 5 items (out of 14 that are listed) of most concern. Each teacher had received a copy of the checklist in our in-services on study skills instruction and had been encouraged to make copies to administer to their students. We gave the teachers self-addressed return envelopes. We asked them to send us their students' responses to the checklist along with an indication of the number of students, their grade level, and the subject of the class in which the checklist was administered.

*5. Analyze the data.* We calculated the percentage of students in each classroom who checked each of the 14 items by dividing the number of students checking that item by the total number of students who had filled out the checklist. We ranked the items for each classroom, the item checked most often receiving a rank of 1, the item checked next most often receiving a rank of 2, and so forth. We then made a master ranking of the items checked most often by elementary, middle, and high school students by averaging the rankings across all the classrooms at each level, weighted by the number of students responding in each classroom.

The top three concerns for elementary students were (1) getting nervous about a test coming up, (2) not understanding what the teacher talked about in class, and (3) coming across words in their reading that they don't understand. The top three concerns for middle or junior high school students were (1) feeling too tired to study, (2) getting nervous about a test coming up, and (3) knowing the answer to the teacher's question but not feeling comfortable to speak up. The top three concerns for high school students were (1) procrastinating instead of studying, (2) feeling too tired to study, and (3) when they write something feeling it is not as good as it could be but not knowing how to make it better.

*6. Interpret and apply the findings.* Our interpretation was that students at different school levels have somewhat different concerns about study and schoolwork, corresponding to the new challenges that confront them at each level of schooling. We also felt that teachers could help their students deal with their concerns more effectively if they first *asked* the students what their main concerns were, rather than assuming or guessing about them.

We now routinely present these results to teachers in our in-services. We point out, however, that each classroom in our sample had somewhat different results. Thus we continue to recommend that teachers, in effect, carry out their own action research by administering the checklist to their students. We point out that teachers can calculate the percentage of students checking each item and then target study skills instruction toward the concerns that were checked by the greatest percentage of their students.

*7. Report the findings.* We prepared tables showing the rankings of the checklist items for each classroom in the sample. We wrote a three-page cover letter describing the study and sent it, along with the tables, to all teachers who had sent us data for our survey. As mentioned above, we also present the findings in each workshop or course we offer.

## EXAMPLE 2. FOSTERING COOPERATIVE LEARNING AMONG ELEMENTARY STUDENTS

**Summary:**   In this project, Patricia Wood (1988), an elementary school teacher, arranged cooperative work groups in her classroom. She and several colleagues carried out observations as students worked on a series of classroom activities. Based on her analysis of the data from each classroom activity, she introduced modifications to subsequent activities and to the cooperative learning procedures used to complete them. Wood found that the modifications, and the students' accumulated practice in working cooperatively, ultimately led to a high degree of success in students' ability to learn cooperatively.

*1. Define the problem.* Wood had supervised a student teacher who conducted an action research project on cooperative learning. Subsequently Wood enrolled in a university course that required her own action research. She selected cooperation as her problem, for four reasons: (1) she perceived the children in her class to be having a difficult time working and playing together cooperatively, (2) she saw the social groups in the class as strongly defined and closed, (3) she had read articles about cooperative activities but had not found time to organize a sequence of lessons for promoting cooperation, and (4) she wanted to continue the thinking about cooperation that she had engaged in earlier when supervising her student teacher.

*2. Select a design.* Wood's design involved isolated cooperative activities with small groups of students for two weeks. Then a framework emerged for the remainder of her project. It consisted of finding at least one block of time each week to introduce a specific cooperation skill, assigning a small-group activity in which children could apply the skill, and debriefing the activity by conducting a class discussion on how the children had worked together. The cooperative activity was scheduled for a time when three other adults were available to assist in data collection—a student teacher, an assistant teacher, and a parent or other staff person in the school.

Examples of Wood's cooperative small-group activities were (1) giving a title to a picture showing an Olympic sport; (2) generating ideas about making a group decision and then creating a list of three jobs that all the students' mothers did; (3) hearing a presentation about the difference between critiquing people's ideas and criticizing the people themselves and about how to include everyone in a group activity, and then designing an imaginary map that included a title, map key, island, and lake; and (4) after a preactivity of listing cooperative comments in a recording of a previous class discussion, cooperatively building a structure that had to include several features (bridge, tunnel, etc.) by using a different medium (Legos, blocks, sand, etc.).

*3. Select a sample.* The sample was Wood's elementary classroom students, who ranged in age from 6 to 8 and included both boys and girls.

*4. Select measures.* All the adult participants in Wood's project had an opportunity to observe the students' cooperative behavior in the small-group activities and then to record the results in ways that would be most helpful in the reflection phase of the research. The data collection consisted of (a) daily recordings noting students' social patterns, (b) anecdotal records of what children did and said during structured group activities, (c) samples of group projects, and (d) tapes of children talking about working together at various times during the semester.

*5. Analyze the data.* After each activity, Wood reflected on the action that occurred. She looked at the data and sought to understand what happened and why it happened in the way that it did. By examining outcomes that contradicted her beliefs about teaching, she was led to question and then to reaffirm her philosophy of teaching and to become more receptive to suggestions and observations from colleagues.

*6. Interpret and apply the findings.* After reflection on each activity, Wood used her impressions to design a new plan of action for the next cooperative activity. For example, the published report describes her reflections following the first activity:

> The picture-titling activity was a disaster. All of the adults were shocked at how challenging this simple task had been. . . . I was confused about what to do next. I hadn't found a curriculum or teacher's guide to give me specific activities or lessons to try. Are there skills that I should teach about cooperation or should children struggle through and discover the process?

Based on these reflections, she had students generate ideas about making a group decision before their next cooperative activity. After this activity, her reflections included these comments:

> I shared my project with another colleague. She helped me realize that I was approaching the problem at a level that was too advanced for this age group (something that I was feeling also). I then read two articles about the impact of children's play on group problem solving. Reencouraged, I decided to continue teaching group skills and roles starting at a more appropriate level.

*7. Report the findings.* Wood's action research project was carried out in part as her project for a university course on preservice and in-service teacher education. She wrote a paper for the course, which along with some later reflections on action research, was subsequently published as a 15-page article in the *Journal of Education for Teaching* (see Chapter References).

## EXAMPLE 3. IDENTIFYING THE CRITICAL FACTORS THAT SUPERINTENDENTS CONSIDER IN ADMINISTRATIVE RESTRUCTURING

**Summary.**   James Martin and George Wilson (1990) conducted semistructured interviews of superintendents in nearby school districts who had carried out a successful restructuring of the district's administrative staff. Martin is a school district supervisor for secondary education, and Wilson is a professor of educational administration. Using a composite list of organizational and environmental factors derived from a literature review, they identified which of these factors were most critical in the superintendents' restructuring efforts. They also made recommendations for superintendents of other districts who are considering administrative restructuring.

*1. Define the problem.* Current pressures to improve schools and the fact that many school administrators are approaching retirement age have led many school districts to adopt some form of administrative restructuring. Martin and Wilson wished to determine the critical factors considered by school superintendents whose school districts are undergoing this process. They believed that this information would help other superintendents consider the critical factors involved in restructuring, and reflect on decisions to restructure, before actually attempting to reorganize the administrative hierarchy.

*2. Select a design.* Martin and Wilson (1990) chose the action research method "because it is the conventional approach for a study which intends to provide information which is 'practical and directly relevant to an actual situation in the working world' " (p. 35). They interviewed superintendents whose districts had undergone administrative restructuring during the superintendent's tenure.

*3. Select a sample.* Eligible western Pennsylvania school district superintendents constituted the sample. Superintendents were considered eligible based on the following factors: (a) the district had completed a successful restructuring of the administrative staff within the tenure of the current superintendent, (b) at least six central office administrators were employed in the district, and (c) the superintendent played a prominent role in the experience.

*4. Select measures.* A semistructured interview was designed. Direct questions and probes were constructed and field-tested, and each interview was recorded on audiotape and transcribed.

*5. Analyze the data.* The interview responses were categorized and then compared with a list of factors that had been identified through a review of literature as being critical to administrative restructuring of a school district. The list included both environmental factors (those that are considered to be "not under the direct control of the superintendent") and organizational factors (those that are considered to be "under the direct control of the superintendent") (Martin & Wilson, 1990, p. 36).

*6. Interpret and apply the findings.* The major environmental factors identified as considerations in administrative reorganization were declining enrollment, local culture, school board influence, and politics. The major organizational factors identified were organizational politics, long-range and strategic planning, and teacher empowerment. Of the 12 reasons that superintendents offered for restructuring, 4 dominated: (a) declining enrollment, (b) increased attention to curriculum, (c) a need to strengthen a particular area of the organization, and (d) existence of a long-range plan that called for restructuring.

Martin and Wilson formulated ten conclusions based on their research, including (a) the finding that few superintendents saw a need to use a consultant for assistance in designing an administrative reorganization plan, (b) the observation that superintendents were aware of the political nature of their positions and of the need to generate a support base for their actions through effective communication with stakeholders, and (c) the recommendation that superintendents engage in more long-range planning and become more proactive in planning for change.

*7. Report the findings.* Martin and Wilson wrote a journal article reporting their study that was published by *Planning and Changing,* a journal that specializes in analyses of current trends in educational administration (see Chapter References). Publication was consistent with their purpose for doing the research, namely, to develop and disseminate guidelines for superintendents considering administrative restructuring within their school districts.

# Differences between Formal Research and Action Research

Although both formal research and action research aim to increase knowledge and understanding, they differ in important ways.

*1. Training needed by the researcher.* Most formal research methods require extensive training to be used properly. Individuals who do quantitative research studies need to be skilled in using various measurement techniques and inferential statistics. Those who do qualitative research studies need specialized skills in collecting and interpreting intensive data on selected cases. Familiarity with formal research methodology comes only with extensive training and experience. By contrast, most education practitioners can carry out action research on their own, in collaboration with colleagues, or with the aid of a research specialist. They do not need advanced skills in research design and interpretation. In the second case example described above, an elementary school teacher was the researcher. In the study by Santa, Isaacson, and Manning (1987), presented later in this chapter, two elementary teachers worked with the school principal and the district curriculum coordinator in designing and carrying out the research.

*2. Goals of the research.* The goals of formal research are to produce knowledge that is generalizable to a broad population of interest and to develop and test theories. Action research, by contrast, is aimed at obtaining knowledge that can be applied directly to the local situation. It also has the goal of contributing to the training and hence the competence of education practitioners. In the second case example, Wood's primary goal was to improve her own teaching by fostering cooperation among her students. Her purpose in publishing her study was primarily to encourage other teachers to use action research to improve their own teaching, rather than to present generalizable findings about cooperative learning in elementary school instruction.

*3. Method of identifying the problem to be studied.* In formal research, problems for investigation usually are identified through a review of previous research. Researchers may choose to study problems that interest them, but they tend to be problems that do not relate to their work responsibilities. In action research, however, educators investigate precisely those problems that they perceive to be interfering with their efficacy, and perhaps that of their colleagues, or that involve important goals they want to achieve in their work. In the third case example, we assume that Wilson, as a supervisor of secondary education, had a personal commitment to improving the procedures by which superintendents design administrative restructuring efforts.

*4. Procedure for literature review.* In formal research, an extensive literature review, focusing on primary source materials, is usually necessary. The review is needed to give the researchers a thorough understanding of the current state of knowledge about the problem being investigated. This knowledge enables researchers to build on the knowledge accumulated by others in designing and interpreting their own research. For action research, researchers need only to gain a general understanding of the area being studied. Hence, a more cursory literature review, focusing on secondary sources, is usually adequate. In the second case example, all of Wood's references appear to be books or reports providing guidelines for conducting action research; none are concerned with cooperative learning. If she had intended her study to be a formal study of cooperative learning, she would have needed to do a thorough review of research in this area before conducting her study.

*5. Sampling approach.* In formal research, researchers aim to select either a random or a representative sample of the population to eliminate sampling bias as a possible factor affecting the results. Action researchers, however, use as subjects the students or clients with whom they typically work. In the first case example, we used as our sample the teachers who chose to send us the results of their use of the Checklist of Student Concerns.

*6. Research design.* Formal research emphasizes detailed planning to control for extraneous variables that can confuse the interpretation of the results. For example, in quantitative research, major attention is given to maintaining similar conditions in experimental and control groups, except for the variable being compared. Rigorous controls also are used in qualitative research, especially in checking the validity and reliability of the data collected. Thus the time frame for carrying out formal research is usually long, with an interval of a year or more between the time the study is designed and when results are obtained and interpreted. Action researchers, by contrast, plan their procedures more loosely, make changes freely during the action phase, of the study if they appear likely to improve the practical situation, and complete the study fairly quickly. Little attention is paid to control of the situation or elimination of sources of error or bias. Because the researchers tend to be personally involved, bias is typically present.

Thus, in the second case example, Wood continued to redesign her study as she obtained and reflected on the results from each cooperative learning activity. However, in the study presented later in this chapter, a more formal design involving inferential statistics was used. So we see that when action researchers wish to obtain generalizable results to be disseminated to a wider audience, their research design approximates that of formal research.

*7. Measurement procedures.* Researchers who do formal studies attempt to obtain the most valid and reliable measures available. As a result, they may first evaluate available measures and conduct a trial run of the measures selected for the research prior to doing the research itself. Action researchers, by contrast, often use convenient measures or standard tests, such as those routinely given in the course of classroom instruction. In the case examples presented above, the only measure utilized was the Checklist of Student Concerns. This measure has not been subjected to extensive testing to determine its reliability or validity. Similarly, the study presented at the end of this chapter used short-answer tests apparently designed by the teachers themselves.

*8. Data analysis.* Formal research often involves complex analysis of data, but raw data are rarely presented. Tests of statistical significance are usually emphasized. In formal qualitative research, the researcher engages in careful, reasoned analysis of intensive case data to determine their consistency with the theory in which the research is grounded. Most action research, however, involves simpler analysis procedures, with a focus on practical significance rather than statistical significance. The raw data may be presented. Also, the subjective opinion of the researchers is often weighted heavily. Except for the study by Santa, Isaacson, and Manning (1987), which involved a test of statistical significance (the $t$ test), all the examples of action research in this chapter involve only descriptive statistics (means and percentages in the first case example) or general observations that are not quantified or grounded in theory (in the second and third case examples).

*9. Application of results.* Researchers who do formal research emphasize the theoretical significance of their findings and implications for further research. They may discuss the practical implications of their results, but this is not a requirement or reflection on the study's merit. In action research, however, the practical significance of the results is of foremost importance. Action researchers report their findings mainly in an effort to clarify how the findings might affect their own work and to inform their colleagues about the possible implications for professional practice. Although colleagues may adopt strategies found to be effective in an action research project, they usually do so without concern for careful replication of the original research procedures.

# When Action Research Is Appropriate

Now that you have read several examples of action research, we would like you to consider doing your own action research to improve your effectiveness as an educator. One situation in which action research is appropriate occurs when you have read the research literature and have arrived at a tentative solution to a problem that has arisen in your work. Now you wish to put the solution into practice. Using action research will enable you to collect your own evidence of the solution's effectiveness. Or perhaps you have not found a satisfactory solution to your problem in the research literature. Instead, you may develop a tentative solution. Action research is a good method for testing the solution to determine how effective it is.

Another common situation is that you and your colleagues will identify a problem of mutual concern. Through action research, you can collaborate to find and test a solution. In their guide for teacher-researchers, Mohr and MacLean (1987) describe their experience in helping teacher-researchers form small groups (four or five teachers) based on common interests. Each group typically included teachers from various grade levels and disciplines. They met regularly; got to know one another and one another's work; and discussed their individual research logs, data, analysis, findings, and drafts of reports. Through this process, both individual and joint action research projects were defined, applied, refined, and reported. Mohr and MacLean documented the positive effects of this process on both teachers' classroom instruction and their planning and research skills.

One situation in which collaborative action research is appropriate involves practitioners working with an education specialist who has formal research training. The article in this chapter by Santa, Isaacson, and Manning (1987) illustrates this situation. Santa, as the curriculum coordinator for a school district, used her research skills to assist the principal and two teachers in designing and reporting the action research carried out in their elementary school.

For action research to be successful, several conditions should be met: the researcher should have sufficient time, a considerable degree of work autonomy, and both the opportunity and commitment to write about the research process and outcome.

Educators usually need release time from some of their normal work responsibilities to carry out an action research project. The time is needed for designing the project, doing it, reflecting on and sharing the findings, and modifying one's work practices according to what has been found. Educators who enroll in graduate degree programs often find it desirable or necessary to obtain a leave from their regular positions during their period of study. Thus it is not surprising that much action research by educators occurs as part of university coursework. Educators who remain on the job typically need release time for an action research project.

Another type of support needed by educators is autonomy to modify their daily routines according to the findings of their action research. For example, some teachers feel constrained from changing their teaching strategies. School or district mandates may require them to use a particular instructional model, or the use of standardized test results to evaluate school and teacher effectiveness may discourage instructional innovation. Both school administrators and the clients of the educational system (students and parents) need to give teachers support for trying out new strategies. Of course, they should also encourage teachers to collect data on the effectiveness of these strategies as part of an action research project.

Finally, the researcher should be committed to writing about the research. Stephen Tchudi (1991), describing the teacher-as-researcher model of action research, notes:

> The teacher-as-researcher is, above all, a *writer*. Such a teacher designs questions about curriculum and teaching, creates trials or experimental lessons and activities, collects a variety of evidence, and *writes up* the findings. The data collected by this teacher/writer/researcher are wide-ranging. . . . While gathering these data, the teacher keeps a learning log, recording and analyzing in the manner of the ethnographic researcher, as a participant observer. (p. 86)

We conclude this chapter by presenting a complete action research study, along with comments by the researcher and our critical review. This study demonstrates that good action research can be designed and conducted simply and can still produce results valuable not only to the researchers themselves but also to their students and to a wider audience of educators.

# Sample Action Research Study:
# CHANGING CONTENT INSTRUCTION
# THROUGH ACTION RESEARCH

## Abstract[1]

Teachers in this Montana school system don't just use action research to try out alternative ways of teaching—they discuss the data later with their students, who gain awareness and control over their techniques for reading and learning.

## Researcher's Comments[2]

I feel that research studies conducted by teachers are the most powerful way to effect change in the educational system. I know that this is a bold claim, but I believe it intensely.

Too often teachers use the same methods year after year, without ever questioning their effectiveness. They don't think enough about what they do or take sufficient time to reflect. Therefore, they don't grow and change.

The solution to this problem of entrenchment is teacher research. Teachers must think of their classrooms as research laboratories and involve their students as research collaborators. In this way, learning about teaching never becomes static. We remain alive as teachers, and even more important, our students begin to think of themselves as researchers, too. When we involve students as research collaborators, they learn about themselves as learners.

This study is one of many that my district's teachers and I have conducted in the classroom. Most have not been formally published because publishing is not our major purpose. We do studies for ourselves and for our students and then share the results among ourselves.

This study, however, was one that needed to be published beyond our district audience. It focused on an instructional problem that is more general, and one that the teachers and I feel passionately about. Using round-robin oral reading as a replacement for teaching students how to learn seems a terrible waste of valuable classroom time. Rather than round-robin reading, students should be learning how to learn. They need many opportunities to explore a variety of learning strategies and to learn which strategies work best for them. The round-robin procedure may help students (or should I say, teachers) get through the material, but it doesn't help students become lifelong learners.

I couldn't let this problem rest. Yet I knew that I couldn't be Ms. Full Charge and stomp into classrooms and tell teachers to change. That simply would not work. Teachers and students had to see the need for change themselves.

I began by talking about the round-robin problem with an elementary principal, Leanna Issacson (one of the coauthors of this article). She, too, was concerned and wanted to change the situation. We placed the names of all sixth-grade teachers in our district into a hat and drew out two names. The rest of the story is in the article. The third author of the article happens to be one of the sixth-grade teachers involved in the study. He also felt that our experiment should have a wider audience than just the teachers in our own district.

Our story is continuing to unfold. For the past few years, I have facilitated a "teacher as researcher" group in my school district. We meet after school in the home economics room of our junior high school. (Treats and coffee are essential.) We begin the year by sharing articles on teachers as researchers. We explore different methodologies, such as case studies, surveys, questionnaires, and action research. Teachers keep a log of their observations and questions, which serves as a springboard for group discussion.

The teachers have undertaken a variety of projects. Some wrote case studies based on observations of one or two students. Others carried out their own action research studies. For example, Sue Harding had her students investigate whether writing improved their problem-solving skills in mathematics. Her students practiced writing and solving one another's word problems. They worked together in reaction groups to revise problems containing unclear questions. Students kept track of their own test scores throughout the semester. Most found that their problem-solving skills improved as they became more adept at writing their own problems.

Sandy Bradford's fourth-graders evaluated several strategies for comprehending and learning social studies material. They wrote their reactions in their journals to each day's strategy and commented about the grades they received on checkup questions. At the end of the experiment students graphed their grades and wrote summaries describing the strategy that was most effective.

In each situation, teachers shared their research with an audience of professional colleagues. All of us have learned that conducting research helps us become scholars of our craft and invigorates our professional lives. Integrating research with the process of teaching provides a powerful tool in our continual search for excellence.

# CHANGING CONTENT INSTRUCTION THROUGH ACTION RESEARCH

Carol M. Santa, Leanna Isaacson, and Gary Manning
SCHOOL DISTRICT 5, KALISPELL, MONTANA

This article focuses on two issues in education. One is the very general problem of how to get teachers involved in the process of evaluating and changing their methods of instruction. The other issue deals with a specific problem in teaching content material at the elementary level.

Our experience has shown that when teachers are involved in action research—studies of a new method in their own classrooms—they become open to varied alternatives. Best of all, when they discuss their experiments with the children who participated, the students become aware of what was actually going on in their learning, of how they learn, and that there are multiple techniques for promoting their own learning.

We have seen action research have this effect in our own school system in the past few years. It began with a study on ways of teaching content material from textbooks. The specific method we were concerned about was the practice of teaching content material through round robin oral reading with interspersed discussion.

## Reading for Content Aloud

Our issue was not with oral reading per se, but with oral reading as the dominant approach to instruction in content areas. It appeared that this classroom method simply did not foster much learning.

The routine begins with the teacher discussing the

C. M. Santa, L. Isaacson, & G. Manning. "Changing Content Instruction through Action Research," *The Reading Teacher*, 40(4), 1987, 434–438. Reprinted with permission of Carol Santa and the International Reading Association.

upcoming topic followed by oral reading in turn taking fashion. Students supposedly follow in their text while listening to their colleague's oral production. Only one person at a time is reading and the time on stage is brief.

Silent reading by everyone seldom occurs before children alternate taking the reading stage. Few children follow the often halting reading and fewer still appear to be listening. On the whole, students seem quite bored by the whole procedure.

The oral reading approach to content instruction is at odds with research on reading comprehension. Leinhardt, Zigmond, and Cooley (1981) found that silent reading practice was related to reading achievement, but oral reading activities were not. Children also learn most effectively when taught how to learn (Baumann and Schmitt, 1986). The readers need to be shown how to use their own background knowledge, how to read for main ideas, how to organize material from their reading, and how to study and write about information gained from their reading.

If teachers restrict content instruction mainly to oral reading followed by discussion, little time remains for showing students how to learn. Moreover, since oral reading is slow and tedious, students do not have as much time to read and learn the content material.

## Changing Instruction

How do we go about changing instructional routines entrenched so deeply within teaching behavior? We knew that change through administrative dictum would simply antagonize teachers. Instead, we wanted somehow to convince teachers that altering their routines would not only make teaching more interesting, but more rewarding by improving student learning.

Therefore, the most sensitive approach seemed to be one that involved teachers as research collaborators. Such tactics had worked well in changing instruction in our junior high and high school (Santa, 1986), so we felt confident that elementary teachers would also approach the problem with an open mind when the issue was seen as part of a research project.

## Classroom Research

We began our collaboration with two of our most talented and respected 6th grade teachers. Together, we developed an instructional plan to validate within each of their classrooms. We wanted our experiments to incorporate some basic principles for learning from text. Namely, the procedure should help students integrate their background knowledge with the content information, encourage active involvement in the material, and help students self monitor their comprehension.

We chose two selections from a chapter in the 6th grade social studies book, *The World and Its People* (Cooper, 1984). The first was a 1,000 word excerpt describing the geography and history of Australia, and the second an 800 word segment about New Zealand. Neither class had read the selections.

For the first part of the experiment, we randomly selected one 6th grade class as the experimental and the second as the control class. We settled on an instructional procedure for the experimental group which combined a variety of strategies currently recommended for content reading instruction (Santeusanio, 1983).

We used the Australia selection with both groups. In an effort to keep instruction similar except for the critical variable of oral reading, the teachers began the lesson in the same way for both experimental and control classes.

The teacher asked the students to list everything they knew about Australia. She wrote the brainstormed information on the board and then categorized it according to topic. For example, some of the topics were jobs, location, and resources.

The categories and information generated in each class were practically the same. Both classes then read the material silently. From this point experimental and control instruction differed.

After silent reading, the control students took turns in round robin fashion reading the material out loud. After

each student read, the teacher led a brief discussion focusing on the information. Oral reading and discussion continued until the section was complete.

When the experimental students completed the silent reading, the teacher quickly demonstrated how to develop two column notes. The students received a blank sheet of paper, and listed the category labels generated in the prereading activity in a spaced column on the left portion of their paper. Next they used the right-hand portion of the paper to list information from their reading about the topic headings. Students included a section for miscellaneous information which did not seem to fit under any of the labels.

They then used these labels as cues to recall information from text. After recalling as much as they could from memory, they reread the selection silently, put the reading aside, and added additional information to their notes.

In both cases, the teachers collected the reading materials and the notes from the experimental class. The time for the completion of the activities for both classes was the same, 45 minutes. The following day, the teachers gave their classes the same test, consisting of 10 short answer questions. Each question required from one to three sentences to answer.

Both teachers outlined content from the reading selection which answered each of the 10 questions. They then compared their outlines and came to an agreement as to the content for each question.

Students received 1 point for each item included in their short answers which matched the outlined materials. The short answer tests were scored by an unbiased third person.

As expected the experimental students performed significantly better than the control students (means = 18.83 and 12.30, $t = 4.03$, $p < .01$).[3]*

## Verifying the Results

Even with these differences between classes, we wanted to make sure that the effects were not merely measures of inherent differences in ability between the two classes, and specific to the passage. Therefore, we repeated the experiment with a different selection and switched the experimental and control classes.

* Numbered notes to articles are supplied by the authors of this text.

The following week, the teachers conducted the second experiment using the next selection in the text, the excerpt on New Zealand. The previous experimental class became the control and vice-versa. The procedures were identical to those in the first study—only the classes and material differed. After a 24 hour delay the students took a 10 item short answer test. The procedure for scoring was identical to the first study.

The pattern of results was similar to the first study, with the experimental group performing better than the control class (means = 15 and 8, $t$ = 4.47, $p$ < .01). The experimental condition produced significantly better results, irrespective of class and passage.

## Why the System Worked Well

We then analyzed why the experimental condition consistently led to improved performance. First, we concluded that students in the experimental group were superior to the control because they were more actively engaged in their reading. The read-recall and read-recall sequence required active participation by everyone. The procedure required more mental effort than the silent reading followed by the round robin oral reading with class discussion.

Second, the experimental students received specific instruction in how to organize their information for learning. The experimenter showed the students how to organize the recalled information into a two column notetaking format with topical headings on the left and details in support of the topics on the right.

Third, the experimental students had opportunities to self monitor their performance. Once they had recalled, they read the material a second time for the specific purpose of filling in additional information in their notes. This read-recall approach provided them a system for deciding what they knew about the information and a procedure for going back and adding to their comprehension.

Thus, the experimental approach incorporated three essential ingredients of content instruction: Students were actively involved in their learning, they received direct instruction in how to read and organize information for learning, and they had a system for self monitoring and modifying their comprehension. As a result, students learned more.

## The Experimental Process Stimulates Participants

While the experiment produced interesting results, the process of experimenting was even more important. We wanted the research to influence both students and teachers. Therefore, our next step was to discuss the results with the students. The teachers informed them of their participation in a teaching study, and asked for their reactions to the two methods.

Practically all students felt the experimental method helped them learn more effectively. Many commented about how much harder they had to work using the experimental procedure and several revealed that taking notes in a free recall manner within the format of two column notes helped them organize and remember the information. Several even mentioned that they might use this technique on their own—quite a breakthrough for these budding adolescents.

We felt that such process discussions are essential if students are going to become more aware of how to learn from content materials. A quick perusal of the literature on metacognition (Baker and Brown, 1984) indicates that many students are not aware of what they do or should do to comprehend and learn information.

Providing them opportunities to experiment with new approaches and then to talk about the merit of such approaches is an essential ingredient of good instruction. Involving students in experiments and using the data as a focus for discussion has helped our students gain more control over their own reading and learning.

## Other Faculty Join In

Once students were aware of the results, we began disseminating our findings to other faculty. The teachers presented their results at faculty and principal meetings. They provided the audience with a theoretical rationale for varying the round robin discussion routine. They talked about the importance of generating and organizing background knowledge, providing all students with opportunities for reading, and developing strategies for students to monitor their own performance. We also summarized the studies in a newsletter sent to each school and placed in faculty lounges.

Soon the effects began to spread. Round robin oral reading no longer is the standard routine in content instruction. In fact, teachers began conducting a host of experiments to validate alternatives.

One teacher learned that having students keep content journals in mathematics improved problem solving. Another discovered that having students take their own classnotes was more effective than studying from notes written by the teacher. A 1st grade teacher found that reviewing a reading lesson by having her students free recall in the form of a language experience lesson promoted long term retention when compared with oral rereading of the selection. Classroom research evolved into an effective way to change instructional routines.

## Guidelines for Conducting Classroom Research

In conducting our experiments, we include some rudimentary controls so that we can feel fairly confident of our results. We try to run our experiments in more than one classroom, and we make an effort to keep instructional time the same for both the experimental and control groups.

So that students as well as teachers can understand the methodology, we keep our experimental designs and statistics simple. Whenever possible we use *t* tests to analyze our data and simple bar graphs to display our results.

Classroom experimentation has evolved into a sensitive and successful way to change instructional routines. Involving teachers in planning, conducting, and report-

ing classroom research not only preserves teacher ownership of ideas but provides convincing evidence that alternative teaching strategies help students learn.

Subsequent to these as well as other classroom based studies, fundamental shifts in instruction have occurred throughout our district. Consequently, our teachers are teaching more and our students are learning more. Everyone wins.

## References

BAKER, LINDA, and ANN L. BROWN. "Metacognitive Skills and Reading." In *Handbook of Reading Research,* edited by P. David Pearson, pp. 353–94. New York, N.Y.: Longman, 1984.

BAUMANN, JAMES F., and MARIBETH SCHMITT. "The What, Why, How, and When of Comprehension Instruction." *The Reading Teacher,* vol. 39 (March 1986), pp. 640–46.

COOPER, KENNETH S. *The World and Its People: Europe, Africa, Asia, and Australia.* Morristown, N.J.: Silver Burdett, 1984.

LEINHARDT, GAEA, NAOMI ZIGMOND, and WILLIAM W. COOLEY. "Reading Instruction and Its Effects." *American Educational Research Journal,* vol. 18 (Fall 1981), pp. 343–61.

SANTA, CAROL M. "Content Reading in Secondary Schools." In *Reading Comprehension: From Research to Practice,* edited by Judith Orasanu, pp. 303–17. Hillsdale, N.J.: Lawrence Erlbaum, 1986.

SANTEUSANIO, RICHARD P. *A Practical Approach to Content Area Reading.* Reading, Mass.: Addison-Wesley, 1983.

# Critical Review

This study provides an excellent example of action research in education. It was initiated and conducted by a district coordinator, a school administrator, and two capable elementary school teachers. It was carried out on a small scale using a simple research design. The results were both statistically significant and of practical value. Based on the results, other teachers adapted the experimental treatment in their own classrooms.

As is often the case in action research, highly capable teachers were the teachers who agreed to participate in the experiment. The question that arises in such studies is "Will this approach work with the average teacher?" The authors give us a partial answer by noting that many other teachers in the district adopted the experimental approach after the study was completed.

The experimental and control group each included only one teacher, so we need to be particularly concerned that the teachers were similar in ability. Otherwise we would not know whether the superior performance of the experimental group students was due to the treatment or to the superior teaching ability of the teacher. The researchers dealt with this problem by having the two teachers reverse use of the experimental and control procedures in their classrooms. If teaching ability was a critical factor, the better teacher would have elicited a better performance from the class, regardless of whether he or she was following the experimental or control procedures. Because each teacher obtained better results with the experimental treatment, the teacher's ability did not appear to affect the results of the study.

Another good experimental control was keeping the instructional time similar for the experimental and control conditions. If students in the experimental group had more time to utilize the reading strategies they were taught in the experimental treatment, we would not know whether their superior test performance was the result of increased time for learning or of the experimental instruction.

A common problem in research reports is inadequate reporting of the types of items used on the criterion test and the possible range of scores. In this study we know that the mean test scores of the experimental students and control students were 18.83 and 12.30, respectively, after the first experimental session; and the means were 15.00 and 8.00, respectively, after the second experimental session. These seem to be substantial group differences, but their significance is unclear. For example, are scores of 18.83 and 15.00 high? We need to know the maximum possible score to answer this question.

Another question is whether the superiority of the experimental group resulted from a few students making unusually large gains or from many students making moderate gains. Reporting standard deviations as well as mean scores would help answer this question. Finally, we wonder about the content of the test items. Were they fact questions, higher-cognitive questions, or a combination of both types? Each type of item is valid, but we need to know which type or types were used so that we can draw appropriate conclusions about the learning outcomes that are facilitated by the experimental procedures.

Both experimental and control students earned lower scores following the second experimental session than they did following the first. This result was not interpreted in the report. Perhaps the second test was more difficult than the first. Another possibility is that one or both tests were not scored reliably. To ensure that the tests were being scored reliably, the researchers would need to demonstrate that different persons could score the tests independently of one another and agree in their scoring.

A major strength of this study, and of action research in general, is that the findings can be translated easily into practice. Virtually any school district can apply the procedures that Santa, Isaacson, and Manning used in their reading program. In fact, they could generalize the procedures easily to improve other areas of their curriculum. By contrast, formal research studies are more rigorous than action research but often produce findings without immediate practical application.

# Chapter References

CAMERON-JONES, M. (1983). *A researching profession? The growth of classroom action research* (ED 266 128). Edinburgh, Scotland: Moray House College of Education, Focus on Teaching Project.

GALL, M. D., & GALL, J. P. (1991). *Study for success teacher's manual,* 4th ed. Eugene, OR: M. Damien.

GOODLAD, J. (1983). The school as workplace. In *Staff development: 1982 yearbook of the National Society for the Study of Education, Part II,* ed. G. Griffin. Chicago: University of Chicago Press, 1983.

LEWIN, K. (1946). Action research and minority problems. *Journal of Social Issues, 2,* 34–46.

MARTIN, J. A., & WILSON, G. (1990). Administrative restructuring: The first step in public school reform. *Planning and Changing, 21*(1), 34–40.

MOHR, M. M., & MACLEAN, M. S. (1987). *Working together: A guide for teacher-researchers.* Urbana, IL: National Council of Teachers of English.

PERRY-SHELDON, B., & ALLAIN, V. A. (1987). *Using educational research in the classroom.* Bloomington, IN: Phi Delta Kappa Educational Foundation.

SANTA, C. M., ISAACSON, L., & MANNING, G. (1987, January). Changing content instruction through action research. *The Reading Teacher,* pp. 434–438.

SIMMONS, J. (1984). *Action research as a means of professionalizing staff development for classroom teachers and school staffs* (ED 275 639). Grand Rapids: Michigan State University.

STEVENS, K. (1986). Collaborative action research: An effective strategy for principal inservice. *Theory into Practice, 25,* 203–206.

TCHUDI, S. (1991). *Planning and assessing the curriculum in English Language Arts.* Alexandria, VA: Association for Supervision and Curriculum Development.

WOOD, P. (1988). Action research: A field perspective. *Journal of Education for Teaching, 14*(2), 135–150.

# Recommended Reading

## GUIDES TO CONDUCTING ACTION RESEARCH

ASSOCIATION FOR SUPERVISION AND CURRICULUM DEVELOPMENT. (1991). The reflective educator. *Educational Leadership, 48*(6).

Fourteen articles in this issue of *Educational Leadership* deal with action research and other current approaches designed to inspire students, teachers, and administrators to engage in "thinking deeply about what we are doing" in education.

BRUNING, J. L., & KINTZ, B. L. (1987). *Computational handbook of statistics,* 3rd ed. Glenview, IL: Scott, Foresman.

This text provides easy-to-follow computational procedures for most of the statistical techniques used in quantitative research. The emphasis is on application, with extensive examples. This is a useful resource for the practicing action researcher.

HUSTLER, D., CASSIDY, A., & CUFF, E. C., eds. (1986). *Action research in classrooms and schools.* Boston: Allen & Unwin.

This book includes six contributions concerning important issues in action research, six case studies of teachers' action research, and several studies based on two large-scale action research projects in Great Britain.

MOHR, M. M., & MACLEAN, M. S. (1987). *Working together: A guide for teacher-researchers.* Urbana, IL: National Council of Teachers of English.

The authors share their experience in conducting teacher-researcher seminars over a period of several years. The book also includes five project reports by schoolteachers who carried out action research in their classrooms.

PERRY-SHELDON, B., & ALLAIN, V. A. (1987). *Using educational research in the classroom.* Bloomington, IN: Phi Delta Kappa Educational Foundation.

This book provides a good overview of the benefits, difficulties, and procedures of action research and includes an extensive bibliography.

WALFORD, G., ed. (1991). *Doing educational research.* New York: Routledge.

This book provides semiautobiographical accounts of the research of 13 major educationists working in the British Isles. The authors reflect on the practical and personal aspects of the research process, illustrating many of the issues that confront both new and experienced action researchers.

## OTHER EXAMPLES OF ACTION RESEARCH

BERTLAND, L. H. (1988). Usage patterns in a middle school library: A circulation analysis. *School Library Media Quarterly, 16*(3), 200–203.

This article describes a school librarian's action research on the use of a computerized circulation program to analyze the usage patterns of a middle school library and to suggest how the data may be used to design the library's future collection management and acquisition policies.

DICKER, M. (1990). Using action research to navigate an unfamiliar teaching assignment. *Theory into Practice, 29*(3), 203–208.

The author, an experienced secondary school teacher in Canada, describes her use of action research methodology in designing and teaching a course in a subject that was new to her. Dicker's article is one of 11 articles in the summer 1990 issue of *Theory into Practice* entitled "Teacher as Researcher," which is devoted to action research.

KULL, J. A., & CARTER, J. (1989–90). Wrapping in the first grade classroom. *The Computing Teacher, 17*(4), 12–13, 52.

The authors describe an action research study in which the researchers recorded what children were doing as they learned to use the software program Logo. The observers discovered that learning Logo in a nondirective manner helped children develop other skills besides programming skills (problem solving, peer tutoring, productive play, etc.).

LOMAX, P., ed. (1990). *Managing staff development in schools: An action research approach.* Philadelphia: Multilingual Matters.

This book contains accounts written by teacher-researchers about action research endeavors aimed at improving management practices in their schools and colleges, particularly in relation to staff development.

## Application Problems

1. Suppose that you are a teacher, and you have decided to carry out some action research in your classroom to improve your students' learning. Briefly list three ways in which you could involve parents in your action research and a benefit of each.
2. Name three people in your institution who could help you design an action research project to improve your practice and one way each of them could help. If possible, include individuals who perform different roles in the institution.
3. Suppose you are a principal and you want to solve a critical problem in your school. You estimate that you can spend about two hours each day for two weeks before you must implement whatever solution you decide is best. You want to choose between two options on how to spend the bulk of that time: (a) do a thorough literature review to identify previous studies concerning the problem or (b) design and carry out your own action research. Name three factors you would consider in deciding which option to choose.

## Chapter Notes

1. The abstract of the article is reprinted here to help you understand the researcher's comments.
2. This commentary was written by Carol Santa.
3. The *t test* is a statistical procedure to determine the likelihood that a difference found between two groups in a sample would be found in the population represented by the sample. The *t* test yielded a *p* value of less than ($<$) .01, which means that we can generalize beyond this sample with confidence. If the experiment were repeated with similar students to those used here, it is quite probable that the experimental group would outperform the control group.

# APPLICATION PROBLEMS: SUGGESTED ANSWERS

## Chapter 2, Locating Educational Information

1. **a.** The 1991–92 edition of *Books in Print* lists the following book in the section on Ability Grouping in Education: Kate, L. G., *et al.* (1990). *The Case for Mixed-Age Grouping in Early Childhood Education,* published by the National Association for the Education of Young Children.

   **b.** Tanner, L. N., ed. (1988). *Critical issues in curriculum: The eighty-seventh yearbook of the National Society for the Study of Education.* Part I. Chicago: NSSE. Chapter IX: Passow, A. H. Issues of access to knowledge: Grouping and tracking.

   **c.** Four articles from the Fall 1987 volume of the *Review of Educational Research* (Volume 57, No. 3) concern ability grouping. The first article, by R. E. Slavin, is entitled "Ability grouping and student achievement in elementary schools: A best evidence synthesis," pp. 293–336. Two responses to Slavin's article follow, the first by E. Hiebert and the second by A. Gamoran. The fourth article is a reply to Hiebert and Gamoran by Slavin. The Fall 1990 volume of *RER* (Volume 60, No. 3) includes another article on ability grouping: R. E. Slavin, "Achievement effects of ability grouping in secondary schools: A best-evidence synthesis," pp. 471–500. While this article does not concern elementary education, you might wish to make the superintendent aware of it if your district is a K-12 district.

   **d.** For each of these preliminary sources, check the subject index for "Ability Grouping."

## Chapter 4, Reviewing Primary Sources and Writing a Report

1. **a.** Newfield, J., & McElyea, V. B. (1983). Achievement and attitudinal differences among students in regular, remedial, and advanced classes. *Journal of Experimental Education, 52*(1), 47–56.

   **b.** Burkhalter, B. B., & Wright, J. P. (1984). Handwriting performance with and without transparent overlays. *Journal of Experimental Education, 52*(2), 132–135.

2. **a.** Weeden, C. L. (1985). The effects of a treatment program on the self-concept of seventh and eighth grade students (University of Mississippi, 1984). Abstract in *Dissertation Abstracts International,* 45(10), sec. A, 3101A.

   **b.** You could have located this study in two ways. The preferred approach would be to look up key words from the problem statement in the Keyword Title Index at the back of the issue. This study is listed under Self-Concept in this index. Another approach would be to check Education Psychology in the Table of Contents. You would find abstracts related to this topic starting on page 3092A. By scanning the references in this section, you would find Weeden's dissertation abstracted on page 3101A. A related dissertation by H. C. Herbert, entitled "The Effects of a Course in Intrapersonal Relationships on the Academic Self-Concept of High Risk College Freshmen," might also be useful. However, upon review you would conclude that this study is somewhat less relevant to your interests, and also it failed to produce significant changes in self-concept.

# Chapter 5, Evaluating Research Reports

1. **a.** The title "Team Teaching Is the Answer" suggests that the researcher is more interested in convincing readers of the value of team teaching than in conducting an impartial study to test its value.
   **b.** Referring to the alternate approach (the lecture method) as "timeworn" indicates bias because it is an evaluative term with strong negative connotations.
   **c.** Stating that the study's purpose was to "demonstrate" the superiority of team teaching indicates bias because it shows that a particular research result was preferred. A more objective approach would be to compare the two instructional approaches with an open mind or to test a hypothesis derived from a theory.

2. **a.** The "hypothesis" does not meet the first criterion that the relationship of the variables to each other should be specified. We do not know whether computer feedback is hypothesized to *increase* or *decrease* students' rate of response and accuracy of response to computer-presented questions.
   **b.** The "hypothesis" does not meet the second criterion, which states that a hypothesis should be grounded in theory or previous research.
   **c.** The "hypothesis" appears not to fit the qualitative research paradigm. Therefore, the third criterion relating to emergent hypotheses does not apply.
   **d.** The "hypothesis" does not meet the fourth criterion because it is not clear that an actual hypothesis is being tested.

3. **a.** To select a simple random sample of 1,000 students you would first assign each of the 19,206 students a number (from 1 to 19,206); using a table of random numbers, randomly select a row or column as a starting point and select all the numbers that follow in that row or column; then proceed to the next row or column and so forth until you have selected 1,000 numbers. (You would need to use five-digit numbers and skip numbers greater than 19,206).
   **b.** To select a systematic sample of 1,000 students you would first assign each of the 19,206 students a number (from 1 to 19,206) and then divide the population size (19,206) by the number needed for the sample (1,000). The result is 19. You would select at random a number, $X$, that is smaller than 19 (i.e., 1 to 18). Starting with the number you obtained, you would select every $X$th name from the population list. If $X$ is 5, for example, you would select the fifth name, the tenth name, the fifteenth name, and so forth until you had selected 1,000 students.
   **c.** To select a sample of 1,000 students stratified on the basis of socioeconomic status (SES) of the schools you would first determine the percentage of the total population that falls in each SES category by dividing the number of students in each category by 19,206. The result would be

| Percentage | Number of Schools | Number of Students | SES Category |
|---|---|---|---|
| 18 | 40 | 3,520 | Upper middle |
| 26 | 54 | 4,968 | Lower middle |
| 32 | 62 | 6,211 | Working class |
| 23 | 44 | 4,507 | Inner city/welfare |
| 99 | 200 | 19,206 | |

You would now have two choices concerning how to proceed. You could divide the sample size, 1,000, by 4 (the number of SES categories), which would give you 250. You could then select 250 students from each SES category, using either random sampling (see a above) or systematic sampling (see b above). Alternately, you could ensure that the proportion of students in each group in the sample is the same as the proportion in the population by multiplying 1,000 by the percentage of students in each group and selecting that number of students from each group. In other words, you would select 180 upper-middle-class students, 260 lower-middle-class students, 320 working-class students, and 230 inner-city/welfare students. (This totals 990 students, so you would need to add 3 more to each group to obtain 999.) You would now use either random or systematic sampling to select the students from each group.

d. To select a cluster sample of about 1,000 students you would use the same number of students in each group as you obtained in c above and then divide each of these numbers by 25, which is the average classroom size, to determine the number of classrooms from each SES category you need to select. The result is 7, 11, 13, and 9, respectively, for the four SES categories listed above. You would then give each classroom a number and randomly select the needed number of classrooms by using a table of random numbers, as described in a above.

4. The accessible population in problem 3 is the total district enrollment, namely, 19,206 students. The results might be generalized to the target population of all students who are in large urban school districts similar in size and socioeconomic distribution to this district.

5. Aspects of the test that should be evaluated include validity as a measure of students' learning of chemistry; reliability; and appropriateness for the sample's level of ability, culture, and so on. The same aspects of the interview procedure should be evaluated, but by using somewhat different procedures.

# Chapter 6, Educational Measures

1. **a.** N
   **b.** L
   **c.** T
   **d.** N
   **e.** T
2. Yes, there is a possibility of bias. The same researcher developed the training program, trained the experimental group, and conducted the interviews of teachers in both the experimental and control groups following the training. There are two main sources of bias. First, the researcher knows which teachers were in the experimental group since he carried out the

training: This knowledge could lead him to obtain different results from the experimental teachers when he conducts the interviews, for example, by asking leading questions or characterizing their responses differently. Second, the researcher is likely to be positively biased toward the training program because he developed it, and thus he may be more favorably inclined toward the experimental teachers when he conducts the interviews.

3. Observer B's approach probably would produce more reliable information than observer A's approach. Observer B's checklist includes a guide to what constitutes a thought question and what does not; thus his judgments are more likely to be consistent over time than those of observer A, who is operating without a guide. In addition, observer B is tallying instances of thought questions for each teacher. This is a more objective measure than the subjective comparison to "the average teacher" that observer A is using. Again, this procedure will lead to higher consistency of observer B's judgments than of observer A's judgments. If other observers were involved, the *interobserver reliability coefficient* would be higher for observers using observer B's approach than for those using observer A's approach.

4. **a.** Content validity
   **b.** Concurrent validity
   **c.** Construct validity
   **d.** Predictive validity

5. **a.** The researchers first need to determine whether the questions used in the semistructured interview schedule are face valid. That is, do they deal with the subject of teaching methods for gifted and talented students and with criteria of students' effectiveness by which to judge these teaching methods? They then need to determine whether the self-reports elicited by the interview questions accurately reflect what the respondents actually did, said, thought, or felt. They can further test the validity of the interview schedule by (i) collecting other sources of evidence and comparing them to the information obtained from the interviews, for example, collecting information from the students themselves about the teaching methods they find helpful in fostering their unique gifts and talents; (ii) checking the connections among the interview questions, the data that were collected, and the conclusions that were drawn from the data; (iii) having some of the interview respondents review the researchers' notes or a draft of the research report as a check of their accuracy; and (iv) doing their own self-reflection to determine their biases and whether they took steps to keep these biases from influencing the data collected.

   **b.** To determine reliability, the researchers should keep careful records of their interview and observation procedures, so other researchers could duplicate their procedures if they wished to. They could do so by specifying in their research report such information as the time line for collecting the data; a description of the outstanding personal and professional characteristics of each teacher, supervisor, and parent who was interviewed; the context in which the measurements were made, for example, the time of day and the location of each interview; the procedures used to gain access to the individuals, for example, how the initial contact was made and what information was provided to elicit agreement to participate; the interview questions that were asked; the methods used to record the data, for example, detailed notes, tape recording, or other means; and whether the data collectors received any training before conducting the interviews. By carefully reporting this information, the researchers would make it possible for an independent reviewer to make his own judgment of the reliability of the interview schedule, that is, the likelihood that the procedures described would lead to the type of data reported by the researcher.

6. **a.** *The Mental Measurements Yearbooks*
   *ETS Test Collection Bibliographies*
   *Tests—A Comprehensive Reference for Assessments in Psychology, Education, and Business*
   **b.** *The Mental Measurements Yearbooks*
   *Test Critiques*
   **c.** Content validity
   **d.** Have a committee of experts in social studies instruction determine whether each item on the test corresponds to an objective in the state curriculum guide and to the content covered in the textbook. The percentage of items that correspond to the guide and textbook can then be determined. Also, the correspondence of the items to particular curriculum guide objectives and textbook content can be recorded to determine whether some objectives and content are oversampled or undersampled.

# Chapter 7, Statistical Analysis

1. **a.** Categorical scores
   **b.** Continuous scores
   **c.** Continuous scores
   **d.** Rank scores
   **e.** Categorical scores
2. **a.** Mean
   **b.** Analysis of variance
   **c.** *t* test
   **d.** Standard deviation
   **e.** chi-square test
   **f.** *t* test
3. **a.** The distribution of scores deviates substantially from the normal curve. Therefore, it is more appropriate to use the median to represent the average score of the sample.
   **b.** Each of the statistical analyses is appropriate.
   **c.** Analysis of variance was not the appropriate statistical test because the three classes of students differed substantially on the pretest. Analysis of covariance is the appropriate test. Beginning-of-year reading test scores would be used as a covariate to adjust statistically the end-of-year test scores to account for the initial differences among the three classes in reading ability.

# Chapter 8, Synthesis of Research Findings

1. The full reference of each document is given here for your information.
   **a.** Bridges, D. (1990). The character of discussion: A focus on students. In *Teaching and learning through discussion,* ed. W. W. Wilen. Springfield, IL: Thomas. This is a professional review.
   **b.** Epstein, J. L. (1988). Parent-teacher conferences. In *Encyclopedia of school administration and supervision,* eds. R. A. Gorton, G. T. Schneider, & J. C. Fisher. Phoenix, AZ: Oryx. This is a professional review.

     c. Anderson, T. H., & Armbruster, B. B. (1984). Studying. In *Handbook of reading research*, ed. P. D. Pearson. New York: Longman. This is a conceptual-methodological critique.

     d. Kulik, J. A., Kulik, C. C., & Bangert, R. L. (1984). Effects of practice on aptitude and achievement test scores. *American Educational Research Journal, 21*(2), 435–447. This is a primary source analysis.

2. **b and c.** Choice *a* is not correct unless the practice test is an identical form of the achievement test because the effect size of .23 for taking a parallel form of the test as a practice test is smaller than .33, the minimum effect size generally considered to have practical significance.

3. Four terms that could be useful as descriptors for locating research syntheses are "literature review," "meta analysis," "literature search," and "bibliography." Check the *Thesaurus of Psychological Index Terms* and the *Thesaurus of ERIC Descriptors* for these terms and ask your librarian for other possible terms to use.

# Chapter 9, Qualitative Research

1. **a.** This is most likely a quantitative study because the data are collected at widely separate, discrete points in time. In qualitative research, by contrast, the data are usually collected on a continuous basis.

     **b.** This is most likely a qualitative study. The researcher's visits to the principal's home probably reflect an interest in understanding the total context of the principal's work life. Quantitative research, by contrast, tends to be much more focused, with relatively little attention on context.

     **c.** This is most likely a qualitative study because of the researchers' interest in identifying multiple perspectives about the program's efforts. Also, the effort to identify hoped-for effects indicates an interest in value orientations, which are a major concern of qualitative research.

     **d.** This is most likely a quantitative study because the research is clearly concerned about the objectivity and precision of the measuring instrument.

2. Qualitative and quantitative researchers could work together with staff development experts to design and implement a program based on adult learning principles. Qualitative researchers then could produce thick descriptions of a trial version of the program in operation and its perceived effects on teachers. Staff developers could use this information to refine the program, and quantitative researchers could use it to identify relevant variables and develop measures of them. Next, the qualitative and quantitative researchers could work together to design and conduct an experiment to test the effectiveness of the program. Program effects would be measured by collecting data on teachers' performance on objective measures. Qualitative researchers could participate in the experiment by collecting interview and observational data on participants' perceptions and on contextual factors. The combination of the qualitative and quantitative data would provide a strong basis for understanding the effects of the experimental staff development program and why predicted effects occurred or failed to occur.

3. The department's interest in policy changes over time suggests the need for a specialist in historical research methods. However, the policies to be studied involved children from migrant worker families, which tend to be from minority cultures. A specialist in ethnographic research methods would be able to study the cultural background of the children, how it differs from the majority culture, and whether the differences are reflected in educa-

tional policies. The department should consider having the study done by a research team that included specialists in historical research and ethnographic research or by a single researcher with training in both research methodologies.

# Chapter 10, Descriptive Research

1. **a.** A questionnaire would be best to measure the parent's monitoring of students' homework. Direct observation would perhaps give more accurate information, but it would be difficult and expensive to collect data.

   **b.** Direct observation would be the best way to measure the aggressive playground behavior of first-grade male students.

   **c.** To measure something as sensitive as teachers' sexual history and attitudes toward teaching sex education, it would be necessary to use interviews.

   **d.** To measure students' level of prereading skills, a test would be appropriate.

# Chapter 11, Causal-Comparative Research

1. It would be unethical to inflict brain damage on young adults to study its effects on their problem-solving performance. Because it is not possible to manipulate experimentally the presence or absence of brain damage, an experiment would not be appropriate. However, causal-comparative research is appropriate because the researcher can obtain a defined sample of brain-damaged adults and a comparison sample of adults similar to the defined sample in other characteristics.

2. Stating the research problem; selecting a defined group; selecting a comparison group; data collection; data analysis.

3. All of the following are possible causal interpretations of the findings that could be correct:

   **a.** Greater activity on the playground causes students to demonstrate a higher level of participation during classroom instruction.

   **b.** A higher level of participation during classroom instruction causes students to exhibit more activity on the playground during recess.

   **c.** Both playground activity and classroom participation could be caused by a third variable, for example, the quality of nutrition.

# Chapter 12, Correlational Research

1. **a.** S-D and R

   **b.** S-D and P

   **c.** D-S and R

   **d.** S-D and R

   **e.** S-S and P

2. **a.** This is a relationship study because it is aimed at learning more about the nature of mathematical aptitude. If the mathematical aptitude measure was being used to determine which students would do best in an advanced mathematics course, it would be a prediction study.

**b.** A serious limitation is that the researcher selected the sample from students in an advanced mathematics course (trigonometry). Since this is an elective course, we can expect that most students who take it will be above average in mathematical aptitude. This factor would restrict the range of mathematical aptitude scores and thus would tend to reduce the correlations between mathematical aptitude and the other measures.

**c.** Common variance is determined by squaring the correlation coefficient. The common variance between MA and VIQ is .29 (.54 squared). That is, 29 percent of the variance measured by these two tests is common. In other words, verbal IQ accounts for 29 percent of the variance in mathematical aptitude. The common variance between MA and logical reasoning is .16 (.40 squared), meaning that logical reasoning accounts for 16 percent of the variance in mathematical aptitude. The common variance between MA and creativity is .09 (.30 squared), meaning that creativity accounts for 9 percent of the variance in mathematical aptitude.

**3. a.** This is a prediction study because the goal is to determine how well high school GPA and the tests of mental maturity and education skills predict GPA in the first year of college.

**b.** The main limitation is that the correlations were computed only for the scores of the 266 freshmen students who successfully completed their first year of college. It would have been better to correlate the prediction variables with the criterion variable for all freshmen who completed at least one college term, even if they subsequently dropped out.

**c.** First-year GPA and H.S. GPA: $.68^2 = .46$, or 46 percent
First-year GPA and CTMM: $.61^2 = .37$, or 37 percent
First-year GPA and EST: $.48^2 = .23$, or 23 percent

**4. a.** No. This conclusion assumes that there is a cause-and-effect relationship between working while in college and degree of personal maturity. Causal inferences cannot be made with a high degree of assurance from correlational data.

**b.** Yes. The correlation of $+.65$ means that the two variables are positively related; that is, an increment in amount of employment is likely to be associated with an increment in personal maturity score.

**c.** No. As in *a* above, this conclusion makes a causal assumption that is not warranted on the basis of the correlational data obtained in this study.

# Chapter 13, Experimental Research

**1. a.** An experimental design, specifically the pretest-posttest control group design, was used.

**b.** Experimental mortality is the major threat to internal validity. Only two cases were lost from the control group, compared with 32 from the experimental group.

**c.** It is likely that the most motivated students in the experimental group completed the spelling program, whereas the less motivated students tended to drop out. The higher mean for the experimental group was probably a combination of learning and motivation. Thus, we cannot be sure how much of the spelling difference (if any) was caused by the spelling program.

**2. a.** This is a quasi-experimental design because pupils were not randomly assigned to the two reading programs. Specifically, the teachers used the pre-post design with nonequivalent groups.

**b.** The major threats to internal validity are (i) *differential selection* because Jones's class was made up of below-average readers and Smith's class contained average and above-average readers; and (ii) *statistical regression* because there is a tendency for scores to regress toward the test mean. Regression would tend to increase the average score for Jones's group and decrease the average score for Smith's group.

   **c.** Differential selection would make the results very difficult to interpret because we would be trying to compare the performance of two groups that are not comparable. Suppose one of the reading series was much better suited for above-average readers than the other. If Smith used this series, the results would probably be very good since the series would be well suited to her children. But if Jones used this series, the results would probably be poor since the series would not be suited to below-average readers. Therefore, the results could be due primarily to which teacher used which series and may tell us nothing about the overall effectiveness of the two series. Statistical regression would tend to increase the apparent gain for Jones's pupils since they were initially below average and decrease the apparent gain for Smith's pupils. Unless a statistical correction is made for regression, the results could be misinterpreted.

**3. a.** The teachers have used a preexperimental design, specifically the one-group pretest-posttest design.

   **b.** This design, since it does not employ a control group, is subject to several threats to internal validity. In this study, the most serious threats are probably history and maturation.

   **c.** Much attention is currently being given to drug and alcohol abuse in most communities and in the media. Students' attitudes may have been affected by information from the media or from personal sources outside of the school program. Because there is no control group to help estimate out-of-school influences on students' attitudes, the teachers cannot determine how much of the change in students' attitudes is due to the school awareness program and how much is due to out-of-school experience.

**4. a.** Regression toward the mean probably occurred.

   **b.** Students in the highest quartile may have made a substantial gain in arithmetic skills, but it may not have been reflected in the posttest scores because of a ceiling effect. That is, the posttest may not have measured the entire range of possible achievement for the particular variables of concern.

# Chapter 14, Evaluation Research

**1.** You can point out that the program coordinator will need to make frequent decisions about the study skills program. For example, what students should the program serve? Are changes needed in the design of program procedures and/or materials? Who should staff the program? Evaluation can provide information that will improve these decisions. Also, the coordinator probably will be held accountable to the funding agency and to various stakeholders for program results. Evaluation can provide objective data about the program's effectiveness, so that the coordinator does not need to rely exclusively on his or others' subjective impressions.

**2. a.** To what extent do the materials achieve the objective of improving students' writing skills?

   **b.** How difficult or easy are the materials for students to understand?

   **c.** Are students willing and able to spend the amount of time that is necessary to use the materials appropriately?

   **d.** How do college faculty members feel about the value of the materials and what are their recommendations for improving them?

    **e.** How do college students feel about the value of the materials and what are their recommendations for improving them?

**3.** You might point out that the school has many programs (e.g., the computer education program, study skills program, school lunch program, and athletic program). Each program can be evaluated for various aspects, such as goals, resources utilized, operating procedures, and management. The principal must decide which program(s) and which aspect(s) need to be evaluated.

**4.** You would not ask what the program's stated goal is, or you would disregard it in designing your evaluation. Instead, you would look at the program's actual effects. You might examine, for example, the program's effects on students' liking, or fear, of swimming after training; possible changes in the attitudes and behavior of other students toward students who participated in the training; needed changes in the maintenance or schedule of the pool following the training program.

**5. a.** Teachers might be concerned about how much time the new classroom management program will take to learn and how much classroom time will be needed to use it.

    **b.** School administrators might be concerned with the cost of training teachers to use the new program and its effects on student on-task behavior.

    **c.** Parents might be concerned with the extent to which their children's self-esteem is positively or negatively affected by the program and whether it has any effect on students' academic achievement.

    **d.** Students might be concerned with possible effects of the program on the level of attention or praise they can expect from their teachers and on the extent of aggressive behavior their classmates might display toward them.

# Chapter 15, Action Research

**1. a.** You could involve some parents as aides to do some of your routine teaching tasks, like grading tests or papers. A benefit is that it would give you more time to design and carry out the action research.

    **b.** You could involve some parents as observers in collecting data about the students before and after you instituted changes in your classroom activities as part of your action research. A benefit is that it would give you practical support and assistance in designing and carrying out the data collection for your research.

    **c.** You could include your students' parents as subjects of your action research. For example, you could interview them about how they interact with their children concerning school and homework and make some suggestions to enhance their contributions to their children's learning. A benefit is that you would have a more lasting impact on the students' learning by showing the parents how to foster it.

**2.** If you are a teacher:

    **a.** Your principal could suggest problems related to curriculum, classroom management, or unique student characteristics that are worthy of study.

    **b.** A district curriculum/research specialist could help you design your action research project.

    **c.** Another teacher who teaches students and/or subjects similar to yours could give you ideas and feedback to help you design your research.

If you are a principal:

**a.** Another principal who has addressed this problem could warn you of possible pitfalls in dealing with it.

**b.** A district curriculum/research specialist could help you select data collection methods appropriate for your research problem.

**c.** A teacher in your school could help you think about the potential impact of your proposed solution on students in your school.

**3. a.** How much time, difficulty, or cost would be involved in modifying the solution, or finding and implementing a better solution, once you put your solution into effect. If time, difficulty, or cost is likely to be high, option (a), a thorough literature review, would help you choose the best solution to implement.

**b.** How much you already know about the problem from your preservice and inservice education, your administrative experience, the reading you have done, and so on. If you already have a good knowledge base in the problem area, a thorough literature review might not be necessary, so option (b) might be preferred.

**c.** How great is the degree of controversy or the range of differing philosophies or viewpoints concerning the problem. Some areas are marked by controversy, for example, whether to use a whole-language or phonics approach to teaching reading or the best way to teach students with different learning styles. If your problem involves such an area, option (a), a thorough literature review, will help you clarify your own position before posing a solution. However, if the problem is less controversial, such as whether higher-cognitive questions are better than knowledge questions to stimulate students' thinking, you may prefer option (b) so that you can focus on designing your own solution (e.g., helping your teachers plan lessons involving higher-cognitive questions).

# COMPUTER SEARCH RECORD FORM

# COMPUTER SEARCH RECORD FORM

_____
**Your Name**

**Purpose of Search:** _____

**Problem Definition:** _____

_____

_____

_____

**Secondary Sources Reviewed:** _____

_____

_____

**Data Base to be Searched:** _____

_____

**ERIC Descriptors or Psychological Index Terms:**

1. _____     9. _____
2. _____     10. _____
3. _____     11. _____
4. _____     12. _____
5. _____     13. _____
6. _____     14. _____
7. _____     15. _____
8. _____     16. _____

**Search 1:** _____

**Search 2:** _____

**Search 3:** _____

**Search 4:** _____

**Search 5:** _____

**Search 6:** _____

Computer Search Record Form

426

# APPENDIX 3

# FORM FOR EVALUATING
# A QUANTITATIVE RESEARCH REPORT

The following are questions to use in evaluating each section of a quantitative research report. For each question we identify the type of information you will need to look for in the report to answer the question and we provide a sample answer. The examples are drawn from our experience in evaluating quantitative research studies.

## Introductory Section

1. Are the research problems, procedures, or findings unduly influenced by the researchers' institutional affiliations, beliefs, values, or theoretical orientation?

    *Information needed.* Find the researchers' institutional affiliation. (This information usually appears beneath the title of the report or at the end.) Also locate any information in the report that indicates their beliefs about education, values, or theoretical orientation.

    *Example.* Most of the researchers' prior work has advocated cognitive models of learning. Therefore, they may have biased their experiment so that the cognitively oriented teaching method came out better than the behaviorally oriented teaching method.

2. Do the researchers demonstrate undue positive or negative bias in describing the subject of the study (an instructional method, program, curriculum, person, etc.)?

    *Information needed.* Identify any adjectives or other words that describe an instructional method, program, curriculum, person, and so on in clearly positive or negative terms.

    *Example.* The researchers described the group of students as difficult to handle, unmotivated, and disorganized. No evidence was presented to support this characterization. This description in the absence of evidence may indicate a negative attitude toward the children who were studied.

3. Is the literature review section of the report sufficiently comprehensive? Does it include studies that you know to be relevant to the problem?

    *Information needed.* Examine the studies mentioned in the report. Note particularly if a recent review of the literature relevant to the research problem was cited or if the researchers mentioned an effort to make their own review comprehensive.

    *Example.* The researchers stated the main conclusions of a previously published comprehensive literature review on the instructional program that they intended to study. They demonstrated clearly how their study built on the findings and recommendations of this review.

4. Is each variable in the study clearly defined?

   *Information needed.* Identify all the variables (also called constructs) that were studied. For each variable, determine if and how it is defined in the report.

   *Example.* One of the variables is intrinsic motivation, which is defined in the report as the desire to learn because of curiosity. This definition is not consistent with other definitions, which state that intrinsic motivation is the desire to learn because of the satisfaction that comes from the act of learning and from the content being learned.

5. Is the measure of each variable consistent with how the variable was defined?

   *Information needed.* Identify how each variable in the study was measured.

   *Example.* The researchers studied self-esteem but did not define it. Therefore, it was not possible to determine whether their measure of self-esteem was consistent with their definition.

6. Are hypotheses, questions, or objectives explicitly stated, and if so, are they clear?

   *Information needed.* Examine each research hypothesis, question, or objective stated in the report.

   *Example.* The researcher stated one general objective for the study. It was clearly stated but did not give the reader sufficient understanding of the specific variables that were to be studied.

7. Do the researchers make a convincing case that a research hypothesis, question, or objective was important to study?

   *Information needed.* Examine the researchers' rationale for each hypothesis, question, or objective.

   *Example.* The researchers showed how the hypothesis to be tested was derived from a theory. They also showed that if the hypothesis was confirmed by the study it would add support to the validity of the theory, which is currently being used in the design of new reading curricula.

# Research Procedures

8. Did the sampling procedures produce a sample that is representative of an identifiable population or of your local population?

   *Information needed.* Identify the procedures that the researchers used to select their sample.

   *Example.* The researchers selected several classes (not randomly) from one school. The only information given about the students was their average ability and gender distribution. I cannot tell from this description whether the sample is similar to students in our schools.

9. Did the researchers form subgroups to increase understanding of the phenomena being studied?

   *Information needed.* Determine whether the sample was formed into subgroups, and if so, why.

*Example*. The researchers showed the effects of the instructional program for both boys and girls; this information was helpful. However, they did not show the effects for different ethnic subgroups. This is an oversight because the program may have a cultural bias that could have an adverse effect on some ethnic subgroups.

10. Is each measure in the study sufficiently valid for its intended purpose?

    *Information needed*. Examine any evidence that the researchers presented to demonstrate the validity of each measure in the study.

    *Example*. The XYZ Test was used because it purportedly predicts success in vocational training programs. However, the researchers presented evidence from only one study to support this claim. That study involved a vocational training program that was quite different from the one they investigated.

11. Is each measure in the study sufficiently reliable for its intended purpose?

    *Information needed*. Examine any evidence that the researchers presented to demonstrate the reliability of each measure in the study.

    *Example*. The researchers had observers rate each student's on-task behavior during Spanish instruction in a sample of 30 classrooms. Interobserver reliability was checked by having pairs of observers use the rating system in the same 5 classrooms. The pairs typically agreed on 90 percent of their ratings, which indicates good reliability.

12. Is each measure appropriate for the sample?

    *Information needed*. Determine whether the researchers reported the population for whom the measure was developed.

    *Example*. The ABC Reading Test was developed 20 years ago for primary grade students. The current study also involves primary grade students, but the test may no longer be valid because students and the reading curriculum have changed so much over the past 20 years.

13. Were the research procedures appropriate and clearly stated so that others could replicate them if they wished?

    *Information needed*. Identify the various research procedures that were used in the study and the order in which they occurred.

    *Example*. The researchers administered three research tests during one class period the day before the experimental curriculum was introduced. The tests, though brief, may have overwhelmed the children so that they did not do their best work. Also, some aspects of the experimental curriculum (e.g., the types of seatwork activities) were not clearly described, and the researchers did not indicate how soon the final research tests were administered after the curriculum was completed.

# Data Analysis

14. Were appropriate statistical techniques used, and were they used correctly?

    *Information needed*. Identify any statistical techniques described in the report.

    *Example*. The researchers calculated the mean score for students' performance on the five tests that were administered. However, they did not give the range of scores (i.e., lowest score and highest score). This would be helpful information because they studied a highly heterogeneous group of students.

# Discussion of Results

15. Do the results of the data analyses support what the researchers conclude are the findings of the study?

    *Information needed.* Identify what the researchers considered to be the major findings of the study.

    *Example.* The researchers concluded that the experimental treatment led to superior learning compared to the control treatment, but this claim was true for only two of the four criterion measures used to measure the effects of the treatments.

16. Did the researchers provide reasonable explanations of the findings?

    *Information needed.* Identify how the researchers explained the findings of the study and whether alternative explanations were considered.

    *Example.* The researchers concluded that the narrative version of the textbook was less effective than the traditional expository version. Their explanation was that the story in the narrative version motivated students to keep reading, but at the same time it distracted them from focusing on the factual information that was included on the test. They presented no evidence to support this explanation, although it seems plausible.

17. Did the researchers draw reasonable implications for practice from their findings?

    *Information needed.* Identify any implications for practice that the researchers drew from their findings.

    *Example.* The researchers claimed that teachers' morale would be higher if administrators would provide more self-directed staff development. However, this recommendation is based only on their questionnaire finding that teachers expressed a desire for more self-directed staff development. The researchers are not justified in going from this bit of data to the claim that teachers' morale will improve if they get the kind of staff development they prefer.

# FORM FOR EVALUATING
# A QUALITATIVE RESEARCH REPORT

The following are questions to use in evaluating each section of a qualitative research report. For each question we identify the type of information you will need to look for in the report to answer the question and we provide a sample answer. The examples are drawn from our experience in evaluating qualitative research studies.

## Introductory Section

1. Are the research problems, procedures, or findings unduly influenced by the researchers' institutional affiliations, beliefs, values, or theoretical orientation?

    *Information needed.* Find the researchers' institutional affiliation. (This information usually appears beneath the title of the report or at the end.) Also locate any information in the report that indicates their beliefs about education, values, or theoretical orientation.

    *Example.* The researchers taught in inner-city schools for many years before doing this study. This experience would give them empathy for inner-city students but also some possible biases about what their typical problems are. Were the researchers able to stay free of preconceptions during data collection?

2. Do the researchers demonstrate undue positive or negative bias in describing the subject of the study (an instructional method, program, curriculum, person, etc.)?

    *Information needed.* Identify any adjectives or other words that describe an instructional method, program, curriculum, person, and so on in clearly positive or negative terms.

    *Example.* The researchers used a qualitative research method known as educational criticism to study a high school football team. This method is inherently evaluative, so it is no surprise that the researchers made many judgments—both positive and negative—about the impact of the team on individual players.

3. Is the literature review section of the report sufficiently comprehensive? Does it include studies that you know to be relevant to the problem?

    *Information needed.* Examine the studies mentioned in the report. Note particularly if a recent review of the literature relevant to the research problem was cited or if the researchers mentioned an effort to make their own review comprehensive.

    *Example.* The researchers completed their literature search prior to data collection. This procedure is not desirable because questions and hypotheses were bound to arise as they collected data. They should have done an ongoing literature search to find out what others have found concerning these emerging questions and hypotheses.

# Research Procedures

4. Did the sampling procedure result in a case or cases that were particularly interesting and from whom much could be learned about the phenomena of interest?

*Information needed.* Identify the procedures that the researchers used to select their sample.

*Example.* The researchers used purposive sampling to select a high school principal who had received several awards and widespread recognition for "turning her school around." She was an excellent case to study, given the researchers' interest in administrators' instructional leadership.

5. Was there sufficient intensity of data collection?

*Information needed.* Identify the time period over which an individual, setting, or event was observed and whether the observation was continuous or fragmented. If documents were analyzed, identify how extensive the search for documents was and how closely the documents were analyzed.

*Example.* The researchers' goal was to learn how elementary-school teachers established classroom routines and discipline procedures at the beginning of the school year. They observed each teacher every day for the first three weeks; this is a good procedure. They assumed, however, that routines and discipline procedures would be explained at the start of the school day, and so they observed only the first hour of class time. The validity of this assumption is questionable.

6. Is each measure in the study sufficiently valid for its intended purpose?

*Information needed.* Examine any evidence that the researchers presented to demonstrate the validity of each measure in the study.

*Example.* The researchers' primary measure was ethnographic observation. They appear to have taken careful notes and studied them extensively prior to writing their ethnographic report. They checked the validity of their statements in the report by having several knowledgeable people in the community they studied review the statements.

7. Is each measure in the study sufficiently reliable for its intended purpose?

*Information needed.* Examine any evidence that the researchers presented to demonstrate the reliability of each measure in the study.

*Example.* The researchers acknowledged the difficulty of determining the reliability of their interviews. Their main concern was whether the interviewees were taking the interviews seriously. They collected data about this possible problem by asking the interviewees several of the same questions on different occasions to see if the responses would be similar. By and large they were.

8. Is each measure appropriate for the sample?

*Information needed.* Determine whether the researchers reported the population for whom the measure was developed.

*Example.* The researchers used the interview method but noted that children in the culture they studied are very uncomfortable with adults asking them questions in a formal setting. The researchers made the children more comfortable by setting up a playlike environment and asking questions unobtrusively as the interviewer and children played.

9. Were the research procedures appropriate and clearly stated so that others could replicate them if they wished?

*Information needed.* Identify the various research procedures that were used in the study and the order in which they occurred.

*Example.* The researchers' main data collection procedure was to ask students questions as they attempted to solve various math problems. The problems and questions are available upon request, so it seems that the study could be replicated.

# Research Results

10. Did the report include a thick description that brought to life how the individuals responded to interview questions or how they behaved?

*Information needed.* Identify how much vivid detail was included in the account of what the individuals being studied did or said.

*Example.* The researchers identified 10 main strategies that mentor teachers used in working with beginning teachers. Unfortunately the strategies were described in rather meager detail, with no examples of what they looked like in practice.

11. Did each variable in the study emerge in a meaningful way from the data?

*Information needed.* Identify all the variables (also called constructs) that were discovered in the study. For each variable, examine how it emerged from the data.

*Example.* The researchers did a careful content analysis of what the students said in the interviews. They looked for repetitive themes in their comments. These themes were the variables. The researchers did a nice job of labeling these variables by using words that the students themselves used.

12. Are there clearly stated hypotheses or questions? And do they emerge from the data that were collected?

*Information needed.* Identify each research hypothesis and question stated in the report. Examine whether and how they emerged from the data.

*Example.* The researchers focused almost entirely on writing a narrative account of the events leading up to the teachers' strike. There was no attempt to develop hypotheses about why these events happened, so that these hypotheses could be tested in subsequent research.

13. Were appropriate statistical techniques used, and were they used correctly?

*Information needed.* Identify any statistical technique described in the report.

*Example.* The researchers studied three teachers' aides and made such comments as "They spent most of their time helping individual children and passing out or collecting papers." Time is easily quantified, so the researchers should have collected some time data and reported means and standard deviations.

# Discussion of Results

14. Were multiple sources of evidence used to support the researchers' conclusions?

    *Information needed.* Identify the researchers' conclusions and how each of them was supported by the data analyses.

    *Example.* The researchers concluded that textbook adoption committees were frustrated by the paucity of written information provided by publishers and their inability to question publishers' representations in person. This frustration was documented by analysis of interviews with selected members of the textbook adoption committees, field notes made by the researchers during committee meetings, and letters written by the chair of the committee to the director of textbook adoption in the state department of education.

15. Did the researchers provide reasonable explanations of the findings?

    *Information needed.* Identify how the researchers explained the findings of the study and whether alternative explanations were considered.

    *Example.* The researchers found that peer coaching did not work at the school they studied, and they attributed its failure to the lack of a supportive context, especially the lack of a history of collegiality among the teaching staff. Another plausible explanation, which they did not consider, is that the teachers received inadequate training in peer coaching.

16. Was the generalizability of the findings appropriately qualified?

    *Information needed.* Identify whether the researchers made any statements about the generalizability of their findings. If claims of generalizability were made, were they appropriate?

    *Example.* The researchers made no claims that the results of their case study could be generalized to anyone other than the teacher who was studied. It is unfortunate that they did not discuss generalizability, because the findings have significant implications for practice if in fact they apply to other teachers. There are not enough data about the teacher's professional training for readers to generalize on their own.

17. Did the researchers draw reasonable implications for practice from their findings?

    *Information needed.* Identify any implications for practice that the researchers drew from their findings.

    *Example.* The researchers found that students who volunteer for community service derive many benefits from the experience. Therefore, they encourage educators to support community service programs for their students. This recommendation seems well grounded in their findings about benefits of community service participation for students.

# NAME INDEX

# SUBJECT INDEX

*Note to reader:* The page, or pages, on which a technical term is first defined or explained are boldfaced in this index. A page number followed by an "n" and a note number indicates a reference to a chapter note that explains the term.